Library of Congress-in-Publication Data
Loom and Doom / by Susan Sleeman
p. cm.
I. Title
                    2016952056

CountrySamplerFiction.com
(800) 282-6643
Antique Shop Mysteries™
Series Creator: Shari Lohner
Series Editor: Shari Lohner, Michelle Ochoa
Cover Illustrator: Bonnie Leick

10 11 12 13 14 | Printed in China | 9 8 7 6 5 4 3 2 1

"**I**'m not sure I can handle all of this," Maggie Watson said, dropping registration papers on the counter of her shop, Carriage House Antiques.

Early morning sun filtered through the front window and illuminated the pages as they fanned out on the rich maple countertop. A single paper floated to the floor, and Maggie bent to retrieve it.

"You *can* handle this, Maggie," shop manager June McGillis said, shifting on her stool. She adjusted the cloisonné ballpoint pen she often wore on a chain around her neck. Maggie's Aunt Evelyn, from whom she'd inherited the shop, had given the pen to June years ago. June's habit of losing pens was legendary. "You're organized and a born leader—perfect skills for the 25-Mile Antiques Sale committee chair. You'll succeed. I know you will."

"Thanks for the vote of confidence. I hope you're right." Maggie quickly scanned her to-do list for the upcoming sale, a new feature of the Somerset Harbor Arts and Music Festival.

Scheduled to begin that day, the festival would run through the Fourth of July weekend. Maggie thought it was exciting that festivalgoers would be able to enjoy the music of local musicians as well as the artistic creations of area residents in Greenway Town Park. The festival had been held every summer for fifteen years, and Somerset Harbor Historical Society president Ruth Harper always chaired the event. This year the committee had added a 25-Mile Antiques Sale, which Maggie had agreed to oversee. Antiques dealers within a twenty-five-mile stretch along the Maine coast were hosting special sales and donating items for a big auction. The auction would take place that night in the Somerset Harbor school gym, and all proceeds would go to the historical society.

"I can't believe it's Friday morning already." Maggie retrieved a box of auction fliers from under the counter. "And it's almost seven. If we have any hope of getting back here in time to open, we should get going."

June slid off her stool, ran a hand over her short strawberry blonde hair, and grabbed her purse. "I can't wait to see what the other dealers have in their inventories. Maybe I'll buy a thing or two."

"Don't get too excited." Maggie shouldered her tote bag. "We have never paid full retail price for an antique before, and I'm not starting now."

"Ah," June said, "but everyone is having a sale, and with five other shops participating, there's bound to be something I want to buy." She cast a sideways glance at Maggie. "Besides, I know you have your eye on that 1840s carpetbag at Carol Hansen's shop."

"But that piece will be sold at our auction, so technically it's not retail. It will cost whatever price the crowd sets."

"Uh-huh." June smirked as they strolled toward the door. "Keep telling yourself that buying it at auction is different if that's what you need to do to justify your purchase."

"Okay, you're probably right." Maggie knew full well that she would make an exception for the bag in Carol's shop, which was similar to one her aunt had once owned.

When Maggie used to visit Somerset Harbor as a child, her Aunt Evelyn would always fill a carpetbag-style satchel with antique items. Then Maggie and her aunt would take turns pulling an item out of the bag and making up a story to go with it. Maggie had journeyed the world in her mind on those lazy summer days, and she still had such fond memories of her aunt's bag that she wanted this one for her private collection as a reminder of those special times.

At the door, Maggie dug out her keys with her free hand, and June stopped near a vignette that she'd set up especially for the sale. June had chosen a summer theme for their selection. A Victorian birdcage hand-painted red, white, and blue served as the centerpiece, and a sunset seascape oil painting was displayed behind it. A rare Victorian-era basket sat off to the side, as if waiting to be taken on a summer picnic. June straightened the beautiful Heywood-Wakefield basket, then stood back to admire it.

"You did an amazing job on that." Maggie pulled open the door, feeling fortunate to have such a talented employee. "Thank you for your hard work."

June settled her sunglasses on her nose. "No thanks needed. You know how much I love creating displays."

A welcome cool breeze drifted in from the harbor as Maggie and June got into Maggie's Jetta.

She drove out to the road and past the town square, where patriotic banners dangled from shop windows and large pots of matching flowers hung from corner streetlamps. "Everything looks so festive. I can't wait."

"You've fit in so well here since you took over the shop that I forget this will be your first time at the festival." June smiled at her. "Especially given that you're overseeing the antiques sale."

"It's no biggie," Maggie said, but it *had* been a challenge to get all of the other antiques dealers to agree on everything. She only hoped they would come through for her, which was why she planned to stop in at each business to check on them this morning.

She parked in the lot near Greenway Town Park and climbed out of the car, pausing to admire the rows of white tents already filled with paintings, sculptures, wood carvings, and many other items handcrafted by area artisans. Streamers fluttered from the tents, and small American flags were strung across the walkways alongside lights that would sparkle into the night.

From what June had told her, the event had grown over the years and had spread to include the neighboring school athletic fields in addition to the town square. The festival was now recognized as the top art fair in the state thanks to Ruth's strong organizational skills. Maggie hoped her own work in the antiques sale portion of the festival would live up to Ruth's exacting standards.

"There's Ruth." June pointed across the lot to the Welcome table at the park entrance.

Ruth's aqua knit top was easy to spot as she worked on setting up the table. When she caught sight of Maggie and June, she waved a cheerful hello, and they hurried across the lot toward her.

Maggie set the fliers on the festively decorated table. "It looks like everything is coming together."

Ruth nodded, then frowned. "Looks that way. But after chairing this event for ten years, I know something will go wrong at the last minute."

"Has something happened?" June asked.

"Nothing so far, but I'm expecting it will." Ruth eyed Maggie "You're not here to tell me about a problem with the antiques sale, are you?"

Maggie shook her head and tapped the fliers. "I'm just dropping these off, and then June and I are going to make a quick stop at each antiques shop to make sure there are no unexpected issues."

"Perfect." Ruth's smile returned, forming dimples in her cheeks. "I appreciate all of your hard work. Thanks to you, the antiques sale has already been a boon to the local economy."

"How's that?" Maggie asked, pleased.

"The Oceanview Hotel is booked up with visitors. Many of the customers said they were here for the antiques. Couldn't pass up a sale, they said."

June elbowed Maggie playfully. "See, I told you the sale was irresistible—even to you."

Maggie chuckled and caught sight of Ina Linton, another member of the historical society, walking toward them. She was petite and fit, and even at seventy-five, she seemed to have no intention of slowing down. Her navy slacks were a perfect complement to her red-and-white striped top and the large straw hat sitting jauntily on her head. Her cotton-white curls peeked out from under the brim.

Ina lifted one foot, clad in a bright white athletic shoe, and waved it at Ruth. "I've got my go-fast shoes on, so put me to work."

"I'm afraid I have some sitting for you to do first," Ruth replied. "I'd like you to staff the visitor table this morning."

Disappointment reigned on Ina's face.

"You're perfect for the job, Ina," Maggie cajoled. "No one knows more than you do about this area. And you always have a smile for everyone. You're the best ambassador I can think of for our town."

"You're a smooth talker, Maggie Watson," Ina said, giving her a wink.

Maggie laughed. "You can use those go-fast shoes tonight when I put you to work at the auction."

"I'll hold you to it." Ina smiled, the skin near her eyes crinkling.

"We need to get going." June gestured at Maggie's car. "Maybe we should have taken my SUV. There'd be so much more room for all the things we're going to buy."

Maggie mocked a stern look similar to one her mother would have used on her years ago.

June grinned and said good-bye to Ruth and Ina, then linked arms with Maggie and propelled her toward the parking lot.

"Help!" Maggie called over her shoulder. "I'm being abducted by a woman on a mission to break the bank."

The women's laughter carried on the breeze, and joy replaced Maggie's earlier anxiety. She loved Somerset Harbor and the people who lived there. She was especially fond of her friends in the historical society. And then there was James Bennett, a local alderman and preservationist who worked to restore historical homes to their original state. He was knowledgeable in history and antiques, and he had been so helpful to Maggie since she'd come to Somerset Harbor. He wasn't hard to look at either, but he and Maggie were just friends—good friends. She'd lost her husband a few years ago, and she wasn't sure she was ready to think of another man in a romantic way. But she couldn't deny that there was something very special about James . . .

"It's a perfect day for a drive." June buckled her seat belt, the sharp click drawing Maggie's thoughts back to the present.

Maggie started her car and eased into the light traffic, then pointed the car north on the coastal highway toward Pelican Cove. The sea always grabbed Maggie's attention on this road. In the bright sunshine, the surging water was stunning as it crashed against the craggy rocks along the road. But it was hard for her to fully appreciate the view. She'd had a close shave on this road around Christmas, and she couldn't help but feel a little anxious each time she made the drive.

Thankfully, June chatted about the sale and antiques all the way to Pelican Cove, providing a welcome distraction. When a small strip mall came into view, Maggie pulled the car into the parking lot of Grandma's Antiques and took a moment to look at the lovely beach across the road. Even this early in the morning, couples strolled arm in arm on the golden sand, and children frolicked in the waves.

"I love the look of this mall," June said. "What a great idea to paint all of the businesses different colors."

Grandma's Antiques, their destination, was painted a bright fuchsia color. Next door, the taffy-and-fudge shop was done in lime green. The clapboard of the T-shirt vendor on the opposite side was covered with such a bright shade of turquoise that it almost hurt to look at it for too long.

"It definitely grabs your attention." Maggie noticed that a police car was parked in front of Grandma's Antiques and a uniformed officer stood talking to the owner, Carol Hansen. "Uh-oh. You don't think something bad has happened, do you?"

"Normally I'd say no," June replied. "But with the way mysteries seem to pop up around you, I wouldn't be surprised."

Maggie shook her head. She might have solved a few mysteries since she'd come to Somerset Harbor, but that didn't mean she found one *everywhere* she went.

"Let's find out what's going on." Maggie grabbed her clipboard and started for the shop, followed closely by June. Gritty sand whipped across the street and into her sandals. She ignored the irritation and focused on the sixty-something woman clad in a bright floral blouse.

As they drew closer, the worried expression on Carol's face became clear.

Maggie reached her and asked, "Is everything okay?"

Carol dabbed a tissue at red-rimmed eyes. "Someone broke into my shop last night."

"I'm so sorry." Maggie's gaze shot to the building, looking for any sign of the break-in. "Did they take anything?" *Please not the carpetbag,* she prayed silently, feeling selfish even as she did.

"I didn't find anything missing." Carol's chin trembled.

"That's good."

"Yes, but still . . ." Carol's tears brimmed over again. "It's a violation of my privacy. Someone was in there doing whatever they pleased with my things." She shuddered. "I'm terrified to be in the shop alone now."

Usually, Carol was open and friendly. To see her frightened and upset was heartbreaking, and Maggie immediately resolved to do whatever she could to help.

"I can call your niece," the officer suggested. "I'm sure Penny would be happy to spend the day with you."

"Thank you, Officer Anderson, but no. I think I'll close up shop for a few days and take it easy."

"Close the shop?" Maggie asked, fighting down panic. If Carol closed because of a break-in, would other shop owners do the same to prevent break-ins of their own? "I want you to feel safe, Carol, and if you must close, I'll understand. But if you do, people will be so disappointed. Some of them have traveled a long way for this part of the festival."

"Really?" Carol asked dubiously.

Maggie pulled a brochure from her clipboard. "See? You're listed in the brochure and in our ads, and the Oceanview Hotel is filled with die-hard antiques lovers eager to drop by all of the antiques shops. I'm sure they've already plotted out their schedules, including a visit to your lovely shop."

Carol nibbled on her lip.

"You should be perfectly safe here," Officer Anderson added. "There will be plenty of people around this weekend, and I'll be walking among the crowd all day."

"If you think so." Her voice still shook, but Carol lifted her chin in resolve.

"Thank you, Carol," Maggie said. "If at any time you feel the need to change your mind, would you please call me? And let me know if there's anything I can do to make you feel more at ease."

Carol nodded and turned to gaze at her shop.

With that problem solved — at least for the moment — Maggie's thoughts switched to the break-in. "Do you have security cameras by any chance?"

"Yes," Carol said. "But the intruder knew about the camera closest to where he was. He covered the lens with a sock."

"That's too bad." Maggie thought for a moment. "If you'd like, I'd be glad to have a look around to see if I can help sort this out." Secretly, she was itching to find out what had happened. *Why would someone go to the trouble of breaking in and not take anything?*

Officer Anderson snorted with amusement. "I suggest you leave the investigating to the police."

"Of course," Maggie said, fully intending to stay out of the officer's way. But once he left, she planned to do a little looking around on her own.

As June often said, mysteries had a way of finding her, and she was never one to turn the other way when one needed solving.

2

With all of the details that still needed to be worked out for the evening's auction, Maggie's day flew by, and she was relieved to find she had time for a burger—grilled to perfection by the high school band boosters—before heading over to the gym to organize volunteers for the auction. She loaded the thick patty with lettuce, pickles, and the special secret sauce a few enterprising parents had developed after years of holding this fundraiser. Maggie took a huge bite, and the tangy, sweet sauce made her hum with appreciation. She could tell why they'd been so successful with burger sales each year. She took her time, savoring each bite while listening to the local accordion trio that was playing on the center stage.

Dressed in patriotic attire, the female octogenarians swayed as they worked their accordions. Small children danced at the base of the stage, and their parents looked on fondly. All too soon, it was time for Maggie to get back to work.

She finished eating and strolled over to Daisy Carter's mini coffee bar. All the other vendors had chosen plain white tents, but not Daisy. Hers had pink stripes and looked as cheerful as she did. As the owner of The Busy Bean coffee shop, Daisy had filled her tent with baked goods and every selection of flavoring a coffee drinker could imagine. She'd set up bright yellow and pink Adirondack chairs and lime-green tables in front of the booth.

Daisy wore clothing as bright as her tent; she was dressed in hot-pink capris and a black-and-pink checked top. Her lipstick matched her capris, and she'd added a pink floral belt to complete the ensemble.

Maggie wound through the chairs to reach the counter. "Will you be able to attend the auction?"

Daisy patted her brown hair, twisted into a sky-high bun. "Depends on business. We've been running ragged all day. If it keeps up, I'll have to stay here."

"A good problem to have."

"Except we'll be up half the night baking." Daisy grinned. "I might even need to get Harry to help."

Maggie giggled at the thought of Daisy's husband—a big, burly fisherman—baking anything. "Well, I hope to see you at the auction."

"Oh, don't worry," Daisy said with a wink. "If I'm there, you'll see me."

Maggie chuckled at her friend's comment and joined the throng of visitors perusing the artwork. She greeted her fellow residents as she walked to the school gymnasium, where Principal Bill Johnson waited at the door.

"Nice night for an auction." His bald head gleamed as he unlocked and pulled open the door.

"I couldn't ask for better weather." Maggie followed him inside.

"Wait here while I turn on the lights." The principal headed for the electrical panel in the equipment room.

She stood in the glow of the exit sign above her head until the lights snapped on, illuminating the large space. At the end of the business day, dealers had dropped by with their antiques, and she and June had displayed them on long tables near the auctioneer's podium.

Maggie's gaze drifted to the carpetbag, and she couldn't resist taking a closer look at it. At the table, she ran her fingers over the flowery carpet remnant, the coarse texture reminding her of the days with her aunt. Her fingers itched to open the chunky wood frame, shaped like a large doctor's satchel, with its ornate lock.

How she longed to create a story to go with the bag. Navy and cream flower designs were woven into the carpet, and a hard bottom gave the bag structure, allowing it to stand on its own.

Maggie heard the door open, and she turned to see fellow historical society member Fran Vosburg enter the gym. Fran's dark hair was pulled back in a ponytail that swung as she hurried across the gymnasium to join Maggie. In her late thirties, Fran was the youngest member of their group, but Maggie often thought she seemed wise beyond her years.

"It's beautiful, isn't it?" Fran asked. She was owner of The Quilt Cupboard, and anything to do with fabric caught her attention. "The stories it could tell."

Maggie nodded. "That's why I want it."

"Then I hope you get it." Fran looked at her watch. "Almost time to open the doors. Do you still want me to register the bidders?"

"Yes, please. Follow me."

Fran settled at a table by the door as Liz Young, another member of the historical society, came in. A sparkly metallic top that she'd paired with black capris brought out the silver streaks in her short blond hair. As Pastor David Young's wife and a licensed psychologist, Liz counseled members of Old Faith Chapel. She had such a warm, inviting personality that Maggie had assigned her to one of the most visible jobs of the event.

"Perfect timing," Maggie said. "I can review the registration process with both of you at one time."

Liz took a seat next to Fran. "There's already a crowd building outside."

"Sounds like we're going to be busy, then." Maggie reviewed the procedure and forms that the bidders needed to fill out. After answering a few questions, she left the pair chatting about their day.

Maggie spotted Ina standing by the door, a big frown on her face.

Concerned there was a problem, Maggie joined her. "What's wrong?"

Ina wiggled her foot. "Still haven't made decent use of my go-fast shoes, and I paid a good bit of money for them."

"Not to worry." Maggie let out a sigh, relieved that nothing was seriously wrong. "I have the perfect job for you."

"What?" Ina asked skeptically.

"I need someone to jot down the numbers of winning bidders. James will serve as our auctioneer, and he will call out the winner's number. Fran and Liz should catch it, but I want to be sure we get it right. You write the number on a note card along with the winning bid amount and deliver it to Fran and Liz." Maggie teasingly wagged a finger at Ina. "You'll have to be meticulous and get the numbers right, but I know you can handle that."

"Of course I can," Ina scoffed as her eyes shone with delight.

Maggie handed Ina a stack of note cards preprinted with the item numbers and their descriptions from her clipboard. "These are in the order that the items will be auctioned tonight, so it'll be easy to keep up."

"You can count on me." Ina gave her a mock salute.

The door opened behind them, and James joined them. "Ladies." He had a ready smile for Ina and Maggie.

"Good to see you," Maggie said.

James glanced around the room. "I'm excited to see all the donated items." His love of historic preservation and antiques made him the perfect choice for auctioneer.

"Let's get you set up with your gavel." Maggie led him to the podium.

He picked up the large gavel they'd borrowed from the city council and hefted it before whacking it on the wooden circle made for that purpose. A loud bang sounded, drawing everyone's attention.

"Feeling powerful, are you?" she asked.

He smacked the gavel against his palm and grinned. "I've been an alderman for some time. Maybe it's time to move up to the next level so I can wield this bad boy more often."

Maggie grinned at him. "I would never have asked you to be our auctioneer if I'd known it would go to your head like this."

"Don't worry. It'll pass," he laughed. "Now what exactly do I have to do?"

She explained the details of his job, making sure he knew that he had to be sure the bidding had stopped before declaring an item sold.

"Sounds easy enough." James turned his focus to the items. "June told me you're going to bid on a carpetbag. If you're winning, should I make sure the bidding is over on that too, or bring down my gavel while you're ahead?"

For a moment she thought he was serious, but then a playful expression came over his face, and she rolled her eyes. "I've got to open the doors. Let me know if you have any serious questions."

She checked on all the workers to be sure they were in place before she approached the door. She wished June could be there to help since she was a hard worker and very good at organizing a group. But June was busy at the shop, along with Maggie's daughter, Emily, who'd come home from college for a few days to help during the big sale.

She pulled open the door to see a big crowd standing outside. "Welcome. Please come in and—"

Maggie's greeting was drowned out as the crowd surged inside, pushed past her, and flooded to the tables to view the items available for bidding. Several people crowded around the carpetbag and inspected it carefully. *Drat.* She'd hoped to be the only one bidding on it, but it was in great condition, and she supposed she should've expected competition.

She circled the room, mingling with customers and answering questions until James announced that the auction would begin in three minutes. Bidders hurried to get the best seats.

The auction began, and bright yellow paddles waved in the air at a frenzied pace. Prices escalated ridiculously fast. At this rate, Maggie wondered how much she would have to pay for the carpetbag. She'd set a budget of $200, but now it looked like the price could go higher.

When it was time to bid on the carpetbag, Ruth handed it to James, who held it up for the crowd to see. Maggie leaned forward with her bidding paddle firmly in hand.

"Item twenty-eight is an 1840s carpetbag in pristine condition," he read from the card June had prepared for the bag. "The vivid pattern is highly sought after, and the leather accents are in excellent condition. Most importantly, the wooden frame is intact with no breaks." He looked up. "I'll start the bid at $125."

Maggie lifted her bidding number into the air.

"I have $125. Do I hear—?"

"One-fifty!" a man with a phone to his ear shouted, waving his paddle marked with the number fifty-two. He leaned in a casual pose against the collapsed set of bleachers, but even at a distance the intensity in his eyes was clear behind his wire-rimmed glasses. He was tall, with thick black hair and bright red tennis shoes, and he looked to be in his early thirties.

"Do I hear a bid of $160?" James asked.

"One-sixty!" Maggie announced.

"One-eighty!" the man called out.

Maggie's heart thumped hard from the thrill of competition, and she didn't wait for James to announce another price. "One-ninety."

The man pushed off the bleachers and shot Maggie a look. "Two-twenty-five."

Maggie stifled a gasp and looked at James, not that he could help her decide if she should bid again. She'd be overpaying for the item, but she couldn't put a price on memories, could she?

"Two hundred twenty-five dollars going once."

"Two-thirty!" she shouted and turned to look at her opponent, but he'd disappeared.

"Aha," she whispered. *He couldn't take the heat.*

"Two hundred thirty dollars going once. Two-thirty going twice." James slammed down the gavel and grinned at her. "Sold to bidder number one for $230."

Maggie felt herself beaming. Part of her wondered what had happened to her competitor and why he'd given up. They had exceeded the value of the item; maybe he'd dropped out because of that. No matter—she now owned the bag, and she had little time to dwell on the purchase or the other bidder with the work she had to do.

She helped with the final items and then moved to the cashier's table located next to the exit. A soft breeze floated in through the open door, cooling Maggie as she sat to collect payments. Bidders started lining up, and she made sure to thank each one for their support.

Bidder number fifty-two advanced on the table and glared at her. A sore loser, she suspected. Not an uncommon thing at an auction.

"Congratulations. Which item did you win?" she asked, pasting a smile on her face.

He dug out his wallet. "Number fifteen."

Maggie ran her finger down the list recorded by Fran and Liz until she found his bidder number next to a pair of metal sprockets. She strolled to the storage area and found the bin containing the items.

One sprocket was about eight inches across with fanlike

teeth lining the edge. The other was eighteen inches or so with a sawtooth edge and crosspieces in the middle. She lifted the bin, sagging under the weight of the wrought-iron pieces. Returning to the counter, she carefully wrapped each item in tissue and then put them in a bag.

Bidder number fifty-two watched her every move like a hawk, as if he thought she wanted to steal that deal out from under him too. She kept her composure and collected his money.

She forced herself to keep smiling as she handed the bag to him. "Thank you for supporting our historical society."

"Right," he said with a snarl. "This auction is rigged. The auctioneer was clearly favoring locals."

Maggie blinked. "What are you talking about?"

"Sure, like you don't know what I mean." He spun with a huff and marched out the door.

Trying to figure out what the bidder meant by his outburst, she watched him walk away but soon lost him in the crowd.

"Well, he seemed like a spoilsport," Fran said.

"Do you know him?" Maggie asked.

Fran shook her head. "He doesn't live in Somerset Harbor."

Maggie knew she shouldn't let the man bother her, but as she collected money from the customers in her line, she continued to feel unsettled. Each time she walked back to the storage area, she checked to see if he was still in the gym. But she suspected if he was as angry as he seemed, he'd have stormed out of the building and left town by now.

She decided a break was in order. Leaning close to Fran she said, "Can you hold down the fort while I step outside for a breath of fresh air?"

Fran nodded.

Maggie meandered outside. The sun had plunged toward the horizon, and the sky was a mix of reds and purples, casting long shadows into the lot. A rock band had taken the music stage, and deep bass notes throbbed through the night. The streetlights illuminated the area, and Maggie's gaze landed on Ruth standing nearby, next to a large portable classroom. A crowd had gathered around the older woman, and she had one hand clasped over her heart.

Ruth stood transfixed, her finger pointing at the area between the classroom and the main building. "He's d-d-dead," she stammered in a rare display of distress. "He's been murdered!"

3

Maggie didn't want to go into the void between the buildings, but she had to see what had put the horrified look on Ruth's face. She inched toward the space and rounded the corner. The first thing she saw was a pair of feet encased in bright red shoes.

Number Fifty-Two?

She faltered but slid closer, trying to see the man's face. His glasses lay on the ground next to him. Blood stained the side of his head. He wasn't moving, and his skin was white, his lips blue.

It was definitely Number Fifty-Two. And it looked like he was dead.

She peered at his chest, looking for any sign that he was breathing. His chest was perfectly still. His hand still held the handle of the bag she'd filled only minutes earlier with the sprockets, but the bag was empty.

Did someone kill him for the sprockets?

Maggie had limited knowledge of the value of such items, but she didn't think they were worth killing over.

Either way, the police needed to be notified. She dialed 911 on her cell phone.

"I need to report a murder," she said, though she didn't know if Number Fifty-Two had truly been killed or if he'd fallen and hit his head on the metal stairs that led up to the portable classroom's door. She added the location and the circumstances, and the operator promised to send an officer right away.

Maggie rejoined Ruth, who hadn't yet regained her composure.

"Maybe you should go inside and sit down," Maggie suggested.

Ruth shook her head. "I can't. I'm a witness, and I need to be here when the police arrive."

"What exactly did you see?"

"The dead man was talking to another guy a few minutes ago, and they were arguing. I walked away, but I forgot my clipboard so I came back. That's when I found the dead man. The guy he argued with wasn't anywhere around, so I want to keep an eye out for him."

Maggie felt her stomach knot. If the other guy had indeed killed Number Fifty-Two, then Ruth had actually seen the killer, and she could be in danger.

"Did this man see you?" Maggie asked.

Ruth shrugged. "I caught a good look at his face, but honestly, I think he was too busy arguing for my presence to register."

Maggie sighed, hoping that was the case. She hated to think that a killer might come after Ruth to keep her from talking. "What did he look like?"

"He's about six feet tall and muscular," Ruth said. "He had stubble on his face like he hadn't shaved in a few days. He wore a cap, but I saw blond hair sticking out underneath. The cap was black with what looked like the letter *P* embroidered on the front, so I'm guessing it's a Portland Sea Dogs cap."

The cap was commonly worn by many of the men in the area who supported the nearest baseball team. "Besides the cap, what else was he wearing?"

"Jeans. Navy T-shirt." Ruth shook her head. "If I'd known this would happen, I would have paid more attention."

"Actually, Ruth, your description is very thorough."

"He was kind of rugged, like he didn't have a desk job but worked with his hands." A big frown drew down her mouth. "Trouble is, I just described most of the fishermen in the area."

"Did you catch any part of their argument?"

Ruth shook her head. "I was too far away to make out their words, but their voices carried and their body language screamed 'angry.'"

"As we wait for the police to arrive, it might help if you keep thinking about the argument. You might remember something."

Ruth nodded. "I am so sorry this man was killed, but I also have to think about the effect it's going to have on the festival. I would hate for people to think it's not safe to attend or not want to come in future years because of it."

Maggie hadn't thought of the wider-reaching effects. "Do you think people will associate the incident with the festival after this year?"

"I think it's a good possibility." Ruth peered at Maggie. "You're so good at solving mysteries. Would you be willing to look into this?"

"I'm not sure I—"

"Please?" Ruth pressed. "With the festival going on, our little police department is already taxed. They barely have enough officers to patrol the festival, much less look into a major crime at the same time. After something like this, they'll want to make sure the festivalgoers feel extra safe, so they'll have patrol to focus on as well as the investigation."

"I see your point." Maggie hated to think of anyone feeling unsafe in her lovely little town. She wanted to get to the bottom of this to be sure that festival attendees would continue to feel welcome at the event for years to come. "I'll do what I can."

Ruth clutched Maggie's arm. "Thank you. Let me know what I can do to help."

Maggie glanced around the area, taking mental notes of the scene. A gray pickup with a door open was parked in a handicap space next to the trailer. A silver Subaru Forester was parked next to it. She jotted down the license plates in the notebook she carried in her purse, ready to share the information with the officer who'd just arrived on scene, closely followed by an ambulance. After parking at the curb, the officer stepped out and settled his cap on his head. Even from this distance, Maggie could tell it was Officer Robert Linton, Ina's nephew and the officer she'd worked with on several mysteries of late.

Officer Linton and the EMT team hurried across the parking lot, the onlookers parting like the Red Sea to let them through. Maggie was glad to see Robert had gotten the call. He took his job seriously, and despite his boyish appearance, he was about Maggie's age, with over twenty years of experience to handle the investigation.

"Maggie." He offered a quick nod of acknowledgement. "I hear you made the 911 call. Tell me what happened."

She told him about seeing Ruth in a state of shock. "I recognize the deceased. He bought a pair of metal sprockets at the auction. I don't remember his name, but his bidder number was fifty-two. The sprockets were in the empty bag that he's still clutching in his hand."

"And he was arguing with a guy right before this," Ruth added, then recounted the details of what she'd witnessed. "The deceased isn't local, nor was the man he argued with. I never saw either of them before today."

"And the other man isn't in the crowd right now?"

Ruth shook her head.

"Okay, good, Ruth. Thanks for your help. Let me get things organized here, and then I'll get a description from you."

The officer joined the EMTs, who were checking the man's vitals—or lack thereof. One of the technicians shook his head at Officer Linton, his expression grim. The officer stared at the dead man for a moment, then shined his flashlight around the area.

"Do you think he was murdered, or is it possible that he fell and hit his head?" Maggie asked.

"At this point, anything I could tell you would be speculation, and I don't want to start rumors." Officer Linton made eye contact, and he didn't need to verbalize his opinion. It lingered in his troubled expression. He clearly suspected foul play.

"I understand," Maggie said.

He pulled out a small notepad and pen. "You said you didn't remember his name, but do you have it and his address listed somewhere in his auction paperwork?"

She nodded. "I'll go get it. Be right back." Maggie squeezed Ruth's arm, then rushed toward the gym.

Despite Officer Linton's care in not starting rumors, Maggie heard rampant speculation as to the man's identity and how he was killed as she made her way inside. A few bidders still stood in line to pay, but they were the only people still in the gym.

Maggie joined Liz and Fran, both still seated at the table. At her approach, they looked up.

"Is it true?" Fran asked. "Was someone *murdered*?"

"We don't know," Maggie answered honestly. "But a man has died."

The situation suddenly hit her, and her legs felt wobbly. She quickly took a seat and reached for the pile of registration forms. She flipped through the stack until she spotted the fifty-second bidder and ran her finger down the page to his name.

Ike Wynne. Maggie recalled that the copy of his driver's license that they had required for registration had listed his age as thirty-three. His death was horrible no matter how she looked at it, but to die at such a young age was even more of a tragedy.

Memories of their heated bidding war came flooding back. He'd been avidly seeking the carpetbag, and Maggie was still surprised that he'd dropped out of the bidding.

Had his bidding been interrupted by the man Ruth saw him arguing with? And did the mystery man have anything to do with the items Ike was interested in?

Too many questions and no answers.

"So Mr. Wynne," she whispered as she stared at his name on the form. "Exactly what were you doing in Somerset Harbor, and why did someone want to kill you?"

Maggie provided Ike's information to Officer Linton, and when she returned to the gym, she found her daughter, Emily, perched on the corner of the cashier's table, chatting with Fran. With all of the excitement, Maggie had forgotten that Emily had planned to stop by after she finished helping at the shop so they could visit the festival together.

Maggie smiled. Despite the terrible turn the day had taken, simply looking at Emily brightened her mood. Her daughter was becoming such a beautiful woman. Emily had gathered her shoulder-length hair back into a ponytail, and its sleek black color gleamed under the gym lights. She wore white shorts with a navy T-shirt. Her feet, encased in sandals, swung back and forth, and she appeared as young and carefree as a teenage girl should be.

"Hello, sweetheart," Maggie said. "How did you get in here without me seeing you?"

"You were busy talking to the police officer." Emily's eyes narrowed. "Is it true? Was someone really murdered here?"

Maggie didn't want to have to discuss such a horrible incident with her daughter, but the news would be better coming from her than a stranger. "It looks like it. Officer Linton just told me that the medical examiner said the victim was hit over the head, and he believed it to be the cause of death."

Fran peered up at Maggie, her eyes dark with worry. "Since the sprockets are missing, do you think Ike could have been hit with one of them?"

"The medical examiner said it was too soon to say, but I

think it's possible." Maggie told Emily about Ike's bidding on the sprockets and the carpetbag.

Fran thought for a moment. "I know he bid against you, but did you know him?"

Maggie shook her head.

"But you do plan to investigate the murder, right?" Emily asked.

"I feel like I have to," Maggie said. "This is the first auction to be associated with our lovely festival, and I'm responsible for everything that happens surrounding it. I couldn't bear to have something so awful tarnish the event for visitors to Somerset Harbor, and Ruth has asked me to look into what happened. Hopefully we can get this sorted out and ensure the safety of everyone here."

"You're a good friend," Fran said. "And if Ruth asked for your help, I know you'll give it your all."

"Mom's the best." Emily smiled at Maggie.

Maggie hugged her daughter's shoulders in reply.

Officer Linton marched into the gym and straight to the table, stopping in front of Maggie. "I'd like to get your full statement now if you're up to it."

"Sure." Maggie took a seat. "What do you need to know?"

He took out his notepad and flipped a few pages. "What can you tell me about the missing sprockets?"

Maggie grabbed an auction brochure that was lying on the table, turned to the sprocket page, and laid it in front of him. "As you can see, they're made of wrought iron from the late 1800s. The value for the lot of two was around seventy-five dollars, but he actually paid ninety for them."

"Not of great value, then," Office Linton mused as he made notes on his pad.

"No. The real value in sprockets like these today is for their use in decorating."

"Either in the steampunk trend or as industrial design, both of which are really popular right now," Emily added, her knowledge of current antique trends delighting Maggie.

"Steampunk?" the officer asked.

Emily nodded. "It's a style inspired by industrial steam-powered machinery from the nineteenth century."

"Okay, so the sprockets probably aren't worth killing over."

"Not likely," Maggie said.

"From what I remember," Fran interjected, "there was only one other person who bid against him for the sprockets, and she didn't appear to be too upset after losing out."

Officer Linton nodded. "It's unlikely that she killed him to get her hands on the sprockets, but I'd still like to talk—"

"I've already gone through the bid slips, and I have her name and number ready for you." Maggie flipped a few pages on her clipboard and pulled out a page where she'd jotted down the information.

Office Linton took the paper and pocketed it. "I've also heard from a few others that you bid against the deceased for a bag of some sort. Is that in your auction book too?"

Maggie nodded, turned to the carpetbag in the brochure, and handed it to him.

He studied the picture and ran his finger over the description. "It says here that the opening bid was $125, but you paid $230. Is it actually more valuable than the suggested bid?"

She shook her head. "We both wanted the bag. It has sentimental value for me. Ike disappeared in the middle of bidding. Also, you should know he was talking to someone on the phone while he was bidding. I suspect he may have been trying to buy the bag for someone else."

"Odd," Officer Linton murmured.

"Telephone bids aren't that odd."

"No, not that. We didn't find a cell phone on him." Officer Linton's forehead furrowed. "Are you positive you saw him talking on a phone?"

"Absolutely." Maggie sat on the edge of her seat. "Do you think his assailant stole the phone? Maybe that's who Ike was talking to, and he had to take the phone to cover his tracks."

"Hard to say at this point." Officer Linton tapped his pen on his notebook. "Could I take a look at the bag that caused the bidding war?"

"Sure. In all the excitement, I haven't had a chance to pay for it, so it's still in the holding area." Maggie led him to the area cordoned off beside the stage.

Emily followed, but Fran remained at the table. Maggie's bag was the only unclaimed item remaining. She lifted it from the bin, and at the touch, memories of her late Aunt Evelyn warmed her heart even in the midst of the difficult moment.

Maggie took the bag to the cashier's table.

Officer Linton opened it, then peered inside and gave the exterior of the bag a careful examination too. "I don't see anything special about it."

"Oh no," Emily warned with humor in her tone. "Never say an antique isn't special to an antiques aficionado."

"I didn't mean it like that." Officer Linton peered sheepishly at Maggie. "I meant it doesn't seem to have anything about it that would be worth killing over. Nothing suspicious."

"No offense taken," Maggie said. "And I agree with you. This whole thing is quite a puzzle to me too."

Emily studied the bag. "You said this is more valuable than the sprockets, right? So maybe the killer was expecting this Ike guy to leave with the carpetbag. When he didn't, the killer thought Ike was hiding it. They got into a fight, and Ike was accidentally hit over the head."

"Perhaps," Officer Linton replied, but he didn't appear to believe it. He flipped over the bag and pointed at the leather nameplate. "Do any of you know anything about a Lavinia Taylor?"

Maggie shook her head. "I don't know any Taylors who live in Somerset Harbor, but I'm relatively new to town."

Officer Linton faced Fran. "What about you, Fran? Do you know of any Taylors around these parts?"

She shook her head.

"Maybe the bag is from Lavinia's single days, and she lived in Somerset Harbor under her married name," Maggie suggested. "Since we're so far removed from that period in history, none of us would know about it."

Officer Linton pointed at the brochure listing for the bag. "Or since it was donated by Grandma's Antiques in Pelican Cove, maybe Lavinia lived near that shop."

The conversation sent Maggie's mind spinning with questions, and she was eager to get started on finding answers about both the murder and the history of the antique.

"It's getting late," she said to Officer Linton. "Is there anything else you wanted to ask before we leave?"

He appraised her for a long moment. "Ruth told me you were going to investigate this incident to try to clear the festival's name."

"Well, 'try' is the operative word. Ruth asked for my help, and I will certainly do what I can."

"I won't bother telling you to leave it to the police because you won't listen, but I want to caution you to be very careful. If Ike was killed because of the bag and you now own it, you could be in danger too. Watch your back." He gave her a pointed look, then tipped his cap and walked away.

"Is he right?" Emily asked. "You might be in danger?"

Maggie waved her hand to downplay any threat. "He's probably overreacting."

Emily nipped her lower lip, something she'd done since childhood whenever she was worried.

"Why don't we head out to the festival now?" Maggie suggested.

Emily released her lip, but her eyes still held concern. "If it's okay with you, I'd rather go back to the house. After working at the shop all day, I'm wiped out and ready to relax at home with you."

"Home sounds good," Maggie agreed. "I want to look up Ike Wynne on the Internet and see what I can find out about Lavinia Taylor too. Since you're better at online research than I am, would you help me?"

Emily perked up. "Sure."

Fran stood. "I'll find Bill and get this place closed up so you can spend more time together."

Maggie smiled at her friend and tapped the carpetbag. "I need to pay for this before I take it home." She withdrew cash from her wallet and counted out the right amount. She wasn't even going to think about what it meant that she'd promised herself she'd only spend $200 on the bag but had withdrawn $300 from the ATM. She suspected she'd been willing to spend that much on the bag right from the get-go, and that went against her frugal nature.

Fran tucked the cash into the box, recorded the purchase, and wrote out a receipt. When she looked up at Maggie, her eyes were narrowed. "Do you think this murder is going to ruin the entire festival?"

"It could do just the opposite. Once people hear about it, they might show up to gawk. That's what I've noticed happens at crime scenes on the news."

Fran nodded. "The festival has withstood several bad incidents over the years, so I suppose it can withstand this."

"I've never heard of anything bad happening at the festival before," Maggie said, confused.

"One year we had such a big storm that the entire area was flooded, and the event had to be canceled. Another year, the company that provided the tents forgot to reserve them, and the artists had to set up without any protection."

"Let me guess. It rained and ruined their work."

"Yep."

"Still, I haven't heard anyone mention either of these things. But I suspect a murder will be talked about for years to come."

Fran sighed. "I suppose so."

"Which is why I have to do my best to find the killer and hope that the reason for murder isn't directly related to the auction. At least that way when people gossip about Ike's death, it won't have anything to do with the security of the event itself."

"But if a sprocket was used to kill him, then it already does," Emily interjected.

"That's speculation at this point. We'll have to wait for the medical examiner to rule on it, and of course, the sprockets will have to be recovered."

"If one of them was used as the murder weapon, what are the odds of that happening?" Fran asked.

"Depends on what they're for, I suppose. If they're important and were bought because they actually do something, then I doubt the killer will discard them."

"Then let's hope the one used to hit Ike is of some value and hasn't been flung into the ocean or something." Fran made a shooing motion with her hands. "Now, off you two go so I can get this place locked up."

Emily picked up the bag, and Maggie linked arms with her daughter again, enjoying every moment of their time together. As they went outside, Maggie braced herself for questions from curious onlookers, but everyone, including Officer Linton, had departed from the parking lot.

Maggie sighed with relief, thankful to be alone with Emily. The temperature had cooled, and the muggy air had thinned. The full moon hung in the sky, the moonbeams shining bright on the parking lot as if nothing horrible had transpired there a few hours earlier.

Emily gestured toward the portable classroom. "Is that where it happened?"

Close enough. Maggie nodded but kept them moving toward the car so Emily wouldn't dwell on the incident. They drove in silence down Wharf Road, which was home to both the historical society's house and The Lobster Quadrille, a fabulous restaurant where Maggie had eaten frequently since coming to town. Visitors still packed the streets, and Maggie had to drive slowly to navigate around the roads closed off for the festival. The city had voted to seal off the downtown area during the festival to encourage visitors to stroll down the road to the local shops and not have to fight the summertime traffic. Maggie had to admit that the plan seemed to be effective. Store owners had displayed merchandise outside their shops, and throngs of people surrounded the tables. As they neared home, Maggie was thankful June was holding down the fort at the shop so she had one less thing to worry about tonight.

They arrived at Sedgwick Manor, the magnificent nineteenth-century Colonial Revival mansion that Maggie now called home. Her late aunt had lived in the three-story house, which was sided in clapboard as was common for the seaside town. Painted a pale yellow with white trim and black shutters, the home was stately and welcoming at the same time.

Together they climbed the front steps to the porch flanked by large columns, and Maggie unlocked the door, which featured a decorative stained glass design in the center panel. Inside, she flipped on the light switch, bringing the Swarovski crystal chandelier to life above them. Sparkling lights danced on the walls and reflected into even the deepest corners of the foyer, casting out shadows.

Emily closed the door, and Maggie secured it after her.

"Why don't I make some popcorn?" Emily suggested.

"That would be perfect," Maggie replied, remembering all the times they'd shared popcorn while Emily was growing up. "I'll be in the office."

Maggie took the carpetbag from Emily and headed to the office.

Every time she entered the room and spotted the flame mahogany pedestal partners desk with its embossed leather blotter, memories of Aunt Evelyn came rushing back. When Maggie had been a child, she had loved snuggling with books in an overstuffed chair placed across from that very same desk while her aunt completed paperwork for the antiques shop.

A contented sigh slipped out. Maggie had come so far from her childhood books to running the antiques shop herself. She set the carpetbag on the desk and pulled the early-twentieth-century embossed desk lamp closer to shine on the bag. Hoping she'd find something on it or stashed inside that would provide a lead on Ike's death, she ran her fingers over every inch of the exterior. Finding nothing out of the ordinary, she opened the middle clasp on the top of the bag and ran her hands over the silk lining. Nothing.

Emily entered the room, bringing with her the scent of freshly popped popcorn. She set a tray that held a large bowl of popcorn and two tall glasses of ice water on the desk. "What are you doing with the bag?"

Maggie explained her actions.

"You sound disappointed." Emily stuffed a handful of popcorn into her mouth.

Maggie dropped into the chair. "A bit, I guess, but I didn't really expect that solving the mystery would be as easy as finding a lead hidden in the bag."

Emily swallowed. "Mind if I take a peek?"

"Go ahead. I'll get started on looking up Ike." Maggie opened her laptop. Once connected to the Internet, she typed *Ike Wynne* into a search engine, then sat back to enjoy the familiar way her daughter's face scrunched up when she was concentrating on a task.

Emily's tongue peeked out at the corner of her mouth, and a look of determination claimed her face. Suddenly, her head popped up. "You're right. The bag doesn't seem to be hiding anything, unfortunately."

Search results appeared on the computer screen, catching Maggie's attention. "Maybe these links will give us something to go on."

Emily grabbed another handful of popcorn and joined Maggie. She munched for a few moments and then said, "The third one down looks promising."

Maggie clicked on the link and was taken to a website for a private investigator named Ike Wynne. "Do you think the victim was a PI?"

Emily pointed at the screen. "Click on the 'About' page and maybe there will be a picture."

Maggie selected the link, which held photos of a business storefront in Portland and information about Ike having been a police officer for five years, but there was no picture of the man himself.

"Darn," Maggie said, her mind already working through the reasons why the site didn't contain a picture.

"I suppose it makes sense that a PI wouldn't want his picture on his website, or people might recognize him when he followed them." Emily popped the last bit of her handful of popcorn into her mouth.

Maggie grabbed a fistful herself and munched on it as she thought about her next course of action. "I have his address from his registration form. If by chance he works out of his house, it should match the office address listed here." She got her notepad and compared the address on it with the one shown on the screen. "It doesn't match."

"Give me the address and I'll use a map site to see if the office and his house are located close together." Emily dusted the salt from her fingers and took over the laptop.

Maggie rattled off Ike's home address and enjoyed more popcorn as Emily worked her magic.

"They're within five miles of each other," Emily announced.

"This might be the right guy, but it's not certain by any means."

Emily snapped her fingers. "I'll search for an image of Ike as a police officer, and then you can compare that to the guy you saw tonight."

"Great idea," Maggie said, thankful for the suggestion.

Emily typed on the keyboard, then swiveled the laptop toward Maggie to display several photographs.

In the middle of the results, Maggie saw a man dressed in uniform. She clicked the picture, and as it opened, she held her breath. The image sharpened and a bolt of adrenaline shot through her veins. She looked up at Emily. "It's him. The victim. He was a cop and then a PI."

Emily's eyes were alive with excitement. "What's next?"

"All I need to do now," Maggie said, her mind whirring with possibilities, "is figure out why a PI was in Somerset Harbor buying antiques, and more importantly, whether or not he was buying them for our elusive killer."

5

The next morning, Maggie walked across the school parking lot beneath the bright sun. The usual cooling breeze from the ocean had all but disappeared. The day was predicted to be a scorcher, and she wanted to get all her work done as early as possible.

She stifled a yawn as she drew near the portable classroom. It was way too early to be up and preparing to clean the gym after a long night of tossing and turning. Unfortunately, the gym wasn't air-conditioned, and her friends would suffer if they postponed the cleanup.

But first she had to make a quick stop.

She approached the blood-spattered patch of gravel near the entrance of the portable classroom and paused to look around. She searched the immediate area, but seeing nothing amiss, she got down on her knees and shined the light from her cell phone into the dark space behind the white lattice skirting of the trailer.

"Why am I not surprised to find you here?" James's voice sounded from above her. Startled, she dropped her phone.

"Goodness! You scared me." She peered up at him, squinting into the rising sun.

He frowned at her. "What if I'd been the killer, returning to the scene of the crime?"

"Then you wouldn't be very smart, now would you?" Maggie joked as she picked up her phone and brushed dirt off the knees of her jeans.

"I suppose you have a point."

"And what was yours? Your point, I mean."

James sighed, clearly frustrated. "That you need to be aware of your surroundings and not let the latest mystery completely consume you."

"I'll try, but I want to get to the bottom of this as soon as possible—*if* it's possible. I guess I let that desire take over and got sidetracked from everything else."

He tipped his head toward the gym. "You mean like forgetting about our friends waiting inside the gym?"

"Exactly." She shoved the phone into her pocket and hurried toward the gym door.

She found Daisy, Ina, Ruth, and Liz all standing in a circle near a refreshment table topped with muffins and drinks from The Busy Bean. They'd been deep in conversation, but the minute she and James came in, the conversation stopped, and they turned to stare at her.

She suspected they had been talking about Ike and speculating on the reason for his murder. Joining the small group, she braced herself for their questions, wishing she had some answers. Other than a game plan for the day, which included delving deeper into Ike's background and trying to discover the purpose of the sprockets, she'd come up with nothing that would help them understand why Ike had been killed.

"About time you rolled out of bed." Daisy wrinkled her nose and grinned. "Help yourself to some goodies before we get to work." Her canary-yellow shirt was in keeping with her vibrant personality, and a vivid red bandana covered her hair to keep it out of her way.

Maggie settled her tote bag on the floor nearby and filled a paper cup with coffee. She eyed lemon muffins with crumbly glazed tops, raspberry scones with the bright red berries marbling the pastry, and cinnamon rolls with sticky caramel drizzled over them. She reached out a hand to pick up a cinnamon roll, then shoved it back into her pocket instead. She'd been indulging in too many sweets lately. Anyway, she'd soon be plenty excited by investigating the murder; she didn't need the sugar buzz on top of that.

Steaming cup in hand, she returned to her friends. "Sorry I'm late. I called the antiques dealers this morning to make sure they didn't want to pull out of the sale, given what happened here last night."

"Do they?" Ruth asked as she took a bite of one of the lemon muffins.

"Not the ones I talked to. Two of them didn't answer, so I'll go by their shops when we finish here." Maggie chose not to go into details of her phone conversations, but the truth was she'd had to reassure several of the shop owners that the murder was unrelated to the 25-Mile Antiques Sale. She took a sip of the rich Colombian brew and smiled at her friends. "Thank you all for coming back to help clean up."

She didn't have to mention the reason why the cleanup hadn't occurred last night as planned. The unanswered questions of Ike's death still hung in the air, and the best way to deal with the mood was to get everyone working.

"No need to thank us," Ruth said. "What do you need us to do?"

"Would you pack up the auction supplies and forms in case we have an auction again next year?" Maggie said to Ruth. "Though I suspect the committee might vote not to include an auction again after last night."

"Hey," Ruth protested, squeezing her arm. "You don't know that. They agreed to continue on with this year's sale, and that's a good sign."

James poured a cup of coffee. "I was wondering about that."

"They called an emergency meeting last night," Ruth said.

"The consensus was that although some people might find continuing with the sale to be insensitive, we'll disappoint so many others who've traveled a long distance if we don't carry on with the event as planned."

"Makes sense to me," Daisy said. "Besides the murder, everything has gone like gangbusters."

"Yes." Ina nodded encouragement. "You did a fabulous job planning, Maggie."

"And executing," Liz said, and then she quickly clapped a hand over her mouth, clearly distraught by her poor choice of words.

"Nice one, Liz." Daisy laughed.

Maggie patted her shoulder. "It's okay, Liz. I know what you meant, and it means a lot to me."

Ruth jumped in. "The auction raised a few thousand dollars for the historical society, so I'd say it was a huge success. We can only pray that the committee agrees to hold another auction in the future and that Maggie will once again chair it and the antiques sale too."

"I appreciate your support," Maggie said, touched.

"We're happy to help you, hon." Daisy's lips curled up at the corners, her vivid red lipstick accentuating her perfectly white teeth. "But we're also going to grill you for details on what you've learned about the man who was murdered."

"Yes, we all want to hear any updates." Ruth pushed up her glasses, and her inquisitive gaze settled on Maggie. "I've already told everyone about the man I saw last night, but have you heard anything more about him or the murder?"

Maggie shook her head. "Nothing I can relate yet. I don't have any facts."

Liz clutched her hand against her chest and peered at Ruth. "What did the man you saw look like?"

"Six feet. Blond hair. He wore a Portland Sea Dogs cap and a blue T-shirt, which he filled out with a very formidable build." Ruth shuddered. "I still can't believe I might have seen the killer."

Liz's eyes widened. "Do you really think that guy's the murderer?"

Ruth shrugged. "The man was arguing with Ike shortly before he was found dead."

"We can't jump to any conclusions," Maggie pointed out. "We need more information."

"I can tell you that the medical examiner has confirmed the manner of death was consistent with being hit on the head with a metal object such as one of the large sprockets," James said. "However, without the item, he can't be certain that a sprocket killed Ike."

Maggie blinked. "How did you . . . ?"

"I have my sources too," James said with a grin.

"Then I suppose we should all be asking if *you've* heard anything else."

James shook his head.

"No mention of Lavinia Taylor?" Maggie pressed.

"Who's that?" Ruth asked.

"Her name is stamped on a leather label on the bottom of the antique carpetbag I bought."

"Before you ask if I knew her, I'm old, but I'm not that old," Ina said with a wink, and the group shared a much-needed laugh. Maggie had a special fondness in her heart for Ina and loved how the older woman could poke fun at herself.

"If the bag is from the 1800s, that means Lavinia could have lived in this area back then." Ruth's strong voice cut through the residual merriment. "But I've looked through a ton of historical records over the years, and I don't remember her name."

The other women murmured in agreement.

"I'd be glad to research the historical society archives for any reference to her," Ruth offered. "But it'll have to wait until after the festival is over."

Maggie beamed at her no-nonsense friend who could always be counted on to take action. "Thank you, Ruth. If I haven't solved this mystery by then, I'd appreciate your help. In the meantime, I'm also going to look into the possibility of her having lived near Pelican Cove, since the carpetbag was donated by the antiques shop there."

"And we can all ask around town," Liz added. "I'll stop by The Quilt Shop to update Fran, and I'm sure she'll ask all of her customers."

"And you know I've already been asking my customers what they know about the murder." Daisy planted a hand on her hip. "I'll add Lavinia to my questions."

"Has your gossip produced any leads?" James asked in jest. He and Daisy were always teasing each other.

"I'll have you know I heard . . ." Daisy's voice contained the hint of drama she often applied liberally to her stories.

The group mock-groaned in unison.

"Okay, fine," she pouted. "I *won't* tell you then that the police have issued an alert for the man Ruth described."

"Not surprising," James said.

"I think the best thing we can do now is clean up this mess and get involved in the festival so we don't have to think about the murder any longer," Liz said with authority.

"But you'll still be thinking about it, right, Maggie?" Ina asked.

"Of course, but there's no need for everyone else to think about something so unpleasant." Maggie clapped her hands, the sound echoing to the rafters. "Let's get started, shall we?"

She handed out assignments, and the cleanup began. Maggie and James strode to a storage room at the back of the gym to get the metal racks for the rental chairs. They each selected a rack and pushed it toward the middle of the gym. Maggie's rack squeaked with each turn of the wheels, making her think of old machinery, which in turn made her think of the sprockets.

"I wish we knew what the sprockets were for," she said to James. "Knowing their purpose might help us connect them to the carpetbag, if indeed they are connected."

"You mean because Ike was trying to buy both items?"

"Yes." She pulled the rack to a stop.

James lined up his rack next to hers. "One of my contractor friends is into industrial antiques and might have some insight about the sprockets. He lives in Pelican Cove. I could arrange for you to meet with him."

"That sounds perfect."

"I'll call him right now." James dug out his phone and dialed.

As he connected with his friend, Maggie crossed the gym to the maintenance closet. The moment she opened the door, the familiar odor of cleaning chemicals assaulted her senses. She sorted through the jam-packed closet and selected the cleanest dust mop, then gave the fluffy mophead a thick coat of dusting spray.

James came to the door, his hand cupped over the phone. "My friend—his name's Gary Keel—is free this afternoon. Any chance you can meet him around two thirty at The Busy Bean?"

Maggie mentally ran through her responsibilities for the day. She might have to juggle lunch breaks at Carriage House Antiques, but a meeting with Gary was too important to miss. "Two thirty would be perfect."

James turned his attention back to his call, and she took the dust mop to the far side of the room. She hoped that by the time she reached the middle of the gym, the others would have stacked the rental chairs and moved them to the door to load into Harry's truck for return.

She pushed the mop across the gleaming hardwood floors and soon noticed Ruth following her lead with another dust mop on the other side of the space. She was thankful for Ruth's help and friendship. Maggie loved that the older woman was so knit into the fabric of the town that she was a fount of information about the local residents and way of life.

Maggie freshened the mop with spray and then continued covering long swatches of the floor. She ran the mop along the closed set of bleachers and noticed a humming noise sounding from underneath them.

She paused to listen.

Nothing. She had probably imagined it. She lifted the dust mop and turned.

The buzz sounded again, like a vibration. She got down on her knees to look under the aged wood but saw nothing in the shadows. She dug out her cell phone and aimed the light under the bleachers. The beam illuminated another cell phone.

Of course. She should have recognized the sound as a phone vibrating against the floor, but why would she have suspected that a phone would be under there?

She thought for a moment. Ike had been talking on a phone during the auction, and Officer Linton said they hadn't found one on him. *Is it possible? Could this be Ike's missing phone?*

The vibrating continued, each hum building Maggie's excitement. Hoping not to find any spiders, she slipped her hand into the space. The top of her hand rubbed along the wood.

Drat. Her hand wouldn't fit in the narrow space. She needed something to fish out the phone. Maggie turned, searched the immediate area, and caught sight of the dust mop she'd leaned against the bleachers. *Perfect.*

She grabbed the handle and shined her light under the bench again. She inserted the wood pole and coaxed the phone—along with several dust bunnies—out from under the seats. She reached out for it but then remembered the crime shows she watched. If this was indeed Ike's phone, then she shouldn't touch it with her bare hands. She nudged it back under the bench for safekeeping and ran across the room to a box of supplies they'd used for the auction.

"Hey there," Ruth said as she swept past. "What's the rush?"

"A lead! I might have a lead on Ike." Maggie dug through the box and found cotton gloves used for handling antiques.

Ruth stood watching as Maggie raced past again, and then she heard the tap of Ruth's tennis shoes following her.

Maggie dropped to the floor, grabbed the now-silent phone with gloved fingers, and woke it up. "Six missed calls," she said. "All since Ike left the building last night. The last two were moments ago."

The phone suddenly vibrated in Maggie's hand. Startled, she fumbled with the phone and barely managed to catch it before it hit the floor. The buzzing continued, and she didn't know what to do.

Think, think, think. Hurry.

If she answered, she might wind up talking to the killer, and she could mess up the investigation. But if she didn't answer, she might miss out on the perfect opportunity to identify Ike's assailant.

She had only seconds to decide.

6

Uncertainty gripped Maggie. She had very few rings left before the call would roll to voice mail . . .

She blew out a breath and connected to the call. Holding the phone next to her ear, she didn't speak, hoping the caller would somehow identify him- or herself.

"Ike? You there?" a gravelly male voice asked.

She didn't respond.

"Ike?"

She couldn't continue her silence or the caller would hang up. "Ike lost his phone last night, and I just found it. My name's Maggie Watson. Who is this?"

"I'm . . . you shouldn't . . . don't . . ." Silence followed.

"Don't what?" Maggie asked.

When there was no reply, she waited, feeling time tick by as slowly as a barnacle inching across one of the boats in the harbor.

One second. Two. Three. Four. Five.

She held out the phone and peered at the screen. The call had been disconnected.

"What happened?" Ruth's eyes were wide with interest.

"I think he hung up." Maggie stared at the phone. "Should I try calling him back?"

"Maybe we should notify the police and let them handle this."

Maggie wasn't sure she wanted to call them yet. She scrolled to the most recent call on the call history and hit redial. The phone rang five times before a recorded message started playing. She held her breath, waiting for the person to identify himself, but the recording told her that the phone's owner hadn't set up his voice mail system. She didn't know who she'd called, and she also couldn't leave a message.

"Maggie?" Ruth asked. "Should I call the police station?"

Maggie nodded, but instead of waiting with Ruth while she made the call, she crossed over to the refreshment table and sat. If the police were on the way, she only had a short window of opportunity to look at the phone and glean any leads she could from it. She grabbed a notepad and pen from her tote bag, then started tapping through the phone. She reviewed the contact list but found it empty. She opened the photo gallery to see if Ike had taken any pictures with the phone. There were none. Next she moved to the email account, but he'd never set it up. She selected the call log and wrote down the phone number she'd previously dialed. She looked for any other recent calls but found none.

She sat back and frowned, then double-checked for outgoing calls. *Nothing.* Either no calls had been made from this phone or Ike had deleted them. She looked up and saw James striding across the gym toward her.

"What's going on?" he asked.

She explained about finding the phone and the call. "There's only one number listed in the call history. I think Ike only used this phone to talk to the man I spoke to."

James leaned against the table. "He could have cleared out the history."

"True, but the phone doesn't have any other personal information in it either. Like the owner's name, emails, photos, things like that."

"It could be a new phone."

"Still, who doesn't have at least one of those things on their phone these days? Even a new one. Especially guys like Ike who are in their early thirties. I have a hard time believing this was his first phone, and the phone company will usually transfer items you want to keep from your old phone to a new one."

"True." James's forehead creased like he was pondering the latest development. "Maybe you shouldn't draw too many conclusions until after the police look at the phone."

"They're great at their jobs, but they aren't going to share details they discover." Maggie looked around the room, hoping to find the answer, but all she saw was Daisy coming toward them.

"You never know," James said. "Things have a way of coming out in small towns."

"What things?" Daisy asked.

"See?" James grinned. "Daisy's the perfect example."

"Somehow I think you're having a laugh at my expense." Daisy's full lips gathered into a pout.

Maggie knew Daisy was joking, but she explained the situation anyway.

"Well, shoot," Daisy said. "All you have to do is tell me what you want to know, and I'll ask around."

"My point exactly." James grinned at Daisy.

She swatted her hand at him, and he responded with a quirk of his mouth. Normally Maggie enjoyed their lighthearted bantering, but today her mind was focused on Ike. She turned her attention back to the phone as Daisy and James joked, but their good humor evaporated when Officer Linton opened the door.

His gaze traveled the space, and when it landed on Maggie, he made a beeline for her. "I hear you found a phone that you think belonged to Ike Wynne."

"Yes." She held up the phone. "When I answered it, the man on the other end said Ike's name, so the odds are good that it was his phone."

"You answered it?" Officer Linton crossed his arms.

"Before you say anything about sticking my nose into police business," she said, "when I found the phone, I had no way of knowing who it belonged to. Then I remembered you'd said Ike's phone was missing, so I didn't touch it without my gloves. And I didn't just snatch it up and answer it. I thought about what I should do. I decided my best course of action was to answer, because I figured whoever was calling might never call back again."

"Hmm." Officer Linton dug latex gloves from his pocket, snapped them on, and took the phone.

"You're not going to find anything of value on it," she said. "I've already looked through it. The only thing on there is the phone number from the incoming call, and you'll also see I dialed that number back after our call was disconnected."

His eyebrows knit together in a deep furrow. "Tell me about the conversation."

She was careful to relay the brief conversation word for word.

He nodded, then turned his attention back to the phone and tapped his finger on the screen. "Hopefully this phone number will pan out."

"What do you mean by 'pan out'?" Daisy asked.

"I mean lead us to the owner."

Daisy tilted her head, reminding Maggie of a puppy casting a quizzical look at its owner. "Why wouldn't you be able to find out the details of the person who owns this one?"

Officer Linton focused on Daisy, a hint of amusement in his expression. "If Ike was engaged in nefarious activities, this phone could be what we in the police world call a burner phone."

Daisy frowned. "Now you've really confused me."

"What I mean is that it could be a prepaid phone. You can purchase these phones in most convenience stores and use them without providing any contact information to the phone company. You simply pay in advance for minutes and data and then buy extra blocks to load onto the phone as needed. You can pay cash for the phone and usage so there's no way to trace the phone back to a particular individual."

"Sneaky," Daisy said.

"And common. They can also be used by people who don't like phone contracts or have small budgets, but when a criminal is planning illegal activities with other criminals, they don't want anyone to trace that information back to them, should their phone be found."

"So you think Ike was a criminal?"

"I didn't say that, Daisy." Officer Linton sighed. "And please don't tell your customers that I did." He eyed her. "Am I clear?"

"Crystal," she replied, but Maggie doubted she would heed his warning.

"Sounds like you think the man who called Ike's phone has a prepaid cell too," Maggie said, drawing his attention from Daisy.

"Could be." The officer eyed Daisy again. "Note, I said it *could be*, not that it *is*."

"I hear you, Robert, but what *is* isn't often all that interesting, and I have a reputation to uphold." Daisy patted her scarf and batted her lashes at Officer Linton until his lips curved up, albeit a fraction.

"Don't worry," James said to the officer. "She's not singling you out. She does this to all of us."

Daisy somehow managed to manufacture an innocent expression.

"Is it too much to hope that you'll share information about Ike with me?" Maggie asked. "Things like his occupation, or if his record search turns up any prior criminal offenses?"

"You know that as much as I'd like to help you out, I can't do that, Maggie."

She grinned. "I know, but I have to keep trying."

"Yes, you do." He shook his head. "Now that we've located Ike's phone," he continued, "I need to ask you to leave the building so we don't disturb any evidence even more than we already have." He pulled out the small notepad where he often jotted case-related information. "If you'll excuse me, I have a few follow-up questions for Ruth."

He strode away, and it took all of Maggie's self-control not to trail after him and listen in on their conversation. She gathered up her things and slung her tote bag over her shoulder. As she left with the rest of her friends, she made a mental note to ask Ruth later about the conversation.

Outside, Maggie shielded her eyes from the searing sun. "I'll let you all know when Officer Linton says we're allowed to finish our cleanup."

"Let's not forget we're all meeting for lunch today," Liz announced.

"Hmm, I don't remember an invite to lunch," James said.

"It was only the ladies of the historical society," Liz said pointedly, "but consider yourself invited now."

"If it's gonna be girl talk . . ."

"Oh no you don't," Daisy said. "You wanted to come to lunch and now you're coming to lunch. You'll have to put up with the girl talk."

Maggie checked her watch. "I need to head over to Grandma's Antiques to talk to the owner, but I should be back in plenty of time."

They split up, and Maggie slid into her car to make the drive along the coastline. She lowered the windows, letting the salty sea air blow through the space and wash out the heat that had built up from being parked in the bright sun.

At Carol's shop, Maggie headed up the boardwalk to the entrance, her sandals snapping on the weathered wood. The police officer from yesterday stood guard out front, and he nodded to Maggie. She hoped he was simply following through on his promise to keep an eye out for Carol and that his presence didn't mean Carol had endured another break-in.

"Have you made any progress on finding the person who broke into Carol's shop?" Maggie asked.

He cocked an eyebrow and lifted his hat to scratch his full head of ginger hair. "You seem awfully interested in this break-in."

"I'm concerned for Carol's well-being."

"There's no need to worry yourself. Our department is handling things, and Carol's fine." He smiled, creasing freckled cheeks.

She could tell he meant it as a way to fend off additional questions. "I'm glad to hear that. Have a good day," she said and slipped into Grandma's Antiques.

Maggie glanced around the space and saw that nothing had changed except that the items for the auction were gone. She noted how dark the lighting was and that the space appeared overcrowded with antiques. Maggie preferred brighter, less cluttered spaces, but Carol ran a successful business, so her customers clearly didn't mind.

On the way to the counter where Carol stood, Maggie paused to look at a lovely display of antique crosses. She fingered a Victorian book chain necklace. The chain boasted a unique blend of cushion-type links with engraved tops and chased sides with flat engraved links. A beautiful gold cross hung from the chain with a stone cameo set at the center of the crossbar.

Carol walked over to Maggie. "It's a lovely piece, isn't it? I bought it from a sweet older lady whose husband bought it for her on a trip to Paris. He passed away twenty years ago, and she's on a fixed income now. What with money not going as far as it used to, she had to sell this piece for much-needed cash. She hated parting with the necklace, but you know how it goes . . ."

Maggie nodded as Carol chattered on. She'd had no idea Carol was such a talker. She took one last look at the necklace, and as she considered buying it, she spotted the price tag—$425. She had to resist gulping; she'd never paid that much for a piece of jewelry in her life.

". . . and I guess it's just been a crazy year for everyone," Carol finally finished, looking expectantly at Maggie.

"How did your day go yesterday?" Maggie asked, not only because she was honestly interested in how the 25-Mile Antiques Sale had impacted Carol's business but also to give Carol an opening to share whether anything else suspicious had happened after the break-in.

"I'm so glad I listened to you and participated in the event," Carol gushed. "I had a record sales day yesterday. I sold furniture, jewelry, glassware, and primitive pottery. Oh, and dishes and linens. Pretty much everything I marked on sale." She jabbed a finger at the counter that was covered with various small items and a stack of big red sale tags. "So I'm marking down a whole new grouping now, and I'm hoping to top that today if I—"

"How wonderful," Maggie interrupted kindly but firmly.

"I hope other shops are doing as well. If this becomes an annual event, you can count on me to participate."

Maggie's heart warmed for a moment, but as Carol rambled on about what she'd do differently next year, the reality returned that this could be the one and only 25-Mile Antiques Sale.

"Oh, about the auction," Carol continued. "I wasn't able to attend last night. My son, you see. His wife is pregnant and not feeling well. And my son can't cook a lick, so I made them dinner, and then he wanted to show me their ultrasound pictures, and—well, you know how things get out of hand, and before you know it, you've run out of time." She pulled in a long breath, then added on the exhale, "How did the auction go?"

"You haven't heard, then?" Maggie asked.

"Heard what?" Carol's eyes were wide.

Maggie told her about Ike.

"Oh my stars!" Carol's hand flew to her mouth, and she stared at Maggie for a moment. "My, oh my, oh my. Murdered, *really*? The poor, poor man. And you said he bought one of my lots?" She shot a worried look around her shop. "Do you think it has to do with me? Or with the break-in? Oh, this is terrible. Just terrible. I wonder if I should go out and tell the officer—"

"Calm down, Carol," Maggie said gently. "We have no reason to believe the murder is connected to your shop."

"But the sprockets—what happened to them? Why are they missing?" Carol's face had paled, and Maggie worried the woman might pass out.

Maggie gestured at a lovely vignette with a pair of Louis XVI parlor chairs. Made of mahogany with a lyre back and carved details, they were clearly from the late 1800s and appeared to have their original blue velvet cushions. "Can we sit down?"

"Yes, that sounds like a good idea." Carol dropped into the nearest chair and twisted her hands together in her lap. "If this has to do with those sprockets . . . I . . . oh my! But no, that can't be right. They weren't worth hardly anything."

"Where did you get them?"

Carol stared ahead, her gaze worried. "I bought them from an older gentleman. He came in about a month ago with the carpetbag and the sprockets. He said he found the items in his attic. He thought they might have some connection to his family since they've lived in that house for a few generations, but he hadn't seen them before and didn't know anything else about them. I only bought the sprockets because I wanted the bag, and he insisted on selling all three items together, so I made him a deal for the lot."

"And you didn't know him?"

She shook her head. "He doesn't live in town, nor is he a regular customer."

"Did he say why he was selling them?"

"The same reason most people sell off their cherished posses-sions. He'd fallen on hard times and had chosen things from the attic that had no sentimental value to him. He also said he was prepared to sell his house if he had to, but I hoped he wouldn't have to do that. He was such a kind gentleman."

"That's so sad. Did you get any contact information from him?" Maggie interjected.

"No."

"Could you describe him to me?"

"Sure, I remember him well because he had this odd mark on his right cheek. I kept thinking it looked like the state of Florida, especially when he smiled." The corner of her mouth turned up, but then straightened again. "I'd guess he was over seventy . . . I mean, I'm sixty-three, and he was older for sure. Much more wrinkled at least, but maybe he was a fisherman. You know how daily exposure to those harsh sea winds can age a person. Oh, and he was short. Thinning gray hair. Round belly. He smelled like mints."

Maggie dug out the picture of Ike that she'd found on the Internet and printed. "Have you ever seen this man in your shop?"

Carol lifted a pair of reading glasses hanging from an antique sterling silver chain around her neck and perched them near the end of her pug nose. She took the picture from Maggie and studied it closely.

She looked up, her eyes troubled above the narrow lenses. "I remember him. He was in last week."

"Do you know which day?"

She tapped her chin and looked up at the ceiling, which

was covered in decorative tin tiles. "Thursday. Yes, Thursday. I remember because right after he left, the shop owner from next door came in, and we went to Willie's Seafood for our weekly lunch. Have you ever been to Willie's place? He only serves fresh seafood, and his chowder is to die for. I get it even on a hot summer day like today. Oh, gosh, now I want a bowl."

"Do you remember what this man was looking at that day?" Maggie asked, trying to get the conversation back on track.

"Come to think of it, he asked about the carpetbag and the sprockets. I had them on display for the auction." She jumped to her feet, rushed to the front of the shop, and stopped near a thick wood-wrapped column with shelves. "I had them here on the shelves, and he spent a good bit of time looking at them, but he didn't act weird or anything. He knew about the auction, and I thought he was probably a guy going from shop to shop to get a good look at all of the lots before the event so he could bid on the ones he liked."

"Could be," Maggie said, but now she couldn't help but wonder if Ike was the person who'd broken into Carol's shop to try to steal the bag and sprockets. "Could I get a look at the video files from your security cameras for that day?"

Carol nibbled on her lip and acted frightened again. "Are you really good at solving mysteries?"

"I do seem to have a knack for it, and I've been lucky enough to solve a few."

"And the video? It will help you find the killer and the person who broke into my shop?"

"I hope so."

Carol waffled for a few moments, then gave a firm nod. "I'll call my younger son who installed the system and get a copy of the files from that day and from the night of the break-in for you."

"How long do you think that will take?" Maggie tried to sound patient; she didn't want to spook Carol into deciding against handing over the files.

"I can try to have it to you when you stop by tomorrow morning, but it depends on my son's schedule. He travels a lot for business. He's a software engineer, and he makes frequent trips to visit the companies he works for." She took a deep breath.

Maggie took advantage of the opening. "Would it be a terrible imposition to ask you to call him now so I know what to expect?"

"Not at all." Carol wound through the tight aisles to pick up a cordless handset from the counter.

Maggie got up and meandered around the shop, noticing the angles of both of the security cameras. Carol had said yesterday that the intruder only covered one of the cameras, and Maggie was hoping the file she received for the other camera would show her a glimpse of the culprit.

Carol concluded her conversation and hung up. "Good news. He's in Portland. He'll drive over after work tonight, and I'll have the file for you in the morning. I had to promise to bake him an angel food cake—it's his favorite—but that means he'll have to come back to eat it, and I'll get to see him again, so it will be worth it."

"Thank you so much, Carol. You may have cracked this investigation wide open."

Carol ran a hand over her hair and preened.

Maggie had only one more question. "The bottom of the carpetbag had a leather tag embossed with the name Lavinia Taylor. Does that name mean anything to you?"

"Taylor . . . I remember seeing that." Carol tapped her chin with the phone's tiny antenna. "Nothing comes to mind. Should it?"

"I thought it might help me find the man who sold the items to you."

"Do you think he's involved in the murder?"

A seventy-year-old man? "Not likely, but he might know why someone else would kill for those sprockets."

Carol gulped, her eyes wide. "Like I said, he didn't know anything about them."

So who had? And why were they worth killing for?

7

Maggie couldn't quit thinking about the mystery man who'd sold the carpetbag and sprockets to Grandma's Antiques as she made her way down the coastal highway to Mills Landing. Despite Carol's ramblings, Maggie thought she still had enough time to visit Tom Owens at Antique Alley to show him the picture of Ike and ask if he'd visited Tom's shop too.

She pulled to the curb by Antique Alley, a white clapboard shop with a long wooden porch painted bright red. On the porch were two white cane rocking chairs and cast-iron urns filled with red flowers spilling over the edges. The sign above the door was made of a hodgepodge of rusty metal letters that on any other type of shop might have looked trashy, but it fit the theme of the antiques shop quite well.

She crossed the porch to the vintage screen door. There was a heavy wood door standing open behind it, and the sound of a fan buzzed in the entrance. As she reached for the door handle, Tom opened it from the other side and came out. Tall and stick thin, his cheeks were ruby red, and he was fanning his face with a French fan embroidered with a beautiful rose and forget-me-not flowers surrounded by an arabesque frame. She suspected retail on the fan was nearly $200, and she would never have been so careless with the mahogany handle.

He dropped into one of the cane rockers and gestured at the other one. "I'll be darned if I'll turn on the air conditioner before noon. Electric bills are going to be the death of my business this summer."

"It has been an unusually warm summer." She settled into

the other rocker, though she hoped not to be there for very long. She still had a lot to do today.

"After the murder last night, I wasn't sure if the sale would continue."

She explained the committee's reasoning for proceeding with the sale.

"I agree with them. It's not like you had any control over what happened in the parking lot." Tom's brow creased. "Was he actually the guy who was bidding against you for that carpetbag?"

"You saw him?"

He nodded.

Maggie's heart rate kicked up. "Do you know him? Have you seen him before?"

"Me? Nah. I didn't recognize him."

"He stopped by Carol Hansen's shop the other day."

"He hasn't been in here, I can assure you of that. And if he lived in Mills Landing, he must have just moved here. I know everyone in town."

Stifling her disappointment at his responses, she pressed on. "The carpetbag had a name embossed on the bottom. Lavinia Taylor. Is that a name you recognize?"

"Maybe, but I can't recall where I heard it." He fanned his face, a pensive look taking hold. Maggie gave him time to think. "I've been involved in researching historical records in the area, and I suppose I could have seen her name then, but I can't be sure."

"The bag was sold to Carol Hansen by an older man. Maybe in his seventies. Short, rotund. Would you know of any Taylors in Mills Landing around that age and fitting his description?"

"I don't know any Taylors, period," Tom said as a pair of women approached his shop. "Time to get back to it." He stood and held the fan over his eyes, shielding them from the blazing sun. "Maybe I'll turn on that air after all. I wouldn't want customers to take off because of the heat."

Maggie rose too. "You have my phone number, right? Just in case you remember anything about the Taylors?"

"Yeah, you gave me your card."

Maggie thanked him for his time. She pondered what to do next as she pulled onto the highway. She certainly needed help in finding as much information as she could about Lavinia Taylor, which meant digging into old records of the area. With Ruth unavailable, who better to help Maggie than the other members of the historical society? They were all busy with the festival too, but not to the extent that Ruth was, so maybe they could find time to help. She'd bring up the subject at lunch and plan from there.

A horn honked behind her, and she realized she'd slowed down nearly to a crawl as she was thinking. She sped up and looked in the mirror again just in time to catch sight of the woman who'd honked at her turning off the road. But her attention soon shifted to a truck she saw roaring toward her car in her rearview mirror. The large gray pickup pulled up within a few feet of her bumper, then fell back before repeating the pattern.

Was the vehicle following her, or did he simply want to pass?

If he *was* following her, she thought it would be prudent to gather as many details as possible about the vehicle. She glanced in the mirror again, noting the truck appeared to be a recent model. The grill was painted a matching color and boasted a black-and-silver decal in the middle. With the large size of the truck, he could have easily run her off the road, but as they continued down the highway, he stayed a good distance back.

She tried to get a look at the driver, but the sun reflected from his windshield, and she couldn't even be sure it was a man. But if it was . . .

Is it Ike's killer?

Her adrenaline kicked up, and she focused on her driving. The two-lane highway had a terrifying drop-off to a craggy shoreline below. At the exit for Somerset Harbor, she sighed with relief and veered her Jetta into town.

The truck trailed after her.

Is he following me?

She looked hard in the mirror, but the bright sun continued to glare off the windshield, leaving her without a view of the driver. She finally reached Shoreline Drive, but with the downtown streets closed due to the festival, she turned onto Wharf Road instead. She slowed for pedestrians strolling across the road, and the truck kept two car lengths between them, which she found odd.

She made her way down the road and passed the school to see if the truck pulled into a parking space so the driver could attend the festival. He continued to follow her. *Enough.* It was time she found out who was driving the truck. In a public place now instead of on the isolated highway, she could afford to take a risk.

When she reached the first available spot that would allow her to escape if needed, she stopped in the road and left her car running. She hopped out, but before she could take more than a few paces, the pickup swung into the other lane and roared past her, sending her stumbling and trying to gain her footing. The driver blew through the intersection, flying past an elderly gentleman with a cane who wobbled dangerously.

Maggie ran to catch hold of the man before he hit the ground. "Are you all right?"

"I'm fine." He shook his head. "These young people need to pay more attention to the rules of the road."

"Young?" she asked with great interest. "Did you see the driver?"

The elderly man pushed up thick glasses and peered at her with gray eyes that were enlarged by his thick lenses. "Briefly."

"What did he look like?"

"White guy. Wore a black baseball cap. Had some kinda logo on it, but I didn't get a good-enough look to make it out."

"Could it have been a *P* like on a Portland Sea Dogs cap?" Hoping it was the same man who'd argued with Ike, she held her breath in wait for the answer.

The older man simply shrugged, and Maggie's excitement dissipated.

"Would you like to report this to the police?" she asked.

He shook his head. "No. Even if we had the plate, they'd just give the guy a ticket and a slap on the wrist." Shaking his head, he toddled off, his cane thumping on the sidewalk.

Maggie quickly asked if anyone nearby had caught the license plate number, but when the drivers she was blocking started blaring their horns, she got back into her Jetta and turned onto a side street. She couldn't be sure the truck was connected to Ike, but if she saw the vehicle again, she'd mention it to the police. Until then, she needed to be careful—extra careful, as she'd promised James.

She drove back to Sedgwick Manor to freshen up for lunch. The moment she walked through the door, she smelled Emily's perfume and suspected her daughter had recently run out the door to relieve June so the shop manager could join the other society members for lunch.

"Hello, Snickers," Maggie said when her loving yet often finicky cat came bounding through the entryway to greet her. "I suspect you're hungry."

He meowed in response, and she walked into the kitchen to pour food into his bowl. He shoved his head under her hand and began wolfing down the food.

"Impatient much?" She chuckled and hurried to her bedroom where she washed up and changed into a sleeveless tank top. In front of the bathroom mirror, she added a touch more makeup than usual.

Snickers came prancing into the room and wound between her legs, rubbing his soft fur against her bare ankles. When she didn't bend over to scratch his neck, he demanded attention with an irritated meow. If ever a cat had sounded indignant, he did.

"Sorry I don't have more time right now, boy, but I have to get ready for lunch."

He meowed again.

"Okay, fine, you're right. I could skip the makeup, but . . ." She'd almost admitted to taking extra care for James, but she stopped before the words escaped. Not that Snickers could repeat them, but saying it aloud made her attraction to James a reality she wasn't yet ready to deal with.

Snickers gave another commanding meow. She relented and bent to stroke her hand over his soft fur, then hurried to the office to grab the carpetbag and place it in a large shopping bag. She wanted to pass the carpetbag around the lunch table to see if her friends had any thoughts about its origins or about Lavinia Taylor.

"Don't worry, Snickers," she said on the way to the sunroom. "I won't forget to come home and feed you dinner."

She left the manor refreshed and ready for lunch, but the sticky heat outside made her feel as if she might instantly melt. She decided to ignore the sun beating down on her and took the path from the manor toward Carriage House Antiques. She paused on the small wooden footbridge that spanned the narrow stream, something she liked to do if she had the time. She took a few deep breaths and listened to the birds chirping in the trees and the soft bubbling of the creek as she gazed over the lush green grass.

The sudden sound of a polka band drifting in from town brought her back to reality, and with a sigh, she shook herself and set off toward her destination. A brisk wind blew in from the harbor and caught the bag, and she gripped it tightly. She slipped into the crowd milling about outside the shop.

She glanced at the long table with a white plastic tablecloth that had been set up in front of Carriage House Antiques. Similar tables were scattered along the streets in town so patrons could rest and sample food from the wonderful dining establishments in the hope that they would stay longer and spend more money.

James sat at the head of the table with June, Fran, and Ruth to his right. An empty chair sat to his left, and Liz and Ina occupied the other chairs. James looked up, caught Maggie's eye, and waved. He never seemed bothered by being the only man at a table filled with women. Others had told her he was a bit of a flirt, but in Maggie's opinion, he was just such a nice guy that women were naturally drawn to him.

Maggie didn't wait for him to pull out a chair for her but took the vacant one. She suspected the other women had intentionally left it empty so she would sit next to him; they were all matchmakers.

"What's in the bag?" Ruth asked in her straightforward tone.

"The carpetbag." Maggie explained her reason for bringing the bag when what she actually wanted to do was take a long drink of the iced tea waiting at her space. "I thought you could look at it now or after we eat and give me any thoughts you might have."

"I'm glad you gave us a choice," Daisy said. "I consider you a dear friend, but I'm not going to let anything interfere with my lobster lunch."

"Hear! Hear!" Fran said, and the group burst into laughter.

Maggie noticed a waitress fighting her way through the crowd as she balanced a tray filled with to-go containers. They'd preordered from The Lobster Quadrille, whose name was taken from *Alice's Adventures in Wonderland*, and the owner had agreed to have a waitress deliver the food to their table. The restaurant made wonderful lobster bisque, but with the summer heat, Maggie had ordered a lobster salad, as had many of the others.

The waitress handed out the containers, and Maggie lifted the lid on her salad. Big chunks of lobster were mixed with grilled corn, scallions, and avocado, all dressed with a light lemon vinaigrette. She quickly offered a silent prayer of thanks for her food and her friends, then slid the fork from its plastic sleeve and dug in.

The lobster paired beautifully with the tangy lemon dressing and the avocado, all of it melting in her mouth and bringing her senses to life. She resisted groaning aloud and savored the mouthful. "The lobster salad is so good."

Liz swallowed a bite. "That's what I have too. So yummy."

"This was a great idea," James said, laying his grilled cod sandwich on his plate. "Good food, good company, and fresh air." He raised his plastic cup. "Here's to Maggie for suggesting it, and to Liz for my belated invite."

Everyone clicked their cups in an informal toast.

"What have you learned about the man who was killed?" Liz asked, forking a large bite of her salad.

"Well, I still haven't been able to confirm this," Maggie said cautiously, "but it looks like he's a private investigator from Portland."

"A private eye!" Ina exclaimed. "What was he doing here, other than trying to buy your bag and the sprockets?"

Maggie swallowed and set down her fork. "That's what I'm trying to find out. I learned this morning that he stopped at Grandma's Antiques in Pelican Cove last Thursday. The owner said he looked at the carpetbag and the sprockets." She dug out Ike's picture and gave it to Liz. "This is what he looked like in case you didn't see him at the auction."

"He was once a police officer too?" Liz asked when she saw the uniform.

"Yes," Maggie said. "Which makes it harder to believe that he'd be into something illegal."

"So why would someone want to kill him?" Ina asked.

"Police officers, or former ones, *can* do bad things," Ruth suggested. "Maybe he was kicked off the force."

"I searched for that kind of information online," James added, "but I couldn't find anything."

Maggie shot him a surprised look. "You did?"

He nodded. "After I left the gym last night. Since you're bound and determined to find his killer, I figured it would be a good idea for me to know the kind of people this Ike might have associated with. I've been trying to get my hands on his client list too. So far I've struck out, but I'll keep trying."

"That's so sweet of you, James," Fran said, and James actually blushed bright red.

To take the attention off him, Maggie switched the subject back to Lavinia. "Ruth volunteered to research Lavinia Taylor, but since she's so busy with the festival, I was wondering if anyone else would have time today to do it."

"Research as in look through old records at the historical society?" Liz asked.

Maggie nodded.

"I have a few hours I could devote to it."

"Me too," Ina offered.

They arranged to meet later, and then the subject changed to excitement for what appeared to be a record-setting crowd filling the street. Maggie was content to finish her salad and listen to her friends.

"June, what is it?" Ina suddenly asked.

Maggie looked at June. Her face was screwed up in concentration. She'd pulled the carpetbag from the plastic bag and had her hand inside the satchel, her focus fixed on it. Her head suddenly popped up, and she met Maggie's gaze.

"You can forget about your other leads for now." Her excited tone captured Maggie's curiosity. "I'm pretty sure I know why Ike wanted this bag so badly."

8

June's face lit with anticipation as she handed the bag back to Maggie. "There's something hidden between the lining and the bottom."

"Hidden?" Maggie's mind was awash with confusion. "Emily and I checked inside the bag last night and didn't feel anything."

"It's thin," June replied. "Barely perceptible."

Maggie ran her fingers carefully over the interior's faded silk lining, pressing harder than she had the last time. But all she detected was the hard bottom and the silk. "I'm not feeling anything."

"Press down near a corner. You can feel the edge of something."

Maggie pushed her fingers into a corner and felt a slight bump. "It's so thin it would have to be paper."

"Or an imperfection in the bottom," James suggested.

June frowned at him. "I'm almost certain there's something inside there."

"There's only one way to find out if she's right," Ina said. "Slice open the lining."

Maggie stared at the decades-old piece and couldn't fathom damaging the fabric on a hunch. "I don't think I could do it."

"What about a seam?" Fran asked. "If there is one, you could open it without ruining the lining."

Maggie checked inside. "The seam runs along the side of the bag."

"Can I look at it?"

Maggie passed the bag across the table.

Fran peered inside. "I'm going to gently turn the lining inside out."

Maggie wouldn't trust herself to mess with the aged silk, but with Fran's textile degree and her extensive sewing experience, Maggie trusted her implicitly.

Fran pressed her lips together as she examined various angles of the fabric, then looked up. "I can open the seam at my shop where I have the right tools to do it."

"That would be wonderful," Maggie said.

"You trust me not to ruin it?"

"Of course. If anyone can do this, it's you."

"Then let's clear the table and go." Fran pushed to her feet.

"Wait!" June protested. "I discovered the hidden item, and I really want to be there to see what it is, but I have to get back to work."

"No problem," Fran said. "I can get my tools, and we can do it at the antiques shop so you can watch."

"Thank you," June said. "I know I probably shouldn't have gotten so invested in this, but I think Maggie's sleuthing is contagious."

"You do spend a lot of time with me." Maggie smiled and stood. "I'll clear your spot, Fran, so you can go pick up whatever you need."

Looking as excited as June, Fran nodded and disappeared into the crowd.

"You all are welcome to join us for the big reveal if you want." Maggie set down the bag to collect their empty containers.

"I have to get back to my duties." Ruth picked up her own lunch containers. "And Liz and Ina are joining me in a few hours to run the raffle."

Ina's lips pursed in a pout. "I wanted to use my go-fast shoes this morning, so I put them on, but now I wish I'd worn stick-in-the-mud shoes so I could stay here and see what you find."

Maggie chuckled.

James rose. "As an alderman, I thought it would be good to take this whole weekend off to help with the festival, so I don't have any official duties until later today. I'd love to see what you find."

"You'll come tell us what it is, right?" Liz asked.

"Of course," Maggie promised. "Before you go, Ruth, could you tell me what Officer Linton was questioning you about this morning?"

"Oh that." Ruth waved a hand. "He wanted to know if I've thought of anything else since last night."

"And have you?"

"Nope."

"Promise me you'll be careful today."

"I don't follow," Ruth said.

"You saw the man arguing with Ike, and he could be afraid you can identify him."

"Oh." Her eyes widened.

"I don't mean to worry you. Just be careful, okay?" Maggie opted not to tell Ruth about the truck that had followed her that morning. No sense in panicking her friend when Maggie couldn't be absolutely certain that the vehicle *had* been following her.

Ruth nodded and then left with Liz and Ina.

"Kind of like the pot calling the kettle black, isn't it?" James said.

"You mean me telling Ruth to be careful?"

He nodded. "Now you know how I feel."

"I can take the bag," June offered when she came back from tossing her items into the trash.

Maggie handed over the carpetbag, then cleaned up the remains of her lunch and Fran's. She and James headed into Carriage House Antiques. The small bell above the door tinkled, and Maggie sighed as cooler air enveloped them.

June had set the bag on the counter and was looking at the computer. Emily stood in the middle of the shop, helping a customer. Maggie overheard her beautiful daughter talking knowledgeably about a seven-inch German doll crafted by

Hermann Steiner. Maggie had enjoyed antiques for years, and she was pleased to have passed along her interest to Emily, who especially loved antique dolls.

"She has the original glass flirty eyes, wig, body, and factory dress." Emily tucked a long strand of hair behind her ear.

"It seems to be in excellent condition. I'll take it," the customer said.

Emily caught Maggie's gaze, and her dark eyes, so like her father's, shone with happiness. Maggie knew she wasn't going to deal in antiques for a career—she was going to nursing school—but a $1,500 sale was something to be proud of.

"Emily's doing a great job. We're lucky to have her this week," June said fondly, and Maggie beamed at her.

Emily escorted her customer toward the counter. Maggie didn't want to seem like a helicopter parent, so she said to James, "We have a lighted magnifying glass in the back. I'll go grab it."

"Why not take the bag back there?" James asked.

"I should stay out here," June answered.

"And I don't want her to miss out on the reveal," Maggie added.

He settled on one of the counter stools. "Watch—with all this fuss, the surprise will end up being paper used to line the bottom or something equally anticlimactic."

"Let's hope not." Maggie strolled through the shop, running a finger over a mahogany English side table with its crossbanded top. She not only liked to look at antiques, especially ones like this one with its tapering fluted legs and spade feet, but she loved to touch the rich wood too.

She slid into the back room, and by the time she'd retrieved the light from their workbench and returned to the front, Emily was saying good-bye to the doll customer and greeting a woman in search of a crystal bowl.

Emily took her to their crystal display near the back of the shop, where June was helping another customer. Maggie clamped the light onto the counter. She felt James watching her from his stool and was so aware of his attention that her hands suddenly felt clumsy. She managed to get the light attached and plugged in as Fran traipsed inside. Maggie positioned the magnifying glass over the bag and turned on the light.

"I thought this might help," Maggie said to Fran.

"Yes, that's great." Fran set a small cloth bag on the counter and took out a tiny seam ripper. "If there's something else you have to do, you may want to do it. I plan to go stitch by stitch so I don't ruin the fabric, and it'll take some time."

"I don't have anything more important than this."

"Then feel free to stay, but please don't hover over my shoulder," Fran said shyly. "I'm already anxious enough, and being watched won't help." She settled on a stool, turned the bag on its side, and pulled out the lining.

The doorbell tinkled as a silver-haired man with stooped shoulders entered.

"I'll go help this customer," Maggie said.

"And I can take a look around at the new antiques," James offered as he rose to his feet. Maggie knew he'd already seen everything she'd recently added, as he stopped by all the time, but he was being considerate of Fran.

Maggie greeted her customer with a broad smile.

"I'm looking for a copper teakettle," the older man said. "My wife's friend said she saw the one I'm looking for, and I was hoping you still had it."

"I haven't been working in the shop today, but let's check our display." Maggie led the man across the shop, and when she caught sight of the kettle, she hurried ahead to pick it up.

A single handle was fastened to the top with a long arched spout on the front. The copper was worn and dented, and green patina colored the ridges. It had dovetail jointing down the side and a maker's mark on the bottom.

She turned to show the kettle to the customer. "Is this what you were looking for?"

"It's perfect. Silvia is going to be thrilled. It's for our fiftieth anniversary."

Maggie thought the teakettle was special but not something she'd choose for a fiftieth wedding anniversary. Sometimes people, often men, needed guidance when making their selections.

"This is a lovely gift," she said with feeling. "But did you know the traditional gift for a fiftieth anniversary is gold?"

He waved a gnarled hand. "That's for the movies and fancy people. No, we recently moved to a smaller home, and the movers lost a box. Inside was a French teakettle passed down through Silvia's family over the years. She was devastated. This one won't be the same, but it'll make her smile, and with her recent health issues, I'll do just about anything to make her happy."

Maggie was in awe of his love for his wife and felt tears welling up. She gave a crisp nod and blinked them back. "Then let's get this wrapped up for you so you can make Silvia's day special."

Working on the end of the counter opposite Fran, Maggie wrapped the package in white paper. For good measure, she added gold ribbon and a bow while the sweet older man watched her.

"You've got a nice shop here," he said.

"I inherited it from my aunt," Maggie said proudly. "She was an amazing woman." She slid the package across the counter. "Is there anything else I can do for you?"

"Keep this a secret." He lifted a finger to his lips and winked.

Maggie laughed and collected his payment. By the time he departed, June was free to help other customers, and Maggie and James rejoined Fran at the counter.

She looked up. "I think the opening is big enough now for

your hand, Maggie. Let's check it before I rip out more stitches."

Maggie carefully put her hand through the small gap and felt along the bottom. "There are papers in here all right."

June clasped her hands. "I knew it!"

"I can't get them out through this opening though." Maggie gently withdrew her hand. "I'll need you to make it bigger, Fran."

"That I can do." Fran took the bag and applied her small seam ripper again while they waited. After a minute, she passed the bag back to Maggie.

Maggie felt for the bottom again and grasped the edge of the papers. "I think I can roll this up and get it out."

She took her time and rolled the paper—no easy feat, since she was doing it with one hand, blindly, and she had to be careful not to damage it. She got her fingers around the roll and slowly lifted her hand out. When the pages were visible, she said, "Someone grab onto the papers so I don't drop them back inside."

Fran wrapped her fingers around the papers below Maggie's hand, and they took their time withdrawing their discovery so they didn't damage either the papers or the lining.

Maggie gently unrolled the papers and was surprised to see it was only one page folded up. She spread out the paper to reveal a large pencil drawing of a Victorian home. In addition to a line drawing of the elevation of the house that showed its location near a cliff by the sea, the interior floor plan was drawn at the bottom and held the measurements of each room. There was also a horse-drawn carriage with a man and woman in the buggy and a footman in the back, facing away from the couple.

"It's an architectural drawing of a house," James said, looking over her shoulder. "The plan would have been used when building the place."

"Likely from before modern blueprints were invented and commonly used," June said. "That was in the mid-1800s."

"Your knowledge constantly amazes me," Maggie said to her friend, and she meant it.

"Look." June pointed at one of the corners. "The edge has been torn off."

"I suspect that's where the owner's name and address were located," James said.

"Do you think someone wanted to hide that information, or was it damaged over time?" Fran asked.

June inspected the edge. "Hard to tell."

"One thing is clear," Fran said. "The drawing is old. Does anyone have a guess on the age?"

"The house is Victorian," James offered.

"The clothing is Victorian too." June leaned over the drawing, as did Maggie.

The woman wore a high-necked Abbington blouse with a cameo brooch and a long walking skirt. Over the top, she wore a simple duster, and a dark coachman hat sat on her head. The man was drawn in Bowden trousers and a Comstock vest. He also sported a coachman hat and a dark frock coat. A silky puff tie completed the look.

Maggie had seen enough to render an opinion. "If we're going on clothes only, I'd say this is from the Victorian era, from 1837 to 1901."

"I concur," June said. "And judging by the size of the house, plus the clothing and carriage, this couple, if they are based on a real couple, was wealthy."

James tapped the footman. "I suspected as much when I saw the servant."

"Do you think the woman is Lavinia Taylor and the man her husband?" Maggie asked.

"That would make sense," James said. "I don't recognize the house, though, so I doubt it's here in Somerset Harbor."

Maggie bent closer to look at a room in the back of the house with a small symbol drawn in the corner. "Is that a heart-shaped padlock?"

James put the drawing under the magnifying glass. "It's definitely a padlock."

"What in the world could that mean?" Maggie asked. "Was there some sort of secret in that room? Perhaps having to do with love since the lock is shaped like a heart?"

"And why was the drawing hidden in the carpetbag in the first place?" June asked. "I mean, why hide an architectural drawing like this at all?"

"My best guess is that it has to do with this padlock symbol," Maggie said. "We need to learn about locks from the 1800s, and I know just the man who can help."

James pointed at the rough edge on the bottom of the paper. "It could also have to do with this missing corner."

"But what?" Fran asked.

Maggie's mind was already racing ahead to things she needed to do. "I aim to find out."

9

James stared at the drawing as if hoping that eyeballing it would make answers pop off the page. Maggie had been doing the same thing, but the fact of the matter was, if it hadn't hit her yet, it wasn't going to. She wished Fran hadn't needed to return to her quilt shop so soon and June wasn't busy helping a customer. It might prove helpful to have them weigh in with more thoughts about the drawing.

She pushed off her stool. "I'm going to call Erwin Arnett."

"He's the locksmith who's an expert in antique keys and locks, right?" James asked.

Maggie nodded. "He helped me with that key we found in the vase at Christmastime." She dug out her cell phone and dialed.

Erwin answered on the first ring.

"Erwin, it's Maggie Watson."

"Maggie! Please tell me you have another mystery to test my brain."

"As a matter of fact, I do. However, this time it's about a padlock shaped like a heart, and I only have a drawing of it on the sketch of a building design."

"Heart-shaped, you say?"

"Yes, and we think the drawing was created in the 1800s, so I thought you might be able to shed some light on this lock, if it actually exists."

"Heart-shaped locks have been common in a myriad of time periods, so I would need to see the drawing to help narrow it down."

"Hold on," Maggie said. "Let me take a quick picture and text it to you."

At his ready agreement, she grabbed her phone and navigated to the camera. Though the lock was small, as she zoomed in on it, she could see it was as intricately drawn as the people. She snapped a few pictures and sent the best one to Erwin.

"Okay," he said. "What I can tell from this picture is that the lock has a movable key cover, and it's thick and less refined, both of which are characteristics of nineteenth-century locks. But that's all I can tell you."

"How about what a lock like this might be used for and why it might be on a house drawing?"

"I have no idea why it would be on the drawing. I've never seen a drawing with a lock on it before. And without knowing the actual size of the lock, I'd be speculating as to its use." Erwin sighed. "I'm sorry I can't be of more help, but if you find the actual lock, I'd love to take a look at it for you."

She thanked him, and as she put her phone away, she noticed James watching her. "I suppose you got the gist of that call."

"The drawing isn't enough for him to be of any help."

She nodded.

"Maybe we're coming at this the wrong way." James ran his finger over the drawing, letting it come to rest on the area behind the house. "The house was built overlooking the ocean, and if we assume that it's located nearby, we might have a chance of finding the actual house."

Maggie nibbled on her lip as she gave his idea some thought. "We could take a drive along the coast to Pelican Cove, where the bag was sold. Maybe the house is located there."

"Maybe," he agreed, but his tone was reserved. "But you have to recognize that my theory could be a long shot. The house could have been torn down long ago to make way for commercial development or even a more modern home."

"True, but what harm would it do to take a scenic drive this afternoon? I've finished everything I need to do for the antiques sale, and I have my cell phone if any of the dealers need to contact me. Can you spare the time?"

"Like I said, I'm off all weekend. I'd be glad to take you on a drive after we talk to Gary."

"It's a beautiful day for a drive," June said as she joined them. "You should take the time to enjoy it."

"You don't mind if I leave you here for a bit?" Maggie asked.

June waved a hand. "I've got plenty of customers to keep me busy, and it's nothing I can't handle. And as long as I have a coffeepot and Emily is around to give me a dinner break, I'm good to go."

"I'll be here until six and can help close," Emily said from where she sat on the stool, looking at her phone. "But then I'm heading back to Standish for the fireworks."

Maggie wished Emily could stay longer, but she had acclimated well to college life and had many friends, for which Maggie was grateful.

"Can you take the carpetbag back to the house when you leave?" Maggie asked in case she didn't make it back to the shop that night. For some reason, she didn't like the idea of leaving the bag in the shop.

"Sure, Mom."

"And how about a hug if I don't see you before you go back to school?"

Emily set down her phone, and Maggie pushed to her feet. She held her daughter close, remembering so many wonderful occasions they'd shared in the past.

"You're acting like you won't ever see me again." Emily extracted herself and flashed a look of independence. "I'll be back to visit soon, you know."

"I know," Maggie said with a wink. "But that doesn't mean I won't hug you just as hard then too."

Emily rolled her eyes, but a little smile crossed her lips as she turned her attention back to her phone.

Maggie grabbed her tote bag and looked at James. "Let's go talk to Gary and take that drive."

Outside, the crowd had thinned. She suspected most people had gone to the park for the raffle. Maggie and James made their way down the street to The Busy Bean. They wove between the tables and the people milling about in front of the coffee shop. The cool ocean breeze always whisked over the area, and on hot days locals vied for the outdoor seats. Today was no exception, even though the breeze had disappeared again and the sun was swelteringly hot.

At the door, James turned to her. "Why don't you grab us a table, and I'll wait for Gary outside to make sure he finds the place?"

She didn't mind sitting in the air-conditioned café, so she nodded and he opened the door for her. The nutty aroma of fresh coffee drifted out on the blessedly cool air. Several tables were filled with fellow residents of Somerset Harbor, but an empty table sat in the back where no one would overhear their conversation. She crossed quickly to it and sat down.

Daisy waved from behind the counter, her face flushed and wisps of hair matted on her forehead. As a former beauty queen, she always took great care with her appearance and had looked picture-perfect at lunch, but she'd clearly been working hard in the interim.

"Can I get you anything, hon?" she called out.

"I'll have a glass of ice water. You can bring it when everyone arrives for the meeting."

Daisy arched an eyebrow, looking like she wanted to ask who Maggie was meeting, but she blew a strand from her face instead and turned her attention back to the espresso machine. Maggie checked the beehive clock on the wall. It was time for their meeting. Perhaps Gary had run into issues with traffic?

With the festival in full swing it would not be surprising.

When he finally walked through the door, he looked exactly as Maggie had expected a contractor with an interest in antique sprockets to look. Tall and brawny with wide shoulders, he wore a plaid shirt with the sleeves rolled up, jeans worn thin at the knees, and a baseball cap. His work boots were scuffed and scarred, and he clomped through The Busy Bean next to James, who was dressed in business casual. They were quite the study in contrasts.

When they reached her, James introduced Gary, who removed his cap and stuck it in his back pocket before he shoved out his hand. Maggie grasped it and wasn't surprised by the rough and callused skin.

She gestured at a chair across from her. "Can I get you a cup of coffee or something else?"

"I came from a jobsite, and with this heat, I could drink a gallon of water."

Daisy appeared with her order pad and pencil. "I'll bring you the tallest glass we have. How about a slice of apple pie to go with that?"

"I'd never say no to pie," Gary said eagerly, "and there's nothing more patriotic on this weekend than apple pie."

"Coming right up . . ." Daisy's words fell off, and she gave him a pointed look.

"Gary Keel."

"He's a contractor from Pelican Cove," Maggie added.

Daisy shot her a questioning look. "You planning on remodeling?"

Maggie shook her head but didn't elaborate. She knew Daisy would try to read too much into anything she might say.

"Gary said he's *really* thirsty," James reminded Daisy. "And I'd love a glass of iced tea."

"Okay, fine." Daisy shoved her pencil behind her ear. "I can take a hint."

"Really?" James teased. "Since when?"

She swatted at him, then gave Maggie a look that said, *I'm going now, but you will tell me what this meeting is about later.*

Maggie dug the auction catalog from her tote bag and flipped to the sprocket page for Gary. "I'm sorry we don't have the actual items for you to look at."

Gary took the brochure and pulled off his glasses to hold the picture close. He studied the page, rotated it a few times, and then set it down. "Interesting."

"What?" Maggie asked.

"I've seen the larger sprocket before. It's common to many industrial machines, but the little one is new to me. I'll have to do some research on it to see if I can determine its use."

"That would be great. I'd really appreciate it." Maggie made sure to offer him a thankful smile.

"Trust me. It's no hardship. I love looking into industrial antiques." Gary stared at the brochure again. "The large sprocket has a traditional sawtooth edge, and it's very common, which might make it hard to pin down. But the angle of the teeth on the smaller one is so unique that it should be easier to figure out its use."

Daisy returned with a tray holding drinks for all and a large slice of warm apple pie for Gary, who dug into it and beamed. "I won't forget how good this is. The next time I pass through town, I'll be sure to stop in."

Daisy looked pleased, but then a shrill timer sounded and she rushed back to the counter.

As Gary consumed his pie and downed his water, they chatted about his love of industrial antiques.

After he'd cleaned his plate, he picked up the brochure again. "I'll get going and report back to you as soon as I have anything worth passing on."

"Thanks again," Maggie said and handed him a business card.

After a quick nod, he headed for the door.

"Ready for that scenic drive?" James asked.

"You bet. Not only will it be nice, but it's probably best to get out of here before Daisy grills us about our meeting with Gary. I'd rather the whole town didn't know about this just yet." Maggie gathered her things and waved good-bye to Daisy on their way out.

"Hope you found out what you needed to know," Daisy called after them.

Maggie nodded but hurried outside. She didn't want this particular bit of information to make it into Daisy's daily gossip.

"My car's parked behind my office." James placed his hand on the small of her back, guiding her.

As they negotiated the throng of people, she caught sight of Gary climbing into a truck very much like the one that had followed her that morning. She couldn't see the plate, but she stopped to stare as he drove off.

"What is it?" James asked.

"Gary. He got in a pickup that looks identical to one that followed me this morning."

James locked gazes with her. "You never mentioned being followed."

"That's because I'm still not entirely sure he *was* following me." She paused. "And I knew it would worry you and everyone else."

"Then you know me well, because it does."

She appreciated his concern, but her mind had moved on to wondering if Gary had any connection to the sprockets and Ike's death.

"I recognize that look, and before you go thinking that Gary is somehow involved, he isn't. I've known him for years. He's a good guy."

Maggie chose not to argue about it. She didn't want to

disparage James's friend when she had no solid reason to do so. "We should get going," she said instead and started off again.

Once they were settled in James's classic black Mercedes, he fixed his attention on the road. Maggie appreciated his vigilance, especially with pedestrians scurrying in all directions. He finally merged his car onto the highway, and his attention drifted to the rearview mirror.

Maggie glanced back and spotted a gray pickup truck in the distance. "Do you see the truck behind us?"

He nodded. "It's a Ford F-250, a very common truck. I personally know many guys who own them, and this could simply be a coincidence."

"Or it could be Gary."

James shot her a quick look, then worked the muscle in his jaw.

"Do you know what kind of truck he drives?" she asked.

James shook his head. "I know he bought a new one a few months ago, and I didn't notice what he was driving today."

Maggie looked back again. "If you quickly change our route, we can see if this truck is following us."

"Already on it." At the next exit, he made a last-minute lane change to leave the highway.

Maggie held on and watched out the back window. The truck slammed on its brakes and turned onto the off-ramp just in time, the tires squealing.

"He's following us, all right." James frowned. "I'm going to pull over ahead, and when I do, can you try to get the license plate number?"

"Yes." She jerked a notebook and pen from her tote bag. She glanced over her shoulder and spotted the grill ornament. "It looks like the same truck that followed me this morning."

"Get ready to write down the plate number." James glanced in the mirror, then swerved onto a scenic lookout on the side of the road and slammed on the brakes. The truck had no choice but to drive on by.

Maggie caught the Maine license number and jotted it down. "Got it. I saw a similar truck near the portable schoolroom the night Ike was killed too, but this isn't the same plate number."

"When we get back to town, we'll go straight to the police department and have them run the plate."

"Agreed, though I'm sure they won't tell us who the truck belongs to."

James met her gaze. "It could lead to Ike's killer."

"Which is why I want the information."

"Okay," James said. "In the event this guy is still hanging around, I'm going to do a U-turn and then make a bunch of quick turns to get back to the highway."

Maggie didn't miss James's saying "this guy" instead of "Gary." She supposed she'd do the same thing if they were discussing one of her friends in relation to a murder.

"Hold on," he said.

She grabbed onto the armrest, and he made several crazy turns in succession.

"I'll need to call you Mario Andretti after this," she joked, but her humor did nothing to lighten the mood in the car.

Once he merged back onto the highway, she settled against the leather seat and placed the drawing on her lap so she could compare it to the houses they drove by. James eased off the gas, and Maggie fixed her focus on homes located close to the wide, sandy beach. They passed a pair of large Dutch Colonial Revivals painted blue with white trim and a quaint white cottage with peeling paint, none of which fit the traditional look of the home they were searching for.

She focused down the road, and her breath caught. "There! Up ahead. That one is big enough, and it could be Victorian."

James slowed even more, and as they pulled up next to the two-story home, Maggie saw that it didn't have a wraparound porch or the multitiered roofline of the home they were looking for.

She didn't need to say anything. James sped up and they finished the drive to Pelican Cove.

"I was sure we'd find the house by now," she said.

"I'd hoped for the same thing."

James slowed his speed to match the posted speed limit, and they crept through the small town. On a normal day, she'd enjoy the unique shops with brightly colored awnings, but today her focus was on finding the house in the drawing. They drove down every street in the small town to no avail.

"Maybe we should check Mills Landing. It's not far from here."

"Sure," James said.

They fell silent as he drove back onto the highway.

Maggie kept her gaze focused out the window. When they arrived in the middle of town without spotting the house, Maggie's hope died. "It's not looking good."

"Don't give up yet," James said. "We have a few more streets to check by the ocean."

Maggie's phone rang, and she dug it from her bag. The number didn't have a name associated with it, meaning the person wasn't in her address book.

"Hello?"

"Maggie, it's Carol Hansen at Grandma's Antiques." Her voice was rushed and breathless.

"You sound upset. Are you all right?"

"No! Just the opposite." Carol's voice teetered higher. "My son helped me find the video, and I looked at it. You'll never believe it, but the man who sold me the carpetbag and sprockets—I know his name."

10

"There!" Maggie exclaimed, momentarily distracted from the news she had just heard. "Sorry, Carol. I'm going to need to call you back. I'll stop by Grandma's Antiques to discuss this with you in person." She disconnected the call and nudged James, pointing. "That's it. The house sitting back from the road."

James slowed almost to a stop, and Maggie saw his eyes narrow as he squinted at it. "Sure looks like it." He clicked on the blinker and made the turn.

Maggie couldn't bear to sit still as they pulled up in front of the home that looked to be an exact match to the one in the drawing, so she jiggled her knees in pent-up anticipation.

James parked in front of the two-story home that was painted a crisp white with a porch wrapping around the entire building. She counted five different peaks in the roof, which she assumed created very interesting rooms inside.

"It's a perfect match to the drawing. It even has the same gingerbread trim," she pointed out. "I'm so glad to see it's been well cared for."

"There's a car in the driveway, so maybe someone's home."

"Let's go find out." Maggie climbed out of the car, and a blustery wind from the ocean caught the drawing, almost ripping it from her hand. She used both hands to hold on, but her hair blew wildly, preventing her from seeing the ground ahead of her.

"Let me take the drawing." James gently pulled it from her hands and folded the flapping paper.

Maggie looked at the ocean, and she was surprised to see

boats bobbing on the whitecaps. "I wouldn't want to be out there today."

James nodded, his expression sobering, and Maggie instantly regretted bringing up the ocean with him. After high school, his fiancée had taken her catamaran out in bad weather and drowned. James wasn't afraid of water, but he had a healthy respect for the damage rough seas could do.

He started for the front door, and Maggie followed. Her hair whipped into her face, and she pulled it back with her hands, holding it in place until she was on the porch, where they were shielded from the heavy gusts.

James rang the doorbell. Maggie combed her fingers through her tangled hair and straightened her shirt.

"Do you know what you're going to say if anyone answers?" James asked.

"No. I thought I'd play it by ear."

Maggie heard footsteps on the other side of the door. She took a deep breath and smiled broadly so the occupant wouldn't be leery of them.

The door opened, revealing a woman who looked to be in her early forties. She hugged the back of the door and poked her head around the edge. Her blond hair was pulled up in a messy bun, leaving strands free to dangle against her round face.

"Can I help you?" she asked, still clinging to the door.

Maggie introduced both of them, then took the drawing from James. "We found this drawing in an old carpetbag and took a drive up the coast to see if we could find the house." She held out the drawing. "We believe it's your house."

The woman opened the door wider to glance at the page, then eyed them skeptically. "It could be our house, I suppose."

"The bag that held the drawing appears to have belonged to a woman named Lavinia Taylor. Do you know anything about her?"

"No. Never heard of her."

Maggie held the drawing closer to the woman and tapped the room layout section of the page. "Can you confirm this is the layout of your house?"

The woman stared at the drawing. "No," she finally said. "Our kitchen is on the opposite side of the house."

"Has your home been updated in a renovation?" James asked, and Maggie was glad he did; she hadn't even considered that possibility.

"Yes," she said.

James looked at Maggie. "If the kitchen was moved, we could be looking at the right house."

"If you'll excuse me," the woman said, "I have something in the oven."

"What about your husband?" Maggie asked. "Could we talk to him?"

"He's busy right now." She firmed her chin. "I'm sorry, but I don't think we can help you." She started to close the door.

Maggie reacted on instinct, shoving her foot into the open doorway. "Please, won't you ask him? It'll only take a minute, and this is so important to us."

The woman seemed to think about it for a moment and then nodded. "I'll be right back." She nudged the door toward them until Maggie withdrew her foot, and then the door closed with a solid thump.

Maggie heard the deadbolt slip into place. "She's apprehensive."

"Do you blame her? Two complete strangers just showed up on her porch and started asking questions about her house, of which they have an old drawing."

"I suppose I'd probably react the same way."

"Are you kidding me?" He grinned. "You'd invite us in and find a way to get involved in the mystery."

"Okay, maybe I would. Let's hope the husband is more like me, then."

The door opened again, and Maggie looked the man over. He was tall and muscular, and he had on jeans and a checked shirt. Not a work-worn kind of shirt like Gary had been wearing, but a casual cotton shirt. His chin was covered in stubble, his hairline was receding, and he had spiked a tuft of hair on the top. There was a distinct dent in his hair, probably from a cap. *Maybe a baseball cap, like the one Ike's killer supposedly wore?*

She let that thought go for the moment, introduced herself and James again, and then held out the drawing. "I know it's a strange request, but we're looking for information about a woman who may have once owned this house. It's imperative that we find out all we can."

The man pointed at the torn corner on the drawing. "Maybe someone tore that off to hide her identity."

"Her name was Lavinia Taylor," Maggie said, undaunted by his surly attitude. "Any chance you know of her?"

He eyed her. "If you're looking for a family connection to this lady, you won't find it through us. We only bought the house two years ago."

"Do you know the name of the people you purchased it from?" Maggie pressed.

"Don't remember."

"Could you check your records?"

"No." The man crossed his arms.

Maggie couldn't help but notice the muscles under his sleeves. Muscles quite capable of hefting a heavy sprocket and hitting someone over the head with it. "It's vitally important that we find Lavinia," she continued as she dug into her pocket for her phone.

"You're not going to find out about her through me. I never heard of her." He reached for the door.

"Please wait. It's a matter of life or death," Maggie said, though she knew it was a slight stretch of the truth.

He arched an eyebrow.

On impulse, she quickly lifted her phone to snap a picture of his face.

He reached out like he might take her phone, then slammed the door in their faces, his expression livid.

"That didn't go so well," Maggie observed to James.

"Why on earth did you take his picture?"

"I had this strange feeling that he might be involved in Ike's death. Ruth may have seen the killer, so I can show the picture to her and see if this was the guy she saw."

"You do realize it's a long shot."

"I do. But what else do we have to go on at this point?"

"For one, now that we have an address, we can review the property records. Those will give us the history of the house and perhaps provide us with another name to research."

"Women didn't often own property back then," Maggie said. "Odds are that the deed was in Lavinia's husband's name only."

"But we can use the surnames to check marriage records."

"The marriage records for this county aren't online, so that will have to wait until Monday. That could be a problem."

"True," he said. "But I'll try to find permits online for this house to see if the kitchen was moved. I also think it's time for you to make copies of the drawing and put the original in a safe place."

She shot him a surprised look. "You think someone might want it? Like the man who followed me?"

"I don't know, but I do know the more you show it around, the more likely the news will spread."

"I was hoping to show it to locals at the festival tonight, so you might be right. Which means storing it at the shop or the manor isn't a good idea."

"I can hold on to it for you if you'd like."

"Perfect," Maggie said, grateful to have his help.

They turned to leave, and Maggie spotted a gray truck pulling to the curb ahead of them. She grabbed James's arm and pointed. "Look."

She felt the muscles in his arm go rigid. "This isn't good."

He dug in his pocket and withdrew the keys for his car, then held them out. "Go to the car while I have a talk with this guy."

Maggie wanted to be the one to chat with the driver, but she knew James would argue, and perhaps in that time, the man would drive off. She took the keys. "Be careful."

He nodded but didn't respond. Soon he was taking long strides toward the truck.

She pulled out her phone so she'd be ready to call 911 if need be. Then she slowly backed toward James's car, keeping a close eye on the truck. As James approached it from the back, the engine suddenly came to life, and the truck roared from the curb, leaving James standing in its wake.

Maggie wished he could have talked to the man, but maybe it was better this way. She was starting to think the trip to the police department that James had suggested earlier would be their safest course of action.

11

Maggie forced the threat of danger to the back of her mind and trusted James to keep an eye out for the truck in the event that it returned to follow them on their drive to Grandma's Antiques. She opened the Internet on her phone and navigated to a Web page of county property records. When the page opened, she plugged in the address of the home from which they'd recently departed. The screen churned for a few moments and then a name popped up.

"The house is owned by Warren and Patricia Duncan." Maggie read through the record. "They bought it ten years ago."

"So the guy lied to us," James muttered.

"But why lie about it? That's what I want to know."

"Does the record list the previous owners?"

"I'll see." She scrolled down the page. "No."

"That's odd," he said. "Maybe the website is set for mobile users and gives less information than you'd see on a full-size computer screen. I'll be glad to look for other records tonight."

"Thank you," she said. "I'm going to search for Patricia and Warren online. If I find a picture of them, I could confirm they're the owners."

James nodded.

She found Warren, and the page opened to reveal several pictures of the man and woman they'd just talked to. When James exited the highway at Pelican Cove and stopped at a light, Maggie showed him one of the clearest pictures.

"No doubt. That's the guy we talked to." James frowned. "But if he is involved in Ike's death, it doesn't explain the truck following us. Warren couldn't be in two places at once."

"Maybe he has a friend watching us."

"That seems far-fetched."

Maggie had to agree, but she wouldn't rule it out until she possessed enough information to do so. She turned her attention back to the road. "When we get to Grandma's Antiques, would you mind waiting in the car?"

"I'm that scary, am I?" He grinned.

"Frightfully so." She laughed.

Maggie opened her car door and got out. "Actually, I need you to stay out here for backup. If I don't return soon, please come get me."

James stepped out too and leaned against the car. "Why would I need to?"

"Carol is very easy to talk to. I could lose the whole day."

"I guess that's the price you have to pay to solve a mystery."

Maggie crossed the road, and as she entered Grandma's Antiques, she noticed the police officer was nowhere in sight.

"His name is Angus," Carol blurted out before Maggie had even closed the door. "The guy who sold me the sprockets and carpetbag."

Maggie joined Carol at the counter. "Angus what?"

"My customer didn't know."

"Okay, back up. What does a customer have to do with this?"

"I was looking at the video file that my son made, and one of my customers came up next to me and said, 'Hey, that's Angus.'"

Maggie was glad to know the man was named Angus, but without a last name and address, she'd still have to do a lot of digging to find him. She was wishing she hadn't suggested James stay in the car. He might have thought of a question to ask Carol like he had at the house they'd found.

Carol crossed her arms and eyed Maggie. "I thought you'd

be more excited to learn his name. I mean, I had to get my son over here. And I'll need to bake for him too."

"I *am* excited, and knowing his name will help since there probably aren't a lot of men named Angus in the area. But it would be even more helpful if I knew his last name or where he lived. Did your customer know anything more about him? Anything at all?"

"When I asked for more information, all he said was that Angus was once a fisherman. That's it." Carol was starting to sound perturbed.

"I'm sorry to keep asking questions," Maggie said to soothe the woman's obviously ruffled feathers. "I just don't want to miss anything."

Carol nodded. She handed over the DVD holding the security video feed for the last month. "Maybe you'll see something on here."

"I appreciate your help," Maggie said again and started for the door. "If you think of anything else, call me."

"I will," Carol promised.

Maggie rejoined James at his car, where the policeman who'd promised to keep an eye out for Carol stood talking to him.

"Officer," she said in greeting.

"This guy is with you?" He tipped his head at James, who was still leaning on the car.

She nodded. "Why?"

"I saw him watching Carol's shop, and it looked mighty suspicious."

"He was waiting for me." She climbed into the car, and James got in after her. "Thank you for looking out for Carol, Officer."

"Just doing my duty, ma'am. You two have a nice weekend."

"Thank goodness you came out when you did," James said. "I thought the guy was going to haul me in for loitering."

"Really?" She buckled her seat belt.

"No, but he was about to make me move along." James backed the car out. "What did you learn?"

She shared the news about Angus and having the video feed for review. "I think I'll use the drive to look for anyone named Angus who might live in the area."

"We can tell the police about him too."

"Yes, of course," Maggie said. When James parked in front of the Somerset Harbor Police Department, she'd come up empty on her search for Angus and was eager to talk to the police about him.

In the shade of a large tree, she and James walked up the sidewalk to the building.

James held the door, and Maggie entered a small foyer with a front counter made of reclaimed wood. The receptionist, Paula Ellis, looked up. She had brown curly hair with blond strands woven throughout. Her mouth was wide, her chin pointy, her gaze hard.

James explained his request to talk with someone about the truck.

"Take a seat," she said brusquely. "All our officers are patrolling the festival, so Chief Cole is the only one here right now. I'll ask if he has time to see you."

Everyone in town knew Paula hoped to become a police officer, but the force had its requisite number of officers on staff, and it was unlikely a slot would open soon. So she'd settled for the receptionist job, but she handled herself like an officer regardless of her title.

James sat, but Maggie remained standing and peered through the window that looked out over the town filled with shoppers. As she gazed at the action, she used her fingers to comb through her hair, which was still tangled from the wind. Soon a side door opened and Chief Rick Cole, a tall, barrel-chested man with thinning hair, appeared.

He smiled at Maggie, crinkling his windburned cheeks. "Ms. Watson."

"Maggie," she insisted and shook his hand, noting it was as chapped as his face. Somerset Harbor officers spent a good deal of time outside, and she'd heard people say that the chief believed in getting down in the trenches with his team to know what was going on in his town. That philosophy, plus his ability to command his team, helped make him a respected leader in the town.

"Come on back to my office and we can talk." He led the way into a large open room holding five desks. Maggie had heard officers refer to it as the bull pen, and she knew in the back of the station away from public view there were two holding cells. They passed a conference room and a small break room to get to the chief's office.

He gestured at two chairs in front of his desk. "Have a seat."

James and the chief both waited for Maggie to be seated before taking their places.

Chief Cole rested his hands on his desk and looked directly at Maggie. "I assume you're here about Ike Wynne's murder."

Maggie was there to report being followed, but she wasn't about to miss an opportunity to ask about the investigation. "Could you give me an update? Especially as it pertains to any forensic evidence you may have found?"

He interlaced his fingers and frowned at her. "I thought you understood the legalities involved in sharing information for an ongoing case."

"I do, but someone has been killed . . ." She stopped talking and let the implication hang in the air.

"And you want to make certain that we're not letting information slip out that needs to be kept confidential." He finished her sentence in a way that she hadn't intended. "Just know that we're working very hard on finding the perpetrator."

"Doing what, exactly?"

He looked like he wanted to sigh. "You know I run a transparent department, and I'm more than happy to share any information that I can. While I'm not at liberty to go into the details of the case, be assured we're working on it."

"But—"

"Rick says he's working on it, so let's leave it at that and tell him why we stopped by," James interrupted.

Maggie's mouth fell open. What was going on with James? He was here to help her out, not defend the chief when she asked a difficult question. She glared at him.

James chortled at her look, and when she gaped at him, he held up a hand. "I'm sorry. Don't get mad. I didn't mean to laugh, but honestly, your expression when you get fired up about something isn't quite as fierce and intimidating as you think."

She felt her face flush.

The chief cleared his throat. "If we could get back on topic."

Maggie could still feel the heat in her face, but she forced herself to shift her focus back to Rick. She quickly told him about the man named Angus. "Since the name is so uncommon, I was hoping you could look him up in your records to locate any possible matches."

He offered Maggie a tight smile. "I'm sorry, I'm afraid I can't do that. Angus hasn't committed a crime. Maybe you can find the information you're seeking on the Internet."

"Perhaps," she said, doing her best to keep her disappointment in check.

"The other reason for our visit is to report a truck that's been following Maggie," James said.

"Following her?" the chief asked, his interest clearly piqued.

Maggie described the incident and pulled a page from her notebook. "Here's the license plate number."

"Now that's something I can act on." Chief Cole slid the paper close to him and dragged out his keyboard tray. His fingers clicked across the keys, and then he sat back to wait for the computer. "See? You didn't even need to bring James along to bully me."

"I didn't—"

The chief interrupted her, grinning. "I know you didn't. I was joking."

"Oh," Maggie said and laughed. "I guess this whole situation has swallowed my sense of humor."

The computer dinged, and his attention shot back to the screen. "Interesting," he said, then shoved the keyboard tray back under the desk and pulled out two notepads from his drawer. He slapped them along with pens onto the desk. "If each of you will write out exactly what happened with the vehicle, I'll open an incident report."

Maggie slid up to the desk and started writing. James took the notepad and balanced it on his knee. When they'd finished, Chief Cole escorted them to the door.

Outside, the sticky air hit Maggie hard. She had planned to spend the evening at the festival, but given the weather, she decided she'd rather stay inside.

"Maggie!" Ruth shouted from down the street as she ran toward them. "Thank goodness I found you."

Apprehension settled in Maggie's stomach. "What is it?"

"I saw the man who argued with Ike. You know . . . the one we think killed him. He was in the park. I looked for a police officer, but they must be spread thin during dinnertime. So I took a picture of the guy and came straight here to report him." Ruth didn't offer to show the picture but ran past Maggie. She opened the front door of the police station and called out, "I found the killer! He's at the park."

Maggie reached Ruth in time to see the receptionist's face light up. She quickly paged the chief to the lobby.

Maggie was so excited that she grabbed Ruth's arm. "Show me the picture."

Ruth took out her phone and displayed the photo.

Maggie took one look and her breath caught. Even though the picture was blurry, she thought she recognized the man.

James rushed over to her. "What is it?"

"You're not going to like this, but the man in the picture . . . it . . . it could be Gary Keel."

12

"It could also be Warren Duncan," James replied.

"And who might that be?" Chief Cole asked as he reached them.

Maggie explained about finding the drawing in the bag and then locating the house.

"And you didn't think this was important enough to tell me about earlier?"

"I'm not sure the carpetbag is connected to Ike's death." Maggie scrolled through her phone to her picture of Warren and held it out to Ruth. "Could this be the guy that you saw arguing with Ike?"

Ruth stared at the screen, her eyes widening. "It could be him." She furrowed her brow. "But now that you mention Gary Keel, it could be him too. I barely know him, so I can't be sure." She wrung her hands together. "I thought it would be so easy to identify this man, but now I wonder how clearly I saw him last night."

"You all seem to know this Gary, but I don't." Chief Cole dug a notepad from his pocket. "What else can you tell me about him?"

"He's a contractor and friend of mine who lives in Pelican Cove," James offered.

"And he's an expert in industrial antiques," Maggie added. "I met with him and asked him to look into possible uses for the sprockets Ike bought at the auction."

Chief Cole scrubbed a hand over his face, and Maggie could see he carried a heavy burden as the chief.

"I've known Gary for ten or fifteen years," James said. "And other than an ugly divorce a few years ago where he was accused of hiding some assets from his ex, he's a stand-up guy. I don't know if he actually hid the assets or not. Just that there was a big to-do about it."

Maggie suspected Chief Cole was considering Gary's character, and hiding assets didn't speak well of him. Still, he was James's friend, so she'd give him the benefit of the doubt for now.

"If you'll give me his address and phone number," the chief said, "I'll personally have a talk with him. If he's not involved, it won't go beyond us."

James dug out his cell phone and gave the number to the chief, who then turned to face Maggie. "I suppose you're already planning to question Keel."

"Of course she is," James said matter-of-factly. "And I plan to be with her."

"It would be best if you'd give me a crack at him first." Chief Cole looked at his watch. "I have a few things to finish up here, and then I'll drive over to Pelican Cove. Probably only take me a few hours."

"I understand," Maggie said. "Will you give me a call to let me know that you've spoken to Gary?"

"Yes, but—"

"I know, you can't tell me what he says. It's okay. And after Warren Duncan slammed the door in my face, I don't think there's any point in me trying to talk to him again, but will you?"

The chief nodded.

She started to say good night, but then a question came to mind. "There's one thing I forgot to ask about earlier. Were you able to confirm that Ike's phone is a prepaid cell?"

"I can't answer that, Maggie."

"Well . . . can you at least say if you *haven't* found out anything new about the phone?"

He paused for a moment, then said carefully, "Officer Linton is often right about his assessments made at a crime scene."

She nodded. "Thank you."

"For what? Telling you Officer Linton does his job well?" The chief suddenly seemed less weary—there was a playful glint in his eye.

"Oh, and fingerprints on the phone," she said. "Did you find any?"

"I think we should end our discussion while you're ahead." Chief Cole glanced at James as he went back inside. "You're a more patient man than I, James Bennett."

"He's right. You are very patient," Maggie said to James.

James grinned. "I try."

"I appreciate it and all of your support. You're a good friend."

"Paula!" the chief called out as he passed her desk. "Get the picture from Ruth's phone and issue an alert for officers to be on the lookout for this guy."

Maggie peered at Ruth. "I'm going to stop by the shop to make a few photocopies. Would you like to walk with us instead of going back to the festival?"

"No," she said. "I'll be fine. But thank you for the offer."

"Are you sure?"

"Paula is notifying the officers. So I feel safe."

"Call me if you need me," Maggie said and turned to James. "Where would you like to meet up before we head to Gary's place later—assuming the chief is able to speak with him as planned?"

"What if we have dinner and go from there?"

"Right, dinner," she said. "We do need to eat."

He quirked up his mouth. "We could do it together, you know. Friends often eat together."

"What if we meet at the festival?"

"Because you want to get there as soon as possible in case Gary or Warren is hanging around."

Maggie cocked an eyebrow. "You're getting to know me well, aren't you?"

"I am at that." James grinned, but she saw something in his eyes that she couldn't quite interpret. "I'll walk you to the shop so you can give me the original drawing to take back to my office."

Maggie nodded and led the way to the antiques shop, where she copied the drawing and handed it to James.

He looked at his watch. "Does dinner in two hours work for you?"

She nodded. "I'd like to try the fish tacos from the Portland vendor in the park."

"Perfect," he said. "See you then."

Maggie wished Emily hadn't left already since she would have loved to spend the next few hours with her daughter. But she could use the time to catch up on paperwork for the shop, which she did before setting off for the park again.

A few hours later, she found James standing in line at the taco vendor. Still, they had to wait nearly thirty minutes for their food, but they were entertained by a very good jazz band while waiting. Maggie hummed along to their rendition of "In the Mood" as James carried their tray across the grassy space, scanning for a place to sit.

"Over there—hurry." He didn't wait for her, but dashed through the crowd like Wile E. Coyote in chase of the Road Runner.

She managed to catch up with him and was rewarded for the crazy slide through the crowd when she saw that he'd gotten a prime table under a tree overlooking the harbor.

"You're a miracle worker." Maggie sat on the painted bench facing the water.

The sun had already started dropping toward the horizon and would set in about an hour. There was a faded line blending the sea and sky, and it was hard to distinguish between the two.

James took a seat next to her, a troubled look on his face. She opened her food container. "What's wrong?"

"The wind's shifted from the south."

"Ah," she said, remembering that when warm southern winds blew over the colder ocean, fog would soon come rolling in and blanket the area. "People around here are used to the fog. I doubt they'll go home because of it."

"You're right." He opened the packaging around his taco. "I was thinking more about the man following you. Fog would be a good cover if he wanted to get close to you."

"Oh . . . yes . . . well . . ." She chose not to think about the possibilities and bit into the soft tortilla filled with flaky fish and spicy tomato salsa. The sauce burned as it went down, but she savored the flavor and took another big bite. She followed it with a long drink of her raspberry lemonade. "I'm sorry about Gary."

"I'm choosing to believe he isn't involved in Ike's murder."

"I'd rather think it was Warren. He wasn't nearly as nice as Gary seems."

They turned their attention to their meal, and several people stopped to talk to them, a common occurrence in their small town. Chief Cole also phoned to tell Maggie that he hadn't found Gary at home. He reluctantly gave his blessing for her to talk to Gary if she happened upon him first. Maggie wondered if the reason the chief couldn't find Gary was because he was the man Ruth had seen at the festival earlier, but she didn't voice her suspicion because she didn't want to upset James.

As predicted, by the time they finished eating, fog had drifted in, cocooning them in a hazy blanket.

"It's going to be slow going to Gary's place," James said. "Are you sure you still want to go tonight after the chief said he wasn't home?"

"If you don't think it's too dangerous to drive, I'd like to at least try. He might be home by the time we get there."

"I've driven in far worse conditions. Let's go." James gestured ahead, and she started down the hill toward his car.

As he drove, James focused fully on the road, and Maggie didn't want to disturb him, so she listened to the wipers swish moisture off the windshield while thoughts of the investigation swam in her head.

She'd made good progress today. When she'd started the day, she didn't have a suspect at all. Now she had Gary, Warren, and the mystery man driving the truck—assuming it wasn't Gary. On top of that, she'd located the house in the drawing.

But then there was Angus. She still needed to figure out how to find him.

James slowed and leaned forward as if to see through the fog. "Gary's driveway is somewhere on the right."

She peered out the window. "I see it. Just ahead."

James made the turn onto a long, narrow drive. A light burned in the front room of the small cottage; otherwise, Maggie might not have even seen the house. James parked in the middle of the drive.

"No vehicle in the driveway," Maggie said, stating the obvious. "Maybe Gary's still not home."

James turned off the engine. "He usually parks in the garage out back."

Maggie climbed out and wished a cooling breeze would pick up and stir the soupy air. She walked down a path of crushed seashells that wound to the front door. She knocked hard on the weather-beaten door and stood back to wait. She heard the faint sounds of footsteps inside.

"Did you hear that?" she asked.

James shook his head. "What?"

"Footsteps. At least it sounded like footsteps, and moving away from the door."

James leaned to the side and looked through a window. "I don't see anyone."

Maggie checked the window on the other side. "Same here." She knocked harder, then pressed her ear to the door. "Nothing. I'm going to check the garage."

James grabbed her arm. "Are you sure you want to go snooping around here?"

"Why not?"

"It's private property for one thing."

"And for another?"

"Gary's my friend, and I don't treat my friends like that."

"What if he's in danger?"

"Do you actually believe he's in danger?"

"I suppose not." She waffled. "I simply want to get to the bottom of Ike's murder."

"Me too, but not at the expense of my friendships."

"Point taken." Maggie looked around, hoping to find another approach or anything to do except get back in the car and drive away.

"We should be going." James started back to the Mercedes and didn't look back to see if she was following him.

She slowly trailed him to the car. Once inside, she peered at him. "I'm sorry if I'm pushing your boundaries with your friend. I'd act the same way with you if it was one of my friends under the gun."

"Apology accepted." He started the car.

As James made a three-point turn, Maggie saw the curtain in the front room stir. "Did you see that? The curtain just moved in the front window."

"Probably the wind," James said.

She nodded, but she'd heard the hum of the air-conditioning compressor and knew the windows weren't open. She also knew she was not going to be able to convince James.

Obviously Gary was home, but he wasn't willing to talk to them. James believed in his friend's innocence, and Maggie wanted to as well. But unfortunately, his actions had just pushed him higher up on her suspect list.

She hoped for James's sake that she was wrong.

13

"Do you want me to drop you off at home?" James asked as he drove down the congested street of Somerset Harbor.

Maggie shook her head. "I still want to ask people about Lavinia and Angus, plus show them the drawing in case the house we found turns out to be the wrong one."

"Do you think it's wrong?"

"No, but it's possible the builder built two identical houses, right?"

"I suppose so. I'm scheduled to judge the junior art category this evening so they can announce the winner in the morning. Not that I know anything about art. I tried to tell the committee that, but they figured with my contracting skills, I must know something about form and function at least." James shook his head. "I suspect they didn't have anyone else to judge."

She laughed. "Good luck with that."

He parked in the school lot and they went their separate ways. As she drew near to the park, where country music rang out from the stage, she decided to focus on longtime residents since she thought they were more likely to know something about the house.

She soon ran into Daniel Simpson, one of Somerset Harbor's oldest occupants. He wore a short-sleeved shirt with the buttons closed at the neck and navy pants held up with striped suspenders. The retired fisherman's face was rough from years of working at sea. His nose was flat and wide, his forehead covered in wrinkles that reminded Maggie of a pug.

"Good evening, Mr. Simpson," Maggie greeted him politely.

"A-yup," he said with conviction and hooked his thumbs in his suspenders. Nearing ninety-five, Daniel was still fit and able to get around. His mind was sharp, and he often declared he'd aged successfully as a result of a lifetime of breathing the salty ocean air.

"I was wondering if I might show you a drawing of a house. I'm hoping you might have seen it on the coast and could tell me where it is."

He nodded, and she held out the picture.

"A-yup. Saw it with my father when I was a kid." His eyes took on a faraway look. "I remember it because it was painted bright colors. I don't remember exactly where it is though."

Maggie wished he could recall the location, but it was exciting that he recognized the house. "Do you know who lived there?"

"Real hoity-toity family. Name was Parson."

"Not Taylor?" she asked as she pulled out her notebook to write down the name.

"Nope."

"Was there anyone in the family named Lavinia?"

"Not that I know of, but then I don't much know the people." He furrowed his bushy eyebrows. "Now my father, if he was alive, he could've told you who lived there. The whole family. He knew everyone up and down the coast."

"Speaking of names, are you familiar with a man in the area with the first name of Angus?"

He nodded. "Knew a fisherman named Angus once. Lived in Seacliff. Short guy, but a powerhouse in the day."

The man in Carol's video was short, so the description seemed to fit.

"Could this Angus be related to Lavinia Taylor?" she asked.

The older man shrugged. "I actually knew the father better than Angus. Their last name was Underwood. Last I heard, which is going on thirty or forty years now, Angus still lives in the family home in Seacliff."

Angus Underwood. The man she was looking for? Living in Seacliff? That didn't jive with the house they'd found in Mills Landing. She entered his name in her notepad. "Have you ever been to the Underwoods' house, or could you tell me how to find it?"

"Me? Nah. I never had a reason to go over there."

As Maggie pocketed her notepad, she was beginning to think that if Angus lived in Seacliff, perhaps that meant she and James hadn't found the right house. She needed to ask James if he'd had a chance to search the property records.

For now, she turned her attention back to Daniel. "Can you think of anyone else I might ask about Lavinia?"

"Did you talk to Daisy Carter? She knows everything that goes on around these parts."

Maggie had kept Daisy up to date as she had with all the women in the historical society, but with both of them being so busy, she hadn't taken time to sit down with Daisy and ask if she'd learned anything in her gossip sessions. Maggie would remedy that immediately.

She thanked Daniel for his time, then hurried toward Daisy's booth. She wound through the thick crowd and spotted Daisy slumped in a chair outside her small booth. Her long legs were splayed out in front of her, and her usually big hair was matted and flat.

"Oh, sweetie," Maggie said. "You look beat."

"I am." Daisy kicked off her sandals and rubbed her feet in the grass. "I don't know why we were so blessed this year with a crowd the size of the Atlantic, but I was totally unprepared."

"I've heard that from everyone." Maggie sat in the bright Adirondack chair next to Daisy. "A good problem to have though, right?"

"Yes, of course." Daisy got a silly look on her face. "But my workers are exhausted, so I might actually have to put Harry to work baking tonight."

Maggie tried to imagine the tough fisherman stoically donning an apron and hairnet, and the thought made her giggle.

"It's no laughing matter." Daisy leaned closer and winked. "And just a heads-up: Don't order anything from my booth tomorrow, just to be on the safe side."

Maggie wrinkled her nose. "Are you really going to rope Harry into helping?"

"Cleaning up and carrying things back to the shop, yes. Baking, no way. I do want to stay open, you know." Daisy slipped one foot back into a sandal. "What have you been up to today?"

Maggie brought her friend up to speed on her activities.

Daisy cast an affronted look at her. "And this is the first I'm hearing of Angus? You should have come to me sooner."

Maggie sat forward. "Then you do know something about him?"

"No, but if you'd told me, I could have subtly asked around for you today."

"Um, Daisy? Subtlety was never really your thing."

Daisy mocked offense with a hand to her chest. "Okay, fine. I may not be subtle, but I could have asked around." She pushed to the edge of her chair. "Would you like me to start now?"

"Yes, please. But don't share the other things I've told you, okay?"

Daisy pretended to twist a key at her lips and toss it away, but Maggie knew the lock was flimsy at best.

"I'd better get back to work." Daisy rose, one hand massaging her lower back. "Catch you later."

Maggie was about to get up too when church secretary Elsbeth Holdridge appeared at her side, her usual sharp gaze zeroing in on Maggie. Her traditional black slacks and white blouse fit her personality to a tee. She often wore a gold chain with glasses dangling from her neck, but tonight she'd replaced it with a pearl necklace.

"Evening, Maggie," she said. "Someone told me you were looking for information about a Lavinia Taylor."

Maggie shot upright in the chair. "I am. Do you know something about her?"

Elsbeth nodded.

"Please sit down and tell me what you know." Maggie patted the chair that Daisy had vacated.

Elsbeth took a seat, her posture stick straight despite the sloping back of the chair. "As you know, it's my job to keep the church records in order. With the church going back to the 1700s, you can imagine what a big task it is."

"Yes," Maggie said, genuinely thankful for Elsbeth's service.

Elsbeth folded her hands on her lap. "Not too long ago, I remember coming across the name Homer Underwood in an old record from 1915. He was listed as a baptism sponsor. Homer is a unique name, and it stuck with me."

"I can imagine."

"I also remember seeing the first name of Homer's mother."

"Was it Lavinia by any chance?" Maggie asked eagerly.

"It was indeed."

Maggie clasped her hands. "I don't suppose you learned that he has a relative named Angus . . . ?"

Elsbeth shook her head. "That's all I know. I hope it's helpful."

"With what Mr. Simpson has already told me about Angus Underwood, all I need to do is prove that this woman's maiden name was Taylor, and Angus is one of her descendants. Once I do that, I'll have the connection I'm seeking—one of them, at least."

"How on earth are you going to do that? I know the name Lavinia sounds unique now, but back in the day, it was fairly common."

"I'll start with a visit to Angus Underwood and hope he knows his ancestors well, assuming I can find him." Maggie got to her feet. "Thank you, Elsbeth. You have been an enormous help."

Maggie headed toward the park entrance. The day's discoveries had put a spring in her step, and she strode down the street with purpose. When she reached the alley behind the municipal building, she ducked down it to avoid the crowds and hurried in the direction of Sedgwick Manor. Thick fog obscured the quaint town and created an eerie feeling. She remembered James's comment about her stalker taking advantage of the low visibility and shivered.

"Stop it," she warned herself, clamping down on her runaway imagination.

The alley exited onto Harbor Street, which was still filled with visitors, so she put her head down and headed the other direction to avoid the crowds. Finally, she found an empty street. As she walked down the sidewalk, an uneasy feeling crept over her again, and she stopped to survey the area. Half expecting to see a madman lying in wait, she scanned the shadows clinging to the shrubs and houses. Leaves on the trees danced in a light breeze, but nothing else stirred. Still, an ominous feeling gnawed at her, and she sped up.

A moment later, the sound of footsteps broke the silence. The heavy footfalls reverberated off the sidewalk as they came closer to her.

Her mind whirled with the vision of a faceless killer chasing after her.

Fear gripped her, and she broke into a jog.

She heard her pursuer pick up speed to match her pace. *Oh no . . . please let me get away . . .*

The sound of additional footfalls reached her ears. Was she being chased by more than one person?

She dared to take a quick look back and saw a flash of movement. Trying to get a better look without tripping, she slowed and squinted into the misty fog rolling in from the ocean. A shadowy figure suddenly emerged from the haze, closer than she'd thought, and headed straight for her.

With a scream, she turned and ran.

Terrified, Maggie sprinted as fast as she could.

"You there, stop!" James's voice boomed through the night.

Maggie glanced over her shoulder again to see the figure pause before changing directions and vanishing into the whirling fog like a shadow.

"James?"

"Maggie!" he called out while racing toward her—at least she assumed it was James.

She waited until she could make out his face, then let out a ragged sigh of relief.

"Are you okay?" he asked.

She nodded. "Did you get a good look at the man?"

"No. Did you?"

She shook her head. "We need to call the police so they can go after him."

James drew out his phone and dialed 911. He reported the incident, and then he pointed to a nearby bench. "Let's sit while we wait for the police to arrive."

They took a seat, and the fog swirled around them like a living, breathing thing.

Maggie still felt unsettled, but she chose not to let the thought of the faceless stalker scare her. "Too bad it's so foggy tonight, or we might have been able to identify the man."

"I suspect if it wasn't this foggy, he wouldn't have tailed you so closely, and I wouldn't have seen him."

She turned to look at James. "And how did you . . . I mean, are you following me too?"

A sheepish look crossed his face.

"James Bennett. You *were* following me."

"I finished judging and saw you take off. I wanted to make sure you got to the shop or home or wherever you were headed in such a hurry safely."

"Home. I was going home to look up Angus Underwood on my computer."

"You learned his last name, then."

She told him about her conversations with Daniel and Elsbeth. "I can't prove he's related to Lavinia Taylor yet, especially with Daniel telling me Angus lives in Seacliff, but I suspect talking with Angus will be enlightening."

"Please tell me you'll wait until tomorrow to go out to talk to Angus."

"Trust me, I'm not going anywhere else in this fog tonight," she said as sirens swelled through the night, white and blue lights straining to cut through the fog.

Before long, Officer Linton pulled up to the curb and lowered his window. "Which way did he go?"

James jabbed a finger at the road the shadowy figure had taken.

"I'll check it out and come back to take your statement." He took off, and his car soon vanished into the haze.

Maggie sighed. "He must be getting tired of coming to my rescue."

"He's a fine officer, and he'll do whatever he needs to do to make sure everyone in town is safe." James grinned. "Even if you do seem to need more attention than others."

"I'm glad you find it funny," she said. She suspected tonight might not be the last time the man would try to tail her. The thought sent a shiver through her, and she noticed the air had turned cool. She dug into her bag for a sweater. Temperatures might have climbed to the nineties earlier in the day, but the average night temps in July were still only in the upper fifties.

Maggie slid her arms into the lightweight cardigan. "Do you think the man saw me asking questions about the drawing and wanted to take it from me?"

"Perhaps." James absently drummed his fingers on his knee. "Though I'm not sure why."

"Maybe he thinks the page is intact, and he wants the information from the missing corner just as we do."

"That sounds logical, I suppose, but unless we figure out what was torn off, we may never know."

Maggie heard tires rolling along the road, and then the headlights from Officer Linton's car broke through the fog. He parked on the other side of the road, and Maggie hurried to meet him as he climbed out of his vehicle.

"No luck, I'm afraid. With the thick fog, that's not surprising." Officer Linton drew out his notepad and pen. "Tell me exactly what happened, and I'll file a report."

Maggie filled him in, and James added details that she missed.

Officer Linton looked up. "You both said you didn't get a good look at the guy, but you must have some thoughts about his identity."

"I'm wondering if it might be the man we met this afternoon." She explained about Warren and Patricia Duncan. "Patricia was marginally friendly, but Warren shut us down and only asked about the missing corner of the paper. I didn't think anything of it at the time—"

"But now you wonder if he was after the drawing not for what you can see, but for what was missing."

"Exactly," she said. "Chief Cole said he would talk to Warren, but I'm not sure he's had time to do so."

Officer Linton flipped his notebook closed. "You haven't

given me much to go on, but I'll file a report anyway. Who knows? If we're lucky, the guy is running through backyards to avoid apprehension, and we'll get a 911 call with his whereabouts." He shoved his notebook into his pocket. "Don't hesitate to call me if—I mean, *when* something else happens."

Maggie caught the hint of a grin as he turned back to his car, and she knew James was right; Officer Linton didn't really mind her "frequent-flier" status.

"I'll walk you home." James's tone brooked no argument, so they set off together.

At the manor's front door, she flipped on the chandelier, and Snickers came trotting across the wooden floor. He let out a loud meow.

"I've left him alone too much lately," she said and bent to sweep the tabby into her arms. He reached out a striped leg and planted it on her shoulder, his sign that he wanted affection. She ruffled his soft fur and received a throaty purr in response. Maggie was grateful for Snickers's company, but she wanted human company tonight too, and Emily had already left for Standish. "Could I interest you in a cup of coffee or tea before you go?"

"Why don't you take a seat, and I'll make us some tea?" he suggested.

"I'm okay, you know. The guy didn't hurt me."

"I know, but you've still had a scare. You relax and let me make it." He didn't wait for a response but headed for the kitchen.

She continued to scratch Snickers under the chin as she strolled through the study to the office. She took a seat at the desk, but she resisted the temptation to open her computer so she could spend a little more time loving on Snickers.

"Did you have a good day?" she asked him, and she got a chipper meow in response. "Mine was . . . interesting."

She settled him on her lap, and he pushed his head under her hand, demanding additional attention. She scratched his ear, but he showed no sign of letting up on his demands. She continued to pet him and let her tension from the chase subside.

James soon joined her, carrying a tray with two cups of tea and chocolate chip cookies she'd baked for Emily's visit. He set the tray on a small table, then sat in a 1930s English Chesterfield leather club chair. The hand-dyed leather showed years of wear, as did the brass arm endcaps.

He handed her a steaming cup. "Maybe it's time to let the police handle the murder investigation."

"Now? When I'm finally getting somewhere?"

"Think about what might have happened if I hadn't decided to follow you tonight."

"We don't know that the man would have hurt me. It's possible he was merely trying to frighten me."

"We don't know that he *wouldn't* have hurt you."

James was right, of course, but she was reluctant to admit that she could be in more danger than she'd originally thought, so she turned to her laptop and typed *Angus Underwood* into an Internet search engine. Results quickly popped up.

She looked at James. "Angus is in a Seacliff phone directory."

"You'll go visit him, then."

"His address is unlisted, so I'll need to call him first." She jotted down his number, then checked the clock. "It's too late to call tonight, but right after church tomorrow, I'll phone him. Maybe . . . just maybe I'll finally learn something that will lead us to Ike's killer."

15

Maggie turned off the video that Carol had provided and headed for the master bedroom located on the manor's first floor. She'd not only gotten a good view of Angus on the tape, but she'd also discovered the thief had stolen a ring from the display cabinet under the counter. She now suspected the break-in was a coincidence and probably had nothing to do with Ike's death. She made a mental note to tell Carol about the theft tomorrow, as she obviously hadn't noticed the ring was missing.

Maggie changed into her pajamas, settled into the big bed, and leaned back against the carved headboard. She pulled up the double wedding ring quilt made by her grandmother, and the soft fabric soothed away the residual unease from the night's drama.

She patted the empty space next to her. "Okay, Snickers. I'm ready for you."

He launched himself into the air and landed with a graceful plop on the bed before settling down to bury his nose under his paw.

"You might be able to sleep," she said to him. "But I need to get my thoughts down on paper, starting with all of my questions so I can empty my brain."

She pulled up her knees and rested her notepad on her lap, tapping her pen on the paper as she considered the things she needed to follow up on.

"Number one. Let's see," she said. "I suppose the most important thing is to give Angus a call." She made a note. "Then I need to find Gary. He may or may not be a suspect, but I need to see if he's actually researching the sprocket, because the fact that he hid from us at his house makes me think he's not." She quickly noted that on her page. "And I suppose it wouldn't hurt to try to research the sprocket too. Don't you think, Snickers?"

At the mention of his name, he opened an eye and peered at her, but he soon scrunched his eye closed again and tucked his paw under his chin as if he'd decided her comment wasn't worth his attention.

Her phone rang, startling her. She grabbed it from the nearby walnut chest and checked for a name on the phone but saw only a local phone number.

"Hello?"

"Hey, Maggie. It's Olive Becker," the caller said. "I hope I didn't wake you."

"No, I'm still up," Maggie replied, wondering why the woman who lived down the street would be calling so late at night. "What can I do for you?"

"I just got back from a late night walk, and I thought I saw someone lurking around your shop. Do you have someone working late? I didn't want to call the police on someone who's supposed to be there."

"No, I don't. What do you mean, lurking?" Maggie asked, tossing her notepad aside.

"When I first saw him, he was in the shadows outside, but now I think he's gone in."

"Did you see him go in?"

"No, but he's not out front any longer. He must have gone somewhere."

"He could have left or . . ." It occurred to Maggie that the prowler might be trying to get inside the house. "I'm going to hang up now, Olive, so I can call the police. Thanks for letting me know." She ended the call and dialed 911. "This is Maggie Watson. I need to report a potential intruder at my antiques shop."

"The shop's address?" the dispatcher asked.

Maggie quickly provided the needed information.

"I have an officer on the way." The dispatcher's voice held a measure of comfort. "Are you at the shop now, and if so, are you in a safe location?"

"I'm inside my home, but it's right next to the shop, and I'm worried he might be coming here next."

"I'll make sure the officer is aware of your situation and that he stops by to update you on anything he finds. I'll also stay on the line with you until the officer arrives at the shop."

"Thank you." Maggie's thoughts drifted to an officer coming to her door while she was dressed in her pajamas. "I can already hear the siren, so I'm fine. Thank you."

Maggie disconnected the call and hopped out of bed. An irritated meow came from Snickers, and he raised his head to glare at her.

"Sorry, buddy," she said on the way to her closet. "I have to get dressed."

She grabbed the first things her hand could find—a pair of navy linen slacks and a short-sleeved knit top in cherry red. As she gazed into the bathroom mirror to comb her hair, she realized the sirens had ceased. *Good.* The officer had arrived at the shop, and it wouldn't be long before she knew if someone had broken in.

She rushed down the hall, and when she reached the breakfast area, she peered through the window of the door where she thought she'd be able to see a snippet of the shop through the trees. However, with the dark of night and the heavy fog cloaking the area, all she could see were the police lights trying to cut through the fog. She stood and waited. Time ticked by. Slowly. She tapped her foot. Something warm brushed against her leg, and she shrieked before realizing it was Snickers.

"You nearly scared me to death." Maggie picked him up and noticed the time on the early-nineteenth-century Scandinavian clock that hung on the wall. "It's been ten minutes since the officer arrived. What do you think is going on?"

Snickers purred and bumped his head against her chin. She petted him and strode to the front door, hoping to see a police car pulling up the drive. Fog and the black of night greeted her instead.

Perhaps the intruder had fled, and the officer was in pursuit. Could he be coming her way?

She settled Snickers on the floor so she could double-check the security of her locks. She tested the deadbolt, then switched off the light so if an intruder did come to the door, he wouldn't see her. She hurried to the side door and then the porch entrance, and she tried those locks as well.

James's words of warning came back to her; she could be in danger. She retraced her steps back to the bedroom and was suddenly very thankful that Emily had returned to school and was safely out of harm's way.

"C'mon, Snickers," she called and heard his claws clicking over the floor. The moment he entered the room, she closed and locked the door to wait for help to arrive.

She heard another siren.

"Is that good or bad news, Snickers?" she asked, suspecting it could only be bad news. "Perhaps I should go out and try to help?" But she knew that would only cause more confusion and work for the police. Instead she leaned her head against the door and listened, feeling the heavy weight of time slowly ticking by. Suddenly, a third siren broke through the night.

"What in the world is going on?" Maggie whispered just as the doorbell rang.

She released the cat and crept from the bedroom to the front door. Peering through the peephole, she saw Officer Linton standing on the porch. Relief flooded her body, and she almost sagged to the floor. She took a few deep breaths to steady herself and opened the door.

It was immediately clear to her that something wasn't right. Officer Linton looked harried, though he was usually a picture of calm. Something was terribly wrong.

"What is it?" she asked. "What's happened?"

"It's Officer Clayton. She responded to the 911 call and found the back door of your shop had been pried open. She entered, and the intruder hit her over the head with a heavy object."

"Oh no!" Maggie exclaimed. "Is Samantha okay?"

"She was knocked unconscious but came to after the responding medic arrived." He clutched his hands together. "The medic says she may have a concussion, but she'll be fine."

Maggie blew out a breath and thought about how badly this could have ended. "Thank goodness dispatch sent multiple cars to the call."

"Actually, only Officer Clayton was dispatched."

"I don't understand. Who called the medics? I heard multiple sirens."

"Officers report their arrival to dispatch, and dispatch starts a timer ticking. If they haven't heard from the officer in the allotted time, another officer is sent out to check on the first officer."

Maggie had never given much consideration to what happened when a police officer responded to a dangerous call. "How wonderful that such a safety net exists."

He nodded gravely. "Nothing appears to be disturbed at the shop, but you should check your inventory to see if anything has been stolen."

"Now?" she asked.

"If you don't mind."

"Not at all." A vision of the intruder creeping into her shop flashed into her mind. "The intruder. What happened to him?"

"We assume he fled after hitting Officer Clayton."

She took a reflexive step back.

"Don't worry," Officer Linton said. "He wouldn't want to hang around after assaulting an officer and face our full-out response."

Another siren cut through the night.

"As you can tell, we're responding in force. You don't mess with one of our own and get away with it." Officer Linton's lips flattened into a grim line.

Maggie nodded, and as she followed Officer Linton to the carriage house, she suspected the intruder had just made a big mistake.

The scene that greeted her at the shop was so foreign to her lovely little town that Maggie came to a stop, gaping. Two patrol cars stood in the middle of the street, their lights still flashing. Lights on an ambulance whirled nearby. Even the local fire truck had responded, as was customary for a medical emergency callout. It might be midnight, but the copious sirens seemed to have awakened the whole town. Many of her friends had already arrived, dressed in all kinds of attire, to check out the commotion and try to make sense of the chaos. Bright yellow crime scene tape had been strung around the area to keep onlookers away from the scene, but Officer Linton lifted the tape for Maggie to duck under.

She locked eyes with June, who stood at the edge of the group outside the police barrier.

"Maggie!" June called out. "Are you okay?"

"Is it all right if she joins me?" Maggie asked.

"Mrs. McGillis is good to approach," Officer Linton called out to the officer at the barricade.

June didn't waste any time in joining Maggie. "You're not hurt, are you?"

"I'm fine, but would you come inside with me to see if you notice anything amiss?"

"Of course."

"Follow me and remove your shoes at the door to keep from contaminating the scene." Officer Linton led the way to the front door.

As Maggie slipped off her shoes, she cast a look around the space. She found nothing out of order after a cursory glance, but she took a longer look. Her gaze traveled over the wide pine floors she loved, past the rustic chandeliers and charming country cottage decor to the vignettes she and June had carefully built.

"Everything looks fine, doesn't it?" June came to stand next to her.

"Like we always leave it at night."

"Maybe Officer Clayton interrupted the intruder before he had a chance to do any damage," June suggested.

Maggie told her about being followed from the festival. "Perhaps the intruder wanted the carpetbag, but he didn't find it because I had Emily take it to the house."

"Or after the questions you asked at the festival, the drawing is now public knowledge and he's looking for that."

Maggie nodded. "I suppose there's only one conclusion I can draw after being followed tonight." She paused and met June's eyes. "Someone has been watching me, and now I'm wondering—for how long?"

16

Morning had dawned bright and was heating up fast. Maggie was glad there was such a nice cross breeze at Old Faith Chapel so they didn't need to turn on the air-conditioning. She walked down one of the two main aisles dividing rows of box pews, which had been common to the early 1700s when the church had been built. She moved into the foyer and peered at her friends standing near the door. The women of the historical society— minus Daisy—had rushed out of the building the moment the service ended and were now in a huddle, deep in conversation. Maggie had seen Daisy slip out right after the sermon ended.

Liz waved, and Maggie crossed the rough-hewn floor that was original to the church. She heard people whisper as she passed by. They were probably discussing the break-in, which was big news for the small town.

She chose not to listen or stop to talk but focused ahead on the clapboard walls that displayed photos of ships and boats from years gone by. Many pictures were from the town's annual Blessing of the Fleet ceremonies and the summer regatta. And no wall of a seaside church would be complete without a memorial to honor those lost at sea. As she passed, Maggie said a prayer for the safety of the many local fishermen and joined the group.

"I'm so glad to see you," Liz said. "We all wondered if you were coming when the service started and you weren't here."

"Especially after last night," Fran added, an earnest expression on her face.

"I tried to be on time, but I had to call the antiques shop owners who are participating in the 25-Mile Antiques Sale."

"But the festival doesn't start until noon today," Ruth said.

"I know, but I wanted to make sure that no other shops had been broken into last night and that the owners were fine with opening today."

"And did any of them have a problem?" June wanted to know.

Maggie shook her head.

"So either Carriage House Antiques was a specific target, or the intruder was targeting businesses in Somerset Harbor," Fran said.

Maggie nodded. "I plan to talk with all the local shop owners this morning to confirm they've had no problems."

Ruth frowned. "I'm sure we would have heard about another break-in by now."

"Not if it hasn't been discovered yet."

"Oh my!" Ina clutched her chest. "I can't imagine opening my shop and finding out some stranger with ill intent had been there during the night, and I don't even own a shop."

"I can't imagine it either," Fran added. "And I *do* own a shop."

"Unfortunately, after last night I can imagine it all too well." Maggie tried not to shudder, but her body refused to cooperate. "If Olive hadn't seen the intruder, I don't know what would have happened."

Fran shuddered. "I can only hope everything at The Quilt Cupboard is okay when I arrive. We put so much of ourselves into our businesses that a break-in feels like a personal attack."

"I'm sure it will be fine." June turned to Maggie and rested an arm around her shoulders. "The important thing is nothing *did* happen, and the shop is all right."

Maggie nodded. "Does anyone know why Daisy ducked out early?"

"She said she still has to catch up on her baking," Liz said. "I plan to head straight over there to help her. Oh, and by the way, we didn't find anything in our search for Lavinia Taylor yesterday. Ina and I made it through all of the records."

"I appreciate your searching, but I have another lead on her." She told her friends about the house she and James had found and about Angus Underwood.

"But the house you found is in Mills Landing."

"It doesn't fit, I know, but Angus's family could have moved over the years. I'll have to ask him about it."

"What's this we hear about James's friend Gary?" June asked.

Ruth sighed. "I'm still not over the shock of learning the killer might be someone James knows. That makes this all hit too close to home. Can we talk about something else?"

Maggie glanced out the window. "I sure hope this weather holds. They're saying rain is forecasted, and the threat of it might keep people indoors."

"Speaking of the festival." Ruth pulled her ever-present clipboard from her tote bag. "I'm still looking for a few volunteers for the afternoon."

"I can help," James offered as he joined them.

"That would be great. Come find me, and I'll put you to work."

"Does everyone else have jobs this afternoon?" Maggie asked.

"I'm not assigned, but I'll do whatever Ruth gives to me," Ina said.

"David and I will be judging the cake decorating contest," Liz said.

"Such hardships you endure for the community." Maggie laughed.

Fran's expression perked up. "I'm going to take some time to enjoy the textile booths, and then I'll be working at The Quilt Cupboard until we close."

"You know where I'll be," June said.

"At the shop," Maggie replied. "I'll do my best to stop by and give you some breaks."

"I've packed my lunch, so you do what you need to do," June said. "I can handle it."

Maggie thanked her friend and checked her watch. "I should get going. I have a long list of things to get done yet today."

In her car, Maggie retrieved her phone and dialed Angus. She'd had to restrain herself from calling him the moment she got out of bed, but it was Sunday after all, and he probably wouldn't welcome an early call.

"Good morning, Mr. Underwood," she said after he answered the phone. "My name is Maggie Watson. I own Carriage House Antiques in Somerset Harbor, and I bought the carpetbag you sold to Carol Hansen at Grandma's Antiques. I was wondering if I might stop by to talk with you about the bag this morning."

"Don't know anything about the bag."

"But you did sell it to Carol, right?"

"Yes, but like I said, I don't know anything about it. My son found it when he was cleaning out the attic, and that's all I can tell you."

"Still, I'd really like to meet with you. Maybe my questions will bring back a memory." When he didn't respond, she added, "I'll bring some delicious muffins from our local coffee shop."

"Well . . ."

"I can pick them up and be there within the hour."

"Fine," he said.

"I'll need your address."

He rattled it off, and Maggie jotted it down.

After they'd hung up, Maggie set out for The Busy Bean at a brisk pace, since Shoreline Drive was still closed to car traffic. With dark, angry clouds above, few pedestrians walked the streets. *Probably won't have much of a turnout for today's festival,* she thought grimly.

Maggie found Daisy standing behind the counter. She still

had on the blue paisley dress she'd worn to church, but now a yellow apron with an embroidered bumblebee that matched the shop logo covered it.

"I need a box of mixed muffins to go," Maggie said breathlessly.

Daisy arched a perfectly plucked eyebrow. "What's your hurry?"

Maggie quickly explained.

"Then don't let me delay you." Daisy reached for a tall display case, and Maggie noticed that her brows were knit with worry.

"What's wrong, Daisy?" Maggie asked.

"Harry told me that his friend Eli Clayton is missing." She finished boxing the muffins, then perched on a stool.

Eli was Officer Samantha Clayton's father. Officer Clayton had been hurt investigating the break-in at the antiques shop the night before. "Missing?" Maggie asked.

"He went out on his boat before church, and when he didn't come home, his wife sent their son out to look for him. Their son found Eli's boat in a small harbor near Mills Landing, but he wasn't on it."

"Oh no." Maggie clutched Daisy's hand. As the wife of a fisherman, Daisy lived with this fear all the time—as did all of the families in town with relatives who daily took to the sea on their boats. "I'm sure the police have already launched their patrol boat. They'll find him."

Daisy smiled, but Maggie could tell it was forced. "With Eli being Officer Clayton's father, the police are on top of the incident."

"What have they found?"

"Nothing yet," Daisy said. "They're heading for his boat now."

"I'll say a prayer for them."

"That's what I've been doing since I heard. I know that's the most important thing, but I wish I could do more." Tears formed in Daisy's eyes, and she pushed to her feet. "No point in sitting around and dwelling on it. Keep busy, I always say."

Maggie picked up the muffins and patted Daisy's hand. "Stay strong and keep me updated, okay?"

She gave a firm nod.

Maggie left the shop, her excitement over getting to talk to Angus dulled by Daisy's news. She hurried down the street and decided to stop by the antiques shop to give June Angus's address—just in case. After the previous night, she didn't want to skip any precautions.

Through the window, she saw June sitting at the counter, her laptop open in front of her. Maggie poked her head inside the door. "I wanted to let you—"

"Oh, Maggie, wonderful," June said. "I have some exciting news for you about Lavinia Taylor."

Maggie didn't want Angus to wait, but she couldn't pass up hearing the news. She entered the shop and closed the door.

June pointed at her computer. "I've been on an ancestry site, and I found Lavinia's family line. Interestingly enough, her descendants have a history of smuggling liquor during Prohibition."

"Do you think that's related to Ike's death?"

June shrugged. "Anything's possible, I suppose. I've also confirmed that Homer Underwood was indeed her descendant and Angus's great-grandfather. Homer had a sister a year younger than he was. She married an Aldrich and had a son and grandson. So Angus should have a present-day connection to the Aldrich family, and I was about to start searching for current information on them."

"Then keep searching. I'll ask Angus about them, and then we can compare notes." Maggie jotted down Angus's address on a scratch pad and slid it across the counter. "This is where I'm going."

June nodded and returned her attention to her computer.

Maggie picked up the muffins and strode to the door. With knob in hand, she turned back. "By the way, have you heard about Eli Clayton?"

June shook her head, and Maggie brought her friend up to date. "I thought you'd like to know so you could pray for him."

June nodded solemnly, and Maggie hated that she'd spoiled June's good mood, but Eli needed all of their prayers.

"Let me know if you hear any news on Eli, will you?" Maggie asked.

"Of course. You do the same."

Maggie left and started down the street.

Suddenly, a man darted out of the shadows and stood in Maggie's path. He wore a Sea Dogs cap pulled low over his face, so it took a moment for his identity to register. When it did, Maggie took a step back.

"I heard you were looking for me," Gary said, a scowl on his face.

17

Maggie stared at Gary, her heart thumping a wild rhythm. *What kind of game is he playing?*

"Were you looking for me?" he asked.

She nodded. "Y-yes. I was."

"I've been out of town, but I finished my research on the sprockets." He lifted a large tote bag, one that was big enough to hold any number of weapons. "Can we go inside so I can lay out my papers?"

Going inside could put June in danger too, but Maggie didn't want to be alone with Gary. If she talked to him in the shop's back room, maybe she could keep June out of harm's way and still not be alone with the man.

She led him inside and introduced Gary to June.

June's eyes widened. "But you're the—"

"We'll be in the back, talking about Gary's discovery." Maggie made a production of setting the muffins on the counter to distract Gary. When he wasn't looking, she mimed for June to call the police.

June subtly nodded her understanding.

Maggie led the way to the back room, her fear making her intimately aware of her surroundings. She felt the warm glow of the antique lights and inhaled the strong cedar oil scent permeating the space. She stared at the wall covered with tools of every description and wondered if she could use any of them to defend herself if necessary.

Gary crossed the room in a lumbering gait, and she resisted the urge to back away, instead leaning on the large worktable because her legs had turned to rubber. She decided she would let him tell her about his discovery and not ask about his possible argument with Ike until the police arrived.

"Hotter than the desert out there." Gary set the bag on the table, then swiped a hand across his face. "Like I said, I finished looking at the sprockets and wanted to come right over." He drew out a few sheets of paper from the bag and set them on the tabletop. The top page held a photograph of the small sprocket with handwritten notes jotted in the margins. "It took a bit longer than I anticipated." He ran his finger over the paper. "I first thought this was for a wooden washing machine, but you see the ridges on the outside?"

She nodded, trying not to show how nervous she felt.

"The angle of the metal told me I was wrong. So I kept searching." He turned the page.

From Maggie's vantage point, it looked like the picture matched the one in the brochure. "That's it, right?" she asked.

Gary nodded and flipped to the next paper. "Ever see one of these?"

Swallowing her apprehension, Maggie picked up the page and studied the wooden item with a cross frame and matching sprocket on the side. A tall wooden structure rose up from the frame and long bar pedals resembling piano keys were located at the bottom. The item was stenciled with the words *Manchester* on one of the crosspieces.

She looked up at Gary. "I suppose I should know what this is, but I don't."

He handed her the next page, which featured the same item, only strands of thread were woven over the top, and what appeared to be the start of a rug was on the other side.

"It's a loom," she said.

"Correct."

"The sprocket fits a loom, then?" she clarified.

"Not just any loom — the Manchester." Gary puffed out his chest, and a satisfied smile tugged at his mouth.

"How can you be so certain you're right?"

He frowned, and she suspected her question had offended him. He reached into the bag and drew out the auction brochure along with a magnifying glass and handed them to her. "Look closely at the sprocket."

She bent over the picture and stared at the black cast iron. "What am I looking for?"

"Do you see how the edges of the sprocket resemble a modern power saw blade except that the teeth are spaced farther apart to carry the rods?"

"Yes."

"The spacing between the teeth is the key. The distance only matches the Manchester loom." Pride rang through his tone. "That plus the fact that the sprocket is circa the late 1800s — when the Manchester loom was manufactured — confirms my theory."

Maggie momentarily pushed aside the thought that he could possibly be Ike's killer. *If James trusts him* . . . "I can't thank you enough for your research. Though I have to say, I have no idea what a sprocket from a weaving loom has to do with the drawing of a home that we found in the carpetbag."

"Perhaps the person who lived in that home owned a Manchester."

"Lavinia Taylor, a weaver?"

"If it helps, I did a little research on looms while I was looking for the sprocket. It wasn't uncommon for a home to have a loom in the early 1800s. Later in the century, fabric became more readily available, and people wove more as a hobby."

"Did you happen upon the value of a loom like this one?"

"Around $500."

"Money wouldn't be a motive for stealing the sprocket to complete a loom that was damaged."

"No," he said. "That wouldn't make sense."

Maggie agreed, though she also knew that murder never made sense.

The doorbell tinkled, and Maggie glanced into the shop to see Officer Linton stride in.

She turned her focus back to Gary. "Listen, Gary, I was looking for you because I wanted to ask you about Ike Wynne. Did you have an argument with him the night he died?"

Gary's mouth fell open and his gaze shot around the room.

Maggie watched him carefully and waited for him to speak, to deny it, to say she was nuts to even suggest it. But he said nothing.

"If you argued and then pushed Ike, everyone will understand it was an accident," she said quietly, hoping to give him the opening if there was anything he needed to confess.

He took a step toward her. Renewed fear pierced her heart, and she quickly backed away, putting the table between them.

"You're afraid of me?" Gary gaped at her. "You think I'm going to hurt you? Wow."

"The only way I can change my opinion is if you tell me the truth. What happened that night?"

His eyes narrowed into snakelike slits. "I . . ."

"Thank you for coming, Officer Linton," June called out, most likely to let Maggie know he'd arrived.

Gary shot a look into the front of the shop, then spun and raced for the back door, whipping it open and fleeing.

A moment later, Officer Linton walked into the back room.

"Gary ran out the back," Maggie said. "He might be our killer. Go after him!"

Officer Linton remained in place with his feet planted wide. "Did he admit to killing Ike, or are you basing your opinion on feelings?"

She lifted her chin. "He didn't deny arguing with Ike."

"Did he admit to doing so?"

"No."

"Then we have no reason to pursue him other than to talk to him. Which we will do."

"But he—"

"He may not be involved at all," Officer Linton interrupted. "We could still be looking at Warren Duncan for this."

"Has anyone talked to him?"

Officer Linton nodded. "Chief Cole. But I can't share what they talked about."

"You said you were still considering him as a suspect, so that means you haven't ruled him out either."

"I suppose it might look like that to you," he said, his answer noncommittal as usual.

"But if it turns out that Gary isn't involved in this, why would he run when you got here?"

The officer shrugged. "Like I said, talking with Gary is the only way we'll have an answer." He shifted on his feet. "Now that we know he's in town, we'll keep an eye out for him."

"So will I."

"Okay then. I'll get back on patrol."

When he was gone, Maggie turned to June, who stood quietly in the doorway. Maggie told June about the sprocket since she doubted June had heard that part of her conversation with Gary.

"Who would have guessed the sprocket was for a loom?" June said.

Maggie nodded, and for the first time she seriously pondered Gary's news. "It's a strong lead, and I was too busy trying to figure out if Gary's guilty to really think about it."

"Perhaps Gary is innocent. Giving you information about the sprocket that could lead you to the killer does seem to point in that direction."

"Or he could be sending me on a wild goose chase so I'll leave him alone."

"That too," June said. "We can do our own research on the Manchester loom. Katie Finnegan at Pins & Needles is a weaver. You should ask her about it."

"Good idea, but first, Angus is expecting me." Maggie grabbed the muffins, made her way to the car, and pointed it toward Seacliff.

She'd hoped to concentrate on the new lead on her drive, but the moment she caught sight of the harbor, her thoughts drifted to Eli. She didn't know Eli well, but she did know he was a kind man who would help anyone at the drop of a hat, and she hated that he was missing at sea. She offered an additional prayer for him and for his family too. She could imagine how terrified they must be.

At the exit for Angus's street, she turned off the highway. She located his house about half a mile down the street, and her hopes plummeted.

The house was a small bungalow with a large porch. Clapboard siding was the only thing it had in common with the drawing. Instead of a second floor, the home had a framed attic with a large porthole window in the middle. The house was clearly Craftsman in design, a style that was popular in the 1920s, so she doubted it was much older than that.

She stared at the house for a few moments, trying to wrap her mind around the fact that the place was not what she'd expected. The front door opened, and the man from Carol's video poked his head out.

Maggie grabbed the muffins and climbed out of her car. By the time she reached the front door, he was appraising her with a wary gaze from the small stoop.

"You must be Maggie Watson," he said.

"I am, and you're Angus."

He nodded, and she held out the muffins.

"Come on in." He led her inside.

Scuffed hardwood covered the floor of the foyer as well as the living room to her right. Built-in cabinets flanked the fireplace, and heavy wood beams crossed the ceiling.

"You have a lovely home," she said. "When was it built?"

"In 1925."

So she'd been right about the age of the house.

Angus gestured to the room opposite the living room. "Let's go to the dining room." He led her to an oak chair sitting by a solid oak table with a heavy pedestal base. "I'll grab some plates from the kitchen."

He disappeared through a swinging door, and she sat and opened the muffins. He soon returned with a pair of Blue Willow plates. He handed one to Maggie, and she almost gasped at how casually he handled what she suspected to be authentic china from the 1800s.

A ding sounded from the kitchen.

"That's the coffeepot. I made a fresh one. Would you like some?"

"That would be lovely."

The moment he left the room, she flipped her plate over and found the telltale maker's mark. The plates had been made by Hulse, Nixon, & Adderley in Staffordshire, England. Only in business for fifteen years, the company had made the pattern between 1853 and 1868. The dishes were much older than Angus's house. *They could have been handed down from his ancestors. Lavinia Taylor perhaps?*

Carrying two mugs of steaming coffee, he entered the room again and set a mug in front of Maggie.

"I love Blue Willow china patterns," she said, hoping to get him talking about the history of the dishes.

"This?" He tapped the edge of his plate, and she realized he had no idea of its value. "Family's been using these dishes for as long as I can remember."

"They've been passed down to you, then?"

"My parents had them when I was born, but I have no idea where they came from before that."

"Perhaps one of their parents?"

He shrugged.

"You don't know if your grandparents owned the plates?"

He took a muffin and removed the paper. "No. My dad's family perished at sea, and he never wanted to talk about them, so we didn't."

Odd. "But still, you must have asked questions."

He shook his head. "Times were different back then. You didn't sass your elders like you see so many kids doing nowadays. Sure, I asked about my grandparents, but my dad only had to tell me one time that he never wanted to talk about them, and I didn't bring it up again."

"What about your mother? Did you ask her?"

"Yeah, but she gave me the same story and confirmed that Dad didn't want to discuss it." Angus shook his head. "I often thought that my dad might have felt responsible for their deaths, but like I said, I never mentioned it." He chomped off a big bite of the muffin.

"What about the Aldriches?"

"The who?"

"The Aldrich family—your great-grandfather's sister married an Aldrich."

His eyes narrowed. "I don't know anything about this woman."

"The genealogy site lists her in your family tree."

"Look, lady," he said, frowning. "I told you I don't know anything about the previous generations."

She'd planned to press him on it, but he seemed genuinely surprised by her line of questioning, so she changed directions. "Tell me about the carpetbag and sprockets you sold to Carol."

"Those old things?" He set down his muffin. "Like I said. My son found them in the back of the attic in an old trunk. I'm cleaning out the place so I can sell it, and I have no use for old junk."

"Did you notice the name on the bottom of the bag?"

"Yeah, Taylor, I think."

"Lavinia Taylor."

"Right, yeah, that's what it said. But I don't know who she is."

"Would it surprise you if I told you she was your great-grandfather's mother?"

"No, I suppose not. Like I said, Dad didn't talk about his family." He frowned again. "All I care about is my son, Shelton. He's my only living relative. I wish he lived here, but he moved to Portland."

Maggie nodded, but she wouldn't let him sidetrack her. "What did your father do for a living?"

"He was a fisherman, like most people around here. Me too."

"Might that have included smuggling liquor during Prohibition?"

Angus crossed his arms and glared at her.

"With Maine being the first state to enact Prohibition," Maggie said, remembering facts she'd learned when researching an old bottle, "smuggling would have been a lucrative career from 1851 until the national repeal in 1933."

"My dad wouldn't have been involved in something like that."

"But he would have known if his family was involved in smuggling. Maybe that's how they died."

Angus shot to his feet and pointed at the door. "You can leave if you're going to slander my family's name!"

"I'm sorry," Maggie said. "I'm only speculating on what the research says."

"Then feel free to speculate on your own." He marched to the door and yanked it open.

At the door, she turned to face him. "I am very sorry, Angus. I didn't mean to offend you, but a man has been murdered, and finding a killer sometimes involves asking tough questions."

"Murder?" Angus roared, scaring birds into flight. "Now you think I'm involved in a *murder*?"

"No no, but the man who was murdered bought the sprockets and bid against me for the carpetbag, so we think his death has something to do with those items."

"Which I once owned," he said, still sounding peeved but lowering his voice as understanding set in.

"Exactly." Maggie took a deep breath. "I've just learned that one of the sprockets was meant for a weaving loom. Do you know anything about a loom that might have been in your family?"

He shook his head and started to close the door.

She dug out her business card and handed it to him. "Will you please call me if you think of anything?"

"I doubt I will since I don't plan to think about it." He closed the door firmly.

"That didn't go so well," Maggie mumbled as she headed for the car. "Not well at all."

When Maggie returned to Somerset Harbor, she parked her car at home and took off on foot to Pins & Needles. She worked her way through the groups of festivalgoers and was about to round the corner when she saw a man with the same build as Gary and wearing a Portland Sea Dogs cap slip into the crowd. She abandoned her plan and hurried after him.

He wove in and out of the people on the sidewalk, but Maggie managed to keep sight of him. When the man suddenly stopped and turned, she caught a good look at his face.

Gary!

He glanced to the side and then took off running. *Drat. He must have seen me.* She pursued him, offering her apologies as she bumped into people in her haste. At the next corner, she saw Officer Linton watching the crowd. She shouted at him to catch his attention.

"Officer Linton! Over there!" she pointed ahead. "It's Gary in the baseball cap."

He pivoted like a precision soldier and took off. As Gary burst through the crowd, Officer Linton appeared in front of him, planting his feet wide. Gary came to an abrupt stop and frantically looked around. She thought he was considering fleeing, but then his shoulders sagged.

"I've been hoping to talk to you, Mr. Keel," Officer Linton said.

Gary turned and eyed Maggie. "I've been out of town until this morning."

"Ask him about the argument," Maggie said to the officer as she tried to catch her breath.

"Perhaps we should all take a walk to the station house," Officer Linton suggested.

Gary looked at his watch. "I'm a bit pressed for time."

"It's only a block away," Officer Linton responded in a tone that Maggie knew he used to handle difficult people.

"I—"

"Right this way." Officer Linton held out his hand.

"Fine." Gary shoved his hands into his pockets.

Officer Linton's hand drifted to his weapon. "I prefer your hands to stay where I can see them."

Gary muttered something under his breath but pulled his hands out and let them hang at his sides. "I was on my way to an appointment, so let's make this quick."

Officer Linton turned to Maggie. "I would like you to accompany us to the station. You can wait in the lobby in case I have any additional questions for you."

"Of course," she said.

Officer Linton walked next to Gary, and Maggie traipsed along after them. Once at the station house, the pair disappeared into the back, and Maggie started pacing in the front lobby. She smiled at Paula. The receptionist responded with a tight smile, which was very cordial for her—especially considering she had to work on a Sunday. With the festival in full swing, Maggie knew the entire police force was working overtime.

The door suddenly popped open, and Gary charged out the door, marching straight for the exit.

"That's it?" Maggie asked. "You're finished?"

Gary adjusted his cap. "I can't see you giving up on this, so I might as well tell you what's going on." He drew her to the side of the room and out of Paula's earshot. "You're right. I argued with Ike, but I didn't lay a hand on him."

"What did you argue about?" Maggie asked.

He took a deep breath, as if collecting his thoughts. "A few years back, when my wife and I were getting a divorce, I hid some assets. Her lawyer hired Ike to find them. When I saw him outside the gym, I gave him a piece of my mind. That's all."

Maggie didn't believe it was that simple. "People have killed for far less. Sounds like a possible motive for murder."

"It might sound that way," he said, his brows narrowing, "but I know where his office is located, so why would I wait two years to kill him?"

She didn't have an answer for that.

"That's the whole story," he said. "If you're looking for something more complicated, I'm afraid I can't help you."

"If it's all that innocent, then why did you run off that night, and why take off when I asked you about it? Seems like only a guilty person would do that."

"Or one who didn't want his teenage daughter to find out he'd done something underhanded to her mother." Gary shook his head. "I love my daughter, and it would humiliate her to learn I tried to hide money from her mother."

As a parent, Maggie knew how far she'd go to protect Emily, and Maggie had to admit she believed him. "Did you follow James and me yesterday?"

"Follow you? Why would I do that?"

"Just answer the question."

"No. I didn't follow you."

"And when we stopped at your house last night and you didn't answer the door?"

"Like I said, I was out of town."

"But I saw the curtains move."

"My daughter's staying with me this week, and she's been taught not to answer the door for strangers."

As much as Maggie hated to admit it because it meant she

still had no answers, she was satisfied with his explanations. At least James would be glad to hear the news.

"Any other questions?" Gary asked wearily.

She shook her head. "I'm sorry for suspecting you, Gary. And I appreciate you researching the sprockets."

He gave a firm nod of his head. "You can repay me by not repeating the story about my wife."

"I won't mention it to anyone," she promised.

He nodded again and took off for the door. Maggie followed him out of the building and resumed her trek to Pins & Needles. Through the shop's sparkling glass door, Maggie saw Katie standing with a customer near a shelf filled with skeins of yarn in every color imaginable. In her midthirties, Katie had long red hair, a round, friendly face, and cheeks covered in freckles. Her white knit top was accented with a navy crocheted scarf that featured a delicate rosette in the front, and Maggie assumed she'd made it herself.

Inside the shop, Maggie peered at a cozy knitting area with its orange checked chairs circling a studded leather trunk that served as a coffee table. Katie had used antiques relating to the business as decorations throughout the shop. One such item was a Mauchline Ware knitting ball that separated into two pieces and held a skein of yarn. The wooden ball had a lacquer finish and was looped to a string that could be worn around the knitter's neck to keep control of the yarn. It sat on a Federal-style mahogany Martha Washington sewing stand with three drawers and rounded sides that opened from the top to store knitting or sewing items.

Katie excused herself from the customer and crossed the room to Maggie.

"I'm surprised you're able to get out of your shop with this weekend's big crowd." Katie flashed her a warm smile.

"You know June can handle just about anything on her own."

"What I wouldn't give to be able to afford my own June." Katie sighed.

Maggie chuckled. "Do you have a minute for a quick question, or would you like me to come back?"

"Now's fine."

Maggie took the Manchester photos from her bag and laid them on the counter. "June told me you're a weaver, and I'm interested in learning about this loom."

Katie picked up the top picture. "A Manchester. I've never seen one in person, but I've read a lot about them."

"Do you know anyone in the area who owns one?"

"No, but I think one was recently sold at a private auction for my weavers guild."

"Do you know who sold it?"

Katie shook her head. "But I can look online at the listing to see if I can figure it out."

"Could you do it now?"

"Sounds urgent."

Maggie leaned in so she wouldn't be overheard. "I think it might provide a lead in the Ike Wynne murder case."

"Oh my. I'll do it right away." Katie turned to her computer terminal. Her fingers flew over the keyboard, but Maggie felt each keystroke like a tick on the clock.

"Okay, I'm on the auction site now." Katie ran her finger over the wheel on her mouse, the scrolling sound echoing through the space. "I see it. The Manchester."

Maggie wanted to race around the counter to look at the screen, but she resisted the urge.

Katie continued, "This particular one was built in 1885. It didn't sell for what I'd have expected." She bent closer to the screen and squinted. "Oh, I see. It's because one of the original main sprockets was missing, and they replaced it with a modern one."

A missing sprocket!

"The loom only went for $350," Katie said. "With the pristine condition of the loom, it should have fetched at least $500 or $600."

Maggie nodded, but the value was irrelevant at this point. "Can you see who sold it?"

Katie nodded, but bit her lip.

"What is it?"

"I don't know if I should share this information with you. Technically, it's—"

"I completely understand," Maggie said. "I don't want to put you in a spot that would make you uncomfortable, but this is very important. Would it help if I promise not to share the name with anyone who doesn't need to know about it?"

Katie nodded and looked at her screen again. "Yes. And I trust you. His name is Hal Aldrich."

"Yes!"

Katie gave Maggie a sideways look, but she didn't care. She'd discovered that a Manchester loom with a missing sprocket had been sold at auction by a man who could be one of Lavinia Taylor's descendants.

Maggie lowered her voice. "Do you have an address for Hal?"

"No, not the exact address, but his profile says he's from Mills Landing."

Maggie could barely stop herself from shouting for joy again. "Can you tell me who bought the loom?"

Katie looked at the monitor again and scrolled with her mouse. "Her name is Felicia Evans. She lives in Portland."

Maggie jotted down the names to be sure she didn't forget them. "Thank you, Katie. This information is priceless."

Katie's brows drew together. "Remember, you said you wouldn't share those names with anyone unless you have to."

"I'll remember," Maggie promised as she headed out the door.

She knew exactly where she would go next. Big drops of rain started to fall, and the crowd had thinned considerably, allowing her to cross the street with ease. Her mind was filled with her discovery, and she nearly stumbled into a large pothole. She lurched to a stop just in time, and that's when she heard someone close behind her.

She turned to see a man, the hood of his black jacket pulled tightly over his head. The dark skies shadowed his face, so she couldn't make it out, but he was of the same physical build as the man who had followed her last night. If that wasn't enough to make her heart race, the fact that it was too warm for a jacket—which meant he could be wearing it to conceal a weapon—set her pulse pounding.

He advanced on her. Step by step.

Terror clutching her heart, she backed away. Her foot dropped into the pothole, and she lost her balance. She flailed out her arms but knew she was going to fall, and with a sinking dread she realized that the mysterious stalker might kill her before she even had a chance to get back on her feet.

"You there! Stop!" James's voice came from down the street.

The man spun. Maggie hit the ground with an "Oof!" and lost sight of him.

She heard footsteps running—one set, then another. James chasing the man, she hoped. She turned and confirmed her suspicion. The man slipped on the wet pavement and went into a crazy skid. James grabbed the man's arm and twisted it up behind him.

Maggie scrambled to her feet.

"Hey," the guy complained. "Let me go."

James ignored his pleas and marched him back toward Maggie. "Are you all right?" James's gaze ran over her from head to toe.

"Fine."

James tightened his grip on the man. "I think a call to the police is in order."

"Wait," the man said. "I didn't do anything wrong. There's no reason for you to hold me like this or call the police."

Maggie glared at the guy. "Then why were you threatening me?"

"I didn't say a word."

"You didn't need to. You were following me with your hand in your pocket. How was I to know whether or not you were carrying a gun?"

"A gun? Are you crazy? No, I don't have a gun."

"I'll confirm that if you don't mind." James patted the man's pockets. "He's telling the truth."

The man shook his head. "Why would you think I had one?"

"You've followed me twice now. If not to hurt me, then why?"

The man arched a brow and watched her for a moment. "I've been trying to find out what happened to Ike. You bought the carpetbag, so I thought you knew about the drawing and had stolen the sprocket."

"Me? You thought *I* killed Ike?"

"Yes."

Maggie shook her head in disbelief. "Who are you anyway?"

"Shelton Underwood."

Maggie's mouth dropped open. "Angus's son?"

He nodded.

"I think it's time you tell us exactly what's going on here," James said. "Let's get out of the road, and you can fill us in."

James kept Shelton firmly in his hold and escorted him to the closest sidewalk.

"It would be nice if you'd let go of my arm," Shelton muttered.

James stared at him. "It would have been nice if you hadn't followed and scared Maggie too, but you did, so my hand stays put until you prove I can trust you."

"Fine," Shelton said. "I hired Ike so—"

"You?" Maggie interrupted. "You're the one who hired him to buy the carpetbag?"

"And the sprockets."

"Explain."

"It's about my dad, you see. He's fallen on hard times and has to sell his house to raise money. One day, I was helping him get ready to put the house on the market and looking for things he might sell, and it wore him out. He took a nap, and I headed up to the attic. I found an old trunk. Since it was locked, I figured it had something valuable in it, so I jimmied the lock."

Maggie could easily imagine the excitement of making such a discovery. "And what did you find?"

"The carpetbag and sprockets, plus my grandfather's old journal." Shelton shook his head in slow, sorrowful arcs. "Turns out my family was smuggling alcohol during Prohibition. By the time the law was repealed, my ancestors had become quite wealthy. But my grandfather didn't like the reputation they'd gained from the smuggling. So he moved to a new town and made up a story about the family perishing at sea. He didn't talk about their past with anyone, not even my dad."

"I wondered about the smuggling and asked your dad about it today," Maggie said. "Either he's good at lying or you didn't tell him."

"I figured at his age there was no point in telling him about it."

"But he sold the carpetbag and sprockets, so he had to know about those at least."

Shelton nodded. "I messed up there. Dad woke up and came up to the attic while I was reading the journal. I shoved it under my shirt and closed the trunk, then took the journal back to Portland to finish reading it. By the time I learned the importance of the bag and the sprockets, he'd sold them."

"And that's when you hired Ike," Maggie said. "Was that you with him on the phone the night of the auction, telling him how high to bid?"

Shelton nodded. "Yes."

"I don't get it," Maggie said. "They aren't worth more than $300 combined, so why hire a PI to find them?"

"The drawing inside the bag is worth more than you can imagine." Shelton took a deep breath before continuing. "When Lavinia Taylor got married, she had the family home built. The journal says she hid something in her carpetbag and if anyone found it, it would help them locate the house."

"I assume you're referring to the drawing, but did the journal say why she hid it in the bag?"

He shook his head. "It does mention a tunnel under the old family house that runs from a secret door in the basement to the cliff—that's how they smuggled the alcohol—so maybe it has to do with that."

"There's a padlock on the drawing. Maybe it's a sign for the tunnel?" Maggie dug a copy from her bag and held it out.

Shelton studied it. "Yeah, that's where the journal says the tunnel is located."

"Okay, so say you use the drawing to find the old house," James weighed in. "I still don't see the value in that."

"My ancestors were engaged in illegal activities. They couldn't use a bank for their smuggling proceeds, so they stored their cash in that tunnel. When my granddad left the family house to become a legitimate fisherman, his cousin stayed behind to carry on the 'family business.' Granddad wrote that his cousin wasn't at all bothered by morals. So Granddad took the bag and kept it so his cousin would always have to wonder if someone might happen upon his smuggling operation. Granddad thought that might motivate his cousin to straighten up."

"Did it?" James asked.

"The journal doesn't say."

"And no one ever told your father about all of this?" Maggie asked.

Shelton shook his head.

"And it sounds like you think the money is still in the tunnel."

"I'm hoping so. Dad could really use it."

Maggie let the news filter through her brain. "How are the sprockets related?"

"The larger one is irrelevant—a way to throw people off the trail if they learn about the tunnel—but the small one is from a weaving loom that belonged to Lavinia."

Maggie thought to mention the recently sold loom with the missing sprocket, but decided she'd hold off until Shelton told the entire story.

"Though the sprocket was made for the loom," Shelton continued, "when it's taken off and pressed into a matching pattern on the tunnel door, it unlocks the door."

Maggie's heart soared at the news until she remembered the sprockets had been missing since Ike's murder.

"It's odd to use a sprocket as a key," James commented.

"It was kind of ingenious if you ask me," Shelton replied. "They could hide the key in plain sight on the loom, and no one would think anything of it."

"So," James said, "thinking the sprocket and bag would make you rich, you hired Ike to buy them back, but why not do it yourself?"

"I told you, I want the money for my dad, but I didn't want anything to be traced back to him. And you know how word travels around small towns. I didn't want it to get back to Dad that I'd bought them and then have to tell him about his family. Besides that, he's a proud old dude and doesn't like to accept help."

Maggie carefully appraised Shelton. "How do we know that Ike didn't find out about the money and was going off on his own with the sprockets, so you killed him?"

"I guess you don't, other than my word that I didn't kill him."

"You don't have an alibi, then."

"I was home alone."

"We'll let the police sort that out." James dug out his phone.

Maggie held up her hand before James could make the call. "But what about the break-ins? First at Grandma's Antiques on Thursday and then my shop last night."

"I didn't do that, if that's your question."

"Do you have an alibi for those nights?"

"Same one. At home alone, sleeping in my own bed."

In other words, no alibi. "What kind of vehicle do you drive?"

"Pickup. Ford F-250."

"You followed me on Friday, then the two of us yesterday," Maggie accused.

"Friday, but not yesterday," he admitted. "I had to work, and I was in Portland all day."

Maggie shot a look at James. His surprised expression said that he was thinking what she was thinking: If Shelton was telling the truth, then it had to be the person who had stolen the sprocket who had tailed them yesterday. And if the story in the journal was true, the man with the tunnel key had a lot of money riding on finding the house. Which meant he'd have no qualms about killing to achieve his goal.

"I need to see the journal," Maggie said.

Shelton reached for his backpack, but James stayed his hand. "I'll get it."

James retrieved an old leather-bound journal. Maggie flipped through it, reading snippets of the entries and confirming Shelton's story.

"Well?" James asked.

"It looks real." Maggie met his gaze. "Time to call the police."

James made the call, and Officer Linton took Shelton to the station for questioning. After she and James had given their statements, they returned to her shop to regroup.

Maggie paced back and forth as she, James, and June tried to figure out what to do next.

"Okay, so what do we know?" June asked.

"This is becoming so confusing I think we need to write it down." Maggie grabbed a sheet of paper from the counter and climbed onto a stool. She wrote the words *house drawing, tunnel, sprockets, smuggling, Angus,* and *Shelton.* "We know that the drawing of the house is the home that has the tunnel. The big question is, where is the house, and who owns it now? Is it the Duncans' place?"

"*If* Shelton's story was true," James said, "I can't imagine the family ever selling the house. Unless, of course, the money is all gone."

"Prohibition ended in . . . what, 1933?" June asked. "That means we're talking about ninety years or so when the other family members could have blown through the money."

"But what family?" James asked.

"The Aldriches," Maggie and June answered at the same time. They laughed, and James sat staring at them.

June explained the discovery of Homer's sister, and Maggie added *Aldrich?* to her list under *tunnel.* "If the money is gone, and the Aldriches don't need to hide their tunnel any longer, they could have sold the house to the Duncans."

"That's what I was coming to talk to you about before Shelton showed up," James said. "I've been digging into property records, and the Duncans bought the house from a Nicholas Ingles."

"How long did he own it?" Maggie asked.

"I'm not sure yet," James replied. "The county only keeps online records dating back to 1980."

"I can search the Aldrich family line to see if Nicholas Ingles is related," June offered.

Maggie noted the name on her paper. "That's going to take time though, right?"

"It could," June said. "All depends on the public information I find online."

"Can either of you think of a faster way to get the address for the Aldrich family home?"

"I assume you've looked in the phone book," James said.

"I can see that you need to ask, but really?" June put her hands on her hips.

James chuckled. "You're right. I shouldn't have doubted you." He became serious again. "The online database is only searchable by property address, so that won't be much help."

Maggie tried to think of a solution, but she came up empty, and it was time to move on. "What about the break-ins?" She added them to her list and told June and James about seeing the thief steal a ring at Grandma's Antiques on the security tape. "Do you think we're missing anything here?"

June's eyes narrowed. "If we are, it's not obvious."

"What about Eli and his boat?" James said. "I know it's kind of far-fetched, but I wondered if his disappearance is related to Samantha getting hurt."

Maggie pictured Eli's boat in the cove and remembered what Daniel Simpson had said about viewing houses from his boat. A vision of the house from the drawing with a tunnel running to the cliff replaced the boat in her mind.

"That's it! I have to go." Maggie grabbed her paper and shoved it into her tote bag.

"Where?" James asked.

"It's a long shot, but I'll let you know if it pans out." She glanced at June. "Call me if you find the Aldriches' address or anything on Nicholas."

And with that, she raced out the door.

20

Maggie rushed to The Busy Bean, barely noticing that the rain had picked up. She slipped inside and headed for Daisy, who was sitting at a back table with Harry. Their faces were somber, their mouths tight. Either Eli had been found and it was bad news, or they still hadn't heard anything yet. Maggie suddenly felt a pang of guilt. Here they were, worried for their friend's life, and she'd shown up to ask a favor.

Maggie couldn't intrude that way. She turned to go, but Daisy called out, "Come join us, Maggie."

She tried to come up with a reason for being there other than to ask a favor as she crossed over to them, but her mind was blank.

Daisy got up. "Sit down, hon, and I'll get you a cup of coffee."

Maggie did as she was bid and looked at Harry. Slightly heavyset, he had golden-brown eyes, dark brown hair, and a short beard. His hands, which fiddled with his cup, were red and rough from his days spent on the ocean.

"Have you heard anything about Eli?" she asked.

"Nothing new."

Daisy returned with the coffee. "The police say it doesn't look like there was any foul play."

"There was no blood found," Harry added, but Maggie could read between the lines. No blood didn't mean no foul play; Eli could have been pushed overboard.

Daisy placed her hand over Harry's. "You know Eli is a strong swimmer. He probably swam to shore and is hiking home."

"We've been up and down that road and we didn't see him."

"He could have taken another route," Maggie offered, though in her heart she suspected he would stay on the coastal highway, and with water temperatures in the fifties, even in July, she doubted his strong swimming would serve him for long. "If it helps, I'm continuing to pray for him."

"Of course that helps, doesn't it, Harry?"

He nodded, but his expression tightened. He got to his feet. "I can't sit here. I need to do something."

"Now hold on, Harry." Daisy stood. "Don't go and do something rash."

"I won't."

"Then tell me what you have planned."

"Maybe I'll take the boat out and look for him."

"The Coast Guard and police are already doing that."

"But they don't know the waters like I do."

"Promise me you'll be careful," Daisy said resignedly.

"Could I tag along with you, Harry?" Maggie asked.

Daisy pivoted to look at Maggie. "On the boat? Whatever for?"

She explained the secret tunnel. "I want to search the coastline to see if I can find the door, and if Harry's going out anyway . . ."

"Now, Maggie—" Daisy began.

"I'd love the company," Harry interrupted. "C'mon. I'll even let you use my binoculars."

She stood, and Daisy put a hand on her arm. "Wait a minute. It's bound to be cold out on the water. Let me pack you a thermos of coffee and something to eat in case it takes longer than you expect."

When Daisy returned with an old plaid thermos from the '50s and a lunch bag, she gave Harry a hug and reminded him to be careful again.

Outside, Harry lifted his face to the sky. "We best be getting out there before the storm rolls in."

Maggie had hoped to stop for more serviceable shoes and a jacket, but she didn't want to delay Harry.

He must have read her mind. "Daisy keeps a few things on the boat including boots that you can wear."

They would be too big, but Maggie would make do. "Thank you, Harry."

He took off with big lumbering strides, and she had to jog to keep up with him and hop aboard his fishing boat before he cast off and set the motor rumbling. She settled into a cracked vinyl seat in the small cabin. As rain pelted the roof overhead, she was glad for the dry shelter of the *Daisy Mae*. She could do without the strong fishy odor of the boat, but she wasn't about to complain.

Harry was the opposite of Daisy — quiet and introspective — so Maggie didn't expect much in the way of conversation, and she sat back for the ride. The steady thrum of the motor and the boat rising and falling over the ocean swells made her eyes droop even though napping was the last thing she wanted to do.

She turned to Harry. "You said I could use your binoculars?"

"They're in the compartment between our seats. Help yourself."

She dug them out, and though they hadn't reached Mills Landing, she focused along the coastline to get used to looking through the binoculars. She enjoyed seeing the variety of architectural styles as they buzzed along at top speed, but she had to look away periodically or the steep swells left her feeling dizzy.

Harry suddenly slowed the boat. "Mills Landing is just ahead."

She peered at the shore, trying not to blink so she didn't miss a thing.

"When I drop anchor, I'll want the binoculars."

She hated to give them up, but looking for Eli was far more important than her mission of searching for an old house. She kept her focus on the shore, where she soon spotted the Duncans' house, giving her their approximate location. She intensified her search on both sides of their house but didn't see another home resembling the drawing.

The boat came to a stop, and she handed the binoculars over to Harry.

"That's Eli's boat," he said and pointed at a well-used white-and-red fishing boat much like his own. Two Coast Guard cutters were anchored nearby, and uniformed men stood on the deck, peering at the water.

"Coast Guard's not going to let us get very close." Harry turned away and started running the binoculars over the area.

She strained to see the coastline, but she couldn't make out the homes well enough to learn anything. *My phone*—she could use her phone's camera to zoom in. She lifted it from her bag and narrowed the camera's focus to the shoreline near the Duncans' home. Seeing the video button next to the picture icon gave her an idea. She would record the area so she could enlarge it on her computer later to take a better look.

Harry anchored the boat in several different locations and spent nearly an hour searching, but there was no sign of Eli. Maggie wasn't surprised. If the Coast Guard hadn't found him, the odds weren't in their favor, but Maggie fully understood Harry's need to search. If one of her friends was missing, she'd move heaven and earth to find him or her.

Harry lowered his binoculars and looked into the distance. "Storm's coming in fast. We need to head back."

"I'm sorry we didn't find Eli."

"Didn't much expect to," he muttered and handed her the binoculars.

She took that to mean he didn't want to continue their conversation, so she watched out the window in silence. The winds picked up, and the ocean swells grew choppier, peppering the windshield with water. With the added spray, Maggie couldn't tell how hard it was raining. When they reached the dock, she was surprised to see the rain hadn't picked up much at all. Still, ominous gray clouds hung in the distance, and they hurried down the sidewalk. She bid Harry good-bye and rushed back to the manor to review the video she'd shot from the boat.

Eager to be out of the rain, she bustled through the sunroom door. Snickers immediately came running.

"Some days I wish I was a spoiled cat like you," she said and marched to the bathroom to towel off and put on dry clothes. Then she hurried to the office and plugged her phone into her computer. She'd taken a total of five videos, and when the files had uploaded, she set them to play. The first two videos were uneventful, but the third one had her on the edge of her chair and enlarging the picture as much as her computer would allow.

"There!" she said to Snickers, who came padding into the room. "Another house that looks like the drawing, and it's only a few miles away from the Duncans' house."

Snickers meowed loudly.

"I have to see it." Maggie checked the local radar on the Internet. "The real storm is still an hour away, which gives me plenty of time."

She ran to the coat hooks in the sunroom and donned her raincoat. Snickers followed, and his meow sounded disapproving.

"I'm sorry I have to leave again, but I'll be back soon, and we can spend time together then."

She set off for Mills Landing. On the highway, the rain picked up despite the radar's prediction, and she was forced to switch the wipers to high.

Maggie crept along the highway, glancing at the fog hovering over the craggy rocks. She could no longer see the steep drop-off to the ocean. When she arrived in Mills Landing, she managed to find the road the Duncans lived on. Between each thump of the wiper blades, she searched for the correct house.

Nearly three miles past their home, she spotted the house that matched the drawing perfectly and pulled to the curb across the road. *If only we hadn't missed this the first time.* She turned off her car and tucked her phone into her coat's zipper pocket to keep it dry.

Outside, the rain and wind buffeted her body, but her focus remained on the house. Once she got up close, she noticed the house had not fared well over the years. The black shutters had grayed and one hung precariously from a corner. White paint peeled in long strips, exposing gray siding, and the porch boards looked like they might collapse at any moment. She was starting to believe the Aldriches had long since abandoned the house.

Only one way to find out.

She knocked hard on the ornate door that showed deep cracks in the wood. Time ticked by, and she listened for footfalls inside, but the only sound she heard was the rain pelting the roof. She knocked again and gave it a few additional minutes.

"No one home," she muttered, but she wouldn't be deterred. She tried to peek through a window that was accessible from the porch, but it was covered by a heavy curtain. She crossed to the other window she could reach from the porch and found the faded brocade curtains pulled tight there too.

Now what?

She took out her phone and entered the address into the county property record search. As she waited for the results, she focused on the door and windows, hoping to see a sign of life.

The search information loaded, revealing the owner was Hal Aldrich.

"Bingo!" This was the house, all right, and she wasn't leaving without a quick search of the property.

She checked the neighboring houses, and seeing no one watching her, she hurried across the front yard, which was covered in weeds and high grass. She darted around the corner and paused to assess the area with wild berry brambles, knee-high grass, and overgrown weeds. Farther ahead, she could see the harbor, but the view today was hazy and gloomy.

The rain picked up, pummeling her face. She bent her head and crept toward the back of the house, where the drawing displayed the heart-shaped lock.

A deep male voice cut through the air behind her. "I suggest you stop right there."

She started to turn but froze when the cold, hard barrel of a gun was shoved into her back.

21

Maggie screamed, and a big, meaty hand clamped over her mouth, sealing it and sending a wave of panic through her body.

"Stop with the screaming, or I'll use this." The man jabbed the gun into her ribs, the sharp angle sending pain reverberating along her side. "Now if you promise not to scream, I'll take my hand away."

Maggie suspected the howling wind and driving rain would mask a gunshot report enough that he could actually get away with shooting her despite the proximity of the nearby homes. She took a few deep breaths through her nose to stem her panic and nodded.

His hand fell away, but the gun barrel moved to her back again. She started to turn.

He stopped her with a firm hand on her shoulder.

"Who are you and what are you going to do with me?" she asked, surprised at how calm she sounded when she was barely keeping herself together.

"That's not important. Give me your phone." She handed it over reluctantly. "Start moving toward the back entrance of the house." He shoved the gun into her side again like a cattle prod.

Maggie stumbled forward. Her foot tangled in a trailing vine. She bent down to free herself as her mind raced to find a way to escape. If she could get far enough ahead of the gunman, she could run. But that wouldn't work. She couldn't outrun a bullet, and with the overgrown vegetation, she wasn't going to run anywhere, even without a gun at her back.

Oh why didn't I tell someone where I was going?

"You're free, now get going," he growled.

She stood up and walked at a snail's pace.

"Faster," he demanded.

"If I speed up, I'll get tangled again."

"I'm finding my way just fine." The gun pressed harder. "You can too."

She upped her pace, but not much. Still, she found herself at the peeling back door in no time. He pushed her against the building and planted his arm across her shoulders while he dug out a key and unlocked the door.

"You had to keep after this, didn't you?" he growled and pushed her inside.

She wasn't about to answer his question; she was busy wishing she hadn't made the trip alone. But she *was* alone, and it was up to her to find a way out. Starting with getting her bearings in the darkness. She squinted to try to make out the area around her, but darkness obscured everything.

"Move to your right so I can close the door," he said.

She felt along the floor with her foot and inched to the side. For a brief moment, the gun left her back.

Run, now! her mind screamed, but she remained in place. She couldn't go running off into the dark. She had no idea what lay ahead of her, and she could trip. She had to get out of the situation alive.

She heard the man fumbling around in the dark before light illuminated the area. She blinked hard and her vision cleared. To her right, a short flight of stairs led up. She closed her eyes to orient herself to the floor plan on the drawing. If the home hadn't been renovated, the stairs would take her to the kitchen.

Once they climbed the stairs, her escape route was a quick left turn. She could come to a quick stop and throw her shoulder into the creep, and he'd go flying down the stairs while she raced down the long hallway to the front door.

"We're going downstairs," he said, annihilating her plans.

The basement hadn't been included in the drawing, giving her no idea of what lay ahead. No idea how to make her escape.

Tears pricked at her eyes, and she scrunched them closed until she was in control of them. She looked down the stairs now in front of her. Only the first three steps were illuminated. The remaining stairs were eerily dark, and she was reminded horribly of the time she'd been locked in the church basement for hours.

"Keep going," he commanded.

She felt ahead with her foot and took the first step. Then another. A shiver seized her body. She wasn't sure if it was from the cold, the dank, musty smell rising up to greet her, or the fear of what awaited her if she was once again trapped in a basement.

Was he going to lock her down there? Kill her?

The questions gave her pause, and he shoved a booted foot into her back, making her arms windmill for balance. "If you're trying to think of a way to best me, you're asking for trouble. Now move!"

She slid her foot forward, letting it drop down to the next step. She heard a click, and a single bulb hanging from the ceiling illuminated the space. She took the remaining stairs and stared in surprise. She'd conjured up a dungeon or otherwise creepy basement, but a finished family room with hand-me-down furniture from the '80s lay before her. An overstuffed sofa and chair were covered in a peach-and-green Southwestern print, and they took up most of the space. Oak tables with dusty glass tops sat nearby, and an old television looked like it might fall off a rickety shelf.

The furnishings didn't fit with the age of the home, and if the family had left the house when Angus's ancestors had departed, that style of furniture wouldn't have been left behind; it hadn't been invented yet. Maggie supposed the furniture could be from renters, but if the tunnel story was true, they certainly wouldn't have rented out the house.

So what is this room for, and who is this guy?

She turned to look at him. He was of medium height and build, with a receding hairline. His eyes, though narrow and mean, bore a strong resemblance to Angus's. *Can this be Hal Aldrich?*

"If I'd known you were coming, I would have cleaned the place up." He laughed nastily.

"No need, Hal," she said, trying his name.

He flinched.

Bingo. "What? You didn't think I'd figure out who you were and that you were the one who killed Ike?"

"You have no proof." His narrow lips thinned below his large, bulbous nose. "Not that you're leaving here to tell anyone."

She had no doubt that he meant it, and a stab of dread replaced her triumph at having guessed the identity of Ike's killer.

"Have a seat while I decide what to do with you." He shoved her toward the big chair.

She perched on the edge, sending a puff of dust into the air, and the musty scent in the room intensified. "The age of your furniture tells me your side of the family didn't leave this house or their past behind."

He looked like he might not answer, then he shrugged. "We haven't lived here since the 1920s, if that's what you're getting at."

"But the furniture . . ."

"We needed something comfy to sit on while we waited for our shipments."

"You're still using the tunnel," she said, but she expected him to deny it.

"Yup."

Well, surprise, surprise. "Obviously you're no longer smuggling liquor."

He lifted his shoulders and preened. "I've made our family a tidy sum by smuggling various items of value over the years."

"And now?"

Hal looked at her long and hard. "Guess it won't hurt to tell you, seeing as you won't be blabbing to anyone once I'm through with you. We've been importing ivory tusks from narwhals out of Canada."

Maggie fought down panic and tried to keep her mind clear. *What does that mean, when he's 'through with' me?* She searched her brain for what she'd once learned about narwhals. She remembered the whales were called the unicorns of the sea due to their spiral ivory tusks that could grow longer than ten feet.

"I didn't know their tusks were valuable," she said to keep him talking, though she suspected the ivory would be worth quite a lot of money.

"Are you kidding? They can sell for thousands of dollars each."

"And because you're smuggling them, I will assume that it's illegal to bring them into the U.S."

His lips twisted into a sneer. "We've made close to $1 million in the last ten years."

"We?"

"My sons and I. Got two boys. They're the ones who turned me on to the tusks. We smuggle them in by boat and store them in the tunnel before finding buyers and transporting the tusks to them."

"I don't understand. How could you use the tunnel if the key you needed to open it has been hidden away in someone's attic all these years?"

"Oh sweetie," he sneered, the endearment full of condescension, "a tunnel needs two entrances to be worth anything, you know. Until recently, we've been using the cliffside entrance to stow shipments and make deals. We never could access the tunnel from in here. But several weeks ago, the mechanism used to open the outer door jammed. My numbskull of a son tried to fix it, but all he did was make the blasted thing worse. Hasn't been very good for business, let me tell you."

"So you set out to take the sprocket for yourself," Maggie interjected. She fought to keep the revulsion from her voice. He sounded so *proud* of his crimes.

"Yup. I heard that Underwood youngster had found it and might be on to us. I've got some connections, and I heard folks talking about that auction over in Somerset Harbor."

"And you went there to kill Ike," she said bluntly.

The sneer vanished as he came closer, raising the gun. Her heart skipped a beat, and she held her breath.

He stopped, the gun still lifted in his hand. "You make it sound like we planned it—like we're killers—but we didn't. I simply asked the guy to hand over the sprockets. Dumb ex-cop thought he could best me and lunged at me. Well, I showed him. Ironic that it was the sprocket that did the job."

"And of course, you needed the sprocket to access the tunnel from inside the house. I'm guessing you had some items of value in there."

A bushy brow lifted. "You figured that part out, did you?"

"With a little help from Shelton Underwood."

Hal shook his head. "Never did understand why his old idiot grandfather turned his back on a great career to live out his life in a tiny house and schlep out to sea everyday to haul in a bunch of fish. That's just plain dumb in my book."

"Some people have morals."

His glare darkened even more. "So do I. It's just that my morals revolve around money."

"If the tunnel is such a secret," she said, trying to keep him talking, "why did Lavinia hide the drawing in her bag?"

"For love." He scoffed. "Can you believe that? Love. Sheesh."

"Love?"

"She was in an arranged marriage but in love with the man who'd designed their house. He oversaw the construction of the home, and he built the tunnel so he could meet with her in secret. Her husband found out about it when the lover drew a heart on the drawing for her as a symbol of leaving his heart in that location. Of course, that ended her affair, but she kept the drawing to remember him by and hid it in the lining of her bag so her husband wouldn't find it." Hal glared at her. "But now someone could find the tunnel by using the drawing, and you're going to tell me where it is so I can get it back. We were always worried that old fool would sell the carpetbag and someone would look a little too close."

"I doubt that anyone could find the house, much less the tunnel," she replied.

"You did."

"Dumb luck."

"Hmm," he said. "I think plenty of people would be able to figure it out. After all, you did, and forgive me for saying so, honey, but you don't seem all that bright to me. I mean, look where you're sitting." He cackled wickedly.

Not in a good place, unfortunately. She was a hostage in the home of a man who demanded she return the drawing, but with everything he'd confessed to her, even if she told him where to find it, he wouldn't let her go.

Then there was James.

If she told Hal that he had the drawing, she'd be putting James's life on the line too.

22

Hal kept his focus and weapon trained on Maggie as he pulled a kerosene lamp from a cupboard and carried it to a nearby wall. He set the lamp on the floor and lifted a picture to reveal an odd-shaped keyhole in the wall. He withdrew the heavy sprocket from his jacket and inserted it into the lock, and suddenly a wide section of the wall started to slide, revealing a solid oak door with heavy wrought-iron hardware.

He gestured for her to join him, grinning maniacally. "Time for you to see what all the fuss is about."

She rose but remained near the sofa. She couldn't let him take her into the tunnel, where she was sure he'd either kill her or leave her to die. He'd already taken away her phone, and she couldn't think of any other way out of her predicament.

He waved the gun. "With or without a bullet, you're going into the tunnel. Doesn't matter to me how you get there."

Her mind racing for a way out, she started toward him. *Please don't let him kill me.*

As she neared him, she thought to shove him out of the way and run—taking her chances with a bullet in the back—but he retreated along the basement wall.

"Open the door," he commanded. "Slowly."

She grabbed the large round ring, the iron cold in her hand, and pulled hard. Large hinges groaned as if in agony.

"Sea air does its best to corrode the hardware," he said. "Can't keep the hinges lubricated enough." He dug in his pocket and pulled out a lighter, then handed it to her. "Get the lamp going."

She stood staring at him.

"Or we can make the trip in the dark. I've done it plenty of times, but I guarantee you won't like it."

She bent down and lit the lamp that was sitting on the ground. Thick black smoke curled up and joined oily stains on the ceiling of the entrance. Hal was going to force her inside, and if someone somehow figured out she'd come to the house, they wouldn't think to look in the wall unless she left a clue for them. She fiddled with the height of the flame to keep Hal's attention and subtly reached into the pocket of her raincoat with the other hand. She drew out one of her business cards that she kept in all of her jackets, then set it on the floor so when he closed the wall, the card would still be visible. She had to hope he wouldn't notice it.

"That's enough. Get going. There are a few steps down, a sharp turn, and a few more steps, and then you'll be in the main section of the tunnel."

She started ahead, holding the light high. The walls and floor were carved from a grayish-brown stone with a metallic luster. She ran her fingers over the rough texture to keep her balance on the wide stairs that were worn smooth from decades of use. As Hal had said, she took four steps and came to an open doorway, then the turn and five additional stairs.

Movement ahead caught her light and she jumped back, startled.

"Ah, I see you've spotted my other guest," Hal said. "No need to worry. He's harmless."

He shoved her forward. She descended the last few stairs, then held the light high. A man stood near a massive door that she suspected opened out to the cliff. She turned to take in the space that appeared to be about thirty feet long, ten feet wide, and ten feet high. Three narwhal tusks lay in an open container near a stack of antique wooden crates, filling the interior wall from floor to ceiling. Hal came to a stop next to them.

She was more curious about the silent man by the door than the crates. The sound of the raging storm barreling against the door grew louder as she got closer to the man and squinted. His face became clear, and a flood of relief washed over her.

She hurried toward him. "Eli! Is that you?"

"Yes," he said, glaring at Hal.

"How did you end up here?"

"Simple," Hal said. "His boat died off the coast. He took a swim and happened to catch us bringing in a shipment. As I said, we've had to bring everything in and out through the house lately." He patted the boxes. "Couldn't risk him reporting us so I asked him to join me like I asked you." He snickered.

"Hal said he's going to kill me," Eli said with disgust. "He's only keeping me alive until the Coast Guard calls off their search. Then he says we'll take a trip out into the ocean."

The knot in her stomach loosened as she realized that with the Coast Guard circling so close, Hal wouldn't risk taking her out to the cliff either. That bought them some time. She turned to face Hal. "Even if the Coast Guard calls off the search, you should know that Eli's daughter is a tenacious police officer, and I can't see her ever giving up."

"Trust me. I've grown quite adept at dealing with law enforcement over the years. One little cop isn't going to stop me." He smiled again, but Maggie thought it looked forced this time. "Now put down the lamp and make yourself comfortable."

She settled the lamp on a ledge and was thankful he didn't plan to leave her in the dark as he had left Eli.

"All I need to know is where you've stored the drawing."

A sudden realization hit her. "It was you who broke into my shop to find the drawing!"

He sneered. "You're just figuring that out now?"

"I still don't see how killing me will help anything. When I don't return, my friends will know my disappearance is related to the drawing and the sprockets, and they'll be relentless in figuring it out."

"I'll take my chances." His eyes narrowed. "Now, where is the drawing?"

He meant to kill her anyway, so why tell him? She shook her head.

He shot across the room. She lurched back, but he whisked past her and put Eli in a chokehold, pressing the gun against the older man's head. "Tell me where it is or Eli doesn't have long for this world."

"Wait!" Maggie was willing to risk her own life, but she wouldn't risk Eli's. "Fine. But if I tell you who has it, you have to promise not to harm them."

"Do you think you're in any position to negotiate?"

"No, but I won't sell out a friend."

"Look," Hal said. "Why would I want to kill someone else and draw more attention to the problem? Tell me who has it, and as long as I can get it without being seen, your friend will be A-okay."

She gritted her teeth and told him that James had the original, but she couldn't shake the feeling that she was betraying him. *What have I done?*

Hal glanced at his watch and started for the stairs. "Assuming your buddy is at the big to-do in town, I should be able to find what I need without incident and be back here in a flash." He glared at her. "You best not be lying to me to buy time, because if you are, Eli gets it when I come back."

"I'm telling the truth."

With that, he spun and ran out of the tunnel.

As soon as Hal was gone, Maggie turned to Eli. "We have to get out of here."

"Trust me," he said. "I've run my fingers over every inch of this place, and there isn't a way out without a key."

"You didn't have a light, though. Now we do," she said hopefully.

"Maybe." Eli scowled. "We could simply wait for Hal to come back and then try to overpower him."

Maggie gave the idea some thought. "We couldn't do it in the stairway—it's too narrow—but maybe when he comes down the last few steps . . . it's a long shot, but it has potential. I'd still like to keep looking for a way out."

"Agreed."

"Okay. We need to move fast and be systematic." Maggie grabbed the light. "Let's start with the sea side of the tunnel. We can signal to the Coast Guard faster than trying to contact the police."

"That door is jammed. And it sounds to me like there's a storm brewing out there. Do you think the Coast Guard's still around?"

"They were an hour ago, and it's the Coast Guard. A little rain doesn't stop them from saving a life."

"Good point. I suppose it wouldn't hurt to take another crack at this door. I didn't have help before." He gave her a small, grateful smile.

Together they picked their way toward the door, where the rocks were slick from the rainwater seeping under the door. A loud clap of thunder echoed through the space, making Maggie jump.

"I can't believe Hal keeps all that cash stashed down here," Eli said. "Must get wet."

"Cash?" she asked, her focus on the lock.

"The boxes on the wall. They're filled with it. He said he can't take his money to the bank, so he lives off the cash."

Ah, so the money is *still here. Just like Shelton said.*

Eli let out a weary sigh. "If only Aldrich had left that sprocket behind, maybe we could have used it to jimmy one of these doors.

He seems like the kind of dim-witted crook who's just riding his luck until it wears out."

Maggie thought of the big metal piece and made a mental note to make sure it found its way into police custody as evidence. *If we manage to get away, that is . . .*

"I think this pretty well settles it. There's no way to force this open." Eli's resigned tone cut through her reverie.

"Okay, then the other door. It wasn't as secure. Just a big lock."

"Yeah, but what do we pick it with?" Eli ran a shaky hand through his sparse hair.

"What if we took a crate apart and used the nails?"

"We could try it."

Maggie carefully made her way across the floor, noting that the puddles of sea water ended a good ten feet from the crates, making it a safe place to store cash. That explained why the boxes showed no signs of water damage.

She set the lantern on the far crate and opened the top of another. Stacks of cash were wrapped in clear plastic vacuum-sealed bags, another way they avoided the dampness of the tunnel.

Eli shook his head. "Can you imagine a day in Hal's life? The wife gets up and needs to go grocery shopping, so she says, 'Honey, can you go into the tunnel and grab me a bag of cash?' It's bizarre."

"It certainly is." Maggie ran her fingers over the edge of the box and discovered nails with rectangular heads, proof the crate was made in the 1800s, when such hand-forged nails were still used. She hated destroying a piece of history, but desperate times called for desperate measures.

"Help me lift this down and empty it out," she said.

Eli joined her and together they set the box on the floor and made quick work of pulling out the bags of money.

"I wonder how much is here," Eli said.

"We'll find that out when we get out of here and the police seize the cash." She tried to sound positive, but with each passing minute, she was sure Hal would come back with the drawing and finish them off.

"Let me have a go at the box." Eli set it on its side, then kicked at the top piece of wood. It didn't budge. He tried it again, and soon one corner let loose, and Eli ripped the side free, exposing the hand-hammered nails.

"I'll hold this steady, and you pound the nails through with my boot," he said excitedly, proffering his heavy, steel-toed workman's boot.

His enthusiasm was contagious, and Maggie started to believe that they were going to get out of this mess alive. She beat on the nails with renewed vigor.

"There," she said, standing back. "Those should pull right out."

Eli got a grip on the nails while Maggie retrieved the lantern.

"Ready to try them?" she asked.

His brow furrowed. "Ready and not ready. What if we fail?"

"We won't fail. We can't. We both have amazing daughters who need us."

"You're right. Let's go."

Maggie headed for the wood door into the house, feeling the warmer air as she drew closer to it. The space was so tight that she had to press herself against the wall to give Eli room while he fumbled with the lock.

Time ticked by. Seconds. Minutes. The lock didn't budge.

A noise came from the other side of the door, and Maggie thought she heard someone talking.

"Stop." Maggie grabbed Eli's hand to keep him still. "Did you hear that?"

"What?"

"Someone's talking out there."

"Hal?"

"I don't know," she whispered and shot Eli a look. "Surely he wouldn't be bringing someone back with him."

The minute her words were out, she knew she was mistaken. He could indeed be bringing help—his sons.

They might not make it out of the tunnel alive after all.

23

Maggie wished she could make out the words of the two men on the other side of the door, but they were too far away. And the pair seemed to be moving around the room, as if taking a tour.

"Should we go back downstairs?" Eli whispered.

"They're not near the door, so I think we're okay for now," she replied. "But be ready to take off if the key is inserted in the lock."

She pressed her ear against the door and heard the voices grow louder. "Oh no. They're coming this way. Their voices are still muffled, so I think the false wall must be closed." She held her breath, waiting to hear the wall sliding open, but she only heard the muffled voices. "If it's Hal, wouldn't he come straight in?"

"Unless you told someone you were coming to this house, who else could it be?"

"Good point," she admitted, and she saw Eli's optimism evaporate from his face. "Maybe James figured out another clue on the drawing," she added quickly to restore his hope. She decided not to mention that she'd studied that drawing dozens of times and had found nothing that might help locate the house.

"Over here!" a voice from the other side of the wall said.

Maggie shot a look at Eli.

His eyes widened. "Should we go back down the stairs?"

Before she could answer, she heard the outer wall slide open. Eli grabbed her arm and pulled her toward the stairs.

Fists pounded on the door, stopping them.

"Maggie!" James's voice came through the wood. "Maggie, are you in there?"

"I'm here!" She raced back to the door. "James? Is that really you?"

"Yes, and I have Robert with me too."

"Be careful!" she cried out. "Hal Aldrich is the killer, and he's coming back here for me and Eli."

"Eli's with you?" Officer Linton shouted.

"Yes! He discovered Hal's smuggling operation, and Hal took him prisoner so he couldn't tell anyone else." Maggie told them about Hal's current mission.

"Are you both okay?" James asked.

"We're fine."

"That's great news!" Officer Linton shouted. "Eli, I'll radio the good news to Samantha and call in backup."

"And send someone to James's office in case Hal's still there," Maggie added.

"I'm pretty sure Robert can handle things from here." Humor brightened James's voice. "We need to concentrate on getting you out of there. I'll look for something to help me pry the door open."

Maggie wanted to ask him to stay by the door and keep talking so she could be sure his voice wasn't simply her imagination, but she preferred that he work on getting the door open.

She turned to Eli instead. "Looks like we'll both be going home soon."

"Thank the good Lord for that."

The joy of being rescued suddenly overwhelmed her, and she gave Eli a big hug. "Worst case, we're stuck in here until they arrest Hal and get the door key from him."

They separated, and she heard what sounded like someone running on the other side of the wall. Then she heard multiple voices. Then silence. Maggie tapped her foot impatiently.

"Okay, stand back," James called out. "Robert gave me a tire iron, and I'm going to try to pry open the door."

Maggie and Eli backed away from the door. She heard a loud thump and the groaning of wood before it cracked with a horrendous splintering noise. A gap opened in the wood, and a shaft of light filtered through the space before the tip of the tire iron poked through and made another pass. Finally, James shoved the door open. She had never been so happy to see him.

He reached out a hand, and she placed hers in the warmth of his palm. "You're freezing," he said as he pulled her from the cavern.

"It's the damp," Eli noted as he followed her. "I've fished for years, and the damp is what gets to my old bones."

James gestured at the stairway to the main floor of the house. "Let's get out of here."

Maggie didn't have to be told twice. She climbed the stairs to the kitchen so she could use the front door and not have to battle the overgrown weeds out back. On the porch, she took a deep breath. The thunderstorm had cleared, and an invigorating breeze washed over her.

Officer Linton strode up the walkway. "Let's go. We've got Hal in custody, and I'll need to take your statements. We can do that at the station."

He didn't wait for them but hurried toward his car.

"We'd better keep up," James said with a grin. "Robert's missing out on the excitement in town, and I for one don't want to be the reason for it."

Maggie chuckled and followed him to the car. Eli joined Officer Linton in the front so he could talk to his daughter on the radio. James sat next to Maggie in the backseat.

"How did you find the house?" she asked.

"The drawing's missing corner." James pulled out a copy of the drawing. He'd jotted numbers on the side that Maggie recognized as latitude and longitude. "I just couldn't let it go, so I did the only thing I could think of. I got the carpetbag from your place—June let me in—and took it to Fran. She reopened the lining for me, mentioning something about how it looked like it had been opened and resewn before she got her hands on it. She didn't know why she hadn't noticed it before. I dug around in there and found the missing corner. It fits the drawing perfectly, and it had the latitude and longitude on it in the artist's handwriting. One of the smugglers must have torn it off to hide the house, and then Angus's grandfather must have saved it and added it in the carpetbag lining with the drawing when he stole the sprocket."

"You're amazing," she said.

Suddenly feeling exhausted, she laid the drawing on her lap and rested her head against the back of the seat. As they drove down the coastal highway, she listened to the joyful exchange between Eli and Samantha over the radio.

Maggie was pleased that they'd solved the murder and reunited a father and daughter in the process.

When they pulled up to the police station, her heart was full of happiness, and she vowed that if she saw Hal inside, she wouldn't let him take it away. But she was spared seeing him when Officer Linton escorted her directly to Chief Cole's office to give her statement. When she finished, they returned her to the lobby, where James waited for her. He looked up from the seat near the corner and beamed at her.

Chief Cole shook her hand. "We owe you a debt of gratitude for finding Officer Clayton's father."

"I'm glad I could help, though it was quite accidental. I think a big part of that gratitude belongs to James for finding both of us."

"Nonetheless, Eli's been rescued, and I know Samantha wants to thank you after she settles her dad at home."

"That's not necessary," Maggie said. "I'm just happy they're back together."

"Don't be surprised if she seeks you out. And I believe this is yours." He handed her the phone Hal had taken from her.

"Thanks, Chief. For everything," she told him, pocketing the phone. She turned to James. "You didn't have to wait."

"I wasn't going to leave you here after everything you've been through." James stood. He had truly become an invaluable friend.

"Thank you."

"So," he said, "are you up for attending the closing of the festival, or would you like me to take you home?"

She didn't want to be alone at that moment. "How about a quick trip home to freshen up and then we meet our friends at the park?"

"Sounds like a plan."

Back at the manor, she quickly washed up and changed out of her filthy clothes. She'd already planned to wear a navy striped top, a red silk scarf, and navy slacks for the Fourth of July celebration, so she would be ready for the festivities in no time.

Humming, she slipped into her clean clothes and added a pair of sandals. Then she grabbed a white sweater and joined James in the library. She found him seated with Snickers purring on his lap. He ran his gaze over her, and the look of admiration in his eyes warmed her heart.

"Very festive." He stood and settled Snickers on the floor.

Maggie felt a moment of guilt over leaving Snickers alone again so soon, but after the confinement in the tunnel, she needed to be in fresh air and around people.

Then she remembered something she needed to do. "Just a minute," she said to James, pulling her newly recovered phone from her pocket.

She dialed Carol Hansen's number. "Hello?" came the older lady's voice.

"Hi, Carol." Quickly she explained about seeing the thief steal the antique ring on the video.

"Oh, that old thing?" Carol interrupted with a laugh. "Of course I knew it was gone. It was just costume jewelry, glass and gilt. It was completely worthless, which is why I didn't report it missing. It just looked flashy. I kept it because I knew a thief who didn't know what he was doing would go for it, and I wouldn't be out any money. Thanks for letting me know, though, dear. Have a lovely evening."

Amused, Maggie hung up and turned back to James. "Now I'm ready."

They strolled down the damp streets toward the park. The setting sun hid behind wispy clouds with no hint of additional storms. Businesses had closed for the night, and only a few people lingered on the streets.

She heard the high school band playing "The Stars and Stripes Forever" in the park, and suddenly the sky lit up ahead of them with a splash of red, white, and blue.

"Looks like the fireworks have started," James said.

"Then our friends are waiting, so we should hurry." She picked up speed, and they soon reached the park entrance.

Lights strung between booths glowed over the area, illuminating visitors who had brought lawn chairs and blankets. The varied colors added to the celebratory atmosphere.

June rose from a yellow chair sitting outside Daisy's booth and waved her arms excitedly.

"She looks like she can't wait to hear about your day," James said.

"And I can't wait to tell her and all the ladies about it."

James took her arm, stopping her. "I know solving a mystery is exciting, but after all the danger you were in today, I want to encourage you to try to be more careful in the future. And perhaps next time you could just let the police handle it?"

She knew he worried about her, and there was no denying that she'd had some close calls. But if her friends needed her help again, she wouldn't let them down.

"Hey," she replied, grinning at him. "I don't go looking for these mysteries. They find me. And you know I can never say no to a friend in need."

"That's what I knew you'd say, Maggie Watson," James said with a chuckle. "Exactly what I knew you would say."

THE PETERSON FIELD GUIDE SERIES

A Field Guide to Rocky Mountain Wildflowers

from northern Arizona and New Mexico
to British Columbia

by

JOHN J. CRAIGHEAD
United States Fish and Wildlife Service,
Montana State University

FRANK C. CRAIGHEAD, JR.
Outdoor Recreation Institute, Washington, D.C.

RAY J. DAVIS
Idaho State College

Color Plates by the Authors
Drawings by
GRANT O. HAGEN *and* EDUARDO SALGADO

Sponsored by the Outdoor Recreation Institute

HOUGHTON MIFFLIN COMPANY BOSTON
The Riverside Press Cambridge

LIBRARY OF CONGRESS CATALOG CARD NUMBER: 63-7093

Second Printing R

The Riverside Press

CAMBRIDGE · MASSACHUSETTS

PRINTED IN THE U.S.A.

Editor's Note

THE western cordillera that forms the ridgepole of the continent extends nearly the full length of North America and then, after a break, continues as the Andes to Tierra del Fuego. No region on earth is richer botanically than this immense master mountain system, and even when things are narrowed down to the area covered by this book, the Rockies from northern Arizona and New Mexico to British Columbia, the number of plants exceeds 5000 species. It would plainly be impossible to treat them all in a single volume smaller than a New York City telephone directory, and even if this could be done the average layman would be unwilling to face such a formidable galaxy. This *Field Guide*, then, is selective, and the more than 590 species covered in its pages are the most representative; they are also those that the traveler is most likely to encounter.

The professional botanist often moves about in a rarefied atmosphere. He might quibble with his colleagues as to whether there are 5000 species of plants in the Rocky Mountain area or 7000, or even more, depending on his views on taxonomy and whether he recognizes certain plants as "good" species or merely forms or variants — in other words, whether he is a "lumper" or a "splitter."

It is less important for the layman to be able to name every last buttercup or every last aster than to place them correctly in their families. As he travels he will find more buttercups and more asters; to remember them all, when even the botanist disagrees about the validity of certain species, is expecting too much. But to know the family and perhaps the genus is a worthwhile accomplishment that makes him a bit more educated than the average tourist who visits a new terrain.

This *Field Guide* is an introduction, stressing things on the family level and in addition giving a good selection of the more distinctive and widespread species. For the others, many of them local and obscure, the reader must resort to the more comprehensive botanical works. However, he will seldom find in the technical publications much of the supplemental information that John and Frank Craighead and Ray Davis have assembled here — particularly wildlife food values and food values for human use. The Craigheads, incidentally, are among the world's foremost authorities on survival in the wilderness. Resourceful brothers, they did the research for and wrote the technical manual *How to Survive on Land and Sea* which was issued by the U.S. Navy to servicemen of World War II.

This, an ecologist's book, is of particular interest to the student of wildlife management. Its unique feature is the linking of the season of bloom with various wildlife phenomena. For example: under the subentry *Flowering season* we find that the Swamp-laurel blooms both where and when mosquitoes are becoming a nuisance. Such facts are often more illuminating than the bald statement "late June to early August," since the Rocky Mountain region is a vertical land where spring and summer ascend the slopes and a flower that blooms in June in the river valleys might not unfold its petals until July or even later at higher altitudes.

We have here a departure from the more stylized treatment that has been used in many of the other *Field Guides* but at the same time one of the most interesting and readable books of the series. We owe the team of Craighead and Davis, who blend the skills of the ecologist and the systematic botanist, our gratitude for the result. To aid identification, there are the authors' color photographs of 209 plants and 118 line drawings by Grant Hagen and Eduardo Salgado. It is an attractive book, a joy to handle, and will have its place in our knapsack on every mountain climb.

ROGER TORY PETERSON

Acknowledgments

THIS *Field Guide* is based on field collections and observations of the authors and on the extensive botanical literature available. A selected bibliography is given in Appendix III.

The late Willis Smith, head of the Biology Department at the Ogden, Utah, high school and seasonal ranger at Grand Teton National Park, suggested a field guide illustrated with colored photographs. He saw and emphasized the need for a popular treatment of the more common flowers of the national parks. His enthusiasm initiated this project in 1946 and it became a reality under the encouragement of Paul Brooks, Editor-in-Chief of Houghton Mifflin Company.

We are indebted to John McLaughlin, Edmund B. Rogers, and Lemuel A. Garrison, superintendents of Grand Teton and Yellowstone National Parks respectively, for permission to collect, to use the park herbariums, and for encouraging us in this undertaking. Carl Jepson, for years Chief Naturalist at Grand Teton park, was especially helpful. The herbariums at Idaho State College and Montana State University were used to make final determinations on all plants photographed, collected, or treated in the text. Dr. Marion Ownbey of the State College of Washington identified some slides and plants for us. Dr. LeRoy H. Harvey of Montana State University helped in determining the occurrence of certain plants in Glacier National Park and checked portions of the manuscript. Appreciation is expressed to Mr. Edwin L. Wisherd, chief of the photographic laboratory of the National Geographic Society, and to his staff for use of photographic equipment and for their help and encouragement.

Special thanks are due Jack E. Schmautz, Range Conservationist in the United States Forest Service, for thoroughly reviewing the manuscript, making many helpful suggestions, and generously contributing information from his long field experience. James Ashley of the United States Fish and Wildlife Service read the manuscript and made helpful suggestions.

Mrs. Alvina K. Barclay and Mrs. Bessy N. Beal helped with the typing. Thanks are due Esther Craighead and Margaret Craighead for hours devoted to proofreading and for invaluable assistance in obtaining and filing color photographs.

Helpful suggestions were made by Roger Tory Peterson, and assistance with the final draft of the manuscript was rendered by Helen Phillips of Houghton Mifflin Company.

The line drawings were executed by Grant O. Hagen and

Eduardo Salgado under direction of the authors. The drawings of *Haplopappus uniflorus*, *Hieraceum albertinum*, and *Senecio integerrimus* on pages 216, 220, and 226 are based on illustrations by John J. Rumely appearing in *Vascular Plants of the Pacific Northwest*, Part 5, *Compositae* (1955) by Arthur Cronquist. We are grateful to the Washington University Press for permission to make use of this material.

With pleasure and humility we acknowledge the help of many botanists and naturalists who contributed to this work through a gradual accumulation of scientific information that in time has become a general pool of knowledge and a basic foundation for a book of this kind.

JOHN J. CRAIGHEAD
FRANK C. CRAIGHEAD, JR.
RAY J. DAVIS

Contents

Editor's Note   v
About This Book   xiii
Glossary   xxvii

Cattail Family: *Typhaceae*   1
Burreed Family: *Sparganiaceae*   2
Pondweed Family: *Najadaceae*   2
Arrowgrass Family: *Juncaginaceae*   4
Arrowhead Family: *Alismaceae*   5
Grass Family: *Gramineae*   6
Sedge Family: *Cyperaceae*   8
Arum Family: *Araceae*   11
Duckweed Family: *Lemnaceae*   13
Rush Family: *Juncaceae*   13
Lily Family: *Liliaceae*   15
Iris Family: *Iridaceae*   34
Orchid Family: *Orchidaceae*   36
Buckwheat Family: *Polygonaceae*   40
Purslane Family: *Portulacaceae*   45
Pink Family: *Caryophyllaceae*   48
Water Lily Family: *Nymphaeaceae*   51
Buttercup Family: *Ranunculaceae*   51
Barberry Family: *Berberidaceae*   64
Bleedingheart Family: *Fumariaceae*   65
Mustard Family: *Cruciferae*   65
Caper Family: *Capparidaceae*   69
Orpine Family: *Crassulaceae*   70
Saxifrage Family: *Saxifragaceae*   72
Hydrangea Family: *Hydrangeaceae*   77
Gooseberry Family: *Grossulariaceae*   78
Rose Family: *Rosaceae*   79
Pea Family: *Leguminosae*   95
Geranium Family: *Geraniaceae*   105
Flax Family: *Linaceae*   107
Spurge Family: *Euphorbiaceae*   108
Sumac Family: *Anacardiaceae*   110
Staff-tree Family: *Celastraceae*   111
Buckthorn Family: *Rhamnaceae*   112
Mallow Family: *Malvaceae*   114
St. Johnswort Family: *Hypericaceae*   115
Violet Family: *Violaceae*   116

ix

Loasa Family: *Loasaceae*   117
Cactus Family: *Cactaceae*   119
Evening Primrose Family: *Onagraceae*   120
Parsley Family: *Umbelliferae*   124
Dogwood Family: *Cornaceae*   132
Wintergreen Family: *Pyrolaceae*   134
Heath Family: *Ericaceae*   139
Primrose Family: *Primulaceae*   143
Gentian Family: *Gentianaceae*   144
Milkweed Family: *Asclepiadaceae*   148
Morning-glory Family: *Convolvulaceae*   149
Phlox Family: *Polemoniaceae*   150
Waterleaf Family: *Hydrophyllaceae*   153
Borage Family: *Boraginaceae*   155
Mint Family: *Labiatae*   161
Potato Family: *Solanaceae*   165
Figwort Family: *Scrophulariaceae*   168
Madder Family: *Rubiaceae*   180
Honeysuckle Family: *Caprifoliaceae*   181
Valerian Family: *Valerianaceae*   184
Bluebell Family: *Campanulaceae*   185
Composite Family: *Compositae*   186

Appendixes
   I. Key to Plants   241
   II. Abbreviated Names of Authors   259
   III. Selected Bibliography   261
Index   265

Illustrations

Plates (grouped between pages 136 and 139)
1. Grasses and Related Plants
2. Lilies and Irises
3. Lilies (Lily Family)
4. False Hellebore, Orchids, and Buckwheats
5. Buckwheats, Purslanes, and Pinks
6. Pink, Water Lily, and Buttercup Families
7. Buttercup Family, Holly-grape, Steershead
8. Whitlow-grass, Sedums, Capers, Syringa, Saxifrages
9. Roses and Related Species (Rose Family)
10. Sticky Geranium; Rose and Pea Families
11. Rose, Pea, and Loasa Families
12. Mallows, St. Johnswort, Violets, Cacti, and Evening Primroses
13. Evening Primrose, Parsley, and Sumac Families
14. Collomia, Orogenia, Dogwoods, Flax, Wintergreens, Heaths
15. Pinedrops, Leafy Spurge, Heaths, Primroses, and Green Gentian
16. Gentian, Phlox, Waterleaf, and Milkweed Families
17. Henbane, Morning-glory, Borages, Horsemint
18. Paintbrushes, Louseworts, etc.
19. Monkeyflowers, Honeysuckle, Elderberry, Valerian, Harebell, Arnica
20. Mints, Bedstraw, Beardtongues, and Composites
21. Mountain Penstemon and Composites
22. Composites (Composite Family)
23. Composites (Composite Family)
24. Composites (Composite Family)

Line drawings
> Text: the 118 drawings are indicated in the Index by the boldface page numbers
> Glossary: 4 pages of illustrations showing (a) types of inflorescences, flowers, and roots, (b) types of leaf margins, and shapes and arrangements, (c) parts of a typical flower, (d) aids in identifying the Compositae

Map of area covered is on page xxxviii

About This Book

THIS *Field Guide* considers the more conspicuous plants of the Rocky Mt. area. It is essentially a guide for the outdoorsman and amateur botanist — the layman who desires information about flowers observed along the highway, near camp, on the bank of a trout stream, in a mountain meadow, or on the exposed slopes of a mountain peak.

There are more than 5000 species of plants in the Rocky Mt. region. Many are of interest purely to the professional botanist and can be specifically identified only on the basis of technical characters. This book deals with more than 590 of the common plant species — a selection of those flowers most conspicuous or most likely to be encountered.

Travelers to Glacier, Yellowstone, Grand Teton, and Rocky Mt. National Parks (abbreviated as G, Y, T, R under *Where found* in the text descriptions) and surrounding areas will find this *Field Guide* particularly useful. It should also prove helpful to university students studying botany, range management, or wildlife; but it is specifically directed to the inquiring sportsman, vacationer, and outdoorsman.

Fishermen, hunters, hikers, mountain climbers, photographers, and campers continually come in contact with the showy plant life that largely characterizes their favorite outdoor haunts. Some plants will have particular significance to each of these individuals. The fisherman who can recognize flowers of streambank and meadow as well as the fish that take his fly will find an ever widening interest in his sport and an ever growing aesthetic appreciation of his environment. He soon can learn to recognize the Bulrush and Common Cattail, which could serve him as emergency food if need be. He discovers that the flowering of the Bitterroot corresponds with the appearance of salmon flies on the stream, thus indicating good fishing. He learns that when the petals of the Yellow Monkeyflower have dropped into the stream and the first asters have appeared the large trout can be more easily enticed to take the dry fly, that the surface water of lakes and slow-flowing streams has then become too warm to yield the fishing it provided earlier in spring. Flowers have thus become clues that tell him things of interest in the out-of-doors. They can inform the climber of his approximate altitude on the mountain, the basic type of rock under his boot; they can tell the naturalist when the elk calves are dropping, when Canada geese eggs are hatching, or when young horned owls will leave the nest. A knowledge of flowers aids one to fuller enjoyment of our mountains, their streams and forests.

Identification of plants has in the past been largely the work of botanists, or scientists trained in related fields, or the pastime of students sufficiently advanced to utilize manuals with artificial analytical keys. A key is an arrangement of contrasting statements whereby one can eliminate all plants except the one at hand. Botanists resort to regional floras, checklists, to monographic or revisionary work of particular plant families or genera, and to herbariums, where an unknown plant can be compared with known specimens to determine its identity. These methods of identifying plants, though basic and essential to the botanist, are beyond the reach of the layman. Today, however, plants are no longer the concern solely of the botanist. Knowledge of plant identification has progressed to the point where the general public can use, appreciate, and enjoy much of the information that the science of taxonomic botany has accumulated and systematized over the years. As human population density increases, as education expands, as opportunity for travel grows, as our interests broaden and our leisure time increases, there becomes an ever greater demand on the part of the public for the sharing of scientific knowledge. It is a responsibility of any science not only to assemble knowledge but to make it available for all who wish to learn.

To make knowledge of wild plants available to the general public, it is necessary to present the material in simplified and readily understood form. This *Field Guide* attempts to do this by: (1) confining the coverage to a comparatively small well-defined region; (2) limiting the plants treated to a selection of conspicuous species; (3) attempting to characterize each plant in such a way that it cannot readily be confused with others in the region; and (4) illustrating the plants so that the book itself serves as a simplified herbarium where unknown plants can be compared with known colored photographs or drawings.

VEGETATION ZONES

The reader with an interest in plants who has done even a little traveling will have observed different types of plants growing in various parts of our country. The more conspicuous trees, shrubs, and grasses characterize certain land areas. For instance, in crossing the United States from east to west the traveler passes through the broadleaf forests into the tall-grass prairies (now largely cultivated crops), thence into the short-grass prairies and on into the Rocky Mts. with their coniferous forests and valleys covered with sagebrush. The plant ecologist has classified the different types of vegetation by what he terms *natural plant communities*. Those plant communities controlled by climate he has called *vegetation*, or *bioclimatic*, *zones;* they represent the climatic climax for a given area. Ten such zones are found in the Rocky Mts. and they can be recognized by one or two key plant species. There is considerable intergradation of zones. Hence any one zone is not always readily discernible to the layman. Each zone attains its characteristic development within certain altitudinal limits, but there are often extensions up or down, depending upon local physiography, aspect, exposure, moisture, and soil conditions. The outdoorsman who learns to recognize the vegetation zones in the Rocky Mts. will soon discover that he can expect to find — even predict — certain flowers in a specific zone. This knowledge helps him locate new flowers as well as to identify unfamiliar ones.

Within the region covered by this book the topography varies from approximately 1000 feet in the lower river valleys to over 14,000 feet on the highest mountain summits. The zones within this altitudinal spread, according to R. F. Daubenmire,* are:

1. Sagebrush-grass (lowest zone)
2. Wheatgrass-bluegrass
3. Fescue-wheatgrass
4. Oak–mountain mahogany
5. Juniper–piñon pine
6. Ponderosa pine
7. Douglas fir
8. Arborvitae-hemlock
9. Spruce-fir
10. Sedge-grass (alpine or highest zone)

Among the flowers treated in this book some will be found in each of the 10 zones. However, without exception all of the plants described can be found in 5 of the zones. These zones are: sagebrush-grass, ponderosa pine, Douglas fir, spruce-fir, and alpine. Since it is within these 5 vegetation zones that most of the Rocky Mt. national parks and monuments are located, this plant life is emphasized in the descriptive text.

PLANT SUCCESSION

We have pointed out that certain species of plants are to be expected in a given vegetation zone and that some of these definitely characterize each zone. Where one or a number of these predominate within a zone they are referred to as *plant communities* or *vegetation types*. The dominant type for which the zone is named represents the *climax type* (the most advanced development in plant life possible under the existing climatic conditions of the zone). The climax vegetation is able to reproduce itself and prevent other plants from dominating the area. It maintains this supremacy by virtue of its adaptations to shade tolerance, water

* "Forest Vegetation of Northern Idaho and Adjacent Washington and Its Bearing on Concepts of Vegetation Classifications," *Ecological Monographs*, Vol. 22 (1952), pp. 301–30.

requirements, etc., that give it a decided advantage over other competing plants. Thus, the climax vegetation if undisturbed by fire, plow, or ax may hold and characterize an area until the climatic cycle changes.

In the spruce-fir zone, for example, the ecologist finds that spruce and fir cover large areas and dominate the forests, but that in addition to these there will be areas of lodgepole pine, of sagebrush, of sagebrush and aspen, of grassland, tamarack, and other types. The outdoorsman, viewing this, finds it pleasing to the eye but probably sees little "rhyme or reason" for the lodgepole pine–aspen stand to his right, the sedge-willow parkland in front, and the spruce-fir forest to his left. One fundamental concept will shed light on this complexity and bring order to his observations. This is the concept of plant succession — that the vegetation on any area evolves, or changes, over a long period of time, and as the vegetation develops the same area becomes successively occupied by different plant communities. Within a zone or region the same final or climax stage results from a series of successive and progressive vegetative stages, whether they start in open water, on bare rocks, or denuded soil. There is a long series of progressive stages in the development of the highest type of vegetation that a climate will support. Gradually the rock, sand, or soil is altered and conditioned by each successive plant stage to the point where the total environment is suitable for the development of the next stage in the series.

Now to return to our outdoorsman looking at the vegetation types about him: the spruce and fir forest to his left represents the highest development of the vegetation in the zone; the lodgepole pine–aspen stand to his right, the sedge-willow parkland in front are vegetation stages developing toward the climax condition. Closer scrutiny of the lodgepole pine–aspen forest reveals only a few young aspen or lodgepole and an abundance of spruce and fir saplings. This tells the plant ecologist that the lodgepole pine and aspen are on their way out. They have prepared the soil so that the spruce and fir can grow, they have created shade so that their own seeds or shoots requiring an abundance of sunlight cannot survive. Consequently, a young forest of spruce and fir will eventually replace the lodgepole and aspen. In much the same way, the process of plant succession occurs from the lowest stage (crustose-lichen) on bare rock to the foliose-lichen stage on a meager substratum, successively through the moss stage, herbaceous plant stage, shrub stage, and subclimax forest stages to the final climax forest.

Each successional stage holds possession of an area and produces profound influences upon the habitat. The plant populations of each stage make conditions suitable for the next community of plants but generally less favorable for their own existence. This developmental process is slow, probably hundreds or even thousands of years. It can be likened to the development of an organism — a dynamic concept of birth, growth, change, and death.

PLANTS AND WILDLIFE

A close relationship exists between plants and animals; so close, in fact, that we can say all animal species, whether they feed on vegetation or on other animals, are dependent directly or indirectly on plant life. Most outdoorsmen recognize that the mule deer and moose are dependent on many types of woody vegetation for food, that the pronghorn and sage grouse largely subsist during part of the year on a single group of plants — the sagebrushes; they know that the ring-necked pheasant thrives on cultivated grain, wild seeds, and berries, and that our waterfowl consume the seeds, leaves, and tubers of aquatic vegetation. So much for general information. The specific plants involved are usually not known by the layman, yet most wild animals show decided preferences for one plant over another. This preference for specific plant foods by various species of game and nongame animals forms a basic tool for managing and preserving our wildlife resources. When we know the food requirements of a wildlife form we can begin to take steps to improve its habitat or to increase or decrease its numbers.

And so the individual with an interest in flowers is unconsciously forming a close relation with the animal forms that use flowering plants as food and cover. Conversely, the sportsmen and outdoorsmen who study, shoot, photograph, or simply observe wildlife are getting close to the plant base that supports animal life. There can be no sharp demarcation of interests. As knowledge grows the interrelation of plants and animals becomes more and more apparent, and from a flower enthusiast or a hunter a naturalist evolves. The professional term is *ecologist*. This book is foremost a treatment of flowers but the reader will find interesting facts about how these plants are utilized. It is hoped that the reader's interest will develop beyond specific identification of flowers to a realization and understanding of plants as an integral part of our wildlife resources.

PLANT FOODS

As our knowledge of western plants increases, we shall probably find that there is scarcely a plant not utilized in greater or lesser degree by wildlife. As yet the food habits of many wildlife species are incompletely known; and even less is known about the quantitative and nutritional value of specific plant foods. We do know, however, that the leaves, stems, twigs, bark, buds, fruits, seeds, roots, and sap of different plants all furnish wildlife with food.

Some plants may supply only leaves or fruits as food and others have scarcely a portion of the plant that is not edible.

The leaves, stems, twigs, and other vegetative parts of plants form the major portion of the diet of our big game species — elk, deer, moose, Rocky Mt. sheep, mountain goats, and pronghorn. Rodents such as ground squirrels, meadow mice, prairie dogs, rockchucks, and also the little mountain pika live largely on vegetation.

Next to the vegetative portion of plants, the seeds probably constitute the major wildlife food source. Rich in carbohydrates, proteins, and vitamins, they make up the entire diet of some of our songbirds and form a large segment of the diet of ducks, geese, grouse, pheasants, and partridges. Small mammals, like the white-footed mouse, kangaroo rat, chipmunk, and jumping mouse, live through the winter on seed caches. The seeds of the grasses are especially valuable, as are also those of many of our so-called "weed plants."

The fleshy fruits of the Rose, Serviceberry, Hawthorn, Mountain-ash, and many others are important items in the diet of grouse, pheasants, songbirds, and small mammals.

Nuts too are utilized, being rich in fat and protein. In some parts of the Rocky Mts. acorns are available, but by far the most important nuts are the pine nuts. Those of the Piñon, Whitebark, Limber, and Single-leaf pines are excellent food sources for birds, squirrels, chipmunks, bears, and humans. The seeds of the spruces, firs, and the Ponderosa Pine are essential to the survival of the chickaree, or pine squirrel, which is so abundant in our coniferous forests.

The underground portion of plants (bulbs, tubers, rootstocks, and stem bases) constitute a large reservoir of food. Here plants store starch that is used for a rapid growth in spring. Much of this food is available only to animals specialized to make use of it. Ducks and geese dive or dabble for some of the smaller aquatic tubers; muskrats excavate and chew the larger roots and rootstocks; pocket gophers, moles, and ground squirrels burrow to roots and tubers of their choice.

The flower, for all its beauty and in spite of its vital role of seed producer, does not escape attention. The flowers of many plants are eaten indiscriminately along with the vegetative parts by grazing animals. The delicate flower morsels of Beargrass, Arrowleaf Balsamroot, Sticky Geranium, Dandelion, and Elk Thistle are specifically sought and eaten by deer, elk, moose, and bears, often to the exclusion of other plants.

Today wild plants still are a source of human food, but they are no longer a vital survival need. They have, except in emergencies, been relegated to the role of luxuries. The interesting and historical uses of many of these wild food-plants are discussed in the text. The authors have eaten the edible plants mentioned and have experimented considerably with the better ones. Nevertheless, we caution the reader with a similar yen for trying these firsthand to start with small amounts of each until he has become experienced in plant identification.

Perhaps as a reversion to earlier and harsher days when primitive man gathered wild plant foods in earnest, modern man is still drawn to the forest and fields to reap the native harvest. He may gather berries for jelly, jam, and wine, green leaves and stems for potherbs, mushrooms for flavoring, roots and tubers for a tasty diet change, and nuts for storage over winter. Somehow this activity leaves him with a sense of well-being, a short-lived but strong feeling of security, of having provided for himself and family from the raw offerings of nature. It brings him close to the earth and living things, but today it is largely a recreational and aesthetic, not an economic, activity, though such simple joys may well prove more fundamental than we realize.

Less than 150 years ago, our wild western plant foods played a vital role in human economy. Animals, the staff of life, fluctuated in numbers, moved from place to place, and were obtainable only through the use of skilled hunting, trapping, and snaring techniques. It was plant food that carried the Indian from periods of animal scarcity to periods of animal abundance. Many of the western Indian tribes at times subsisted largely on plant foods, and all tribes resorted to this ever-present easily secured food source as an emergency ration in times of famine. A vast lore of practical plant knowledge was passed from Indian generation to generation. This knowledge was a key factor in their survival. Our information of the nutritional and medicinal value of native plants has stemmed largely from facts obtained from the Indian. No doubt much valuable information was left unrecorded, but enough is known so that we can safely state that the Indian was a superb botanist and that few useful plants grew in his tribal territory which he could not recognize and put to use. Among all native peoples knowledge concerning which plants could be safely eaten and which ones could not must have evolved through the process of trial and error. It can safely be assumed that many a hungry individual succumbed to eating death-camases, Poison-hemlock, and Rocky Mountain Iris before it became an established fact that these plant roots and tubers were poisonous and such closely related ones as the blue Camas, Yampa, and Biscuitroot were highly nutritious.

When the white man moved westward he first depended upon the Indian to show him which plants were edible and in time he learned to recognize and use these himself. Members of the Lewis and Clark expedition traded with the Indian tribes for plant food and in their most trying period they, like the Indian, resorted to plants as an emergency ration. It was this food that carried them through. The mountain men, explorers, and pioneers who followed in the wake of the Lewis and Clark expedition learned to recognize the Bitterroot, Biscuitroot (or Cous), Yampa, Camas, Wild Hyacinth, Arrowhead, Sego Lily, and probably a host of others. Those individuals and expeditions that took off into the wilderness without such knowledge were severely handicapped from the start. A review of the ill-fated expeditions for which any record exists indicates that this inability to fall back on the plant resource as emergency food was often the difference between success and disaster. It played a little-heralded but determining role in early western history. Legendary figures, men around whose lives and activities western history was made — Meriwether Lewis, William Clark, George Shannon, John Colter, Hugh Glass, Truman Everts — are only a few of those who at one time or another owed their lives to the sustenance and strength received from wild plant foods. With the passing of the buffalo, the destruction of the Indian's way of life and his confinement to reservations, the plowing of the prairie, logging of the forests, and harnessing of the rivers, little remains of the primitive West. The plants that nourished the Indian and the early white man are, however, still abundant; but no longer a key to survival. Instead they are a tangible aesthetic reminder of one of the most remarkable feats of mankind — the conquering of the West.

POISONOUS PLANTS

The poisonous properties of some plants are discussed under *Interesting facts*. In the Rocky Mt. region one need have little fear of poisoning from eating berries. Baneberries (*Actaea*) and nightshade berries (*Solanum*), though poisonous, are distasteful and thus not likely to be eaten in sufficient quantity to cause harm. Those wishing to experiment with edible roots and tubers should accurately identify the plants in this guide before eating them.

It may surprise the reader to learn that a good many western-range plants contain poisonous compounds that in greater or.lesser degree are harmful to livestock. Many of these are well known to stockmen; others described in this book may not be. Poisonous plants grow intermingled with good forage plants and are thus readily available to grazing animals. Most of these are not sufficiently palatable to be selected and eaten in preference to more desirable species. On good ranges, where a choice of forage exists, animals tend to avoid toxic plants. On overgrazed lands, where hungry animals feed on whatever they can get, including poisonous species, danger from poisoning is greatest. Under such conditions sufficient quantities can be consumed to cause injury, even death, and resultant financial losses. Some plants are poisonous to certain animals and apparently do not affect others. Likewise, a plant poisonous under one set of conditions may be safely eaten under another.

FINDING PLANTS

Knowledge of the flowering season of the various plant species is a help in finding and identifying plants. Such information in the text descriptions has been treated in generalities because of the considerable extent of latitude and the variations in altitude within the area covered. These factors of course affect the flowering season. Therefore, it would not be possible to give specific flowering dates for a number of localities. For this reason certain helpful phenological information has been included. These data correlate plant development (usually first flowering) with seasonal animal activities occurring at the same time, and they tend to alter correspondingly with differences in latitude and altitude; or, in other words, with climatic differences. For example, it is more accurate to express a flowering date over a large area by saying that a particular flower first appears when Canada geese are hatching than to say it first appears in bloom around the middle of May. Moreover, some animal activities are more readily observed than the flowering of certain plants; so such observations help to indicate when one should look for the plants concerned. Conversely, the outdoorsman will find it helpful to know that when a certain conspicuous plant is blooming he can expect to observe interesting associated animal activities.

CLASSIFYING AND NAMING PLANTS

The identification, naming, and classifying of plants is of ancient origin. Primitive man early learned to recognize and identify plants useful and vital to his very existence. In time he gave names to these. As the knowledge of plants increased throughout the ages, man then sought to systematize this knowledge. The Greeks classified plants on the basis of whether they were trees, shrubs, or herbs. To this crude system was later added knowledge based on sexual and numerical parts of plants. Following this classification, form relationship was added, and this in turn gave rise to the phylogenetic system which predicates that present-day plants have slowly evolved from more primitive forms.

Botanists have thus gradually developed our system of plant classification. They have also devised a method of naming plants within this system. This is called *taxonomy*. Plant taxonomy is the science of collecting, describing, naming, and classifying plants on the basis of principles that have developed as botanical knowledge has grown.

In order to understand how plants are named and identified one must have a general knowledge of plant taxonomy. Taxonomy as we know it today is based on the hypothesis that there are relationships between plants and that these relationships are genetical in character. It is assumed that present-day plants have evolved from less complex ancestors. On this basis plants have been placed in categories that presumably group genetic affinities in phylogenetic sequence. Thus plants are grouped into units in the order of their structural complexity. Those treated in this book are so grouped; the less complex ones occur first in the sequence and progress to the more complex or so-called "highly developed" plants. With the exception of families Hydrangeaceae and Grossulariaceae, they are arranged according to the system devised by C. G. de Dalla Torre and H. Harms in *Genera Siphonogamarum ad Systema Englerianum Conscripta* (Leipzig: Engelmann, 1900–1907).

The categories of classification in the plant kingdom are:

1. Division	8. Subfamilies, or tribes
2. Subdivisions	9. Genera
3. Classes	10. Subgenera, or section
4. Subclasses	11. Species
5. Orders	12. Subspecies
6. Suborders	13. Varieties
7. Families	14. Forms

In this book we are concerned largely with the family, genus, and species.

The *family* represents a more natural unit of classification than the higher categories. Most plant families have definite characters common to their respective members and thus are readily recognized as natural groupings. For example, a member of the Mustard or the Grass family has sufficient characters in common with other members so that one has little difficulty in recognizing a mustard or a grass as belonging to its respective family category.

Each family is composed of one or more genera. A *genus* is a category including those plants within a family that have more characters in common with each other than with plants of other genera within the family.

The *species* is the basic unit. It has been variously defined. For the purpose of plant identification, however, it is sufficient to know that a species represents a closely related group of plants — a population — to which a specific name can be given distinguishing it from all other plants or plant populations. This basic unit must fit into the *binomial system* of nomenclature. That is, it must have a Latin name consisting of two parts, the *generic* and the *specific names*. The first word (a noun) designates the genus and the second (an adjective describing the noun) the species. Together they form the plant's name, which serves to distinguish the plant from all other plants on earth. There are sound advantages to this system. Foremost, the scientific name constitutes an internationally accepted name that practically eliminates ambiguity and misunderstanding.

To take an example, many English names have been applied to the same plant. The lily *Erythronium grandiflorum* is known in the Rocky Mts. as Dogtooth Violet, Fawnlily, Glacier Lily, Snow Lily, and Adders-tongue. Also, the same common name is used in different areas to designate very different plants. The name Beargrass in Arizona refers to a woody cactus-like plant in the genus *Nolina*. In Idaho, a beautiful, liliaceous flower with grass-like leaves, in the genus *Xerophyllum*, is called Beargrass. In Florida, a member of the genus *Yucca* is called Beargrass, and none of these three plants is a grass at all. Without the scientific name the plant in question cannot accurately be traced in the literature and further information gained about it. Even in conversation we cannot be sure we are talking about the same plant species unless the scientific name is referred to. This immediately places the plant in a systematized category of genetic relationships. Each plant species thus has a definite place in a complicated system and, like a filing card, can be relatively easily found within that system. Common English names show no relationship and belong to no system. Therefore the layman who feels he has no need for scientific terms is nevertheless *strongly urged to learn the scientific name* and to look for and learn generic relationships, in order to build for himself a system of plant knowledge rather than an unrelated smattering of names. The Dogtooth Violet then becomes a lily differing in specific structural ways from other genera of lilies but similar to them in having certain characteristics that distinguish all lilies as belonging to the family Liliaceae. In other words, the amateur botanist soon learns that despite color differences all lilies look much alike, usually having their petals and sepals in series of threes and having six stamens, and a superior ovary with three carpels.

Taxonomic botanists are not yet able to agree on the number of species within certain genera occurring within a definite geographic area. This is partly due to the fact that some botanists tend to split the species down to the most minute details and others tend to lump them. Many genera of western plants are now in the process of being revised by taxonomists, and it is hoped that eventually some agreement will be reached on the number of species that should be listed under any given genera.

At the present time there appear to be many superfluous names in a large number of the genera treated in this *Field Guide*. The authors have used Harrington's *Manual of Plants of Colorado*, Moss's *Flora of Alberta*, and Davis' *Flora of Idaho* (see Appendix III for fuller details) and attempted to reduce the synonyms as much as possible, using these three books as a basis. In this way the approximate number of species has been designated for each genus, but it should be recognized that this number might not be generally accepted by all taxonomic botanists and that it will be subject to change as new monographs appear. For the common names of plants treated in the text, the authors relied primarily on *Standardized Plant Names*, 2nd ed. (1962), prepared for the American Joint Committee on Horticultural Nomenclature by its editorial committee, Harlan P. Kelsey and William A. Dayton.

To identify an unknown plant one must first find where it belongs in the classification system. This might seem like a tedious, hopeless task, and it would be if he had to trace his plant through the thousands described in a regional flora. However, when in a book such as this one all plants except those of a given area are eliminated, and these are reduced to the relatively few common plants likely to be encountered by the amateur, and are illustrated in a way so the plant family can readily be detected, then identification becomes a more simple, satisfying hobby.

HOW TO USE THIS BOOK

Students who have intimately observed flowers and systematically collected plants, or have had basic courses in taxonomic botany, will know how to use this book.

Beginners should familiarize themselves with the family groups, recognizing that flowers can be identified by their similarities as well as by their differences. When a plant has been carefully examined or collected for identification, the observer can leaf through the illustrations until he finds the picture most resembling it. With this procedure he has reduced the possibilities to a few genera. Reference to the text should confirm the species or reduce the possibilities to a few closely related species.

The beginner who is serious about his hobby will find that he will accumulate a fund of systematized knowledge about plant identification if he follows the well-established procedure used by professional botanists:

First, the plant should be run through the "Key to Plants." (In using a botanical key the plant in question should be studied carefully. A hand lens will be useful with small flowers. Note the number of sepals, petals, stamens, ovaries or divisions in an ovary, and parts of the style, and the position of these parts on the flower. Also note whether any of the parts are united or partly united. Observe the position, shape, and size of the leaves on the plant, as well as the size and general nature of the plant itself.)

Turn to this key (p. 241) and notice the series of numbered pairs of contradictory statements. From your plant, decide which of the first pair of statements it fits (pairs may be separated by several pages). Under this choice you will again find two opposite statements. Choose the proper one and continue doing so until the genus name of the plant is found. Ignore the alternate description and its succession of choices each time an identifying character is arrived at. This process may be likened to traveling along a marked road that repeatedly forks. If the signs are correct and the directions are always carefully followed, the traveler will arrive at the desired place. If his observations and choices are not accurate, he may become lost. The simpler forms of plants such as ferns, pines, junipers, etc., are merely keyed out; *only the plants bearing flowers* are discussed in this book.

Second, turn to the page cited in the Key for detailed species description (if the text has more than one species within a genus it will be necessary to look at all the inclusive pages for the genus). Compare the botanical characteristics of the plant specimen with those given in the text. If the species is not described in detail, read the section on *Related species*.

Third, the specimen should be compared with the colored plates or line drawings that illustrate the genus arrived at in the keying process. One or more species in the genus will be illustrated.

It is not essential to use the Key. An unknown flower can be compared first with the illustrations. If it accurately matches an illustration you have identified your plant. If it closely resembles but does not match the illustration, turn to the text page indicated and compare the unknown plant with the detailed written descriptions and the briefer descriptions under *Related species*.

The beginner must realize there are several thousands of inconspicuous plants not treated in this *Field Guide*. He can feel confident, however, that the more conspicuous showy plants can be identified by following the procedures outlined above.

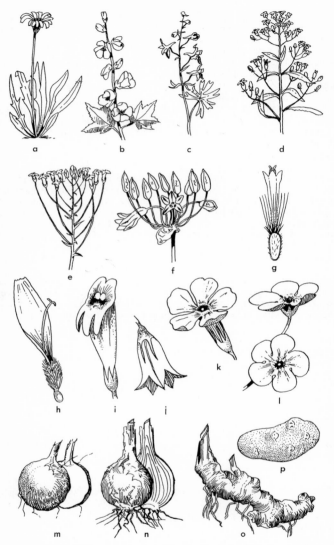

Types of inflorescences, flowers, and roots: a, scapose; b, spike; c, raceme; d, panicle; e, corymb; f, umbel; g, diskflower; h, rayflower; i, tubular; j, campanulate; k, funnel-form; l, rotate; m, corm; n, bulb; o, rhizome; p, tuber.

Glossary

Abortive. Imperfectly formed, rudimentary, or barren.

Achene. A small, dry, and hard, one-seeded, indehiscent (non-splitting or gaping) fruit.

Acuminate. Long-tapering at outer end.

Acute. Sharp-pointed, but less so than acuminate.

Alternate. Not opposite each other.

Annual. Of only one year's duration.

Anther. The part of the stamen which contains the pollen.

Appressed. Lying close and flat against.

Aquatic. Pertaining to water; growing in water.

Awn. A slender bristle-like organ.

Axil. The upper angle formed by a leaf or branch with the stem.

Axillary. Borne at or pertaining to an axil.

Barbed. Furnished with rigid points or short bristles, usually reflexed, like the barb of a fishhook.

Barbellate. Finely barbed.

Basal. At the base, such as leaves at base of plant, or seeds attached at base of ovary.

Beaked. Ending in a beak or prolonged tip.

Berry. A fruit that is wholly soft and pulpy.

Bidentate. Having two teeth.

Biennial. Of two years' duration.

Bipinnate (leaf). Twice-pinnate (or twice-compound).

Blade. The flat expanded part of a leaf.

Bloom. A waxy coating, such as on a fruit or leaf.

Bract. A modified leaf, usually small, near the base of a flower or flower cluster, or a spore case.

Bristle. A stiff hair or any similar outgrowth.

Bulb. An underground leaf bud with fleshy scales or coats. (The onion is an example.)

Calyx. The outer of two series of floral leaves, individually called sepals.

Campanulate. Bell-shaped.

Capillary. Hairlike in form, as fine as hair or slender bristles.

Capitate. Shaped like a head; collected into a head or dense cluster.

Capsule. A dry dehiscent (splitting or gaping) fruit, composed of more than one carpel.

Carpel. A simple pistil (ovary) or a division of a compound pistil.

Caudex. An upright underground stem living over from year to year. Usually the top dies back to the ground each winter.

Cell. A seed-bearing cavity of an ovary or a pollen cavity of an anther. A microscopic unit of living things.

Chartaceous. Papery in texture.

Chlorophyll. Green coloring matter of plants.

Ciliate (foliar organs). Beset on the margin with a fringe.

Circinate. Coiled from the tip downward.

Clavate. Club-shaped; thickened toward the apex.

Cleft. Cut about halfway to the midvein.

Compound. Composed of two or more similar parts joined together.

Cone. The dry, multiple fruit of pines, spruces, firs, etc., that bear the seeds.

Confluent. Running together; blended into one.

Conic. Cone-shaped.

Connivent. Converging or coming together, but not united.

Cordate. Heart-shaped with the point upward.

Corm. The enlarged fleshy base of a stem, bulblike but solid.

Corolla. The inner of two series of floral leaves, individually called petals.

Corymb. A convex or flat-topped flower cluster with stems arising at different levels.

Creeping (stems). Growing flat on or beneath the ground and rooting.

Cyme. Usually a flat inflorescence with the central flowers blooming.

Deciduous. Falling away at the close of growing period.

Decompound. Divided more than once, or compounded.

Decumbent. Reclining, but with the tips ascending.

Dehiscent. Opening spontaneously and allowing the contents to be discharged.

Dentate. Toothed, especially with outwardly projecting teeth.

Digitate. Diverging, in manner as the fingers spread.

Discoid. Heads of composites composed only of tubular flowers; rayless; like a disk, or the yellow center of a daisy after the white rays have been plucked.

Diskflower. The central flowers of a head of a composite, which are tubular and lack a flattened extension. (Example: tiny yellow flowers making up the center of a daisy.)

Dissected. Cut or divided into numerous segments.

Divided. Cleft to the base or to the midrib (leaf).

Drupe. A simple fruit, usually indehiscent (nonsplitting), with fleshy exterior and bony nut or stone (such as cherry or peach).

Elliptic. With the outline of an ellipse; usually narrowly ovate.

Entire. Without divisions, lobes, or teeth.

Types of leaf margins, and shapes and arrangements: a, entire; b, undulate; c, serrate; d, lobed; e, filiform; f, linear; g, lanceolate; h, ovate; i, obovate; j, reniform; k, alternate; l, opposite; m, imbricate; n, whorled; o, sessile; p, compound.

Evergreen. Bearing green leaves throughout the year.
Exserted. Prolonged past surrounding organs.

Fascicle. A close bundle or cluster of like organs.
Fibrous. Composed of or resembling fibers.
Filament. The stalk of a stamen.
Filiform. Threadlike.
Foliate. Leaflike.
Follicle. A dry fruit, derived from one carpel, splitting along one side.
Fruit. Seed-bearing structure of a plant; ripened ovary.
Funnel-form, Funnel-shaped. Expanding gradually upward, like a funnel.

Galea. The hooklike upper part of some corollas.
Glabrous. Devoid of hairs.
Gland. A secreting cell, or group of cells.
Glandular. With glands, or glandlike.
Glaucous. Covered or whitened with a waxy bloom.
Globose. Spherical or nearly so.

Head. A dense cluster of stalkless or nearly stalkless flowers on a very short support or receptacle.
Heartwood. The inner wood of a tree that has ceased to carry sap.
Herb. A plant with no persistent woody stem above ground.
Hyaline. Thin, translucent, and not colored.
Hybrid. A cross between two species.
Hypanthium. A cup-shaped, enlarged receptacle, usually bearing the sepals, petals, and stamens, and enclosing the ovules when mature.

Imbricate. Overlapping (as shingles on a roof).
Immersed. Growing wholly under water.
Incised. Cut sharply and irregularly, more or less deeply.
Indehiscent. Not splitting open.
Inferior. Lower or below; outer or anterior. Inferior ovary, one that is below the petals and stamens.
Inflorescence. The mode of arrangement of flowers on a plant.
Intercostal. Between the ribs.
Involucre. A whorl of bracts (modified leaves) subtending a flower or flower cluster.
Irregular. A flower in which one or more of the organs of the same series are unlike the rest.

Keel. Two united anterior petals, as in the Pea family.

Laciniate. Cut into narrow segments.
Laminate. Composed of layers.

Lanceolate. Lance-shaped; considerably longer than broad, tapering upward from the middle or below.

Latex. The milky sap of certain plants.

Leaflet. One of the divisions of a compound leaf.

Ligulate. Possessing ligules.

Ligule. The elongated part of some flowers of the Composite family. The thin collarlike growth at juncture of the sheath and blade in grasses.

Linear. Long and very narrow, with parallel margins.

Lip. One of the divisions of a two-lipped corolla or calyx; the odd petal in the orchid flower.

Lobed. Cut halfway or less to the center with outer points blunt or rounded.

Loment. A legume constricted and usually breaking crosswise into one-seeded joints.

Neutral. Flowers lacking pistil; not fertile.

Nut. An indehiscent (nonsplitting) one-seeded fruit with a hard or bony pericarp (wall).

Nutlet. A small, hard, mostly one-seeded fruit, remaining closed.

Oblong. Longer than broad, with sides nearly parallel, or somewhat curving.

Obovate. The broad end upward.

Obtuse. Blunt, or rounded.

Ocrea. A sheathing stipule.

Opposite (leaves and branches). Pairs oppose each other at each node.

Oval. Broadly elliptic.

Ovary. The part of the pistil containing the seeds.

Ovate. In outline like a longitudinal section of a hen's egg (broadest below middle).

Ovoid. Shaped like a hen's egg.

Ovule. A body in the ovary which becomes the seed.

Palmate. Diverging radiately like the fingers.

Panicle. A compound (branched) flower cluster of the racemose (elongated) type.

Papillate. Beset with nipple-like or pimple-like projections.

Pappus. The modified calyx limb — the hairs, awns, or scales at base of the corolla or the tip of the achene (fruit) in the Composite family.

Parasitic. Growing on and deriving nourishment from another living plant.

Parietal. Borne on or pertaining to the wall of the ovary.

Parted. Cleft nearly, but not quite, to the base.

Pedicel. The stalk of a single flower in a flower cluster.

Peduncle. The stalk of a flower or flower cluster.

Perennial. Lasting from year to year.

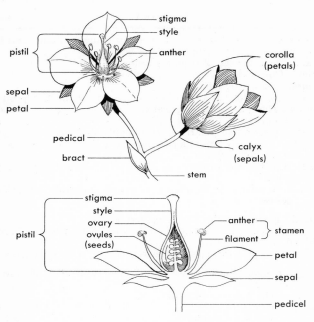

cross section of flower

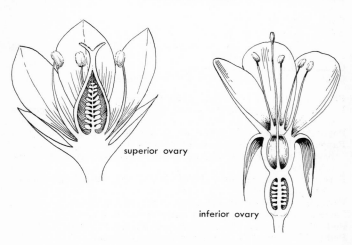

superior ovary

inferior ovary

Parts of a typical flower.

Perianth. The calyx and corolla together; term especially used when calyx and corolla cannot be distinguished.

Petal. One of the modified leaves of the corolla (usually colored).

Petiole. The leafstalk.

Pinnate (leaf). Compound, with the leaflets arranged on each side of a common petiole.

Pinnatifid. Pinnately cleft.

Pistil. The central organ of a flower containing the macrosporanges (ovules).

Pistillate. Female; bearing seed-producing organs only.

Placenta (pl. ae). That portion of the ovary from which seeds are borne.

Plumose. Feathery.

Pod. Any dry and dehiscent (splitting or opening) fruit.

Pome. A core fruit (apple-like).

Prostrate. Lying flat upon the ground.

Puberulent. Covered with fine, short, almost imperceptible down.

Pubescence (pubescent). Hairs, usually soft and downy.

Raceme. An elongated flower cluster along a single stalk with each flower pedicelled and youngest at the top.

Racemose. In racemes, or resembling racemes.

Rachis. An axis bearing close-set organs; the axis of a compound leaf or of a spike or raceme.

Radiate. Composed of many rayflowers.

Rayflower. A type of flower found in the composites that has a flattened, elongated, and colored extension of the corolla. (Example: the white "petals" of a daisy.)

Receptacle. The end of the flower stalk, bearing the floral organs; or, in composites, bearing the flowers; also, in some ferns, an axis bearing sporanges.

Regular. Having the members of each part alike in size and shape.

Reniform. Kidney-shaped.

Revolute. Rolled backward from both sides.

Rhizome. An underground stem producing leaves on the upper side and roots on the lower.

Rootstalk. A rootlike stem growing underground from which regular stems may grow up into the air.

Rosette. A cluster of leaves or other organs in a circular form, usually at the base of a plant.

Rotate (corolla). Wheel-shaped; flat and circular in outline.

Runner. A filiform or very slender stem growing along the ground and sending (at intervals) roots down and leaves up.

Saccate. Possessing a sac or pouch.

Sagittate. Shaped like an arrow head, with lobes pointing backward.

Saprophyte. A plant that grows on dead organic matter.

Scale. A minute rudimentary or vestigial leaf.

Scape. A stem rising from the ground, naked or without ordinary foliage.

Scapose. Bearing or resembling a scape.

Scarious. Thin, dry, and translucent, not green.

Scorpioid. Coiled up in the bud and unrolling as it expands.

Seleniferous. Containing selenium.

Sepal. One of the modified leaves of a calyx at outside of flower.

Serrate. Having teeth pointing forward.

Sessile. Without a stalk.

Sheath. A tubular envelope; like the lower part of the leaf in grasses.

Shrub. A low woody plant that usually branches at the ground level.

Simple. Of one piece; opposed to compound.

Sinus. The notch between two blades.

Spathe. A large, concave bract enclosing a flower cluster, like the white portion of the Calla Lily.

Spike. An elongate flower cluster, with stalkless or nearly stalkless flowers.

Spikelet. A small spike.

Spine. A sharp woody or rigid outgrowth from the stem, leaf, etc.

Spinulose. Bearing very small spines.

Sporange. A sac in which spores are produced; a spore case.

Spore. A single cell or a small group of undifferentiated cells, each capable of reproducing a plant.

Spreading. Diverging nearly at right angles; nearly prostrate.

Spurred. Possessing a hollow saclike or tubular extension of a floral organ.

Stamen. The organ of a flower which bears the microspores (pollen grains).

Stigma. That part of a pistil through which fertilization by the pollen is effected.

Stipules. The appendages on each side of the base of certain leaves.

Stoma (pl. stomata). An opening in the epidermis of a leaf.

Style. The usually attenuated portion of the pistil connecting the stigma and ovary.

Sub. A prefix meaning somewhat or almost.

Taproot. A stout vertical root that continues the main axis of the plant.

Tendril. A thread-shaped process used for climbing.

Terete. Same as cylindrical, but may include tapering.

Ternate. Divided or arranged in threes.

Tomentose. Densely woolly, with matted hairs.

Toothed. Toothlike projections, especially on margins.

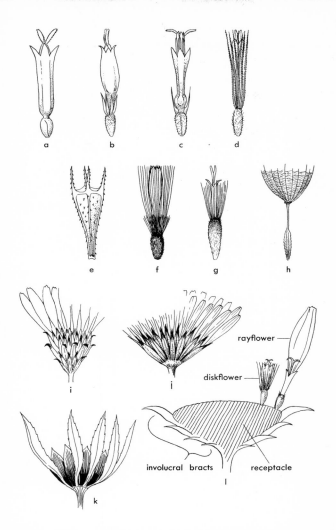

Aids in identifying Compositae: a, pappus lacking; b, pappus of awns; c, pappus of deciduous awn scales; d, pappus of long scales; e, barbed pappus; f, pappus of numerous capillary bristles (pappus double); g, pappus of numerous capillary bristles (pappus simple); h, pappus bristles plumose; i, involucral bracts graduated in length; j, involucral bracts about equal; k, involucral bracts unequal and leafy; l, cross section of composite flower head.

Tree. A woody plant of large size and with a single stem (trunk) for some distance above the ground.

Trifoliate. Leaves in threes.

Tuber. A thickened and short underground branch, having numerous buds.

Tubercle. A small tubelike prominence or nodule.

Tubular. Tube-shaped, or composed of diskflowers.

Turbinate. Top-shaped.

Twining. Ascending by coiling round a support.

Umbel. Flat-topped or convex flower cluster, with all the pedicels (stalks) arising from same point.

Undulate. Wavy, or wavy-margined.

Unisexual. Having only one kind of sex organs; applied also to flowers having only stamens or pistils.

Vascular bundles. Vessels or tubes for conducting fluids.

Verticillate. Arranged in whorls.

Villous. Bearing long, loose, soft hairs.

Viscid. Sticky.

Whorl. A group of three or more similar organs, radiating from a node; a verticil.

Wing. Any membranous extension.

A Field Guide to
Rocky Mountain
Wildflowers

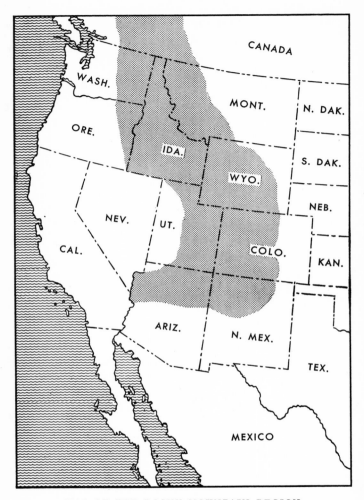

MAP OF THE ROCKY MOUNTAIN REGION

The shaded areas indicate the mountain and intermountain regions covered by this book. However, a number of the plants described will be found in isolated mountain ranges not included in the shaded portions. References in the text to the Rockies and the Rocky Mountain region are synonymous.

COMMON CATTAIL   *Typha latifolia* L.
Pl. 1

Family: Typhaceae (Cattail).

Other names: Cattail Flag, Broadleaf Cattail.

Description: This cattail with flat straplike leaves (3–6 ft. long) and a spongy, jointless, unbranched stem is not easily confused with any other plant except those of the same genus. At top of the 4- to 8-ft. unbranched stem is a dense raceme of minute brown flowers. Lower 2–8 in. of this inflorescence is a dense, sausagelike cluster of female flowers. Immediately above are the male flowers, which shed their yellow pollen in early summer, then blow away and leave bare upper part of stem protruding above female flowers.

Related species: In *T. angustifolia* the spike of the male flower does not adjoin female spike on stem, usually being separated by about 1 in.; leaves are very narrow.

Flowering season: Late May to July, but brown fruits persist on plant until late fall and frequently throughout winter.

Where found: G, Y, T, R. Always found in wet places, growing in mud or water, and seldom above 6000–7000 ft. Common in most areas of world except arctic regions. There are 4 species of *Typha* in U.S.; only 2 in Rocky Mts.

Interesting facts: *Latifolia* means broad-leaved. This is truly the outdoorsman's plant. Lower part of stem and the roots contain nearly pure starch. Rootstock is easily pulled up and can be eaten raw, or roasted in hot coals; can be gathered throughout the year, and in deep snow country seldom freezes so solid that it can't be pulled or dug with a pointed stick. In some places the leaves are used for weaving mats. Female flowers make an excellent tinder. The "fuzz" will explode into flame with a spark from pyrite or flint and steel. Early settlers used the down for bedding. Down is useful as insulation against cold under emergency conditions; stuffed into boots it will prevent frostbite. The core of the large rootstocks was dried and ground into meal by Indians and early settlers. New shoots are edible and taste like cucumber. Cattail is widely used in dry bouquets and as a home decorative motif.

Muskrats and geese feed on rootstocks, new shoots, and stem bases. Elk utilize shoots in early spring. Cattails serve as nesting cover for marsh wrens, red-winged blackbirds, and many kinds of waterfowl and shorebirds. No other plant in the Rocky Mt. region is so desirable as roosting cover for ring-necked pheasants. Extent and distribution of this plant are important factors in determining the number of pheasants that can winter in a given area.

BURREED *Sparganium simplex* Huds.   **Pl. 1**

Family: Sparganiaceae (Burreed).

Description: A water plant with grasslike leaves and conspicuous globose heads of small flowers. To the layman it looks like a large erect grass with white blossoms. Stem is stout and erect, and some leaves are triangular-keeled. Male and female flowers are in separate heads about ½ in. broad; male heads at top and female below. Flowers lack true sepals and petals, but these are replaced by scales.

Burreeds could be confused with cattails (*Typha*) during their early growth, but later the flowers of cattails appear in long terminal spikes and those of burreeds are in round heads, mainly at side of stems. Unlike cattails, burreeds seldom form extensive beds.

Related species: (1) *S. eurycarpum* is a coarse plant, 3–7 ft. tall; found over most of N. America. (2) *S. angustifolium* is a weak-stemmed plant; normally floats on water and leaves usually not keeled.

Flowering season: July and Aug. When broods of half-grown common mergansers are seen on rivers, Burreed is in full bloom.

Where found: G, Y, T, R. Generally in still or slow-moving water, or sometimes on mud. Flowers protrude above water, but leaves usually float if water is shallow. Found from B.C. to Labrador, south to Iowa, Georgia, Minnesota, Colorado, and California. In mts. it grows almost to timberline. There are about 20 species of *Sparganium* distributed over temperate and cold regions of both hemispheres; about half occur in Rocky Mt. area.

Interesting facts: *Simplex* means simple, unbranched. Burreed seeds are eaten by ducks and marsh birds but muskrats utilize the entire plant. It is eaten occasionally by moose and deer. The tubers and bulbous stem base of some species were consumed by Indians.

PONDWEED *Potamogeton pectinatus* L.

Family: Najadaceae (Pondweed).

Other names: Sego Pondweed, Fennel-leaf Pondweed.

Description: This underwater plant attains a length of 1–3 ft. and is minutely divided with stringlike branches and leaves. Leaves are 2–6 in. long, and are usually alternate on stem. Flowers minute, green, and arranged in dense spikes, which mature into clusters of small dark-colored seeds.

The submerged growth and threadlike nature of this pondweed make it unlikely that it will be confused except with a few other species of *Potamogeton*. These various species can be separated only on very technical characters.

Related species: (1) *P. natans* has heart-shaped, floating leaves; (2) *P. richardsonii*, found in still water, has leaves all submersed and ribbonlike or lanceolate; (3) *P. epihydrus* has flattened stems, elliptic floating leaves and ribbonlike submersed leaves. These 3 plants common throughout Rocky Mts.

Flowering season: July and Aug.

Where found: G, Y, T, R. Mainly in shallow water of lakes, ponds, and slow-moving streams. Probably the most abundant of all pondweeds; found over most of N. and S. America and in Eurasia. Currently around 80 species of *Potamogeton* known; about 25 are in Rocky Mt. area.

Interesting facts: *Pectinatus* means comblike. This is a plant with which the waterfowl enthusiast should be familiar; this pondweed probably supplies more food for our ducks and other waterfowl than any other single plant. The tubers, seeds, rootstocks, and even stems and leaves are consumed. It grows so dense that at times it almost clogs streams, canals, and ditches. Some pondweeds may go for years without flowering, then blossom profusely. The reasons for this irregularity are not known.

Pondweed (*Potamogeton pectinatus* L.)

ARROWGRASS   *Triglochin maritima* L.

  Family: Juncaginaceae (Arrowgrass).

  Other names: Podgrass, Goosegrass, Sourgrass.

  Description: A slender, unbranched plant, reaching a height of 1–3 ft. Leaves are basal, 6–18 in. long, narrowly linear, and appear grasslike. Unlike true grasses, however, Arrowgrass leaves are fleshy and flat on one side and round on the other. Upper portion of stem extending above leaves is densely covered with a spikelike raceme of small greenish flowers.

Arrowgrass (*Triglochin maritima* L.)

    Arrowgrass could be confused with the Flowering Quillwort (*Lilaea subulata*) and *Scheuchzeria*, except that these others do not have a long raceme of flowers standing above the leaves.

  Related species: *T. palustris* is scarcely half the size of *T. maritima*.

  Flowering season: June and July.

  Where found: Y, T, R. Saline, marshy areas. Occurs from Alaska to Labrador, south to New Jersey, Iowa, Mexico, and California; also Europe and Asia. There are about a dozen species of *Triglochin*, mainly in Mediterranean region; only 2 in Rockies.

Interesting facts: *Maritima* means of the sea. Arrowgrass is reported to contain considerable amounts of hydrocyanic acid. Animals feeding on the green leaves or on hay containing this plant have been killed in a very short time. The plant is most likely to prove toxic when growing under drought conditions. On the other hand, seeds of Arrowgrass were parched and ground for food by western Indians. Roasted seeds were also used as a substitute for coffee. Plant parts that contain hydrocyanic acid are heated or roasted in order to eliminate the poison. Cashew nuts, for example, are treated in this way to make them edible. A few other cyanogenetic plants dangerous to livestock under certain conditions are common Sorghum, Sudan Grass, and wild chokecherries (*Prunus*).

ARROWHEAD *Sagittaria cuneata* Sheld.   **Pl. 1**
    Family: Alismaceae (Arrowhead).
    Other names: Swamp Potato, Duck Potato, Wapato (Indian), and *S. arifolia.*
    Description: A perennial bog or water plant 6–30 in. tall, characterized by basal, distinctly veined, arrow-shaped leaves on long leafstalks. Leaves about 2–8 in. long and ⅔ as wide.

Arrowhead (*Sagittaria cuneata* Sheld.)

If water is deep enough, blades of leaves do not develop, and only the long, slender leafstalks show. Flowers arranged in whorls near top of flowering stalk have 3 green sepals and 3 conspicuous white petals; uppermost are male flowers, lower female.

There is no other plant in the Rocky Mts. likely to be confused with this one except other species of *Sagittaria*.

Related species: *S. latifolia* is a larger plant, basal lobes of leaves are divergent, and seed has a horizontal beak about $\frac{1}{16}$ in. long; found throughout Rocky Mts.

Flowering season: July and Aug. First blooms about time young spotted sandpipers are running about and young Audubon's warblers are leaving nest.

Where found: Y, T, R. Ponds, shallow water of lakes, slow-moving streams. Occurs from sea level to around 7500 ft. in mts., and is found over most of N. America, except se. U.S. About 30 species of *Sagittaria* are scattered over N. Hemisphere, but perhaps only 3 occur in Rockies.

Interesting facts: *Cuneata* means wedge-shaped. Many species of *Sagittaria* have nutritious starchy tubers at the ends of the long narrow rootstocks. When under water, these can be loosened by sticks or by digging with toes. The freed tubers are readily gathered when they rise to the water's surface. The tubers are slightly bitter raw, and have about the same texture as a potato. They taste like water chestnuts when boiled or roasted. Arrowhead is highly esteemed by the Chinese, who cultivate it. Lewis and Clark found these tubers constituted the chief vegetable food of Indians along the lower Columbia. The exploring party consumed large quantities of Wapato while wintering at the mouth of the river. This plant has commercial possibilities.

GREAT BASIN WILD RYE   Pl. 1
Elymus cinereus Scribn. & Merr.

Family: Gramineae (Grass).

Other names: Buffalo Rye, Ryegrass, and *E. condensatus* for Rocky Mts.

Description: This is the most common bunchgrass of large size seen along highways, railroad tracks, and hillsides. A tall, coarse grass 3–6 ft. high, growing in bunches often 1 ft. or more across at base. Leaves are flat, about $\frac{1}{2}$ in. or more wide, and 1–3 ft. long. There is a single, erect, dense spike of flowers 5–8 in. long at end of each stem.

Related species: (1) *E. canadensis* grows 3–5 ft. tall; head is nodding and covered with bent stiff awns about 1 in. long. (2) *E. glaucus* is about same height but heads are erect, more slender, and awns are soft and $\frac{1}{2}$ in. long or less.

Flowering season: July and Aug.

Where found: G, Y, T, R. Dry to medium-moist soil of plains, valleys, and in mts. to around 8000 ft. Found from Saskatchewan to B.C., south to California and New Mexico. Approximately 45 species of *Elymus* are native to north temperate region; about 20 in Rocky Mt. area, of which 3 are quite common.

Interesting facts: *Cinereus* means ash-colored. Although this grass is very coarse, it is eaten by wildlife, especially during winter when other food is covered by snow. Elk feed on it freely at this time of year, but it is poor forage. It is palatable to horses and cattle in spring. In late summer and fall the heads are filled with grain, and animals such as chipmunks and ground squirrels fell the stalks in order to gather and store the seeds. This plant is a close relative of the cultivated rye.

FOXTAIL BARLEY   *Hordeum jubatum* L.   Pl. 1

Family: Gramineae (Grass).

Other names: Squirreltail, Ticklegrass.

Description: This attractive perennial grass grows in bunches and is quickly noticed because the flower head is densely covered by very slender reddish-golden awns. These awns are 1–2 in. long, minutely barbed on sides, and become rigid and brittle when mature. Flower head looks like a miniature fox tail, and hence the name. Grass bunches are 4–5 in. across at base and 1–3 ft. high, with flower spikes 2–4 in. long. Spikes usually curve downward or to one side.

Related species: (1) A common species, *H. pusillum*, is an annual grass about 1 ft. tall, grows in dry soil, and has stiff, short awns about ½ in. long; (2) *H. brachyantherum* is common in mt. meadows.

Flowering season: July and Aug. Mature fruiting head is conspicuous until snow flies.

Where found: G, Y, T, R. Alkali, damp to wet soil of meadows, roadsides, pastures, and waste places. Occurs from Alaska south to Maryland, Texas, Mexico, and California. Grows in mts. to around 9000 ft. There are about 20 species of *Hordeum* in temperate regions of both hemispheres; about half occur in Rocky Mt. area.

Interesting facts: *Jubatum* means crested. This plant is sometimes used ornamentally; however, it is a troublesome weed, and crowds out more desirable plants. When eaten by animals, pieces of the barbed awns may work into the gums, sides of mouth, and into the digestive tract and cause irritation and inflammation. They also work their way into the ears and eyes, sometimes causing blindness and even death. Foxtail Barley is an agent leading to necrotic stomatitis in bighorn sheep, deer, and elk — a disease that at times has caused great losses of elk on winter feeding grounds. While elk feed, the awns pierce the mouth tissues, then a bacterium penetrates into the lesions and the disease follows a well-defined course, usually causing death. A number of grasses have barbed awns, including a near relative — cultivated barley — Brome Grass, Needle-and-Thread Grass, and others.

SEDGE   *Carex nebraskensis* Dewey   **Pl. 1**
   Family: Cyperaceae (Sedge).
   Other names: Nebraska Sedge.
   Description: This grasslike plant is usually bluish green in color, has sharp-angled, triangular stems, and attains a height of 10–40 in. Leaves are 4–16 in. long and often ¼ in. or more broad. Old, dry leaves of previous year persist on lower part of stem. At top of plant are 1 or 2 spikes of male flowers with dark scales and reddish-brown anthers. Below these are 2 to 5 spikes of female flowers, spikes being brown and broader than male spikes.
   Sedges generally can be distinguished from grasses by their solid, triangular stems instead of round, hollow stems. Leaves are usually in 3 rows on stem, leaf sheaths are not split, and anthers are attached at base instead of center.
   Related species: Three are quite common in our area: (1) *C. amplifolia* is found growing in water or mud and attains a height of 3 ft. or more; (2) *C. geyeri* grows in medium-dry soil — commonly in Lodgepole Pine forests, where it forms a dense cover — flowers soon after snow melts; (3) *C. festivella* has a single dark-colored head, forms distinct clumps of plants, and grows in open, medium-dry places.
   Flowering season: July and Aug.
   Where found: G, Y, T, R. Wet to boggy soil of meadows, around springs and along streams in the open. Found from South Dakota to B.C., south to California and New Mexico, in valleys and mts. up to 9000 ft. *Carex* is one of our largest genera, with nearly 800 species; more than 100 species occur in Rocky Mts.
   Interesting facts: *Nebraskensis* means from Nebraska. The young shoots and tender leaf bases of almost all sedges are sweet and furnish a tasty nibble for the hungry outdoorsman. Being widespread and available, they rate high as emergency food. Elk feed considerably on young sedge shoots in early spring and also seek out tender basal parts of the mature plant. *Carex geyeri* is such an important elk food that it has received the common name of Elk Sedge. Muskrats feed extensively on the sedge stem base and ducks utilize the seeds. Sedges are one of the staple foods of black and grizzly bears in spring.
   The outdoorsman with a preference for swamps and marshes will find that he can readily make a soft insulated bed by cutting clumps of sedge leaves and laying them as he would fir boughs.

·

COTTON-SEDGE *Eriophorum angustifolium* Roth

Family: Cyperaceae (Sedge).

Other names: Cotton-grass.

Description: Usually noticed when mature, for at this time a large terminal tuft of "wool" or "cotton" is conspicuous. This grasslike plant has stiff, obscurely triangular stems 1–2 ft. high. At the top grow spikes of inconspicuous flowers; from these, silky white hairs ⅛–1 in. long develop and form the "cotton" ball. Leaves are flat and grasslike.

This plant could easily be confused with grasses or other sedges, but when the cottonlike growth develops it is quite distinctive.

Related species: *E. gracile* has V-shaped leaves.

Flowering season: June and July.

Where found: G, Y, T, R. Wet or boggy soil, or sometimes in shallow water, from Alaska to Greenland, south to Maine, Illinois, New Mexico, and Washington. Grows in valleys and to about 9000 ft. in mts. There are about 20 species of *Eriophorum;* only 3 or 4 occur in Rockies.

Interesting facts: *Angustifolium* means narrow-leaved. Long hairs, produced on many plants, aid in seed dispersal. Common

Cotton-sedge (*Eriophorum angustifolium* Roth)

cotton seeds are covered with such hair; milkweed, thistle, and other seeds have a tuft of them at top of seed. In Cotton-sedge the hairs develop at base of ovary and correspond to sepals and petals in other plants.

Bulrush (*Scirpus acutus* Muhl.)

BULRUSH   *Scirpus acutus* Muhl.

Family: Cyperaceae (Sedge).

Other names: Tule, Clubrush, Giant Bulrush, Roundstem Bulrush.

Description: A dark green, round-stemmed, willowy plant with no leaves except some sheaths around stem base. These characteristics distinguish most bulrushes from all other large water plants. Stems are stiff and firm, ½ in. or more in diameter near base and 3–9 ft. tall, with clusters of erect brown bristly flower spikes near top. A single stemlike bract appears just under flowers. Bulrushes usually grow in dense patches in mud or shallow water and cover large areas.

Plants in our area most likely to be confused with this *Scirpus* are other species of this genus.

Related species: (1) *S. validus* has soft, weak stems and drooping flower clusters; (2) *S. americanus* seldom grows more than 3 ft. tall, is slender, and has grasslike leaves on lower part of stem; (3) *S. paludosus* has large flower clusters and 2 leaflike bracts immediately beneath, which make the flowers appear to be terminal. These species occur throughout most of temperate N. America.

Flowering season: July and Aug.

Where found: Y, T. Alaska to Newfoundland, south to North Carolina, Texas, and California. Grows from sea level to elevation of about 8000 ft. There are about 200 species of *Scirpus* distributed over most of the earth; approximately 20 occur in Rockies.

Interesting facts: *Acutus* means sharp-pointed. The strong, pithy stems dry and often do not decay for a year or more. They were used by the Indians in weaving mats, and the modern duck hunter can weave them into meshed wire to make an excellent waterfowl blind. Rootstocks of this species were eaten raw by Indians or were used to make bread. The stem bases and young shoots are crisp and sweet. New shoots form in autumn and make a welcome snack for the hunter who has forgotten his lunch. Various species of bulrush have been used by people throughout the world to stave off starvation in famine times. Bulrushes form a buffer against wind and wave action, thus permitting other aquatic plants to grow in an otherwise unfavorable environment.

Like the Common Cattail, Bulrush furnishes nesting cover for red-winged blackbirds, marsh wrens, coots, least bitterns, ducks, and Canada geese. It is a staple food of muskrats and is used in the construction of their houses. Seeds are consumed by waterfowl.

YELLOW SKUNKCABBAGE Pl. 1; p. 12
Lysichitum americanum H. & S.

Family: Araceae (Arum).

Other names: American Skunkcabbage.

Description: This is the only plant in the region with a conspicuous flowering stalk bearing at the top a bright yellow, partly rolled flower-covering called a spathe (see Plate 1). Inside this the thick stalk bears hundreds of minute flowers. Plant has a thick vertical rootstock, from which grows a cluster of leaves 1–5 ft. long and 4–16 in. broad. Flowering stalk, 8–12 in. long, protrudes from among leaves.

There is no mature plant in our area likely to be confused with this, but the young Skunkcabbage leaves can be confused with those of poisonous False Hellebore (*Veratrum viride*). Latter has pleated leaves that are stalkless on an elongated stem.

Flowering season: The distinctly scented flowers appear at first sign of spring, before leaves begin growth. Look for Skunk-

Yellow Skunkcabbage (*Lysichitum americanum* H. & S.)

cabbage when migrating birds begin to arrive in spring. At height of the blooming, bald eagle is nesting and steelhead are arriving on the spawning beds.

Where found: G. Marshes and wet woods, mainly along our western coast from Alaska to California, but extending inland at low elevations, to w. Montana. Only species in our area.

Interesting facts: *Americanum* means American. There is a difference of opinion whether there are 1 or 2 species of *Lysichitum* in the world. Some botanists believe our plant is same species as the one found on eastern coast of Russia (*L. kamtschatcensis*); others claim that these are 2 distinct species.

Yellow Skunkcabbage is eaten by black bears throughout the warmer months. All of the plant — leaves, roots, and fruit — is consumed. Crystals of calcium oxalate, in all parts of this plant, produce a stinging, burning sensation in the mouth when chewed raw. Heat breaks or rearranges crystals in the starch so that the plant can be eaten with no unpleasant effect. By roasting and drying the root the Indians were able to use this plant, as well as the eastern Skunkcabbage (*Symplocarpus foetidus*), for food. A flour was prepared from the starch. The young green leaves (cabbages) usually can be eaten after being boiled in several changes of water. At times even repeated boilings will not remove the stinging property. This plant is related to taro, the staple food of the Polynesians. Like the Skunkcabbage, taro contains crystals of calcium oxalate. Native peoples throughout the world use members of the Arum family for food, and quite independently they have discovered that drying or heating removes the stinging properties.

DUCKWEED   *Lemna minor* L.
Family: Lemnaceae (Duckweed).
Other names: Lesser Duckweed.
Description: These are minute green plants that float on still or sluggish water, often covering and coloring the whole surface of a pond. Individual plants are flat, egg-shaped, and ⅛–¼ in. long. Single white root about 1 in. long grows from lower surface. Occasionally produces almost microscopic flowers and seeds, but normally a bud forms in cleft at edge of this plant and breaks loose to form a new plant. This method of reproduction, known as budding, is found in a number of other plants.

These plants could be confused with other genera of same family, but presence of a single root is distinctive of *Lemna*.
Related species: *L. trisulca* is elongated in shape; new plant remains attached to parent plants by a long stalk. This species, like *L. minor*, is widely distributed.
Flowering season: Latter part of July to first part of Aug.
Where found: Y, T. Throughout N. America, Europe, and Asia, except coldest parts. Grows from sea level up to timberline. There are about 8 species of *Lemna* distributed over the earth; at least 3 occur in Rocky Mt. area.
Interesting facts: *Minor* means smaller. As its common name indicates, this is an important duck food, particularly in warm regions, where it is extremely abundant. Entire plant is consumed.

WIREGRASS   *Juncus balticus* Willd.   p. 14
Family: Juncaceae (Rush).
Other names: Rush, Baltic Rush.
Description: This looks like a small-sized Bulrush with a cluster of purplish-brown flowers (on short stalks) that appear to come directly out of the side of the main stalk. Stems are leafless, unbranched, 8–36 in. tall, and ¹⁄₁₆–⅛ in. thick near base. Coarse, branching, underground rootstocks give rise to dense mats of green stems.

The wiregrasses are most likely to be confused with the bulrushes (*Scirpus*), but latter have bristles for flower parts and wiregrasses have 3 sepals and 3 petals that are dry, paperlike, and purplish brown in color. Wiregrasses produce seed pods containing several small seeds in each pod; bulrushes have only 1 seed to a flower.
Related species: Some of these species bear flowers in obviously terminal clusters. Among these are: (1) *J. bufonius*, a small delicate annual; (2) *J. saximontanus*, with flowers borne mostly

singly on densely clustered branches; and (3) *J. mertensianus*, with flowers that occur in dense single heads. These plants extend throughout Rocky Mt. area.

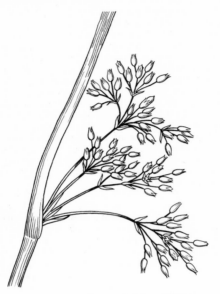

Wiregrass (*Juncus balticus* Willd.)

Flowering season: Latter part of June to first part of Aug.
Where found: G, Y, T. In damp to wet soil, usually in saline situations. It and its varieties grow from lowest valleys up to around 9000 ft. Found over most of N. America, except in se. U.S.; also occurs in S. America and Eurasia. There are about 225 species of *Juncus* distributed over most of the earth; nearly 40 grow in Rocky Mt. area.
Interesting facts: *Balticus* means of the Baltic. This plant is consumed by livestock when it is young, but as it matures it becomes so stiff and woody that there is little food value. Various species of wiregrass are abundant throughout the pine woods of the South, where it is common practice to burn the old stalks each season so that livestock can readily feed on the fresh new growth as it appears. Many of the western Indians used it in weaving baskets and mats. With excessive and improper irrigation, *J. balticus* will increase and displace more valuable sedges and grasses in mt. meadows and valleys.

NODDING ONION   *Allium cernuum* Roth   **Pl. 2**

Family: Liliaceae (Lily).

Other names: Wild Onion, Garlic, Leek.

Description: This onion grows 6–18 in. tall from elongated bulbs and can be told from other onions by the nodding umbel. There are several grasslike basal leaves extending ½–¾ the length of plant. Stalk has distinct bend in it so that umbel of 25 to 40 flowers faces sideways or downward. Stamens longer than the white or pink sepals and petals.

Wild Hyacinth (*Brodiaea douglasii*) might be mistaken for this plant (see Plate 3) but it has sepals and petals united for about ⅓ their length, forming a cup; in onions each one is separate. These are the only 2 groups of plants with the flowers in umbels which are likely to be confused. Some of the death-camases (*Zigadenus*) can be puzzling before they flower, but bulbs do not have an onion smell and emerging leaves are sharply creased.

Related species: (1) Siberian Chive (*A. schoenoprasum* L.) has round, hollow leaves like the common cultivated onion and the flowers are rose-colored or lavender; see illus. below; (2) in

Nodding Onion (*Allium cernuum* Roth) and
Siberian Chive (*A. schoenoprasum* L.)

Shortstyle Onion (*Allium brevistylum* Wats.)

A. textile the bulb is covered with layers of netlike fibers, and flowers are white; (3) in *A. acuminatum* the bulb is covered with paperlike layers, and flowers are pink; (4) Shortstyle Onion (*A. brevistylum* Wats.) usually has more than 2 leaves shorter than stem; stamens are shorter than the pink sepals and petals; see illus. above. All these species occur throughout Rocky Mts.

Flowering season: Flowers begin opening about middle of June and continue at higher elevations until first part of Aug.

Where found: G, Y, T, R. Grows in dry to moist soil in valleys, open hillsides, and ridges. In mts. found as high as 9000 ft. Extends from New York across s. Canada and n. U.S. to B.C., then south in mts. to Mexico. There are perhaps 50 different species of onions in Rocky Mt. area.

Interesting facts: *Cernuum* means nodding. There are about 300 species of onions in the world, and all have the distinctive odor and taste of onions, which is caused by the presence of volatile sulphur compounds in all parts of the plant. Onions, garlic, leek, chives, and shallot all belong to this genus. Most of them are valuable for food and flavoring, some species are grown for ornamental purposes, and in warmer climates some are noxious weeds.

Wild onions were used extensively by Indians, and Lewis and

Clark found them a welcome addition to a meat diet. The bulbs are utilized by bears and ground squirrels; elk and deer graze the early spring herbage. Onions add considerably to camp cooking and improve the flavor of wild game for some people. When eaten by milk cows they impart a disagreeable flavor to the milk. The dried stem and seed pods of some species persist well into winter and indicate to an observant woodsman that emergency food can be obtained only a few inches below the ground surface.

WILD HYACINTH   *Brodiaea douglasii* Wats.   **Pl. 3**
   Family: Liliaceae (Lily).
   Other names: Cluster-lily, Bluedicks.
   Description: This plant is characterized by blue, tubular-shaped flowers occurring in an umbel at the top of a slender leafless stem. Flowers are about 1 in. long, with 5 to 15 in an umbel. Stems, arising from coated bulbs, are 1–3 ft. tall and normally several grow together. The few inconspicuous leaves are grasslike, basal, and somewhat shorter than stem.

   Wild Hyacinth might be confused with Nodding Onion (*Allium cernuum*) and with blue Camas (*Camassia quamash*),

Wild Hyacinth (*Brodiaea douglasii* Wats.)

but petals of both these plants are separate instead of united into a tube. Flowers of blue Camas form a raceme instead of an umbel (see Plate 2). The blue Camas bulb is layered like an onion; Wild Hyacinth's is solid.

Related species: *B. hyacinthina* has white flowers and occurs only in western part of our region.

Flowering season: Late April to early July. Look for it when Camas is in bloom, about time young magpies are leaving nest.

Where found: G, Y, T, R. Dry to moist soil, often in rocky areas, meadows, or open woods of valleys, hills, and in mts. to around 9000 ft. Like Camas, grows in patches covering considerable area. Can be found from Montana to B.C., south to California and Utah. There are about 20 species of *Brodiaea*, all confined to w. N. America; most of them occur in California, but 2 are found in Rocky Mt. area.

Interesting facts: *Douglasii* means plant is named for David Douglas. The corm of this plant is edible, and was used by the Indians and early white settlers. The Nez Percé Indians were particularly fond of it. It can be gathered in considerable quantities and eaten either raw or cooked. When boiled it has a sweet, nutlike flavor and is perhaps one of the tastiest of our edible bulbs. The tender seed pods make an excellent green. Bulbs of the other brodiaeas are also edible. Deer feed on the early spring growth and the corms are a favorite food of grizzly bears.

SEGO LILY   *Calochortus nuttallii* Torr.   **Pl. 3**

Family: Liliaceae (Lily).

Other names: Mariposa Lily, Star Tulip, Butterfly Tulip.

Description: A white tuliplike flower with a triangular cup-shaped appearance. Flowers are few and showy, base of petals being yellow and marked with a crescent-shaped purple band or spot. This plant generally grows on dry open plains and hillsides. Possesses a few grasslike leaves, a thin-coated bulb, and like most members of the Lily family it has 3 sepals, 3 petals, and 6 stamens. Stems attain a height of 8–20 in.

This is the only sego lily of the Rocky Mt. area that has white flowers and does not have 3 thin wings running length of seed pods.

Related species: (1) Purple-eyed Mariposa (*C. nitidus* Dougl.), Plate 3, is very similar to *C. nuttallii* except it lacks the basal crescent-shaped spot and 3 thin longitudinal wings develop on seed pod; found from Montana to Washington, south to Nevada. (2) *C. macrocarpus* has purple petals with green central stripe; ranges from Montana to B.C., south to California and Nevada. (3) *C. elegans* has greenish-white petals bearing a purple mark at base, and inner surface of petals is very hairy.

Flowering season: Blooms in June and early July, first appearing when young golden eagles are feathering and their parents are busy hunting rodents, and prairie falcons are fledging.

Where found: Y, T, R. Grows on dry well-drained plains and hillsides at low elevations. Look for it among sagebrush or on gravel slopes and terraces. Sego Lily ranges from New Mexico and Colorado to Dakotas, west to Idaho and California. The genus, of 57 species, is found in w. U.S., Canada, and as far south as Guatemala; 9 species occur in Rockies, some restricted to mts. and others to plains and valleys.

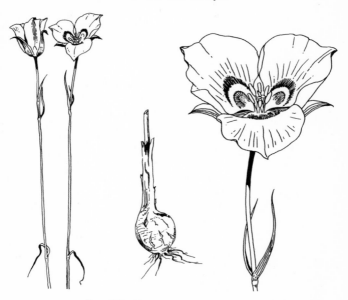

Sego Lily (*Calochortus nuttallii* Torr.)

Interesting facts: The species name *nuttallii* means named for Thomas Nuttall. The Sego Lily is the state flower of Utah. The bulbous root, about the size of a walnut, is sweet and nutritious, and was used as food by the Indians. The Mormons, during their first lean years in Utah, consumed the bulb in large quantities. As an emergency food it can be eaten cooked or raw. Boiled, it tastes like a potato. The Indians frequently ground it and made bread from the starchy meal. The name Sego is of Shoshonean origin. Other members of the genus contain starchy tubers that are edible. Bears and rodents consume the tubers, and the seed pods are avidly eaten by domestic sheep and probably by bighorn sheep. However, the leaves and stems dry up quickly and the plant has little forage value.

Camas (*Camassia quamash* [Pursh] Greene)

CAMAS   *Camassia quamash* (Pursh) Greene   **Pl. 2**

Family: Liliaceae (Lily).

Other names: Camash, Swamp Sego.

Description: This has bright blue flowers that form a showy spikelike raceme. The 3 sepals and 3 petals are similarly colored, and there are 6 stamens. Camas is 1–2 ft. tall, with an unbranched stem and basal grasslike leaves ½–¾ in. broad arising from an ovate bulb about 1 in. wide.

It might be confused with death-camases (*Zigadenus*) — see Plate 2 and p. 32 — before and after flowering, but when in bloom the small yellowish flowers of death-camases are in sharp contrast to the large, bright blue or occasionally white flowers of Camas. Can be distinguished from Wild Hyacinth (*Brodiaea douglasii*) by its distinct rather than united sepals and petals (see Plate 3).

Related species: (1) *C. scilloides* occupies the Mississippi Valley;

(2) *C. leichtlinii*, (3) *C. howellii*, and (4) *C. cusickii* are mainly confined to western states.

Flowering season: From middle of April to middle of June, depending on altitude. At peak of flowering, cow elk have dropped calves and mule deer are just beginning to give birth to fawns.

Where found: G, Y, T. Found in wet meadows and stream-banks. The genus is strictly N. American, ranging from s. Alberta and B.C. south to California and Utah. There are about 6 species, all but 1 confined to West.

Interesting facts: *Quamash* is an Indian name. The bulb of this plant is starchy and nutritious; it can be eaten at any season but is best in autumn. The boiled bulbs are potato-like in flavor but slightly slimy or gummy and less mealy than potatoes. They can be baked, roasted, dried, or eaten raw. Indians cooked them in rock ovens. The Camas probably played a more significant role in early western history than any other plant. It formed the chief vegetable diet of the Indians of the North-west, trappers, and early settlers. Members of the Lewis and Clark expedition used the Camas extensively and at times were entirely dependent on it as food. The bulbs of this plant enticed the Nez Percés, under Chief Joseph, to leave their reservation along the Clearwater River in Idaho and go south to collect them. This infraction started the Chief Joseph War, which was one of the most brilliant campaigns waged by the American Indians in defense of their homelands. Elk, deer, and moose reportedly graze the plant in early spring. Because Camas grows so luxuriantly in places, frequently giving a bluish tint to acres of meadowland, it has inspired many place names, such as: Camas, Idaho; Camas Prairie, near Grangeville, Idaho; and Camas Hot Springs, Montana.

QUEENCUP *Clintonia uniflora* (Schult.) Kunth   **Pl. 3**
  Family: Liliaceae (Lily).
  Other names: Beadlily, One-flowered Clintonia.
  Description: The flowers are white, about 1 in. broad, and there is usually just 1 at the end of a slender stalk some 3–8 in. tall. Leaves are almost basal, bright green, lance-shaped, longer than flowering stalk, and 2 to 5 together. Fruit a blue, globose or pear-shaped berry. This plant has slender, creeping stems that spread just below ground surface. Leaves, flowers, and fibrous roots form at stem nodes, enabling plant to spread over con-siderable area.

  Queencup flowers might be confused with those of Fairybells (*Disporum trachycarpum*) and Wakerobin (*Trillium ovatum*), but these have leaves along stem (see Plates 3, 2).

  Flowering season: Latter part of May until July. Dolly Varden trout are beginning to migrate to upstream spawning beds.

Where found: G. Moist to wet soil, usually in forest shade, especially under conifers, but sometimes among shrubs and along streams. A hill and mt. plant, it grows from Alaska to California, east to Idaho and Montana. There are 6 species of *Clintonia:* 2 of w. U.S., 2 of e. U.S., and 2 of e. Asia. Queencup the only species in Rockies.

Interesting facts: *Uniflora* means 1-flowered. Ruffed grouse are fond of the blue berries.

FAIRYBELLS   *Disporum trachycarpum* (Wats.) B. & H.   **Pl. 3**

    Family: Liliaceae (Lily).

    Other names: Mandarin.

    Description: The inconspicuous white to greenish-yellow bell-shaped flowers are borne at ends of the branches. Flowers are about ½ in. long, droop on slender stalks, and are usually hidden by leaves. Leaves are ovate to oblong, 1–3 in. long. Stems are 1–2 ft. tall, branched and leafy at top, and arise from thick, rough, underground rootstocks. Fruit is a globose, lobed, velvet-skinned orange-yellow berry.

    This plant is usually confused with Twisted-stalk (*Streptopus amplexifolius*) and False Solomonseal (*Smilacina racemosa*), but latter has unbranched stems, and flowers of Twisted-stalk are at base of leaves and not at ends of branches as in Fairybells. See also illustrations, p. 29 and Plate 2.

    Related species: *D. oreoganum* has an oval, narrow, reddish-

Fairybells (*Disporum trachycarpum* [Wats.] B. & H.)

orange berry; leaves are usually heart-shaped; found from Montana to B.C., south to Oregon and Colorado.

Flowering season: April, May, and June. Start looking for it when the more conspicuous Dogtooth Violet first appears in bloom.

Where found: G, Y, T, R. Rich damp soil of woods and canyons, from our mt. valleys up to around 8000 ft. Grows from Alberta to B.C., south to Oregon, Arizona, and New Mexico. There are about 15 species of *Disporum* native to N. America and e. Asia; 2 species occur in Rocky Mt. area.

Interesting facts: *Trachycarpum* means rough-carpeled. Hikers, campers, fishermen, and mountain climbers often wonder whether the luscious-looking berries of this plant are poisonous or edible. They are not poisonous, have a sweet taste, and were eaten raw by Blackfoot Indians. Rodents and ruffed and spruce (Franklin's) grouse utilize the berries.

DOGTOOTH VIOLET

Pl. 2

Erythronium grandiflorum Pursh

Family: Liliaceae (Lily).

Other names: Fawnlily, Glacier Lily, Snow Lily, Adders-tongue.

Description: The only yellow lily in our area with 2 large, shiny, oblong basal leaves. One to several nodding flowers occur on long, usually naked stem. Narrow sepals and petals are strongly recurved. Each plant originates from a solid, deep-seated bulb.

It can be confused with Yellow Fritillary (*Fritillaria pudica*), since the two bloom about the same time (see Plate 3). Yellow Fritillary, however, has 2 to 6 linear leaves, and petals are not recurved.

Related species: Three species occur in Rocky Mts.; differences are so slight that many botanists believe they belong together.

Flowering season: At low elevations, first appears in early April soon after snow recedes, and blooms for about a month. When the Dogtooth Violet begins to flower, mating calls of saw-whet owls can be heard and mule deer are beginning to fawn. Climbs mts. with the season, so to speak, blooming later at higher elevations. At 8000 to 9000 ft., height of flowering season is early July, when white-tailed ptarmigan, gray-cheeked rosy finch, and water pipit are nesting, and it may still be found in mid-Aug.

Where found: G, Y, T, R. Found growing at various altitudes, following the melting snowline from valleys to subalpine canyon cirques of 12,000 ft. Look for it on rich, moist soil along stream-banks, in shaded woods, and in subalpine meadows. Frequently occurs in large patches. Genus has about 15 species, all but 1 N. American. There are several distinct species of *Erythronium* along Pacific Coast area; 3 in Rocky Mt. region. Dogtooth Violet is found from Montana to B.C., south to California and Colorado.

Interesting facts: *Grandiflorum* means large-flowered. The bulb of the Dogtooth Violet was boiled and eaten by the Indians or dried for winter use. Leaves were used as greens. The fresh green seed pods taste like string beans when boiled. The bulb of the purple-flowered Dogtooth Violet of Europe and Asia was collected by the Tartars and boiled with milk or broth. The bulbs are eaten by both black and grizzly bears and are gathered and cached for winter use by some of the small rodents. The green pods are avidly eaten by deer and elk, bighorn sheep, and probably by Rocky Mt. goats.

LEOPARD LILY   *Fritillaria atropurpurea* Nutt.   **Pl. 3**

Family: Liliaceae (Lily).

Other names: Purple-spot Fritillaria, Tiger Lily, Purple Fritillary.

Description: The color is distinctive enough to set this flower apart from all others in Rocky Mt. area. Broadly bell-shaped flowers are dull purplish brown, with greenish-yellow spots. Flowers vary from 1 to 4, hang downward, and are about 1 in. wide. Unbranched stem grows to height of 8–30 in., with grasslike leaves on upper portion.

Related species: Only plant likely to be confused with this is another species of leopard lily (*F. lanceolata*). However, this plant has a flower about twice as large, and the leaves are lance-shaped instead of linear and grasslike.

Flowering season: Latter part of April, through May and June. First appears about time dandelions reach height of blooming and cover fields with golden color.

Where found: Y, T, R. Rich, damp soil of valleys and open woods, and in mts. to near timberline. Occurs from North Dakota to Washington, south to California and New Mexico. There are about 50 species of *Fritillaria* scattered over N. Hemisphere; only 3 are in Rocky Mts.

Interesting facts: *Atropurpurea* means dark purple. This flower is easily overlooked because it hangs downward and effectively hides the colorful stamens and inner surfaces of sepals and petals. The starchy corms, as in the case of the Yellow Fritillary, are edible and are still eaten by western Indians and Eskimos.

YELLOW FRITILLARY   **Pl. 3**
Fritillaria pudica (Pursh) Spreng.

Family: Liliaceae (Lily).

Other names: Yellowbell.

Description: This plant usually has a single golden-yellow flower whose stalk is bent so that the flower lies sidewise or hangs downward. Sepals and petals similar, 3 each, and ½–¾ in. long, forming bell-shaped structure. There are 6 stamens. Plant

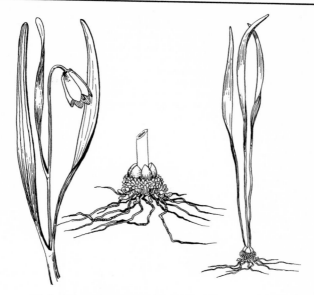

Yellow Fritillary (*Fritillaria pudica* [Pursh] Spreng.)

grows from a starchy corm and is 3–8 in. tall, with unbranched stem and 2 to 6 narrow leaves.

This flower may be confused with the Dogtooth Violet (*Erythronium grandiflorum*, see Plate 2), and with buttercups (*Ranunculus*, see Plate 6). Latter have many stamens and pistils and flower is open and saucer-shaped.

Flowering season: One of earliest flowers of spring, commencing to bloom the middle of March in valleys and continuing until late June in higher mts. When Yellow Fritillary blooms, meadowlarks are returning in numbers, pink-sided juncos arrive, sage grouse are displaying on the strutting grounds, and Canada geese are laying eggs.

Where found: G, Y, T, R. Found in sagebrush areas, dry hillsides, and mts. to elevation of 9000 ft. Distributed from Montana to B.C., south to California and New Mexico. Only 3 species in Rocky Mt. region.

Interesting facts: *Pudica* means bashful. This flower changes color as it ages: the brilliant orange-yellow hue fades to a dull red in later stages of development. The fleshy corm from which the plant grows is pitted, flattened on upper surface, and looks like a large drop of candle wax. It is surrounded by 30 to 50 true Solomonseal (*Polygonatum commutatum*) of e. U.S. has a starchy, fleshy rootstock that is edible when cooked and has a parsnip-like taste. Ruffed grouse utilize the berries of both the False and true Solomonseal.

WILD LILY-OF-THE-VALLEY   Pl. 1
Smilacina stellata (L.) Desf.

Family: Liliaceae (Lily).

Other names: Wild Spikenard, Solomonplume, False Solomonseal.

Description: Characterized by an unbranched leafy stem terminating in a raceme of 3 to 15 white flowers. Plant is 1–2 ft. tall, with lance-shaped leaves folded along midrib and usually terminated in long pointed tips. Grows from a slender underground rootstock and, like False Solomonseal (Plate 2), generally forms dense patches. Globose berries are green with black or brown stripes.

The sharp-pointed leaves, usually folded on midrib, and flowers in a raceme instead of a panicle distinguish this plant from other species of *Smilacina* in the Rockies.

Flowering season: May, June, and July. At low elevations blooms in early May when morels can be gathered.

Where found: G, Y, T, R. Moist soil in both open and shaded areas, especially along valley streams and in mts. up to about 9000 ft. Occurs from B.C. to Labrador, south to Virginia, Texas, and California. Only 2 species in our area.

Interesting facts: *Stellata* means starry. This plant is related to the European Lily-of-the-Valley commonly cultivated in gardens. The young shoots and leaves can be used as a green. Elk eat the green leaves and stems.

TWISTED-STALK   *Streptopus amplexifolius* (L.) DC.

Family: Liliaceae (Lily).

Other names: White Mandarin, Liverberry.

Description: The small whitish flowers are borne in the leaf axils on very slender stalks that have a distinct joint, or kink, near the middle; hence the name Twisted-stalk. Usually a branching plant 2–4 ft. high, with ovate leaves 1–2 in. broad. Ovary in each flower usually develops into a bright red, oval berry about ½ in. long.

This plant is most apt to be mistaken for False Solomonseal (*Smilacina racemosa*) and Fairybells (*Disporum trachycarpum*), but can be distinguished from these by sharp bend in flower stalk.

Flowering season: May, June, and July. Robins are busy feeding young when this flower comes into bloom. Waterleaf and Holly-grape will be flowering before this flower appears.

Where found: G, Y, T, R. Grows only where soil is moist or

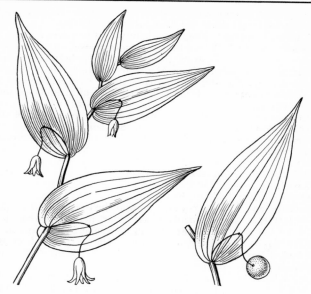

Twisted-stalk (*Streptopus amplexifolius* [L.] DC.)

wet; can stand considerable shade, so is usually found in woods, about boggy areas, and along streams. Occurs in valleys and to about 9000 ft. in mts. Widely distributed over most of N. America except in hotter areas. Other species of this genus found widely distributed over temperate N. America, Europe, and e. Asia. This the only species in Rocky Mts.

Interesting facts: *Amplexifolius* means clasping-leaved. The berries were eaten by Indians and are utilized by ruffed grouse.

FALSE ASPHODEL   *Tofieldia glutinosa* (Michx.) Pers.   **Pl. 3**
Family: Liliaceae (Lily).
Other names: Scottish Asphodel.
Description: The creamy-white flowers are about ¼ in. broad and borne in terminal clusters on stems that are normally bunched together. Roots are fibrous and matted. Plant varies in height 4–20 in., is unbranched, with tufts of grasslike basal leaves, or with leaves only on lowest part of stem. Leaves usually ⅓–⅔ as long as stem. As flowers get older and seeds ripen, raceme of flowers may elongate from ½ to 3 in.

False Asphodel probably looks as much like the death-camases (*Zigadenus*) as any other plant in the Rockies. However, these latter always grow from bulbs; False Asphodel has a short basal rootstock and flower is much daintier.

Flowering season: June through July, to first part of Aug.

Where found: G, Y, T. Primarily in open, wet, boggy areas of mts., but occurring from prairies up to timberline. It, and varieties of it, occurs from Alaska to Newfoundland, south to North Carolina and California. About a dozen species of *Tofieldia* occur in N. Hemisphere and mts. of S. America; only 2 in our area.

Interesting facts: *Glutinosa* means sticky. A species of *Tofieldia* grows in n. England and in Scotland. Quite likely the common name of Scottish Asphodel, applied to our species, derives from this fact.

WAKEROBIN   *Trillium ovatum* Pursh   **Pl. 2**

Family: Liliaceae (Lily).

Other names: Trillium, Birthroot.

Description: A single-flowered, unbranched plant 8–16 in. tall, characterized by 3 broadly ovate, short-petioled leaves near top of the stem. They are 2–5 in. long and almost as broad. Flower is 1–2 in. across, on an erect stalk that arises from the whorl of leaves. The 3 conspicuous white petals gradually turn pink, then rose-colored with age.

A plant that might be confused with the trilliums is the Bunchberry (*Cornus canadensis*), Plate 14. These two plants have same general appearance, but Wakerobin has only 1 flower with 3 petals; Bunchberry has a central cluster of minute flowers surrounded by 4 large white bracts that are often mistaken for 4 petals.

Related species: Flower of our other species of *Trillium* (*T. petiolatum*) is dark purple and stalkless; leaves are long-petioled.

Flowering season: Latter part of March to June. As soon as snow disappears, Wakerobins push out of earth and in a few days are blooming. Male red-winged blackbirds are defending nesting territories.

Where found: G. Damp woods or boggy areas in partial shade. Grows from lowest valleys to about 7000 ft. Found from Montana to B.C., south to California and Colorado. There are about 25 species of *Trillium*, all native of temperate N. America and e. Asia; 2 in Rocky Mts.

Interesting facts: *Ovatum* means ovate. Wakerobins are eagerly watched for because they are among the first harbingers of spring wherever they grow. This is one of the few wild plants that make excellent cut flowers and remain fresh for days. In this respect it has commercial possibilities. The thick underground rootstalks were used by Indians during childbirth; hence the name Birthroot. The plants are sometimes cooked for greens.

FALSE HELLEBORE *Veratrum viride* Ait.   **Pl. 4**
  Family: Liliaceae (Lily).
  Other names: Cornlily, American Hellebore, Green Hellebore; sometimes erroneously called Skunkcabbage.
  Description: A large, coarse, leafy-stemmed plant that usually grows in dense patches and attains a height of 3–6 ft. The numerous flowers are yellowish green, about ½ in. broad, arranged in a large, dense panicle at top of plant. Stems unbranched, often 1 in. thick at base, and almost completely hidden by large leaves. Leaves broadly oval, 4–12 in. long, with very coarse, parallel veins.
  Related species: Only other mature plant of our area likely to be identified with this is another species of *Veratrum* (*V. californicum*), which, however, is larger and has white flowers, and lower branches of the panicle tend to be erect instead of drooping.
  Flowering season: June, July, and first part of Aug.
  Where found: G. Wet meadows and open areas of our valleys, and in mts. to about 9000 ft. Occurs from Alaska to Maine, south to North Carolina and Oregon. There are about 15 species of *Veratrum* native to N. Hemisphere.
  Interesting facts: *Viride* means green. False hellebores contain several alkaloids used medicinally to slow the heartbeat and lower blood pressure. Indians used it in this way and probably taught its use to early settlers. It is fatal if taken in large quantities. Livestock, deer, and elk are sometimes killed by eating the roots and new shoots, though such loss is not great because animals usually avoid eating the plant. The seeds are poisonous to chickens and may likewise affect other bird life. The poison decreases as the plant matures, and after the foliage has frosted and dried it is apparently quite harmless to livestock. The plants are dried, powdered, and sold as the garden insecticide hellebore. Elk bed down and make wallows in the moist meadows and seepage areas where this plant abounds.

BEARGRASS *Xerophyllum tenax* (Pursh) Nutt.   **Pl. 1**
  Family: Liliaceae (Lily).
  Other names: Basket-grass, Squawgrass, Bearlily, Elkgrass.
  Description: The small white flowers form a large dense conical raceme that at a distance appears as a strikingly large flower on a tall slender stem. No other white flower in the region appears so conspicuously large. Flowering stalk is from 2 to 3 ft. tall and plants often grow in patches, enhancing beauty of whole landscape. At base of stalk is a large tussock of long grasslike leaves that are tough and sharp-edged.
    When not in flower this plant can be mistaken for a true grass, even though it is a member of the Lily family. Presence of a dried or fresh-flowering stalk helps to place it in proper family.

Flowering season: Does not flower each year, perhaps only every 5 to 7 years. Thus, some seasons there will be few blooms and other years almost every plant will flower. At lower levels, starts flowering in June and continues blooming at higher elevations until Sept. When Beargrass flowers young mountain bluebirds are fledging.

Where found: G, Y, T. Open woods, mt. slopes, and alpine meadows, where large white flowers contrast strikingly with varied greens of Lodgepole Pine, Alpine Fir, and Engelmann Spruce. Genus is found solely in N. America. but there is only 1 other species (*X. asphodeloides*), and this occurs in e. U.S. Beargrass found from Montana to B.C., south to Wyoming and California.

Interesting facts: *Tenax* means holding fast, tough. The flowers, flowering stalks, and tender seed pods are avidly eaten by small rodents and game animals, especially elk. The leaves remain throughout winter and Rocky Mt. goat exhibits a strong preference for this food during the cold-weather months. The tough grasslike leaves, however, are unpalatable to all other big game species and to livestock, seldom being utilized even as an emergency food. Bears reportedly eat the white succulent leaf base in spring. The spruce mouse and possibly other mice eat the entire basal stem and thus kill the plant. Leaves are slick and when stepped on pull out from the sheath so suddenly that on steep slopes even an experienced woodsman may find his feet literally "yanked out from under him."

The leaves when dried and bleached were used by the Indians of the Northwest for making clothing and fine baskets.

MOUNTAIN DEATH-CAMAS   *Zigadenus elegans* Pursh

Family: Liliaceae (Lily).

Other names: Poison Camas, White Camas, Poison Sego, Wandlily.

Description: This is 1–2 ft. tall, with grasslike leaves and dull whitish flowers arranged in a raceme. Leaves occur on lower part of unbranched stems. Flowers are about ⅜ in. long, with 6 stamens, and 3 sepals and 3 petals colored so much alike that flower appears to have 6 petals.

The larger flowers distinguish Mountain Death-camas from Death-camas (*Z. paniculatus* [Nutt.] Wats.), Plate 2, and other species of *Zigadenus*.

Related species: (1) *Z. gramineus*, (2) *Z. venenosus*, and (3) *Z. paniculatus* are more poisonous than *Z. elegans* and cause most poisoning in livestock. Can be distinguished by technical characters. However, *Z. paniculatus* is found in dry soil of hills and desert areas, and *Z. gramineus* and *Z. venenosus* are found in wet or damp soil. All have whitish flowers with conspicuous gland spots at base of petals.

Flowering season: June, July, and, at higher elevations, Aug. Flowers soon after the true Camas (*Camassia quamash*). When the grasslike leaves of Death-camas (*Z. paniculatus*) emerge, great blue herons are beginning to nest and male red-winged blackbirds are defending territories.

Where found: G, Y, T, R. Moist soil of meadows, streambanks, woods, and ledges, from 6000 to 12,000 ft. in mts. Distributed from Alaska to Minnesota, west to Nevada and south to New Mexico. About 8 species occur in Rocky Mts.; other species of this genus are distributed over most of temperate N. America and some occur in Asia.

Mountain Death-camas (*Zigadenus elegans* Pursh)

Interesting facts: *Elegans* means elegant. This genus contains alkaloids poisonous to both man and livestock. Sheep are frequently affected, since they seem to eat the plants more readily than other animals do. Hogs are said to be immune to the poison. Poisoning usually occurs in early spring because the death-camases appear before most other range plants and their succulent leaves are available. One of the more poisonous species (*Z. gramineus*) requires only ½ pound per hundredweight to produce fatal results, whereas less toxic species take about 6 pounds of green plant per hundredweight of animal. The death-camases should not be confused with the true Camas, which formed a staple food of the Indians of the Northwest. The flowers are quite different; however, the Indians occasionally mistook bulbs of the two, since both plants may grow together in meadows. It is difficult to distinguish death-camases from onions (*Allium*), sego lilies (*Calochortus*), fritillarias (*Fritillaria*), and wild hyacinths (*Brodiaea*) when these edible plants are only a few inches high. However, a combination of leaf characters and a cross section of the bulbs or corms is diagnostic at any stage in the development of these plants.

ROCKY MOUNTAIN IRIS   *Iris missouriensis* Nutt.   **Pl. 2**
Family: Iridaceae (Iris).
Other names: Flag, Fleur-de-lis, Snake-lily, Water Flag.
Description: This iris usually bears from 1 to 4 variegated violet-blue flowers about 2–3 in. long. Grows to height of 1–2 ft. from a coarse, irregular, underground rootstock. There may be several narrow swordlike leaves from base and 1 to 2 from stem, often as long as stalk itself. The 3 sepals are dilated and spreading or reflexed; 3 petals are narrower and usually erect.
Not likely to be mistaken for any other plant.
Flowering season: From mid-May in lower valleys and well through July in mts. Iris are blooming when eggs of ring-necked pheasant are hatching.
Where found: G, Y, T, R. Found in open wet meadows from lowest valleys to about 9000 ft. in mts. Distributed from North Dakota to B.C., south to California and New Mexico. Only 1 species occurs in Rocky Mt. area; 8 others are confined to Pacific Coast. Blue Flag (*I. versicolor*) and a number of other species are native to e. U.S. Genus *Iris* is found in N. America, Europe, Asia, and N. Africa, and numerous cultivated forms are almost world-wide.
Interesting facts: *Missouriensis* means of Missouri. The rootstocks contain the poison irisin, which is a violent emetic and cathartic. Seeds when eaten cause violent "burning" of mouth and throat and this persists for several hours. Roots were ground by the Indians, mixed with animal bile, then put in the gall bladder and warmed near a fire for several days. Arrow points were dipped in this mixture, and it is reported by old Indians that many warriors only slightly wounded by such arrows died within 3 to 7 days.
There is little likelihood of confusing the rootstock with any edible root because of the strong, acrid, disagreeable flavor. Fibers from the leaves of the Oregon Iris (*I. tenax*) were used by Indians in making lines and nets. The irises have no forage value either to livestock or game. They are a good indicator of water close to the ground surface. In some of the dry mt.

country of Oregon, holes are dug where iris grow, and these fill with water and are used by livestock. The iris (fleur-de-lis) is the emblem of France.

GRASS-WIDOWS   Pl. 2
Sisyrinchium inflatum (Suksd.) St. John
  Family: Iridaceae (Iris).
  Other names: Purple-eyed Grass.
  Description: The flowers are about 1 in. wide, bright pinkish purple, and are grouped 1 to 4 in an umbel. Umbel is enclosed at base by 2 bracts generally exceeding flowers in height. These plants usually grow in tufts with stems 6–24 in. tall. Grasslike leaves are scattered along stem, basal ones reduced to sheaths. Roots are fibrous. Plant usually conspicuous, because it blooms early and grows in bunches, often coloring meadows purplish.
  Grass-widows could possibly be confused with shootingstars (*Dodecatheon*), but these grow singly and all their leaves are basal and not grasslike (see Plate 15). *S. inflatum* is the only large, purple-flowered species; others are blue or yellowish and less than ½ in. wide.
  Flowering season: April and May. Grass-widows appear soon after snow disappears. Blooming signifies it is time to be out of doors and begin looking for edible mushrooms such as the morels, wrinkled saddle-shaped helvellas, and puffballs.
  Where found: Moist to wet soil of meadows, grassy hillsides, and open woods, mainly in our valleys or low hills. Occurs from B.C. to Idaho, south to California and Nevada. Possibly 6 species of this genus in Rocky Mts., but many more common names have been applied to these plants.
  Interesting facts: *Inflatum* means inflated.

BLUE-EYED GRASS   Pl. 2
Sisyrinchium sarmentosum Suksd.
  Family: Iridaceae (Iris).
  Other names: *S. halophyllum* and *S. idahoense*.
  Description: The 1 to 5 flowers at the top of the stem have 3 sepals and 3 petals colored pale blue to bluish purple. They are ⅜ in. long, generally with yellow center. Stems are about 5–12 in. tall, generally tufted, and distinctly flattened and sharp-edged.
  Blue-eyed Grass can be distinguished from most others by its flat stem, grasslike appearance, and similarly colored sepals and petals. Difficult to separate from some other species of this genus; considerable difference of opinion among botanists as to whether differences are sufficient to justify giving them different names.
  Flowering season: May to July, depending on elevation.

ℛ. Usually found growing in wet open
...eys to about 8000 ft. in mts. Extends
...C., south in mts. to California and New
...about 60 species of this genus in N. America
...not more than 6 in Rocky Mt. area.

...s: *Sarmentosum* means bearing runners. This
...named. The outdoorsman may at first fail to
...rasslike plant with its tiny flowers amid the exten-
...ery of a mt. meadow; but suddenly a sparkle of blue
ca...his eye and he halts his walk to gaze admiringly into
the ...ue eyes of the meadow. With interest aroused and
observation sharpened, he looks about him and sees at every
turn the Blue-eyed Grass.

FAIRYSLIPPER *Calypso bulbosa* (L.) Oakes   Pl. 4
Family: Orchidaceae (Orchid).
Other names: Venus-slipper, Calypso.
Description: The only pink or rose single-flowered orchid in
the area. Possesses a single broad basal leaf, a sheathed stem,
showy drooping flower, and a marble-sized corm. Like all
orchids, consists of 3 sepals and 3 petals, central petal different
from others, being saclike and called the lip. Filaments and
style are united to form a central column.
   Fairyslipper is unique among orchids of the area, though it
could possibly be confused with the shootingstars (*Dodecatheon*);
latter, however, distinguished from orchids by having numerous
basal leaves, and sepals and petals in 5's instead of 3's (see
Plate 15). Mountain Ladys-slipper (*Cypripedium montanum*
Dougl.), Plate 4, is a larger plant, with spiraled bronze-colored
sepals and petals and an inflated white lip.
Flowering season: First appears in late May, soon after snow
melts, and can be found until late June. A dry spring shortens
flowering season.
Where found: G, Y, T, R. Grows in evergreen forests at
5000–8000 ft. Look for it in wet or boggy coniferous woods, or
on or near decayed stumps and logs. Prefers deep shade. Occurs
from Alaska to Labrador, south to New York, Minnesota,
Arizona, and California; also in Europe. Only species of genus
occurring in Rocky Mts.
Interesting facts: *Bulbosa* means with bulbs. Though individual
orchids are seldom abundant in any locality in the Rockies, the
Orchid family is one of the largest, if not the largest, family in
the world — having 8000 to 10,000 different species. Orchids
are most abundant in tropical rain forests. They are adapted
for cross pollination by insects, and have become so dependent
upon insects for pollination that many of them cannot produce
seeds unless certain insects visit them to carry the pollen from
one flower to another. Even when seeds are produced, they

frequently will not germinate unless stimulated by
of certain fungi. Thus orchids are rare, and each one
lessly picked further reduces the chance of a new orchid co
to life.

Spotted Coralroot (*Corallorhiza maculata* Raf.)

SPOTTED CORALROOT   *Corallorhiza maculata* Raf.   **Pl. 4**
   Family: Orchidaceae (Orchid).
   Other names: Mottled Coralroot.
   Description: This is a saprophytic member of the Orchid family,
characterized by brownish-purple coloring and absence of leaves
and green color. Raceme of flowers varies in length 4–8 in.
Individual flowers are about ½ in. long, with a conspicuously
white lip spotted with crimson. Stems unbranched, 6–24 in. tall,
and arise in clumps from thick and knotted rootstalks.

   Most of the coralroots can be told apart only on technical
characters. Members of the Indianpipe and Broomrape families
can be confused with them because they too lack leaves and
green color (chlorophyll). In Orchid family, however, flower
parts arise from top of ovary; in other two families flowers
originate beneath ovary.

Coralroot (*C. striata* Lindl.), Plate **4**,
.cept lip is not 3-lobed and flowers are
instead of spotted.

from middle of May at lower elevations
n mts.

, Y, T, R. In decaying plant material in moist
ver most of N. America, except southern states.
y restricted to N. America, but some members
urope, Cent. America, and n. Asia; 6 species in
.ts.

Inter...ing facts: *Maculata* means spotted. Coralroot illustrates the degeneracy of plants that live off the products of others. In the long process of evolution it has lost its chlorophyll, which enables other plants to make their own food from carbon dioxide, sunlight, and water. Its leaves have disappeared and its roots have been greatly reduced. Part of the stem is underground and performs some of the functions of a true root. The underground stem is composed of short, thick, fleshy fibers, repeatedly divided into short, blunt branches and densely interwoven like coral; hence the name Coralroot. This plant is intimately associated with a fungus that decays stumps, logs, roots, leaves, and other organic matter. Coralroot is entirely dependent on this fungus for food.

WHITE BOG-ORCHID   Pl. **4**
Habenaria dilatata (Pursh) Hook.

Family: Orchidaceae (Orchid).
Other names: Leafy White Orchid, Bog-candle, Scent-bottle.
Description: The dense spike of waxy white flowers contrasting with the bright green leaves attracts the attention of the passer-by. Unbranched stem varies from nearly 1–2 ft. in height, with upper portion densely covered with flowers that are spurred. Remainder of stem produces linear to lance-shaped leaves up to 6 in. long. There are several varieties of this species, and only on technical characters can they be separated.

This plant can be confused with several other orchids in the Rockies. Ladies-tresses (*Spiranthes romanzoffiana*), a very similar orchid, has flowers arranged in a spiral. The irregular petal called the "lip" does not have distinct spur at base as in White Bog-orchid.

Related species: (1) *H. hyperborea* is 1–3 ft. tall and has greenish-colored flowers; (2) *H. obtusata* has 2 orbicular leaves spreading on ground; (3) *H. unalascensis* has 2 to 4 lanceolate leaves at base of stem, then many scalelike bracts above. All occur throughout Rocky Mt. area.
Flowering season: May be found in flower during June, July, and early part of Aug., depending on altitude and latitude.
Where found: G, Y, T, R. Occurs in wet soil of swamps, bogs,

banks of springs around 10,000 ft., and found New Jersey, Minnesota, California, species in Rockies; other species of the genus occur to cold regions of Europe, Asia, and N. America.

White Bog-orchid (*Habenaria dilatata* [Pursh] Hook.)

Interesting facts: *Dilatata* means expanded. The radishlike tubers of this orchid are gathered and eaten by Indians of the Northwest and Eskimos. When boiled for about half an hour they taste like frozen potatoes. Generally speaking, orchids are rare and should not be used as food except in extreme emergencies. Bulbs of all N. American orchids are reported to be edible.

LADIES-TRESSES *Spiranthes romanzoffiana* Cham. **Pl. 4**
    Family: Orchidaceae (Orchid).
    Other names: Pearltwist.
    Description: The small white flowers appear in a dense terminal spike, usually in 3 rows that partially spiral about the stem. Plants are 4–20 in. tall, bright green and fleshy-appearing, with narrowly lance-shaped leaves on lower part of stem.

and streams. Grows from Alaska to New Mexico. Eight temperate

39

flower when
. habitat.

marshes, meadows, salt
woods. Occurs from Alaska
New York, Wisconsin, Arizona, and
. There are about 25 species of
over most of the earth; only 2 in Rock-

facts: The generic name is derived from *speira*, a
and *anthos*, a flower, and refers to the distinct flower
arrangement. This spiral arrangement is comparable to spiraling in other plants. Spiral growth in trees is not uncommon and becomes especially evident where spiral cracks form. Vines and tendrils spiral about supporting objects. This spiraling is due to uneven growth of the cells, which causes the stem to twist. *Romanzoffiana* means plant is named for Count Romanzoff.

UMBRELLA PLANT *Eriogonum heracleoides* Nutt. Pl. 4
Var. *subalpinum* (Greene) St. John
  Family: Polygonaceae (Buckwheat).
  Other names: Wild Buckwheat, Indian Tobacco.
  Description: Compound umbels of small cream-colored flowers develop at ends of almost leafless stalks 4–16 in. tall. These umbels give this plant its characteristic umbrellalike appearance. Flowering stems arise from dense clusters of leaves and woody branches that mat over the ground. Leaves vary from lance shape to linear and are green above, white below. Scape has a whorl of leaves above middle. Flower heads, often rose-colored as they begin to develop, turn cream-colored as they mature. Perianth may then turn rose again.
  The many species are extremely difficult to distinguish.
  Related species: (1) *E. dendroideum* is an annual with narrow leaves, very fine branches, and awn-tipped floral-envelope lobes; (2) *E. deflexum* is also a fine-branched annual, but leaves are round, perianth lobes not awn-tipped; (3) *E. alatum*, a coarse perennial up to 3 ft. tall, has 3 longitudinal wings on seeds; (4) *E. ovalifolium* has silvery-colored oval to round leaves beneath a leafless, nearly 1-ft.-tall stalk terminating in a round, dense head of yellowish flowers; (5) *E. umbellatum* possesses a branched woody base, compound umbels of yellow flowers, oval to orbicular basal leaves; (6) Sulphurflower (*E. flavum* Nutt.), Plate 5, is similar to *E. umbellatum* but with elongated leaves. These plants all occur over most of Rocky Mt. area.

Flowering season: Latter part of May, through J
this when young red-tailed hawks are leaving nest.
Where found: Y, T. In open areas of dry soil from foothills
higher valleys to around 9000 ft. Common in sagebrush. This
plant, or varieties of it, occurs from Alberta to B.C., south to
Nevada and Colorado. There are about 150 different species of
Eriogonum, all native to N. America; 50 or more occur in
Rocky Mts.

Interesting facts: *Heracleoides* means heracleum-like. Throughout the West, wherever there is considerable difference in soil
type, soil and air moisture, exposure, land slope, or salinity,
there tend to be different species or varieties of *Eriogonum* growing under these varied conditions. In the course of time each
has adapted to the specific habitat and in doing so has changed
sufficiently from the parent stock to become a recognizable
species or variety. The seeds of the eriogonums are gathered by
chipmunks and white-footed mice. Umbrella Plant is a preferred forage plant of domestic sheep in sw. Montana and se.
Idaho.

MOUNTAIN-SORREL *Oxyria digyna* (L.) Hill   Pl. 5
Family: Polygonaceae (Buckwheat).
Other names: Alpine-sorrel.
Description: A member of the Buckwheat family, 6–12 in. tall,
with round or kidney-shaped fleshy leaves on long leafstalks
arising from the basal portion of a scaly stem. Small, greenish
to crimson flowers are arranged in dense panicled racemes.
Fruit is thin and flat, with an encircling wing indented at both
ends. Fruit usually bright rose-colored, and more conspicuous
than flowers.

Mountain-sorrel can be confused with the docks (*Rumex*), but
the round or kidney-shaped leaves readily distinguish it.
Flowering season: From latter part of June through Aug.,
depending upon elevation.
Where found: G, Y, T, R. In shady, wet, or moist places,
generally on mt. slopes, ledges, and rock crevices. Ranges from
about 6000 to 11,000 ft., being found as far south in mts. as
California and New Mexico. Circumpolar in distribution, occurring in n. Europe, Asia, and N. America. Only species of the
genus *Oxyria*.

Interesting facts: The name *Oxyria* comes from the Greek word
oxys, meaning sour; the acid-tasting leaves are pleasingly sour.
Species name *digyna* means 2 carpels and refers to these female
parts of the flower. The plant is used in salads and as a potherb.
Growing high in the mts., it makes a welcome addition to the
rationed diet of the mountain climber. It is rich in vitamin C
and is valued by native peoples as a scurvy preventative and
cure. Mountain-sorrel is eaten by elk.

olygonum bistortoides Pursh   **Pl. 4**
Buckweat).
, Snakeweed, Knotweed.
...er, swaying plant with a white or pinkish
...mall flowers. From a distance flower spike
...f cotton. It has narrow tapering leaves, basal
...med, upper ones stalkless and smaller; and a
..., snakelike root.
...ass (*P. viviparum*) is similar, but the root is not so
...and the flower spike usually contains bulblets, and is
rath... ...oose and slender.

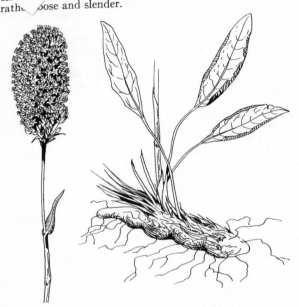

American Bistort (*Polygonum bistortoides* Pursh)

Related species: (1) *P. convolvulus* has a slender, twining stem up to 5 ft. long and heart-shaped leaves; (2) *P. aviculare*, a prostrate plant with lance-shaped leaves, often grows as a weed in dooryards or in dry places. These plants can be found over most of U.S.

Flowering season: Makes first appearance in valleys in early June and has disappeared by mid-July. At higher elevations in mts. starts flowering in early July and lasts into Aug.

Where found: G, Y, T, R. From valley floors to above timberline, in wet meadows, along streambanks, in mt. and among rock debris at high elevations. Found from and B.C. to California and Mexico. Genus occurs through world, but is rare in tropics. Of about 150 species, approximately 35 are in Rocky Mt. area.

Interesting facts: *Bistortoides* means resembling *P. bistorta.* The root of various species of bistort has been used as an emergency food by the Russians, Chinese, Japanese, Europeans, Eskimos, and North American Indians. The Cheyenne and Blackfoot Indians used it in soups and stews. Rootstocks are starchy and slightly astringent when eaten raw. Boiled, they are somewhat sweeter but are best roasted on coals; then they have a sweet nutty flavor. The roots are eaten by black and grizzly bears and rodents, the foliage by deer and elk.

WATER LADYSTHUMB

Polygonum natans (Michx.) Eat.   **Pl. 5**

Family: Polygonaceae (Buckwheat).
Other names: Water Pepper, Smartweed.
Description: This plant catches the eye with its bright pink terminal spike of flowers, generally arising above a cluster of floating leaves. Commonly grows semisubmerged in shallow water but may also grow on mud. Small pink flowers form dense, ovoid, or short-cylindric spikes ½–1½ in. long. Stems branch at base, may grow 3 ft. or more long, and are covered by pointed, elliptic leaves 2–5 in. long.

This species can be distinguished from others by its bright pink flowers, forming short, terminal spikes, and by lack of hairs and glands on the flowering stem.

Flowering season: Latter part of June to mid-Sept. Flowers at time broods of young Barrow's goldeneye ducks begin to appear on beaver ponds and sloughs.

Where found: Y, T, R. Shallow water of ponds, lakes, and slow-moving streams, or at borders of such areas. In summer when ponds recede, these plants may be found on dried mud. Occur from the plains to around 8000 ft., and can be found from Alaska to Quebec, south to Pennsylvania, New Mexico, Mexico, and California. There are almost 50 species of *Polygonum* in Rocky Mts.

Interesting facts: *Natans* means floating. Water Ladysthumb is a good example of the way many plants will vary with the habitat. Normally this is a prostrate plant, but when stems are lying on mud they root at the nodes and these land stems tend to assume an erect position, producing narrower and more pointed leaves than those floating in water. Also, the land plants are more hairy than the water plants. The plant propagates by seeds and rootstock; the seeds are an important duck food.

CURLYDOCK   *Rumex crispus* L.
   Family: Polygonaceae (Buckwheat).
   Other names: Narrow-leaved Dock or Yellowdock, Spurdock.
   Description: A smooth, dark green plant whose leaves have curly or wavy margins and whose greenish flowers give rise to conspicuous reddish-brown fruits having the general appearance of coffee grains. It is 1–3 ft. tall, arising from a fleshy, yellow root. Leaves, mostly basal, are 6–12 in. long, lance-shaped, with slightly heart-shaped base. Small greenish flowers arranged in whorls in panicled racemes. The 3 inner sepals enlarge and become winglike in fruit.
   This species can be confused with Mexican Dock (*R. mexicanus*), but latter has narrow, flat, glaucous leaves with a pointed or slightly rounded base.
   Related species: Two native species commonly found in sagebrush in early spring are (1) *R. acetosella* and (2) *R. paucifolius*. They are generally smaller than *R. crispus* and flower panicles turn decidedly red with age. Calyx of *R. acetosella* does not develop into wings in fruit and some of the basal leaves are usually arrowhead-shaped. Basal leaves of *R. paucifolius* are on long leafstalks. (3) *R. maritimus* is an annual with minute spines around edges of lobes of perianth. (4) *R. venosus*, a hair-

less perennial from underground spreading rootstock, wings almost 1 in. wide.

Flowering season: Mainly during June, but because reddish brown fruits are more conspicuous than small green flowers this plant becomes particularly noticeable in fall.

Where found: Y, T, R. Curlydock, a native of Europe and Asia, was introduced and has become established, often as a troublesome weed, over most of temperate N. America. Found in moist soil along roads, irrigation ditches, in pastures, cultivated fields, and waste land from valleys to around 6000 ft. in mts. Other species of this genus are almost world-wide. There are 16 species in Rocky Mt. area.

Interesting facts: *Crispus* means curled. The root was formerly a medicinal drug, used as a laxative and tonic, and sold under the name yellowdock. The early spring leaves are cooked for food, often along with dandelion leaves, and the mixture is known as "greens." The leaves and stems of some of our native species have a pleasantly sour taste imparted by oxalic acid and can be eaten raw or cooked. If consumed in large quantities, this green may act as a laxative.

Sheep Sorrel (*R. acetosella*) is a summer food of ruffed grouse and Canada geese. It is probably sought by both black and grizzly bears.

SPRINGBEAUTY *Claytonia lanceolata* Pursh   **Pl. 5; p. 46**
Family: Portulacaceae (Purslane).
Other names: Groundnut.

Description: One of the first conspicuous white or pink flowers to appear in spring. Possesses 1 pair of opposite stem leaves, usually 1 basal leaf, and grows from a round tuberlike corm. Each flower has 2 sepals, 5 petals, 5 stamens, and 1 pistil with a 3-cleft style.

A plant that may be confused with this is *C. megarrhiza*, which, however, has a thick carrotlike root and leaves all basal; a rare plant, found only in alpine regions (9000–12,000 ft.). The related Lewisia (*Lewisia pygmaea*), Plate 5, is distinguished by having 6 to 8 petals, and a 2-cleft style.

Related species: (1) *C. cordifolia*, a fleshy perennial from slender rootstocks, has heart-shaped basal leaves and 1 pair of broad stem leaves; (2) *C. chamissoi*, a perennial that produces runners, has several pairs of stem leaves; (3) *C. perfoliata* is an annual with only 1 pair of stem leaves, these united about stem. All 3 common throughout Rocky Mt. area.

Flowering season: At low altitudes it begins flowering in early April, ending in mid-May. Height of season is early May. At high altitudes found flowering until mid-Aug., but reaches its height in mid-July.

Where found: G, Y, T, R. Grows in moist soil from valleys to

Springbeauty (*Claytonia lanceolata* Pursh)

alpine regions (10,000–11,000 ft.). Look for it along wood borders, mt. parks, alpine meadows, and below snowbanks. Occurs throughout Rocky Mt. region. Some 50 species of *Claytonia* are widely distributed over the earth; about 15 species occur in Rockies.

Interesting facts: *Lanceolata* means lance-shaped. The corms, fleshy taproots, stem, and leaves of many of the claytonias are edible, and have been used as food by people throughout the world. None are known to be harmful. Tubers of Springbeauty were eaten by Indians. Raw, they have a pleasant radishlike taste. Boiled tubers have taste and texture of baked potatoes. Springbeauty is grazed by deer, elk, and sheep during early spring. The tubers are eaten by rodents and are especially prized by grizzly bears, and the leaves and flowers are utilized by elk.

Pl. 5

BITTERROOT   *Lewisia rediviva* Pursh
    Family: Portulacaceae (Purslane).
    Other names: Redhead Louisa, Rockrose.
    Description: The only conspicuous white to pinkish flower that appears to be leafless. Actually, the numerous leaves appear almost as soon as the snow melts, and usually wither before flowering time. They are fleshy, almost round in cross section,

1–2 in. long, and arise from a fleshy root cro
flower is 1–2 in. broad, on a 1–3 in. stem. There are 6
like sepals, 12 to 18 elliptic petals, and many stamens.
slender conical bud is characteristic. Lewisia (*L. pygmaea*
[Gray] Robins.), Plate 5, is smaller, with 6 to 8 petals.

Flowering season: Latter part of April through June and into
July. Hen pheasants and mallards are incubating eggs when
buds of Bitterroot first appear; when it is in full bloom Canada
geese are undergoing a postnuptial molt and are flightless.

Where found: Y, T. Usually found in rocky, dry soil of valleys,
or on foothills, stony slopes, ridges, and mt. summits to about
8000 ft. Distributed from Montana to B.C., south to California
and Colorado, being especially abundant in w. Montana. There
are 6 species in Rocky Mt. area.

Interesting facts: *Rediviva* means brought to life. Its striking
beauty and historical significance make the Bitterroot a fitting
state flower for Montana. Captain Meriwether Lewis first
collected the plant in the Bitterroot Valley of w. Montana in
1806. It seems probable that the Lewis and Clark expedition
used the starchy root as food, although it was not until the
return trip that the plant was specifically noted. It was collected, carried to Washington, D.C., and turned over to
Frederick Pursh, a noted British botanist, who named it
Lewisia in honor of the explorer.

The Indians located the roots in early spring by the small
tufts of elongated leaves. At this time they are tender and
nutritious, since the stored starch has not yet been utilized by

Bitterroot (*Lewisia rediviva* Pursh)

... roots were dug in large quantities
... outer root covering readily peels off,
... re that can be boiled, baked, or powdered
... boiled it has a jellylike appearance. The
... ll as the Indians were fond of it; reservation
... er and prepare it in the manner of their

... name *rediviva* refers to the plant's ability to
... gor after the root has been dried for weeks, or even
... Bitterroot is bitter, as its common name implies; this
tas... gely disappears when the root is cooked. The Bitterroot
River, Bitterroot Valley, and Bitterroot Mts. of w. Montana
were named after this plant.

SANDWORT *Arenaria obtusiloba* (Rydb.) Fern.   **Pl. 5**
   Family: Caryophyllaceae (Pink).
   Other names: Sandywinks.
   Description: A low mat-forming plant with clustered stems
bearing small solitary white and green flowers; sepals 5, petals 5,
and longer than the sepals, stamens 10, pistil 1 with 3 styles.
Leaves linear, generally less than ¼ in. long, with a prominent

Ballhead Sandwort (*Arenaria congesta* Nutt.)

Flowering season: June, July, and, at higher elevations, Aug. Flowers soon after the true Camas (*Camassia quamash*). When the grasslike leaves of Death-camas (*Z. paniculatus*) emerge, great blue herons are beginning to nest and male red-winged blackbirds are defending territories.

Where found: G, Y, T, R. Moist soil of meadows, streambanks, woods, and ledges, from 6000 to 12,000 ft. in mts. Distributed from Alaska to Minnesota, west to Nevada and south to New Mexico. About 8 species occur in Rocky Mts.; other species of this genus are distributed over most of temperate N. America and some occur in Asia.

Mountain Death-camas (*Zigadenus elegans* Pursh)

Interesting facts: *Elegans* means elegant. This genus contains alkaloids poisonous to both man and livestock. Sheep are frequently affected, since they seem to eat the plants more readily than other animals do. Hogs are said to be immune to the poison. Poisoning usually occurs in early spring because the death-camases appear before most other range plants and their succulent leaves are available. One of the more poisonous species (*Z. gramineus*) requires only ½ pound per hundredweight to produce fatal results, whereas less toxic species take about 6 pounds of green plant per hundredweight of animal. The death-camases should not be confused with the true Camas, which formed a staple food of the Indians of the Northwest. The flowers are quite different; however, the Indians occasionally mistook bulbs of the two, since both plants may grow together in meadows. It is difficult to distinguish death-camases from onions (*Allium*), sego lilies (*Calochortus*), fritillarias (*Fritillaria*), and wild hyacinths (*Brodiaea*) when these edible plants are only a few inches high. However, a combination of leaf characters and a cross section of the bulbs or corms is diagnostic at any stage in the development of these plants.

ROCKY MOUNTAIN IRIS   *Iris missouriensis* Nutt.   **Pl. 2**
 Family: Iridaceae (Iris).
 Other names: Flag, Fleur-de-lis, Snake-lily, Water Flag.
 Description: This iris usually bears from 1 to 4 variegated violet-blue flowers about 2–3 in. long. Grows to height of 1–2 ft. from a coarse, irregular, underground rootstock. There may be several narrow swordlike leaves from base and 1 to 2 from stem, often as long as stalk itself. The 3 sepals are dilated and spreading or reflexed; 3 petals are narrower and usually erect.
  Not likely to be mistaken for any other plant.
 Flowering season: From mid-May in lower valleys and well through July in mts. Iris are blooming when eggs of ring-necked pheasant are hatching.
 Where found: G, Y, T, R. Found in open wet meadows from lowest valleys to about 9000 ft. in mts. Distributed from North Dakota to B.C., south to California and New Mexico. Only 1 species occurs in Rocky Mt. area; 8 others are confined to Pacific Coast. Blue Flag (*I. versicolor*) and a number of other species are native to e. U.S. Genus *Iris* is found in N. America, Europe, Asia, and N. Africa, and numerous cultivated forms are almost world-wide.
 Interesting facts: *Missouriensis* means of Missouri. The rootstocks contain the poison irisin, which is a violent emetic and cathartic. Seeds when eaten cause violent "burning" of mouth and throat and this persists for several hours. Roots were ground by the Indians, mixed with animal bile, then put in the gall bladder and warmed near a fire for several days. Arrow points were dipped in this mixture, and it is reported by old Indians that many warriors only slightly wounded by such arrows died within 3 to 7 days.
  There is little likelihood of confusing the rootstock with any edible root because of the strong, acrid, disagreeable flavor. Fibers from the leaves of the Oregon Iris (*I. tenax*) were used by Indians in making lines and nets. The irises have no forage value either to livestock or game. They are a good indicator of water close to the ground surface. In some of the dry mt.

country of Oregon, holes are dug where iris grow, and usually these fill with water and are used by livestock. The iris (fleur-de-lis) is the emblem of France.

GRASS-WIDOWS   Pl. 2
Sisyrinchium inflatum (Suksd.) St. John

Family: Iridaceae (Iris).

Other names: Purple-eyed Grass.

Description: The flowers are about 1 in. wide, bright pinkish purple, and are grouped 1 to 4 in an umbel. Umbel is enclosed at base by 2 bracts generally exceeding flowers in height. These plants usually grow in tufts with stems 6–24 in. tall. Grasslike leaves are scattered along stem, basal ones reduced to sheaths. Roots are fibrous. Plant usually conspicuous, because it blooms early and grows in bunches, often coloring meadows purplish.

Grass-widows could possibly be confused with shootingstars (*Dodecatheon*), but these grow singly and all their leaves are basal and not grasslike (see Plate 15). *S. inflatum* is the only large, purple-flowered species; others are blue or yellowish and less than ½ in. wide.

Flowering season: April and May. Grass-widows appear soon after snow disappears. Blooming signifies it is time to be out of doors and begin looking for edible mushrooms such as the morels, wrinkled saddle-shaped helvellas, and puffballs.

Where found: Moist to wet soil of meadows, grassy hillsides, and open woods, mainly in our valleys or low hills. Occurs from B.C. to Idaho, south to California and Nevada. Possibly 6 species of this genus in Rocky Mts., but many more common names have been applied to these plants.

Interesting facts: *Inflatum* means inflated.

BLUE-EYED GRASS   Pl. 2
Sisyrinchium sarmentosum Suksd.

Family: Iridaceae (Iris).

Other names: *S. halophyllum* and *S. idahoense*.

Description: The 1 to 5 flowers at the top of the stem have 3 sepals and 3 petals colored pale blue to bluish purple. They are ⅜ in. long, generally with yellow center. Stems are about 5–12 in. tall, generally tufted, and distinctly flattened and sharp-edged.

Blue-eyed Grass can be distinguished from most others by its flat stem, grasslike appearance, and similarly colored sepals and petals. Difficult to separate from some other species of this genus; considerable difference of opinion among botanists as to whether differences are sufficient to justify giving them different names.

Flowering season: May to July, depending on elevation.

Where found: G, Y, T, R. Usually found growing in wet open areas from lowest valleys to about 8000 ft. in mts. Extends from Manitoba to B.C., south in mts. to California and New Mexico. There are about 60 species of this genus in N. America and West Indies; not more than 6 in Rocky Mt. area.

Interesting facts: *Sarmentosum* means bearing runners. This flower is well named. The outdoorsman may at first fail to notice the grasslike plant with its tiny flowers amid the extensive greenery of a mt. meadow; but suddenly a sparkle of blue catches his eye and he halts his walk to gaze admiringly into the blue eyes of the meadow. With interest aroused and observation sharpened, he looks about him and sees at every turn the Blue-eyed Grass.

FAIRYSLIPPER *Calypso bulbosa* (L.) Oakes   **Pl. 4**

Family: Orchidaceae (Orchid).

Other names: Venus-slipper, Calypso.

Description: The only pink or rose single-flowered orchid in the area. Possesses a single broad basal leaf, a sheathed stem, showy drooping flower, and a marble-sized corm. Like all orchids, consists of 3 sepals and 3 petals, central petal different from others, being saclike and called the lip. Filaments and style are united to form a central column.

Fairyslipper is unique among orchids of the area, though it could possibly be confused with the shootingstars (*Dodecatheon*); latter, however, distinguished from orchids by having numerous basal leaves, and sepals and petals in 5's instead of 3's (see Plate 15). Mountain Ladys-slipper (*Cypripedium montanum* Dougl.), Plate 4, is a larger plant, with spiraled bronze-colored sepals and petals and an inflated white lip.

Flowering season: First appears in late May, soon after snow melts, and can be found until late June. A dry spring shortens flowering season.

Where found: G, Y, T, R. Grows in evergreen forests at 5000–8000 ft. Look for it in wet or boggy coniferous woods, or on or near decayed stumps and logs. Prefers deep shade. Occurs from Alaska to Labrador, south to New York, Minnesota, Arizona, and California; also in Europe. Only species of genus occurring in Rocky Mts.

Interesting facts: *Bulbosa* means with bulbs. Though individual orchids are seldom abundant in any locality in the Rockies, the Orchid family is one of the largest, if not the largest, family in the world — having 8000 to 10,000 different species. Orchids are most abundant in tropical rain forests. They are adapted for cross pollination by insects, and have become so dependent upon insects for pollination that many of them cannot produce seeds unless certain insects visit them to carry the pollen from one flower to another. Even when seeds are produced, they frequently will not germinate unless stimulated by the presence of certain fungi. Thus orchids are rare, and each one thoughtlessly picked further reduces the chance of a new orchid coming to life.

Spotted Coralroot (*Corallorhiza maculata* Raf.)

SPOTTED CORALROOT *Corallorhiza maculata* Raf.   **Pl. 4**
  Family: Orchidaceae (Orchid).
  Other names: Mottled Coralroot.
  Description: This is a saprophytic member of the Orchid family, characterized by brownish-purple coloring and absence of leaves and green color. Raceme of flowers varies in length 4–8 in. Individual flowers are about ½ in. long, with a conspicuously white lip spotted with crimson. Stems unbranched, 6–24 in. tall, and arise in clumps from thick and knotted rootstalks.

  Most of the coralroots can be told apart only on technical characters. Members of the Indianpipe and Broomrape families can be confused with them because they too lack leaves and green color (chlorophyll). In Orchid family, however, flower parts arise from top of ovary; in other two families flowers originate beneath ovary.

Related species: Striped Coralroot (*C. striata* Lindl.), Plate 4, is similar-appearing, except lip is not 3-lobed and flowers are conspicuously striped instead of spotted.

Flowering season: From middle of May at lower elevations until last of July in mts.

Where found: G, Y, T, R. In decaying plant material in moist shady forests over most of N. America, except southern states. Genus largely restricted to N. America, but some members occur in Europe, Cent. America, and n. Asia; 6 species in Rocky Mts.

Interesting facts: *Maculata* means spotted. Coralroot illustrates the degeneracy of plants that live off the products of others. In the long process of evolution it has lost its chlorophyll, which enables other plants to make their own food from carbon dioxide, sunlight, and water. Its leaves have disappeared and its roots have been greatly reduced. Part of the stem is underground and performs some of the functions of a true root. The underground stem is composed of short, thick, fleshy fibers, repeatedly divided into short, blunt branches and densely interwoven like coral; hence the name Coralroot. This plant is intimately associated with a fungus that decays stumps, logs, roots, leaves, and other organic matter. Coralroot is entirely dependent on this fungus for food.

WHITE BOG-ORCHID   Pl. 4
Habenaria dilatata (Pursh) Hook.

Family: Orchidaceae (Orchid).

Other names: Leafy White Orchid, Bog-candle, Scent-bottle.

Description: The dense spike of waxy white flowers contrasting with the bright green leaves attracts the attention of the passer-by. Unbranched stem varies from nearly 1–2 ft. in height, with upper portion densely covered with flowers that are spurred. Remainder of stem produces linear to lance-shaped leaves up to 6 in. long. There are several varieties of this species, and only on technical characters can they be separated.

This plant can be confused with several other orchids in the Rockies. Ladies-tresses (*Spiranthes romanzoffiana*), a very similar orchid, has flowers arranged in a spiral. The irregular petal called the "lip" does not have distinct spur at base as in White Bog-orchid.

Related species: (1) *H. hyperborea* is 1–3 ft. tall and has greenish-colored flowers; (2) *H. obtusata* has 2 orbicular leaves spreading on ground; (3) *H. unalascensis* has 2 to 4 lanceolate leaves at base of stem, then many scalelike bracts above. All occur throughout Rocky Mt. area.

Flowering season: May be found in flower during June, July, and early part of Aug., depending on altitude and latitude.

Where found: G, Y, T, R. Occurs in wet soil of swamps, bogs, banks of springs and streams. Grows from lowest valleys to around 10,000 ft., and found from Alaska to Greenland, south to New Jersey, Minnesota, California, and New Mexico. Eight species in Rockies; other species of the genus occur in temperate to cold regions of Europe, Asia, and N. America.

White Bog-orchid (*Habenaria dilatata* [Pursh] Hook.)

Interesting facts: *Dilatata* means expanded. The radishlike tubers of this orchid are gathered and eaten by Indians of the Northwest and Eskimos. When boiled for about half an hour they taste like frozen potatoes. Generally speaking, orchids are rare and should not be used as food except in extreme emergencies. Bulbs of all N. American orchids are reported to be edible.

LADIES-TRESSES *Spiranthes romanzoffiana* Cham.   **Pl. 4**
  Family: Orchidaceae (Orchid).
  Other names: Pearltwist.
  Description: The small white flowers appear in a dense terminal spike, usually in 3 rows that partially spiral about the stem. Plants are 4–20 in. tall, bright green and fleshy-appearing, with narrowly lance-shaped leaves on lower part of stem.

Ladies-tresses are very easily confused with White and Green Bog-orchids (*Habenaria*), but flowers of these have a spur lacking in Ladies-tresses. Also, flower spikes are slender, comparatively loose, and long; in Ladies-tresses they are thick, dense, usually not over 1–4 in. long, and spiraled.

Flowering season: July and Aug. Begins to flower when mosquitoes are numerous in the swampy, wet habitat.

Where found: G, Y, T, R. In bogs, marshes, meadows, salt flats, thickets, and occasionally open woods. Occurs from Alaska to Newfoundland, south to New York, Wisconsin, Arizona, and California; also in Ireland. There are about 25 species of *Spiranthes* scattered over most of the earth; only 2 in Rockies.

Interesting facts: The generic name is derived from *speira*, a spiral, and *anthos*, a flower, and refers to the distinct flower arrangement. This spiral arrangement is comparable to spiraling in other plants. Spiral growth in trees is not uncommon and becomes especially evident where spiral cracks form. Vines and tendrils spiral about supporting objects. This spiraling is due to uneven growth of the cells, which causes the stem to twist. *Romanzoffiana* means plant is named for Count Romanzoff.

UMBRELLA PLANT *Eriogonum heracleoides* Nutt.　　**Pl. 4**
Var. *subalpinum* (Greene) St. John

Family: Polygonaceae (Buckwheat).

Other names: Wild Buckwheat, Indian Tobacco.

Description: Compound umbels of small cream-colored flowers develop at ends of almost leafless stalks 4–16 in. tall. These umbels give this plant its characteristic umbrellalike appearance. Flowering stems arise from dense clusters of leaves and woody branches that mat over the ground. Leaves vary from lance shape to linear and are green above, white below. Scape has a whorl of leaves above middle. Flower heads, often rose-colored as they begin to develop, turn cream-colored as they mature. Perianth may then turn rose again.

The many species are extremely difficult to distinguish.

Related species: (1) *E. dendroideum* is an annual with narrow leaves, very fine branches, and awn-tipped floral-envelope lobes; (2) *E. deflexum* is also a fine-branched annual, but leaves are round, perianth lobes not awn-tipped; (3) *E. alatum*, a coarse perennial up to 3 ft. tall, has 3 longitudinal wings on seeds; (4) *E. ovalifolium* has silvery-colored oval to round leaves beneath a leafless, nearly 1-ft.-tall stalk terminating in a round, dense head of yellowish flowers; (5) *E. umbellatum* possesses a branched woody base, compound umbels of yellow flowers, oval to orbicular basal leaves; (6) Sulphurflower (*E. flavum* Nutt.), Plate 5, is similar to *E. umbellatum* but with elongated leaves. These plants all occur over most of Rocky Mt. area.

Flowering season: Latter part of May, through July. Look for this when young red-tailed hawks are leaving nest.

Where found: Y, T. In open areas of dry soil from foothills and higher valleys to around 9000 ft. Common in sagebrush. This plant, or varieties of it, occurs from Alberta to B.C., south to Nevada and Colorado. There are about 150 different species of *Eriogonum*, all native to N. America; 50 or more occur in Rocky Mts.

Interesting facts: *Heracleoides* means heracleum-like. Throughout the West, wherever there is considerable difference in soil type, soil and air moisture, exposure, land slope, or salinity, there tend to be different species or varieties of *Eriogonum* growing under these varied conditions. In the course of time each has adapted to the specific habitat and in doing so has changed sufficiently from the parent stock to become a recognizable species or variety. The seeds of the eriogonums are gathered by chipmunks and white-footed mice. Umbrella Plant is a preferred forage plant of domestic sheep in sw. Montana and se. Idaho.

MOUNTAIN-SORREL *Oxyria digyna* (L.) Hill   **Pl. 5**
Family: Polygonaceae (Buckwheat).
Other names: Alpine-sorrel.
Description: A member of the Buckwheat family, 6–12 in. tall, with round or kidney-shaped fleshy leaves on long leafstalks arising from the basal portion of a scaly stem. Small, greenish to crimson flowers are arranged in dense panicled racemes. Fruit is thin and flat, with an encircling wing indented at both ends. Fruit usually bright rose-colored, and more conspicuous than flowers.

Mountain-sorrel can be confused with the docks (*Rumex*), but the round or kidney-shaped leaves readily distinguish it.

Flowering season: From latter part of June through Aug., depending upon elevation.

Where found: G, Y, T, R. In shady, wet, or moist places, generally on mt. slopes, ledges, and rock crevices. Ranges from about 6000 to 11,000 ft., being found as far south in mts. as California and New Mexico. Circumpolar in distribution, occurring in n. Europe, Asia, and N. America. Only species of the genus *Oxyria*.

Interesting facts: The name *Oxyria* comes from the Greek word *oxys*, meaning sour; the acid-tasting leaves are pleasingly sour. Species name *digyna* means 2 carpels and refers to these female parts of the flower. The plant is used in salads and as a potherb. Growing high in the mts., it makes a welcome addition to the rationed diet of the mountain climber. It is rich in vitamin C and is valued by native peoples as a scurvy preventative and cure. Mountain-sorrel is eaten by elk.

AMERICAN BISTORT   *Polygonum bistortoides* Pursh   **Pl. 4**

Family: Polygonaceae (Buckwheat).

Other names: Bistort, Snakeweed, Knotweed.

Description: A slender, swaying plant with a white or pinkish plumy cluster of small flowers. From a distance flower spike looks like a tuft of cotton. It has narrow tapering leaves, basal ones long-stemmed, upper ones stalkless and smaller; and a thick, twisted, snakelike root.

Serpentgrass (*P. viviparum*) is similar, but the root is not so elongated and the flower spike usually contains bulblets, and is rather loose and slender.

American Bistort (*Polygonum bistortoides* Pursh)

Related species: (1) *P. convolvulus* has a slender, twining stem up to 5 ft. long and heart-shaped leaves; (2) *P. aviculare*, a prostrate plant with lance-shaped leaves, often grows as a weed in dooryards or in dry places. These plants can be found over most of U.S.

Flowering season: Makes first appearance in valleys in early June and has disappeared by mid-July. At higher elevations in mts. starts flowering in early July and lasts into Aug.

Where found: G, Y, T, R. From valley floors to above timberline, in wet meadows, along streambanks, in mt. canyons, and among rock debris at high elevations. Found from Montana and B.C. to California and Mexico. Genus occurs throughout world, but is rare in tropics. Of about 150 species, approximately 35 are in Rocky Mt. area.

Interesting facts: *Bistortoides* means resembling *P. bistorta*. The root of various species of bistort has been used as an emergency food by the Russians, Chinese, Japanese, Europeans, Eskimos, and North American Indians. The Cheyenne and Blackfoot Indians used it in soups and stews. Rootstocks are starchy and slightly astringent when eaten raw. Boiled, they are somewhat sweeter but are best roasted on coals; then they have a sweet nutty flavor. The roots are eaten by black and grizzly bears and rodents, the foliage by deer and elk.

WATER LADYSTHUMB

Pl. 5

Polygonum natans (Michx.) Eat.

Family: Polygonaceae (Buckwheat).

Other names: Water Pepper, Smartweed.

Description: This plant catches the eye with its bright pink terminal spike of flowers, generally arising above a cluster of floating leaves. Commonly grows semisubmerged in shallow water but may also grow on mud. Small pink flowers form dense, ovoid, or short-cylindric spikes ½–1½ in. long. Stems branch at base, may grow 3 ft. or more long, and are covered by pointed, elliptic leaves 2–5 in. long.

This species can be distinguished from others by its bright pink flowers, forming short, terminal spikes, and by lack of hairs and glands on the flowering stem.

Flowering season: Latter part of June to mid-Sept. Flowers at time broods of young Barrow's goldeneye ducks begin to appear on beaver ponds and sloughs.

Where found: Y, T, R. Shallow water of ponds, lakes, and slow-moving streams, or at borders of such areas. In summer when ponds recede, these plants may be found on dried mud. Occur from the plains to around 8000 ft., and can be found from Alaska to Quebec, south to Pennsylvania, New Mexico, Mexico, and California. There are almost 50 species of *Polygonum* in Rocky Mts.

Interesting facts: *Natans* means floating. Water Ladysthumb is a good example of the way many plants will vary with the habitat. Normally this is a prostrate plant, but when stems are lying on mud they root at the nodes and these land stems tend to assume an erect position, producing narrower and more pointed leaves than those floating in water. Also, the land plants are more hairy than the water plants. The plant propagates by seeds and rootstock; the seeds are an important duck food.

Curlydock
(*Rumex crispus* L.)

CURLYDOCK   *Rumex crispus* L.

Family: Polygonaceae (Buckwheat).

Other names: Narrow-leaved Dock or Yellowdock, Spurdock.

Description: A smooth, dark green plant whose leaves have curly or wavy margins and whose greenish flowers give rise to conspicuous reddish-brown fruits having the general appearance of coffee grains. It is 1–3 ft. tall, arising from a fleshy, yellow root. Leaves, mostly basal, are 6–12 in. long, lance-shaped, with slightly heart-shaped base. Small greenish flowers arranged in whorls in panicled racemes. The 3 inner sepals enlarge and become winglike in fruit.

This species can be confused with Mexican Dock (*R. mexicanus*), but latter has narrow, flat, glaucous leaves with a pointed or slightly rounded base.

Related species: Two native species commonly found in sagebrush in early spring are (1) *R. acetosella* and (2) *R. paucifolius*. They are generally smaller than *R. crispus* and flower panicles turn decidedly red with age. Calyx of *R. acetosella* does not develop into wings in fruit and some of the basal leaves are usually arrowhead-shaped. Basal leaves of *R. paucifolius* are on long leafstalks. (3) *R. maritimus* is an annual with minute spines around edges of lobes of perianth. (4) *R. venosus*, a hairless perennial from underground spreading rootstocks, has seed wings almost 1 in. wide.

Flowering season: Mainly during June, but because reddish-brown fruits are more conspicuous than small green flowers this plant becomes particularly noticeable in fall.

Where found: Y, T, R. Curlydock, a native of Europe and Asia, was introduced and has become established, often as a troublesome weed, over most of temperate N. America. Found in moist soil along roads, irrigation ditches, in pastures, cultivated fields, and waste land from valleys to around 6000 ft. in mts. Other species of this genus are almost world-wide. There are 16 species in Rocky Mt. area.

Interesting facts: *Crispus* means curled. The root was formerly a medicinal drug, used as a laxative and tonic, and sold under the name yellowdock. The early spring leaves are cooked for food, often along with dandelion leaves, and the mixture is known as "greens." The leaves and stems of some of our native species have a pleasantly sour taste imparted by oxalic acid and can be eaten raw or cooked. If consumed in large quantities, this green may act as a laxative.

Sheep Sorrel (*R. acetosella*) is a summer food of ruffed grouse and Canada geese. It is probably sought by both black and grizzly bears.

SPRINGBEAUTY   *Claytonia lanceolata* Pursh   **Pl. 5;** p. 46
  Family: Portulacaceae (Purslane).
  Other names: Groundnut.
  Description: One of the first conspicuous white or pink flowers to appear in spring. Possesses 1 pair of opposite stem leaves, usually 1 basal leaf, and grows from a round tuberlike corm. Each flower has 2 sepals, 5 petals, 5 stamens, and 1 pistil with a 3-cleft style.

A plant that may be confused with this is *C. megarrhiza*, which, however, has a thick carrotlike root and leaves all basal; a rare plant, found only in alpine regions (9000–12,000 ft.). The related Lewisia (*Lewisia pygmaea*), Plate 5, is distinguished by having 6 to 8 petals, and a 2-cleft style.

Related species: (1) *C. cordifolia*, a fleshy perennial from slender rootstocks, has heart-shaped basal leaves and 1 pair of broad stem leaves; (2) *C. chamissoi*, a perennial that produces runners, has several pairs of stem leaves; (3) *C. perfoliata* is an annual with only 1 pair of stem leaves, these united about stem. All 3 common throughout Rocky Mt. area.

Flowering season: At low altitudes it begins flowering in early April, ending in mid-May. Height of season is early May. At high altitudes found flowering until mid-Aug., but reaches its height in mid-July.

Where found: G, Y, T, R. Grows in moist soil from valleys to

Springbeauty (*Claytonia lanceolata* Pursh)

alpine regions (10,000–11,000 ft.). Look for it along wood borders, mt. parks, alpine meadows, and below snowbanks. Occurs throughout Rocky Mt. region. Some 50 species of *Claytonia* are widely distributed over the earth; about 15 species occur in Rockies.

Interesting facts: *Lanceolata* means lance-shaped. The corms, fleshy taproots, stem, and leaves of many of the claytonias are edible, and have been used as food by people throughout the world. None are known to be harmful. Tubers of Springbeauty were eaten by Indians. Raw, they have a pleasant radishlike taste. Boiled tubers have taste and texture of baked potatoes. Springbeauty is grazed by deer, elk, and sheep during early spring. The tubers are eaten by rodents and are especially prized by grizzly bears, and the leaves and flowers are utilized by elk.

BITTERROOT *Lewisia rediviva* Pursh **Pl. 5**
    Family: Portulacaceae (Purslane).
    Other names: Redhead Louisa, Rockrose.
    Description: The only conspicuous white to pinkish flower that appears to be leafless. Actually, the numerous leaves appear almost as soon as the snow melts, and usually wither before flowering time. They are fleshy, almost round in cross section,

1–2 in. long, and arise from a fleshy root crown. Expanded flower is 1–2 in. broad, on a 1–3 in. stem. There are 6 to 8 petal-like sepals, 12 to 18 elliptic petals, and many stamens. Long slender conical bud is characteristic. Lewisia (*L. pygmaea* [Gray] Robins.), Plate 5, is smaller, with 6 to 8 petals.

Flowering season: Latter part of April through June and into July. Hen pheasants and mallards are incubating eggs when buds of Bitterroot first appear; when it is in full bloom Canada geese are undergoing a postnuptial molt and are flightless.

Where found: Y, T. Usually found in rocky, dry soil of valleys, or on foothills, stony slopes, ridges, and mt. summits to about 8000 ft. Distributed from Montana to B.C., south to California and Colorado, being especially abundant in w. Montana. There are 6 species in Rocky Mt. area.

Interesting facts: *Rediviva* means brought to life. Its striking beauty and historical significance make the Bitterroot a fitting state flower for Montana. Captain Meriwether Lewis first collected the plant in the Bitterroot Valley of w. Montana in 1806. It seems probable that the Lewis and Clark expedition used the starchy root as food, although it was not until the return trip that the plant was specifically noted. It was collected, carried to Washington, D.C., and turned over to Frederick Pursh, a noted British botanist, who named it *Lewisia* in honor of the explorer.

The Indians located the roots in early spring by the small tufts of elongated leaves. At this time they are tender and nutritious, since the stored starch has not yet been utilized by

Bitterroot (*Lewisia rediviva* Pursh)

the developing flower. The roots were dug in large quantities with a pointed stick. Outer root covering readily peels off, leaving a white fleshy core that can be boiled, baked, or powdered to form meal. When boiled it has a jellylike appearance. The mountain men as well as the Indians were fond of it; reservation Indians still gather and prepare it in the manner of their ancestors.

The specific name *rediviva* refers to the plant's ability to return to vigor after the root has been dried for weeks, or even months. Bitterroot is bitter, as its common name implies; this taste largely disappears when the root is cooked. The Bitterroot River, Bitterroot Valley, and Bitterroot Mts. of w. Montana were named after this plant.

SANDWORT   *Arenaria obtusiloba* (Rydb.) Fern.   **Pl. 5**
     Family: Caryophyllaceae (Pink).
     Other names: Sandywinks.
     Description: A low mat-forming plant with clustered stems bearing small solitary white and green flowers; sepals 5, petals 5, and longer than the sepals, stamens 10, pistil 1 with 3 styles. Leaves linear, generally less than ¼ in. long, with a prominent

Ballhead Sandwort (*Arenaria congesta* Nutt.)

midvein. Old leaves clothe the stem bases and help form the mat (see Plate 5). *A. obtusiloba* can be confused with other members of the genus and with White Phlox (*Phlox multiflora*) and Carpet Phlox (*P. hoodii*), but these plants have 5 instead of 10 stamens.

Related species: (1) *A. lateriflora* has ovate to oblong leaves, with 1 to several flowers on a stem. (2) Ballhead Sandwort (*A. congesta* Nutt.) arises from a woody underground stem, is 4–12 in. tall, and flowers are congested into a many-flowered head; found in the higher mt. valleys to above timberline; see illus., p. 48.

Flowering season: July and early Aug.; at height of blooming when the more conspicuous Moss Campion colors high alpine regions.

Where found: Y, T. In alpine regions from 10,000 to 12,000 ft. on rocky outcrops, talus slopes, and sandy well-drained soil. Extends from Labrador to Alaska, south to New Mexico and California. Often associated with limestone formations. Members of the genus are found throughout north temperate zone. Sixteen species in Rocky Mt. area.

Interesting facts: *Obtusiloba* means blunt-lobed.

FIELD CHICKWEED *Cerastium arvense* L.   **Pl. 5**

Family: Caryophyllaceae (Pink).

Other names: Mouse-ear Chickweed, Meadow Chickweed.

Description: Grows 3–12 in. tall, on weak, leafy stems. Sometimes occurs singly or scattered, but more often in densely matted patches. Flowers are white, from ¼ to ½ in. across when fully expanded, and each of the 5 petals is deeply notched and at least twice as long as sepals. Leaves are opposite, narrow, almost 1 in. long, and usually glandular and short-hairy.

This plant is difficult to distinguish from some other members of the Pink family, but its separate sepals, lack of stipules, deeply 2-cleft petals, and long, cylindric capsule help identify it. Also, fact that it is a perennial and stems are usually erect helps separate it from other chickweeds.

Related species: (1) *C. beeringianum* has prostrate stems and petals only slightly longer than sepals; (2) *C. nutans* is an annual with flowers on long stalk hooked at summit. Both plants range throughout Rocky Mts.

Flowering season: Blooms from April to late Aug., depending largely on altitude.

Where found: G, Y, T, R. Usually in calcareous or salty soils, and sandy or gravelly sites in dry situations. Ranges from plains and valleys to 11,000 ft. in mts., and is distributed in cold and temperate regions of Asia, Europe, and N. and S. America. Six species in Rockies.

Interesting facts: The genus name came from the Greek word *kerastes*, horned, referring to the long slender capsule, which is often curved; *arvense* means of the fields. The chickweeds in general are troublesome weeds, especially in lawns.

MOSS CAMPION   *Silene acaulis* L.   Pl. 6

Family: Caryophyllaceae (Pink).

Other names: Cushion Pink, Dwarf Silene, Catchfly.

Description: A mossy, cushionlike plant with numerous small pink flowers. The cushionlike beds, composed of many narrow opposite leaves, are 1 in. or so high and often 1 ft. or more across. Flowers are about ¼ in. across. Rarely are they white.

No other *Silene* can be confused with this cushion-forming plant. When white (rarely), it could be confused with White Phlox (*Phlox multiflora*), but latter has larger flowers and longer leaves. Pink phloxes growing at lower elevations look very much like Moss Campion, but have fused instead of separate petals.

Related species: (1) *S. alba*, a large, coarse, branching plant has tubular white flowers about 1 in. long; flowers in masses, usually found along roadsides and fence rows. (2) *S. menziesii*, about 1 ft. tall, has flowers singly at base of upper leaves. (3) *S. drummondii* has a tubular calyx about ½ in. long and white or purplish petals about same length. These 3 plants occur throughout Rocky Mts.

Flowering season: First appears in early July on southern exposures where the sun has melted the snow; by mid-Aug. has generally completed its short span of activity. When it is in full bloom, the water pipit, white-crowned sparrow, and the gray-crowned rosy finch are laying eggs.

Where found: G, Y, T, R. Grows at high altitudes (9000–12,000 ft.), in alpine meadows, on stony ground, talus slopes, and high exposed ridges. Grows best on chalk formations. Moss Campion is found throughout Rocky Mt. region, and in similar situations in e. U.S., Canada, Alaska, Europe, and Asia. Genus *Silene* contains approximately 250 species, of which about 25 occur in Rockies.

Interesting facts: *Acaulis* means stemless. The Moss Campion, like the Purple Saxifrage, is a circumpolar flower that owes its wide distribution to the Pleistocene glaciers. It beautifies the Scottish highlands, peaks of the Alps, and tundras of the north country. In the Teton-Yellowstone area it is frequently found growing side by side with the blue Forget-me-not. The mosaic of color formed by the two brilliant dwarf flowers personifies the beauty of the mountain flora. At times the White Phlox forms a third member. Growing thus together, they appear to be a single cushion of varicolored flowers — the red, white, and blue symbolizing the complete freedom that comes to all outdoor lovers in the vastness of the mts.

YELLOW PONDLILY *Nuphar polysepalum* Engelm. **Pl. 6**
Family: Nymphaeaceae (Water Lily).
Other names: Pondlily, Cowlily, Spatterdock, Wokas (Indian).
Description: A large-leaved water plant with bright yellow waxy blossoms which hardly can be confused with any other plant in the region. Blossoms vary in diameter 3–5 in.; round to oval leaves may be 4–12 in. long.
Flowering season: From latter part of June through most of Aug. First look for these flowers when frogs are numerous and noisy in beaver ponds and cow moose are dropping their calves. It will still be blooming when ducks are flocking in late summer.
Where found: G, Y, T, R. Leaves and flowers will be found floating on surface of quiet streams, ponds, and shallow lakeshores. Occurs in valleys and to almost 10,000 ft. in mts., extending from Alaska to Black Hills of South Dakota, south to Colorado and California. Only 1 species in West and about 5 in U.S.
Interesting facts: *Polysepalum* means many sepals. This is a flower the fisherman knows. Generally it tells him the water is too deep for hipboots. Large leaves serve as excellent cover for trout and other fish and quite likely function as natural insulators, helping to maintain low water temperatures. The huge, yellow, scaly rootstocks twist along the pond floor like prehistoric serpents, and in the black depths of a beaver pond they create an atmosphere of awe and strangeness that is reinforced by the sharp crack of a beaver's tail in the stillness of evening.

The large seeds were collected by Indians, roasted, and eaten like popcorn, which they resemble in taste. The Indians called them Wokas, and this name is used today. Ducks eat the seeds, and the large scaly rootstocks are sometimes eaten by muskrats and frequently used in the construction of their lodges. Indians consumed the rootstocks in time of famine. Related species in Europe and Asia are used for food.

MONKSHOOD *Aconitum columbianum* Nutt. **Pl. 7**
Family: Ranunculaceae (Buttercup).
Other names: Aconite, Wolfbane.
Description: The beautiful purple-blue blossoms, often 1 in. long, are on long stalks and form a loose raceme. Sepals and petals similar in color; one of the sepals develops into a hoodlike cap or helmet supposedly similar to those worn by medieval monks. It covers the other flower parts; hence the name Monkshood. Slender plant grows 2–5 ft. tall, with alternate leaves 2–6 in. broad, nearly round in outline. They are incised almost to the base into 3 to 5 divisions, each of which is again variously toothed and cleft. Largest leaves are at base of stem, decreasing in size as they go up.

Monkshood is often confused with larkspurs (*Delphinium*), which it closely resembles (see Plate 7). However, these have 1 sepal forming a distinct, tapering spur instead of a hood. In early growth, leaves can be mistaken for those of geraniums (*Geranium*).

Flowering season: From latter part of June to first part of Aug. Beaver kits are splashing about in ponds when it first blooms.

Where found: Y, T, R. In wet meadows, near springs, and along streams, often growing in large patches. Ranges from about 6000 to 9000 ft. in elevation; extends from Montana to B.C., south to California and New Mexico. There are about 80 species, most of them occurring in temperate zone of Asia, but some are found in Europe and about 15 species in N. America; only 1 species occurs in Rocky Mts.

Interesting facts: *Columbianum* means of Columbia and refers specifically to the Columbia River. All parts of these plants are poisonous — they contain the alkaloids aconitine and aconine. Roots and seeds are especially poisonous. The leaves are most toxic just before flowering time, and unfortunately it is at this stage that they are most likely to be eaten by livestock. In general, however, the plant causes negligible cattle loss on the range because the quantity usually eaten is insufficient to produce death. The drug aconite, obtained from these plants, is used as a heart and nerve sedative.

BANEBERRY   *Actaea arguta* Nutt.

Family: Ranunculaceae (Buttercup).

Other names: Snakeberry, Chinaberry.

Description: A perennial herb with an erect, branched stem, 1–3 ft. tall, and a large basal leaf, mostly ternately compound. Leaflets are 1–3 in. long, thin, ovate, and sharply incised and toothed. Small white flowers form dense racemes. Sepals fall off as flower opens. Fruit (a glossy, oval, white or red berry, ¼–½ in. long) is more conspicuous than flower. No other berry in the area closely resembles it.

The white flower of Baneberry superficially resembles that of White Clematis (*Clematis ligusticifolia*), but latter is a woody vine and its flowers are in a head instead of a raceme. Marshmarigold (*Caltha leptosepala*) and Globeflower (*Trollius laxus*) might possibly be confused with Baneberry, but these have much larger flowers and simple instead of compound leaves. See Plates 6, 7.

Related species: Our western plant may not be distinct from the eastern Baneberry (*A. rubra*).

Flowering season: May and June to first part of July, but fruit may remain until mid-Aug. Look for first flowers at about time aspens have leaved and are giving definite appearance of foliage. Ruffed grouse hens will be incubating, some males still

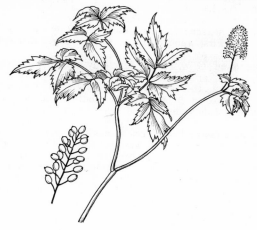

Baneberry (*Actaea arguta* Nutt.)

drumming. Berries will be colored when huckleberries are ripe.
Where found: Found in moist or wet places, often in shaded areas, along streams, about springs and boggy areas. Occurs from valleys to about 9000 ft. in mts. and found from Alberta to Alaska, south to California and New Mexico. There are 6 to 7 species of this genus, confined to temperate regions of N. Hemisphere; only 1 in Rocky Mt. area.
Interesting facts: *Arguta* means sharp-toothed. The white fruit appears to be made of china, and so the name Chinaberry. Red, white, and pink forms of berries are mildly poisonous, apparently acting upon the heart. The rootstock is a violent purgative, irritant, and emetic. Some birds apparently can eat the berries without ill effects.

ANEMONE   *Anemone globosa* Nutt.   **Pl. 6**
    Family: Ranunculaceae (Buttercup).
    Other names: Windflower, Globose Anemone, and *A. tetonensis*.
    Description: A slender-stemmed, deep purple-red flower, sometimes varying to greenish yellow, with divided and lobed basal leaves. Like all anemones, it has colored sepals but no petals; numerous stamens and pistils.
    A. globosa is most often confused with *A. cylindrica*, but latter is usually much more than 1 ft. tall, and the head of seeds is cylindric in shape and ¾ in. or more long. *A. globosa* is generally less than 1 ft. tall, and head of seeds is globose or ovoid in shape.

Related species: *A. parviflora*, with basal leaves wedge- or fan-shaped and lobed, is found throughout Rockies.

Flowering season: Appears about mid-July and found until mid-Aug. First appears about time young red-tailed hawks leave nest.

Where found: G, Y, T, R. Found only in high valleys and mts. of our area, or in colder part of w. N. America. Ranges from Alaska to Saskatchewan, south to California and New Mexico. Genus *Anemone* contains about 85 species (Abrams), widely distributed over earth; 14 in Rocky Mt. area.

Interesting facts: The generic name is derived from the Greek word *anemos*, wind; the flowers supposedly opened at the command of the spring breezes. *Globosa* means globose. Several species of *Anemone* contain anemonin, a poison affecting the central nervous system. American Indians used Anemone roots for treating wounds and attributed to them powerful healing qualities. They have little forage value, being occasionally eaten by deer and elk.

PASQUEFLOWER   *Anemone patens* L.   Pl. 6

Family: Ranunculaceae (Buttercup).

Other names: Prairie Anemone, Windflower, Blue Tulip, American Pulsatilla, Wild Crocus, and *A. ludoviciana*.

Description: The beautiful cup-shaped Pasqueflower has no petals, only sepals colored purple, violet, or occasionally white. Flower, 1–1½ in. across, usually appears singly at end of stem, which is 2–16 in. tall, with several clustered on a branching root crown. Leaves silky, mainly basal, are dissected into narrow linear divisions. As the seeds ripen the styles persist, becoming long and feathery. Stem continues to elongate after flowers bloom.

Besides other anemones, the plant most likely to be confused with the Pasqueflower is Sugarbowl (*Clematis hirsutissima*), which noticeably differs in having several pairs of opposite leaves instead of one pair of leaflike bracts.

Flowering season: Starts blooming in early March at low elevations and continues to bloom until June in higher mts. The early tourist who sees these flowers will find them one of many interesting sights lost to those who get out-of-doors at a later, more mild season.

Where found: G, Y, T, R. Moist soil of meadows, fields, and woods from 4000 to 9000 ft. This plant, or varieties of it, occurs from Alaska south to Washington, Illinois, and Texas. Western pasqueflowers considered a distinct species by some botanists. Fourteen species occur in Rocky Mts.

Interesting facts: *Patens* means spreading. This is the state flower of South Dakota. The plant contains a volatile oil used

Pasqueflower (*Anemone patens* L.)

in medicine as an irritant. Both the acridity of the plant and the fine hairs that cover it tend to make it a poor forage food. Domestic sheep have died from overfeeding on this plant.

BLUE COLUMBINE   *Aquilegia coerulea* James   Pl. 6

Family: Ranunculaceae (Buttercup).

Other names: Colorado Blue Columbine.

Description: The showy flowers of this columbine are 1–3 in. broad, with sepals varying from white to deep blue and petals from white to cream. Basal portion of each petal extends backward between the petal-like sepals, forming 5 straight, slender spurs 1–2 in. long. These spurs immediately distinguish this genus of flowers from others. Plant varies in height 8–24 in., with leaves mostly basal and on long stalks. Leaves compound; leaflets deeply 2- to 3-cleft and round-lobed.

Leaves and stems resemble those of meadowrues (*Thalictrum*), but flowers are so distinctive that there is little likelihood of mistaking these plants in the flowering stages. Larkspurs (*Delphinium*) are distinguished by having only single spur on each flower (see p. 59).

Related species: (1) *A. formosa* has deep red sepals with the expanded part of petals yellow and spurs red; (2) *A. flavescens* has a pale yellow flower.

Flowering season: From mid-June to mid-Aug.

Where found: Y, T, R. In moist to wet soil, from 6000 to 11,000 ft. in mts. Thrives on rockslides and outcrops but also found in shady aspen groves and ravines. Distributed from Montana to cent. Idaho, south to Arizona and New Mexico. Other species of columbines are found in temperate Asia, Europe, and N. America as far south in mts. as Mexico. Nine species occur in Rockies.

Interesting facts: *Coerulea* means blue. This columbine is the state flower of Colorado. Plants may cover considerable area in the higher mts., the large, brilliant blue and white blossoms making an inspiring sight. As one goes north or west from Colorado the blue color becomes less pronounced, until finally the flowers are almost pure white or cream. (Those found at high altitudes are generally more colorful than those at lower elevations.) Columbines are not important forage plants, but on overstocked range domestic sheep graze them heavily, and all species are becoming rare in areas where they were once abundant.

MARSHMARIGOLD *Caltha leptosepala* DC.   **Pl. 6**

Family: Ranunculaceae (Buttercup).

Other names: White Marshmarigold, Cowslip, Meadowbright, and *C. rotundifolia*.

Description: A large white buttercup-like flower of subalpine regions, 1–2 in. across, with numerous yellow stamens that give it a conspicuous yellow center. Plant has large, ovate, shiny, dark green leaves, all basal.

The flower could be linked with the Dryad (*Dryas hookeriana*), which also has large white-petaled flowers, but that is a woody plant growing on dry stony ground (see Plate 9). Bitterroot (*Lewisia rediviva*) is a low white or pink flower distinguished from the Marshmarigold by its linear leaves and fact that it grows in dry locations (see Plate 5).

Flowering season: First appears in late May to early July. In higher alpine meadows found into mid-Aug.

Where found: G, Y, T, R. Grows in subalpine regions of 7000–10,000 ft. A water-loving plant, carpeting mt. streambanks and wet meadows from Alberta to B.C., south to Oregon, Arizona, and New Mexico. There are about 15 species of *Caltha* found in colder regions of both hemispheres; this the only one in Rocky Mts.

Interesting facts: *Leptosepala* means with slender sepals. The Marshmarigold (*C. palustris*) of e. U.S. was used as a potherb by the Indians, though cattle have reportedly been killed by eating it. Its close relative in the West, however, was too bitter to be used as food. Although the western species is believed to be poisonous to cattle, elk consume it in large quantities.

CLEMATIS *Clematis columbiana* (Nutt.) T. & G. **Pl. 7**
 Family: Ranunculaceae (Buttercup).
 Other names: Virgin's Bower, Bellrue.
 Description: A slender, semiwoody climbing vine that may attain a length of 10–12 ft. Flowers are 2–3 in. broad, occur singly in axils of leaves, and have no petals; but sepals are petal-like, lavender-blue. Leaves are opposite and compound, with 3 broadly ovate leaflets 1–2½ in. long. The styles at top of ovaries enlarge greatly, become feathery, and carry seeds for long distances in wind.

No other plant in Rockies is likely to be mistaken for this one.
 Flowering season: Latter part of April through July. First look for it when meadows and fields are covered with dandelions. At height of blooming, magpies will be incubating and some young may be a week old. Some vines will still be blooming when Rabbitbrush is in full bloom and most other flowers have gone.
 Where found: G, Y, T, R. In dry to moist soil of woods and thickets, from valleys to around 8500 ft. in mts. Occurs from Alberta and B.C. south to Oregon, Utah, and Colorado. More than 100 species of *Clematis* are scattered over most of earth; only 3 or 4 found in Rockies. Several exotic species, hybrids, and forms are cultivated under many different names.
 Interesting facts: *Clematis* is derived from the Greek *klema*, a vine branch; *columbiana* means of Columbia. Clematis exhibits a type of growth characteristic of many climbing plants. A vine must depend on other objects or plants for support. The leaf-stalks of the leaves wrap themselves around twigs and branches and in this way support the vine. When a leafstalk touches something, growth is slowed on the side of the leafstalk in contact. The other side of the structure continues to grow normally, causing the leafstalk to form 1 to several circles about the object it touches. The feathery plumelike styles that carry the seeds make excellent tinder. A spark from flint or pyrite struck into a ball of the "fuzz" will quickly ignite it. The out-doorsman can learn to recognize both the White and the purple-flowered Clematis in late summer and early winter from its feathery seed carriers. The American Indians and early western settlers chewed *C. ligusticifolia* as a remedy for colds and sore throats.

SUGARBOWL *Clematis hirsutissima* Pursh **Pl. 7**
 Family: Ranunculaceae (Buttercup).
 Other names: Leather Flower, Old-man's Whiskers, Vase Vine, Clematis.

Description: The nodding, dull purple, sugarbowl-shaped flower, about 1 in. long and ¾ in. broad, is borne singly at the end of each stem. This early-blooming herbaceous perennial has un-branched, clustered stems 1–2 ft. tall. Leaves are opposite and pinnately decompound. Each flower produces numerous seeds, the styles of which become feathery, attaining a length of 2½ in.

Sugarbowl is easily confused with Pasqueflower (*Anemone patens*), but it has opposite stem leaves and Pasqueflower does not. Sugarbowl might also be confused with Anemone (*Anemone globosa*) and possibly with Leopard Lily (*Fritillaria atropurpurea*), but flower of latter is mottled with green-yellow, and leaves are alternate and simple.

Flowering season: Latter part of April through May and June.

Where found: Y, T, R. In moist open areas of plains, hills, and woods to about 8000 ft. in mts. More than 100 species of *Clematis* occur over the globe; only 3 or 4 found in Rockies.

Interesting facts: *Hirsutissima* means very hairy. The feathery, elongated styles of this plant aid greatly in the distribution of its seeds and make an even more attractive house decoration than do the flowers. Indians used the plant medicinally.

WHITE CLEMATIS   *Clematis ligusticifolia* Nutt.   **Pl. 7**

Family: Ranunculaceae (Buttercup).

Other names: Virgin's Bower, Pipestem.

Description: A semiwoody vine often attaining height of 30 ft. and almost hiding the trees and shrubs over which it grows. Small flowers are about ⅓ in. across but occur in such profusion they impart a white color to whole mass of growth. Later in season the seeds develop long, feathery, tan-colored tails, which again give entire plant a tan or whitish color.

The great masses of flowers distinguish this plant from the other species of *Clematis* with which it could be confused.

Flowering season: Blooms from May to Aug., exhibiting this extended flowering because of continued growth of vine.

Where found: G, Y, T, R. Growing over bushes and trees along rivers, creek banks, and canyon bottoms from Alberta and B.C. south to California and New Mexico. More than 100 species of *Clematis* distributed over most of the earth; only 3 or 4 found in Rockies.

Interesting facts: *Ligusticifolia* means ligustium-leaved. White Clematis is occasionally grown as an ornamental, and a decoction of it was formerly used by Indians for colds and sore throats. The feathery seed tails, when bunched together, form a "fuzz" that ignites almost instantly when a spark from knife and pyrite is struck into it. A hunter whose feet are cold will experience immediate relief if he stuffs this insulating fuzz into his boots to substitute for inner soles.

LARKSPUR   *Delphinium nelsoni* Greene   **Pl. 7**
  Family: Ranunculaceae (Buttercup).
  Other names: Low Larkspur, Nelson's Larkspur.
  Description: Larkspur has 3 to 10 rich blue-purple flowers about
  ½–¾ in. long. Sepals as well as petals are colored, upper sepal
  prolonged into a slender, tubular spur that protrudes sidewise
  from flower. Plant is 6–24 in. tall, generally with unbranched
  stem, and grows from fascicle of fleshy, tuberlike roots. The
  few leaves are basal and on stem, round in outline but greatly
  dissected.

Larkspur (*Delphinium nelsoni* Greene)

The leaves of Larkspur can be confused with those of geraniums (*Geranium*) and columbines (*Aquilegia*), but the flowers
of these two genera are quite distinctive. Geraniums have no
spur and columbines have 5 spurs. See Plates 10, 6.
Related species: (1) *D. bicolor* arises from a cluster of woody,
fibrous roots; otherwise similar to *D. nelsoni;* only occurs in
northern and western part of Rocky Mts. (2) *D. occidentale*
grows 3–6 ft. tall, has deep blue flowers; but a variety of this
plant, *cucullatum*, has spotted flowers; neither blooms until
midsummer and both are common throughout Rocky Mts.

Flowering season: From April to July. When they are beginning to bloom, sparrow hawks are defending territories.

Where found: Y, T, R. Found in valleys, foothills, and on dry ridges and flats to 10,000 ft. in elevation. Especially abundant in sagebrush, extending from Black Hills of South Dakota to Wyoming, Idaho, and south through most of Utah and Colorado. There are about 2 dozen species of *Delphinium* in Rocky Mt. region. Other species of larskpurs, numbering about 150, are found in Asia, Europe, N. America, and the western part of S. America.

Interesting facts: *Nelsoni* means named for Aven Nelson. Larkspurs, with their spikes of blue, purple, pink, or white blossoms, form a riot of color from spring until late summer. However, their beauty is deceiving, because they are poisonous to cattle and are responsible for the greatest cattle loss on national forest range land. Grubbing or soil sterilants are the only effective control measures known to date. There are authentic reports of a hundred or more head of cattle being killed in a local area within the span of a few days. Cattle apparently eat the plant because of the pleasant acidity of its leaves; greatest losses occur when Larkspur is grazed early in spring. The poisonous principles are alkaloids, mainly delphinine. To be affected mortally, an animal must eat about 3 per cent of its body weight of the green plant. Interestingly, Larkspur is nontoxic to domestic sheep, even in force-feeding trials, and thus sheep are sometimes used to help eradicate Larkspur on cattle range. Elk appear to avoid some of the larkspurs in early spring when the new leaves are forming, but feed heavily on them in late summer and fall. After blooming, the plants apparently lose their toxicity. A tincture of delphinine is used externally to kill parasites.

ALPINE BUTTERCUP *Ranunculus adoneus* Gray Pl. 6

Family: Ranunculaceae (Buttercup).

Other names: Mountain Buttercup.

Description: Found only around timberline and above in mts. It is a perennial, usually 4–12 in. tall, with bright yellow flowers ½–1 in. broad and sepals sometimes tinged on back with purple. Stems clustered together and clothed at base by old dead leaf bases. There are 1 to 3 flowers on a stem, and later 50 to 70 seeds, forming an ovoid head.

A similar plant, Subalpine Buttercup (*R. eschscholtzii*), grows in the same environment but has the 3 primary divisions of the leaves once-lobed or middle one unlobed; whereas Alpine Buttercup has 3 primary divisions of leaves twice-divided into linear segments.

Flowering season: July and Aug.

Where found: Y, T, R. Wet soil near snowbanks, from 9500 to

11,500 ft. Occurs from Wyoming to Idaho, south to Nevada and Colorado. There are approximately 300 species of *Ranunculus*, mainly in polar and temperate regions of N. Hemisphere; however, extend into tropics in higher mts. About 40 species occur in Rocky Mts.

Interesting facts: *Adoneus* means resembling the genus *Adonis*. This buttercup, growing at high elevations, is exposed to severe climatic conditions. The summer season is short, the temperature frequently falls below freezing at night, and winds and frost reduce available soil moisture. Forced to grow and mature quickly, the plants seem to spring up as if by magic, blooming almost as soon as snow melts. In fact, they can be found growing under the edges of snowdrifts, sometimes pushing up through 2–3 in. of snow and ice. Heat given off during respiration of a growing plant is sufficient to melt a hole 1 in. or so in diameter. Foliage is eaten by deer, elk, pikas, and rockchucks; seeds by mice and chipmunks. Most buttercups are toxic to some degree, and some are quite poisonous to livestock.

WATER BUTTERCUP *Ranunculus aquatilis* L. Pl. 7

Family: Ranunculaceae (Buttercup).

Other names: White Watercrowfoot, White Buttercup, and *Batrachium flaccidum*.

Description: The white flowers are almost ½ in. broad and usually protrude above water surface. Leaves are finely dissected into threadlike divisions. The stems are entirely submersed in water, but the flowers generally protrude. Plants often grow in dense patches.

When not in flower, this plant could easily be mistaken for water milfoils (*Myriophyllum*) or members of the Pondweed family (Najadaceae), but none of these have conspicuous white flowers.

Flowering season: From May until well into Aug. This long flowering season is regulated by water temperature. Cold water coming off mt. snowbanks delays flowering and thus extends season.

Where found: Y, T, R. Submersed in water of shallow ponds, lakes, and streams, or on mud that has recently been covered by water. Occurs in the Old World, and distributed over most of N. America. Approximately 300 species of *Ranunculus*, mainly in polar and temperate regions of N. Hemisphere; however, extend into tropics in higher mts. About 40 species occur in Rocky Mts.

Interesting facts: *Aquatilis* means aquatic. Presence of this plant often indicates good fishing, for its dense growth provides an excellent habitat for development of water insects and crustaceans. These in turn furnish food for fish. Water Buttercup is used as food by ducks and Canada geese.

SAGEBRUSH BUTTERCUP   Pl. 6
Ranunculus glaberrimus Hook.

Family: Ranunculaceae (Buttercup).

Other names: Crowfoot, Early Buttercup.

Description: The first buttercup to appear in spring, blooming in valleys or mts. just as quickly as the snow recedes. A bright shiny yellow flower, turning white with age; has both entire and divided leaves, and thickened fibrous or fleshy roots. Stems are 1- to several-flowered, petals 5, stamens and pistils numerous.

Many species of buttercups are difficult to distinguish, especially in mt. areas, where growth variations are frequent. Of these the Sagebrush Buttercup is the only one possessing both entire and divided leaves. Familiarity with this plant will help you to recognize other buttercups. Whether they are white, yellow, or pink, they have a family resemblance.

Related species: (1) Alpine Buttercup (*R. adoneus*) has a larger flower and leaves parted into linear lobes; see Plate 6. (2) *R. alismaefolius* grows 1–2 ft. tall, has entire leaves, and is found in moist to wet situations. (3) Water Buttercup (*R. aquatilis*), with white petals and finely divided leaves, usually grows submerged in water; see Plate 7.

Flowering season: First appears at low elevations as early as latter part of March, when sage grouse are strutting. By early May flowering is about over in valleys, but plant can be found blooming later at higher elevations. When this harbinger of spring is in full bloom it gives the sagebrush flats a golden hue;

Sagebrush Buttercup
(*Ranunculus glaberrimus* Hook.)

eggs of great horned owls are hatching, rockchucks are coming out of hibernation, cock pheasants have established crowing territories, and ruffed grouse are drumming. In Yellowstone Natl. Park it is the first showy flower to greet black and grizzly bears as they emerge from their deep sleep of winter.

Where found: Y, T, R. Found growing at various altitudes throughout Rocky Mt. region, extending from Montana to B.C. and south to California and Colorado. Look for it on the sagebrush flats in early spring, and in the moist mt. meadows in midsummer. The genus, about 300 species, is found throughout U.S., Europe, and Asia; about 40 species occur in Rockies.

Interesting facts: The generic name *Ranunculus* means little frog; *glaberrimus* means smoothest. Buttercups generally prefer moist meadows and marshes but some are found on dry sites and a few are fully aquatic. "Buttercup" is derived from a fancied resemblance of the gleaming petals to a cup of butter.

Buttercups as a group are poisonous. Bitter Buttercup, or Cursed Crowfoot (*R. sceleratus*), is a species of our area containing principles so acrid and poisonous that a small portion of the leaf, if eaten, will cause stomach pain. Applied to the skin, it causes inflammation and blisters. The volatile toxic principle is rendered harmless by drying or boiling. Bitter Buttercup is particularly poisonous to cows but will affect sheep and horses as well. Sagebrush Buttercup is an important spring food of blue grouse, and probably is utilized by other wildlife.

GLOBEFLOWER   *Trollius laxus* Salisb.   Pl. 7

Family: Ranunculaceae (Buttercup).

Other names: White Globeflower and *T. albiflorus*.

Description: The creamy-white or yellow flowers lack conspicuous petals, but the sepals are enlarged, colored, and look quite like petals. Blooms are 1–1½ in. broad, with numerous light-colored stamens and many dark green ovaries. Stems, usually clustered together, vary in height from 6 to 20 in. and most of them bear a single terminal flower. Leaves are palmately lobed, sharply toothed, and 1–3 in. broad.

Globeflower is most likely to be confused with the Marshmarigold (*Caltha leptosepala*) and with Candle Anemone (*Anemone cylindrica*). Leaves of Marshmarigold are not lobed and only slightly toothed, if at all. *A. cylindrica* has greenish-white sepals and palmately lobed leaves, divided into linear segments but not toothed. Also, *Trollius* flowers do not have a whorl of leaflike bracts below; *Anemone*'s do.

Flowering season: Latter part of May, through July. White-tailed ptarmigan are beginning to nest; grayling are spawning.

Where found: G, Y, T, R. Wet meadows, edges of ponds, streams, and boggy areas, from around 6000 ft. to above timberline. Ranges from Alberta to B.C., south to Washington and Colorado; also eastern part of N. America. There are about 15 species of *Trollius* in N. Hemisphere; only 1 species in Rocky Mts.

Interesting facts: *Laxus* means loose. A similar-appearing globeflower (*T. europaeus*) is found in the Alps and Scandinavian countries. The mountain traveler in these parts will welcome it as an old friend.

HOLLY-GRAPE *Mahonia repens* (Lindl.) G. Don   Pl. 7

Family: Berberidaceae (Barberry).

Other names: Oregon Grape, Creeping Barberry, Mountain Holly, and *Berberis repens*.

Description: This has clusters of bright yellow flowers that develop into dark bluish-purple berries. Flower has 6 petal-like sepals and 6 petals. Compound leaves leathery and evergreen, with 3 to 9 oval leaflets spine-toothed around edge. These hollylike leaves characterize the holly-grapes; sometimes turn bright red in fall. A low shrub, seldom grows more than 1 ft. tall, but stem is usually greatly elongated just under soil surface. New plants arise at intervals along this underground stem. Stem wood is yellow.

The spiny leaflets are so diagnostic that the only other plants likely to be confused with this one are other species of *Mahonia*. However, stems of these other species are taller and erect.

Related species: (1) *M. aquifolium* has erect stems, 1–6 ft. tall, and shiny leaflets. (2) *M. nervosa* has 9 to 19 leaflets forming a long, compound leaf; otherwise, very similar to *M. repens*. First two species only occur in western part of Rockies.

Flowering season: Latter part of April to July. First flowers appear when Narrowleaf Cottonwood buds open and about time young bald eagles hatch.

Where found: G, Y, T, R. Found in moderately dry soil of woods and hills. Occurs from valleys to around 9000 ft. and extends from Alberta to B.C., south to California and Texas. About 35 other species occur throughout temperate N. America, Andes of S. America, and Asia; 6 occur in Rockies.

Interesting facts: *Repens* means creeping. This species of holly-grape often is not separated by botanists from *M. aquifolium*, the state flower of Oregon. Ripened berries can be eaten raw, but are quite sour. The juice, sweetened with sugar, tastes much like grape juice. The camper will find this a refreshing drink. It makes a fine jelly. The red or green leaves provide attractive Christmas decorations. The dried yellow stems and roots are the official drug berberis, used as a bitter tonic. The Indians used it in this way and also made a yellow dye from the wood for dyeing clothing and for basketwork. Holly-grape is a poor forage plant, utilized sparingly by deer and elk. The berries are eaten by black bears. A number of species of this family are planted as ornamental shrubs. One of these, the common Barberry (*Berberis vulgaris*), with spines on the stems, is the alternate host for the black stem rust of wheat. The fungus causing this disease lives on the wheat during summer, and results in enormous losses to the farmer. It then winters on the old wheat stems and in the following spring attacks the barberry, where spores are produced which then reinfect wheat plants. The overwintering fungus cannot attack wheat directly but must first develop on the barberry.

STEERSHEAD   *Dicentra uniflora* Kell.   Pl. 7

Family: Fumariaceae (Bleedingheart).
Other names: Bleedingheart, Squirrelcorn.
Description: This striking flower resembles a steer's head turned upside down, but is so tiny it can be readily overlooked. It has 4 petals, inner 2 being broad at base, narrowed and attached at apex; outer 2 narrow and elongate, growing first upward, then curving outward and down, and usually terminating below base of flower. These outer petals have rounded sacs at their bases. Blossoms vary from white to pinkish in color and come singly at top of a leafless stalk 2–4 in. tall. Leaves are basal and greatly dissected; plant has a carrotlike, fleshy root.

Steershead might be confused with the Dutchmans-breeches (*D. cucullaria*), but flowers of latter are borne in racemes and plants are much larger. Golden Corydalis (*Corydalis aurea* Willd.) is closely related to Dutchmans-breeches; however, the former has yellow flowers and fibrous rather than tuberous roots.
Flowering season: April and May. They begin to appear soon after snow disappears at lower elevations.
Where found: Y, T. Look for this plant in sagebrush, among foothills, below ledges, and in places where soil is loose and sliding. Ranges from Wyoming to Washington, south to California and Utah. There are about 15 species of *Dicentra*, all of N. America and e. Asia; only 2 species in Rockies.
Interesting facts: *Uniflora* means 1-flowered. Steershead, along with other members of the genus, contains alkaloids poisonous to animals. Losses are not great, however, because the plants are small and not very palatable. The poison is probably cucullarine. This poisonous alkaloid is found in the closely related Dutchmans-breeches, which also has been known to kill cattle. Plants are most poisonous to livestock during early spring.

WHITLOW-GRASS   *Draba densifolia* Nutt.   Pl. 8

Family: Cruciferae (Mustard).
Other names: Draba, Rockcress.
Description: This little perennial alpine flower grows in dense tufts. Flowers are yellow, about ⅜ in. broad, and form racemes. Flowering stalks attain height of 1–6 in., with flowers often

densely massed together. Stems branch along ground and the ends are densely covered with narrow linear leaves not more than ¼ in. long. Old leaves of previous years persist on older parts of stems.

Drabas generally can be distinguished from other members of the Mustard family by their oval-shaped, flattened pods containing several seeds in each half. Bright yellow flowers arising from cushion of leaves distinguishes them from other high-mt. plants. "Cruciferae" is derived from "crucifix," or "cross." Flowers have 4 sepals and usually 4 petals that form a cross.

Related species: (1) *D. nemorosa*, a small spring annual with yellow flowers; (2) *D. reptans*, similar but has white flowers; (3) *D. aurea*, a perennial with broad leaves on flowering stems; (4) *D. oligosperma*, also a perennial, has only narrow basal leaves. All these plants common throughout Rockies.

Flowering season: Latter part of June to first part of Aug. Look for it when the conspicuous Alpine Sunflower (*Hymenoxys grandiflora*) is in bloom.

Where found: Y, T. This whitlow-grass can be found only near timberline and above, on ridges and mt. sides. Occurs from Montana to Washington, south to California and Utah. There are around 200 species of *Draba* distributed over arctic and temperate regions and in higher mts. of tropics; about 50 species occur in Rocky Mts.

Interesting facts: *Densifolia* means densely leaved. The mountain climber and hiker will find mat-forming or cushion plants clinging to the rock crevices and surfaces where there is very little soil. There are 4 of these in the Rocky Mt. region that will readily attract his attention: the Moss Campion with its red flowers, the blue flowers of the Forget-me-not, the white of the White Phlox, and the yellow of the alpine drabas.

WALLFLOWER   *Erysimum capitatum* (Dougl.) Greene

Family: Cruciferae (Mustard).

Other names: Treacle-mustard, Prairie-rocket.

Description: The bright yellow flowers, sometimes tinged with orange, occur in a dense raceme, and are about ½ in. long. Narrow leaves vary from linear to lanceolate, and the 4-angled, slender pods may attain length of 4 in. This plant lives 2 or occasionally 3 years, and attains a height of 1–3 ft., with little or no branching.

The various species of wallflowers are difficult to tell apart, but dense cluster of large flowers and the angled pods readily distinguish them from other genera.

Related species: (1) *E. wheeleri* has orange- or maroon-colored petals, and plant is restricted to s. Rockies; (2) *E. repandum* is a widespread annual with petals about ¼ in. long.

Flowering season: Latter part of May until first part of Aug.

Will be blooming at high altitudes by time ice leaves lakes.
Where found: Y, T, R. On open, dry flats and hillsides, from
lowest valleys to about 9500 ft. in mts. This flower, with
several minor varieties, occurs from B.C. to Indiana and south to
Texas and California. There are about 80 other species, widely
distributed in temperate zone of N. America, Europe, and Asia;
7 species in Rockies.

Wallflower (*Erysimum capitatum* [Dougl.] Greene)

Interesting facts: *Capitatum* means headlike. This plant belongs
to the Mustard family, having watery and pungent or acrid
juice. Mustard of commerce is the ground seeds of some members of the family. They contain a glycoside that hydrolyzes
to oil of mustard. The peppery taste of watercress, radish,
horseradish, and turnips, so characteristic of the family, is due
to this chemical. The dried seeds of many of the mustards will
impart a pleasant flavor if mixed with biscuit or bread dough.
Other members of the family include many flowers of our
gardens, noxious weeds of our fields, and such crop plants as
cabbage, rutabaga, rape, and cauliflower. Leaves and stems
eaten by pikas and rockchucks; probably grazed by elk and
bighorn sheep at elevations of 8000–9500 ft.

Watercress (*Rorippa nasturtium-aquaticum* [L.] S. & T.)

WATERCRESS   *Rorippa nasturtium-aquaticum* (L.) S. & T.
    Family: Cruciferae (Mustard).
    Other names: Pepperleaf.
    Description: A floating, prostrate plant that grows in cold water or in mud. Dense cluster of green leaves forming clumps or mats and numerous white threadlike roots are more characteristic than the inconspicuous small white flowers. Leaves have from 3 to 9 segments, terminal one the largest (see illus.).

    Watercress can be confused with the other cresses, but these either have yellow flowers and usually do not grow directly in water or, if they have white flowers and are found growing in water, they will stand erect, whereas Watercress will be floating or prostrate. Bittercress (*Cardamine breweri*) is one of the confusing white-flowered erect species; leaves are mostly pinnate, with 3 to 7 leaflets.

    Related species: (1) *R. sinuata*, a perennial from creeping root-stocks, has petals longer than sepals; (2) *R. islandica*, an annual or biennial, has petals about same length as sepals. Both are common over w. U.S.

    Flowering season: May to July, and occasionally Aug.

    Where found: G, Y, T, R. In springs and clear streams, from lowest elevations to around 8000 ft. in mts. This plant, a native of Europe, was brought to this country and cultivated, has escaped, and is now found over most of America. About 50 species of *Rorippa* are scattered over earth but chiefly in N. Hemisphere; about 10 species are in Rockies.

Interesting facts: *Nasturtium-aquaticum* means water-cress. Watercress, along with other members of the Mustard family, has an acrid sap containing sulphur compounds which is biting to the taste. Leaves and young stems of this plant are used in salads, garnishes, and are eaten as a relish. It has been known and eaten since ancient times. Xenophon highly recommended it to the Persians; the Romans considered it a good food for those with deranged minds; and in w. India it is prized by the Mohammedans. Commercial mustard and horseradish are products of this family, and the cabbage, kale, cauliflower, turnip, rape, and radish are all members of the Mustard family.

Every trout fisherman should know this plant — the floating mats form excellent cover for fish and harbor a wide variety of trout foods such as fresh-water shrimp, snails, and numerous aquatic insects.

ROCKY MOUNTAIN BEEPLANT   Pl. 8
Cleome serrulata Pursh

Family: Capparidaceae (Caper).

Other names: Spiderflower, Pink Cleome, Stinkweed.

Description: This member of the Caper family is a much-branched annual 2–5 ft. tall, with alternate trifoliate leaves. Numerous pink flowers, sometimes fading to white, occur in dense racemes. Seed pods develop while flowers on same stem are still blooming. After flowering the ovary stalks elongate, separating the pods considerably. Flowers may vary in length from ¼ to ½ in., with elongated ovary protruding on a long slender stalk.

Beeplant could be confused with Clammyweed (*Polanisia trachysperma*), but this has long bright purple stamens and is so densely covered with glands and hair that it is sticky or clammy to the touch.

Related species: (1) Yellow Beeplant (*C. lutea* Hook.), Plate 8, has yellow instead of pink flowers. (2) *C. platycarpa* also has yellow flowers, but an ovate-oblong pod instead of a long, linear one; only occurs in w. Rockies.

Flowering season: Latter part of July through Aug.

Where found: Y, T, R. Prairies, sandy areas, roadsides, and waste places to about 6000 ft. Widespread from Indiana to Saskatchewan and Washington, south to California and New Mexico. There are numerous other species of this genus, occurring mainly in tropics of America and Africa; 4 species in Rocky Mt. area.

Interesting facts: *Serrulata* means finely saw-toothed. The plants of this genus have a pungent taste much like mustard and a disagreeable smell that is distinctive. Indians boiled and ate the leaves and flowers of Beeplant. The family name, Capparidaceae, comes from the genus name of the goat (*Capra*). This animal and the plants of this family are supposed to resemble each other in odor.

ROSECROWN   *Sedum rhodanthum* Gray   **Pl. 8**
Family: Crassulaceae (Orpine).
Other names: Red Orpine, Stonecrop.
Description: A dense cluster of rose-colored flowers is at the top of the stem and superficially resembles red clover. Flowers are small, arranged in close racemes in axils of upper leaves. Stems usually clustered on stout rootstocks, unbranched, 6–15 in. tall, and densely leaved, except for lower part of stems. Leaves oblong or narrower, ½–1 in. long, and somewhat fleshy.

This plant is most likely to be confused with Roseroot (*S. rosea*) since the two grow in the same locations and look much alike. However, flowers of Roseroot arranged in flat flower heads instead of clusters in leaf angles, and petals dark

Rosecrown
(*Sedum rhodanthum* Gray)

purple and narrow instead of rose and lanceolate as in Rosecrown.

Related species: *S. debile* has an erect root, yellow flowers, and
broad, opposite leaves; common throughout U.S.

Flowering season: Latter part of June to Aug.

Where found: Y, T, R. Often among rocks in moist to wet
soils of meadows and streambanks, from near timberline to
considerably above it. Ranges from Montana to New Mexico
and Arizona. There are about 300 species of *Sedum*, mainly in
N. Hemisphere, but some are found in tropics and below the
equator in higher mts.; about a dozen species occur in Rocky
Mt. area.

Interesting facts: *Rhodanthum* means rose-flowered. Rosecrown
belongs to a family of largely succulent herbs. Because of their
low and fleshy habit of growth, many are used in rock gardens
and as house plants. Some are called Stonecrop because they
can grow on rock with little soil. Members of this genus are
eaten as potherbs or salads in Europe and Asia. Roseroot is
utilized in this manner by Greenlanders.

STONECROP   *Sedum stenopetalum* Pursh   Pl. 8

Family: Crassulaceae (Orpine).

Other names: Orpine, Yellow Stonecrop.

Description: This member of the Orpine family is a tufted
perennial 4–8 in. tall. Flowers are yellow, occasionally tinged
with purple, ¼–½ in. across, and arranged in dense clusters on
short branches at top of plant. Narrow, fleshy leaves vary in
color from green to reddish brown and are ¼–½ in. long. They
are mainly crowded near base of flowering stems or on sterile
branches. Bunched, fleshy leaves readily distinguish this plant
from other genera in Rocky Mts.

Other species of this genus can be distinguished only on
technical characters. Flowers may be confused with Ivesia
(*Ivesia gordoni*), but this has large pinnately compound leaves.

Flowering season: Latter part of June to Aug. Will appear
when White Phlox (*Phlox multiflora*) is at peak and seed pods
of Yellow Fritillary (*Fritillaria pudica*) are fully developed.
Young ravens are fledging at this time.

Where found: G, Y, T, R. On rocks or rocky dry soil, from
lowest valleys to about 9000 ft. Occurs from Saskatchewan to
B.C., south to California and New Mexico. Most species of
this genus occur in north temperate zone, but a few cross
the equator and go south into Andes. There are about 300
species of *Sedum;* about a dozen species occur in Rocky Mt. area.

Interesting facts: *Stenopetalum* means narrow-petaled. Many
members of the Orpine family are fleshy, succulent plants,
with a waxy covering that largely prevents water loss. Because
of this adaptation they can survive in extremely dry situations.

When sufficient water is present they grow and flower, but when it becomes scarce they may lie dormant for long periods, resuming growth when moisture is again available. Some of the strangest and most bizarre forms in the plant kingdom belong to this family.

JAMES BOYKINIA *Boykinia jamesii* (Torr.) Engl. **Pl. 8**

Family: Saxifragaceae (Saxifrage).

Other names: Purple Saxifrage.

Description: Boykinia has reddish-purple to dark pink flowers about ½ in. long, arranged in close panicles. Leaves usually kidney-shaped, about 2 in. broad, toothed around edge, and mainly basal or on lower part of stem. Stems attain a height of 3–12 in. and grow in dense clusters from thick, rough, branching rootstocks.

There are other members of this genus that resemble James Boykinia, but they have white petals. Saxifrages have long, narrow styles, and these too, with one exception, have white or yellowish petals that readily distinguish them from James Boykinia.

Flowering season: July and Aug. Young horned owls are learning to fly and hunt around their cliff nests when this flower first blooms.

Where found: Y, T, R. In cracks on face of perpendicular cliffs and rocky areas, from around 7000 ft. in mts. to well above timberline. This plant, or a variety of it, is found from Alberta to B.C., south to Nevada and Colorado. *Boykinia* is a N. American and e. Asiatic genus of about 8 species; only *jamesii* occurs in Rocky Mt. area.

Interesting facts: *Jamesii* means named for Edwin James. This plant will grow on the face of granite cliffs wherever there is a crack large enough for the roots to take hold. Roots slowly decompose the rock by chemical action; the dead plant parts gradually decay and form organic food materials for new growth. In time the crack is enlarged by this slow process and the action of freezing and thawing of water. By such processes, many species of plants break down base rocks to form soil. The mountain climber meets this plant on intimate terms. Protruding from a sheer rock face, it tells him that above is a crevice that will take his piton and secure his rope. There is evidence that this plant is eaten by elk and deer when it is accessible.

STARFLOWER *Lithophragma parviflora* (Hook.) Nutt. **Pl. 8**

Family: Saxifragaceae (Saxifrage).

Other names: Woodland-star, Prairie-star, Fringe-cup.

Description: This has a slender, unbranched stem 8–20 in. tall, arising from pink-tinged underground bulblets. The 3 to 6 flowers at summit of stem have white or pinkish petals ¼–½ in.

long, and deeply cleft into 3 to 5 divisions. Leaves are ¾–2 in. broad, mainly basal, almost round in outline, but variously cleft and parted.

This member of the Saxifrage family could easily be confused with members of the Pink family, but the latter seldom have petals cleft into more than 2 divisions.

Related species: (1) *L. bulbifera*, with bulblets instead of flowers at base of some of the leaves, and (2) *L. tenella*, without bulblets at base of stem leaves, occur throughout Rockies. Bloom earlier than *L. parviflora*.

Flowering season: April through June. Appears about same time as more conspicuous Arrowleaf Balsamroot. Tree swallows are selecting nesting hollows and magpies and golden eagles nest building when they first bloom.

Where found: G, Y, T, R. The starflowers are usually found in rich, medium-dry soil, from lowest valleys to about 9000 ft. in mts. Distributed from Alberta and B.C. south to California and Colorado. There are only about a dozen species of starflowers, all of which are native to w. N. America; 3 species in Rockies.

Interesting facts: *Parviflora* means small-flowered. One of the early spring flowers, its delicate deeply cleft petals present a starlike appearance. Slender stems invisible from a distance make the "little white stars" appear suspended in a sky of green. The bulblets are eaten by rodents, the introduced chukar, and probably by gray (Hungarian) partridges.

GRASS-OF-PARNASSUS *Parnassia fimbriata* Koenig Pl. 8

Family: Saxifragaceae (Saxifrage).

Other names: Fringed Parnassia, Rocky Mountain Parnassia.

Description: The white flower, about ¾ in. across, is readily recognized by its conspicuously fringed petals. United, gland-tipped, sterile stamens alternate with fertile ones. Slender unbranched stems, 6–8 in. tall, are clustered on short, thick rootstock. One small, bractlike leaf at about middle of stem contrasts with several heart- or kidney-shaped basal leaves on long leafstalks.

Several members of the Pink and Saxifrage families could be confused with this plant, but a careful check on the characters given above will help distinguish them.

Related species: (1) *P. parviflora*, with unfringed petals almost as long as sepals, is also found throughout Rockies. (2) Wide-world Parnassia (*P. palustris* L.) has unfringed petals considerably longer than the sepals; see illus., p. 74.

Flowering season: July and Aug. Look for it when Monkshood is in bloom.

Where found: G, Y, T, R. This striking plant is found about springs, along streambanks, and in boggy areas, generally where there is shade. Occurs in mts. from about 5000 ft. to timberline, and found from Alaska to Alberta, south to n. California and

Wideworld Parnassia
(*Parnassia palustris* L.)

Colorado. Other species of this genus well distributed over temperate and frigid regions of N. Hemisphere. Six species in Rocky Mt. area.

Interesting facts: The genus name derives from Parnassus, a mt. in Greece sacred to Apollo and the muses. *Fimbriata* means fringed.

PURPLE SAXIFRAGE *Saxifraga oppositifolia* L.

Family: Saxifragaceae (Saxifrage).

Other names: Twinleaf Saxifrage.

Description: A small, wine-colored alpine flower with clustered fleshy leaves growing in dense tufts. Each stem bears a single flower. Numerous tiny leaves form rosettes on slightly woody stem and are opposite one another.

No other saxifrage is like it, and the only alpine flower that could possibly be confused with it is *Astragalus tegetarius*, rather readily distinguished by its pealike flower and compound leaves.

Related species: (1) Brook Saxifrage (*S. arguta* D. Don), with large, round basal leaves coarsely toothed, bears flowers in open panicle on long slender stem; see illus. opposite. (2) Yellowdot Saxifrage (*S. bronchialis* L.) has bunched, entire, linear, spine-

Purple Saxifrage (*Saxifraga oppositifolia* L.)

Brook Saxifrage (*Saxifraga arguta* D. Don) and Yellowdot
Saxifrage (*S. bronchialis* L.)

tipped leaves, white petals purple-spotted; see illus., p. 75.
(3) Diamondleaf Saxifrage (*S. rhomboidea* Greene) has conspicuous basal leaves and a single headlike cluster of white
flowers at top of leafless stem 2–12 in. tall; see illus. below.
All are common in Rockies.

Flowering season: Early July to Aug.

Where found: G, Y, T. Grows on exposed ridges at 9000–
11,000 ft. Look for it on talus slopes and among rock debris. A
plant of arctic regions; Wyoming is as far south as it occurs in
U.S. Also a native of the Alps. The genus, of about 250 species,
is widespread in America, Europe, and Asia; about 25 species
occur in Rockies.

Diamondleaf Saxifrage (*Saxifraga rhomboidea* Greene)

Interesting facts: *Oppositifolia* means opposite-leaved. The
Purple Saxifrage of the Alps is identical with the Purple Saxifrage of the Rockies. How could this tiny plant, separated by
thousands of miles of land and water, be the same? How could
it have reached two such widely separated areas? The answer
is perhaps that the continental ice sheets carried it southward
from the Arctic, and as they slowly receded northward they left
the Purple Saxifrage isolated on the mt. peaks of Europe and

America. There, in a high-mt. arctic environment, it remained unchanged, so that today botanists cannot differentiate between those growing in the Alps, Rockies, or arctic regions.

SYRINGA *Philadelphus lewisii* Pursh   Pl. 8
  Family: Hydrangeaceae (Hydrangea).
  Other names: Lewis Syringa, Mock-orange, Indian Arrowwood.
  Description: A shrub characterized by clusters of conspicuous white flowers with numerous bright yellow stamens. Flowers, 1–2 in. across, emit a fragrant perfume that can be smelled for some distance. Syringa branches considerably and attains a height of 3–10 ft. Leaves are opposite, ovate in outline, 1–3 in. long. Hillsides are sometimes so densely covered by this plant that the blooms impart to landscape an appearance of being snow-covered.
  In the far West it could be confused with the Pacific Dogwood (*Cornus nuttallii*), whose numerous small flowers in a dense head are surrounded by white bracts; this gives appearance of single white flower, lacking bright yellow provided by stamens of Syringa.
  Related species: *P. microphyllus*, a smaller shrub attaining height of 4–6 ft. with smaller flowers (½ in. broad), occurs in s. Rockies.
  Flowering season: Latter part of May, through July. Reaches height of blooming about time Chinook salmon are running up mt. streams of Idaho.
  Where found: G. Medium-dry to moist soil along streams, hillsides, and in mts. to around 7000 ft. Grows from cent. Montana to B.C., south to California. Of about 50 species of *Philadelphus*, native to north temperate zone, only 2 occur in Rockies.
  Interesting facts: This beautiful plant, first discovered and collected by Captain Meriwether Lewis in 1806, has been appropriately selected as the state flower of Idaho. The name *Philadelphus* pays honor to an Egyptian king, and the species name *lewisii* honors the scientist-explorer. Syringa is used extensively in landscape plantings. This shrub frequently occurs with such other woody plants as Chokecherry, Serviceberry, Snowbrush, and Mountain Maple (*Acer glabrum*) — all favorite deer foods. Since Syringa is not normally a preferred deer food, the big-game manager uses the degree of deer utilization on this plant as a rough index to the condition of range browse. Where Syringa has been heavily browsed, the range man knows that the winter deer population is probably high. In parts of Washington and localized areas in Montana, however, both deer and elk show a decided preference for it. The straight stems of the plant were used by Indians in making arrows.

GOLDEN CURRANT   *Ribes aureum* Pursh

    Family: Grossulariaceae (Gooseberry).

    Other names: Buffalo Currant, or Missouri Currant, Clove Bush.

    Description: This shrub has tubular-shaped, golden-yellow flowers ½–¾ in. long. They form racemes in axils of leaves and have a pleasing spicy odor; hence the common name Clove Bush. Stems attain height of 3–10 ft. with leaves 3- to 5-lobed, often toothed, 1–1½ in. broad, and sometimes broader than long. Fruit, in diameter about ¼ in., may be yellow, red, or black.

    This shrub could easily be mistaken for other currants or gooseberries, but lack of prickles on stems, and long, bright yellow flowers help distinguish it from other *Ribes* in Rockies.

    Related species: (1) *R. inerme* has prickly stems; (2) *R. viscosissimum* lacks prickles but leaves, young twigs, and black berry are covered with stalked glands; (3) *R. cereum* lacks prickles and stalked glands but has a white or pink tubular flower and reddish berries. All are common in Rockies.

    Flowering season: Last of April to first part of June. Look for the berries in Aug. and Sept.

    Where found: G. Moist soil along fence rows, streams, waste places, and foothills. Ranges from Saskatchewan to Washing-

Golden Currant (*Ribes aureum* Pursh)

ton, south to California and New Mexico. There are about 100 species of *Ribes*, native mainly to N. Hemisphere, but extending into mts. of S. America. More species occur on Pacific Coast than anywhere else; about 25 species in Rocky Mts.

Interesting facts: *Aureum* means golden. The genus *Ribes* includes both wild and cultivated currants and gooseberries. Many of our wild species are excellent to eat, either fresh, cooked, or made into jellies and jams. Indians added them to their pemmican, a concentrated food produced by mixing dried buffalo meat and sometimes fruit with rendered fat. The mixture was poured into bags or molded into loaves.

Blister rust fungus, which kills the 5-needled pines, must spend one stage of its life cycle on some species of *Ribes* before it can spread to the pines. By destroying the *Ribes* in or near our forests, the life cycle is broken and spread of blister rust controlled.

Birds, black bears, and rodents utilize the fruit, and the forage is browsed by deer and elk when more palatable food is not available. The Sticky Currant (*R. viscosissimum*), Squaw Currant (*R. cereum*), and Western Black Currant (*R. petiolare*) are more important browse plants, mainly because of their wide distribution, large production of leafage, and general availability to game species.

SERVICEBERRY *Amelanchier alnifolia* Nutt. **Pl. 11**

Family: Rosaceae (Rose).

Other names: Shadberry, Shadblow, Juneberry.

Description: Our most common early white-flowering shrub, varying from 3 to 20 ft. in height. The 5 white petals are narrow, usually twisted, and about ½ in. long. Flowers form in lateral racemes so numerous as to outline the shrub in white against the surrounding darker vegetation. Leaves, 1–2 in. long, oval in outline, are toothed above middle or sometimes all around. Fruit, dark blue to purple when ripe, sweet and edible, in diameter may be ¼ to almost ½ in.

Serviceberries, though thornless, can be confused with hawberries (*Crataegus*), which have spines 1 in. long. Chokecherries (*Prunus*), also confused with serviceberries, have a single stone in fruit; serviceberries contain several small soft seeds.

Flowering season: May and June. Under favorable conditions individual bushes may be in bloom for as long as a month. About time this shrub blooms, new velvety antlers of moose are developing and Rocky Mt. bighorn ewes are lambing.

Where found: G, Y, T, R. Moist soil along streams, and in mts. to about 7500 ft. Small, bushy varieties grow on fairly dry hillsides. Serviceberry distributed from Alberta to B.C., south to California and New Mexico; about 25 species occur in north temperate zone, but only this and its varieties grow in Rocky Mts.

Interesting facts: *Alnifolia* means alder-leaved. Some people enjoy eating the berries, others find they taste too mealy and sweet. At any rate, they were a staple in the diet of Indians, who dried and pressed them into cakes for winter use. They made pemmican by pounding the dried berries together with dried buffalo meat. This was then mixed with fat and made into cakes. Pemmican, with or without fruit, is still unsurpassed as a camping ration. Serviceberries make an excellent pie, delicious jelly and wine. The entire plant is so palatable to such wildlife forms as deer, elk, moose, mountain sheep, mountain goats, rabbits, and rodents that it is one of the first shrubs to be eliminated or drastically retarded on overbrowsed ranges. Pheasants, grouse, black bears, and other wildlife eat the berries. It also furnishes valuable browse for livestock and the buds are a staple winter food of ruffed grouse. In winter, Serviceberry can be distinguished from Chokecherry, Bitter-cherry (*Prunus emarginata*), Mountain Maple (*Acer glabrum*), and other similar-appearing shrubs by its alternate buds with imbricate, ciliate-margined scales.

RIVER HAWTHORN   *Crataegus rivularis* Nutt.

Family: Rosaceae (Rose).

Other names: Western Black Hawthorn, Thornapple, Haw.

Description: This shrub or small tree furnishes food and cover to upland game and is well known to outdoorsmen, even if only by the general name of Thornbush. May attain height of 25 ft.; is well armed with sharp, slender spines 1 in. or more in length. In May, appears white, with sweet-scented flowers about ¾ in. broad, and in fall is again conspicuous with clusters of black or dark purple fruit, each fruit in diameter about ¼ in. These resemble small-sized apples, to which they are closely related.

Larger red fruits of Red Haw (*C. columbiana*) readily distinguish it from River Hawthorn. Nevertheless, it would be useless for the layman to try to distinguish the different haw-thorns, because even experts cannot agree on them. They are often confused with entirely different plants, such as the serviceberries (*Amelanchier*), cherries (*Prunus*), Mountain-ash (*Sorbus scopulina*), and Squaw-apple (*Peraphyllum ramosissimum*); however, none of these have sharp, woody spines. When in fruit hawthorns are sometimes confused with wild roses; but hawthorns have simple leaves, roses have pinnately compound leaves.

Flowering season: Latter part of April to first part of June. Look for it when the more conspicuous flowers of Serviceberry are in bloom. First flowering occurs when wood ducks begin laying.

Where found: T. Moist soil along streams and pond borders, and in hills to about 8500 ft. Often grows in thickets, and in fall its red leaves may color large areas of countryside. Extends from Wyoming and Idaho south to Nevada, Arizona, New Mexico. Some botanists recognize about 300 species of *Crataegus*, scattered over most of the earth but mainly concentrated in e. U.S. Other, equally competent, botanists would cut this number in half; 8 species in Rockies.

River Hawthorn (*Crataegus rivularis* Nutt.)

Interesting facts: *Rivularis* means of brooksides. The spines of hawthorns are actually modified plant stems. In contrast, thorns of some other plants are modified leaves.

Hawthorn fruit, collected in large quantities by the Indians, was eaten fresh, or dried and mixed into pemmican for winter use. Early settlers used it for jelly and jam, and it is still gathered for this purpose. Birds avidly feast upon the ripe fruit in fall, and in winter dried fruits still clinging to the branches, or frozen ones beneath the trees, serve as starvation foods to carry many forms of wildlife through critical winter periods. The fruits are high in sugar but low in fats and protein. Ring-necked pheasants and cottontail rabbits seek impenetrable hawthorn thickets for cover and food. Hawthorn thickets are preferred nesting and roosting sites for black-billed magpies. Wood ducks show a preference for this fruit. It is consumed by black bears and probably by grizzlies. Rodents consume the seeds.

DRYAD   *Dryas hookeriana* Juss.   **Pl. 9**
   Family: Rosaceae (Rose).
   Other names: Alpine Avens, White Mountain-avens, Alpine Rose, and *D. octopetala.*
   Description: The largest white-flowered, mat-forming plant of the alpine zone. A dwarf, shrubby plant with simple, toothed, leathery leaves and solitary flowers 1 in. or more broad, consisting of 8 to 9 petals. Like most of the Rose family, it has numerous stamens. Leaves are strongly revolute, hairy-white, and prominently veined beneath; stem is woody.
      No plant in its high rocky environment can be readily confused with the Dryad. The White Phlox (*Phlox multiflora*), Plate 16, forms mats but is not woody, has narrow grasslike leaves, bears 5 instead of 8 petals. Marshmarigold (*Caltha leptosepala*), Plate 6, has succulent stem and grows in moist areas.
   Related species: Mountain-avens (*D. drummondii* Richards.), Plate 9, with broad ovate petals, yellow instead of white, is found only in our n. Rockies.
   Flowering season: Blooms throughout July and into Aug.
   Where found: G, Y, T, R. Found only at high elevations (10,000–11,000 ft.) on exposed gravel slopes and ridges. Forms evergreen carpets over boulders and rocky debris, growing most profusely on limestone sites. Dryad is found throughout high peaks of Rocky Mts. from Colorado to Alaska and in arctic America. A plant of the far north, being widely distributed in Iceland, Greenland, and Spitsbergen; also a common flower in Alps and mountainous areas of England, Scotland, Ireland, Europe, and Asia. There are about a half-dozen species of *Dryas*, all in colder areas of N. Hemisphere; only 2 occur in Rocky Mts.
   Interesting facts: *Hookeriana* means named for Sir William J. Hooker. A true alpine flower, it is an excellent example of a plant adapted to arctic conditions. Low woody growth serves as a protection against wind and snow; rolled leaves prevent rapid evaporation and, being evergreen, they convert water, sunlight, and carbon dioxide into food as soon as the snow disappears. With these advantages the large short-stemmed flower matures quickly, producing many seeds to insure survival of a few in the harsh environment. Once established, a plant slowly extends itself year after year by producing new shoots to carpet the surrounding rocks. Dryad has been found to possess root nodules as do legumes, and like this group of plants it fixes nitrogen.

STRAWBERRY   *Fragaria vesca* L.   **Pl. 9**
   Family: Rosaceae (Rose).
   Other names: Earth Mulberry and *F. americana.*
   Description: Strawberries are low, perennial herbs, spreading by means of runners. Flower has 5 white petals and about 20

stamens. Leaves are basal, composed of 3 coarsely toothed leaflets, 1–2½ in. long. Numerous seeds develop on each receptacle, which organ enlarges greatly; becomes juicy, and usually turns red upon ripening. Seeds are on surface of "fruit," and stems, when in fruit, usually are longer than leaves.

When not in bloom or fruit, the Strawberry can be confused with Barren Strawberry (*Waldsteinia idahoensis*), which has yellow flowers and lacks runners.

Related species: *F. virginiana* has the seeds sunk in pits in fruit, and stems are shorter than leaves; varieties of *F. virginiana* (*ovalis, glauca, platypetala*) occur throughout Rocky Mts.

Flowering season: Starting early in May and continuing throughout summer. Begins to flower about time Audubon's warblers return in numbers, and fruit is ripe when first Sego Lilies bloom.

Where found: G, Y, T, R. Moist soil of woods, open meadows, and along streams, from lowest valleys to timberline. Our varieties extend from Alaska south in mts. to California and New Mexico; 2 species occur in Rockies. Other strawberries are found in temperate zone of Europe, Asia, N. America, and south into Andes.

Interesting facts: *Vesca* means weak. Strawberry derived its name from a practice of laying straw around the cultivated plants to keep the fruits from becoming soiled in wet weather. From a botanical point of view, a fruit is a ripened ovary, so the Strawberry fruits are the small brown seeds. The delicious, juicy part that we eat is the enlarged flower receptacle, a false "fruit."

Many wild strawberries possess a flavor and sweetness not equaled by the cultivated varieties. The wild varieties also make a more tasty jam. Indians not only utilized the berries but made a tealike beverage from the leaves. The berries are eaten by ruffed grouse, robins, turtles, small rodents, black and grizzly bears, and a host of other wildlife species.

LONG-PLUMED AVENS   *Geum triflorum* Pursh   Pl. 11

Family: Rosaceae (Rose).

Other names: Oldman's Whiskers, Prairie-smoke, and *Sieversia ciliata*.

Description: A russet-pink-colored flower whose stem bends over, causing flowers to hang downward. Sepals and bracts usually pink but may be green or purple; the 5 petals show combinations of white and pink. Plant may vary in height from 6 to 24 in. and arises from stout rootstock, which is covered with old leaf bases. Leaves are hairy, mainly basal and fernlike in appearance, pinnately compound and then dissected. As plant matures, the styles elongate ¾–1½ in., and become featherlike.

Related species: (1) *G. rossii* has yellow flowers and the styles do not elongate and become feathery; (2) *G. macrophyllum* has a few large leaflets and the styles are jointed and bent near middle. These plants common in Rockies.

Flowering season: Throughout May and until first part of July. Seeds with the feathery styles may be found until late summer. First flowers about time earliest nesting Swainson's hawks are laying eggs and American bison are calving.

Where found: Y, T, R. Medium-dry plains, hillsides, and ridges to over 8000 ft. Distributed from New York westward along northern states to B.C., then south in mts. to California and New Mexico. Most other members of this genus are found in temperate parts of N. Hemisphere, but some range throughout mts. of S. America, and 1 species is found in Africa. There are 6 species in Rocky Mt. area.

Interesting facts: *Triflorum* means 3-flowered. The seeds of this plant are wind-dispersed by means of the long feathery style, which acts as a sail. Other plants whose seeds are scattered in the same way are the anemones, species of *Clematis*, and the mountain mahoganies (*Cercocarpus*). The fernlike leaves are one of the first green things to appear as the snow recedes. Indians boiled the roots to make a beverage; it tastes very much like weak sassafras tea.

MOUNTAINSPRAY   *Holodiscus discolor* (Pursh) Maxim.   **Pl. 10**

Family: Rosaceae (Rose).

Other names: Oceanspray, Rock-spirea, Creambush.

Description: This is a much-branched shrub 3–15 ft. tall, which during the flowering season is a complete mass of tiny creamy-white flowers. Leaves are ovate, toothed, or lobed, 1–3 in. long, and dark green above but often almost white beneath.

The shrubs most commonly confused with Mountainspray are the ninebarks (*Physocarpus*). Bark of ninebarks becomes loose and peels in long strips. Mountainspray has prominently ribbed shoots and twigs; ninebarks do not.

Related species: (1) *H. dumosus* and (2) *H. glabrescens* are both much smaller than *H. discolor*. *Dumosus* is very hairy on undersurface of leaves; *glabrescens* has glands. Both are often considered as varieties of *H. discolor*.

Flowering season: June to Aug.

Where found: G, R. Streambanks and moist woods, canyons, and hills from valleys to around 7000 ft. in mts. This shrub, or varieties of it, occurs from Montana to B.C., south to California and New Mexico. There are about a half-dozen species of *Holodiscus*, all natives of w. N. America and mts. of n. S. America; 2 species occur in Rockies.

Interesting facts: *Discolor* means of different colors. This shrub is only browsed lightly by domestic animals, deer, and elk but on overutilized game ranges it crowds out better forage plants. Its small dry fruits were eaten by Indians. It is a popular ornamental for home plantings.

IVESIA   *Ivesia gordonii* (Hook.) T. & G.   Pl. 9
   Family: Rosaceae (Rose).
   Other names: Horkelia.
   Description: The yellow flowers grow in dense clusters at the ends of unbranched stems and are about ⅛ in. broad. Sepals are usually longer and hide the petals. Plant grows in dense clumps from coarse, woody, branching root crowns, with almost leafless stems 2–10 in. tall. Basal leaves are numerous, 2–8 in. long, pinnately compound, with each leaflet divided and also usually toothed, giving it the appearance of a narrow fern leaf.
   When not in fruit or flower this plant is easily confused with Long-plumed Avens (*Geum triflorum*); see Plate 11. However, the styles of latter are long and featherlike and petals pinkish or white; styles of *Ivesia* are slender and petals yellow.
   Related species: (1) *I. baileyi*, with leafy stems and white or cream petals, and (2) *I. tweedyi*, with golden-yellow petals longer than the sepals, occur only in northwestern part of Rockies.
   Flowering season: Latter part of June to first part of Aug.
   Where found: Y, T, R. Medium-dry to moist soil, often among rocks, of hillsides and ridges from around 7000 ft. to well above timberline. Can be found in high mts. from Montana to Washington, south to California and Colorado. *Ivesia* is a western American genus of about 20 species; approximately a half dozen occur in Rocky Mt. area.
   Interesting facts: *Gordonii* means plant is named for George Gordon. Most members of the Rose family have numerous stamens; *Ivesia* has only 5, the closely related *Horkelia* 10, and *Potentilla* 20 or more.

SILVERWEED   *Potentilla anserina* L.   p. 86
   Family: Rosaceae (Rose).
   Other names: Goosegrass, Cinquefoil, Fivefingers.
   Description: A perennial herb with bright yellow flowers, long creeping runners, and basal tufts of pinnately compound leaves. Leaflets toothed and silvery white beneath. In 1 variety, also silvery above. Flowers, about ½ in. broad, are solitary, on stalks 1–4 in. tall.
   Flowers of this genus are much alike, but presence of long runners readily separates Silverweed from others. All usually have 20 stamens or more.
   Related species: (1) *P. palustris* is the only red-flowered species in Rockies; (2) *P. norvegica* has a very leafy inflorescence and petals about as long as sepals; (3) *P. diversifolia* has pinnate

basal leaves not dissected or whitish beneath; (4) *P. plattensis*, though similar, has leaflets dissected into narrow divisions.

Flowering season: May, June, and July. First appears about time young mallards are hatching.

Where found: G, Y, T, R. In moist or wet, often saline, soil; along river and lake shores, in open areas from Alaska to Newfoundland, south to New Jersey, Nebraska, New Mexico, and California. Also occurs in Europe and Asia. Can be found from our lowest valleys to around 8000 ft. There are approximately 300 recognized species of this genus at present, widely distributed over north temperate zone. Some botanists have divided them into many more, as well as dividing the genus into 6 separate genera. Thirty species in Rocky Mt. area.

Interesting facts: *Anserina* means of geese. The long narrow roots taste like parsnips or sweet potatoes when boiled or roasted, and are nutritious. The larger, older plants with bigger root systems should be sought. This plant exhibits an interesting type of reproduction. At nodes or joints on the runners, roots are sent into the soil and leaves develop. When the older plant portions die the newer ones that have formed on the runners are separated and become individual plants. This growth habit protects the plant from overgrazing; hence it is

Silverweed (*Potentilla anserina* L.)

often found near livestock waterholes and along heavily grazed
streambanks after other associated plants have disappeared.

Shrubby Cinquefoil (*Potentilla fruticosa* L.)

SHRUBBY CINQUEFOIL *Potentilla fruticosa* L. **Pl. 9**
    Family: Rosaceae (Rose).
    Other names: Yellow Rose, Fivefingers.
    Description: A much-branched shrub 1–5 ft. tall, with bright
yellow flowers about ¾ in. broad. Bark is brown and shreds off
in long strips. Leaves are pinnately compound and may or may
not be evergreen, depending on locality. Leaflets 3 to 7 in
number, narrow and leathery.
    The shrub is not likely to be confused with any other plant of
the Rockies, although the novice might mistake it for Bitterbrush (*Purshia tridentata*) on first acquaintance.
    Flowering season: Latter part of June to first part of Aug.
Starts to flower when green-tailed towhees are laying.
    Where found: G, Y, T, R. Damp to wet saline soil of plains
and hills to around 9000 ft. Found from Alaska to Labrador,
south to New Jersey, Minnesota, New Mexico, and California.
Upwards of 300 species of *Potentilla*, mostly restricted to N.
Hemisphere; of 30 species in Rocky Mt. area, only this one
becomes a good-sized shrub.
    Interesting facts: *Fruticosa* means shrubby. Though not
preferring it, both domestic and wild animals browse this
plant, and because it retains its leaves during winter, it fur-

nishes nourishment for big game animals during this critical period. In overgrazed areas, this shrub is eventually eaten until severely stunted or killed. Stockmen and wildlife biologists use this as one of the indicator plants in determining range conditions. When indicator plants are overbrowsed the stockmen know that the better forage plants are generally in even more critical condition and that less desirable forage plants are invading the range. This in turn means there are more livestock on the range than it can support. In the case of game ranges, heavily browsed cinquefoils indicate an over-population of big game. The wildlife biologist may accordingly recommend a reduction through increased hunter harvest. Thus, to a trained observer the presence or condition of a plant may have far-reaching significance.

CINQUEFOIL *Potentilla gracilis* Dougl. **Pl. 11**
Ssp. *nuttallii* (Lehm.) Keck
    Family: Rosaceae (Rose).
    Other names: Fivefingers.
    Description: Many bright yellow roselike flowers about ½ in. broad borne at ends of branches. Stems are clustered together, branched at top, and attain a height of 1–2 ft. Leaves mostly

Cinquefoil (*Potentilla gracilis* Dougl. var. *pulcherrima* [Lehm.] Fern.)

basal and digitately compound, with about 7 toothed leaflets. There are many varieties of *P. gracilis;* see illus. opposite for *P. gracilis* Dougl. var. *pulcherrima* (Lehm.) Fern.

Potentillas, though easy to recognize, are extremely difficult to differentiate as to species. They are allied to the strawberries (*Fragaria*) and some species look enough like them to be confused.

Flowering season: June and July. Becomes conspicuous as flowers of Bitterbrush fade and die.

Where found: G, Y, T, R. Moist soil of meadows and open woods, and along streams from low valleys to around 8000 ft. One of our most common cinquefoils; distributed from Alaska to Alberta, south to Colorado and California. Only 30 of some 300 species of *Potentilla* occur in Rocky Mts.

Interesting facts: *Gracilis* means slender. A number of potentillas contain tannic acid and have been used medicinally as astringents. Though widely distributed, the cinquefoils have little forage value. They withstand heavy grazing and trampling and frequently are used to indicate range conditions. *P. gracilis* and some of the other species of potentillas are eaten by elk and the Rocky Mt. goat.

CHOKECHERRY *Prunus melanocarpa* (Nels.) Rydb. **Pl. 10**

   Family: Rosaceae (Rose).

   Other names: Black Chokecherry.

   Description: A large shrub or small tree up to 25 ft. tall. When in bloom, covered with long racemes of many small white flowers that later give rise to dark round fruits or cherries, each containing a single large hard stone. Fruit in diameter about ⅜ in. Leaves elliptic and 1–4 in. long, with fine teeth around edges.

   The plant most likely to be mistaken for this is the Serviceberry (*Amelanchier alnifolia*), which, definitely a shrub, is generally much smaller; flowers in short rather than long clusters, and fruit tufted on top and containing several soft seeds within.

   Related species: (1) *P. pensylvanica* (bearing flowers in umbels) and (2) *P. americana* (similar but with spiny branches and inner face of calyx lobes densely woolly) occur only in southeastern part of Rockies.

   Flowering season: May and June. Begins to flower about time Serviceberry has completed flowering and when young ravens are on the wing. In full bloom when young prairie falcons are about to fledge.

   Where found: G, Y, T, R. Moist soil along creeks in valleys and on hills and mt. sides to about 8000 ft. Can be found from North Dakota to B.C., south to California and New Mexico. There are about 100 species in the genus *Prunus*, and though mainly occurring in north temperate zone some extend into

Africa and Andes of S. America; only 3 or 4 species in Rocky Mts.

Interesting facts: *Melanocarpa* means black-fruited. Choke-cherry is edible, but when not fully ripe it puckers the mouth. The cherries are commonly gathered for jelly or wine making. Indians ate them fresh and also dried them in cakes for winter use. Members of the Lewis and Clark expedition used them when other food was scarce, and several of the Astorians grate-fully consumed them at a time when they were weak from starvation. Mountain man Hugh Glass reportedly sustained himself on wild cherries after being frightfully mauled by a grizzly bear. Many birds feed on Chokecherry. In the fall the pheasant or grouse hunter knows he is quite likely to find feeding birds among the cherry trees. The stems and leaves are eaten by mountain goats. Chokecherries are close relatives of peaches, plums, prunes, apricots, and almonds. Though the seeds are nutritious, they, like peach kernels, contain cyano-genetic poison. In spring and early summer the leaves of Chokecherry can be poisonous, especially to domestic sheep. Cases of livestock poisoning from eating wild cherry leaves are common. The leaves contain the glucoside amygdalin, which, when acted upon by the proper enzyme in the leaf or animal, produces hydrocyanic acid (HCN), also called prussic acid. The twigs and buds of Bittercherry (*P. emarginata*) serve as winter browse of deer, elk, and moose. Bears seek out the thickets when the fruits are ripe. Indians used the stem and bark to make a tea. The leaves are among the first to turn color in the fall.

BITTERBRUSH   *Purshia tridentata* (Pursh) DC.   **Pl. 9**

Family: Rosaceae (Rose).

Other names: Antelope Brush, Brittlebrush.

Description: A much-branched evergreen shrub 2–10 ft. tall, commonly growing with sagebrush and in spring densely covered with light yellow, roselike flowers. Flowers almost ½ in. broad, and quite fragrant. Leaves, numerous and small, averaging in length about ½ in., are characteristically wedge-shaped, with 3 teeth at broad outer end, and are green above but whitish beneath.

The shrub most likely confused with this is the Cliff Rose (*Cowania stansburiana*), occurring in southern part of Rocky Mt. area. The two are known to hybridize in Utah. However, leaves of Cliff Rose normally are pinnately divided instead of 3-toothed at apex.

Flowering season: May to first part of July. Flowers about time sage grouse eggs are hatching and first broods of young birds are seen.

Where found: Y, T, R. Dry soil of valleys, hills, and mts. to around 9000 ft. Found from Montana to B.C., south to California and New Mexico. Over large areas, closely associated with sagebrush. There are only 2 species of *Purshia*, and though both grow in w. U.S., only Bitterbrush occurs in Rocky Mts.

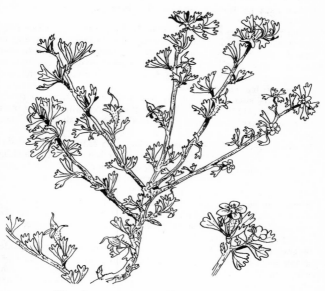

Bitterbrush (*Purshia tridentata* [Pursh] DC.)

Interesting facts: *Tridentata* means 3-toothed. Bitterbrush branches growing next to rocks, or near the soil, may be in full bloom while the rest of the plant is still in bud. This is due to the higher temperature of air caused by heat absorption and reflection from rocks or soil. The plant responds to these localized differences.

Bitterbrush is important to wildlife, being a favored browse of elk, moose, deer, antelope, mountain sheep, and livestock. On overgrazed land this shrub is severely pruned back by grazing animals. Because of this, its vigor and growth can be and are used as an indicator of range conditions. Small rodents so relish the seeds that a very high percentage of the annual crop is either eaten or cached. White-footed mice often store as much as 2 and 3 pounds of seed in a single cache. Fortunately, the plant often forms roots and new branches where old stems touch the earth, thus assuring reproduction even if all seeds are consumed. It usually does not sprout after fire, and this hazard may eliminate it over large areas.

ROSE *Rosa woodsii* Lindl. Pl. 9

Family: Rosaceae (Rose).

Other names: Wild Rose, Fendler Rose, and *R. neomexicana* and *R. arizonica*.

Description: This is a shrub 3–10 ft. tall, usually with prickly, branched stems. The pink flowers, varying from 1½ to 2½ in. broad, are composed of 5 sepals, 5 petals, and numerous stamens and pistils. Flowers commonly grow in clusters on young side branches arising from the old wood. Pinnately compound leaves are toothed.

There is such variation in roses, they hybridize so freely, and have created such divergent opinion among botanists that to separate many of them is a difficult task for the amateur.

Related species: (1) *R. gymnocarpa*, with calyx lobes and disk that fall off the "fruit," enters only northern part of Rockies; (2) *R. nutkana*, with only 1 to 3 flowers in a cluster on very short lateral branches and foliage that is glandular and resin-scented, occurs throughout Rockies.

Flowering season: Latter part of May, through June and July. Look for this rose to bloom first when Sticky Geranium (*Geranium viscosissimum*) is at its height and coloring large areas in light pink shades.

Where found: G, Y, T, R. In moist soil of draws, hillsides, along streams, and in open valleys. Found growing in the open, often forming thickets; along streams it mingles with other shrubs and trees. Occurs from valleys to about 7000 ft. Found from Saskatchewan to B.C., south to California and New Mexico. There are well over 100 species of wild roses, and an enormous number of cultivated varieties scattered over large part of the earth. Ten species occur in Rockies.

Interesting facts: *Woodsii* means named for Alphonse Wood. Many rose hips, or "fruits," can be eaten raw or made into jelly. They adhere to the plant over winter and can be picked and eaten when other fruits are unavailable. The Indians and early settlers used them as food, as do also the rural inhabitants of Europe and Asia. They are an important winter wildlife food for pheasants, grouse, and quail, and are eaten by black bears in the fall. The cultivated Multiflora Rose, widely planted by conservationists, provides food and cover for upland game. Cultivated roses are largely hybrids propagated by grafting. The petals of *R. gallica* are distilled or extracted, and the resulting oil, attar of rose, is used to make perfume and in medicine serves as an astringent and flavoring agent.

THIMBLEBERRY *Rubus parviflorus* Nutt.   **Pl. 9**
  Family: Rosaceae (Rose).
  Other names: White-flowering Raspberry, Salmonberry.
  Description: An erect shrub 2–6 ft. tall, with white flowers, shreddy brown bark, and large 5-lobed leaves almost round in outline. They are 2–8 in. broad; green and shiny above, lighter beneath. Usually there are several white flowers together, each 1–1½ in. across. These give rise to juicy, edible red berries whose appearance closely resembles the wild red raspberries but whose flavor is more insipid.

  Thimbleberry is most likely to be confused with Wild Red Raspberry (*R. idaeus*). The stiff, erect growth, lack of prickles on stem, and larger size of Thimbleberry flowers and leaves easily separate it.

  Related species: (1) *R. spectabilis*, found in n. Rockies, has reddish-purple flowers and yellow or occasionally reddish berries; (2) American Red Raspberry (*R. idaeus* L.), with red fruit, white flowers, and fine prickles on stem (see illus. below), and (3) *R. leucodermis*, with black berries, long, arching stems, and undersurface of leaves white, are both widespread in Rockies.

American Red Raspberry (*Rubus idaeus* L.)

Flowering season: May, June, and July. When this plant is flowering, the young mountain bluebirds are hatching.

Where found: G, Y, T, R. Along streams and in moist places, often in partial shade, from lowest valleys to around 8000 ft. in mts. Extends from Alaska to Ontario, south to New Mexico and California. There are hundreds of species of *Rubus* distributed throughout the world, but largely concentrated in north temperate zone; 15 species in Rocky Mt. area.

Interesting facts: *Parviflorus* means small-flowered. This berry illustrates the type known to science as a "multiple fruit." Each section of the berry develops from an ovary, and all parts adhere loosely together to form the whole fruit. The fruit structure when ripe readily separates from the cone-shaped white receptacle. This is in contrast to the Strawberry, in which the receptacle becomes juicy and enlarges, and the ovaries develop into hard seeds on the outside. Thimbleberry plants are eaten by both mule and white-tailed deer, and the berries are consumed by both black and grizzly bears.

MOUNTAIN-ASH   *Sorbus scopulina* Greene   **Pl. 10**

Family: Rosaceae (Rose).

Description: A compound-leaved shrub 3–15 ft. tall, with large, almost flat-topped clusters of small whitish flowers. Flower clusters are about 6 in. broad. Later in season they give rise to distinctive bright orange-red clusters of fruit. Large compound leaves are composed of 11 to 17 toothed leaflets that are glossy, elliptic to oblong in outline, and about 2 in. long.

Shrubs most likely to be mistaken for this are the elders (*Sambucus*), which, however, have opposite compound leaves and only 5 stamens in each flower; see Elderberry, Plate 19, and Elder, p. 183. Mountain-ash has alternate leaves and many stamens in each flower.

Related species: *S. sitchensis*, found from Alaska south to Oregon and Montana, has only 7 to 11 blunt-tipped leaflets, and the stipules are persistent.

Flowering season: Latter part of May until well into July. Berries can be gathered during fall and winter.

Where found: G, Y, T, R. Moist to wet soil of hills and mts. to around 9000 ft. Look for it in canyons, along streams and moist seepage areas. Often grows in dense thickets. Distributed from Alberta to B.C., south to California and New Mexico. There are only about a dozen species of *Sorbus*, all native to N. Hemisphere; 3 species in Rockies.

Interesting facts: *Scopulina* means of rocks. The tender twigs are eaten by domestic stock and wild game. Moose browse it heavily in winter. The fruits persist on the tree throughout the winter and are consumed by grouse, cedar waxwings, grosbeaks, and in the fall are consumed by bears. They were gathered by the Indians and though bitter were eaten fresh or dried. Peoples in distant places such as Europe, Asia, and Kamchatka collect and eat the ripe berries. In lean years the dried berries are ground into a meal. Early white settlers often made them into jellies and jams. They have a high carbohydrate content, contain considerable tannin, and are low in fat and protein. The berries are decorative and last well inside the house.

SPIREA *Spiraea splendens* Koch
Family: Rosaceae (Rose).
Other names: Bridal Wreath, Meadowsweet.
Description: A much-branched shrub 2–7 ft. tall, with dense clusters of minute pink flowers at ends of branches. Numerous stamens in each flower and, being much longer than the petals, they are quite conspicuous. Leaves oval or ovate in outline, minutely toothed, and averaging in length about 1 in.
Related species: (1) Pink Spirea (*S. douglasii* Hook.), Plate 10, occurring in northern part of Rocky Mts., is often confused with this shrub. However, sepals are soon reflexed and flowers occur in elongated, sometimes leafy, clusters; in *S. splendens* the sepals are erect and clusters of flowers usually globose. (2) The white-flowered *S. betulifolia* sometimes crosses with the pink-flowered species and produces combinations of characters.
Flowering season: Latter part of June through July. Blooms about time young long-eared owls leave nest.
Where found: G, Y, T. Moist soil of woods, along streams, and in mts. to about 8000 ft. Found from Alberta to B.C., south to California and Wyoming. Of approximately 75 species of *Spiraea* distributed over N. Hemisphere, only about a half-dozen species occur in Rockies.
Interesting facts: *Splendens* means splendid. The genus *Spiraea* has furnished many species of beautiful shrubs for ornamental plantings. Most of them, with snowy-white blossoms completely covering the bushes, are conspicuous in public parks and private gardens. Some species of *Spiraea* form dense cover and are used as roosting sites by ring-necked pheasants. The mature fruits are dry pods. Indians brewed a tea from the stem, leaves, and flowers of some species.

MILKVETCH *Astragalus alpinus* L.
Family: Leguminosae (Pea).
p. 96
Other names: Alpine Vetch, Rattleweed, Locoweed.
Description: The flowers are yellowish white and variously marked with purple. They are almost ½ in. long, appearing at first in dense racemes, but as fruit matures the stem elongates, separating pods and flowers. Elliptic pod is usually black-hairy, about ½ in. long, and hangs downward. Slender stems

may be 4–15 in. long, and erect, ascending, or prostrate. Bright green, compound leaves have 15 to 23 elliptic, blunt leaflets.

There are hundreds of species of *Astragalus* in the U.S., many in Rocky Mts. It is impossible to differentiate them here. Lack of tendrils helps to separate them from true vetches (*Vicia*). Large number of leaflets on a leaf and fact that all the stamen filaments but one are grown together and form a papery sheath around the ovary distinguish this genus from most of the others in the Pea family.

Related species: (1) *A. tegetarius* is a prostrate, mat-forming plant with purple flowers and spinulose-tipped leaflets; (2) *A. calycosus* is a small, tufted plant with small pink flowers and all-basal leaves; (3) *A. drummondii* occurs in large clumps, grows 1½–3 ft. tall, and has a dense raceme of white flowers that are pendulous; (4) *A. agrestis* is purple, the calyx not black-hairy; blooms early. These species common in Rockies.

Flowering season: June, July, and Aug.

Where found: G, Y, T, R. Moist soil of forests, wet areas along creeks, bogs, and near snowbanks. It, or its varieties, can be found from foothills to above timberline. Extends over tem-

Milkvetch (*Astragalus alpinus* L.)
Crazyweed (*Oxytropis besseyi* [Rydb.] Blank.)

perate and into arctic areas of Europe and N. America, where it comes as far south as New England in East and to New Mexico in West. There are about 1500 species of *Astragalus*, mainly in N. Hemisphere, but they also extend throughout mts. into S. America; perhaps 100 occur in Rocky Mt. area.

Interesting facts: *Alpinus* means alpine. Some species of *Astragalus* are poisonous or seleniferous; others are among the best domestic sheep feeds. Although the roots, pods, and peas of quite a few species of *Astragalus* were eaten by Indians of various tribes, it is not recommended that they be tried by the novice. The pods were eaten raw or boiled.

LOCOWEED *Astragalus purshii* Dougl. **Pl. 10**

Family: Leguminosae (Pea).

Other names: Milkvetch.

Description: This locoweed is a low-tufted grayish plant 3–8 in. tall, with racemes of dense white to cream-colored flowers almost 1 in. long. Tips of inner petals are purple. Flowering stalks and compound leaves are almost equal in length. Pods are short, thick, curved, and densely covered with long woolly hairs.

Locoweed is the most common *Astragalus* in the Rockies that has whitish flowers about 1 in. long and most, or all, of its leaves basal. There are varieties of this species that have purple flowers. *Astragalus* is closely related to the locoweeds of the genus *Oxytropis;* see Crazyweed (*O. besseyi* [Rydb.] Blank.), Plate 10 and opposite. The keel (lower petals) of *Oxytropis* is abruptly contracted into a distinct beak; keel of *Astragalus* flowers is not beaked.

Flowering season: Latter part of April to June. Look for early blooms when ground squirrels appear in spring, and starlings are selecting nesting hollows.

Where found: Y, T, R. Dry soil of plains and hills and rocky ridges in mts. to about 7000 ft. Grows from Saskatchewan to B.C., south to California and Colorado. Of 1500 species of *Astragalus* known, about 100 occur in Rocky Mts.

Interesting facts: *Purshii* means named for Frederick Pursh. A number of the plants of this genus possess an alkaloid that is poisonous to animals. Others have the ability to absorb from shale soils sufficient quantities of selenium to produce the "loco disease" in stock, especially in horses. Animals do not ordinarily eat large quantities of these plants unless other food is scarce or the range overgrazed. Once started they often acquire the habit, selecting them even when other food is available. If selenium is present in the soil, loss of stock may result. The disease is well described by the Spanish word *loco*, meaning crazy. In the early stages a horse becomes dull, listless, unsteady in gait; and may suddenly run away or jump into fences, gates, and other obstacles. In the later stages the animal loses weight rapidly, ceases to eat, and dies. The closely related locoweed *Oxytropis lamberti* is poisonous to domestic animals. In severe poisoning cases the animal becomes blind, is unable to walk, and dies in convulsive spasms. This plant is found on prairies and dry plains mainly east of the Continental Divide. Its flower stalks are longer than the leaves.

WILD LICORICE   *Glycyrrhiza lepidota* Nutt.   **Pl. 11**
  Family: Leguminosae (Pea).
  Other names: American Licorice.
  Description: A perennial herb, 1–3 ft. tall, arising from deep, creeping stems. Greenish-white flowers are about ½ in. long, and occur in dense racemes. These flower stalks arise from axils of leaves; leaves consist of 11 to 19 lance-shaped leaflets that are about 1 in. long. Mature fruit is a conspicuous brown pod, about ½ in. long, densely covered with hooked spines. Burlike pods remain on plant until late fall.
      Cocklebur (*Xanthium strumarium*) is the only plant with which this might be confused after the fruit is formed, but it has simple, heart-shaped leaves several inches broad.
  Flowering season: June through first part of Aug. Blooms about time young ruffed grouse are quail size and can fly well.
  Where found: G, Y, T, R. Cultivated ground, waste places, roadsides, prairies, gravelly river bottoms, and moist mt. draws up to around 7000 ft. Usually grows in patches, frequently in heavy clay and saline soil. Occurs from Saskatchewan to B.C., south to California and Mexico. There are about 15 species distributed over Eurasia, N. America, southern part of S. America, and Australia; this the only one in Rockies.
  Interesting facts: *Lepidota* means with small scurfy scales. Most of the licorice of commerce comes from the rootstocks of *G. glabra*, which contains glycyrrhizin, considerable sugar, and other chemicals. It is used in medicine as a mild laxative, a demulcent, and a flavoring agent to mask the taste of other drugs. It is also used in confections, root beer, and chewing tobacco. Our native wild species was chewed raw by the Indians or used as flavoring, and contains almost as many valuable properties as the plants imported from Spain or Russia, but high labor costs make its commercial use prohibitive. In the very early stage it is quite poisonous to livestock.

SWEETVETCH   *Hedysarum occidentale* Greene   **Pl. 11**
  Family: Leguminosae (Pea).
  Other names: Sweetbroom, Northern Sweetvetch.
  Description: The stems are 1–2 ft. tall and clustered on the top of a thick taproot. Flowers are reddish purple, about ¾ in. long, and form long, dense racemes at top of plant. Large leaves are pinnately compound.

Hedysarum is most commonly confused with *Astragalus*, but the two genera can easily be distinguished when pods are present. *Astragalus* pods are shaped somewhat like those of a garden pea, but the pods of *Hedysarum* are constricted between the seeds so that each section appears almost round.

Related species: (1) *H. boreale* can be distinguished by not having sections of pod winged; *H. occidentale* does. (2) *H. sulphurescens* has yellow flowers and winged pod sections.

Flowering season: Latter part of June to first part of Aug. By the time it blooms in mts., bighorn sheep have moved their lambs to the lush alpine meadows.

Where found: G, Y, T. Dry and often rocky soil of open areas, from the plains to about 8500 ft. Grows from Montana to Washington, south to Utah and Colorado. There are about 70 species of sweetvetch, most of them growing in Europe and Asia; about 5 species occur in Rocky Mts.

Interesting facts: *Occidentale* means western. The roots of this plant are nourishing, have a sweet licorice-like taste, and were eaten by the Indians. The pods are eaten by rodents to such an extent that it is often difficult to find a single pod containing mature seeds. Mountain goats are rather fond of the entire plant. The roots of *H. boreale* were gathered in early spring and again in the fall by Indians and trappers in the Northwest. In the Rocky Mts. it offers the mountain climber a tasty nibble.

LODGEPOLE LUPINE *Lupinus parviflorus* Nutt. **Pl. 11**
Family: Leguminosae (Pea).
Other names: Bluebonnet, Quakerbonnet, Wolfbean.
Description: Plants with long spikes of blue pealike flowers growing in mts. are likely to be lupines. Lodgepole Lupine has flowers generally less than ¼ in. long, and leaves palmately compound.

If the plant grows only in mts. and has flowers light blue to almost white in color and leaves composed of 5 to 11 leaflets fairly broad and widest above middle and bright green on both sides, it is probably *L. parviflorus*.

Flowering season: Latter part of June until first part of Aug. First blooms about time young ruffed grouse are learning to fly.

Where found: Y, T, R. Moist soil of pine and aspen woods, open hillsides and meadows, from the hills to around timberline. Found from South Dakota to Idaho, south to Utah and Colorado. Of approximately 200 known lupines about 50 species occur in Rocky Mts.

Interesting facts: *Parviflorus* means small-flowered. Many of the lupines are poisonous to stock during late summer and early fall. The majority of other plants that are poisonous are most harmful in spring and early summer. As the pods and seeds ripen they produce alkaloids that can be fatal if eaten in sufficient quantities. The plants are again safe for feed after the seeds are ripe. Some of the lupines are fit for human consumption, but the species are so difficult to distinguish that it is wise to refrain from eating them. Many species of mice feed on the roots and seeds. Both black and grizzly bears eat seeds, pods, and roots; elk consume the flowers and seed pods.

BLUEBONNET *Lupinus sericeus* Pursh   **Pl. 11**
   Family: Leguminosae (Pea).
   Other names: Lupine, Quakerbonnet, Wolfbean.
   Description: The attractive flowering stalks of lupines color extensive fields as well as roadside borders. Flowers of this lupine are blue or mostly blue, ⅓ in. long or slightly more, and in dense terminal racemes. Stems are diffusely branched, vary from 1 to 2 ft. in height, and are clumped together on a coarse, branching root crown. Leaves are palmately compound, with 5 to 9 narrow leaflets, which may vary in length 1–2 in.
      The palmately compound leaves, with edge of leaflets entire, distinguish lupines from other similar-appearing plants in Rocky Mt. area. Very difficult to separate the different species.
   Related species: (1) *L. laxiflorus*, with a distinct spur on upper side of calyx and the upper corners of wing petals hairy; (2) *L. pusillus*, an annual with mostly 2 seeds in a pod; and (3) *L. caespitosus*, with basal leaves about as long as flowering stalk. All widespread in Rockies.
   Flowering season: June to first part of Aug.
   Where found: Y, T. Dry to moist soil of valleys, and in mts. to around 7000 ft. This lupine and its varieties are found from Saskatchewan to Montana and Oregon, south to Arizona and New Mexico. There are perhaps 200 species of lupines, chiefly in N. and S. America, but a few occur in Mediterranean region of Old World; about 50 species in Rocky Mts.
   Interesting facts: *Sericeus* means silky. The name Lupine comes from *lupus*, a wolf, because at one time it was erroneously thought that lupines robbed the soil. Instead it is now known that bacteria in the nodules on the roots are able to take nitrogen from the air and use it in making plant food. Thus, these plants, along with other members of the Pea family (including peas, beans, clover, and alfalfa), actually enrich the soil in nitrogen. The Texas Bluebonnet (*L. subcarnosus*) is the state flower of Texas.

SWEETCLOVER *Melilotus officinalis* (L.) Lam.
   Family: Leguminosae (Pea).
   Other names: Yellow Sweetclover, Honeyclover, Yellow Melilot.
   Description: A much-branched biennial herb 2–5 ft. tall, with light yellow flowers about ¼ in. long that occur in long loose racemes. Compound leaves are trifoliate, with toothed margins.
      Sweetclover can hardly be distinguished from White Sweet-

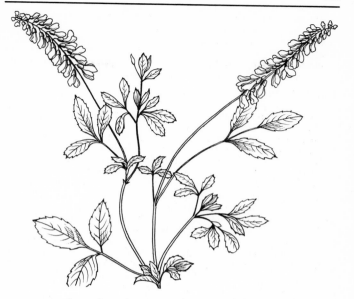

Sweetclover (*Melilotus officinalis* [L.] Lam.)

clover (*M. alba*) until the flowers open; then the respective yellow and white flowers readily separate them. The true clovers (*Trifolium*) are much smaller plants, more leafy, and flowers are arranged in heads or short, dense spikes.

Related species: *M. indica* has very small (⅛ in. long) yellow flowers and leaf margins only toothed above middle.

Flowering season: June, July, and early Aug. Blooms about same time as Fireweed and continues to be conspicuous until cool days and nights announce arrival of fall.

Where found: G, Y, T, R. Moist or fairly dry soil of fields, roadsides, and waste places up to about 8500 ft. Sweetclover was introduced from Europe, escaped cultivation, and is now naturalized and widely scattered over most of temperate N. America. There are about 20 species of *Melilotus* found in Europe, Asia, N. Africa, and N. America; only 2 species occur in Rockies.

Interesting facts: *Officinalis* means official. Sweetclover is planted for forage. It contains a chemical, coumarin, which imparts a peculiar flavor and odor to the plant. If Sweetclover is used for hay or silage and allowed to spoil, the coumarin breaks down into a toxic substance preventing the clotting of blood in animals that eat it. Affected animals may bleed to death from minor wounds because the prothrombin content of the blood is reduced to the point where the blood cannot clot. White Sweetclover is a desirable bee plant, imparting a pleasant flavor to honey. Both Sweetclover (*M. officinalis*) and White Sweetclover (*M. alba*) are favorite feed for mule deer.

FALSE LUPINE   *Thermopsis montana* Nutt.   **Pl. 11**

Family: Leguminosae (Pea).

Other names: Golden Pea, Buckbean, Mountain Thermopsis, Buffalo Pea.

Description: Attains a height of 1–4 ft., terminating in a long raceme of golden-yellow flowers, each flower being ½–¾ in. long. These plants usually occur in patches, for they spread by underground stems. Compound leaves are trifoliate, with leaflets mainly oval and 1–3 in. long. At the base, where leaf is attached to stem, are 2 large leaflike stipules.

False Lupine is easily confused with true lupines (*Lupinus*); however, the 3 leaflets, instead of 5 or more as in lupines, are fairly diagnostic. False Lupine also has all stamens distinct instead of united together as in true lupines. In the clovers (*Trifolium*), stamens are also united but flowers are in a head instead of a raceme. Most of the vetches (*Vicia*) and sweet peas (*Lathyrus*) have terminal leaflet modified into a tendril.

Related species: (1) *T. rhombifolia* is usually 1 ft. or less tall, has broad leaflets, and seed pods are curved in an approximate half circle. (2) *T. divaricarpa* has seed pods spreading out from stem; in *T. montana* they are strictly erect.

Flowering season: Latter part of April, May, and June.

Where found: Y, T, R. Damp or wet soil of plains, hills, and mts. to around 8000 ft. This plant is found from Montana to Washington, south to California and Colorado. There are about 20 species of *Thermopsis* native to Asia and N. America; 3 species occur in Rockies.

Interesting facts: *Montana* means of mountains. False Lupine can withstand drought and trampling, and is sufficiently unpalatable to game and livestock to thrive when more palatable plants on the same range are heavily overgrazed. Under such conditions it reproduces and spreads and better forage plants are crowded out, fail to spread, or may eventually be killed.

CLOVER   *Trifolium longipes* Nutt.

Family: Leguminosae (Pea).

Other names: Longstalk Clover, Trefoil.

Description: This perennial long-stalked clover grows 4–12 in. high and has flowers that form dense heads and with age hang downward. Flowers vary in color from purple to pink, or yellowish, and are about ½ in. long. The 3 leaflets, characteristic of most clovers, vary in length ⅓–2 in.

There are a number of clovers (*Trifolium*) in our area, but *T. longipes* is one of the most common. All can be distinguished from the sweetclovers (*Melilotus*), false lupines (*Thermopsis*), lupines (*Lupinus*), and lotuses (*Lotus*) by their dense heads of flowers, and from Alfalfa (*Medicago sativa*) by having straight or nearly straight pods instead of coiled ones.

Flowering season: Latter part of May, June, and July.

Clover (*Trifolium longipes* Nutt.)

Where found: Y, T, R. Wet meadows, along streams, and in mts. to about 9000 ft. This species, or varieties of it, occurs from Montana to Washington, south to California and Colorado. There are upwards of 300 species of clovers, mainly in north temperate zone, but a few are native to s. Africa and S. America. About 40 native species occur in Rocky Mts.

Interesting facts: *Longipes* means long-footed. The clovers are among our most valuable forage crops. A high-protein content makes them very nutritious. The roots of this as well as other legumes are inhabited by the bacteria (*Rhizobium*, *Azotobacter*) which fix atmospheric nitrogen into organic compounds that enrich the soil and can be used by other plants. In addition to our wild native species we grow the Red, Alsike, White, Strawberry, Crimson, Ladino, and Persian Clovers for pasture, silage, or hay. Clovers are important summer food of ruffed and sage grouse and Canada geese and when available are preferred forage of deer, elk, and black and grizzly bears. Various species of clover were eaten raw or cooked by American Indians.

BIGHEAD CLOVER   Pl. 10
Trifolium macrocephalum (Pursh) Poir.

Family: Leguminosae (Pea).

Other names: Trefoil.

Description: Huge flower head of this clover is very distinctive and conspicuous. It may be ¼ to ½ as long as entire flower stem, and is usually round or oval in outline. Individual flowers are pale yellow to pinkish and about 1 in. long. Stems are stout and 3–10 in. long.

Flowering season: Latter part of April and May. In bloom when many birds are migrating northward.

Where found: Dry, often rocky soil, usually among sagebrush or under yellow pine. Can be found in valleys and foothills from Idaho to Washington and California. There are upwards of 300 species of clovers, mainly in north temperate zone, but a few are native to s. Africa and S. America. About 40 native species occur in Rocky Mts.

Interesting facts: *Macrocephalum* means large-headed. The introduction of clovers into customary crop rotations in the 16th century revolutionized agricultural practices throughout the world. They not only furnish excellent forage but also enrich the soil in nitrogen. So great is the variety of cultivated clovers that one can be obtained that will grow well in most any agricultural area.

When seeking a "4-leaf clover," look for the Bighead Clover: it has 3 to 9 such leaflets on each leaf instead of the usual 3 of other clovers. This plant is cooked as a green in some areas.

AMERICAN VETCH   *Vicia americana* Muhl.

Family: Leguminosae (Pea).

Other names: Wild Pea.

Description: A prostrate or climbing vine with 2 to 6 bluish-purple flowers on stalks that originate from the axils of leaves. Leaves are pinnately compound, with terminal leaflets developed into tendrils that wrap around solid objects and support plant in an upright position. Stems are slender, square, and 1–4 ft. long.

Vetches (*Vicia*) and sweet peas (*Lathyrus*) are the 2 genera of leguminous plants that climb by means of tendrils, but the different species can only be distinguished by technical characters.

Related species: (1) *V. cracca* is a perennial with bluish-purple flowers all on 1 side of stem and reflexed; (2) Vetch (*V. villosa* Roth), Plate 10, an annual or biennial covered with long tangled hairs, has racemes of flowers that are also 1-sided. These species occur throughout Rockies.

Flowering season: June to early Aug. First appears about time cow moose are dropping their calves.

Where found: G, Y, T, R. Moist soil of open woods and plains, and in mts. to about 7000 ft. Distributed from New Brunswick to B.C., south to California, Texas, and Virginia. There are about 150 species of *Vicia*, some of them occurring on all continents. Perhaps 10 species occur in Rocky Mts.

Interesting facts: *Americana* means American. The tender seeds and young stems of vetches are eaten by American Indians as well as by other peoples throughout the world. White-tailed deer feed upon these plants and they are a favorite food of domestic sheep. The European bean *V. faba* is one of the most ancient of cultivated plants.

STORKSBILL   *Erodium cicutarium* (L.) L'Hér.

    Family: Geraniaceae (Geranium).

    Other names: Cranesbill, Filaree, Pinkets, Alfilaria.

    Description: A prostrate, mat-forming plant with 2 to 10 small pink flowers on upright leafless stalks, above pinnately dissected and toothed leaves. Seed pods strikingly resemble stork heads,

Storksbill (*Erodium cicutarium* [L.] L'Hér.)

with the bill generally pointing downward at an angle due to a crook at top of flower stalk. Flower has 5 petals and 5 sepals.

No other plant in Rocky Mt. area is likely to be mistaken for this when in fruit because of peculiar stork-bill shape.

Flowering season: April to Aug., if there is sufficient moisture. In full bloom when American magpies have completed nest building and are laying eggs.

Where found: Y, T. Dry plains, valleys, and foothills; also often found in moist places. Storksbill, introduced from Europe, is now established over most of U.S. There are about 60 species of *Erodium*, chiefly in Mediterranean region; only 1 in Rockies.

Interesting facts: *Cicutarium* means cicuta-like. Because Storksbill is able to adapt to a wide range of moisture conditions, it has been able to crowd out many native plants. Also, its seeds germinate in the fall, thus allowing the young plants to renew growth in early spring. This manner of growth provides both late fall and early spring forage for livestock. It is a highly nutritious food and a very important component of the California and Arizona annual range type. Other plants that have similarly been introduced and spread are the Russian Thistle, the Tumbling Mustard, wild Morning-glory, Downy Brome Grass, and *Halogeton*, poisonous to livestock. Young Storksbill plants can be eaten as greens, either cooked or raw.

STICKY GERANIUM   Pl. 10
Geranium viscosissimum Fisch. & Mey.

Family: Geraniaceae (Geranium).

Other names: Pink Geranium, Cranesbill.

Description: A common, conspicuous, pink-flowered plant 1–2 ft. tall, clumped together on a deep woody root. Flowers are about 1 in. broad, usually pink to rose-purple, with dark veins. Leaves are mostly basal, on long stalks; and 2–4 in. broad, 5- to 7-lobed, with the lobes themselves dissected. The style of the ovary elongates to about 1 in. when in fruit and resembles a crane's bill. With a little imagination one can also see resemblance to a rocket ship, the red-tipped pistils forming the exhaust tubes.

Geranium leaves look much like those of the larkspurs (*Delphinium*) and monkshoods (*Aconitum*), but are distinguished by gland-tipped hairs. Flower is symmetrical; these other flowers are not, having sepals modified into either a distinct spur or a hood.

Related species: (1) *G. richardsonii* (very similar plant but with white flowers) and (2) *G. carolinianum* (annual plant with pink flowers ½ in. broad or less) occur throughout Rockies.

Flowering season: May, June, and July, reaching peak of flowering when the tall larkspurs first bloom and young mountain bluebirds have left their nests and are on the wing.

Where found: G, Y, T. Plentiful in medium-dry to moist or

Sticky Geranium (*Geranium viscosissimum* Fisch. & Mey.)

even wet soil of open woods, roadsides, creek banks, and meadows. Ranges from valleys to 9000 ft. in mts.; from Alberta to B.C., south to California and Colorado. There are approximately 200 species of *Geranium* well distributed over the earth in both temperate zones; 9 species occur in Rockies.

Interesting facts: *Viscosissimum* means sticky. Our household geraniums planted in window boxes, pots, and gardens, belong to the same family but to a different but equally large genus, *Pelargonium*. Between the two groups they furnish many shades of colorful garden flowers, and various perfumes. Sticky Geranium is a valuable forage plant, abundant over much of the western range land. It constitutes a major food item for elk and deer during spring and summer and also is consumed by black bears and probably grizzlies at this time. Moose will select the flowers and upper leaves in preference to other vegetation.

BLUEFLAX *Linum lewisii* Pursh   **Pl. 14**
  Family: Linaceae (Flax).
  Other names: Lewis Flax, Prairie Flax.
  Description: The sky-blue saucer-shaped flax flowers are borne on stems so slender that they continually sway, even when

there is no apparent breeze. Flowers are ½–1 in. across when fully opened and the flower stalks bend downward. Petals drop off after 2 or 3 days. Occasionally a flower is white instead of blue. Several stems (8–24 in. tall) arise from a woody crown. Leaves numerous, very narrow, ½–1 in. long, and almost cover stem.

The plant most often confused with this is the Harebell (*Campanula rotundifolia*), but its 5 petals are united, forming a bell (see Plate 19); 5 petals of Blueflax are entirely separate. Common cultivated flax looks like this one but is an annual and this is a perennial.

Related species: (1) *L. kingii*, seldom much over 1 ft. tall, has yellow flowers with distinct styles; widespread in Rockies. (2) *L. rigidum* is similar but larger and styles are united except at top; occurs from Canada to Texas east of Continental Divide.

Flowering season: June, July, and first part of Aug.

Where found: G, Y, T, R. These plants favor dry plains, hills, and open ridges, often among sagebrush. Blueflax grows from lowest valleys to around 8000 ft. and is distributed from Alaska to Saskatchewan, south to California and Mexico. About 100 species are found in subtropic and north temperate zones; 5 species occur in Rockies.

Interesting facts: *Lewisii* means named for Captain Meriwether Lewis. If you question your identification of this plant, try twisting one of the stems. It should behave like a piece of string and not readily break. The long tough fibers in the stem are quite characteristic. Cultivated flax also has similar fibers, from which linen thread and cloth are made. Much of the wrapping around Egyptian mummies was made from flax. The stems of numerous wild plants contain fibers that the Indians used for making cordage, varying from ropes to fishing lines. A few other western plants utilized in this way are the nettle, Indian hemp, milkweed, yucca, spruce, and tamarack. Linseed oil, obtained from flax seed, is used in paints, varnishes, linoleum, oilcloth, and printer's ink. In medicine it serves as a laxative, an applicant for burns and scalds, and a poultice. When eaten, Blueflax causes drowsiness in livestock.

LEAFY SPURGE   *Euphorbia esula* L.   **Pl. 15**

Family: Euphorbiaceae (Spurge).

Other names: Leafy Euphorbia, Wolfs-milk, Tithymal.

Description: This grows in dense patches attaining a height of 1–3 ft., the stems branched and covered with numerous narrow leaves. Near the top are many umbels of minute, inconspicuous, imperfect flowers enclosed in a broad, calyx-like, bell-shaped whorl of bracts often mistaken for a yellowish-green flower.

Leafy Spurge can be distinguished from any other *Euphorbia* by its size and numerous leafy branches. May be mistaken for Butter-and-Eggs (*Linaria vulgaris* Hill), Plate 18, prior to the

Leafy Spurge (*Euphorbia esula* L.)

appearance of the large snapdragon-like flowers on this latter plant. However, Leafy Spurge has a milky juice and *Linaria* does not.

Related species: (1) The garden escapee *E. cyparissias* seldom grows much over 1 ft. tall and stems are densely covered with very narrow leaves; (2) *E. serpyllifolia* is a fine-stemmed, prostrate annual of circular growth.

Flowering season: Appears to flower throughout summer, for involucres surrounding the flowers develop in May and persist throughout Aug. after true flowers have gone and seeds developed.

Where found: Introduced from Europe, it has now become spottily established over much of temperate N. America. Habit of spreading by underground stems as well as seeds makes it a noxious weed. Frequents moist roadsides, cultivated fields, and pastures. There are about 1600 species of *Euphorbia*, mainly of the tropics and dry, hot areas. In desert environment, many resemble cactus plants; can readily be distinguished from cacti by their milky juice. Fourteen species occur in Rockies.

Interesting facts: *Esula* means acrid, sharp. Most of the Spurge family have a milky, acrid juice (latex). In the rubber tree this latex is made into the rubber of commerce. Many members of this family are used as ornamentals (poinsettia), some as drugs (caster-oil bean), some as food (tapioca roots), and many are poisonous. Leafy Spurge is among this latter group, since it may irritate the skin and cause inflammation and blisters. It can even result in loss of hair to animals coming in frequent contact with it. If eaten in quantity, it causes death. Honey derived from the flowers of some spurges is mildly poisonous. Leafy Spurge is difficult to control with herbicides.

POISON-IVY　　*Rhus radicans* L.

　Family: Anacardiaceae (Sumac).

　Other names: Poison-oak and *Toxicodendron radicans*.

　Description: An erect, strict-growing shrub, 2–6 ft. tall, or in e. America also a climbing vine. Shiny leaves are composed of 3 leaflets, each ovate in outline, 2–4 in. broad and borne near end of stems. The small, greenish-white flowers occur in dense clusters in leaf axils. Fruit is a whitish drupe about ⅜ in. broad. These often identify plant when leaves have fallen. In autumn, leaves vary in color from dark and light green to brilliant shades of red.

Poison-ivy (*Rhus radicans* L.)

The plant most often confused with this is the Virginia Creeper (*Parthenocissus quinquefolia*), which has 5 leaflets on each leaf instead of 3.

Related species: (1) Poison-oak (*R. diversiloba*) occurs along Pacific Coast area and has oakleaf-shaped leaflets; (2) Poison Sumac (*R. glabra*), found east of the Mississippi River, is a shrub with large compound leaves, each with 9 or more long leaflets; (3) Squawbush (*R. trilobata* Nutt.), Plate 13, has 3 leaflets to a leaf and these are broad at outer end.

Flowering season: May and June. Will be in bloom when steelhead are at peak of their spring run.

Where found: Y, T, R. Moist creek banks and rocky crevices in woods, plains, valleys, and foothills. This plant has been divided into several species and varieties by certain authors, but some form of it is found in most areas of s. Canada, U.S., and Mexico; 3 species occur in Rockies.

Interesting facts: *Radicans* means rooting. To most people this shrub is poisonous to touch. Individuals vary in their susceptibility to it. The toxic oil (urushiol) is slightly volatile and produced in all parts of the plant. If even minute quantities come in contact with the skin it generally produces inflammation, swelling, and blisters. Unless aware of your degree of susceptibility, do not touch the plant and beware of burning it in a fire. The "smoke" can cause severe eye inflammation and even blindness. If you are exposed to it, repeated washings with warm water and laundry soap will often remove the oil. Applications (before or after exposure) of 5 per cent ferric chloride dissolved in equal parts of alcohol and water usually prevent the irritating effects. In an emergency, the tannin from boiled tea leaves will bring relief. Birds eat the fruits.

The Sumac family, to which Poison-ivy belongs, contains many plants with poisonous or caustic juices. The effects of Poison Sumac and Poison-oak on humans are similar to those of Poison-ivy. The fruits of some other species of *Rhus*, however, such as Squawbush, are edible and used to make refreshing beverages. The Cashew nut of Cent. and S. America is deadly poisonous if eaten raw, but roasting destroys the toxic hydrogen cyanide.

MOUNTAIN-LOVER *Pachistima myrsinites* (Pursh) Raf. p. 112
Family: Celastraceae (Staff-tree).
Other names: Oregon Boxwood, Myrtle Boxleaf, Mountain-hedge.
Description: An evergreen shrub with the appearance of a loosely branched boxwood; grows to a height of 8–30 in. Often occurs in dense patches under trees. Leaves thick, numerous, opposite, oval, and ½–1 in. long, with edges of upper half slightly toothed. Flowers small, numerous, in clusters in leaf angles, and brownish to yellowish red in color. They are not

Mountain-lover (*Pachistima myrsinites* [Pursh] Raf.)

conspicuous, but leaves are attractive both in summer and winter.

It is not likely to be confused with other plants, and no other species of *Pachistima* occur in Rockies.

Flowering season: May and June. Blooms soon after aspen leaves appear and when elk and mule deer are moving from winter ranges to high country.

Where found: G, Y, T, R. Rich, moist soil of hills and mts., mainly under open stands of aspen and Lodgepole Pine. Growing from foothills to around 8000 ft., it is found from Alberta to B.C., south to California and New Mexico. There are only 2 species in this genus, 1 in West, the other occurring in East.

Interesting facts: *Myrsinites* means myrtle-like. This shrub is often gathered for winter decorations because the rich green-colored leaves readily withstand drying. It provides winter forage for elk and mule and white-tailed deer and is sufficiently palatable to be eaten the year round. Pink-sided juncos nest under its shade and protection.

SNOWBRUSH   *Ceanothus velutinus* Dougl.

    Family: Rhamnaceae (Buckthorn).

    Other names: Mountain-laurel, Deerbrush, Tobacco-brush, Sticky-laurel, Soapbloom.

    Description: A bright glossy-green bush with large clumps of small white flowers that look like patches of new-fallen snow.

Flowers (composed of 5 sepals, 5 petals, and 5 stamens) are in large clusters in leaf angles. An erect or usually an ascending brushy shrub, 3–8 ft. tall, characteristically growing in dense patches. Leaves are evergreen, thick, finely toothed around edges, oval, 1–2 in. broad, dark green and often sticky above, but very light-colored beneath.

When not in flower or fruit, Snowbrush can be confused with chokecherries (*Prunus*). However, its bark is grayish, or dull green, and that of chokecherries is often brownish red and shiny. Entire plant is pleasantly aromatic.

Related species: (1) *C. fendleri* is a thorny shrub occurring in s. Rockies. (2) *C. sanguineus* has thin deciduous leaves; current twig growth is green and older twigs and stems are generally reddish; occurs in w. Rockies.

Flowering season: Look for this flower when clouds of Lodgepole Pine pollen first appear.

Where found: G, Y, T, R. Moist soil of hills and mts. to 8500 ft. Often occurs in draws and on open face of hills, becoming rapidly established on burned-over mt. slopes. Distributed from South Dakota to B.C., south to California and Colorado. *Ceanothus* is an American genus of about 60 species, most of which grow in California; 6 occur in Rocky Mts.

Interesting facts: *Velutinus* means velvety. Snowbrush is

Snowbrush (*Ceanothus velutinus* Dougl.)

browsed by elk, deer, and moose because of its palatable twigs and evergreen leaves. In winter and early spring it may form a considerable portion of their diet. Overbrowsing on this shrub is an indication of too many animals in the wintering area. During the hunting season deer often seek shelter and comparative safety in dense patches of Snowbrush. It is difficult, at times almost impossible, to stalk or surprise a deer hiding in such a retreat. The weary hiker who has fought his way up a hillside of dense Snowbrush on a hot day will forever remember it. Snow depresses the bushes so that they have a permanent downhill bend. One can slide down over them, but only with difficulty can they be negotiated uphill. Redstem Ceanothus (*C. sanguineus*) is also an excellent winter browse for deer and elk.

Many species of *Ceanothus* contain saponin, a poisonous glucoside. Found in the flowers and fruits, it gives them soaplike qualities. The Indians and early settlers used the flowers as a substitute for soap; hence the common name Soapbloom. Poison from the flowers appears to have no ill effect in the digestive tracts of game animals and livestock, since it must enter the bloodstream direct to take effect. Some species of *Ceanothus* are nitrogen-fixers.

MOUNTAIN HOLLYHOCK   Pl. 12
Iliamna rivularis (Dougl.) Greene

Family: Malvaceae (Mallow).

Other names: Maplemallow, Globemallow, and *Sphaeralcea rivularis*.

Description: When you see pinkish-white to rose-purple flowers in dense spikes blooming on a plant that though smaller looks like the garden Hollyhock, you have probably found the Mountain Hollyhock. A perennial herb growing in large coarse clumps 3–6 ft. tall. Leaves are maple-like, 2–6 in. broad, toothed, and 3- to 7-lobed. Flowers are 1–2 in. broad and start blooming at bottom of the spikes. Sepals less than 1 cm.

Other members of the Mallow family might be confused with this one. However, any approaching size of smallest of the mountain hollyhocks have lobed leaves cut almost to midrib.

Related species: *I. longisepala* has sepals 1 cm. long or longer.

Flowering season: June, July, and first part of Aug. Young Cooper's hawks are hatching when this plant begins to bloom.

Where found: G, Y, T, R. Rich, moist soil, along streams, in canyons, on roadsides, and in open areas. Grows from lower foothills to almost 9000 ft., and is distributed from Alberta to B.C., south to Nevada and Colorado. There are about 6 more species in this genus, most of which are found in w. N. America; 3 occur in Rocky Mt. area.

Interesting facts: *Rivularis* means of brooksides. Ripe fruit of this plant, as well as that of most other members of the

Mallow family, breaks into sections somewhat like an orange. Each section may contain 1 to several seeds. Mountain Hollyhock makes an attractive garden plant and can be readily established by collecting and planting the seeds. The stems of some hollyhocks were chewed as gum by the Indians. Tiny hairs on the ripe fruit are irritating to the skin.

SCARLET FALSEMALLOW
Pl. 12
Sphaeralcea coccinea (Pursh) Rydb.
Family: Malvaceae (Mallow).
Other names: Scarlet Globemallow.
Description: This plant exhibits a cluster of tomato-colored, hollyhock-like flowers about ½ in. broad and borne at top of stems only 4–12 in. tall. Stems are tufted and arise from a woody taproot. Leaves, grayish green in color, are 3- to 5-parted or cleft almost to base.

Members of the Mallow family are difficult to separate. However, members of this genus are characterized by having starlike branched hairs on the fruit. Scarlet Falsemallow is one of the smallest mallows growing in Rocky Mts.
Related species: (1) *S. leptophylla*, with silvery leaves (upper ones entire), occurs in s. Rockies; (2) *S. munroana*, with leaves about as broad as long and coarsely toothed, is found in n. and w. Rockies.
Flowering season: May to first part of July.
Where found: Y. Dry soil of plains, valleys, and foothills, primarily in e. Rockies. Look for it on roadsides. Found from Alberta to e. Idaho, south to Arizona and Mexico. There are about 50 species of *Sphaeralcea* located in drier areas of N. and S. America, Africa, and Australia; about a half dozen occur in Rocky Mts.
Interesting facts: *Coccinea* means scarlet. The Mallow family has a distinctive flower, for the numerous stamens cohere, forming a tube around the pistil. This tube is usually fused to the lower part of the 5 petals. Cotton, hollyhocks, mallows, okra, and many garden flowers belong to this family. Some members of this genus are readily eaten by mule deer and mountain sheep.

GOATWEED   *Hypericum perforatum* L.
Family: Hypericaceae (St. Johnswort).
Other names: St. Johnswort, Klamathweed.
Description: Flowers are about ¾ in. broad, with numerous stamens extending up beyond other flower parts, and are borne in clusters at end of opposite branches. Grows rather stiffly erect and 1–5 ft. tall, arising from a woody, branched rootstock. Leaves are opposite, 1 in. or less long, oblong, and exhibit either colorless or black spots on their surfaces.

There is no other genus of plants in the Rockies likely to be confused with *Hypericum*, but the different species are difficult to distinguish.

Related species: (1) St. Johnswort (*H. formosum* HBK.), Plate 12 — one of our native species conspicuous in mt. areas from 8000 to 10,000 ft. — has a loose, elongated inflorescence instead of the dense flat-topped inflorescence of Goatweed; (2) *H. majus* is an annual whose petals are about as long as sepals. Both plants common throughout Rockies.

Flowering season: June to Sept.

Where found: Moist to fairly dry soil in pastures, roadsides, waste places, and fields from lowest areas to around 7000 ft. This pernicious weed, introduced from Europe, is now scattered and is still spreading over much of Canada and U.S. There are about 300 species of *Hypericum*, occurring over most of the earth but concentrated in subtropics; only about a half dozen occur in Rocky Mts.

Interesting facts: *Perforatum* means with holes. When noxious weeds as well as insects have reached our country from foreign shores, we have in some cases been able to control them by securing some of the native parasites that held them in check at home. A beetle (*Chrysolina gemellata*) that feeds on Goatweed in Europe was brought to America. After it was determined that it would not feed on our crop plants, small colonies of this insect were planted on clumps of Goatweed and are now helping to control the undesirable weed. This principle of biological control is being successfully applied to the alfalfa weevil, and to the control of the European corn borer.

White-skinned animals when feeding on the leaves of Goatweed develop scabby sores and a skin itch. This is a phototoxic response, and is so specific that black and white animals develop sores only on the white parts of the skin.

VIOLET   *Viola adunca* Sm.   **Pl. 12**

     Family: Violaceae (Violet).

     Other names: Purple Violet, Blue Violet.

     Description: Violets look like miniature pansies. This one is blue to violet in color, ¼–½ in. long, with lower petal developed backward from the base, forming a spur or sac about half as long as flower. Plant appears to have no stem when it starts flowering, but before season is over the stem may be as long as 8 in. Leaves are ovate and ¾–1½ in. long.

     Related species: (1) *V. nephrophylla* is a purple violet without stems, the leaves arising directly from the root crown. (2) Yellow Violet (*V. nuttallii* Pursh), Plate 12, has bright yellow flowers and lance-shaped leaves. Some of the violets can be separated on flower color (yellow, bronze, mottled, etc.), and on shape of leaves. (3) *V. praemorsa* has simple long-stemmed leaves oval or elliptic in shape; flowers are yellow with outer surface of upper petal often bronze-colored, and entire plant more or less pubescent.

Flowering season: May, June, and July. When plant in full bloom, crows are incubating, wood ducks beginning to nest.

Where found: G, Y, T, R. Moist to wet soil, by streams, springs, and boggy areas, often in shade. Found over most of temperate N. America. There are probably more than 300 species of violets distributed over most of the earth; only 25–30 in Rockies.

Interesting facts: *Adunca* means hooked. The name Violet is misleading since the various species belonging to the genus *Viola* range from white, blue, violet, and yellow to flowers exhibiting various combinations of these colors.

The first flowers to bloom on a violet plant have petals, and are the showy blossoms familiar to most; but they seldom bear seeds. The flowers produced later in the season usually lack petals, are greenish, are borne next to or under the ground, and are seldom seen. They do not open, so are self-fertilized and bear the seeds. Leaves of the yellow Pansy Violet (*V. pedunculata*) were eaten as greens by California Indians. Another violet, *V. esculenta* of e. N. America, has earned the name Wild Okra because of its use in making soups. Probably most of the "blue" violets can be used in this way.

TEN-PETALED BLAZINGSTAR   p. 118
Mentzelia decapetala (Pursh) U. & G.

Family: Loasaceae (Loasa).

Other names: Stickleaf, Eveningstar, Sandlily, Moonflower.

Description: As its name implies, this plant has 10 or more petals composing the large, terminal, white, or very pale yellow blossoms. These are 2–4 in. broad when fully expanded and there are about 200 stamens in each flower, the outer filaments broadened and petal-like. This coarse, usually 1-stemmed plant, 1–4 ft. tall, has lance-shaped leaves, 2–6 in. long, deeply cut around edges. Entire plant covered with short barbed hairs that catch on clothing; hence the name Stickleaf.

This plant can be distinguished from other members of the Loasa family by the large size and color of the flowers that have 10 petals instead of 5 as in most other species.

Related species: *M. albicaulis*, a small annual with shiny white stems, is distributed throughout Rockies.

Flowering season: July, Aug., and Sept.

Where found: Y. Dry soil of plains, valleys, and foothills from Alberta to Idaho, south to Oklahoma and Mexico. Grows in open areas where soil is rocky, sandy, or has been disturbed. Frequently seen along roadsides, *Mentzelia* is an American genus of about 60 species, most abundant in w. N. America; about a dozen species occur in Rockies.

Interesting facts: *Decapetala* means 10-petaled. This flower opens at night and closes during the day. Cool air and lack of

Ten-petaled Blazingstar (*Mentzelia decapetala* [Pursh] U. & G.)

light cause the inside of the petals to grow faster than the outside; thus the petals bend outward and the flower opens. Light and warmth cause the outside of the petals to grow faster, and so the flower closes. This alternate opening and closing of flowers occurs only while the petals are growing, ceasing when they have matured.

BLAZINGSTAR   *Mentzelia laevicaulis* (Dougl.) T. & G.   **Pl. 11**
   Family: Loasaceae (Loasa).
   Other names: Stickleaf, Sandlily, Eveningstar.
   Description: The 5 long petals of Blazingstar, lemon-yellow in color, open only at night, then close in the morning. Fully expanded flower is 2–4 in. wide. The plant, a coarse, branching perennial, 1–3 ft. tall and almost as broad, has leaves that often stick to clothing because their surface is covered with barbed hairs. Leaves lance-shaped, deeply pinnately cleft, and 2–7 in. long; alternate on stem but often opposite on flowering branches.
   This plant may be confused with others of the same family, but color, large size of flower, and fact that it is a perennial separate it from most of them. Perennials generally have deeper and more extensive root systems than annuals, and remains of previous year's stems and leaf bases are usually evident.

Flowering season: Latter part of June to first part of Aug. Look for it when Sego Lily is in bloom.

Where found: Y, T. Dry, gravelly, or sandy soil of plains and foothills to about 6000 ft. Watch for it along roadsides, road-cuts, and where soil has been disturbed. Found from Montana to Washington, south to California, Nevada, and Utah. There are about 60 species in this genus, located in N. and S. America; about 12 in Rockies.

Interesting facts: *Laevicaulis* means small-stemmed. The oily seeds of the White-stem Blazingstar (*M. albicaulis*) are parched and then ground into meal by the Indians. This species occurs in the dry plains and hills of the Rocky Mt. area.

PLAINS CACTUS   *Opuntia polyacantha* Haw.   Pl. 12

Family: Cactaceae (Cactus).

Other names: The name prickly pear is applied to cactus plants with flat jointed stems such as this one; those with round jointed stems are called chollas.

Description: The large waxy yellow blossoms of prickly pear add a special lush spring beauty to the dry areas where they grow. These plants are succulent, fleshy-stemmed perennials without leaves, or with the leaves small and soon falling off. Stems composed of 1 to several flattened, oval joints, each 2–5 in. long and covered with clumps of long barbed spines and numerous fine bristles.

The various species of *Opuntia* are difficult to separate but the genus *Opuntia* can be distinguished from other members of the Cactus family by the presence of jointed stems and barbed spines that arise from bristly cushions.

Related species: (1) *O. fragilis* (with elongated, almost round stems) and (2) Cactus (*O. rhodantha* Schum.), Plate 12 (with deep orange-pink to red flowers and only 3 to 4 stout spines in a cluster), are also common in Rockies.

Flowering season: May, June, and early July. Blooms early when spring rains are still occasional and snow water has not left the surface soil. In full bloom when young burrowing owls leave nest.

Where found: Y, T, R. More than 250 species of *Opuntia* distributed from B.C. to tip of S. America. Cactus family contains about 120 genera and around 1200 species, all native to the Americas; reach their greatest development in Mexico, but have been introduced and thoroughly established in Australia, and are cultivated as ornamentals in various parts of the world. Seven species in Rockies. Found in driest, hottest localities from lowest areas to around 6000 ft. This species distributed from Alberta to B.C., south to Arizona and Texas.

Interesting facts: *Polyacantha* means many-spined. Cacti are adapted to withstand periods of drought. They drop their leaves to prevent loss of water through transpiration; develop tissue for storing water when the supply is plentiful, and the plant itself is coated with a dense layer of wax to prevent the evaporation of stored water.

The fruits of many opuntias are not only edible but quite tasty eaten either raw or cooked. Some make excellent jellies or candy. If fruits are eaten raw, care should be taken to remove the clumps of spines by peeling away the outer rind. A bitter juice can be extracted from the stems of many opuntias that in an emergency can be used as a source of water. None are known to be poisonous.

CLARKIA　*Clarkia pulchella* Pursh　　　　　　　　**Pl. 12**
　　Family: Onagraceae (Evening Primrose).
　　Other names: Pink-fairies, Deerhorn, Ragged-robin.
　　Description: This attractive annual has clusters of deep rose-lavender blossoms ½–1 in. broad that superficially resemble a cluster of miniature oak leaves. Petals are 3-lobed, and borne on top of the elongated ovary. Stigma has 4 broad, generally white lobes. Plant varies in height from 6 to 20 in., with narrow leaves 1–3 in. long.

　　Clarkia is easily confused with Fireweed (*Epilobium angustifolium*) but is smaller and more slender. Seeds of Fireweed possess tufts of silky hairs, and each flower is borne on a distinct stalk. Clarkia has neither of these characteristics.
　　Related species: *C. rhomboidea*, a more slender and strict-growing plant, has rose-purple unlobed petals about ¼ in. long.
　　Flowering season: Latter part of May to July. In full bloom when fledgling prairie falcons are learning to fly.
　　Where found: Moderately dry sites, often where the soil is disturbed, from the valleys and foothills to around 6000 ft. Found from B.C. south to s. Oregon and east to South Dakota. Of 7 species of *Clarkia* — all of w. N. America — only 2 occur in Rocky Mts.
　　Interesting facts: *Pulchella* means beautiful. The genus *Clarkia* was named after Captain William Clark of the Lewis and Clark expedition. These explorers first collected it along the Clearwater River in Idaho on their return trip to the East after successfully exploring the Northwest country and reaching the Pacific Ocean via the Clearwater and Columbia Rivers. During a favorable season it will flower so profusely that entire hillsides are given a pinkish cast.

FIREWEED　*Epilobium angustifolium* L.　　　　　　　**Pl. 13**
　　Family: Onagraceae (Evening Primrose).
　　Other names: Great Willow-herb, Blooming-sally, Willowweed.
　　Description: With bright pink or lilac-purple blossoms, measuring almost 1 in. across, this is one of the most attractive plants of the mt. area. The 4-petaled flowers form an elongated raceme,

the lower flowers blooming first, the upper later. As a result, plant may have long seed pods, above these open flowers, with tip of stem still in bud. Stems mostly unbranched, 1–7 ft. tall and covered with many lance-shaped leaves 2–6 in. long. Frequently grows in large patches.

Plants most likely to be confused with this are other members of the Evening Primrose family. However, the large size of this plant is usually quite distinctive.

Related species: (1) Broad-leaved Fireweed (*E. latifolium* L.), Plate 13, looks like a miniature Fireweed; has smooth, fleshy leaves and is found in moist sites in arctic-alpine zone. (2) *E. paniculatum* is a much-branched annual growing on dry flats; epidermis of stem shreds off, and petals are about ⅛ in. long. (3) *E. suffruticosum* is semiwoody at base, arises from spreading underground rootstocks, and has yellow petals. (4) *E. adenocaulon*, found in moist to wet soil, is 1–3 ft. tall, much-branched above, and has small pink to white flowers. All are common in Rockies.

Flowering season: June, July, and Aug. Young bald eagles are making their first flights from nest when this flower begins to bloom. At high altitudes may still be blooming when Sept. elk-hunting season opens.

Where found: G, Y, T, R. Moist, rich soil, in open woods, prairies, hills, and especially along streams, in damp places, and on disturbed ground. Occurs from lowest valleys to as high as trees will grow on mts. and found over all but eastern portion of N. America, and in Europe and Asia as well. Perhaps 100 species of *Epilobium* are scattered over most of the earth, except in tropics; 25 species occur in Rockies.

Interesting facts: *Angustifolium* means narrow-leaved. The numerous long pods produce a multitude of minute seeds, each tufted with long silky hairs that act as parachutes for distributing them by wind. When the soil is disturbed, as by forest fire or cultivation, this plant invades, becomes established, helps cover the scar. It is called Fireweed because of this and the flower's resemblance to a flame. The young leaves and shoots are edible and can be boiled as a potherb. Fireweed is also a very valuable range forage plant, eaten by both livestock and game species such as deer and elk. It is a favorite forage of grizzly bears.

EVENING PRIMROSE   *Oenothera caespitosa* Nutt.   **Pl. 12**
Family: Onagraceae (Evening Primrose).
Other names: Sandlily, Rockrose, Morning Primrose, Gumbo Primrose.
Description: When you see a large white flower close against the ground, 2–4 in. broad, composed of 4 petals that turn pink to red as they mature, you may have found the Evening Primrose. This plant does not have a stem; however, calyx tube extending

Primrose
(*Oenothera heterantha* Nutt.)

from petals to ovary may be 2–4 in. long and at first glance be
mistaken for a stem. Leaves, clustered about root crown, are
pinnately cleft, 2–6 in. long, and their stems are winged r
base. Flowers open at night, remaining open during day as w

There are several evening primroses that could be confus
with this one, but lack of a stem, together with the large wh
flowers that change to pink or red, is quite characteristic
Varieties of this plant occur which are difficult to separate.
Related species: (1) *O. scapoidea*, a small annual with leaves
mainly basal, has small yellow flowers in racemes. (2) *O. flav*
a perennial from a fleshy taproot, has leaves that are all bas
and form a rosette; yellow petals are about ⅔ in. long, ag
to purplish. (3) Primrose (*O. heterantha* Nutt.) is similar, wit
yellow petals not aging to purplish; see Plate 13 and illus. above
(4) *O. pallida*, a perennial from underground spreading roo:
stocks with white stems, becomes 1–2 ft. tall; petals are whit
and about 1 in. long. These plants all common in Rockies.
Flowering season: Latter part of May, June, and July. Look
for it about time Shrubby Cinquefoil first blooms.
Where found: Y, T, R. Dry soil of stony slopes, steep areas
(such as roadbeds where soil is slipping), sandy places, and on

ridges. This plant and its varieties occur from plains and valleys to about 8000 ft., and from Saskatchewan to Washington, south to California and New Mexico. Botanists now recognize upwards of 200 species of *Oenothera*, mainly of temperate N. and S. America; we have 25 in Rockies.

Interesting facts: *Caespitosa* means in tufts. About the turn of the last century, Hugo De Vries, a Dutch botanist, imported several species of evening primroses and grew them in his garden. Eventually, from the seeds of these plants he secured a number of new types, and from this work he formulated the theory of evolution by mutation. The Evening Primrose is eaten by white-tailed deer. Birds and small rodents consume the seeds.

YELLOW EVENING PRIMROSE *Oenothera rydbergii* House
Family: Onagraceae (Evening Primrose).
Other names: *O. strigosa.*
Description: A coarse, stiffly erect plant, 1–4 ft. tall, with delicate yellow blossoms ½–1 in. wide that open in evening and close when sun rises. The 4 petals are at top of calyx tube, and flowers are about 1 in. broad. Ovaries of flowers are in axils of

Yellow Evening Primrose (*Oenothera rydbergii* House)

upper leaves; calyx forms a tube 1–2 in. from top of each ovary.

This plant is most likely to be confused with *O. hookeri*, but flowers of latter are about twice the size of flowers of this one. **Flowering season:** July and Aug. In bloom about time young sparrow hawks and goshawks are leaving their nests. **Where found:** Y, T. Moderately dry to moist soil in open areas, along roadsides, fences, and in disturbed soil, from the plains to about 7500 ft. Distributed from Minnesota and Kansas west to Washington and Oregon; 25 species occur in Rockies. **Interesting facts:** *Rydbergii* means named for Per Axel Rydberg. The seeds of several species of *Oenothera* were eaten by the Indians, and an eastern species (*O. biennis*) was cultivated for its edible roots, which are tasty and nutritious when boiled.

WATER-HEMLOCK   *Cicuta douglasii* (DC.) C. & R.
  Family: Umbelliferae (Parsley).
  Other names: Poison-hemlock, Cowbane.
  Description: A stout herb 2–7 ft. tall, with compound umbels of small white flowers. Leaves are 1 to 3 pinnately compound and may vary in length 4–16 in., with saw-toothed leaflets.

Water-hemlock (*Cicuta douglasii* [DC.] C. & R.)

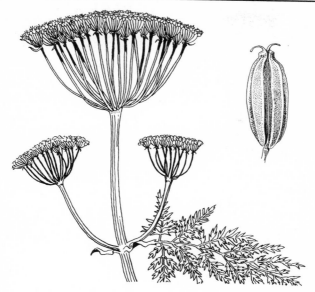

Loveroot (*Ligusticum filicinum* Wats.)

Surest identifying characteristic is the leaf venation. Veins terminate at notches rather than at tips of teeth on leaf margins.

This plant has white flowers in compound umbels without conspicuous bractlets at base of umbel; fruit with longitudinal corky ridges; leaves large, compound, and scattered along stout stem. Plant grows from thickened tubers. If base of stem just above root is cut lengthwise, many transverse chambers divided by pithy walls will be seen. This will not be found in other members of family.

Poison-hemlock (*Conium maculatum*) can quite easily be confused with Water-hemlock and with Loveroot (*Ligusticum filicinum*). Leaves of Poison-hemlock are much more finely divided, seeds are grooved on inner surface, plant grows chiefly on dry ground, stems are purple-spotted, and leaf veins terminate at tips of teeth on leaf margins. Loveroot (*L. filicinum* Wats.) has leaves finely divided into linear segments, the basal leaves large and long-stemmed; fruit narrowly winged; see illus. above.

Related species: *Cicuta bulbifera*, a smaller and more slender plant with bulblets in leaf axils, occurs in n. Rockies.

Flowering season: Middle of June to late Aug. Still blooming

when elk antlers begin to harden and bulls rub off the "velvet."
Where found: Y, T, R. Marshy places, along streams, and
about springs from lowest valleys to around 8000 ft. in mts.
Distributed from Alaska to Alberta, south to Arizona and New
Mexico. There are about 8 poorly differentiated species of
Cicuta which are circumboreal; only 2 occur in Rockies.
Interesting facts: *Douglasii* means named for David Douglas.
This is a violently poisonous plant. It is reported that a piece
of tuber the size of a walnut is sufficient to kill a full-grown cow.
Both black and grizzly bears utilize many members of the
Parsley family. It is not yet known whether bears eat the stem
and tubers of Water-hemlock or, if not, how they differentiate
this species from nonpoisonous members of the family with
apparently similar smell and taste. Cases of human poisoning
by Water-hemlock are numerous. It is quite likely that a
close relative of this plant, Poison-hemlock, was the source
of the poison Socrates was forced to drink because he dared
to speak his beliefs. The Parsley family contains some of the
most edible as well as some of the most deadly poisonous plants.
No members of this family should be eaten until accurately
identified, and even then only sampled cautiously until proved
safe.

COW-PARSNIP   *Heracleum lanatum* Michx.   **Pl. 13**
    Family: Umbelliferae (Parsley).
    Other names: Cow-cabbage, Masterwort, Hercules-parsnip.
    Description: A coarse, hairy, perennial herb, 3–8 ft. tall, with
compound leaves and numerous white, or slightly pinkish,
flowers. These form a compound umbel, flat on top, and sometimes almost 1 ft. across. Leaves are composed of 3 leaflets,
coarsely toothed, each ovate in outline and 4–12 in. broad.
    There are a number of plants with white flowers in com-
pound umbels, especially in the Parsley family, but the large
coarse leaves of this plant will distinguish it from others.
    Flowering season: Latter part of May, June, and first part of
July. Look for first flowering when air over the Lodgepole
forests is filled with clouds of pollen.
    Where found: G, Y, T, R. Rich, damp soil of prairies and mts.,
especially along streams and in open woods. Occurs over most
of temperate N. America, large sections of Siberia, and on
Kurile Is. Found from sea level to around 8500 ft. There are
about 60 species of *Heracleum;* only 1 occurs in the Rockies
and 2 in N. America.
    Interesting facts: It is probable that the genus name *Heracleum*
comes from Hercules, the demigod; *lanatum* means woolly.
The plant is readily eaten by domestic animals and big game,
especially elk. Black bears eat the succulent stem, and there
is evidence that grizzlies consume this and other members of

the Parsley family during the spring. It is very palatable to domestic sheep and its presence in abundance indicates little or no sheep-grazing. This species is used as food by Indians and Eskimos and formerly had wide use in medicine. The sweet, succulent young stems can be peeled and eaten raw or cooked. The juice and hairs of the outer "skin," if left on the face and mouth, may cause blisters. No members of the Parsley family should be used as food until correct identification is certain. Somewhat similar-appearing species are deadly poisonous.

WYETH BISCUITROOT   Pl. 13
Lomatium ambiguum (Nutt.) C. & R.

Family: Umbelliferae (Parsley).

Other names: Desert Parsley, Whiskbroom Parsley, Cous.

Description: A plant of dry areas whose small yellow flowers are borne in compound umbels. Primary rays of the umbel are slender, unequal in length, and ½–3 in. long. The 1 to several stems often are purplish in color, may vary in height 6–24 in., and arise from thick fleshy roots. Leaves greatly divided into narrow segments with base of their stalks broadened so as to sheath the stem.

The plant smells and tastes like parsley, and, though this character will help to place Wyeth Biscuitroot in the proper family and separate it from some other plants that may be confusing, it does not help with those in the same genus. These can only be distinguished by technical characters. A number of species of *Lomatium* are called Biscuitroot.

Related species: (1) *L. grayi* has leaves cut up into almost hairlike divisions and are all basal or nearly so; large umbel of yellow flowers is on a stalk 1–2 ft. tall. (2) *L. simplex* is quite similar except leaves are much less dissected, the ultimate divisions being like blades of grass. Both plants are common in Rockies.

Flowering season: Latter part of April to latter part of June.

Where found: Y, T. Dry plains and hills from w. Montana to B.C., south to Oregon and Colorado. Thirty species occur in Rocky Mt. area.

Interesting facts: *Ambiguum* means ambiguous. There are several closely allied species of *Lomatium* possessing thick, fleshy roots, and known to the Indians as Cous, or Cows. As far as known none are poisonous, and species such as Mountain Biscuitroot (*L. montanum* C. & R.), see illus., p. 128, Biscuitroot (*L. macrocarpum* [H. & A.] C. & R.), Plate 13, and *L. cous* are quite edible. These roots were an important source of plant food and served as one of the Indians' chief articles of trade. They were gathered in large quantities and either eaten raw or ground into meal and shaped into flat cakes. Sometimes

Mountain Biscuitroot (*Lomatium montanum* C. & R.)

the cakes were large enough to be strapped to saddles and carried on long journeys. In the journals of Lewis and Clark there are several entries about trading beads, buttons, and trinkets for Cous roots or cakes. The roots are sought and eaten by pocket gophers, mice, and bears. Grizzlies seek the roots of the various species of lomatiums in early spring, apparently locating them through sense of smell.

DESERT-PARSLEY *Lomatium dissectum* (Nutt.) M. & C. **Pl. 13** Var. *multifidum* (Nutt.) M. & C.

Family: Umbelliferae (Parsley).

Other names: Carrotleaf, Fernleaf Lomatium, Biscuitroot.

Description: The small yellowish or purplish flowers of Desert-parsley come in large compound umbels and give rise to oval, flattened fruits about ½ in. long. Stems cluster from top of a large, aromatic, fleshy taproot, and attain a height of 1–5 ft. Leaves are basal as well as on the stem, and may be 1 ft. or more long. They are dissected 3 or 4 times into linear divisions; this gives them appearance of a large carrot or parsley leaf (see Plate 13).

This is the only member of the Parsley family in the Rocky

Mt. area that has a carrotlike leaf and is a large coarse plant, with fruit ½ in. long. Easily recognized because it blooms in early spring long before other large members of the family. Look for a large early-flowering, carrot-leaved plant.

Flowering season: May and June. It will be flowering along with Arrowleaf Balsamroot and when Canada goose eggs are hatching, red-tailed hawks incubating.

Where found: G, Y, T. Dry rocky soil of valleys and hills, and in mts. to about 7500 ft. Frequently encountered at base of rock cliffs and outcrops. There are about 80 species of *Lomatium*, and all, with 2 exceptions, are confined to w. N. America; 30 species occur in Rockies, Desert-parsley being one of the largest, the others ranging in size down to an inch or two in height.

Interesting facts: *Dissectum* means many times parted. Many plants of the Parsley family produce a volatile oil that gives them a characteristic odor and flavor. Among them are dill, anise, carrot, myrrh, parsnip, parsley, caraway, and celery. The roots of many species of *Lomatium* were used as food by the Indians. They were eaten raw, baked, or roasted. A bread flour was ground from the roots. Some taste like parsnips while others have a sweet nutty flavor. *L. cous* formed an important food of the Indians of the Northwest. Lewis and Clark purchased roots of *L. geyeri* from the Indians in order to feed their men. Lomatiums grow and reach maturity in early spring and are important spring forage plants for livestock, deer, elk, antelope, and rodents.

OROGENIA   *Orogenia linearifolia* Wats.   Pl. 14

Family: Umbelliferae (Parsley)

Other names: Turkey Peas, Indian Potato, Snowdrops.

Description: Short, slender-stemmed perennial from a deep-seated roundish tuber. Seldom over 5 in. high, with 2 to 3 basal leaves ternately divided into linear leaflets. Umbel of small white flowers emerging before the leaves.

Related species: *O. fusiformis* has spindle-shaped rather than globose tuber.

Flowering season: April and May, blooms as snow recedes.

Where found: T, R. Rich moist soil of mt. valleys at 6000 to 7000 ft. Montana to Washington, south to Utah and Colorado. Only 2 species in Rockies.

Interesting facts: *Linearifolia* means linear-leaved. This is one of the first spring flowers to appear in the high mt. valleys. It frequently emerges through the melting snowbanks, thus earning the local name of Snowdrops. Indians ate the tubers; raw they have a potato-like flavor. Tubers are also consumed by pocket gophers and the Uinta ground squirrel and probably utilized by other species of ground squirrels.

YAMPA   *Perideridia gairdneri* (H. & A.) Mathias   **Pl. 13**

    Family: Umbelliferae (Parsley).

    Other names: False Caraway, Squawroot, and *Carum gairdneri.*

    Description: The stems are slender, usually solitary, and may vary in height 1–3 ft. They grow from tubers and are surmounted at branched top by compound umbels of small white flowers. Leaves mostly compound, with narrow and grasslike leaflets 1–6 in. long; often by flowering time these have withered and dried up. Though not a conspicuous plant, it is one that every outdoorsman will find well worth knowing.

    Cicuta bulbifera (see p. 125) is very similar, but has bulblets in the leaf axils. The roots are poisonous.

Yampa (*Perideridia gairdneri* [H. & A.] Mathias)

Related species: (1) *P. bolanderi* and (2) *P. parishii* are impossible to distinguish from this one except on technical characters. However, tall slender stems with very narrow, long leaves and compound umbels of small white flowers will distinguish *P. gairdneri* from most members of Parsley family.

Flowering season: Middle of June to last of Aug. In full bloom when grizzly bears are rapidly putting on "winter fat."

Where found: Y, T. Look for this plant in meadows, open hillsides, and aspen woods, and in areas where soil is damp, at least during early summer. Ranges from Alberta to B.C., south to California and New Mexico, extending from lower valleys to around 8000 ft. There are about 9 other species of *Perideridia*, all native to w. U.S. except 1 eastern plant; 3 species in Rocky Mt. area.

Interesting facts: *Gairdneri* means named for Gairdner. Yampa, one of the finest wild plant foods of the Rocky Mt. region, has a parsnip flavor, raw; cooked it is sweet and mealy. Though this plant was known by different names among the various Indian tribes, all collected the fleshy roots for food and trade. Lewis and Clark used it, as did the explorers and mountain men who followed them. To the outdoorsman it offers a tasty addition to camp meals or subsistence food, should he run short on rations. The small sweet-potato-shaped tubers should be washed and scraped before boiling. They may be dried, stored, then ground into flour. Care should be exercised to identify this plant correctly before eating it. In cross section, 7 longitudinal, faceted starch segments easily identify the root. Eat only a small quantity until sure you have the right plant. Rodents, especially pocket gophers, readily eat the roots. Grizzly bears and probably black bears consume them before going into hibernation.

WATER-PARSNIP *Sium suave* Walt. Pl. 13; p. 132

Family: Umbelliferae (Parsley).

Other names: Water-parsley.

Description: A water-loving perennial plant with compound umbels of small white flowers. Both the umbels and umbellets are subtended by numerous narrow bracts. This plant is 2–5 ft. tall, with pinnately compound leaves, their leaflets lance-shaped and toothed, with base of leafstalk broadened so as to sheath the stem. Roots are fibrous.

A number of plants with compound umbels belonging to the Parsley family could be easily confused with Water-parsnip, and they can be separated only on technical characters. Water-hemlock (*Cicuta douglasii*), a very similar-appearing plant, lacks bracts at base of main umbel and has different leaf venation and thickened roots; see p. 124.

Flowering season: Latter part of June to first part of Aug.

Where found: Y, T, R. Look for this in low swampy ground, along streams and borders of lakes and ponds. Occurs over most of temperate N. America, except southeastern part. There are about a dozen species of *Sium*, but only 1 occurs in Rockies.

Interesting facts: *Suave* means sweet. The stem and leaves of this plant are poisonous and they will kill cattle. However,

Water-parsnip (*Sium suave* Walt.)

stock do not ordinarily eat them, so the loss is not great. The roots are reported to be edible in late fall, but the plant so closely resembles the virulently poisonous Water-hemlock (*Cicuta douglasii*) and *C. bulbifera* that it should be considered unsafe to eat.

BUNCHBERRY *Cornus canadensis* L.   **Pl. 14**
   Family: Cornaceae (Dogwood).
   Other names: Dwarf Cornel, Crackerberry.
   Description: Bunchberry appears to have 1 white flower, about 1 in. broad, at end of the stem, but this is in reality 4 large white bracts beneath and surrounding a cluster of small whitish-purple flowers. These individual flowers later give rise to a dense cluster of bright red fruits; hence name Bunchberry. Grows 4–12 in. tall, and has an apparent whorl of several broad leaves near top of stem, with pairs of reduced ones below.
   Most commonly confused with this is *Anemone piperi*, but it has deeply toothed leaves and Bunchberry leaves are smooth around edges. Wakerobin (*Trillium ovatum*) might be mistaken for this, but it has 3 white petals rather than 4 white bracts (see Plate 2).

Flowering season: May to July. In full bloom when Dolly Varden trout begin their spawning runs.

Where found: Y, T, G. Moist to wet woods, meadows, and bogs, from sea level up to around 8000 ft. Occurs from Alaska to Greenland, south to New Jersey and Minnesota, and in our western mts. south to New Mexico and California. Also occurs in e. Asia. There are about 40 species of *Cornus*, native to N. Hemisphere; only 3 in Rockies. Other 2 are tall shrubs, not herbs.

Interesting facts: *Canadensis* means of Canada. The flowering dogwoods of the East and South, as well as the Pacific Dogwood (*C. nuttallii*), are close relatives of this plant. The flowers are similar, though the plants vary greatly in size. The fresh fruits of Bunchberry were eaten raw by various Indian tribes. *Cornus* fruits contain a hard 2-celled stone with 2 seeds. The top of the fruit is scarred from the remains of the calyx. The berries are a favorite fall food of ruffed grouse and the leaves are important in the summer diet. It is a preferred food of white-tailed deer and probably is eaten also by mule deer.

RED-OSIER DOGWOOD *Cornus sericea* L.　　　　**Pl. 14**

Family: Cornaceae (Dogwood).

Other names: Red-stemmed Dogwood, Cornel, Kinnikinnick (erroneously), and *Cornus stolonifera*.

Description: A reddish-barked, slender shrub with flat-topped cymes of small white-petaled flowers. May attain a height of 15 ft. or more, with few to many stems in a clump, the new growth strikingly red in color. The entire, opposite leaves vary in length 1–3 in. and are about ⅔ as wide. Small bunched fruits are white or bluish in color, with a single stone.

　　Several species of manzanita (*Arctostaphylos*) could easily be confused with Red-osier Dogwood. These shrubs, however, have leathery, evergreen, alternate leaves, and the petals of the flower are united; *Cornus* petals are separate.

Related species: (1) *C. nuttallii*, occurring in w.-cent. Idaho, has flower in a head surrounded by 4 large, white, petal-like bracts that are notched on outer ends; (2) *C. florida* of e. U.S. is very similar, but bracts are pointed instead of notched.

Flowering season: June to Aug.

Where found: G, Y, T, R. Along creeks, in meadows, and in boggy places, from valleys up to 7500 ft. This species, and its various forms, cover most of temperate N. America except se. U.S. and the grass prairies. There are many forms and varieties of this shrub, all of which have been considered distinct species. Present tendency is to group them. There are, however, around 40 species of *Cornus*, mainly of north temperate zone; 3 occur in Rocky Mts.

Interesting facts: *Sericea* means silky. This shrub was confused by the early mountain settlers with the eastern Kinnikinnick because both of them have red bark. This mistake still persists, even though the latter plant is a member of the Heath family and *Cornus* a member of the Dogwood family.

The stem wood is very tough, and was used by the Indians in making bows. The strong, nearly perfect Y-shaped crotches make excellent slingshots and cooking racks and kettle hangers. The fruits are edible and were eaten by various tribes. They are, however, of more value as wildlife food, being available in early winter and being of sufficient protein, fat, and carbohydrate content to be nourishing. Pheasants, grouse, and bears readily feed on the berries as other food sources become scarce. Rabbits as well as moose, deer, and elk are fond of the twigs and winter buds. These are highly palatable and nutritious and Red-osier Dogwood suffers from overbrowsing on winter ranges of both moose and elk. *C. florida* is the state flower of Virginia.

PRINCE'S PINE   *Chimaphila umbellata* (L.) Bart.   **Pl. 14**
Var. *occidentalis* (Rydb.) Blake
Family: Pyrolaceae (Wintergreen).
Other names: Pipsissewa, Wintergreen, Waxflower.
Description: This is the most common *Chimaphila* in the Rockies. It is a semishrubby evergreen arising from long, woody underground stems and standing 6–14 in. tall, with a cluster of waxy white to pink flowers well above the leaves. Leaves are numerous, leathery, pale beneath; dark green and shining above. They are lance-shaped, 1–3 in. long and broadest above middle, with finely toothed edges. There are 10 stamens; the purple anthers open by pores. Stamens look like spokes in a wheel, with pistils as the hub.

Most members of the Wintergreen family have leaves only at base of the stem. Prince's Pine, whose stems are densely covered with leaves, is an exception.
Related species: Another less common species (*C. menziesii*) is distinguished from this by having leaves broadest below middle.
Flowering season: Latter part of June, July, and first part of Aug. Look for it soon after young snowshoe hares start scurrying about. In full bloom when huckleberries are ripe.
Where found: G, Y, T, R. Moist woods, particularly coniferous stands, and along mt. streams, from lower hills up to around 8000 ft. Distributed from Alaska to Alberta, south to California and New Mexico. There are 6 to 8 species of *Chimaphila*, mainly in N. America and ne. Asia; 2 in Rocky Mt. area.
Interesting facts: The name *Chimaphila* comes from two Greek words meaning winter-loving. *Umbellata* means umbrella-like; *occidentalis* means western. The plant contains glucosides and a volatile oil that are used in medicine as an astringent

and tonic. The plants are used for Christmas decorations.
Indians prepared a beverage by boiling the leaves and roots.

PINK PYROLA   *Pyrola asarifolia* Michx.   **Pl. 14**
 Family: Pyrolaceae (Wintergreen).
 Other names: Alpine Pyrola, Bog Pyrola, Wintergreen.
 Description: The flowers are pink to purplish, waxy, hang
downward, are almost ½ in. broad, and come in racemes at
the top of a graceful leafless stalk 8–16 in. tall. As in Prince's
Pine, the stamens open by terminal pores. Leaves are evergreen, leathery, and near base of stem; they are almost round,
in diameter 1–3 in., and often brownish beneath and dark
green above.

Once classified as 3 species, these are now usually considered
variations of the same plant.

 Related species: (1) In Rockies *P. bracteata* is easily confused
with this one, but its leaves are mostly longer than broad and
have an acute tip. (2) The flowers of Green Pyrola (*P. chlorantha*
Sw.) are greenish white and leaf blades are roundish, not mottled,
and usually shorter than leafstalks; see illus. below. Woodnymph (*P. uniflora* L.) is widely distributed throughout Rocky

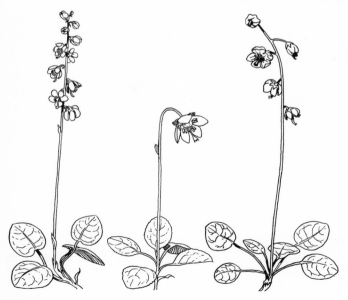

Pink Pyrola (*Pyrola asarifolia* Michx.), Woodnymph (*P. uniflora* L.),
and Green Pyrola (*P. chlorantha* Sw.)

Mts.; readily distinguished from other pyrolas by having only single flower on a stem; see illus., p. 135.

Flowering season: Latter part of June, July, and first part of Aug. Look for Pink Pyrola when the more conspicuous Monkshood is in bloom.

Where found: G, Y, T, R. Wet soil of bogs, stream courses, and around springs, mostly in shady areas and particularly under coniferous stands. Found from plains and lower hills up to around 9000 ft. and distributed from Alaska to Newfoundland, south to New York, Minnesota, New Mexico, and California. There are perhaps 20 species of *Pyrola*, mainly native to temperate N. America but also extending into tropics; 9 species in Rocky Mt. area.

Interesting facts: *Pyrola* is derived from the name *pyrus*, or pear tree, because of resemblance of the leaves of this plant to those of the pear; *asarifolia* means leaves like asarum leaves.

PINEDROPS *Pterospora andromedea* Nutt. **Pl. 15**
    Family: Pyrolaceae (Wintergreen).
    Other names: Giant Birds-nest.
    Description: Pinedrops appears to be all stem with whitish flowers hanging downward like bells. Stems unbranched, purplish brown, sticky-hairy, and 1–4 ft. tall, terminating in a long raceme of flowers each ¼–⅜ in. broad. Leaves are reduced to narrow scales on lower part of stems, and lack green coloring material (chlorophyll) by which ordinary plants manufacture food. Old stalks quite conspicuous; tall, dark brown, naked stem terminates in a long cluster of pendulous, brown, dried ovaries.

    Some of the saprophytic orchids (*Corallorhiza*) could easily be confused with this plant. However, their flowers are irregular in shape; flowers of Pinedrops are regular.

    Flowering season: Latter part of June, July, and Aug. Blooms at time young goshawks, nesting in conifer forests, are leaving their nests.

    Where found: G, Y, T, R. Chiefly under coniferous forests on dry to medium-moist soil with an abundance of decaying plant material. Can be found on plains and in mts. up to about 8500 ft., from Alaska to Labrador, south to Pennsylvania, Michigan, Mexico, and California. The only species placed in this genus. Indianpipe (*Monotropa uniflora*) closely related.

    Interesting facts: *Andromedea* means like Andromeda. The roots of this plant form coarse, irregular masses, intimately associated with fungi that decay fallen plant material, changing it into usable food. Pinedrops utilizes this food; unlike most plants, it cannot make its own. The attractive flowering stalks can be gathered in late summer and fall and used as floral decorations.

Plates

Plate I

GRASSES AND RELATED PLANTS

1. **COMMON CATTAIL,** *Typha latifolia* L.   p. 1
   Note the straplike leaves, sausagelike flower cluster.
        Cattail Family

2. **BURREED,** *Sparganium simplex* Huds.   p. 2
   Looks like a large grass with globose heads of white
   blossoms.   Burreed Family

3. **ARROWHEAD,** *Sagittaria cuneata* Sheld.   p. 5
   Note the arrow-shaped leaves, 3-petaled white
   blossoms.   Arrowhead Family

4. **GREAT BASIN WILD RYE**   p. 6
   Elymus cinereus Scribn. & Merr.
   A tall, coarse grass with an erect dense spike of
   flowers.   Grass Family

5. **YELLOW SKUNKCABBAGE**   p. 11
   Lysichitum americanum H. & S.
   Note the bright yellow, partly rolled flower-
   covering (spathe).   Arum Family

6. **FOXTAIL BARLEY,** *Hordeum jubatum* L.   p. 7
   Flower head (dense reddish-golden awns) suggests
   miniature fox tail.   Grass Family

7. **SEDGE,** *Carex nebraskensis* Dewey   p. 8
   A bluish-green grasslike plant with triangular stems
   (see text).   Sedge Family

8. **BEARGRASS,** *Xerophyllum tenax* (Pursh) Nutt.   p. 31
   Note the large conical flower cluster, grasslike
   leaves.   Lily Family

9. **WILD LILY-OF-THE-VALLEY**   p. 28
   Smilacina stellata (L.) Desf.
   Note the cluster of small white flowers at end of an
   unbranched leafy stem. Smaller than *S. racemosa*
   (Plate 2), has fewer flowers; stamens shorter than
   perianth; berries green, with black or brown stripes.
        Lily Family

Plate 2

LILIES AND IRISES

1. **DOGTOOTH VIOLET**   p. 23
    Erythronium grandiflorum Pursh
      A small yellow lily with 2 shining basal leaves.
                                                    Lily Family

2. **CAMAS,** *Camassia quamash* (Pursh) Greene   p. 20
        A hyacinth-like spike of bright blue flowers (differs
      from Wild Hyacinth by distinct, not united, petals
      and sepals).   Lily Family

3. **DEATH-CAMAS,** *Zigadenus paniculatus* (Nutt.) Wats.   p. 32
        Has whitish flowers with conspicuous gland spots at
      base of petals. Other species have smaller flowers.
                                                    Lily Family

4. **FALSE SOLOMONSEAL,** *Smilacina racemosa* (L.) Desf.   p. 27
        Has cluster of small whitish flowers at end of un-
      branched leafy stem. Note the large ovate leaves.
      See *S. stellata* (Plate 1).   Lily Family

5. **WAKEROBIN,** *Trillium ovatum* Pursh   p. 30
        Note the 3 broad leaves, 3 large white petals.
                                                    Lily Family

6. **NODDING ONION,** *Allium cernuum* Roth   p. 15
        Note the grasslike (leeklike) leaves, nodding flower
      clusters.   Lily Family

7. **ROCKY MOUNTAIN IRIS,** *Iris missouriensis* Nutt.   p. 34
        Unmistakable (typical flag or fleur-de-lis). Only
      species in Rocky Mt. area.   Iris Family

8. **GRASS-WIDOWS**   p. 35
    Sisyrinchium inflatum (Suksd.) St. John
        Grows in tufts; bright pink-purple blossoms, grass-
      like leaves.   Iris Family

9. **BLUE-EYED GRASS,** *Sisyrinchium sarmentosum* Suksd.   p. 35
        Note the small blue flowers, flat stem, grasslike
      appearance.   Iris Family

Plate 3

LILIES (LILY FAMILY)

1. **LEOPARD LILY,** *Fritillaria atropurpurea* Nutt.   p. 24
    The dull purplish-brown flowers spotted with
    greenish yellow are distinctive.

2. **YELLOW FRITILLARY**   p. 24
    Fritillaria pudica (Pursh) Spreng.
    A single yellow bell-shaped flower that hangs down-
    ward. Lacks broad shining leaves of Dogtooth
    Violet.

3. **WILD HYACINTH,** *Brodiaea douglasii* Wats.   p. 17
    Note blue tubular-shaped flowers at top of slender
    leafless stem. Leaves grasslike and basal.

4. **QUEENCUP,** *Clintonia uniflora* (Schult.) Kunth   p. 21
    A single broad white flower with 2 to 5 lance-shaped
    leaves.

5. **PURPLE-EYED MARIPOSA**   p. 18
    Calochortus nitidus Dougl.
    A white tuliplike flower on a slender stem.

6. **SEGO LILY,** *Calochortus nuttallii* Torr.   p. 18
    Similar to Purple-eyed Mariposa but larger.

7. **FALSE ASPHODEL,** *Tofieldia glutinosa* (Michx.) Pers.   p. 29
    Dainty white flowers growing in bunches.

8. **FAIRYBELLS,** *Disporum trachycarpum* (Wats.) B. & H.   p. 22
    White to greenish-yellow flowers droop and are
    generally hidden by broad leaves. Fruit is bright
    orange-yellow.

Plate 4

FALSE HELLEBORE, ORCHIDS,
AND BUCKWHEATS

1. **FALSE HELLEBORE,** *Veratrum viride* Ait. p. 31
   A large conspicuously leafy-stemmed plant with a
   dense cluster of yellowish-green flowers. Leaves 4–
   12 in. long, with coarse, parallel veins. Lily Family

2. **MOUNTAIN LADYS-SLIPPER** p. 36
   Cypripedium montanum Dougl.
   Larger than Fairyslipper, with bronze-colored
   sepals and petals and inflated white lip.
   Orchid Family

3. **FAIRYSLIPPER,** *Calypso bulbosa* (L.) Oakes p. 36
   Only pink single-flowered orchid in area.
   Orchid Family

4. **LADIES-TRESSES,** *Spiranthes romanzoffiana* Cham. p. 39
   A spiral of small white flowers in a dense terminal
   spike. Orchid Family

5. **STRIPED CORALROOT,** *Corallorhiza striata* Lindl. p. 38
   A spike of conspicuously striped brownish-purple
   flowers. Orchid Family

6. **WHITE BOG-ORCHID** p. 38
   Habenaria dilatata (Pursh) Hook.
   A long dense spike of white flowers. Note stout,
   leafy stem. Orchid Family

7. **SPOTTED CORALROOT,** *Corallorhiza maculata* Raf. p. 37
   Similar to Striped Coralroot but with a 3-lobed
   white lip spotted with crimson Orchid Family

8. **UMBRELLA PLANT,** *Eriogonum heracleoides* Nutt. var. p. 40
   subalpinum (Greene) St. John
   Note umbrellalike appearance of clustered cream-
   colored flowers. Buckwheat Family

9. **AMERICAN BISTORT,** *Polygonum bistortoides* Pursh p. 42
   Flower spike looks like a tuft of cotton on slender
   stem. Buckwheat Family

Plate 5

BUCKWHEATS, PURSLANES, AND PINKS

1. **SULPHURFLOWER,** *Eriogonum flavum* Nutt.   p. 40
   Similar to Umbrella Plant but bright yellow and
   with longer leaves.   Buckwheat Family

2. **MOUNTAIN-SORREL,** *Oxyria digyna* (L.) Hill   p. 41
   Note raceme of greenish to crimson flowers and
   kidney-shaped leaves.   Buckwheat Family

3. **WATER LADYSTHUMB**   p. 43
   Polygonum natans (Michx.) Eat.
   A pink spike of flowers above a cluster of floating
   leaves. Generally grows in water.
                                             Buckwheat Family

4. **LEWISIA,** *Lewisia pygmaea* (Gray) Robins.   p. 47
   Similar to Springbeauty but has 6 to 8 petals and
   a 2-cleft style.   Purslane Family

5. **SPRINGBEAUTY,** *Claytonia lanceolata* Pursh   p. 45
   A pink or white flower with 2 sepals, 5 petals, and
   a 3-cleft style, blooming in early spring.
                                             Purslane Family

6. **BITTERROOT,** *Lewisia rediviva* Pursh   p. 46
   A conspicuous short-stemmed white to pinkish
   flower that appears to be leafless.   Purslane Family

7. **SANDWORT,** *Arenaria obtusiloba* (Rydb.) Fern.   p. 48
   A low mat-forming plant with small white and
   green flowers. Note 10 stamens. Grows at high
   elevations.   Pink Family

8. **FIELD CHICKWEED,** *Cerastium arvense* L.   p. 49
   White flowers with deeply notched petals. Gener-
   ally growing in densely matted patches.
                                             Pink Family

Plate 6

PINK, WATER LILY, AND
BUTTERCUP FAMILIES

1. **MOSS CAMPION,** *Silene acaulis* L.   p. 50
   A mossy cushion plant with numerous small pink
   flowers. Grows at high elevations.   Pink Family

2. **YELLOW PONDLILY,** *Nuphar polysepalum* Engelm.   p. 51
   Note large cup-shaped yellow blossoms and large
   floating leaves. Grows in water.   Water Lily Family

3. **ALPINE BUTTERCUP,** *Ranunculus adoneus* Gray   p. 60
   A bright yellow buttercup found only at high
   elevations.   Buttercup Family

4. **SAGEBRUSH BUTTERCUP**   p. 62
   Ranunculus glaberrimus Hook.
   First buttercup to appear in spring. Note both
   entire and divided leaves.   Buttercup Family

5. **MARSHMARIGOLD,** *Caltha leptosepala* DC.   p. 56
   A large white buttercup-like flower with large shiny
   basal leaves. Grows at high elevations.
                                        Buttercup Family

6. **PASQUEFLOWER,** *Anemone patens* L.   p. 54
   A violet or purple (occasionally white) cup-shaped
   flower with dissected basal leaves and 1 pair of
   leaflike bracts.   Buttercup Family

7. **BLUE COLUMBINE,** *Aquilegia coerulea* James   p. 55
   Note that the basal portion of the 5 petals form
   5 straight, slender spurs.   Buttercup Family

8. **ANEMONE,** *Anemone globosa* Nutt.   p. 53
   A purple-red to greenish-yellow flower. Note the
   divided and lobed basal leaves, and whorl of leaflike
   bracts below the flowers.   Buttercup Family

Plate 7

BUTTERCUP FAMILY, HOLLY-GRAPE, STEERSHEAD

1. **SUGARBOWL,** *Clematis hirsutissima* Pursh   p. 57
   Looks like Pasqueflower, but has opposite stem
   leaves.   Buttercup Family

2. **MONKSHOOD,** *Aconitum columbianum* Nutt.   p. 51
   Sepals and petals similar in color; 1 sepal forms a
   hoodlike cap, or helmet. Stem leaves numerous.
   Buttercup Family

3. **LARKSPUR,** *Delphinium nelsoni* Greene   p. 59
   Upper sepal prolonged into a slender, tubular spur.
   Few basal leaves.   Buttercup Family

4. **WATER BUTTERCUP,** *Ranunculus aquatilis* L.   p. 61
   Note white flowers and finely dissected leaves.
   Grows in water.   Buttercup Family

5. **GLOBEFLOWER,** *Trollius laxus* Salisb.   p. 63
   Creamy-white or yellow buttercup-like flower with
   palmately lobed, sharply toothed leaves. Note
   absence of leaflike bracts below the flowers.
   Buttercup Family

6. **CLEMATIS,** *Clematis columbiana* (Nutt.) T. & G.   p. 57
   A slender climbing vine with lavender-blue flowers
   occurring singly in axils of leaves. Buttercup Family

7. **WHITE CLEMATIS,** *Clematis ligusticifolia* Nutt.   p. 58
   A climbing vine with small white flowers that occur
   in clusters.   Buttercup Family

8. **HOLLY-GRAPE,** *Mahonia repens* (Lindl.) G. Don   p. 64
   Note cluster of bright yellow flowers and leathery
   hollylike leaves. A low shrub.   Barberry Family

9. **STEERSHEAD,** *Dicentra uniflora* Kell.   p. 65
   A tiny flower that blooms in early spring and looks
   like a steer's head (upside down).
   Bleedingheart Family

Plate 8

WHITLOW-GRASS, SEDUMS, CAPERS, SYRINGA, SAXIFRAGES

1. **WHITLOW-GRASS,** *Draba densifolia* Nutt.   p. 65
   A mass of small yellow flowers arising from a dense
   tuft of stems and leaves. Note 4 petals and 4 sepals.
                                         Mustard Family

2. **ROSECROWN,** *Sedum rhodanthum* Gray   p. 70
   A dense cluster of rose-colored flowers, superficially
   resembling red clover. Note the numerous oblong,
   fleshy stem leaves.   Orpine Family

3. **STONECROP,** *Sedum stenopetalum* Pursh   p. 71
   Note yellow flowers and cluster of fleshy basal
   leaves varying in color from green to reddish brown.
                                         Orpine Family

4. **GRASS-OF-PARNASSUS,** *Parnassia fimbriata* Koenig   p. 73
   A white flower with conspicuously fringed petals.
                                         Saxifrage Family

5. **ROCKY MOUNTAIN BEEPLANT**   p. 69
   Cleome serrulata Pursh
   A much-branched leafy plant with numerous pink
   flowers. Note some seed pods developing while
   flowers on same raceme are blooming. Caper Family

6. **SYRINGA,** *Philadelphus lewisii* Pursh   p. 77
   A shrub having conspicuous white flowers with
   numerous bright yellow stamens. Hydrangea Family

7. **STARFLOWER**   p. 72
   Lithophragma parviflora (Hook.) Nutt.
   Note the white petals are deeply cleft into 3 to 5
   divisions. Leaves mainly basal.   Saxifrage Family

8. **JAMES BOYKINIA,** *Boykinia jamesii* (Torr.) Engl.   p. 72
   Has reddish-purple to dark pink flowers and kidney-
   shaped leaves arising from a thick branching rootstock.   Saxifrage Family

9. **YELLOW BEEPLANT,** *Cleome lutea* Hook.   p. 69
   Similar to Rocky Mountain Beeplant but with
   yellow flowers.   Caper Family

Plate 9

ROSES AND RELATED SPECIES
(ROSE FAMILY)

1. **ROSE,** *Rosa woodsii* Lindl.   p. 92
   Note pink flowers with numerous stamens and
   pistils. Stems are prickly and the leaves compound
   and toothed.

2. **DRYAD,** *Dryas hookeriana* Juss.   p. 82
   The largest white-flowered, mat-forming plant
   growing at high elevations. Note toothed leathery
   leaves.

3. **MOUNTAIN-AVENS,** *Dryas drummondii* Richards.   p. 82
   Similar to Dryad but with yellow flowers.

4. **STRAWBERRY,** *Fragaria vesca* L.   p. 82
   Note 5 white petals and basal leaves divided into
   3 coarsely toothed leaflets.

5. **THIMBLEBERRY,** *Rubus parviflorus* Nutt.   p. 93
   An erect shrub 2–6 ft. tall, with white flowers and
   large 5-lobed leaves.

6. **SHRUBBY CINQUEFOIL,** *Potentilla fruticosa* L.   p. 87
   An erect branched shrub with broad yellow flowers.
   Note pinnately compound leaves.

7. **BITTERBRUSH,** *Purshia tridentata* (Pursh) DC.   p. 90
   A much-branched shrub with small light yellow
   flowers. Note wedge-shaped leaves.

8. **IVESIA,** *Ivesia gordonii* (Hook.) T. & G.   p. 85
   Note cluster of yellow flowers on unbranched stems
   and narrow fernlike basal leaves.

Plate 10

STICKY GERANIUM; ROSE AND PEA FAMILIES

1. **MOUNTAIN-ASH,** *Sorbus scopulina* Greene   p. 94
   Shrub with alternate compound leaves and large
   flat-topped flower clusters. Bright orange-red fruit.
                                                    Rose Family

2. **STICKY GERANIUM**   p. 106
   Geranium viscosissimum Fisch. & Mey.
   Pink-flowered plant, clumped on a woody root.
   Note gland-tipped hairs on leaves.   Geranium Family

3. **CHOKECHERRY,** *Prunus melanocarpa* (Nels.) Rydb.   p. 89
   A large shrub or small tree with white flowers in
   long pendent clusters.   Rose Family

4. **MOUNTAINSPRAY,** *Holodiscus discolor* (Pursh) Maxim.   p. 84
   A shrub bearing a mass of tiny whitish flowers.
   Note ribbed twigs.   Rose Family

5. **PINK SPIREA,** *Spiraea douglasii* Hook.   p. 95
   A shrub with dense clusters of minute pink flowers.
   Stamens longer than petals.   Rose Family

6. **VETCH,** *Vicia villosa* Roth   p. 104
   A vine with bluish-purple flowers with pinnately
   compound leaves terminating in tendrils.
                                                    Pea Family

7. **LOCOWEED,** *Astragalus purshii* Dougl.   p. 97
   Note the grayish color of plant and the white
   flowers with inner petals purple-tipped. Lower
   petals not beaked.   Pea Family

8. **CRAZYWEED,** *Oxytropis besseyi* (Rydb.) Blank.   p. 97
   Red pealike flowers. Note lower petals form a
   distinct beak.   Pea Family

9. **BIGHEAD CLOVER**   p. 104
   Trifolium macrocephalum (Pursh) Poir.
   Huge flower head often ½ as long as flower stem.
   Leaflets 4-leaved.   Pea Family

Plate 11

ROSE, PEA, AND LOASA FAMILIES

1. **CINQUEFOIL** p. 88
   Potentilla gracilis Dougl. ssp. *nuttallii* (Lehm.) Keck
   Yellow roselike flowers; leaves digitately compound.
   Rose Family

2. **SERVICEBERRY,** *Amelanchier alnifolia* Nutt. p. 79
   An early white-flowering shrub. Note the short
   flower clusters. Stem lacks thorns. Rose Family

3. **LONG-PLUMED AVENS,** *Geum triflorum* Pursh p. 83
   Note downward-hanging flowers and fernlike basal
   leaves. Rose Family

4. **LODGEPOLE LUPINE,** *Lupinus parviflorus* Nutt. p. 99
   Note long spike of small blue pealike flowers.
   Palmately compound leaves composed of 5 to 11
   leaflets. Pea Family

5. **WILD LICORICE,** *Glycyrrhiza lepidota* Nutt. p. 98
   Has a dense raceme of greenish-white flowers and
   leaves with 11 to 19 leaflets. Pea Family

6. **FALSE LUPINE,** *Thermopsis montana* Nutt. p. 102
   Long raceme of golden-yellow flowers. Note fernlike stipules at leaf base. Pea Family

7. **BLUEBONNET,** *Lupinus sericeus* Pursh p. 100
   Note lavender-blue flowers, clumped stems, and
   palmately compound leaves with 5 to 9 leaflets.
   Pea Family

8. **SWEETVETCH,** *Hedysarum occidentale* Greene p. 98
   Has dense raceme of reddish-purple flowers. Pods
   constricted between the seeds; pods of *Astragalus*
   not constricted. Pea Family

9. **BLAZINGSTAR,** *Mentzelia laevicaulis* (Dougl.) T. & G. p. 118
   A large 5-petaled lemon-yellow flower with numerous stamens. Leaves deeply cleft and covered with
   barbed hairs. Loasa Family

Plate 12

MALLOWS, ST. JOHNSWORT, VIOLETS, CACTI, AND EVENING PRIMROSES

1. **MOUNTAIN HOLLYHOCK**   p. 114
   Iliamna rivularis (Dougl.) Greene
   Note pink hollyhock-like flowers and maple-like
   leaves.   Mallow Family

2. **SCARLET FALSEMALLOW**   p. 115
   Sphaeralcea coccinea (Pursh) Rydb.
   Cluster of tomato-colored flowers with 3- to 5-
   parted grayish-green leaves which are distinctive.
                                              Mallow Family

3. **ST. JOHNSWORT,** *Hypericum formosum* HBK.   p. 116
   Has a loose elongated inflorescence of yellow
   flowers. Grows at high elevations. *H. perforatum*
   is a larger plant and grows only at low altitudes.
                                         St. Johnswort Family

4. **YELLOW VIOLET,** *Viola nuttallii* Pursh   p. 116
   Note bright yellow flowers and lance-shaped leaves.
                                              Violet Family

5. **VIOLET,** *Viola adunca* Sm.   p. 116
   Flowers blue to violet, leaves ovate.   Violet Family

6. **CACTUS,** *Opuntia rhodantha* Schum.   p. 119
   Large orange-pink to red waxy blossoms growing
   from a fleshy stem of oval joints.   Cactus Family

7. **PLAINS CACTUS,** *Opuntia polyacantha* Haw.   p. 119
   Large, yellow, waxy flowers and fleshy, jointed
   stems.   Cactus Family

8. **EVENING PRIMROSE,** *Oenothera caespitosa* Nutt.   p. 121
   A large white stemless flower with clustered leaves.
                                      Evening Primrose Family

9. **CLARKIA,** *Clarkia pulchella* Pursh   p. 120
   Note 3-lobed deep rose-lavender petals and petal-
   like stigma of 4 white lobes.
                                      Evening Primrose Family

Plate 13

EVENING PRIMROSE, PARSLEY, AND SUMAC FAMILIES

1. **FIREWEED,** *Epilobium angustifolium* L.   p. 120
   Note 4-petaled flowers forming a long raceme, the
   lower flowers blooming and fruiting before upper
   ones.   Evening Primrose Family

2. **BROAD-LEAVED FIREWEED,** *Epilobium latifolium* L.   p. 121
   Similar to Fireweed but a shorter plant, with fleshy
   leaves.   Evening Primrose Family

3. **COW-PARSNIP,** *Heracleum lanatum* Michx.   p. 126
   Note compound flat-topped umbel of white flowers
   and the large coarsely toothed leaves.
                                              Parsley Family

4. **WATER-PARSNIP,** *Sium suave* Walt.   p. 131
   A compound umbel of small white flowers with
   bracts at base of main umbel.   Parsley Family

5. **DESERT-PARSLEY**   p. 128
   Lomatium dissectum (Nutt.) M. & C. var. *multifidum*
   (Nutt.) M. & C.
      Note compound umbel of small yellowish flowers
   and large carrotlike leaf.   Parsley Family

6. **YAMPA,** *Perideridia gairdneri* (H. & A.) Mathias   p. 130
   A compound umbel of small white flowers on a
   slender stem bearing long, narrow leaves.
                                              Parsley Family

7. **WYETH BISCUITROOT**   p. 127
   Lomatium ambiguum (Nutt.) C. & R.
      Note bright yellow flowers in compound umbels
   and greatly divided leaves that sheath the stem.
                                              Parsley Family

8. **BISCUITROOT**   p. 127
   Lomatium macrocarpum (H. & A.) C. & R.
      Similar to Wyeth Biscuitroot but leaves not so
   narrowly segmented.   Parsley Family

9. **PRIMROSE,** *Oenothera heterantha* Nutt.   p. 122
   A low-growing perennial with long taproot, sessile
   yellow flowers, and a rosette of basal leaves. Note
   stamens are unequal in length.
                                      Evening Primrose Family

10. **SQUAWBUSH,** *Rhus trilobata* Nutt.   p. 111
    Note 3 leaflets broad at outer ends.   Sumac Family

Plate 14

COLLOMIA, OROGENIA, DOGWOODS, FLAX, WINTERGREENS, HEATHS

1. **COLLOMIA**, *Collomia linearis* Nutt.   p. 150
   Note dense cluster of pink tubular flowers in axils
   of leafy bracts.   Phlox Family

2. **OROGENIA**, *Orogenia linearifolia* Wats.   p. 129
   Seldom more than 5 in. high; has umbel of tiny
   white flowers.   Parsley Family

3. **BUNCHBERRY**, *Cornus canadensis* L.   p. 132
   Note 4 large white bracts surrounding a cluster of
   small whitish-purple flowers, whorl of broad leaves
   below the flowers.   Dogwood Family

4. **RED-OSIER DOGWOOD**, *Cornus sericea* L.   p. 133
   A shrub with reddish bark and cymes of white-
   petaled flowers.   Dogwood Family

5. **PINK PYROLA**, *Pyrola asarifolia* Michx.   p. 135
   Pink to purplish waxy flowers hanging downward
   from a slender leafless stalk. Basal leaves are evergreen and leathery.   Wintergreen Family

6. **BLUEFLAX**, *Linum lewisii* Pursh   p. 107
   Sky-blue saucer-shaped flowers borne on very
   slender stems.   Flax Family

7. **PRINCE'S PINE**, *Chimaphila umbellata* (L.) Bart. var.   p. 134
   occidentalis (Rydb.) Blake
   Note waxy white to pink flowers, shiny leathery
   leaves, and the stamens appearing like spokes in a
   wheel.   Wintergreen Family

8. **BLUEBERRY**, *Vaccinium ovalifolium* Sm.   p. 140
   A low erect shrub with inconspicuous flowers, alternate leaves, and bluish-purple berries.   Heath Family

9. **CREEPING WINTERGREEN**   p. 139
   Gaultheria humifusa (Graham) Rydb.
   A creeping evergreen shrub with small flowers,
   alternate leaves, and red fruits. Leaves and berries
   have a wintergreen flavor.   Heath Family

Plate 15

PINEDROPS, LEAFY SPURGE, HEATHS, PRIMROSES, AND GREEN GENTIAN

1. **PINEDROPS,** *Pterospora andromedea* Nutt.   p. 136
   No green coloring; tall, sticky-hairy, purplish-brown stems with downward-hanging whitish flowers.   Wintergreen Family

2. **LEAFY SPURGE,** *Euphorbia esula* L.   p. 108
   Note bell-shaped whorl of yellowish-green bracts, numerous leafy branches, and milky juice.
                                                    Spurge Family

3. **MOUNTAIN HEATH**   p. 142
   Phyllodoce empetriformis (Sw.) D. Don
   Umbels of pink, urn-shaped flowers above a low evergreen shrub with needlelike leaves, often in mats.   Heath Family

4. **SWAMP-LAUREL,** *Kalmia polifolia* Wang.   p. 140
   Note pink saucerlike flowers on red stalks and opposite leathery leaves with inrolled edges.
                                                    Heath Family

5. **KINNIKINNICK,** *Arctostaphylos uva-ursi* (L.) Spreng.   p. 139
   Note ovate to roundish leathery leaves on a trailing or matted plant; bark reddish and peeling, fruits red, flowers pink or white.   Heath Family

6. **PARRY PRIMROSE,** *Primula parryi* Gray   p. 143
   A large, rank-smelling alpine plant with blood-red, funnel-form flowers and a rosette of large basal leaves.   Primrose Family

7. **SHOOTINGSTAR**   p. 143
   Dodecatheon pauciflorum (Dur.) Greene
   Note "shooting star" effect of rose-purple backward-flaring petals and forward-projecting stamens; stem is single and leaves basal.   Primrose Family

8. **GREEN GENTIAN,** *Frasera speciosa* Dougl.   p. 144
   A tall heavy-stemmed plant densely covered with greenish-white flowers and lance-shaped leaves; flowers wheel-shaped.   Gentian Family

Plate 16

GENTIAN, PHLOX, WATERLEAF, AND MILKWEED FAMILIES

1. **MOUNTAIN GENTIAN,** *Gentiana calycosa* Griseb.   p. 146
   A deep blue bell-shaped flower, with numerous opposite stem leaves and but a single flower on a stem.   Gentian Family

2. **WHITE PHLOX,** *Phlox multiflora* Nels.   p. 152
   A low, mat-forming plant with white to lilac-colored flowers; leaves opposite, short, and smooth. *P. hoodii* has hairy-woolly leaves.   Phlox Family

3. **WESTERN FRINGED GENTIAN**   p. 146
   Gentiana thermalis Kuntze
   Large bluish-purple bell-shaped flowers with fringed petals.   Gentian Family

4. **LONG-LEAVED PHLOX,** *Phlox longifolia* Nutt.   p. 152
   Similar to White Phlox but with larger flowers and longer leaves.   Phlox Family

5. **JACOBS-LADDER,** *Polemonium pulcherrimum* Hook.   p. 153
   Note violet-blue corolla with white or yellow tube.
                                           Phlox Family

6. **SCARLET GILIA,** *Gilia aggregata* (Pursh) Spreng.   p. 150
   Has brilliant red (normally), trumpet-shaped flowers and dissected leaves.   Phlox Family

7. **SILKY PHACELIA,** *Phacelia sericea* (Graham) Gray   p. 154
   Note dense spike of purple flowers, protruding stamens, silvery-silky dissected leaves.
                                       Waterleaf Family

8. **PINK MILKWEED,** *Asclepias speciosa* Torr.   p. 148
   A large plant with dense umbels of pink to whitish flowers. Note reflexed petals and milky juice in stem and leaves.   Milkweed Family

9. **WATERLEAF,** *Hydrophyllum capitatum* Dougl.   p. 153
   Distinguished by globular heads of white to purplish-blue flowers, large pinnately divided leaves. Note that stamens extend beyond petals.
                                       Waterleaf Family

10. **SKY PILOT,** *Polemonium viscosum* Nutt.   p. 152
    A funnel-shaped flower with orange anthers, compound leaves, and skunklike smell.   Phlox Family

Plate 17

HENBANE, MORNING-GLORY, BORAGES, HORSEMINT

1. **HENBANE,** *Hyoscyamus niger* L.   p. 165
   A coarse, clammy, downy plant with clasping leaves and bell-shaped flowers about 1 in. long; vase-shaped seed capsules are sharp-pointed.
              Potato Family

2. **MORNING-GLORY,** *Convolvulus arvensis* L.   p. 149
   A twining plant of fields with funnel-shaped flowers about 1 in. across and alternate 2-lobed leaves.
            Morning-glory Family

3. **MOUNTAIN BLUEBELL**   p. 159
   Mertensia ciliata (James) G. Don
   A leafy plant with drooping tubular-shaped flowers and stamens attached to corolla tube; leaves alternate and smooth.   Borage Family

4. **GROMWELL,** *Lithospermum incisum* Lehm.   p. 158
   A many-stemmed plant with yellow flowers in upper leaf axils; corolla lobes fringed, taproot fleshy.
              Borage Family

5. **FORGET-ME-NOT,** *Myosotis alpestris* Schmidt   p. 160
   Wheel-shaped blue flowers with a yellow center, lance-shaped, softly hairy leaves; not mat-forming; seeds without barbed prickles.   Borage Family

6. **BLUEBELL,** *Mertensia oblongifolia* (Nutt.) G. Don   p. 160
   Similar to Mountain Bluebell, but plant shorter and flowering in early spring.   Borage Family

7. **ALPINE FORGET-ME-NOT**   p. 156
   Eritrichium elongatum (Rydb.) Wight
   A dwarf alpine cushion plant with small, brilliant blue flowers (occasionally white) and long soft white hairs covering stem and leaves.   Borage Family

8. **HOUNDSTONGUE,** *Cynoglossum officinale* L.   p. 155
   A stout, tall, branching plant with a disagreeable odor; bears racemes of reddish-purple flowers, or burs when mature.   Borage Family

9. **HORSEMINT,** *Monarda menthaefolia* Benth.   p. 163
   A mint with large, round, rose to purple flower heads surrounded by leaflike bracts; stems square, usually unbranched; leaves bright green and opposite.
              Mint Family

Plate 18

PAINTBRUSHES, LOUSEWORTS, ETC.

1. **OWL-CLOVER,** *Orthocarpus tenuifolius* (Pursh) Benth.   p. 173
   An annual plant that looks like the yellow paintbrushes (*Castilleja*). Note 2 lips of corolla do not
   differ greatly in size.   Figwort Family

2. **SPLITLEAF PAINTED-CUP,** *Castilleja rhexifolia* Rydb.   p. 170
   Note highly colored bracts, which appear to be the
   flowers; 2 lips of corolla differ greatly in size. *C.
   rhexifolia* has narrow, usually entire leaves. Leaves
   of *C. linariaefolia* are generally divided.
                                      Figwort Family

3. **INDIAN PAINTBRUSH,** *Castilleja miniata* Dougl.   p. 170
   This has lanceolate, mostly entire leaves.
                                      Figwort Family

4. **EARLY PAINTBRUSH,** *Castilleja chromosa* Nels.   p. 170
   Leaves deeply cleft into spreading lobes which are
   linear or linear-lanceolate. An early-blooming
   species.   Figwort Family

5. **YELLOW PAINTBRUSH,** *Castilleja sulphurea* Rydb.   p. 168
   Note yellow bracts and hairy grayish-colored leaves.
                                      Figwort Family

6. **BUTTER-AND-EGGS,** *Linaria vulgaris* Hill   p. 172
   Dense raceme of yellow-orange flowers with spur at
   base of corolla; numerous linear leaves.
                                      Figwort Family

7. **ELEPHANTHEAD,** *Pedicularis groenlandica* Retz.   p. 176
   Note dense spike of pink, elephant-head flowers
   and the pinnately divided leaves.   Figwort Family

8. **YELLOW MONKEYFLOWER,** *Mimulus guttatus* DC.   p. 172
   Yellow red-spotted snapdragon-like flowers. Note
   smooth toothed leaves and hollow stems. Plant
   generally 2–18 in. high.   Figwort Family

Plate 19

MONKEYFLOWERS, HONEYSUCKLE, ELDERBERRY, VALERIAN, HAREBELL, ARNICA

1. **MUSK PLANT,** *Mimulus moschatus* Dougl.   p. 172
   A short-stemmed perennial with yellow funnel-
   form corolla; grows in wet soil.   Figwort Family

2. **RED MONKEYFLOWER,** *Mimulus lewisii* Pursh   p. 172
   A large rose-red snapdragon-like flower marked by
   2 bright yellow patches in the funnel-form throat;
   stamens 4. Usually grows a foot or more high, in
   patches near water.   Figwort Family

3. **DWARF MONKEYFLOWER**   pp. 172, 173
   Mimulus nanus H. & A.
   A small annual with almost stalkless reddish-purple
   flowers up to ¾ in. long; favors bare areas and
   loose soil.   Figwort Family

4. **HONEYSUCKLE,** *Lonicera ciliosa* (Pursh) Poir.   p. 182
   A climbing woody vine with whorls of yellow or
   orange trumpet-shaped flowers; berries bright red,
   leaves dark green above, whitish and waxy below.
   Honeysuckle Family

5. **ELDERBERRY,** *Sambucus coerulea* Raf.   p. 183
   Treelike plant or shrub with opposite compound
   leaves, flat-topped white flower clusters, and blue
   berries; stems hollow and pithy.
   Honeysuckle Family

6. **VALERIAN,** *Valeriana dioica* L.   p. 184
   A tall plant with dissected stem leaves, small white
   or pink flower clusters; flower saucer-shaped,
   5-lobed, with 3 stamens.   Valerian Family

7. **HAREBELL,** *Campanula rotundifolia* L.   p. 185
   Violet-blue, bell-shaped flowers that hang down
   from slender tall stems bearing long alternate linear
   leaves.   Bluebell Family

8. **ARNICA,** *Arnica cordifolia* Hook.   p. 193
   A single-stem plant with yellow composite flowers
   and opposite, heart-shaped, slightly hairy leaves;
   usually growing in Lodgepole or aspen woods.
   Composite Family

Plate 20

MINTS, BEDSTRAW, BEARDTONGUES, AND COMPOSITES

1. **MINT,** *Mentha arvensis* L.   p. 162
    Note irregular flowers clustered in axils of leaves,
    square stem, opposite leaves.   Mint Family

2. **GIANT-HYSSOP,** *Agastache urticifolia* (Kuntze) Rydb.   p. 161
    Characterized by dense terminal spike of purplish
    to whitish flowers on stems 2–5 ft. tall, opposite
    leaves.   Mint Family

3. **BEDSTRAW,** *Galium boreale* L.   p. 180
    Distinguished by 4-angled stems, whorled leaves,
    and numerous small, white, saucer-shaped flowers.
                                    Madder Family

4. **BLUE PENSTEMON,** *Penstemon cyaneus* Penn.   p. 178
    Leaves and stem smooth; corolla sky-blue, with
    purplish tube.   Figwort Family

5. **PARROTS-BEAK,** *Pedicularis racemosa* Dougl.   p. 175
    Flowers white, leaves linear and double-toothed.
                                    Figwort Family

6. **ALBERT'S PENSTEMON,** *Penstemon albertinus* Greene   p. 178
    Note bright green leaves, blue-violet flowers.
                                    Figwort Family

7. **CRESTED BEARDTONGUE**   p. 178
    Penstemon eriantherus Pursh
        Leaves and stem hairy; corolla glandular-hairy
        and lilac-purple.   Figwort Family

8. **ARROWLEAF BALSAMROOT**   p. 197
    Balsamorhiza sagittata (Pursh) Nutt.
        The long-stalked arrow-shaped leaves with silvery-
        gray hairs distinguish this plant.   Composite Family

9. **BLANKETFLOWER,** *Gaillardia aristata* Pursh   p. 212
    Note orange- to purplish-red diskflowers and yellow
    rayflowers; diskflowers are elongated and covered
    with hairs.   Composite Family

Plate 21

MOUNTAIN PENSTEMON AND COMPOSITES

1. **MOUNTAIN PENSTEMON** pp. 177, 178
   Penstemon montanus Greene
   A lavender-flowered penstemon with stiff serrate
   leaves and woody stem; grows on high dry sites.
   Figwort Family

2. **BALSAMROOT,** *Balsamorhiza hookeri* Nutt. p. 197
   Yellow sunflower-like flowers arising from clumps
   of incised green leaves that are glandular and hairy.
   Composite Family

3. **SHOWY DAISY,** *Erigeron speciosus* (Lindl.) DC. p. 210
   A daisy with hairy bracts, narrow lilac rayflowers,
   and tubular, yellow diskflowers; leaves numerous,
   often 3-nerved, with fringed leaf margins.
   Composite Family

4. **CUTLEAF DAISY,** *Erigeron compositus* Pursh p. 208
   Each stem terminates in a single head of flowers,
   diskflowers being yellow and rayflowers white, pink,
   or blue; greatly dissected leaves mostly basal and
   divided into 3's. Composite Family

5. **SALSIFY,** *Tragopogon dubius* Scop. p. 232
   A yellow dandelion-like flower on stems having
   grasslike clasping leaves; conspicuous ripened seed
   heads 2–3 in. across; milky juice. Composite Family

6. **ALPINE SUNFLOWER** p. 221
   Hymenoxys grandiflora (T. & G.) Parker
   A stout low alpine plant with enormous sunflower-
   like heads 2–3 in. broad. Leaves gray, woolly, and
   dissected. Composite Family

7. **ALPINE ASTER,** *Aster alpigenus* (T. & G.) Gray p. 195
   A dwarf perennial found in high mts., often slightly
   cottony and bracts often purplish.
   Composite Family

8. **TOWNSENDIA,** *Townsendia sericea* Hook. p. 232
   Flower head is large compared to rest of plant;
   rayflowers rose-purple, diskflowers yellow; stems
   2 in. high or less, borne among a heavy clump of
   leaves. Composite Family

Plate 22

COMPOSITES (COMPOSITE FAMILY)

1. **SUNFLOWER,** *Helianthus annuus* L.   p. 218
   Note the brownish diskflowers and ovate leaves, rough to the touch. Other species of *Helianthus* (with exception of *H. petiolaris*) have yellow diskflowers.

2. **HELIANTHELLA**   p. 217
   Helianthella quinquenervis (Hook.) Gray
   Smaller than *Helianthus annuus* and leaves 5-nerved. The rayflowers are pale yellow and bracts are ovate and soft; in contrast, bracts around flower head of *Helianthella uniflora* are lance-linear and firm and rayflowers are bright yellow.

3. **LITTLE SUNFLOWER**   p. 216
   Helianthella uniflora (Nutt.) T. & G.
   A sunflower-appearing plant with bright yellow rayflowers and lance-linear bracts; leaves more or less 3-nerved.

4. **GOLDENEYE,** *Viguiera multiflora* (Nutt.) Blake   p. 234
   Looks like a small sunflower but has slender branching stems and an enlarged, rounded receptacle. Blooms in late summer.

5. **WESTERN CONEFLOWER**   p. 225
   Rudbeckia occidentalis Nutt.
   Characterized by a head of dark tubular diskflowers, absence of rayflowers.

6. **PUSSYTOES,** *Antennaria rosea* Greene   p. 190
   Mat-forming plant, gray-green and woolly; bracts pearly white to rose-colored and appear to be the flowers.

7. **RABBITBRUSH,** *Chrysothamnus nauseosus* (Pall.) Britt.   p. 202
   Lacks rayflowers, has yellowish involucral bracts; branches are covered with matted, white-woolly hairs.

8. **BEGGARTICKS,** *Bidens cernua* L.   p. 198
   Note yellow rayflowers and base of lance-shaped leaves encircling stem.

9. **GOLDENROD,** *Solidago occidentalis* (Nutt.) T. & G.   p. 227
   Note the numerous small flower heads characteristically not on 1 side of curved branches only. *S. elongata* has flower heads on 1 side of branches.

Plate 23

COMPOSITES (COMPOSITE FAMILY)

1. **THICKSTEM ASTER,** *Aster integrifolius* Nutt.   p. 196
   A stout plant with broad clasping leaves and heads
   of violet-purple rayflowers and orange-yellow diskflowers.

2. **GUMWEED,** *Grindelia squarrosa* (Pursh) Dunal   p. 213
   A yellow-flowered branched composite with sticky
   flowers and leaves; tips of narrow bracts recurved.

3. **PARRY TOWNSENDIA,** *Townsendia parryi* D. C. Eat.   p. 231
   Note large solitary aster-like head, with violet
   rayflowers. Bracts of flower head long-pointed.

4. **SOW-THISTLE,** *Sonchus uliginosus* Bieb.   p. 228
   Flowers of yellow rayflowers only, leaves cut,
   toothed, and prickly-edged; milky sap throughout.

5. **CONEFLOWER,** *Ratibida columnifera* (Nutt.) W. & S.   p. 224
   Flower head of diskflowers is shaped like a thimble,
   and purplish brown; 3 to 7 yellow or purplish rayflowers at base of cone.

6. **RUDBECKIA,** *Rudbeckia laciniata* L.   p. 225
   A composite with large dark cylindrical heads of
   diskflowers and conspicuous orange or yellow rayflowers; leaves pinnately cleft.

7. **WOOLLY YELLOWDAISY**   p. 211
   Eriophyllum lanatum (Pursh) Forbes var. *integrifolium* (Hook) Smiley
   Ray- and diskflowers yellow, on long slender stems;
   plant white-woolly, basal parts woody.

8. **BLUE-FLOWERED LETTUCE**   p. 223
   Lactuca pulchella (Pursh) DC.
   Lavender-blue rayflowered heads appear single at
   ends of branches; leaves narrow and long, juice
   milky.

9. **ENGELMANN ASTER**   p. 197
   Aster engelmannii (D. C. Eat.) Gray
   A tall plant with large ragged heads of white or
   slightly pinkish rayflowers about 1 in. long; smooth-
   edged lance-shaped leaves.

Plate 24

COMPOSITES (COMPOSITE FAMILY)

1. **MULES-EARS,** *Wyethia amplexicaulis* Nutt.   p. 235
   One to 5 large yellow flowering heads on a stalk;
   long, glossy leaves very numerous.

2. **WHITE WYETHIA,** *Wyethia helianthoides* Nutt.   p. 236
   Similar to above but rayflowers are white or cream-
   colored.

3. **BRISTLE THISTLE,** *Carduus nutans* L.   p. 199
   Flower heads nodding; involucral bracts sharp,
   stiff, and conspicuous. Stem winged by leaf bases.

4. **BULL THISTLE,** *Cirsium vulgare* (Savi) Airy-Shaw   p. 206
   Note upper leaf surface covered with short stiff
   hairs. Stem edged with leaflike tissue.

5. **SPOTTED KNAPWEED,** *Centaurea maculosa* Lam.   p. 200
   Numerous branches bearing a single head of pink-
   purple flowers. Finely divided leaves.

6. **ELK THISTLE,** *Cirsium foliosum* (Hook.) DC.   p. 204
   Cluster of white to purple flowers at top of plant;
   succulent stem tapers little from bottom to top.
   Leaves and stem grayish green.

7. **DUSTY MAIDEN,** *Chaenactis alpina* (Gray) Jones   p. 201
   A dusty-looking plant with flesh-colored tubular
   flowers and much-dissected leaves.

8. **RUSHPINK,** *Lygodesmia grandiflora* (Nutt.) T. & G.   p. 223
   A branched rushlike plant with pink flower heads.

KINNIKINNICK *Arctostaphylos uva-ursi* (L.) Spreng. **Pl. 15**
    Family: Ericaceae (Heath).
    Other names: Manzanita, Bearberry, Hog Cranberry.
    Description: A prostrate, matted evergreen shrub with reddish peeling or scaling bark, and small white to pink, urn-shaped, 5-parted waxy flowers in short racemes. Numerous, leathery, ovate leaves are ½–1 in. long and fruit is a bright red, roundish berry about size of a pea.

    Plants most likely to be confused with this are the species of *Gaultheria*, but flowers of these shrubs grow singly from leaf axils, and fruits and leaves have a wintergreen flavor. See Creeping Wintergreen (*Gaultheria humifusa* [Graham] Rydb.), Plate 14.
    Related species: *A. patula*, occurring in s. Rockies, is an erect shrub with creamy-white to yellowish-brown berries.
    Flowering season: May and first part of June. Starts to flower when tree swallows return and is in full bloom when eggs of Canada geese begin to hatch. Berries are well formed but green when young of the Colorado chipmunk are seen scampering about.
    Where found: G, Y, T, R. Dry, open woods, often on gravelly or sandy soil. In the West, typically associated with Ponderosa Pine forests. Found on sand dunes along seashore, and up to and above timberline in mts. Often an indicator of poor soil. Kinnikinnick and its varieties are circumpolar, being found in arctic N. America as well as in Europe and Asia. Extends south to Virginia, Illinois, New Mexico, and California. Other manzanitas are less widely distributed, being largely confined to N. America. About 40 species of *Arctostaphylos* occur in w. N. America and are especially abundant in our Pacific Coast states; 4 in Rocky Mt. area.
    Interesting facts: *Uva-ursi* means bear's grape. The leaves and twigs are eaten by deer and mountain sheep during fall and winter and the berries by black bears, rodents, songbirds, turkeys, and grouse. The Indians used the leaves as an adulterant for tobacco, and our drug establishments gather them for their medicinal value. They are used as an astringent, tonic, and a diuretic. They contain two glucosides (arbutin and ericolin), as well as gallic and tannic acids. The tannin extracted from the Kinnikinnick leaves was used in curing pelts, and in Russia the plant is still an important source of tannin. Kinnikinnick is a valuable ground cover for checking soil erosion on watersheds.
    The berries remain on the plants over winter and are eaten by Indians and Eskimos. Raw, they have a bittersweet flavor and pucker the mouth. When boiled, they become much sweeter and serve as food in an emergency. The evergreen leaves and bright orange or red berries are frequently used as

Christmas decorations. Early pioneers and Indians mixed about equal parts of the dried leaves of Kinnikinnick with the dry inner bark of Red-osier Dogwood to make a smoking tobacco.

SWAMP-LAUREL *Kalmia polifolia* Wang. **Pl. 15**
    Family: Ericaceae (Heath).
    Other names: Pale-laurel, American Laurel.
    Description: A low branching shrub, 6–24 in. tall, with bright pink or rose flowers that usually come 2 to 10 together on slender, red stalks. The 5 petals are united to form a flattish saucerlike corolla ½–¾ in. broad. Stamens lie in depressions or small pouches. Leaves are leathery, evergreen, oval, up to 1 in. long, and waxy white beneath.
    This plant is not likely to be confused with anything else in our mts. It somewhat resembles Mountain Heath (*Phyllodoce empetriformis*), but the leaves are larger and the flowers saucer-shaped rather than urn-shaped.
    Flowering season: Latter part of June to first part of Aug. Mosquitoes are becoming a nuisance both where and when this plant blooms.
    Where found: G, Y, T, R. Bogs and wet soil along streams in colder portions of N. America. Occurs from Alaska to Greenland, south to Pennsylvania, Minnesota, and in mts. of West to Colorado and California. To see this beautiful flower in Rocky Mt. area generally you must climb to timberline. *Kalmia* is a N. American genus of about 8 species, but Swamp-laurel the only one in Rockies.
    Interesting facts: *Polifolia* means gray with leaves of polium. Some botanists consider the western plant to be different from the eastern plant (*K. occidentalis*), and so give it a distinct name. The two intergrade into each other so nicely that this distinctness is doubtful. All parts of Swamp-laurel but the wood contain a poisonous substance, andromedotoxin. Cattle and sheep as well as humans have been poisoned by eating or chewing the laurels. At times honey derived from the nectar of the flowers is poisonous. The laurels are closely related to the rhododendrons so widely used as ornamentals. *K. latifolia* is the state flower of Pennsylvania.

BLUEBERRY *Vaccinium ovalifolium* Sm. **Pl. 14**
    Family: Ericaceae (Heath).
    Other names: Oval-leaf Whortleberry, Huckleberry, Bilberry.
    Description: A low erect shrub with alternate leaves and small, solitary, inconspicuous pink or white flowers, stem much branched, branches grooved and often reddish. Leaves are elliptic, entire, glabrous above, glaucous beneath. Fruit is bluish or purple, almost black at maturity.
    Related species: This can be confused with members of the

same genus. (1) Big Whortleberry (*V. membranaceum* Dougl.) has oval serrate leaves; see illus. below. (2) *V. occidentale* has white or pink flowers, often in clusters, attached to woody portion of stem; *V. ovalifolium* has flowers originating from green nonwoody terminal portion of stem. (3) *V. oreophilum* is usually less than 1 ft. high, has brownish stems and blue-black berries. (4) Grouse Whortleberry (*V. scoparium* Leiberg) has slender greenish, broomlike branches, bright red berries, and is especially conspicuous in Lodgepole forests of Yellowstone Natl. Park; see illus. below.

Big Whortleberry (*Vaccinium membranaceum* Dougl.) and Grouse Whortleberry (*V. scoparium* Leiberg)

Flowering season: June and July, depending upon elevation. In bloom when coyote pups leave the den.
Where found: Y, T, G. Common in Lodgepole forests and other sites where the soil is acid. Found throughout n. Rocky Mts. from 6000 to 9000 ft. Extends from Alaska to Oregon, eastward to Idaho, Montana, and Wyoming. Genus *Vaccinium* widely distributed in N. Hemisphere and occurs in mt. regions of tropics. It is composed of approximately 60 to 70 species; about 15 occur in Rocky Mts.

Interesting facts: *Ovalifolium* means oval-leaved. The sweet, pleasant-flavored berries of this plant and other blueberries were used extensively by the Indians and probably are more sought after by wild-fruit harvesters than any other berry in the Rockies. They are delicious raw and make excellent jam, jelly, and pies. They have a distinct penetrating odor. Some species are grown commercially.

The berries of all species are eaten by grouse, ptarmigan, rodents, marten, coyotes, and many other birds and mammals. They form a staple food of both black and grizzly bears during July, Aug., and Sept. Berries ripen first in the valleys, later at higher altitudes. Bears move up the mts. to take advantage of the ripening fruit, subsisting entirely on these for days at a time. They consume the leaves with the berries, and because their digestive tracts are better adapted to digest flesh than vegetation the leaves and many of the berries pass through the bear intact. During a poor berry season, grizzly bears will travel as much as 10 to 15 miles daily between berry patches and other sources of food. Deer and elk consume the leaves and tender current growth.

MOUNTAIN HEATH   Pl. 15
Phyllodoce empetriformis (Sw.) D. Don
   Family: Ericaceae (Heath).
   Other names: Heather, Heath, Pink Mountain-heather.
   Description: A small evergreen shrub often growing in mats, with umbels of bright pink urn-shaped flowers on long, slender stalks. Entire plant attains a height of only 8–20 in., with branches that appear much like miniature firs or spruces. Leaves numerous, linear, and about ½ in. long.
   Related species: There is another species, *P. glanduliflora*, whose general appearance is similar, but flowers are yellow and whole flower cluster is densely glandular and hairy.
   Flowering season: Latter part of June to first part of Aug. Blooms at high altitudes soon after mountain climbers invade the peaks and ice leaves the high lakes.
   Where found: G, Y, T. Moist to wet soil of our higher mts., from a short distance below timberline to well above it. Can be found from Alaska to Alberta, south to California and possibly Colorado. There are about 8 species of *Phyllodoce*, occupying colder parts of N. Hemisphere; 2 occur in Rockies.
   Interesting facts: *Empetriformis* means empetrum-like. Often people are amazed to see these plants in flower, for the needle-like leaves and over-all appearance suggest our evergreen cone-bearing trees. These plants, however, always bear flowers, never cones. Our Mountain Heath is well known to the mountain climber and is a close relative of Scotch Heath and the heathers of the Old World. The leaves are revolute, an adapta-

tion to reduce water loss through evaporation. Alpine plants, like desert plants, must conserve water when the water in the soil is frozen.

SHOOTINGSTAR Pl. 15
Dodecatheon pauciflorum (Dur.) Greene
>**Family:** Primulaceae (Primrose).
>**Other names:** American Cowslip, Birdbills.
>**Description:** The flowers quickly arouse the interest of even the most casual observer. They are in terminal umbels and usually hang downward when fully expanded. Petals are bright rose-purple, ½–1 in. long, and flare backward over ovary and part of pedicel. Fused stamens form a beak pointing downward. Plant is a perennial herb with simple, basal leaves and flowering stalks 6–16 in. tall.

Shootingstar could be confused with several other members of the Primrose family, but the reflexed petals are quite distinctive. At times flowers are found whose petals are white rather than rose-purple.
>**Related species:** (1) *D. jeffreyi* is a larger and stouter plant, the anthers with very short filaments. (2) *D. dentatum* is the only shootingstar in Rockies whose leaves are coarsely toothed; flowers are white. Both occur in n. and w. Rockies.
>**Flowering season:** Latter part of April through July. Starts blooming when sparrow hawks are screaming and defending their nesting territories, and red-tailed hawks are laying eggs. Tells the fisherman it is time to try his luck with the steelhead as they migrate to spawning beds.
>**Where found:** G, Y, T, R. Moist to wet soil in open places of plains, hills, and mt. sides. Has been collected from our lowest valleys up to nearly 12,000 ft. in mts., and from Saskatchewan to B.C., south to California, Arizona, and Colorado. There are about 30 species of *Dodecatheon* found mainly in w. N. America; several in e. U.S. and about same number in e. Asia. Five species occur in Rocky Mt. area.
>**Interesting facts:** The genus name comes from two Greek words, *dodeka* (twelve) and *theoi* (gods). *Pauciflorum* means few-flowered. Elk and deer eat the plant in early spring when green forage is still scarce. California Indians roasted the roots and leaves of the Henderson Shootingstar (*D. hendersonii*). It is quite likely that other species could be used as emergency foods.

PARRY PRIMROSE *Primula parryi* Gray Pl. 15
>**Family:** Primulaceae (Primrose).
>**Other names:** Alpine Primrose.
>**Description:** The only large blood-red flowering plant 6–18 in. high with funnel-form flowers found in the Rockies in alpine and subalpine regions. Very rank-smelling, and possesses large

smooth green leaves 4–12 in. long, growing in a rosette at base of stem. Flowers are borne in an umbel of 3 to 12 flowers, and each flower has a bell-shaped calyx, 5-parted funnel-form corolla, 5 stamens opposite corolla lobes, and 1 pistil. Considerably larger than any other Rocky Mt. primrose.

The shootingstars (*Dodecatheon*), though somewhat resembling the Parry Primrose, are immediately distinguished by their reflexed corolla lobes and forward-projecting anthers, a combination that gives the "shooting star" appearance.

Related species: (1) *P. incana* has lilac-colored flowers and stem and leaves are whitish; (2) *P. angustifolia* is purple-flowered but stem and leaves are green. Both plants smaller than Parry Primrose.

Flowering season: Found in bloom from about mid-July to mid-Aug. You may expect to find it in bloom when Monkshood and Fireweed first appear at lower elevations.

Where found: T, R. Found growing from 8000 to 12,000 ft. Most abundant above timberline at head of glaciated canyons. Look for it in wet or damp areas, usually on banks of mt. streams, at edges of melting snowfields, and in moist recesses formed by overhanging rocks. Found in Rocky Mt. region from Montana to New Mexico, west to Nevada and Idaho. The genus, of around 150 species, is found in e. and w. U.S., Europe, Asia, India, and Japan; well represented in Alps and Himalayas. Six species in Rocky Mts.

Interesting facts: *Parryi* means named for Charles C. Parry. The Parry Primrose is one of the largest alpine flowers in the region. It is a favorite flower with mountain climbers, who find it growing tall and upright in places where other flowers are stunted and matted from the harsh environment. The red hue of the Parry Primrose is due to one of the anthocyanins. These chemicals give color to many flowers, fruits, leaves, and stems. They impart a red coloring when in an acid medium and change to purple and blue as the medium becomes alkaline.

GREEN GENTIAN   *Frasera speciosa* Dougl.   **Pl. 15**

Family: Gentianaceae (Gentian).

Other names: Deertongue, Monument Plant, Giant Frasera, Elkweed, and *Swertia radiata*.

Description: A biennial. First-year growth is a cluster of long-stalked, straplike leaves. This cluster is quite distinctive and, once learned, is not easily confused with other plants. Mature plant consists of a single, coarse, erect, unbranched stem, 2–5 ft. tall, bearing numerous greenish-white flowers spotted with purple. Flowers borne on long stalks from axils of upper leaves, and are ½–¾ in. broad. Stem densely covered with lance-shaped leaves that may be 1 ft. long at base of plant but decreasing in size toward top. When viewed in its entirety this is not a striking plant, but when individual wheel-shaped flowers are closely observed its unusual beauty is revealed.

The Green Gentian is not usually confused with other plants because of its strict upright habit and pattern of growing in fields or open woods, where it stands out conspicuously.

Related species: (1) *F. fastigiata* is also a large plant but it has light blue flowers; (2) *F. albicaulis* has white, clustered stems less than 2 ft. tall. Both plants occur only in w. Rockies and westward.

Flowering season: June, July, and first part of Aug. First blooms when young robins are beginning to feather.

Where found: Y, T, R. Medium-dry to moist soil of open areas, from around 6500 to above 10,000 ft. in mts. Scattered from Montana to Washington, south to California and New Mexico. Four species occur in Rocky Mt. area.

Interesting facts: *Speciosa* means showy. It is reported that the Indians ate the fleshy root of this plant, but the root of *F. carolinensis* has been used as an emetic and cathartic in medicine and most members of the Gentian family are used medicinally. Elk and cattle find the Green Gentian palatable and eat it along with other spring plants. They particularly prefer the

Green Gentian (*Frasera speciosa* Dougl.)

young basal leaves, generally eating them before the flowering stalk appears. The brown sturdy stalk of this plant can be seen standing erect, resisting the drifting snow until late winter.

MOUNTAIN GENTIAN *Gentiana calycosa* Griseb. Pl. 16

Family: Gentianaceae (Gentian).

Other names: Blue Gentian, Pleated Gentian.

Description: An erect bell-shaped flower, deep blue in color, usually with but a single flower on a stem 4–15 in. tall, and possessing opposite, ovate leaves.

The other common perennial gentians in the region do not occur in the high mts., and they usually have more than 1 flower on a stem. No other high-mt. flower is likely to be confused with it.

Flowering season: First appears late in July and blooms throughout Aug., and into Sept. Still conspicuous when mountain bluebird and blackbirds begin to congregate in flocks.

Where found: G, Y, T. Found growing from 7000 to 10,000 ft. Look for it on rocky outcrops, moist slopes, streambanks, and mt. bogs. Ranges from Montana to B.C., south to California and Utah. Twenty species occur in Rocky Mt. area.

Interesting facts: *Calycosa* means cuplike. The Mountain Gentian is well named, for it and its relatives are at home in the Alps, Himalayas, and Andes, as well as the high Rockies. The Stemless and Carved Gentians of the Alps are so similar to *G. calycosa* that they could easily be mistaken for our Mountain Gentian, as could some of the blue-flowered species that climb the Himalayas to a height of 16,000 ft. In Europe and Asia gentians were sought for their medicinal value, since the gentians contain a clear bitter fluid that is supposed to have a tonic effect. Early settlers used some of our American gentians in this way.

WESTERN FRINGED GENTIAN Pl. 16
Gentiana thermalis Kuntze

Family: Gentianaceae (Gentian).

Other names: Feather Gentian, Rocky Mountain Fringed Gentian.

Description: The flowers are bluish purple, 1–2 in. long, with just 1 flower at the end of each stem. The 5 petals are fringed around edge. Plant is an annual, 4–16 in. tall, usually branched only near base. Leaves are basal or opposite on stems.

There are several species of gentians in the Rockies that might be confused with this plant, but none of the annual plants have purple flowers 1 in. long. Perennial species usually have more than 1 flower on a stem.

Related species: (1) Pleated Gentian (*G. affinis* Griseb.) is more graceful, has a narrow funnel-form corolla with pleated sinuses and linear calyx lobes (see illus. below); (2) *G. strictiflora* is a slender annual with numerous flowers crowded together. These can be found throughout Rocky Mts. (3) *G. romanzovii* has yellowish-white flowers spotted or streaked with purple and are almost 2 in. long; occurs in e. and cent. Rockies.

Flowering season: Latter part of June to Aug. Starts to bloom at about same time as the Beargrass and Mountain Death-camas. Young sharp-shinned hawks are hatching at this time. Continues to bloom until flowers are gone and many birds are beginning to migrate south. Still conspicuous when bull elk begin to bugle in early Sept.

Where found: Y, T, R. Wet soil of meadows, along streams, and especially about warm springs and pools; hence its specific name. Occurs from foothills up to around 13,000 ft., and distributed from the Mackenzie area south to Idaho, Arizona, and New Mexico. There are about 300 species of gentians, occurring mainly in mountainous and cooler parts of the earth; 20 occur in Rockies.

Interesting facts: *Thermalis* means of warm areas. In 1926 the Western Fringed Gentian was adopted as the official flower for

Pleated Gentian (*Gentiana affinis* Griseb.)

Yellowstone Natl. Park. It was an excellent choice because its rich-colored blossoms can be found throughout most of the tourist season. Gentians will always welcome the mountain climber, for whether he climbs in the Himalayas, Alps, or Andes he will meet them in his hazardous ascents.

PINK MILKWEED *Asclepias speciosa* Torr.   **Pl. 16**
Family: Asclepiadaceae (Milkweed).
Other names: Silkweed, Butterflyweed, Common Milkweed.
Description: A coarse perennial 2–6 ft. tall, with pink to whitish flowers almost 1 in. broad. These are arranged in dense spherical umbels 2–3 in. broad, and are borne on stalks arising in angles of upper leaves. Petals are reflexed and the leaves are opposite, thick, lance-shaped, and almost 1 ft. long. Flowers give rise to a rough, showy pod about 3 in. long filled with flat seeds tufted with long silky hairs. Entire plant contains a thick milky juice, hence the name.

No other plant in the Rockies is likely to be confused with this one when in bloom.

Related species: (1) *A. capricornu* is a small plant about 1 ft. tall, with erect or only slightly spreading petals and leaves occurring at irregular intervals; (2) *A. subverticillata* has linear, whorled leaves and white flowers; (3) *A. tuberosa* has orange to red flowers.

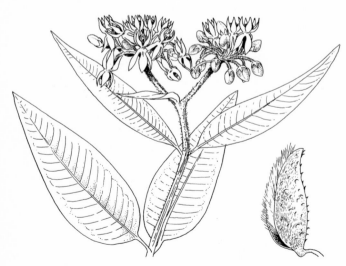

Pink Milkweed (*Asclepias speciosa* Torr.)

Flowering season: June and July.

Where found: G, R. Moist soil of fields, roadsides, along fence rows, and in waste places. Grows in valleys and prairies from Minnesota to B.C., south to California and Texas. There are just under 100 species of *Asclepias*, mostly natives of New World; 7 or 8 species occur in Rocky Mts.

Interesting facts: The name *Asclepias* comes from *Asklepios*, the Greek god of medicine; *speciosa* means showy. The milkweeds have been used in medicine for centuries. The milky sap, called latex, occurs in a special series of branching tubes in the tissues. Its composition varies in different groups of plants. In the rubber tree, latex contains a high percentage of rubber, in the poppy it is the source of opium, in the Upas tree of the tropics it is poisonous and is used by the natives to treat their arrows. In the cow trees of Venezuela latex is nutritious and is used as food much like ordinary milk. In the Banyan tree and other figs it is used to make sticky "bird lime" for trapping various species of birds. Young shoots, leaves, buds, flowers, and pods of Pink Milkweed as well as other milkweeds are used as food by both whites and Indians. Plant parts should be boiled in several changes of water. Young shoots are best; they look and taste somewhat like asparagus. In the early growing stages this plant can be confused with dogbanes (*Apocynum*). The latter contains bitter and poisonous glucosides. Milkweeds and the closely related dogbanes contain tough fibers similar to those found in the flax plant. Strong string or cord can readily be twisted from the fibers. The silky seed hairs are used by the goldfinch for nest building. The Pink Milkweed is poisonous to cattle and horses. It is often cut with hay and such hay may be dangerous to use as livestock feed.

MORNING-GLORY *Convolvulus arvensis* L.   Pl. 17

Family: Convolvulaceae (Morning-glory).

Other names: Bindweed, Glorybind.

Description: A trailing or twining plant with white or pinkish flowers that are funnel-shaped and about 1 in. broad and usually occur 1 to 2 in leaf axils. Alternate leaves have 2 lobes projecting outward and downward at base. Plant forms dense patches and, in cultivated fields, may cover acres of land, largely preventing growth of field crops.

Related species: *C. sepium* is easily confused with this one, but has bracts larger instead of smaller than the calyx.

Flowering season: Latter part of May through July.

Where found: Y. Moist soil of fields, along roadsides, and in waste places, especially where soil has been disturbed. This weed, introduced from Europe, has scattered over much of N. America. There are around 200 species of *Convolvulus* distributed over most of the earth; only 4 or 5 in Rocky Mts.

Interesting facts: *Arvensis* means of fields. The Morning-glory is one of the most serious field weeds in Idaho. The common garden Morning-glory, the Moonflower, and the Sweet Potato are close relatives of this plant. *Ipomoea leptophylla* and *I. pandurata* possess huge deep-seated roots. Though not particularly palatable or nutritious, they were dug by Indians and roasted in times of famine.

COLLOMIA   *Collomia linearis* Nutt.   **Pl. 14**

Family: Polemoniaceae (Phlox).
Other names: Tiny Trumpet.
Description: The flowers are dark to light pink, tubular, and ¼–½ in. long; form dense clusters in axils of leafy bracts at top of stem or branches. Plant is a slender annual, usually unbranched, at least on lower part of stem, and attains height of 4–8 in.

Several flowers in the Phlox family can be confused with this one, but the slender, tubular, pink flowers, narrow undivided leaves, and compact, leafy-bracted cluster of flowers are fairly distinctive.
Related species: (1) *C. grandiflora* is a larger plant and has salmon-colored to yellowish flowers about 1 in. long; (2) *C. debilis*, occurring on western slope of n. Rockies at high altitudes, is a prostrate perennial with lavender flowers.
Flowering season: Latter part of May to first part of Aug.
Where found: Y, T, R. Medium-dry to moist soil of open prairies, valleys, and in mts. up to around 8000 ft. This plant a native of w. N. America, but now scattered over most of e. N. America. There are about 15 species of *Collomia*, all native to w. N. America and S. America; about 10 species in Rockies.
Interesting facts: The name of this genus comes from the word *kolla*, meaning glue; *linearis* means linear. The seeds of this plant contain an unusual quantity of mucus in their outer covering. When these are dropped into water the mucus diffuses and forms a smokelike cloud around the seeds.

SCARLET GILIA   *Gilia aggregata* (Pursh) Spreng.   **Pl. 16**

Family: Polemoniaceae (Phlox).
Other names: Skyrocket, Foxfire, Polecat Plant.
Description: The brilliant red coloring immediately attracts attention. Blossoms usually numerous and normally red, but sometimes vary to pink, orange, and even white. Trumpet-shaped flowers are ¾–1½ in. long. Plant is a biennial. It attains a height of 1–3 ft., and has considerably dissected leaves.

The flower could be confused with the flower of Honeysuckle

(*Lonicera ciliosa*), but this grows on a climbing vine; see Plate 19. Odor from crushed upper leaves is distinctly that of skunk, hence the common name Polecat Plant. Other members of this family, such as the Sky Pilot (*Polemonium viscosum*), have a skunk smell but blossoms are purple, not red.

Related species: (1) *G. congesta* is a white-flowered perennial with dissected leaves which is 1 ft. or less tall. (2) *G. sinuata* is an annual with a rosette of divided leaves and stem leaves reduced upward; lilac to white funnel-form flowers are about ⅛ in. long and occur on long stalks. These common throughout Rockies.

Scarlet Gilia (*Gilia aggregata* [Pursh] Spreng.)

Flowering season: May, June, and July. Blooms about time young ravens leave nest. On any one locality it remains in bloom for about a month.

Where found: Y, T, R. Dry soil of valleys, hillsides, and mt. ridges. Watch for it among the Big Sagebrush from Montana to B.C., south to California and New Mexico. Found from lowest valleys up to about timberline. Thirty species occur in Rockies.

Interesting facts: *Aggregata* means clustered. It is reported to contain saponin, a chemical allied to soap, and poisonous.

However, sheep eat the plant without ill effects. Scarlet Gilia is one of our showy plants that characteristically grow in extensive patches. During a favorable year dandelions literally blanket meadows and low hills in brilliant yellow hues; blue Camas from a distance will give the appearance of a lake; White Wyethia looks like the last of winter's snow, pocketed in a narrow valley; and Scarlet Gilia, like the embers of a dying fire amid the gray sage, is the most spectacular of all.

WHITE PHLOX   *Phlox multiflora* Nels.   **Pl. 16**
   Family: Polemoniaceae (Phlox).
   Other names: Rockhill Phlox, Spreading Phlox.
   Description: Distinguishing the various phlox species is difficult, but all are characterized by symmetrical blossoms with long tubes and 5 spreading petals. The style is divided into 3 parts. White Phlox is a low, mat-forming plant with white to lilac-colored flowers that develop singly at ends of branches and are about ¾ in. long. Main branches of stems are woody and prostrate, and may be 1 ft. long. Growing along these are short, upright, herbaceous branches, covered with linear leaves.
   Related species: (1) *P. hoodii* is a white or bluish-flowered, mat-forming perennial of valley floors and foothills. (2) Long-leaved Phlox (*P. longifolia* Nutt.), Plate 16, is upright rather than mat-forming, and has longer leaves than White Phlox has, and generally larger and pink flowers. (3) *P. kelseyi* has bright blue or lilac flowers.
   Flowering season: Latter part of May through July, depending on elevation. Blooms when young red squirrels first start climbing about and reaches its height when the green-tailed towhees have eggs and young pink-sided juncos are feathering.
   Where found: Y, T, R. Dry to medium-moist soil of open forests, ridges, and grassy areas from foothills up to around timberline. Found from Montana to Idaho, south to Nevada and New Mexico. There are approximately 45 species of *Phlox* native to N. America and ne. Asia; about half occur in Rockies.
   Interesting facts: *Multiflora* means many flowers. Cultivated phlox is an excellent example of what can be done by intelligent plant breeding. The numerous varieties of phlox that adorn our flower gardens, giving them an array of color and perfume, have all been produced from wild species.

SKY PILOT   *Polemonium viscosum* Nutt.   **Pl. 16**
   Family: Polemoniaceae (Phlox).
   Other names: Skunkweed, Jacobs-ladder, Greek Valerian.
   Description: A purple, broadly funnel-shaped flower with orange anthers and compound leaves. Each leaf contains 30

to 40 whorled, roundish leaflets and is somewhat sticky. Crushed plant has an unmistakable skunk smell.

P. confertum is most likely to be confused with *P. viscosum*, but it is distinguished by having narrow instead of broad funnel-shaped flowers. The Silky Phacelia (*Phacelia sericea*) generally grows at lower altitudes and has small plumelike flowers with greatly exserted stamens. The Alpine Harebell (*Campanula uniflora*) has entire, lance-shaped leaves and no disagreeable odor.

Related species: (1) *P. delicatum* has flat, opposite leaflets with upper ones confluent; stems are delicate and extend little above leaves; (2) *P. occidentale* is a strict-growing plant 2–3 ft. tall, with upper leaves markedly reduced in size; (3) Jacobs-ladder (*P. pulcherrimum* Hook.), Plate 16, has violet-blue corolla with white or yellow tube. These plants common throughout Rockies.

Flowering season: Begins flowering in June and July and a few late bloomers can still be found in mid-Aug.

Where found: G, Y, T, R. Grows on highest peaks from 9000 to 12,000 ft. Look for it in protected rock crevices. Sky Pilot is found throughout Rocky Mt. peaks from Montana to Washington, south to Arizona and Colorado. The genus, of about 25 species, extends throughout temperate regions of Europe, Asia, and N. and S. America; about 10 polemoniums in Rocky Mt. region.

Interesting facts: *Viscosum* means sticky. The hiker who inadvertently steps on the Sky Pilot is trailed by a powerful skunk odor that keeps pace with him as he climbs, lingers unpleasantly close at lunch time, and will haunt him in his tent or sleeping bag if he fails to place his shoes a safe distance away. In some plants this odor serves as a protection against grazing animals. The Sky Pilot has little forage value, but is utilized to some extent by domestic sheep.

WATERLEAF *Hydrophyllum capitatum* Dougl. **Pl. 16**

Family: Hydrophyllaceae (Waterleaf).

Other names: Woolen-breeches, Cats-breeches, Pussyfoot.

Description: Waterleaf has broad, fleshy, pinnately divided leaves and globular heads of white to purplish-blue flowers closely resembling a cat's paw. Stamens are longer than rest of flower and form talons of the cat's paw. Leaves usually greatly surpass heads of flowers in height; plant itself grows 4–16 in. tall.

Of the 4 species of waterleaf in the West, this is the only one that has the flowering stalk shorter than stalk of leaf, and it is also smallest of the group.

Related species: *H. fendleri* grows 1–3 ft. tall and has white to violet corollas a little longer than calyx.

Flowering season: May and June. Blooms about time first Canada goose goslings hatch and take to the water.

Where found: Y, T, R. Moist, rich soil, most often in shade, from valleys up to around 9000 ft. Look for it in gullies, canyons, and open forest areas from Alberta to B.C., south to Oregon and Colorado. There are 8 species of *Hydrophyllum*, 4 in eastern and 4 in western part of N. America. Three occur in Rocky Mt. area.

Interesting facts: *Capitatum* means in heads. This plant has developed a thick, fleshy root system filled with food and water. Large food reserve allows plant to make a vigorous early growth in spring, when water is plentiful. As it rains, water is caught and held in the cavity of the leaf; hence the name Waterleaf. After seeds are formed, the plant yellows and dies back to the soil line, but the fleshy roots remain alive throughout the drought and heat of summer, to start the plant again the next season. The young shoots as well as the roots of various species of *Hydrophyllum* were cooked and eaten by the Indians. It offers a succulent spring food for elk; deer, and bear and is often heavily grazed. By the time this early spring plant is in flower, other range plants have advanced far enough so that cattle can be permitted to graze them.

SILKY PHACELIA   *Phacelia sericea* (Graham) Gray   **Pl. 16**

Family: Hydrophyllaceae (Waterleaf).

Other names: Scorpionweed, Purple Fringe.

Description: The brilliant purple flowers form dense spikes on upper ¼ to ½ of the stem. Purple stamens protrude from corolla like long hairs. This plant has from 1 to several unbranched stems 5–18 in. tall, clustered on a branching root crown. Leaves both basal and on stem, silvery-silky, 1–5 in. long, and much dissected.

The long stamens, dissected leaves, perennial habit, and the silvery-silky hair covering the plant help to distinguish it from other members of the genus *Phacelia*. At first glance may also be confused with some of the lupines (*Lupinus*) or with Horsemint (*Monarda menthaefolia*), but on closer observation one will see that petals of *Phacelia* are all alike, whereas those of lupines and Horsemint are dissimilar. Also, stem of Horsemint is square.

Related species: (1) *P. leucophylla* has lilac to white flowers; whole plant is grayish with hair; stems are clustered on a woody root crown and grow 6–20 in. tall. (2) *P. ivesiana* is an annual that grows 2–10 in. tall, and whitish corolla is longer than stamens. (3) Franklin Phacelia (*P. franklinii* [Brown] Gray) grows 1–2 ft. tall, has lavender-colored flowers and hairy-glandular stem; see illus. opposite. (4) *P. linearis* has blue

Franklin Phacelia (*Phacelia franklinii* [Brown] Gray)

saucer-shaped flowers, with narrow and mostly sessile leaves. These species common in Rockies.

Flowering season: June, July, and first part of Aug. Reaches height of blooming about time young golden eagles make their first flight from the nest and trumpeter swan cygnets are about half grown.

Where found: G, Y, T, R. Found in dry to moist soil of open areas along roads, on hillsides and mt. ridges from around 6000 ft. in elevation up to well above timberline. Those who ride or hike the high trails in our national parks and forests will see and recognize this plant. Can be found from Alberta to B.C., south to California and New Mexico. Twenty-two species occur in Rockies.

Interesting facts: *Sericea* means silky. *P. ramosissima* was used for greens by California Indians. Elk and other big game graze Silky Phacelia during the summer months. The early spring growth of *P. leucophylla* is heavily utilized by elk and to some extent by deer and mountain goats. Probably grazed by grizzlies.

HOUNDSTONGUE *Cynoglossum officinale* L. **Pl. 17**
  Family: Boraginaceae (Borage).
  Other names: Beggars-lice, Dogbur, Woolmat.
  Description: A stout, branching biennial, 1–3 ft. tall, bearing many racemes of reddish-purple flowers approximately ¼ in.

long. Each flower gives rise to 4 flattened nutlets that are densely covered with barbed prickles when mature. Leaves are numerous, oblong to lance-shaped in outline, and velvety to the touch, being covered with soft white hairs.

Houndstongue is easily confused with Alkanet (*Anchusa officinalis*) and Henbane (*Hyoscyamus niger*) but differs in that it develops burs that catch to clothing and hair, whereas latter plants do not.

Related species: *C. boreale* is a perennial covered with stiff hair, and has oval leaves and few flowers; grows in Canadian Rockies and eastward.

Flowering season: Blooms from June to Aug.

Where found: Y, T. Watch for this plant along dry roadsides, waste places, hillsides, and sandy areas. Naturalized from Europe, it has scattered over much of temperate N. America. There are about 75 species of *Cynoglossum* of wide distribution; 1 in Rocky Mt. area.

Interesting facts: *Officinale* means official. This plant, though poisonous, is seldom eaten by animals because of its disagreeable odor and taste. It contains cynoglossine and consolidin, which are sometimes used medicinally to relieve pain.

ALPINE FORGET-ME-NOT   Pl. 17
Eritrichium elongatum (Rydb.) Wight

Family: Boraginaceae (Borage).

Other names: Dwarf Forget-me-not and *E. argenteum*.

Description: A dwarf alpine cushion plant bearing a mass of brilliant blue or occasionally white flowers scarcely ¼ in. broad. Leaves and stems are covered with long soft white hairs that give the cushion a grayed appearance. Entire plant is seldom more than 4 in. high.

Tufted Phlox (*Phlox caespitosa*) is blue and forms cushions, but lacks soft white hairs on stem and leaves. When flowers of Alpine Forget-me-not are blue it will not easily be confused with any other plant growing above timberline; when they are white, it could be confused with White Phlox (*Phlox multiflora*), Plate 16, which also forms cushions but has larger flowers and longer leaves.

Related species: *E. howardii* can be distinguished by its short instead of long hairs.

Flowering season: Early July to Aug. The pika is busily harvesting a winter supply of mt. plants and curing them in "haystacks" when this flower is in full bloom.

Where found: Y, T, R. Found growing only at high altitudes, 9000 to 12,000 ft. Look for it on exposed ridges and mt. crests. Extends throughout Rocky Mt. region from Montana to Oregon and south to New Mexico. Genus consists of about 30 species, found in cooler regions of N. Hemisphere; dwarf forget-me-nots similar to ours beautify high peaks of Alps. Two dwarf forget-me-nots occur in Rocky Mt. region.

Interesting facts: *Elongatum* means elongate. Perhaps no flower gives the mountain lover more joy than this little blue gem, radiant in its setting of sparkling mica or feldspar. Its beauty cheers the weary climber, and its presence tells him that he is nearing the summit. It forces him to stop and consider how such delicate beauty survives the cold and storms of the mts., why such a lovely thing is hidden from the eyes of most men. Somehow he feels that it has partly answered the reason for his climbing — the purpose of his efforts.

Stickseed (*Hackelia floribunda* [Lehm.] Jtn.)

STICKSEED *Hackelia floribunda* (Lehm.) Jtn.
    Family: Boraginaceae (Borage).
    Other names: Tall Stickseed, False Forget-me-not.
    Description: A stout, erect plant, 2–5 ft. tall, with numerous small, bright blue flowers with yellow centers. Each flower gives rise to 4 small nutlets with rows of barbed prickles down the edges; hence the name Stickseed.
    Plants in the genera *Cryptantha, Myosotis, Anchusa,* and

Lappula could all be confused with this one, but its rows of barbed prickles, small blue flowers, and perennial habit are a combination of characteristics distinguishing it from other plants.

Related species: *H. patens* has a white flower spotted with blue, is about ⅓ in. broad, and plant branches and grows 1–2 ft. tall; occurs in n. and w. Rockies.

Flowering season: June and July. Seeds become a nuisance about time Soapberry (*Elaeagnus canadensis*) ripens and turns red.

Where found: Y, T, R. Moist to medium-dry soil from our foothills to around 8000 ft. Watch for it along streams, in brushy copses, and on hillsides. Distributed from Saskatchewan to B.C., south to California and New Mexico. There are about 35 species of *Hackelia* widely distributed; about 10 in Rockies.

Interesting facts: *Floribunda* means free-flowering. On the nutlets near the outer end of the prickles are 2 barbs that allow the prickles readily to enter clothing or fur of animals but retard their being pulled back out. In this way the seed is transported and the plant becomes established long distances from its original home. It clings in great numbers to wool shirts, socks, or trousers.

GROMWELL *Lithospermum incisum* Lehm.   **Pl. 17**

Family: Boraginaceae (Borage).

Other names: Puccoon, Indianpaint, and *L. angustifolium*.

Description: A many-stemmed plant 4–18 in. tall, bearing bright yellow flowers in upper leaf axils. Earlier flowers have a slender tube, often more than 1 in. long, and 5 spreading lobes. Later flowers are smaller and paler in color, and on some the corolla never opens. Stems clustered on a short fleshy taproot and leaves are numerous, linear, and ½–2 in. long.

Gromwell could easily be mistaken for other plants of the Borage family, but large size of flower, its bright yellow color, and fact that the lobes are somewhat fringed fairly well distinguish it.

Related species: (1) Wayside Gromwell (*L. ruderale* Lehm.) has a large woody taproot with many unbranched stems 10–20 in. tall; flowers are pale yellow, about ⅓ in. long, and almost hidden in axils of upper leaves; see illus. opposite. (2) *L. arvense* is an annual or biennial 10–20 in. tall, with simple stems or a basal clump; flowers are white and nutlets gray or brown. Both plants common in Rockies.

Flowering season: May to July. Blooms about time sage grouse lay their first clutch of eggs.

Where found: Y, T, R. Dry soil of plains, foothills, and ridges

Wayside Gromwell (*Lithospermum ruderale* Lehm.)

in mts. up to around 7000 ft. Look for it in dry open areas from B.C. to Manitoba, south to Illinois, Texas, and Arizona. There are about 40 species of *Lithospermum*, mainly confined to N. Hemisphere and S. America; only about a half-dozen species in Rockies.

Interesting facts: *Incisum* means incised. This genus was used by the Indians throughout the West as a medicine and food. Interest in these plants has recently been revived as a possible source of modern drugs. This has been the history of the use of many of our drug plants. Western Indians cooked and ate the roots of this plant.

MOUNTAIN BLUEBELL   Pl. 17
Mertensia ciliata (James) G. Don
    Family: Boraginaceae (Borage).
    Other names: Tall Chimingbell, Cowslip, Languid-ladies.
    Description: A large leafy, branching plant, 1–4 ft. high, with light blue, drooping, tubular-shaped blossoms. Unopened blossoms have a pink cast. Leaves alternate, hairless, and smooth. Flower parts (sepals, petals, stamens) are all 5 each, with stamens attached to corolla tube. Corolla is usually 3 to 5 times

as long as calyx. The only smooth-leaved bluebell usually more than 2 ft. high, and can be distinguished from other species in this area with little trouble.

Bluebells are sometimes confused with the penstemons (*Penstemon*), but can be distinguished from the latter by having regular, bell-shaped or tubular flowers instead of irregular 2-lipped ones.

Related species: There are 2 small bluebells (mostly under 1 ft. in height) common in Rockies: (1) *M. alpina* grows at timberline and above, blooms in midsummer; (2) Bluebell (*M. oblongifolia* [Nutt.] G. Don), Plate 17, blooms in valleys and foothills early in spring.

Flowering season: Blooms from early June at lower altitudes to middle of Aug. in higher parts of its range. Height of blooming occurs in mid-July.

Where found: Y, T, R. Found growing from 5000 to 12,000 ft. but is mainly subalpine. Look for it along mt. streambanks and in damp mt. parks. Usually grows in clumps or in pure stands, but will also be found growing with Red Monkeyflower. Mountain Bluebell occurs throughout Rocky Mt. region from Montana to Oregon, south to Nevada and New Mexico. Genus contains about 45 species, mostly native to N. Hemisphere; about 35 occur in Rocky Mts.

Interesting facts: *Ciliata* means fringed. Mountain Bluebell covers large grassy meadows or parks among the spruce and fir trees. Such meadows are favorite summer range of elk bands that not only graze the bluebells but bed down among their leafy stems and pendent flowers. Young elk calves come into the world under the protective covering of this tall plant. Deer and bears feed on the entire plant, and domestic sheep are particularly fond of it. The rockchuck utilizes it throughout the summer and the pika (or rock rabbit) cuts, dries, and stores it for winter use.

FORGET-ME-NOT *Myosotis alpestris* Schmidt   **Pl. 17**

Family: Boraginaceae (Borage).

Description: The flowers are sky-blue with a yellow center, wheel-shaped, and hardly ¼ in. across. Slender stems 4–12 in. tall and densely clustered together, sometimes in clumps 1 ft. or more across. Leaves lance-shaped or narrower, and softly hairy.

This flower could easily be confused with those of *Eritrichium*, *Lappula*, and *Hackelia*. Unlike latter two, however, plants of *Myosotis* genus do not produce barbed prickles on seed and they are not gray cushion-forming plants like Alpine Forget-me-not (*Eritrichium elongatum*). This is the only perennial *Myosotis* in Rockies growing at a high elevation.

Related species: (1) *M. verna* is an erect hairy annual with white, or sometimes bluish, flowers; found in valleys and foot-hills. (2) *M. laxa* is a perennial bright blue, yellow-centered flower growing in water; grows 10–25 in. tall.

Flowering season: Latter part of June to first part of Aug. When it is in bloom cow elk are slowly migrating with their small calves to higher summer ranges.

Where found: G, Y, T. Moist soil of our high mts. Begin to look for it before reaching timberline, and from then on up into alpine meadows and ridges. Grows from Alaska to Alberta, south to Colorado and Oregon; also in n. Europe. There are about 30 species of *Myosotis* widely scattered, mostly in high mts. and cooler portions of the earth; about a half-dozen species in Rocky Mts.

Interesting facts: The genus name comes from two Greek words signifying mouse ear; this pertains to the shape and hairiness of the leaves of some species. *Alpestris* means nearly alpine. This plant and the Alpine Forget-me-not are two flowers you are sure to remember when you see them in their natural surroundings of jagged peaks, snowfields, talus slopes, and matching blue sky. You will agree that they are well named, forget-me-not.

GIANT-HYSSOP *Agastache urticifolia* (Kuntze) Rydb.   **Pl. 20**
    Family: Labiatae (Mint).
    Other names: Horsemint.

Description: Most members of the Mint family have square stems, opposite leaves, and are aromatic. Giant-hyssop is no exception to this rule. Stems are 2–5 ft. tall, clustered on a branching rootstock, and bear dense, thick, terminal spikes of purplish to whitish flowers. Leaves are ovate to triangular in outline, toothed, and about 2 in. long. The 4 stamens in each flower are much longer than corolla, upper pair being longer than lower and the 2 pairs bent so they cross.

    Several members of the Mint family could be confused with this plant, but its large size and dense terminal spikes of flowers are fairly distinctive. Most mints have their flowers in axils of leaves.

Related species: *A. foeniculum*, mainly east of Continental Divide, is a plant 1½–2 ft. tall with blue flowers and lower surface of leaf white with hairs.

Flowering season: Middle of June to first part of Aug. First blooms about time young ospreys are leaving their nests.

Where found: Y, T, G. Moist soil of open hillsides, canyons, and mt. valleys, from foothills to around 8500 ft. Found from Montana to B.C., south to California and Colorado. *Agastache* is a N. American genus of around 10 species; 3 or 4 of these in Rockies.

Interesting facts: *Urticifolia* means nettle-leaved. This plant is one of the few members of the Mint family eaten by both domestic and wild animals. In the Rockies, it is the most important forage plant in the Mint family. The seeds are sought by our smaller birds and were also eaten by the Indians. The leaves of other species are used to make beverages.

Mint (*Mentha arvensis* L.)

MINT   *Mentha arvensis* L.   **Pl. 20**
 Family: Labiatae (Mint).
 Other names: Fieldmint.
 Description: This is a plant with small light blue, light pink, or even white flowers clustered in axils of leaves. Stems are slender, square in cross section, 1–3 ft. tall, and grow in patches from underground branching rootstocks. Leaves ovate, finely toothed, opposite, and dotted with small depressed glands. There is great variation in this plant, partly due to environment in which it is growing.
 The square stems and opposite leaves are characteristic of the Mint family, as is also the irregular flower with 2 lips (the upper entire or 2-lobed, the lower 3-lobed).
 Related species: (1) *M. piperita* and (2) *M. spicata* have flowers

in terminal spikes instead of in clusters in leaf axils. *M. piperita* has its leaves on distinct short stalks and spike of flowers is almost ½ in. thick; *M. spicata* has leaves that are almost stalkless and spike is about ¼ in. thick. These have both escaped from cultivation and are widespread.

Flowering season: July, Aug., and first part of Sept. Look for it when the Mountain Hollyhock and Monkshood come into bloom and fledgling dippers (water ouzels) are leaving their nests.

Where found: G, Y, T, R. Wet soil of streambanks, about springs and bogs, and in wet woods from lowest elevations to around 9000 ft. in mts. This plant, or variations of it, occurs over a large part of temperate N. Hemisphere. There are perhaps 30 species of mints; only 3 species of *Mentha* in Rockies.

Interesting facts: *Arvensis* means of fields. Members of the Mint family in general have glands that secrete oils so volatile they evaporate without leaving a spot on paper or fabrics. Some of them are used in perfume, as flavoring agents, and in medicine. Menthol is derived from a variety of *M. arvensis*, spearmint from *M. spicata*, and peppermint from *M. piperita*. The leaves of all three plants, lightly steeped in hot water, make delicious beverages. They can also be used for making jelly or mint juleps.

HORSEMINT *Monarda menthaefolia* Benth. Pl.17

Family: Labiatae (Mint).

Other names: Beebalm, Wild Bergamot, Lemon Mint.

Description: Horsemint has round flower heads 1–3 in. broad, surrounded by leaflike bracts and composed of rose to purple flowers, growing at ends of square stems. Flowers are about 1 in. long, the 2 stamens still longer. Stems usually unbranched, bunched together on branching rootstock, and are 1–3 ft. tall. Leaves opposite, ovate, or lance-shaped and entire plant finely pubescent or hairy.

  Horsemint could be confused with other members of the same genus, but the large terminal heads of flowers, unbranched stems, and bright green leaves are quite distinctive.

Related species: *M. pectinata* is an annual, 6–15 in. tall, with 2 or more heads of flowers on a stem; occurs from Great Plains to e. and s. Rockies.

Flowering season: Latter part of June to first part of Aug. Look for it about time Mountain Hollyhock blooms and young magpies are flying.

Where found: G, Y, R. Medium-dry to moist soil of our valleys, prairies, and mts. to around 7000 ft. Occurs from Manitoba to Alberta, south to Arizona and Texas. There are around 15 species of *Monarda*, all native to N. America; 3 or 4 occur in Rockies.

Interesting facts: *Menthaefolia* means mint-leaved. The leaves of this plant are used in making tea, for flavoring in cooking, and as a potherb. The antiseptic drug thymol is present in the volatile oils of *Monarda*. Horsemint is eaten by cattle and game but is not particularly relished by horses.

Skullcap (*Scutellaria galericulata* L.)

SKULLCAP   *Scutellaria galericulata* L.

Family: Labiatae (Mint).

Other names: Marsh Skullcap.

Description: This has very slender square stems 1–3 ft. tall, with a single dull blue flower in axil of each of the opposite, upper leaves. Flowers almost ¾ in. long, tubular, and abruptly enlarged and curved near middle; though usually blue, occasionally pink or white. Leaves lance-shaped, toothed around edge, and in length may vary 1–2½ in.

The skullcaps are most likely to be confused with the penstemons (*Penstemon*), but flowers of penstemons do not occur singly in axils of the ordinary leaves.

Related species: (1) *S. angustifolia* has an entire, narrow leaf, sometimes slightly toothed; flowers are bright blue; (2) flowers of *S. lateriflora* occur in axillary racemes.

Flowering season: June to Aug. Blooms about time young spotted sandpipers hatch and begin to run about.

Where found: Y, T, R. In wet or boggy places, often in shallow water. Look for Skullcap among cattails, tules, sedges, and other bog plants. Can be found from Alaska to Newfoundland, south to Pennsylvania, New Mexico, and California. There are about 100 species of *Scutellaria* widely distributed over the earth; about a half-dozen species in Rockies.

Interesting facts: *Galericulata* means helmet-like. Several of the skullcaps, including this one, contain a crystalline glucoside (scutellarin) that has long been used in medicine. It is an antispasmodic, used in cases of nervousness.

HENBANE *Hyoscyamus niger* L. Pl. 17

Family: Solanaceae (Potato).

Other names: Black Henbane, Hogbean, Stinking Nightshade, Insane Root.

Description: The flowers are bell-shaped, about 1 in. long, and are often partially hidden by the leaves. The greenish or purplish-yellow petals are veined with deep purple. This coarse, fetid, leafy plant attains height of 1–3 ft. The numerous stalkless leaves are lanceolate or ovate in outline, irregularly lobed, and 3–8 in. long. Whole plant clammy and downy to the touch. Vase-shaped seed capsules with their sharp-pointed tips are quite characteristic. Stem while growing longer continues to flower near top. At the same time, old flowers below may already have formed seeds.

Henbane is most likely to be confused with Alkanet (*Anchusa officinalis*) or Houndstongue (*Cynoglossum officinale*), Plate 17; smaller flowers of these seldom grow more than ½ in. long. Their fruits consist of 4 small, hard nutlets; Henbane develops an urn-shaped capsule (½–¾ in. long) containing numerous dark brown pitted seeds.

Flowering season: Latter part of May until well through July.

Where found: Y, T. Dry roadsides and waste places from valleys well up into mts. Henbane, a native of Europe, has escaped cultivation in this country and is now scattered over our northern states and adjoining Canada. There are about 15 species of *Hyoscyamus*, mainly from the Mediterranean region; only 1 species in Rockies.

Interesting facts: *Niger* means black. Henbane is very poisonous, but is seldom eaten because of its fetid odor and unpleasant taste. Cattle have been poisoned by eating this plant, and chickens as well as children have been poisoned by eating the seeds. The alkaloids scopolamine and hyoscyamine, together with the glucoside hyoscypicrin, are extracted from Henbane. They are used as sedatives for insomnia, mania, spasms, and pain. In some places this plant is cultivated for its medicinal value. It has at times been used as a substitute for opium and was collected during World War II as a source of atropine. The dried seed pods make striking winter bouquets.

Groundcherry (*Physalis subglabrata* M. & B.)

GROUNDCHERRY   *Physalis subglabrata* M. & B.

    Family: Solanaceae (Potato).

    Other names: Bladdercherry, Poppers.

    Description: A branching perennial, 8–20 in. tall, with pale yellow flowers that are darker in the center, about ¾ in. broad, bell-shaped, and occur singly in the axils. Calyx enlarges to a paperlike balloon or bladder; it may reach width of 1 in., and encloses the small tomato-like fruit. Leaves ovate to ovate-oblong, usually less than 3 times longer than broad.

    No other plant in the Rockies is likely to be confused with one of the groundcherries, but there is considerable difference of opinion about the various species of this genus.

    Related species: (1) *P. lobata* has violet to purple saucer-shaped flowers; (2) *P. fendleri* is covered with tiny branched hairs (use a lens); (3) *P. longifolia* has linear to lanceolate leaves, usually 4 to 5 times as long as broad. These plants are in e. and s. Rockies and eastward.

    Flowering season: June and July. Inflated calyx sometimes persists until fall frosts kill top of plant. Fruits often conspicuous during hunting season.

Where found: Moist to medium-dry soil of cultivated and waste land, as well as along roadsides and fence rows. Found from Vermont west to Washington, south to Texas and Florida; also occurs in Europe. There are about 100 species of *Physalis*, most of which occur in N. and S. America; about a half dozen in Rockies.

Interesting facts: *Subglabrata* means almost hairless. One species of *Physalis* (*P. alkekengi*), known commonly as Chinese Lanterns, is grown in flower gardens for its decorative, bladdery, red calyx. The sweet berries of many species are eaten raw or made into jam or pies.

BLACK NIGHTSHADE *Solanum nigrum* L.

Family: Solanaceae (Potato).

Other names: Deadly Nightshade, Poisonberry.

Description: A much-branched annual herb, 1–3 ft. tall, with white wheel-shaped flowers about ¼ in. broad, composed of a 5-lobed calyx, a 5-lobed corolla, and 5 stamens. These flowers

Black Nightshade (*Solanum nigrum* L.)
and (upper right) Bittersweet (*S. dulcamara* L.)

give rise to round berries, diameter about ⅛ in., at first green but black at maturity. Leaves are lance-shaped, or broader, and may be smooth or slightly lobed around edge.

Black Nightshade is most commonly confused with the Cut-leaved (or Three-flowered) Nightshade (*S. triflorum*), but this plant has pinnately lobed leaves and greenish-yellow berries when ripe.

Related species: (1) Bittersweet (*S. dulcamara* L.) is vinelike, has purple flowers and red fruit; see illus., p. 167. (2) *S. rostratum* is an annual with long yellow spines and yellow flowers. (3) *S. carolinense* is a perennial that has prickles on stems and on main veins of lower leaf surfaces; flowers are purple. These 3 plants are widespread over temperate N. America.

Flowering season: From June to frost in fall. The growing stem keeps producing new flowers, so it is possible to see flowers and ripe fruit on same plant.

Where found: Y, T, R. Moist to medium-dry, sandy or loamy soil, in fields, waste places, and open areas. Introduced from Europe, it can now be found as a weed over most of U.S. and s. Canada. There are more than 1000 species of *Solanum* scattered over the earth, being most abundant in tropics and subtropics; about a dozen species in Rocky Mts.

Interesting facts: *Nigrum* means black. All parts of this plant contain a poisonous alkaloid, solanine. It is more abundant in the unripe berries, and if eaten may cause paralysis and death in both humans and livestock. Cooking is reported to destroy the solanine. It naturally decreases to nontoxic amounts in ripe fruit. The berries are used in pies, jams, and preserves. *S. dulcamara* is a favorite winter food of ring-necked pheasants. This plant is closely related to the garden Potato (*S. tuberosum*).

YELLOW PAINTBRUSH *Castilleja sulphurea* Rydb. Pl. 18

Family: Scrophulariaceae (Figwort).

Other names: Indian Paintbrush, Painted-cup, Squaw-feather.

Description: The flowers occur in dense spikes at the top of unbranched stems. They may be 1 in. or less long, but are not readily noticed because hidden by the ovate yellow bracts, which are usually mistaken for the flowers. Stems clustered on a woody root crown, and vary in height 4–16 in. Leaves lanceolate, usually entire and smooth. Galea long and slender, often nearly equaling the corolla tube.

Related species: *C. flava* has leaves grayish with hair and mostly parted into linear segments; bracts are yellow; galea is short, rarely ½ length of corolla tube.

Flowering season: May, June, and July, depending on elevation at which it is growing.

Where found: G, Y, T. Moist to medium-dry soil of plains,

foothills, and up well toward timberline in mts. Occurs from
Montana to Idaho, south to Nevada and Colorado. There are
about 200 species of *Castilleja*, practically all native to the
Americas, and chiefly found in w. U.S.; 24 found in Rocky Mt.
area.

Interesting facts: *Sulphurea* means sulphur-colored. Most
botanists have difficulty in positively identifying many of the
species of paintbrushes because they look so much alike. For
the public in general there are 2 kinds — red and yellow.
Various shades of yellow and red will be found as well as pink,
white, and orange, but all are readily recognized as paintbrushes. They resemble a ragged brush dipped in paint; hence
the name.

Wyoming Paintbrush (*Castilleja linariaefolia* Benth.)

WYOMING PAINTBRUSH *Castilleja linariaefolia* Benth.
   Family: Scrophulariaceae (Figwort).
   Other names: Paintbrush, Indian Paintbrush, Painted-cup,
Wyoming Painted-cup.
   Description: This plant appears as a brilliant red flower.
Actually, flowers themselves are not attractive, but surrounding

bracts and upper leaves are highly colored. Flowers are about 1 in. long, tubular, yellowish green, at times tinged with scarlet; occur in dense clusters at ends of branches, with red or scarlet leaflike bracts below each of them. Calyx more deeply cleft below than above. These bracts usually extend well beyond blossoms. Leaves narrow and grasslike, or cut into narrow segments. Plant grows 1–3 ft. tall.

The Indian paintbrushes of the Rockies can be distinguished from most other plants by their colored bracts. The owl-clovers (*Orthocarpus*) are an exception. However, these are annuals, and all but 1 of our castillejas are perennials.

Related species: (1) *C. exilis* is a slender annual 1–2 ft. tall, growing in boggy areas; (2) Indian Paintbrush (*C. miniata* Dougl.), Plate 18, has lanceolate, mostly entire leaves, and the flowers are 1¼ in. long or longer; (3) Splitleaf Painted-cup (*C. rhexifolia* Rydb.), Plate 18, has narrow to ovate, usually entire leaves, and flowers 1 in. or less long; (4) Early Paintbrush (*C. chromosa* Nels.), Plate 18, has linear or linear-lanceolate leaves, the lateral lobes much narrower than the midblade. All 4 species have bright red bracts. *C. miniata*, *C. chromosa*, and *C. rhexifolia* found in mts.

Flowering season: June, July, and first part of Aug. Look for this flower about time first young magpies leave nest.

Where found: Y, T, R. Dry to moist soil of plains and mts., from lowest valleys to around 9000 ft. Distributed from Montana to Oregon, south to Mexico. There are about 200 species of *Castilleja*, practically all native to the Americas, and chiefly found in w. U.S.; 24 in Rocky Mt. area.

Interesting facts: *Linariaefolia* means linear-leaved. This plant is a semiparasite, making only a portion of the food it requires. Its roots grow into the soil until they touch roots of other plants, such as the sagebrush. They then penetrate the tissues of this host plant to steal part of their food. Throughout the ages the paintbrushes have so developed this habit that they can now scarcely live without the aid of other plants. Wyoming Paintbrush is the state flower of Wyoming. In full bloom it colors the landscape.

BLUE-EYED MARY   *Collinsia parviflora* Dougl.

　　Family: Scrophulariaceae (Figwort).
　　Other names: Blue-lips, Blue-eyes.
　　Description: A weak, slender annual, 2–12 in. tall, with flowers about ¼ in. long, very irregular, 2-lipped, and blue (often with the upper lip white). Flowers grow on very slender stalks, with 1 to 5 in axils of leaves. Leaves simple, opposite, or sometimes whorled.

　　This plant could be confused with speedwells (*Veronica*), but latter have wheel-shaped and almost regular 4-lobed corollas.

Related species: (*C. grandiflora*) can be separated only on technical characters.

Flowering season: April to July. Appears soon after snow recedes.

Where found: G, Y, T, R. Moist to semi-dry, open, or shaded areas, from lowest elevations to around 7500 ft. in mts. Common on disturbed areas. Occurs from Michigan to B.C., south to California and New Mexico. *Collinsia* is a N. American genus of plants found mainly in western part of continent; 2 species in Rocky Mts.

Blue-eyed Mary (*Collinsia parviflora* Dougl.)

Interesting facts: *Parviflora* means small-flowered. Many small annual plants, such as Blue-eyed Mary, are able to grow on deserts and dry hills because they flower, seed, and die before the winter moisture has left the soil. The mature seeds lie dormant during winter, germinating to form new plants as soon as the snow melts. Some other annuals, such as Chess, Jim Hill Mustard, and Storksbill germinate in the fall when the rains come, then overwinter as young plants. This not only gives them an even earlier start in the spring, but provides a longer growing period before the summer drought occurs.

YELLOW MONKEYFLOWER   *Mimulus guttatus* DC.   **Pl. 18**
  Family: Scrophulariaceae (Figwort).
  Other names: Wild Lettuce.
  Description: A perennial plant with bright yellow, irregular, snapdragon-like flowers that are red-spotted in the throat, and may vary in length ½–1½ in. Leaves opposite, oval, and irregularly toothed around edge. Stems hollow, and 2–18 in. tall.
    This plant is easily confused with other monkeyflowers as well as with Butter-and-Eggs (*Linaria vulgaris* Hill), Plate 18, but latter has linear leaves and a spur at base of corolla. Musk Plant (*M. moschatus* Dougl.), Plate 19, could be confused with smaller forms of Yellow Monkeyflower, but it has sticky, long-haired leaves and stems and grows low and decumbent.
  Related species: (1) Dwarf Monkeyflower (*M. nanus* H. & A.), Plate 19, is a small annual with almost stalkless, reddish-purple flowers up to ¾ in. long; favors bare areas and sliding or loose soil. (2) *M. floribundus* is a weak-stemmed annual with a funnel-form yellow corolla marked with red. These 2 plants common throughout Rockies.
  Flowering season: May into Aug. First look for it when Scarlet Gilia appears. Still in bloom in Sept. when Rocky Mt. whitefish begin to spawn, bull elk are bugling, and beaver have made their winter food caches.
  Where found: G, Y, T, R. Moist to wet soil along streams and about springs and seepage areas and on beaver dams. Grows from lowest valleys to almost timberline. Most common monkeyflower in Rockies. Can be found from Alaska to Montana, south to California and New Mexico. There are about 80 species of *Mimulus*, widely scattered but concentrated in w. U.S.; about 20 occur in Rocky Mts.
  Interesting facts: *Guttatus* means speckled. The appearance of many plants varies considerably, depending on the environment in which they are growing. Yellow Monkeyflower is no exception, for at low elevations, in deep rich soil by the side of a spring or stream, this plant may grow to be almost 2 ft. tall, with huge blossoms nearly 2 in. long. The same plant near timberline may be only 2–3 in. tall and the blossoms ½ in. long or less. In the alkaline sinter about the hot pools at Old Faithful Geyser, the plant may also be only 2 in. high. The Indians and early white settlers used the leaves of this plant for greens, eating them fresh, like lettuce. They are slightly bitter. Muskrats show a decided preference for this plant, utilizing it throughout the summer.

RED MONKEYFLOWER   *Mimulus lewisii* Pursh   **Pl. 19**
  Family: Scrophulariaceae (Figwort).
  Other names: Lewis Monkeyflower.
  Description: A large snapdragon-like plant with numerous rose-

red flowers distinctly marked by 2 bright yellow patches in the funnel-form throat. Grows from 1 to 2½ ft. high and usually in clumps or patches. Stems slender and hairy, leaves finely toothed and opposite. Flowers irregular; petals united into a 5-lobed corolla with lower lobes arranged in form of 2 lips.

The other rose-colored monkeyflower (Dwarf Monkeyflower, *M. nanus* H. & A., Plate 19) in the Rocky Mt. area grows only a few inches high. Red Monkeyflower could possibly be confused with some of the purple or pink penstemons (*Penstemon*); but these have narrow tubular flowers, and blossoms of this monkeyflower are 1 in. broad. It also differs from the penstemons in having 4 stamens; penstemons have 5, one of which is sterile and usually flattened or bearded at tip.

Flowering season: Blooms from latter part of June through Aug. By time this flower first appears, most of the cutthroat trout in small streams along which it grows have finished spawning. When last red petals drop, the cutthroat are moving down higher mt. streams to deeper waters, where they winter.

Where found: G, Y, T, R. Occurs only in wet places, normally at elevations of 5000–10,000 ft. Abundant in mt. canyons. Look for it along banks of mt. streams, where it will often form extensive pink patches. Ranges from Alberta to B.C., south to California and Utah. This genus has world-wide distribution. There are about 80 species of *Mimulus* widely scattered, but most numerous in w. U.S.; about 20 occur in Rocky Mts.

Interesting facts: *Lewisii* means named for Captain Meriwether Lewis. Toward the end of the flowering season, the pink corollas dropping into the water of streams and ponds paint their surfaces with solid layers of colorful blooms. Smaller pockets make natural fingerbowls, outrivaling the rose-petaled ones at court banquets. The common name Monkeyflower refers to the "grinning face" of the variously colored flowers and their resemblance to the masks worn by comic actors of the early stage. The plant has little forage value, receiving only occasional use by mountain sheep, elk, and deer.

OWL-CLOVER   Pl. 18
Orthocarpus tenuifolius (Pursh) Benth.

Family: Scrophulariaceae (Figwort).

Other names: Goldtongue.

Description: An erect annual plant that superficially looks very much like the paintbrushes. May be branched or unbranched, 4–16 in. tall, with dense spike of yellow flowers (often purple-tipped) at top, interspersed and partly hidden by purple-tipped bracts. Leaves linear and linear-lobed, numerous, overlapping, and abruptly transformed into bracts in flower spike.

This owl-clover might be confused with the yellow paintbrushes (*Castilleja*) and louseworts (*Pedicularis*), but the 2 lips of corolla do not differ greatly in size, whereas in *Castilleja* the upper lip much exceeds lower lip.

Related species: *O. luteus* is the most common species in West; has a minute hook at end of corolla.

Flowering season: May to Aug. Will be in bloom when young blue grouse are flying.

Where found: Y, T, R. Moderately dry soil of plains and hills, usually in open areas. Occurs from Montana to B.C., south to Oregon. *Orthocarpus* is a genus of about 25 species, mainly confined to w. N. America; about a half dozen occur in Rocky Mt. area.

Interesting facts: *Tenuifolius* means slender-leaved. The small yellow petals of the flowers and the bicolored bracts are conspicuous. In the paintbrushes, which they somewhat resemble, it is generally the colorful bracts that are first seen and give them their most distinctive coloring. All the species are ranked as poor livestock forage and have little value for wildlife.

FERNLEAF   *Pedicularis bracteosa* Benth.

    Family: Scrophulariaceae (Figwort).

    Other names: Lousewort, Bracted Lousewort, Wood Betony.

    Description: A tall spikelike plant with numerous pale yellow

Fernleaf (*Pedicularis bracteosa* Benth.)

flowers and fernlike basal leaves. Possesses irregular flowers crowded on a leafy bracted spike, and is 1–2 ft. tall.

Related species: (1) *P. siifolia* could be confused with it, since it has deeply pinnatified leaves; but flowers have a distinct sharp beak and those of *P. bracteosa* are blunt at top. (2) Another spikelike plant possessing fernlike leaves is *P. groenlandica*, but it has purplish-red flowers. (3) *P. crenulata* has white or purplish flowers, with upper lip of corolla curved but not beaked; leaves are linear and doubly toothed; occurs in mt. meadows. (4) Parrots-beak (*P. racemosa* Dougl.), Plate 20 and below, has upper lip of corolla prolonged into a distinct beak; corolla white, leaves double-toothed.

Parrots-beak (*Pedicularis racemosa* Dougl.)

Flowering season: First appears in lower canyon regions about July 1, and is found blooming in Aug. at higher elevations. Young screech and saw-whet owls are leaving their hollow-tree nests about time this flower starts to bloom.

Where found: G, Y, T, R. Grows at altitudes of 6000–9500 ft., being most common in canyon regions and moist woods, parks, and meadows 7000–9000 ft. Found from Alberta to B.C., south to Oregon and Colorado. There are almost 500 species of *Pedicularis* in temperate regions of Europe, Asia, N. America, and extending into Andes of S. America; 9 species occur in Rockies.

Interesting facts: *Bracteosa* means with bracts. Fernleaf is one of the few plants hardy enough to raise its head a foot or more above the protective ground at high altitudes. Its strong, thick stem withstands the constant wind and the sudden gusts that keep most high-altitude plants huddled in protective crevices or flattened against the earth. Thus it is frequently seen silhouetted against the clouds, defying the wind and rain. The common name Fernleaf refers to the characteristic fernlike leaves. The green shoots and flowering heads are eaten by elk, but in general this species has little forage value.

ELEPHANTHEAD *Pedicularis groenlandica* Retz. **Pl. 18**

Family: Scrophulariaceae (Figwort).

Other names: Little Red Elephant, Elephant Flower, Fernleaf.

Description: When you see a dense spike of small reddish-purple to pink flowers, each unmistakably resembling an elephant's head with the trunk curving out and up, you are undoubtedly looking at Elephanthead and seeing pink elephants. Unbranched stems usually clustered together, and vary in height from 8 to 24 in. Leaves lance-shaped in outline, but pinnately divided, then lobed and toothed, giving appearance of a fern leaf.

Related species: There is no other flower in the Rockies shaped like an elephant's head; however, *P. hallii* is similar and could be mistaken for this except that upper lip of corolla is short and straight, not slender and curved like an elephant's trunk.

Flowering season: Latter part of June to first part of Aug. Occurs around open beaver ponds soon after goldeneye ducks bring forth their young.

Where found: G, Y, T, R. Wet soil of bogs, meadows, and along streams and lakeshores, often growing in shallow water, and usually in open places. Occurs in Rocky Mt. area from around 5500 ft. elevation to above timberline, and can be found from Alaska to Labrador, south to Saskatchewan, New Mexico, and California. There are almost 500 species of *Pedicularis* in temperate regions of Europe, Asia, N. America, and extending into Andes of S. America; 9 species occur in Rockies.

Interesting facts: The name *Pedicularis* is from the Latin *pediculus*, a louse, and deriving from an old superstition that eating these plants increased the lice on cattle. The species name, *groenlandica*, means of Greenland, but it is doubtful that this plant grows there. Inhabitants of the Kurile Is. make a substitute tea from the leaves of one species, and the yellow roots of an arctic species (*P. lanata*) taste somewhat like young carrots and may be eaten raw or cooked. Elk graze Elephanthead in early summer.

BUSH PENSTEMON
Penstemon fruticosus (Pursh) Greene

Family: Scrophulariaceae (Figwort).

Other names: Beardtongue.

Description: Often grows in dense patches, is 6–20 in. tall and covered with racemes of large, bright, lavender-blue blossoms. Flowers are tubular in shape, about ½ in. broad and 1½ in. long. Most of the flowers occur on 1 side of stem. Leaves are opposite, vary in shape, and are often lustrous.

This flower could be confused with some of the other penstemons and with foxgloves (*Digitalis*), but its large flowers and shrublike growth are usually enough to separate it.

Related species: (1) *P. procerus* and (2) *P. rydbergii* are common plants of Rockies that have purplish-blue flowers, nonglandular flower clusters, and grow 6–20 in. tall. *P. procerus* has flowers about ⅓ in. long; *P. rydbergii* about ⅔ in. long. (3) *P. deustus* is a white-flowered semishrubby plant with toothed leaves. (4) *P. bridgesii* has bright scarlet flowers; only found in s. Rockies. (5) Mountain Penstemon (*P. montanus* Greene), Plate 21, is low and shrubby, with sharply serrate leaves; looks like a small edition of Bush Penstemon.

Bush Penstemon (*Penstemon fruticosus* [Pursh] Greene)

Flowering season: May to first part of July.

Where found: Y, T. Moist ledges and rocky slopes in forest openings, up to around 9000 ft. This plant, or varieties of it, is found from Alberta to B.C., south to Oregon and Wyoming. There are about 250 species of *Penstemon*, and most of these occur in w. U.S.; 60 species occur in Rocky Mts., and they are among our most attractive flowers.

Interesting facts: *Penstemon* was originally written *Pent-stemon*, meaning 5 stamens. The flowers have 4 fertile stamens, and a 5th, represented by a long sterile filament, often densely covered with hair. *Fruticosus* means shrubby.

You can learn to recognize penstemons by their general appearance just as you recognize a bird in flight by a sum of characteristics rather than by detailed markings. The presence of the sterile 5th stamen will confirm your judgment.

LITTLE PENSTEMON   *Penstemon procerus* Dougl.

Family: Scrophulariaceae (Figwort).

Other names: Small-flowered Penstemon, Beardtongue.

Description: The stems of this perennial plant are clumped together, are 4–20 in. tall and topped with dense whorled clusters of small bluish-purple blossoms. Flowers tubular, less than ½ in. long, and may have as many as 25 in a cluster. Corolla, as in all penstemons, is irregular and 2-lipped. There are 5 stamens, 1 of which is sterile and so modified that it resembles a beard; hence the name. Leaves opposite, basal, and lance-shaped.

The various species of *Penstemon* are confusing; not many people can distinguish all of them.

Related species: (1) The tall, large-flowered Blue Penstemon (*P. cyaneus* Penn.), Plate 20, with its sky-blue corolla and purplish tube, is readily located in the sagebrush and along roadsides. (2) Also occurring on dry sites such as high talus slopes is the lavender-flowered Mountain Penstemon (*P. montanus* Greene), Plate 21. (3) Albert's Penstemon (*P. albertinus* Greene), Plate 20, has bright green leaves, serrate to entire, with bright blue to blue-violet corolla. (4) Flowers of the Crested Beardtongue (*P. eriantherus* Pursh), Plate 20, are glandular-hairy and lilac-purple; stems and leaves are also pubescent.

Flowering season: June and July. Little Penstemon first appears when bighorn sheep are lambing.

Where found: Y, T, R. Moist soil of meadows, open timbered slopes, and mt. ridges, from foothills to timberline. Found from s. Alaska to Oregon and Colorado. There are about 250 species of *Penstemon*, and most of these occur in w. U.S.; 60 species occur in Rocky Mts.

Interesting facts: *Procerus* means tall. The penstemons are among our most beautiful wildflowers, their colorful array of red, white, blue, purple, and lavender blossoms often quilting the mts. with color. Some species are highly palatable to domestic sheep and wildlife.

Mullein
(*Verbascum thapsus* L.)

MULLEIN   *Verbascum thapsus* L.

Family: Scrophulariaceae (Figwort).

Other names: Woolly Mullein.

Description: The stems are very coarse, somewhat woody, unbranched, and 2–8 ft. tall. Upright stems first attract attention; later, bright yellow flowers occur in long dense, spikelike racemes, and are ½–¾ in. broad. A biennial, but the dead plants persist beyond 2nd year, standing like brown skeletons. Some of these dead stems are straight and true, others bent and twisted into odd distorted shapes. Entire plant covered with a mat of branching hairs, making it velvetlike to the touch. Leaves somewhat elliptic and very hairy, the basal ones 4–16 in. long, but those of stem gradually reduced upward.

Related species: *V. blattaria* is a tall, hairless or glandular, green, slender plant with conspicuous yellow or white flowers; widespread in America.

Flowering season: Latter part of June, July, and Aug.

Where found: Y, T, R. Dry, gravelly, or sandy waste areas, roadsides, railroad grades, and occasionally occurring in open forests. This is an introduced weed from Europe but now covers most of temperate N. America from sea level to around 8000 ft. There are about 250 species of *Verbascum*, all native to Europe and Asia, especially southern parts; about a dozen established as weeds in America, but only 2 in Rockies.

Interesting facts: *Thapsus* means from Thapsus, an ancient town of North Africa on the Mediterranean. The leaves of this plant are gathered for medicinal purposes. They contain chemicals used in lotions to soften the skin and in medicines to soothe inflamed tissues. The seeds in the egg-shaped capsules are a source of winter food for small birds, being available when other food is covered by snow. Elk will eat the dry leaves and stems on overused winter ranges where preferred foods are not available. The 1st-year plants make an attractive house plant and in some parts of the country they are dug in late winter, potted, and placed where their soft greenery serves as a reminder that spring is "around the corner."

BEDSTRAW   *Galium boreale* L.   **Pl. 20**
  Family: Rubiaceae (Madder).
  Other names: Cleavers, Northern Bedstraw.
  Description: A slender, erect branching perennial, 8–24 in. tall, with numerous small, white, saucer-shaped flowers and 4-sided stems. Leaves are linear to lance-shaped, and often occur 4 in a whorl. Whole plant is more or less covered with minute, stiff, barbed hairs that catch one's clothing; hence the name Cleavers.
  The 4-angled stems, whorled leaves, and numerous small white flowers distinguish the bedstraws from other plants. Some of the different species of bedstraws, however, can only be separated on technical characters.
  Related species: (1) *G. aparine* is an annual with 6 to 8 leaves to a whorl and usually several flowers in a cyme. (2) *G. triflorum* is a perennial from slender, creeping rootstocks; stems are long, reclining, and bristly; 1 to 4 flowers on stalks in the leaf angles. These 2 species common throughout Rockies.
  Flowering season: June, July, and Aug. When it first blooms cow moose are hiding out with their week- to two-week-old calves; often secrete themselves in places where Bedstraw grows.
  Where found: G, Y, T, R. This bedstraw thrives in damp soil, chiefly in open woods, but also in meadows and open hillsides from lowest elevations to 9000 ft. It, or variations of it, occurs in Eurasia and throughout N. America, except se. U.S. There are around 300 species of bedstraws and they occur over most of the earth; 11 found in Rockies.
  Interesting facts: *Boreale* means northern. To some extent ducks and geese feed on the bedstraws. It is also a preferred food of white-tailed deer. It is probable that the common name

comes from using the dried plant as a substitute for straw in mattress ticking. At any rate, in lieu of evergreen branches it makes a comfortable camp bed. A purple dye is produced from roots of most of the bedstraws. The Madder family, to which they belong, is one of the large families of plants. The members are mainly tropical — coffee, quinine, ipecac, and other commercial products being obtained from them.

TWINFLOWER   *Linnaea borealis* L.

Family: Caprifoliaceae (Honeysuckle).

Other names: American Twinflower.

Description: A slender, trailing, mat-forming evergreen with short, upright, leafless branches that divide into 2 at top, each bearing a dainty bell-shaped pink or white flower with a pleasing fragrance. Corolla is nearly equally 5-lobed, and 2 of the 4 stamens are longer than others. Because blossoms are paired, plant is called Twinflower. Leaves oval or round and about ½ in. long.

No other plant is likely to be confused with this one.

Flowering season: G, Y, T, R. June, July, and first part of Aug. First appears when adult Canada geese are undergoing their summer molt and are flightless.

Where found: G, Y, T. In wet soil, along streams, about ponds,

Twinflower (*Linnaea borealis* L.)

springs, and in boggy areas, usually in shaded places. Grows
from lowest elevations to around 9000 ft., and it, or its varieties,
occurs in cooler portions of both Eurasia and N. America. On
this continent it occurs as far south as West Virginia, west to
Minnesota, New Mexico, and California. There are only 2 to 3
species of *Linnaea* (depending on the botanist naming or
classifying); only 1 occurs in Rockies.

Interesting facts: The genus *Linnaea* was named by Gronovius
in honor of Carolus Linnaeus of Sweden, the man largely responsible for the binomial system of naming plants and animals.
This system assigns a generic and specific name to a plant and
these two Latin words constitute the species name. It is fitting
that Twinflower bears Linnaeus' name because it is reported to
have been his favorite flower. *Borealis* means northern.

HONEYSUCKLE   *Lonicera ciliosa* (Pursh) Poir.   **Pl. 19**
   Family: Caprifoliaceae (Honeysuckle).
   Other names: Orange Honeysuckle.
   Description: A trailing or climbing woody vine with whorls of
trumpet-shaped flowers at ends of the branches. These yellow or

Red Twinberry (*Lonicera utahensis* Wats.) and
Twinberry (*L. involucrata* [Richards.] Banks)

orange blossoms are 1 in. or more in length, and give rise to bright red berries. Leaves are opposite, oval, 1–3 in. long, upper surface dark green, lower surface whitish and waxy. Bases of uppermost leaves are united around stem.

There is no other plant in the Rocky Mt. area likely to be confused with this.

Related species: Both (1) Red Twinberry (*L. utahensis* Wats.) and (2) Twinberry (*L. involucrata* [Richards.] Banks) are erect shrubs with yellow flowers; see illus. opposite. *L. utahensis* lacks conspicuous bracts and has red juicy berries slightly united; *L. involucrata* has black berries surrounded by dark red bracts. Both are common in Rockies.

Flowering season: Latter part of May to mid-July.

Where found: G, Y. Moist soil of canyons, hillsides, and woods, from Montana to B.C., south to California. There are more than 150 species of *Lonicera*, mainly of N. Hemisphere; 5 species in our area. Many are widely grown as ornamentals and are valued for fragrance of their flowers.

Interesting facts: *Ciliosa* means fringed. This plant looks so much like the miniature Trumpet Honeysuckle grown in gardens that at first glance it might be thought to have escaped into the woods. Its berries, like those of Twinberry (*L. involucrata*) and Red Twinberry (*L. utahensis*), are edible, though not tasty enough to be widely sought. Ruffed grouse and black and grizzly bears utilize them.

ELDER *Sambucus pubens* Michx.

Family: Caprifoliaceae (Honeysuckle).

Other names: Scarlet Elder, Elderberry.

Description: A large shrub, 3–10 ft. tall, with easily broken stems filled with pith. Small white flowers are arranged in globular clusters 2–3 in. across. Later in season, flowers give rise to small bright red to amber berries.

Elder is most likely to be confused with Mountain-ash (*Sorbus scopulina*), but this shrub has alternate compound leaves and elders have opposite compound leaves. Different species of elders are difficult to distinguish; this one, with reddish berries, hairy undersurface of leaves, and smaller, rounded flower clusters, probably will not be confused.

Related species: (1) Elderberry (*S. coerulea* Raf.), Plate 19, is treelike, has flat-topped flower clusters and blue berries; (2) *S. melanocarpa* is smaller, has rounded flower clusters, and produces black berries. Both occur throughout Rockies.

Flowering season: June and July. Berries are ripe in late Aug. and early Sept.

Where found: G, Y, T, R. Moist to wet soil along streams, in woods and open areas, from valleys to around 10,000 ft. Occurs from B.C. to Newfoundland, south to Georgia, Iowa, Colorado, and California. Of about 40 species of *Sambucus*, well distributed both in temperate zones and tropical mts., some half dozen occur in Rockies.

Interesting facts: *Pubens* means hairy. The plant is browsed by domestic animals; the current growth is browsed by elk and deer. Berries are consumed by many species of birds, including the ruffed and blue grouse. They are regularly sought by bears. The bark and leaves have been used in medicine as a purgative and diuretic; the ripened berries are used in making wine and jelly; and are nutritious, having a relatively high fat and protein as well as carbohydrate content. *S. coerulea* produces an abundance of blue to purple berries that make the finest jelly of all our elderberries. Outdoorsmen frequently fashion a whistle from the easily hollowed stem, and with it an experienced hunter can imitate a bugling elk and call it to within shooting distance.

VALERIAN   *Valeriana dioica* L.   **Pl. 19**
    Family: Valerianaceae (Valerian).
    Other names: Tobaccoroot, Wild Heliotrope, and *V. acutiloba*.
    Description: The small white, or occasionally pink, flowers are borne in clusters at ends of the branches. Corolla is saucer-

Valerian (*Valeriana dioica* L.)

shaped, 5-lobed, and there are 3 stamens. When seed is ripe it is crowned with 5 to 15 spreading, feathery bristles. Stems are slender, 10–18 in. tall, and are clustered together on spreading rootstocks. There are several basal leaves, usually undivided; but the 2 to 4 pairs of opposite stem leaves are dissected.

At first glance one might confuse this plant with some of the bedstraws (*Galium*), but the dissected leaves and size of this plant will distinguish it.

Related species: (1) *V. obovata* is a coarse plant 1–4 ft. tall, with a fleshy taproot; (2) *V. capitata* has bell-shaped corollas. These plants common in Rockies.

Flowering season: May, June, and July. First blooms about time young red-tailed hawks are feathering out, but before they are able to fly.

Where found: G, Y, T, R. Moist to wet soil in mts., usually in open areas or woods, often below snowbanks. It and its variations occur from the hills to almost timberline, and from Canada south through mts. to Arizona and New Mexico. There are about 200 species of *Valeriana* found in north temperate zone and S. America; about a dozen occur in Rockies.

Interesting facts: *Dioica* means 2 sexes of flowers. This plant and *V. officinalis*, cultivated as a drug plant, are sources of the drug valerian, which is used as a mild stimulant, an antispasmodic, and for treatment of nervous disorders. It also is a close relative of the Garden Heliotrope, since both belong in the same genus. Indians cooked the large unpleasant-tasting taproot of *V. obovata* in rock ovens. The roots of all the valerians have a characteristic foul odor. Elk and other big game species eat the leaves and stems and they are utilized by domestic sheep and other livestock.

HAREBELL   *Campanula rotundifolia* L.   **Pl. 19**

Family: Campanulaceae (Bluebell).

Other names: Bellflower, Bluebell, Scotch Bluebell.

Description: The flowers are violet-blue, bell-shaped, about ¾ in. broad, hang downward from slender, perennial stems 8–20 in. tall, and are usually clustered together on a branching rootstock arising from a taproot. Basal leaves are round to ovate, and early withering; the alternate stem leaves are linear and 1–3 in. long.

One of the plants most commonly confused with this is the Blueflax (*Linum lewisii*), which, however, is saucer-shaped, with separate petals (see Plate 14); petals of Harebell are fused together.

Related species: (1) *C. parryi* attains height of 4–12 in. and has linear basal leaves 1–2 in. long, fringed with white hairs; (2) *C. uniflora* has a simple, erect flower on a 2–4 in. stem, with leaves lacking pronounced white hairs.

Flowering season: Latter part of June, July, and Aug. A few of these plants will be found blooming into Sept. hunting season, and they reach height of flowering about time young mallards make their appearance on ponds and streams.

Where found: G, Y, T, R. Dry to moist soil of open hillsides, prairies, and valleys, often among sagebrush, from lowest elevations to around 10,000 ft. Can be found from Alaska to Newfoundland, south to New Jersey, Iowa, Texas, California; also occurs in Eurasia. There are about 300 species of *Campanula*, mainly in north temperate and arctic zones; only about a half dozen are native to Rockies.

Interesting facts: *Rotundifolia* means round-leaved. Many names have been applied to this plant because of its variations in different environments. In deep, rich, moist soil, the plant may reach a height of 2 ft. or more, with thin, almost hairless foliage and numerous flowers; in alpine situations, it may attain a height of only 4–5 in. and produce but a single flower on a stem. In dry situations, the leaves tend to be hairy, short, and stiff. This phenomenon of environmental variation occurs in many plants. The tendency among botanists today is not to segregate and name separately plants that have grown differently because of different environments. This same plant is found in Scotland; hence the common name Scotch Bluebell.

YARROW   *Achillea lanulosa* Nutt.

Family: Compositae (Composite).

Other names: Milfoil, Tansy.

Description: A flat-topped plant bearing numerous minute white flowers in small heads often clustered at about the same level, although flower-bearing stems arise at different heights along main stem. Plant is a perennial herb with a strong odor and grows to a height of 1–3 ft. The numerous leaves pinnately dissected into 5 divisions have a fernlike appearance. One variety, *alpicola*, is only 3–10 in. tall; it has dark brown to black bracts around the flower heads and is found only at and above timberline. Heads of Yarrow are composed of 2 kinds of flowers: rayflowers, with elongated, strap-shaped corollas spaced around the outside; and diskflowers, with short, tubular corollas located in center of head. Flowers generally white, but occasionally pink or yellowish.

Yarrow could be confused with the dogfennels (*Anthemis*) and dusty maidens (*Chaenactis*). However, flower heads of Yarrow are only about ⅛ in. broad; those of these other plants are as much as ¾ in. across.

Flowering season: May to Sept. First flowers about time young blue grouse are hatching. Still blooming in early Sept. when hawks begin to migrate.

Where found: G, Y, T, R. Almost everywhere in dry to moder-

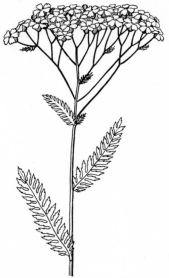

Yarrow (*Achillea
lanulosa* Nutt.)

ately moist soil, but not in deep shade and wet meadow. Grows
from lowest valleys to well above timberline, and is found over
most of N. America, although originally a western plant. The
European Yarrow (*A. millefolium*) has been introduced and is
now widespread; it can hardly be distinguished from our native
plant. There are perhaps 75 species of *Achillea*, most of them
native to the Old World; only 2 species occur in Rockies.
Interesting facts: *Achillea* is the name given to a plant that
Achilles used to cure the wounds of his soldiers; it quite possibly was closely related to our Yarrow. *Lanulosa* means
woolly. A decoction of this plant is used medicinally as a
stimulant and tonic. The Indians used Yarrow for medical
treatments. When eaten by cattle, its imparts a disagreeable
flavor to the milk; however, neither sheep nor cattle utilize
it unless forced to.

FALSE DANDELION   *Agoseris glauca* (Pursh) Dietr.   p. 188
  Family: Compositae (Composite).
  Other names: Goat Chicory, Mountain Dandelion, *Troximon
glaucum.*
  Description: This looks like the common Dandelion, having a
single head of yellow flowers, a basal rosette of large leaves,
and a leafless flowering stalk 4–25 in. tall. Corolla of each

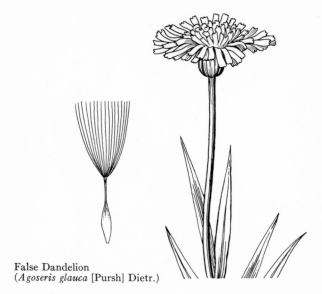

False Dandelion
(*Agoseris glauca* [Pursh] Dietr.)

flower is flat, elongated, and with or without lobes at outer end. They have no true calyx, but this is replaced by numerous hairlike bristles. Seeds have long beaks.

The different varieties and species of false dandelions usually can only be told apart by technical characters and by use of a microscope or a good hand lens. They can be confused with the true dandelions (*Taraxacum*), but these have minute spines or short hard processes on the seeds; in *Agoseris*, seeds reasonably smooth and stems less fleshy.

Related species: (1) *A. heterophylla* is a small annual found in western part of Rockies; (2) *A. aurantiaca* is found throughout Rockies and is characterized by deep orange to brown flowers, which often turn pink on drying.

Flowering season: May to July, or well into Aug. at higher elevations. Starts blooming almost a month after first true dandelions appear; some species will still be blooming in Sept.

Where found: G, Y, T, R. Moderately dry to moist, or even wet soil of meadows, roadsides, and open areas in mts., at almost all elevations. This species, or some of its many varieties, occurs from Manitoba to B.C., south to California and New Mexico. There are about 25 species of *Agoseris*, all natives of N. and S. America; about a dozen occur in Rocky Mt. area.

Interesting facts: *Glauca* means with waxy covering. This plant has lactiferous vessels, and when the tissues are broken a thick, milky juice exudes. This substance turns thicker and dark upon continued exposure to the air. It contains a certain amount of rubber but not in sufficient amounts to make it commercially valuable. The solidified juice of *Agoseris* was chewed as gum by western Indians. The plant is moderately grazed by livestock, domestic sheep being especially fond of it.

Pearly Everlasting (*Anaphalis margaritacea* [L.] B. & H.)

PEARLY EVERLASTING *Anaphalis margaritacea* (L.) B. & H.
 Family: Compositae (Composite).
 Other names: Life-everlasting, Indian Tobacco.
 Description: The flowers are in dense clustered heads. Each head is surrounded by many pearly-white bracts, with the small pale yellow flowers in center. Leaves numerous, narrow, lance-shaped, 2–5 in. long. Lower leaf surfaces and stems are covered with white woolly hairs, giving whole plant a silvery appearance. Stems are usually clumped and 1–3 ft. tall.

The plants most likely to be confused with this are the

pussytoes (*Antennaria*) and cudweeds (*Gnaphalium*). However, Pearly Everlasting is much larger than most pussytoes and does not have creeping stems or tufts of basal leaves. Cudweeds are densely woolly on upper surface of leaves as well as over entire plant.

Flowering season: Latter part of June, July, and into latter part of Aug. First look for it about time wild strawberries ripen.

Where found: G, Y, T, R. Dry to moist soil in foothills, and in mts. almost to timberline. This plant, or variations of it, occurs over most of Canada and south to North Carolina, Minnesota, New Mexico, and California. Also occurs in e. Asia and has been introduced into Europe. There are about 25 species of *Anaphalis*, chiefly native to Asia; this the only one in Rocky Mt. area.

Interesting facts: *Margaritacea* means pearly. Pearly Everlasting has been transplanted from the wild into flower gardens. This plant dries out like strawflowers and makes attractive long-lasting bouquets and decorations.

PUSSYTOES　　*Antennaria rosea* Greene　　　　　　**Pl. 22**

Family: Compositae (Composite).

Other names: Catspaws, Everlasting, Ladies-tobacco.

Description: The stems are 2–12 in. tall, surrounded with basal rosettes of leaves and capped with clusters of flower heads. Each head less than ⅛ in. across and surrounded by a number of conspicuous, dry, pearly-white to rose-colored bracts. Flowers themselves very inconspicuous, for there are no ray-flowers present. The cluster of flower heads may be ¾ in. across. These plants are mat-forming, gray-green, woolly perennials, often covering an area of several feet.

Plants most likely to be confused with the pussytoes are the Pearly Everlasting (*Anaphalis margaritacea*) and the cudweeds (*Gnaphalium*), which do not form mats or have tufts of basal leaves.

Related species: (1) *A. dimorpha* grows about 1 in. tall; flowers in early spring and forms gray patches that may cover many feet of ground. (2) *A. luzuloides* grows 6–24 in. tall and is not a mat-forming plant, the stems being clustered on a woody, branched root crown. Both species common throughout Rockies.

Flowering season: Latter part of May to first part of Aug. Blooms about time young coyote pups begin to play outside their dens.

Where found: G, Y, T, R. Dry to moist soil of prairies, valleys, and mt. sides, to about 9000 ft. Found from Saskatchewan to B.C., south to California and New Mexico. There are perhaps 25 species native to north temperate zone and S. America; about 20 in Rocky Mt. area.

Pussytoes (*Antennaria rosea* Greene)

Interesting facts: *Rosea* means rose-colored. Many of the species of *Antennaria* will produce seed without fertilization. The plants are usually distinctly male or female, and in some species the male plants are rare, or even unknown. Flowers picked soon after blooming can be kept intact into winter. At times they are dyed and used where long-lasting flower decorations are desired. Gum prepared from the stalks of some species of *Antennaria* was chewed by western Indians. Deer utilize some species, but in general antennarias are poor forage plants. Extensive growths of *A. dimorpha* are an indicator of poor range conditions.

BURDOCK *Arctium minus* Schk. p. 192
  Family: Compositae (Composite).
  Other names: Clotbur.
  Description: The flowers are tubular, purple to white, arranged in heads about 1 in. across. Around outside of head, or bur, are slender bracts hooked at tip. These flowers are borne on a coarse, branching, biennial herb, 2–6 ft. tall, with leaves up to 10 in. wide and 1 ft. long. Mature plant is covered with nearly round burs that fall apart when ripe.

The plant most likely to be confused with this is the Cockle-bur (*Xanthium strumarium*), but burs on it are longer than broad and do not break up when mature. Also, Cocklebur leaves are very rough and sharp to the touch; Burdock leaves are smooth and velvety.

Flowering season: Latter part of Aug. to first part of Oct.

Where found: G. Moist soil of roadsides and waste places from lowest elevations to around 6500 ft. This plant, a native of Europe and Asia, has been introduced as a weed over most of U.S. and s. Canada. There are only 4 or 5 species of *Arctium*, all native to Eurasia, but because the burs are readily dissemi-nated all species have become widely distributed; only 2 species in Rockies, difficult to distinguish.

Interesting facts: *Minus* means smaller. The Burdock has been used for centuries in medicine as a tonic, and is still used as a diuretic. Various species are used for food in many parts of the world. The young leaves can be eaten as greens, the young stems peeled and eaten raw or cooked, and even the cooked roots can be used. To most Americans it is just a noxious weed whose burs become matted in clothing and in the hair of domestic animals, irritating their skin. When one tries to pull

Burdock (*Arctium minus* Schk.)

them out, the burs break up and each small part often has to be removed separately. This characteristic has made them particularly effective for the pranks and bur fights of childhood.

ARNICA   *Arnica cordifolia* Hook.   **Pl. 19**
   Family: Compositae (Composite).
   Other names: Heartleaf Arnica, Leopard's Bane.
   Description: A single-stem plant with a head of yellow flowers about 2 in. across. Plant is 8–24 in. tall and basal and lower leaves are heart-shaped, 1–3 in. long, and opposite. Leaves and stems slightly hairy.
   Arnicas are most likely to be confused with the sunflowers (*Helianthus*) and balsamroots (*Balsamorhiza*). These, however, are usually 2 or more times as large as the arnicas, or grow in dense bunches rather than singly or in small clumps.
   The different species of *Arnica* vary considerably in size and shape, but all have at least their lower leaves opposite, and (with 1 or 2 exceptions) have both rayflowers and diskflowers present in all heads.
   Related species: (1) A quite common alpine clumped arnica is *A. rydbergii;* flower heads smaller than in *A. cordifolia*, often with 3 on a stem that has 2 to 4 opposite pairs of leaves. (2) *A. longifolia* is a densely tufted plant with 5 to 12 pairs of leaves on each stem. (3) *A. parryi* lacks the conspicuous rayflowers around the head. These are common species in Rockies.
   Flowering season: Latter part of May through July. Blooms about time Swainson's hawks and Audubon warblers return in spring. Ruffed grouse can still be heard drumming in the woods when and where this arnica appears.
   Where found: G, Y, T, R. Moist soil, usually in open woods, especially under stands of Quaking Aspen and Ponderosa and Lodgepole Pines. Occurs from the foothills to around 9000 ft. This species, or varieties of it, occurs from Alaska to Michigan, south to California and New Mexico. There are about 30 species of *Arnica* in temperate N. Hemisphere, most of them in w. U.S.; 14 occur in our area.
   Interesting facts: *Cordifolia* means heart-leaved. This arnica is an official drug plant; all the parts may be used but the flowers are most potent. If the drug from it is given orally or intravenously, it causes a rise in body temperature. Applied externally as a salve to cuts it aids in keeping down infection. It is not an important forage plant but is grazed by mule deer.

BIG SAGEBRUSH   *Artemisia tridentata* Nutt.   p. 194
   Family: Compositae (Composite).
   Other names: Wormwood, Mugwort.
   Description: This is the common, much-branched, gray-green shrub, 2–10 ft. tall, that covers many of our inter-

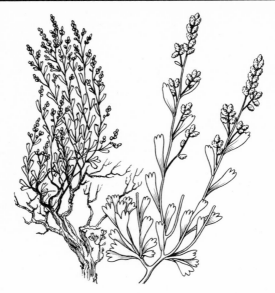

Big Sagebrush (*Artemisia tridentata* Nutt.)

mountain valley floors. Bark on old stems shreds in long strips. Leaves evergreen, aromatic, usually somewhat wedge-shaped, with 3 teeth at the end, and covered with silky-silvery hair. Flowers are minute, and occur in inconspicuous silver-green heads.

In Rockies, the sagebrushes are often confused with Grease-wood (*Sarcobatus vermiculatus*) but this latter plant is spiny. Many other species of *Artemisia* are herbs; this one can be distinguished from those that are shrubs by its large size and the leaves with 3 terminal teeth. This plant should not be confused with the Garden Sage (*Salvia officinalis*), used as a flavoring agent; they are not closely related.

Related species: (1) *A. biennis* is a green annual or biennial weed 2–3 ft. tall; (2) *A. ludoviciana* is a silvery-colored peren-nial herb 1–3 ft. tall; (3) *A. spinescens* is a gray spiny shrub, 1–3 ft. tall; (4) *A. cana* is a silvery-colored shrub with all or nearly all leaves linear and toothless. All are common species in Rockies.

Flowering season: Aug. and Sept., during which time its pollen fills the air and is a common cause of hay fever. Flower-ing of Big Sagebrush heralds end of summer.

Where found: Y, T, R. Dry soil of valleys and hills, sometimes almost to timberline. Extends from North Dakota to B.C., south to California and New Mexico. There are over 100 species of *Artemisia* in north temperate zone and in S. America; about 20 occur in Rocky Mt. area.

Interesting facts: *Tridentata* means 3-toothed. When white men first came to our western valleys, they found grass and sagebrush growing together, but apparently the grass predominated and young brush plants had a difficult time getting started. Overgrazing by cattle and sheep has gradually killed the grasses and these have been replaced by Big Sagebrush, which these animals do not readily eat. Sagebrush is, however, a very valuable wildlife food, being heavily utilized by antelope and sage grouse and browsed by elk, mule deer, and moose, particularly in late winter and early spring. It is high in fat content and best utilized by wildlife when consumed with other browse and grasses. Its abundance and availability undoubtedly save many animals from being winter-killed. It also furnishes cover and nest and den sites for a host of smaller animals. Large areas of sagebrush are now being burned over and the land planted back to grass. If carried too far, this practice could be detrimental to some species of wildlife. Soils over large areas in the West are too saline for Big Sagebrush to grow in, but Greasewood thrives. Our early settlers soon learned to select farmland where the Sagebrush, not Greasewood, grew. Over large parts of the West sagebrushes furnish the only fuel for fires; it burns rapidly, with an aromatic smell. Even green plants will readily burn. Volatile oils with a pleasant sage odor can be extracted from the leaves. Indians extracted a light yellow dye.

SHOWY ASTER *Aster conspicuus* Lindl.

Family: Compositae (Composite).

Other names: Michaelmas Daisy.

Description: A large-headed aster with 15 to 35 blue or violet rayflowers, yellow diskflowers, and many large leaves toothed around edges. Plant usually much branched at top and may vary from 1 to 3 ft. in height. Involucral bracts in 5 rows.

Asters and daisies (*Erigeron*) are difficult to distinguish. Usually the asters are later-blooming, larger, and have several series of green bracts surrounding the head and overlapping like shingles on a roof. Trained botanists have difficulty in identifying the different species of asters.

Related species: (1) *A. frondosus* is a small annual with very short, inconspicuous rayflowers; (2) *A. canescens* has a distinct taproot, leaves toothed and slightly spiny. These plants common in Rockies. (3) Alpine Aster (*A. alpigenus* [T. & G.] Gray), Plate 21, is a dwarf perennial found in high mts. (4)

Thickstem Aster (*A. integrifolius* Nutt.), Plate 23 and below, is a stout fibrous-rooted perennial with broad clasping leaves, and an elongated inflorescence. The heads of violet-purple rayflowers and orange-yellow diskflowers are not easily confused with other asters. Involucre and upper stem are glandular.

Flowering season: Latter part of June through most of Aug.

Where found: G, Y, T. Moist, rich soil, usually in open woods, from foothills to around 9000 ft. in mts. Found from Montana

Thickstem Aster (*Aster integrifolius* Nutt.)

to B.C., south to Oregon and Wyoming. There are around 250 species of asters, mainly in N. America but some extend to S. America and the Old World; in Rockies, perhaps 35 species.

Interesting facts: *Conspicuus* means prominent. Because they are late-blooming, asters have been called Michaelmas Daisies and Christmas Daisies. In mild seasons in temperate regions they can be found blooming up to this winter date. The big-game and waterfowl hunter will find them blooming in the Rockies until snow falls. Elk consume it in fall and winter.

ENGELMANN ASTER *Aster engelmannii* (D. C. Eat.) Gray **Pl. 23**

Family: Compositae (Composite).

Other names: White Aster.

Description: A strict-growing plant 2–6 ft. tall, with large ragged heads composed of diskflowers surrounded by 9 to 15 white or slightly pinkish rayflowers that may be 1 in. long. Numerous more or less lance-shaped leaves, 2–4 in. long, that are smooth around edge; stems have few to many short branches at top.

Flowering season: Latter part of June to first part of Sept. Look for this aster about time Goldenrod begins to bloom. Will still be blooming when mule deer are completing the molt from their "red" summer pelage to the gray-brown winter coat.

Where found: G, Y, T, R. Moist to wet soil, usually in wooded areas but sometimes in open; from foothills to around 9000 ft. Found from Alberta to B.C., south to Nevada and Colorado. There are around 250 species of asters, mainly in N. America but some extend to S. America and the Old World; in Rockies, perhaps 35 species.

Interesting facts: *Engelmanni* means named for George Engelmann. The leaves, stems, and flowers of many species of aster are consumed by our big game animals. The leaves of several species were boiled and eaten by various Indian tribes.

ARROWLEAF BALSAMROOT **Pl. 20**
Balsamorhiza sagittata (Pursh) Nutt.

Family: Compositae (Composite).

Other names: Bigroot, Big Sunflower.

Description: In spring, Arrowleaf Balsamroot often colors dry hillsides a golden yellow. The nearly leafless stalks attain a height of 8–24 in. and usually terminate in a head of flowers varying 2–4 in. across. Large, bright yellow rayflowers surround tubular diskflowers. Arrow-shaped leaves have long stalks, are as much as 1 ft. long and 6 in. wide, and are covered with a dense mat of silvery-gray hairs.

Arrowleaf Balsamroot can be confused with the true sunflowers (*Helianthus*) and other closely related plants. However, clumps of large leaves and naked stems arising from thick taproot, combined with silvery appearance, usually distinguish it from sunflowers. This species of *Balsamorhiza* can be told from others in Rockies by its smooth-edged leaves; others have at least some of their leaves variously toothed or incised.

Related species: (1) *B. incana* has incised leaves whitened with soft cottony hairs; only occurs in w. Rockies. (2) Balsamroot (*B. hookeri* Nutt.), Plate 21, has incised leaves that are green but glandular and hairy; common in Rockies.

Flowering season: Latter part of April to first part of July. Blooms early, first appearing when aspens start to leaf and ruffed grouse are drumming. It is becoming conspicuous when American magpie is laying eggs and is in full bloom when bighorn sheep are lambing.

Where found: G, Y, T. Dry soil of valleys and hills, and in mts. to around 8000 ft. Found from South Dakota to B.C., south to California and Colorado. There are about a dozen species of *Balsamorhiza*, confined to w. N. America, principally to the 3 Pacific Coast states; about half these species occur in Rockies.

Interesting facts: *Sagittata* means arrow-leaved. Indians ate the young tender sprouts, large roots, and the seeds — either raw or cooked. The roots are resinous, woody, and taste like balsam. Elk and deer graze the young tender shoots. Both the leaves and flower heads are a preferred spring food of bighorn sheep. Horses are especially fond of the flowering heads, and the entire plant is important forage for livestock. It can withstand heavy grazing.

BEGGARTICKS *Bidens cernua* L.　　　　　　　　**Pl. 22**

Family: Compositae (Composite).
Other names: Sticktights, Bur-marigold, Spanish Needles.
Description: The blossoms are bright yellow and look like small sunflowers. There are 6 to 8 rayflowers on a head. These plants,

Beggarticks (*Bidens cernua* L.)

however, only attain a height of 6–30 in. Leaves are lance-shaped and toothed, opposite, and often completely encircle stem at their base. You may first notice this plant when you tediously pick the small, flattened seeds off your clothing. Seeds have 2 projecting spines, or teeth, covered with backward-pointing barbs; hence the name *Bidens* (2 teeth).

The beggarticks could easily be confused with many flowers in the Composite family, except for presence of the 2 teeth at top of seeds. This character usually distinctive. Only species of *Bidens* common in Rockies which has simple leaves with either smooth or toothed edges; others have either compound leaves or leaves dissected into narrow divisions.

Related species: (1) *B. tenuisecta* has inconspicuous rayflowers and leaves greatly dissected; (2) *B. vulgata* has leaves with 3 to 5 lanceolate or broader leaflets. These common throughout Rockies.

Flowering season: Latter part of July to first part of Oct. The sticking seeds are a sign of approaching fall.

Where found: Y, T. Wet or boggy soil, from lowest elevations to around 7000 ft. Can be found from B.C. to New Brunswick, south to North Carolina, Missouri, and California. There are about 200 species of *Bidens* widely distributed over the earth; only about a half dozen occur in Rockies.

Interesting facts: *Cernua* means nodding. Nature has evolved many ways for the dispersal of seed, the result being to give each plant a better chance to spread and survive. Outdoorsmen pick up and grudgingly carry hundreds of the prickly Beggartick seeds on their socks and trousers. By doing so they help to spread the very pests they abhor.

BRISTLE THISTLE *Carduus nutans* L.   **Pl. 24**
    Family: Compositae (Composite).
    Other names: Musk Thistle, Nodding Thistle.
    Description: A spiny plant with alternate deeply lobed leaves; stem generally winged by the down-curved leaf bases. Flower heads 1–1½ in. broad; generally solitary and nodding at ends of branches. Involucral bracts are sharp, stiff, and conspicuous, especially before flower head has fully opened. *Carduus* easily confused with *Cirsium*, but stem of latter is not winged by the leaf bases.

Related species: *C. acanthoides* can be distinguished from *C. nutans* by narrower involucral bracts and erect flower heads.

Flowering season: July and Aug.; in full bloom when water level drops in mt. streams and rivers and trout readily take dry flies.

Where found: G. Roadsides, waste areas, and where land has been heavily grazed. More than 100 species native to Europe, Asia, and N. Africa; 2 species occur in Rockies, both introduced from Europe.

Interesting facts: *Nutans* means nodding. This introduced plant is a noxious weed difficult to control. It is attractive to butterflies and is visited by numerous species of nectar-seeking insects.

SPOTTED KNAPWEED *Centaurea maculosa* Lam. **Pl. 24**
Family: Compositae (Composite).
Other names: Spotted Star-thistle.
Description: A biennial or short-lived perennial plant with numerous branches bearing a single head of pink-purple flowers about ¾ in. high. Flowers are all tubular, marginal ones enlarged. Bracts around heads have dark, finely divided tips. Stem attains height of 1–3 ft. and has many leaves finely dissected into linear divisions.

This plant can be distinguished from other species of *Centaurea* by its finely divided leaves. May be confused with some of the asters (*Aster*), but these do not have around the flower heads bracts that are dissected at tips.
Related species: (1) *C. solstitialis* has bracts around flower heads with long, sharp spines. (2) *C. picris* is a perennial from widespreading underground stems; has numerous small heads of purple flowers, many narrow leaves, and plant may cover large areas in dense patches; one of our noxious weeds.
Flowering season: From June to Oct. Frequently greets the sportsman when he stoops to retrieve his first ring-necked pheasant of the season.
Where found: Introduced from Europe and is well established in the East. Rapidly spreading over w. N. America, establishing itself along roadsides, in pastures, fields, and waste places. Though approximately 400 species of *Centaurea* are well distributed over the earth, less than a dozen occur in Rocky Mt. area.
Interesting facts: *Maculosa* means spotted. Some of the species of *Centaurea* are cultivated flowers such as Bachelorsbuttons, Basketflower, and Scabiosa. Others are noxious weeds such as St. Barnaby's Thistle (*C. solstitialis*) and Brown Knapweed (*C. jacea*). The various species in this genus are diversified in habit of growth, foliage, and flowers.

MORNING-BRIDES *Chaenactis douglasii* (Hook.) H. & A.
Family: Compositae (Composite).
Other names: Dusty Maiden, False Yarrow, Bride's Bouquet.
Description: The flowers are small, tubular, white to flesh-colored, and form heads about ½ in. broad. A dusty-looking plant, with 1 to several stems 4–18 in. tall, coming from a taproot. Leaves very much dissected, and larger ones form a basal rosette near ground.

This plant is often confused with Yarrow (*Achillea lanulosa*) or Dogfennel (*Anthemis cotula*), but these plants have rayflowers as well as diskflowers; Morning-brides has only diskflowers. Various species of *Chaenactis* look much alike and are difficult to distinguish.

Related species: (1) *C. stevioides* is a low annual, 2–10 in. tall, with grayish pinnately cleft leaves; (2) Dusty Maiden (*C. alpina* [Gray] Jones), Plate 24, is a small dusty-looking alpine perennial, 2–4 in. tall, with only basal leaves.

Flowering season: Throughout June to first part of Aug. First appears about time Larkspur reaches its height of blooming and prairie falcons are feathering.

Where found: Y, T. Dry to medium-moist soil, along roadsides, waste places, and hillsides, especially where soil has been disturbed. Grows from lowest valleys to timberline, and can be found from Montana to B.C., south to California and New Mexico. There are about 33 species of *Chaenactis*, approximately ⅓ occurring in Rocky Mts. and the rest westward to Pacific Ocean.

Interesting facts: *Douglasii* means named for David Douglas.

GOLDEN-ASTER *Chrysopsis villosa* (Pursh) Nutt. p. 202

Family: Compositae (Composite).

Other names: Goldeneye.

Description: This usually has a cluster of stems 8–24 in. tall, branched at top, with a head of yellow flowers terminating each branch. Both ray- and diskflowers are yellow, and heads are about ½ in. broad. Leaves numerous, vary from narrow to oblong, are quite hairy, and are stalkless or stemmed, depending on the variety. Seeds tipped with hairy bristles.

This plant looks like an *Aster*, but the rayflowers are yellow instead of white, purple, or blue. It is not sticky to the touch and this distinguishes it from Gumweed (*Grindelia squarrosa*), with which it is often confused.

Flowering season: Latter part of June to Aug.

Where found: G, Y, T. Dry to medium-moist soil in open areas, sandy river bottoms, roadsides, and hills, from valleys and plains to around 8000 ft. Occurs from Saskatchewan to B.C., south to California and Texas. There are about 20 species of *Chrysopsis* native to N. America; most of them grow in dry or sandy soil. There is now a tendency to take the old-named species in Rockies and make them varieties under *C. villosa;* using this system, we have only 1 species, with several varieties.

Interesting facts: *Villosa* means soft-hairy. Both the ray- and diskflowers of the Golden-aster are yellow, but in many true asters, daisies, and other plants the diskflowers in the center of the head are yellow but the rayflowers around the outside

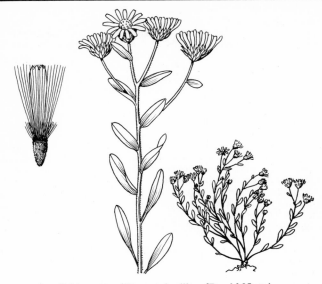

Golden-aster (*Chrysopsis villosa* [Pursh] Nutt.)

of the head are purple or blue. We do not know why a plant manufactures a chemical of one color at one spot and a few cells away makes an entirely different chemical of another color. This phenomenon enables plants to exhibit a wide range of color and color combinations.

RABBITBRUSH *Chrysothamnus nauseosus* (Pall.) Britt.   **Pl. 22**
Family: Compositae (Composite).
Other names: False Goldenrod, Goldenbush.
Description: This is a conspicuous, bushy, goldenrod-like plant growing 2–3 ft. tall. Lacks rayflowers; diskflowers yellow. Has a pappus of hairlike bristles, and involucral bracts yellowish and in vertical rows. Woody wide-spreading branches are covered with matted, white-woolly hairs.
Related species: (1) *C. parryi*, with bracts prolonged into green herbaceous tips, has flowers in leafy terminal racemes; (2) *C. viscidiflorus*, a low, green, desert shrub with little or no hair, has narrow leaves, usually twisted. Both plants common throughout Rockies.
Flowering season: A late-season plant, first blooming about mid-July and continuing into Sept. At height of blooming, pronghorn antelope fawns are about half the size of doe.

Where found: Y, T. Common on dry hills, plains, and road-sides. Look for it growing with sagebrush or on overgrazed eroded soil. At height of season it casts a golden hue over large areas. Extends length of Rocky Mts. from Canada to Mexico. Genus *Chrysothamnus* is composed of about 15 species, all native to w. N. America, with range similar to that of Rabbitbrush; 5 occur in Rocky Mt. area.

Interesting facts: *Nauseosus* means heavy-scented. Rabbit-brush is a useful tool to the conservationist. Since it thrives on poor soil it is an indicator that the land is poor, has been allowed to erode, has been overgrazed, or in other ways has been neglected. Because it can thrive where other plants cannot live, it is frequently the most conspicuous plant on waste areas. It serves as a reserve food for antelope, jackrabbits, mountain sheep, and mule deer, and is an important winter browse for elk. The plant contains rubber, but extraction is not yet commercially profitable.

CANADA THISTLE *Cirsium arvense* (L.) Scop.
    Family: Compositae (Composite).
    Other names: Creeping Thistle, Cursed Thistle.
    Description: A perennial, spiny-leaved plant bearing numerous heads of pink-purple flowers and arising from deep-seated,

Canada Thistle
(*Cirsium arvense* [L.] Scop.)

spreading rootstocks. Stems usually 1–6 ft. tall, and grow in dense patches. As each seed matures, it develops long silky hairs which make it airborne.

The spiny leaves and stems of this thistle separate it from most other plants, and its spreading rootstocks, giving rise to dense patches sometimes covering an acre or more of land, are characteristic only of this species of *Cirsium*.

Related species: (1) *C. undulatum* has rose or rose-purple flowers and leaves that are white-woolly on both sides; (2) *C. brevistylum* similar but consistently white-flowered.

Flowering season: June to Aug. In full bloom when young meadowlarks are flying.

Where found: Y, T. Cultivated fields, meadows, pastures, roadsides, and waste places. Occurs in mts. to around 7500 ft. Introduced from Eurasia, it is now found over most of s. Canada and n. and w. U.S. There are about 200 species of *Cirsium* in north temperate zone, of which around 50 are native to N. America; about 20 occur in Rocky Mts.

Interesting facts: *Arvense* means of fields. This noxious weed has overrun thousands of acres of valuable farmland, making them worthless for growing crops. Its underground rootstocks are so deep they can usually obtain plenty of moisture. They spread in every direction, sending up new shoots, and one plant may cover an area of 20 ft. or more. Plowing and cultivation only cut up and scatter these rootstocks, thus starting new plants and points of infestation. It is quite resistant to herbicides.

ELK THISTLE *Cirsium foliosum* (Hook.) DC.   **Pl. 24**

Family: Compositae (Composite).

Other names: Everts' Thistle.

Description: This plant is usually seen in mt. meadows, standing above other vegetation. Thick, leafy, unbranched, succulent stems vary from 2 to 3 in. up to 4 ft. in height, and taper little from bottom to top. White to purple flowers are clustered at top of plant in heads 1–2 in. broad. Leaves are toothed or deeply dissected; upper ones often extend above flower heads. Entire plant covered by relatively weak spines and has a silvery to grayish-green appearance.

Thistles are our only plants whose leaves are covered with long spines; *C. foliosum* the only species in Rockies that grows in wet mt. meadows and has stems almost as thick at top as at bottom.

Flowering season: June to first part of Aug. First blooms about same time as Green Gentian and, like it, stands out above other smaller plants. Grizzly bear cubs are losing their milk teeth and supplementing their milk diet with other foods.

Where found: G, Y, T, R. Moist to wet soil, usually in open meadows from valleys to about 8000 ft. Found from Saskatchewan to B.C., south to California and New Mexico. There are about 200 species of *Cirsium* in north temperate zone, of which around 50 are native to N. America; about 20 occur in Rocky Mts.

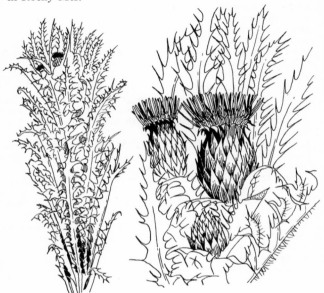

Elk Thistle (*Cirsium foliosum* [Hook.] DC.)

Interesting facts: *Foliosum* means leafy. The fleshy roots and stems were used as food by the Indians. In 1870 Truman Everts, a member of the first party of white men to make a thorough exploration of Yellowstone Natl. Park, became separated from his companions in the vicinity of Yellowstone Lake. A near-tragic mishap occurred when his horse threw him and he lost his mount and broke his spectacles. Being extremely nearsighted, he thought his time had come. Lost and unable to obtain wild game, he was slowly starving to death, when in desperation he ate the root of this thistle and subsisted principally on it until rescued a month later. The peeled stems are tender and have a sweet delicate taste. Cooked as a green it is a welcome addition to any camp meal. In an emergency it is a safe bet to try eating the stems or roots of any of the thistles; among the more palatable ones are the Wavyleaf

Thistle (*C. undulatum*) and Short-styled Thistle (*C. brevistylum*). Elk Thistle is a favorite early summer food of elk and black and grizzly bears.

BULL THISTLE   *Cirsium vulgare* (Savi) Airy-Shaw   **Pl. 24**
Family: Compositae (Composite).
Other names: Common Thistle, Bur Thistle, Spear Thistle, and *C. lanceolatum*.
Description: A wide-branching biennial, 2–5 ft. tall, covered with sharp spines, and large heads of purple flowers. In 1st year only a flat rosette of leaves appears, and not until 2nd year do the flowering stalks develop. Lance-shaped leaves are up to 8 in. long, and deeply cut and dissected.

This is our only thistle with upper leaf surface covered with short stiff hairs. A strip of leaflike tissue running down stem edgewise from base of one leaf to next is also armed with sharp spines.
Flowering season: July to Sept. First blooms about time half-grown Uinta ground squirrels are seen scampering around meadows and crossing highways.
Where found: G, Y, T. Grows in medium-dry to fairly wet soil along roadsides, in pastures, and in waste places, from lowest elevations to around 8000 ft. This weed, introduced from Eurasia, is now established over most of N. America. There are about 200 species of *Cirsium* in north temperate zone, of which around 50 are native to N. America; about 20 occur in Rocky Mts.
Interesting facts: *Vulgare* means common. The seeds of this plant have thickened rings of tissue with long silky hairs, which when ripe are wind-carried by this "down" until they reach moist air. The rings then absorb water, swell, and break loose from seeds, dropping them to moist soil below, where there is a favorable chance for growth. Thistledown makes an excellent tinder. Like cattail down, it will burst into flame from a pyrite spark. The camper or explorer intending to spend some time in the wilderness will do well to gather a pocketful of plant down as he comes upon it. When his matches are wet or spent he can start fires with this, using the pyrite on his matchcase or cigarette lighter.

HAWKSBEARD   *Crepis acuminata* Nutt.
Family: Compositae (Composite).
Other names: Tapertip.
Description: The yellow flowers form numerous cylindrical heads up to ½ in. long. One to few stems from a taproot attain a height of 8–30 in. Leaves, mostly basal or on lower part of stem, are lance-shaped and dissected into narrow divisions. Hair imparts gray color to plants.

The following combination of characters helps to distinguish the hawksbeards from other genera in Composite family: presence of only rayflowers in a head, the milky juice, yellow flowers, leaves on stem, fact that they are perennials, seeds with silky, bright, white hairs at top, and not flattened. They are commonly confused with false dandelions (*Agoseris*), but can be distinguished most readily by their branched and leafy stems.

Related species: (1) *C. runcinata*, found in moist, often alkaline meadows, is green and usually hairless, with most of the leaves forming a basal rosette; (2) *C. modocensis* is a gray-colored plant with hairs on lower parts yellow and on flower heads black.

Hawksbeard (*Crepis acuminata* Nutt.)

Flowering season: Latter part of May through July. Silky white seed hairs as conspicuous as flowers, and seen in July.

Where found: Y, T. Dry to moist soil in open areas, roadsides, and stony hillsides, from valleys to around 8000 ft. Ranges from Montana to Washington, south to California and New Mexico. Around 200 species of *Crepis* are widely scattered over the earth, but only about a dozen are native to America; others have been introduced, for about this many occur in Rocky Mt. area alone.

Interesting facts: *Acuminata* means tapering at end. Forage plants vary considerably in their palatability to different animals. Sheep quite often eat plants not utilized by cattle, horses, deer, or elk. The hawksbeards are especially palatable to domestic sheep, and overgrazing has nearly eliminated hawksbeard from many western ranges.

The common name Hawksbeard refers to the resemblance of the silky seed hairs to the bristles protruding around a hawk's beak.

Cutleaf Daisy (*Erigeron compositus* Pursh)

CUTLEAF DAISY   *Erigeron compositus* Pursh   **Pl. 21**
  Family: Compositae (Composite).
  Other names: Fleabane.
  Description: The flowers are in heads varying from ½ to 1 in. across, with numerous yellow, tubular diskflowers surrounded by many white, pink, or blue rayflowers. The few to many stems arising from a taproot are usually under 1 ft. in height,

varying 1–10 in.; each stem terminates in a single head of flowers. Greatly dissected leaves are mostly basal, and divided into 3's two or three times.

Daisies are usually much smaller than the similar-appearing asters (*Aster*) and bracts around flower heads are generally in a single series (or 2 series at most) instead of 3 or more. Usually daisy rayflowers are narrower and more numerous than those of asters.

Related species: (1) *E. aphanactis* is a yellow-flowered daisy without rayflowers, or with very short ones; (2) *E. annuus*, a large, branching annual weed, is 2–5 ft. tall, with inconspicuous white rayflowers; (3) *E. simplex* is an alpine daisy with a single head about 1 in. broad on each stem. These common throughout Rockies.

Flowering season: May, June, and July. Begins to bloom about time yellow Mules-ears reaches height of blooming.

Where found: G, Y, T, R. Dry, rocky or sandy soil from foothills to above timberline. This plant, or varieties of it, is found from Alaska to Greenland, south to Quebec, Colorado, Arizona, and California. There are approximately 200 species of *Erigeron* well distributed over temperate regions of the earth, and of these about 135 species are native to N. America, centering mainly in mt. areas; about 50 species occur in Rockies.

Interesting facts: *Compositus* means compound. The daisies vary in palatability to game and livestock but generally are poor forage. The Cutleaf Daisy increases with overgrazing and is used as an indicator of range abuse. It becomes especially abundant on overused cattle ranges.

COULTER'S DAISY *Erigeron coulteri* Porter   p. 210
   Family: Compositae (Composite).
   Other names: Fleabane.
   Description: This plant often covers alpine meadows. It has 1 to 3 flower heads, ¾–1½ in. broad at top of each stem. Rayflowers are white or light purple; diskflowers, yellow. The 1 to several stems in a cluster are from 4 to 24 in. tall. Lance-shaped leaves, both basal and on stem, are hairy; sometimes lower ones are toothed. Thin green bracts around flower heads are also hairy, the hairs with black "crosswalls" toward base.
   Flowering season: Latter part of June to first part of Aug. Starts to bloom about time young water pipits leave nest and young white-crowned sparrows are hatching.
   Where found: G, Y, T, R. Damp to wet soil about springs, in meadows, and along streams, 6000–10,000 ft. in mts. Occurs from Wyoming to Oregon, and south to California and New Mexico. There are approximately 200 species of *Erigeron* well distributed over temperate regions of the earth, and of

Coulter's Daisy (*Erigeron coulteri* Porter)

these about 135 species are native to N. America, centering mainly in mt. areas; about 50 species occur in Rockies.

Interesting facts: *Coulteri* means named for J. M. Coulter. Climbers, campers, and hunters who go into alpine country will surely encounter this daisy.

SHOWY DAISY   *Erigeron speciosus* (Lindl.) DC.   **Pl. 21**

Family: Compositae (Composite).

Other names: Oregon Fleabane.

Description: In general the daisies can be distinguished from asters by numbers of rows of bracts surrounding the flower head (1 row in daisies, or 2 at most). Bracts of Showy Daisy are hairy. Rayflowers around edge of head are numerous (65–150), narrow, and usually blue to lilac; the tubular diskflowers are yellow. Few to many stems arise from a woody, branching root crown, 6–30 in. tall. Each stalk may bear 1–12 heads about 1 in. broad. Numerous leaves, lance-shaped or narrower; lower tend to fall off as season advances. Leaf margins fringed and leaves often 3-nerved.

Flowering season: Latter part of June to first part of Aug. Blooms about time first wild strawberries ripen.

Where found: Y, T, R. Dry to moist soil in open areas or open woods, from foothills to nearly 9000 ft. It, or varieties of it, is distributed from Alberta to B.C., south to New Mexico. There are approximately 200 species of *Erigeron* well distributed over temperate regions of the earth, and of these about 135 species are native to N. America, centering mainly in mt. areas; about 50 species occur in Rockies.

Interesting facts: Many of the erigerons have a ragged worn-out look even when first in bloom. This characteristic has given them their name of *Erigeron*, which means soon becoming old; *speciosus* means showy. Some of them when picked and laid aside for a day are scarcely recognizable. The showy flower parts wither up and in their place are the white or brown bristly hairs of the spent flower.

WOOLLY YELLOWDAISY *Eriophyllum lanatum* (Pursh) Forbes
Var. *integrifolium* (Hook.) Smiley   **Pl. 23**

    Family: Compositae (Composite).

    Other names: Woolly Eriophyllum.

    Description: The variety *integrifolium* is the most common member of this genus in the Rocky Mt. area. This plant is white-woolly in appearance, somewhat prostrate and woody at

Woolly Yellowdaisy (*Eriophyllum lanatum* [Pursh] Forbes
var. *integrifolium* [Hook.] Smiley)

the base, and has yellow heads of both ray- and diskflowers. These heads ½–¾ in. broad. May be from 1 to several branched stems 4–24 in. tall, usually long and slender.

In the genus *Eriophyllum* both the ray- and diskflowers are yellow, lower part of plant is semiwoody, stems and leaves are densely covered with white-woolly hair, and seeds lack terminal hairs or bristles.

Flowering season: May, June, and July. First appears about time young sparrow hawks leave their nesting hollows and learn to fly. In full bloom when ravens are fledging.

Where found: Y, T. Dry soil in open areas of foothills and mts. to about 8000 ft. Found from Yellowstone Natl. Park in Wyoming to B.C. and California. This genus has 11 generally recognized species, but with exception of this species all occur in sw. U.S.

Interesting facts: *Lanatum* means woolly. The woolly mat of hairs on this plant and on many others, like Big Sagebrush, Pussytoes, and Mullein, helps to prevent evaporation of water from the leaves. Plants with this characteristic can grow in extremely dry locations. The cacti and many euphorbias accomplish the same thing by secreting a heavy layer of wax over the plant surface. Many of our common trees and shrubs shed their leaves to check water loss when the life of the plant is threatened by drought.

BLANKETFLOWER *Gaillardia aristata* Pursh   **Pl. 20**
    Family: Compositae (Composite).
    Other names: Brown-eyed Susan.
    Description: Blanketflowers have 1 to several stems, 8–30 in. tall, with sunflower-looking heads 2–3 in. across. Orange- to purplish-red diskflowers are surrounded by yellow rayflowers. Leaves are on lower part of stem, are lance-shaped, up to 6 in. long, and sometimes variously toothed.

Gaillardia is the only genus of plants in the Rockies that has the receptacle of the flowering heads covered with stiff hairs. Others either naked, as in common Dandelion (*Taraxacum officinale*), or covered with bracts, as in the sunflowers (*Helianthus*). This species of *Gaillardia* the only perennial one with yellow rayflowers and lobes of diskflowers elongated and covered with hairs.

Related species: (1) *G. pinnatifida* is a perennial, with at least some leaves pinnately parted; (2) *G. pulchella* an annual plant. Both occur only in s. Rockies.

Flowering season: June to first part of Aug. First appears when Bitterroot is in bloom and elk are calving.

Where found: G, Y, T. Medium-dry to moist soil, in open areas from foothills to about 8000 ft. Found from Saskatchewan to B.C., south to Arizona and New Mexico. There are about a dozen species of *Gaillardia*, all native to w. N. America except

1 species in S. America; Blanketflower only species of genus in n. Rocky Mts.

Interesting facts: *Aristata* means bearded. This plant has been domesticated and is now grown in flower gardens over a large part of the earth. It often escapes again as a wild plant in a new country, but usually does not become established because it is crowded out by native plants that are better adapted to the environment.

GUMWEED *Grindelia squarrosa* (Pursh) Dunal   **Pl. 23**

Family: Compositae (Composite).

Other names: Gumplant, Resinweed, Tarweed.

Description: A ragged-looking, yellow-flowered, branched composite that grows 6–30 in. high. Numerous flower heads are about 1 in. across when fully expanded, and surrounded by several series of narrow bracts, whose tips are usually recurved. Leaves numerous, usually more or less toothed; base of upper leaves partly clasp around stem, lower leaves often fall off by flowering time.

The heads of this plant, and usually leaves also, are very sticky. This fact, plus presence of yellow ray- and diskflowers and the recurved bracts, helps to distinguish it from Woolly Yellowdaisy (*Eriophyllum lanatum*), the golden-asters (*Chrysopsis*), sunflowers (*Helianthus*), beggarticks (*Bidens*), and many other somewhat confusing composites.

Related species: (1) *G. fastigiata* is a perennial, flower heads lack rayflowers; (2) *G. aphanactis* is an annual plant. Both occur mainly in s. Rockies.

Flowering season: July, Aug., and first part of Sept.

Where found: Y, T. Dry soil of roadsides and open areas of plains, valleys, foothills, and mts. to about 8000 ft. One of first plants to invade disturbed or denuded areas, and often becomes a serious weed in range land. Occurs from Minnesota to B.C., south to California and Texas. There are about 50 species of *Grindelia*, all native to w. N. and S. America; about 10 occur in Rocky Mt. area.

Interesting facts: *Squarrosa* means parts spreading. This plant was used by the Indians as a medicine, and was known by the early Jesuit missionaries. At the present time, the young leaves and flowering heads are gathered and dried, and an extract prepared for use in medicine as a sedative, antispasmodic, and expectorant. The plant is also used to treat cases of poison-ivy. Indians used the leaves as a substitute for tea and also chewed them.

MATCHBRUSH *Gutierrezia sarothrae* (Pursh) B. & R.

Family: Compositae (Composite).

Other names: Snakeweed, Broomweed.

Description: A shrubby plant sending up many slender, herbaceous, brittle stems, 8–24 in. tall, which bear at the top

numerous branches terminating in small heads of yellow
flowers. Heads, only about ⅛ in. broad, bear both ray- and
diskflowers. Leaves numerous and very slender.

This plant is most commonly confused with goldenrods
(*Solidago*) and rabbitbrushes (*Chrysothamnus*). Goldenrods
do not have a taproot and woody base, as does Matchbrush;
rabbitbrushes lack rayflowers.

Flowering season: Aug. and Sept.

Where found: Y, T. Dry soil of open areas, plains, valleys,
and foothills, from Saskatchewan to Montana and Oregon,
south to California and Mexico. There are between 20 and 25
species of *Gutierrezia*, largely confined to western parts of both
N. and S. America. Questionable whether there is more than
1 good species in Rocky Mts.

Interesting facts: *Sarothrae* means named for a fancied resemblance to *Hypericum sarothra*. Matchbrush, if consumed
in large quantities, can be poisonous to livestock. Ordinarily
it is not eaten when better forage is available. However,
when overgrazing occurs and the more palatable plants are
killed out, Matchbrush fills in the open spaces and may cause
trouble on the range.

STEMLESS GOLDENWEED   *Haplopappus acaulis* (Nutt.) Gray
Family: Compositae (Composite).
Other names: Aplopappus, *Stenotus falcatus*.
Description: This goldenweed is a yellow-flowered composite
that grows in dense patches, has mainly basal leaves and
numerous slender flowering stalks that attain a height of only
2–6 in. Yellow ray- and diskflowers form single heads ½–1 in.
across. Leaves narrow, ½–2 in. long, and rigid and rough to
the touch. Old leaves from previous years densely clothe
lower portions of stems.

Other plants that may be confused with this one are the
Woolly Yellowdaisy (*Eriophyllum lanatum*), Golden-aster
(*Chrysopsis villosa*), groundsels (*Senecio*) and several other
species of *Haplopappus*. If you note carefully that this goldenweed is an herb (no wood above ground), has rayflowers as
well as diskflowers, forms dense patches of growth, and has
leaves harsh and rough to the touch instead of being sticky or
soft, you should be able to distinguish it.

Related species: (1) *H. macronema* is a shrub with branches
densely white-woolly and with heads lacking rayflowers;
(2) *H. spinulosus* has most of its leaves pinnately cleft and
bristle-tipped. Both widespread in Rockies.

Flowering season: Latter part of April to the first part of
July.

Where found: Y, T. Found only in driest soil, usually rocky
hilltops and ridges, from lowest elevations to around 8500 ft.
Distributed from Saskatchewan to Idaho, south to California

Stemless Goldenweed (*Haplopappus acaulis* [Nutt.] Gray)

and Colorado. There are about 150 species of *Haplopappus*, all native to N. and S. America; about 30 occur in Rockies. **Interesting facts:** *Acaulis* means stemless. This plant has a branching rootstock. A taproot goes deep into the ground, but near the surface it branches, spreading out for 1 ft. or so, and develops fibrous roots. Flowering stems arise from these, forming a dense mat over the soil. *H. heterophyllus*, found in the Southwest, contains a toxic substance (tremetol) that causes trembling in domestic sheep if eaten regularly for a few days.

GOLDENWEED p. 216

Haplopappus uniflorus (Hook.) T. & G.

Family: Compositae (Composite).

Description: A perennial plant with single terminal head of yellow flowers about ¾ in. broad. Both ray- and diskflowers present. The 1 to few stems are clustered on a fleshy taproot and are 3–12 in. tall. Leaves mainly basal, lance-shaped in outline, and often toothed. Stem leaves alternate and greatly reduced in size.

This plant is often confused with the arnicas (*Arnica*) and with other species of *Haplopappus*. However, arnicas have mainly opposite leaves; Goldenweed has basal or alternate leaves. It is difficult to distinguish the various species of *Haplopappus*.

Goldenweed (*Haplopappus uniflorus* [Hook.] T. & G.)

Flowering season: May to July.
Where found: Y, T. Moist to wet, usually saline soil of open meadows and streambanks from valleys to around 8000 ft. Found from Saskatchewan to Montana and Oregon, south to California and Colorado. There are about 150 species of *Haplopappus*, all native to N. and S. America; approximately 30 occur in Rocky Mt. area.
Interesting facts: *Uniflorus* means 1-flowered.

LITTLE SUNFLOWER   Pl. 22
Helianthella uniflora (Nutt.) T. & G.
    Family: Compositae (Composite).
    Other names: Aspen Sunflower.
    Description: At a casual glance this looks like a true sunflower. Attains height of 1–3 ft., and several stems are usually clustered together. Yellow flower heads are mostly solitary at ends of branches, and are 1½–2½ in. across. Leaves are lance-shaped, up to 6 in. long, and rough to the touch.
    This plant is confused with the true Sunflower (*Helianthus annuus*) and Goldeneye (*Viguiera multiflora*); see Plate 22. Sunflower is a coarse annual with stem and leaves rough-hairy.

Goldeneye is a slender-stemmed perennial with stem and leaves relatively smooth-hairy. Seeds of Little Sunflower are flat and 2-edged; seeds of other two round or angled but not flattened.

Related species: Helianthella (*H. quinquenervis* [Hook.] Gray), Plate 22 and p. 218, is distinguished from *H. uniflora* by fact that bracts around flower head are ovate or broadly lanceolate; also, rays are pale yellow, bracts on upper part of flower head are soft, flower head itself is larger than that of *uniflora*, and upper leaves are stalkless, the lower long-stemmed. In contrast, bracts around flower head of *H. uniflora* are lance-linear to sometimes linear-oblong, rays are bright yellow, and bracts on upper part of flower head are firm. Leaves of *H. uniflora* generally more or less 3-nerved; those of *H. quinquenervis* 5-nerved.

Flowering season: June through first part of Aug. Appears among aspens when very small ruffed grouse chicks are seen and western tanagers are incubating eggs.

Where found: Y, T, R. Medium-dry to moist soil of open areas or open woods, often associated with aspen trees. Occurs from valleys to around timberline, and can be found from Montana to B.C., south to Oregon, Nevada, and New Mexico.

Little Sunflower (*Helianthella uniflora* [Nutt.] T. & G.)

Helianthella (*Helianthella quinquenervis* [Hook.] Gray)

There are about a dozen species of *Helianthella*, all native to w. N. America; about half occur in Rocky Mt. area. **Interesting facts:** *Uniflora* means 1-flowered. The flowers, leaves, and stems of this plant are readily eaten by livestock and big game animals. The flower heads are quite palatable to elk, but an abundance of these plants on elk summer ranges indicates overuse of other forage plants.

SUNFLOWER   *Helianthus annuus* L.   **Pl. 22**
   Family: Compositae (Composite).
   Other names: Common Sunflower.
   Description: An annual, branching composite, attaining a height of 1–8 ft. Reddish-purple or brownish diskflowers and yellow rayflowers form a head 3–5 in. across. Leaves are rough to the touch, 2–10 in. long and about half this broad. Stem rough-hairy.
   The genera *Wyethia*, *Helianthella*, *Balsamorhiza*, *Arnica*, and *Viguiera* are all confused with the Sunflower. Through a hand lens, seeds of true Sunflower appear 4-angled and have 2 flat awns that when young point upward at top. Among

our annual species, this is the largest. Can generally be distinguished from *Helianthella quinquenervis* and *Helianthella uniflora* by its ovate leaves.

Related species: (1) *H. tuberosus*, a perennial from underground tubers, attains a height of 3–15 ft. and has leaves 1–3 in. broad on distinct stalks; (2) *H. maximiliani* is similar but smaller, leaves lack distinct stalks and are lanceolate or narrower, seldom more than 1 in. broad. It is found in dry open places, often in waste land; (3) *H. nuttallii* has narrow lanceolate leaves with stalks and grows in wet or damp sites.

Flowering season: July, Aug., and Sept. Still blooming in early Sept. when blue-winged teal are migrating and mule deer fawns are losing their spots.

Sunflower (*Helianthus annuus* L.)

Where found: Y, T, R. Dry to medium-moist soil in open areas, waste places, abandoned fields, and roadsides. This plant, once native to West, has now spread over most of U.S. In mts. found to about 7000 ft. Of approximately 60 species of *Helianthus*, all native to N. and S. America, only about a dozen grow in Rocky Mts.

Interesting facts: *Annuus* means annual. This plant, the state flower of Kansas, can be a weed as well as a valuable and useful crop plant. French explorers found the Indians cultivating this plant along the shores of Lake Huron. In cultivation it has been bred until it often attains a height of 20 ft., with flower heads 1 ft. across. It makes good silage, the seeds are used as poultry feed, and a high-grade oil is expressed which is used for cooking, in margarine, and in paints. Seeds of this sunflower and others were used as food by American Indians. They also obtained fiber from the stems, a yellow dye from the flowers, and oil from the seeds. Tubers of two other species, Jerusalem-artichoke (*H. tuberosus*) and Maximilian Sunflower (*H. maximiliani*), were eaten raw, boiled, or roasted. The tuberous-thickened roots of *H. nuttallii* are sought by grizzly bears in the spring and early summer.

HAWKWEED   *Hieracium albertinum* Farr

Family: Compositae (Composite).

Other names: Woolly Weed and *H. scouleri* (American authors).

Description: A perennial plant, usually growing 1–3 ft. tall, with only yellow rayflowers present, these forming heads about ½ in. across. Plant covered with long, spreading, yellow hairs which, though mostly black at base, give plant a

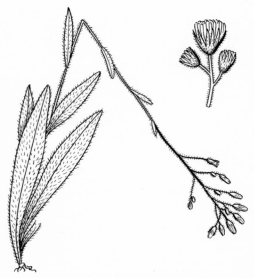

Hawkweed (*Hieracium albertinum* Farr)

yellowish cast. Leaves, mainly on lower part of stem, narrowly lance-shaped, and 3–8 in. long.

The hawkweeds are most often confused with the hawksbeards (*Crepsis*). Both contain milky juice, but hawkweeds have yellowish or brownish bristles from top of seeds; pappus of hawksbeards is white. Presence of long yellow hairs over the plant, together with yellow flowers, helps to separate this hawkweed from others.

Related species: (1) *H. albiflorum* has white flowers; (2) *H. gracile*, a small alpine plant usually less than 1 ft. tall, has heads covered with black hairs. Both common in Rockies.

Flowering season: Latter part of June to first part of Aug.

Where found: G, Y, T. Dry to moist soil of fields and open woods, from foothills to around 9000 ft. Occurs from Alberta to B.C., south to Oregon and Utah. Not more than 300 species of *Hieracium* should be recognized, and probably considerably fewer. They are fairly well scattered over temperate regions of the earth; about a dozen occur in Rockies.

Interesting facts: *Albertinum* means named for Alberta, Canada. *H. albertinum* is very palatable to domestic sheep and is one of the first forbs to disappear when sheep use becomes heavy. It is probably utilized by bighorn sheep at higher altitudes. The milky juice was coagulated and used as chewing gum by the Indians. Most of the species of this genus occurring in the Rocky Mts. are palatable to livestock and game animals.

ALPINE SUNFLOWER   Pl. 21
Hymenoxys grandiflora (T. & G.) Parker

Family: Compositae (Composite).

Other names: Mountain Sunflower, Alpine Goldflower, Sun God, Old-Man-of-the-Mountain, *Rydbergia grandiflora*.

Description: This plant, found above timberline, has large sunflower-like blossoms. It is a stout, low alpine with enormous yellow heads 2–3 in. broad. Woolly, narrow leaves are once- or twice-dissected.

Related species: There are 2 mt. sunflowers in Rocky Mt. region: (1) *H. brandegei* has smooth shiny leaves instead of gray woolly ones, and they are not dissected; (2) *H. acaulis* has entire leaves all basal. *H. grandiflora* is so conspicuously the largest bloom in high mts. that it cannot be confused with anything else.

Flowering season: First appears about mid-July, and if season is wet can be found until mid-Aug.

Where found: Y, T, R. Confined to regions mostly above timberline, 10,000–11,000 ft. Look for it on dry, well-drained slopes and exposed ridges. Grows profusely on limestone. Found in alpine regions throughout Rocky Mts., from Montana to Utah and New Mexico. The genus, of about 15 species, is found in both e. and w. U.S.; 4 species occur in Rocky Mt. area.

Interesting facts: *Grandiflora* means large-flowered. Sun God is a fitting name for this large goldenheaded flower. Appearing to spring out of bare rock, these flowers absorb sunshine from the rarified air and take on the color of their sun god. It is not an infrequent sight to see thousands of them covering a rocky ridge, all facing the rising sun. "Compass Flower" might be an appropriate name, for they do not follow the sun around but continue facing east. The direction that any large number face is a far better indication of east than moss on a tree as an indication of north.

GAYFEATHER   *Liatris punctata* Hook.

Family: Compositae (Composite).

Other names: Blazingstar, Button Snakeroot.

Description: The usually brilliant purple flowers are borne in dense spikes 2–10 in. long. Stems are unbranched, normally clustered, arise from a round underground corm, and are 8–30 in. tall. Numerous leaves, almost covering stem, are linear, 1–2 in. long, and covered with resinous dots.

It may be confused with the ironweeds (*Vernonia*), Joe-pye-weed (*Eupatorium maculatum*), and the brickellias (*Brickellia*). However, heads of purple rayflowers forming dense spikes will distinguish it. These characteristics, plus presence of featherlike bristles on seeds, separate this plant from most other species of *Liatris*.

Related species: *L. ligulistylis*, a plant of Colorado mts. and eastward, has broad leaves, and bristles on seeds are not feathery.

Flowering season: Latter part of July until frost.

Where found: R. Dry soil of open, often sandy, areas of prairies and foothills from Alberta to Michigan, south to Arkansas, New Mexico, and Mexico. Occurs mostly east of Continental Divide. There are about 30 species of *Liatris*, all native to temperate N. America, and all from Rocky Mts. and eastward; only this 1 species at all common in Rockies, but 1 other does occur in Colorado.

Interesting facts: *Punctata* means with translucent dots. Gayfeather usually grows from an underground structure called a corm. The stem enlarges considerably and forms a bulblike growth containing reserve food. A corm is solid; a bulb is actually a modified bud, made up of layers of scale and fleshy and true leaves as in an onion. Other common plants with corms are of genera *Gladiolus*, *Trillium*, and *Cyclamen*. If suitable for human consumption, the reserve food in a corm can be utilized, as is the case with this plant. Indians prepared and ate the roots.

BLUE-FLOWERED LETTUCE Pl. 23
Lactuca pulchella (Pursh) DC.
    Family: Compositae (Composite).
    Other names: Blue Lettuce, Larkspur Lettuce, Chicory Lettuce.
    Description: In this plant only rayflowers form the blue to lavender flower heads, ½–¾ in. broad. Usually only 1 stem grows in a place and it is 1–4 ft. tall. However, underground rootstocks spread over large areas. Leaves narrow, 2–12 in. long, lower ones often lobed. When injured, plant exudes a milky juice.
    Chicory (*Chichorium intybus*) is most likely to be confused with this, but larger flower heads of Chicory are borne 1 to 3 in axils of leaves. In Blue-flowered Lettuce, flower heads appear singly at ends of branches; can be distinguished from other species of *Lactuca* by its large blue flowers.
    Related species: (1) *L. ludoviciana* is a biennial that attains height of 1–5 ft., with heads of yellow flowers about 1 in. high; usually grows in damp locations. (2) *L. scariola* is similar but will grow in dry locations; numerous flower heads are only about ½ in. high. Both plants common throughout Rockies.
    Flowering season: Latter part of June to first part of Sept.
    Where found: Y, T. Medium-dry to moist soil in fields or thickets of prairies, valleys, and in mts. to about 7000 ft. Found from Alaska to Minnesota, south to Missouri, New Mexico, and California. About 50 species of *Lactuca* are native to Eurasia, Africa, and N. America; only about a half dozen occur in Rockies.
    Interesting facts: *Pulchella* means beautiful. This plant is considered a noxious weed because its underground rootstalks spread through the soil for many feet, giving rise to roots and stems at short intervals. Once it is established in tilled soil, plowing and cultivation merely cut the rootstalks, scattering pieces to form new plants that survive even under adverse conditions. Practical methods of eradication are to treat with chemical weed killers, or continually to cut the underground stems before the leaves can expand. This prevents the plant from manufacturing food and it starves to death. Other noxious weeds of the Rockies that grow the same way are Canada Thistle, Spotted Knapweed, Morning-glory, Whitetop, and Quackgrass. In general milky-juiced plants should not be eaten, but this plant, like Pink Milkweed and Salsify, is an exception. Gum from the roots of Blue-flowered Lettuce was used as a chewing gum by Indians, and the young plants and leaves of several other species of *Lactuca* were eaten as greens.

RUSHPINK   *Lygodesmia grandiflora* (Nutt.) T. & G.   **Pl. 24**
    Family: Compositae (Composite).
    Other names: Skeleton Plant.
    Description: A sparsely to moderately branched rushlike plant,

4–20 in. tall with alternate linear leaves and pink flower heads terminating the branches. Head of rayflowers superficially resembles some members of the Pink family (Sandwort and Field Chickweed, see Plate 5, and Moss Campion, see Plate 6). Stem and leaves of Rushpink exude a milky juice when cut or bruised; the pinks do not.

Related species: (1) *L. spinosa* has spine-tipped branches; (2) *L. juncea* is similar to *L. grandiflora* but flower heads as well as leaves are smaller.

Flowering season: May and June. Look for it when the more conspicuous opuntias are in full bloom.

Where found: Open, dry places in the valleys and foothills. About a half-dozen species in w. U.S. and Mexico; 4 occur in Rockies.

Interesting facts: *Lygodesmia* is derived from the Greek *lygos*, meaning pliant twig, and *desme*, bundle; *grandiflora* means large-flowered. This plant has no forage value. Indians boiled the leaves with meat.

CONEFLOWER   *Ratibida columnifera* (Nutt.) W. & S.   **Pl. 23**

Family: Compositae (Composite).

Other names: Prairie Coneflower.

Description: The receptacle looks like a slender sewing thimble, ½–1½ in. long and covered with purplish-brown, tubular diskflowers. At the base are 3 to 7 yellow or purplish rayflowers ¾–1½ in. long, and often reflexed. Stems usually clustered, branching, 1–4 ft. tall, lower part covered with leaves that are dissected, or narrow and smooth-edged.

This plant tends to be mistaken for members of the genus *Rudbeckia*, but in *Ratibida* the head of flowers is narrower and shorter, and seeds are flattened and have 2 sharp edges; in *Rudbeckia* they are 4-angled and not flattened.

Related species: *R. tagetes* is a much smaller plant, with a globular or ellipsoid receptacle and length of rayflowers seldom exceeding ½ in. Chiefly a plant of the plains.

Flowering season: July to Sept.

Where found: R. Dry to moist soil in open areas of plains, valleys, and foothills from Alberta to Minnesota, south to Arkansas, New Mexico, and Mexico. Has been introduced locally both east and west of its natural range. Only 5 species make up this genus, and they are principally native to the central states; 2 of them range into Rocky Mt. area.

Interesting facts: *Columnifera* means columnar. The leaves and thimble-like flower heads were used by Indians as a substitute for tea.

WESTERN CONEFLOWER   Pl. 22
Rudbeckia occidentalis Nutt.
> **Family:** Compositae (Composite).
> **Other names:** Niggerthumb, Niggerhead.
> **Description:** Coneflowers are characterized by dark brown or
> black cylindrical heads, in diameter nearly 1 in. and sometimes
> 2½ in. long. Heads densely covered with dark, tubular disk-
> flowers; rayflowers absent. There may be 1 to several stems in a
> bunch, often branched above, and 2–6 ft. tall. Alternate leaves
> are ovate in outline, sometimes 10 in. long, and mainly on lower
> half of stem. Upper ones are stalkless, with rounded or heart-
> shaped bases. The large, dark cylindrical heads and lack of
> rayflowers make it unlikely that this plant will be confused with
> others.
> **Related species:** (1) *R. hirta* and (2) Rudbeckia (*R. laciniata*
> L.), Plate 23, have conspicuous orange or yellow rayflowers, but
> *hirta* has toothed or smooth-edged leaves, *laciniata* has leaves
> greatly pinnately cleft. Both plants widespread in Rockies.
> **Flowering season:** Latter part of June to Aug.
> **Where found:** Y, T. Moist soil of streambanks and woodlands,
> but especially associated with aspen groves. Found in mts.
> from 5000 to 8000 ft. Ranges from Montana to Washington,
> south to California and Colorado. There are perhaps 25 native
> species of *Rudbeckia* in N. America, 3 of which occur in Rocky
> Mt. area.
> **Interesting facts:** *Occidentalis* means western. Since livestock
> and even big game animals will not usually eat this plant, large
> patches of it may indicate overgrazing or soil disturbances. As
> the more palatable forage species are eaten down until they die
> out, the nonedible ones gradually take their place. Other weedy
> plants of this type are *Antennaria*, *Achillea*, *Agastache*, and
> *Senecio*.

GROUNDSEL   *Senecio integerrimus* Nutt.   p. 226
> **Family:** Compositae (Composite).
> **Other names:** Squaw-weed, Butterweed, Ragwort.
> **Description:** The yellow ray- and diskflowers form heads that
> are ¼–½ in. across. From 5 to 30 heads are congested at end
> of stem, with stalk of top flower usually shorter than others.
> Stems mostly single, 8–30 in. tall, with cluster of large leaves at
> base followed by progressively smaller leaves above. Entire
> young plant generally covered with cobweb-like hairs that often
> fall off as plant matures.
> The genus is characterized by a pappus of numerous nearly
> white bristles and by a single series of equal-length scales about
> flower head, these often surrounded at base by a number of
> narrow bracts.
> Groundsel is most apt to be confused with the arnicas

(*Arnica*), but the lower leaves of latter are opposite; in Ground-sel they are alternate. This species can usually be separated from other species of *Senecio* by fact that its upper leaves are reduced in size, terminal head is lower than the others, and it has loose cobweb-like hairs when young.

Groundsel (*Senecio integerrimus* Nutt.)

Related species: (1) *S. vulgaris* is an annual weed without ray-flowers. (2) *S. hydrophilus*, a waxy bog plant, is very similar to *S. integerrimus*, but it lacks hair and has smooth-edged rather than toothed basal leaves. Grows 2–5 ft. tall and has lance-shaped leaves that are reduced upward. (3) *S. triangularis*, a plant of the open woods, has numerous small heads of yellow flowers and triangular-shaped leaves not tapering at base; stem is leafy to top, 1–5 ft. tall, and much branched. (4) *S. werneriae-folius*, (5) *S. resedifolius*, and (6) *S. fremontii* are found in rocky places at high elevations. *Werneriaefolius* has smooth-edged leaves; *resedifolius* and *fremontii*, tooth-edged leaves. These 6 species common throughout Rockies.

Flowering season: May to first part of July. First appears about time male sage grouse cease their courtship displays and no longer congregate regularly on their strutting grounds.

Where found: G, Y, T. Medium-dry to moist soil of open areas, draws, prairies, and in mts. to near timberline. Occurs from

B.C. to Saskatchewan, south to Iowa, Colorado, and California. There are probably considerably more than 1000 species of *Senecio* widely distributed over the earth; about 40 occur in Rocky Mt. area.

Interesting facts: *Senecio* comes from the Latin *senex*, old man, and undoubtedly refers to the hoary pubescence and the white pappus; *integerrimus* means most entire. The genus *Senecio* probably contains as many, if not more, species than any other in the plant kingdom. S. Africa and S. America boast more species than other large areas of the world. Groundsel contains alkaloids poisonous to cattle and horses but is not often consumed in quantity.

YELLOWWEED   *Solidago elongata* Nutt.

Family: Compositae (Composite).

Other names: Goldenrod and *S. lepida*.

Description: These plants are often seen in small patches, their large clusters of yellow flowers being characteristically on 1 side of curved branches. Small heads are composed of both ray- and diskflowers. Leaves are alternate, hairy, numerous, 2–5 in. long, elliptic, triple-veined, and may be either toothed or smooth around edge. Plants reach height of 1–6 ft.

Goldenrods could be confused with the hawkweeds (*Hieracium*), hawksbeards (*Crepis*), or groundsels (*Senecio*), but the numerous small flower heads (a little over ⅛ in. broad) separate the goldenrods from these other 3 groups of flowers.

Related species: The different species of *Solidago* are difficult to distinguish. (1) Goldenrod (*S. occidentalis* [Nutt.] T. & G.), Plate 22, has resinous small dots over the leaves, and flowers do not grow only on 1 side of curved branches but in an open panicle; (2) *S. multiradiata*, a plant of high mts., grows 3–16 in. tall, with leaves mostly basal, and those on stem few and reduced. Both plants common throughout Rockies.

Flowering season: Latter part of July to Sept.

Where found: Y, T. Moist soil along fence rows, highways, open waste places, open woods, and up to around 8000 ft. Scattered from B.C. to Quebec, south to Minnesota, Colorado, and California. There are almost 100 species of *Solidago*, mainly native to N. America but a few occur in S. America and Eurasia; about a dozen species occur in Rocky Mts.

Interesting facts: *Elongata* means elongate. This is our most common woodland goldenrod. When you see it in full bloom, you may know that summer has passed its peak, and that fall is at hand; one can almost feel the clear, crisp atmosphere of the beautiful "Indian summer" days ahead. Goldenrods are of little value as forage foods. They contain small quantities of rubber, which with selective breeding could probably be increased.

Milk-thistle (*Sonchus asper* [L.] Hill)

MILK-THISTLE *Sonchus asper* (L.) Hill

  Family: Compositae (Composite).

  Other names: Prickly Sow-thistle, Sow-thistle.

  Description: Heads of yellow rayflowers soon give rise to seeds topped with long, silky, white hairs. This gives whole head the appearance of a ball of cotton about ½ in. broad. Stems are often hollow, branched above, and vary in height 6–40 in. An annual plant, it is variously cut, toothed, and prickly around edge of leaves.

  This plant is most likely to be confused with the true thistles (*Cirsium*), but presence of milky sap throughout the plant and heads composed entirely of rayflowers will indicate a milk-thistle.

  Related species: (1) *S. arvensis* is a perennial with wide-spreading underground stems; yellow flower heads may be 1–2 in. broad; a common weed in Rockies. (2) Sow-thistle (*S. uliginosus* Bieb.), Plate 23, is similar to *arvensis* but lacks spreading gland-tipped hairs on involucre.

  Flowering season: July to Oct.

  Where found: Y, T, R. Introduced from Europe, now widely distributed; found in moist to wet soil of waste places, farms, and mts. up to around 7500 ft. Four species occur in Rocky Mt. area.

Interesting facts: *Asper* means rough. Milk-thistle is just one of numerous weeds that have been carelessly imported from other continents. After its introduction by the white man, the American Indians learned to use it as greens. It is eaten in salads or cooked as a potherb by peoples in many parts of the world.

DANDELION *Taraxacum officinale* Weber

Family: Compositae (Composite).

Other names: Common Dandelion, Blowball.

Description: Heads of yellow rayflowers on leafless, hollow stalks that vary in height from 2 to 20 in. average about 1 in. across. Lance-shaped leaves, forming a basal rosette, are variously lobed and cut and are 2–15 in. long. Plant filled with milky sap.

True dandelions are difficult to distinguish from the false dandelions (*Agoseris*), but they have very rough seeds, and green bracts around flower heads are in 2 unequal series; seeds of *Agoseris* are almost smooth, and bracts are nearly equal in length.

Related species: Three native dandelions occur in high mts. of Rockies: (1) *T. eriophorum*, with seeds red or reddish purple at maturity; (2) *T. lyratum*, with black or blackish seeds; and (3) *T. ceratophorum*, with straw-colored to brownish seeds at maturity.

Flowering season: From early spring until late fall, but most blooms open in May, turning lawns, pastures, and meadows a brilliant yellow. When Dandelion is near full bloom, Canada goose goslings are hatching.

Where found: G, Y, T, R. Almost everywhere in moist to wet soil of fields, thickets, and open woods. Close to 1000 species of *Taraxacum* have been described, but conservative botanists now recognize around 50; in Rockies there are about a half dozen.

Interesting facts: *Officinale* means official, referring to drug plants. Dandelion is a native of Eurasia, but the ease with which the seeds are scattered has made it probably the most universal of plants. It is also a serious weed in lawns, pastures, and meadows, where it tends to crowd out other plants. The large, fleshy root is an official drug, and for centuries has been used as a tonic, diuretic, and mild laxative. The tender young leaves are prepared as a potherb by peoples throughout the world, and the roots are used in salads, the flowers for making wine. Although an intruder, this plant is perhaps one of our best wildlife food sources. The flowers and leaves of the Dandelion are a favorite spring and summer food of Canada geese and ruffed grouse, and are utilized at these seasons by elk, deer, black and grizzly bears, and porcupines. Other species of grouse and probably many other forms of wildlife feed on this widely distributed plant.

HORSEBRUSH   *Tetradymia canescens* DC.
  Family: Compositae (Composite).
  Other names: Spineless Horsebrush.
  Description: An intricately branched shrub 8–36 in. tall, with cylindrical flower heads usually with 4 yellow diskflowers in each head. These heads are borne on short stalks and densely cover entire top of plant. Narrow alternate leaves, young twigs, and flower heads are silvery-colored because of dense growth of woolly hair.

Horsebrush (*Tetradymia canescens* DC.)

This shrub is most likely to be confused with rabbitbrushes (*Chrysothamnus*). Rabbitbrushes definitely green in color in spite of hair on them; Horsebrush definitely silvery white in color.
Related species: (1) *T. spinosa* has rigid, spreading, or recurved spines and stems white-woolly; (2) *T. glabrata* has weak spines, if any, and plant has little or no hair.

Flowering season: June to first part of Aug.

Where found: Y, T. Dry soil of plains and foothills up to around 6500 ft. Occurs from B.C. to Montana, south to New Mexico and California. There are only about a half-dozen species of *Tetradymia*, and all occur in w. N. America; 4 are in Rocky Mt. area.

Interesting facts: *Canescens* means becoming gray. Horsebrush stands up under and often above the snow, so when other food is scarce, this shrub is browsed by both domestic and wild animals. *T. canescens* and *T. glabrata* are the 2 principal plants causing bighead malady in domestic sheep. They are most toxic in spring during their early growth, and on poor range are eaten when sheep are being trailed to shearing corrals and summer ranges.

PARRY TOWNSENDIA *Townsendia parryi* D. C. Eat.   **Pl. 23**

    Family: Compositae (Composite).

    Other names: Giant-aster.

    Description: The most noticeable thing about this plant is the large size of its flower heads (1–2 in. broad) in comparison to rest of plant. Rayflowers are blue-lavender, the diskflowers yellow.

Parry Townsendia (*Townsendia parryi* D. C. Eat.)

The 1 to few stems vary in height 2–12 in., are usually un-branched, and each stem is topped by a single flower head. Leaves, broadest at outer end, are 1–2 in. long and usually over half of them form a basal rosette near ground.

Tendency to confuse this plant with the asters (*Aster*) and daisies (*Erigeron*), but single large heads at the ends of short unbranched stems will distinguish this *Townsendia* from these other plants. Townsendias have long flat scales at top of seeds; *Aster* and *Erigeron* have hairlike bristles.

Related species: (1) Townsendia (*T. sericea* Hook.), Plate 21, with a branching root crown and stems 2 in. tall or less, has heads about 1 in. across borne among a heavy clump of leaves. (2) *T. incana* has very narrow leaves; entire plant is white from hair, and rayflowers are white or rose. *T. sericea* widespread and extends above timberline in mts.; *T. incana* mostly confined to s. Rockies.

Flowering season: Latter part of June to frost in fall. Blooms first about time nighthawks are incubating eggs and young pink-sided juncos are becoming well feathered.

Where found: Y, T. Dry soil of hillsides and rocky ridges of mts. to timberline. Found from Alberta to Oregon and Colorado. There are about 15 species of *Townsendia* native to w. N. America; over half occur in Rockies.

Interesting facts: *Parryi* means named for Charles C. Parry.

MEADOW SALSIFY   *Tragopogon pratensis* L.

Family: Compositae (Composite).

Other names: Goatsbeard, Oysterplant.

Description: The round, white seed heads, 2–3 in. across, forming when plant matures, are more conspicuous than the flowers. They look like huge ripened dandelion seed heads and are formed by development of long seed stalks. At top of each stalk, featherlike growths form miniature umbrellas. Flower heads are composed of numerous yellow rayflowers; the narrow green bracts at base of heads are as long or shorter than rayflowers. Stems attain a height of 1–4 ft., have many grass-like clasping leaves (especially on lower part), and single heads of flowers, 1–2 in. across.

Related species: (1) Salsify (*T. dubius* Scop.), Plate 21, has yellow flowers and bracts 1–2 in. long around flower heads; these are distinctly longer than the flowers and increase in length up to 3 in. when plant fruits. (2) Oysterplant (*T. porri-folius* L.) has purple flowers and bracts 1 in. long that extend beyond flowers; see illus. opposite. All the species contain milky juices.

Flowering season: June and July, but the seeding heads may be seen throughout Aug. In full bloom when red-shafted flicker and European starling have young.

Oysterplant (*Tragopogon porrifolius* L.)

Where found: Y, T. Medium-dry to moist soil along roadsides, fence rows, and waste places from lowest elevations to about 7000 ft. Meadow Salsify was imported, escaped from cultivation, and is now found in most parts of temperate zones. There are about 50 species of *Tragopogon*, all native to Eurasia and Africa; 3 of these have been introduced into Rockies.

Interesting facts: *Tragopogon* derives from the Greek *tragos*, goat, and *pogon*, beard; *pratensis* means of meadows. The large, fleshy taproots of these plants are used for food, since they are nutritious, and when cooked taste like parsnips, though some say somewhat like oysters. The salsifies were cultivated in Europe, introduced in America by the early colonists, spread rapidly, and were soon used by the Indians as food. The Indians chewed the coagulated juice of the several species of *Tragopogon*. As the juice is considered a remedy for indigestion, it is quite possible that they were more interested in its medicinal properties than in its use as a gum or confection. The round white seed heads make striking flower decorations for the home and will last a considerable time if carefully handled and sprayed.

Goldeneye (*Viguiera multiflora* [Nutt.] Blake)

GOLDENEYE　*Viguiera multiflora* (Nutt.) Blake　　**Pl. 22**
Family: Compositae (Composite).
Description: This goldeneye looks like a small-sized sunflower,
but the plant is slender-stemmed and more branching than
the sunflowers. Both ray- and diskflowers are yellow, forming
heads 1–1½ in. broad. The several stems from a taproot attain
a height of 1–4 ft. Leaves are broadly to narrowly lance-shaped,
slightly toothed, and 1–3 in. long.

This plant is often confused with the sunflowers (*Helianthus*),
the little sunflowers (*Helianthella*), the beggarticks (*Bidens*),
and the coneflowers (*Ratibida*). However, the receptacle of
Goldeneye is enlarged and rounded, whereas these other plants
have flat, or almost flat, receptacles — except the coneflowers.
Leaves of coneflowers are all alternate; those of Goldeneye are
all opposite, except uppermost ones.
Flowering season: Latter part of July to first part of Sept.
About time Goldeneye first blooms, goldeneye ducks have
broods of young that are half adult size and mallards are
leading young ones still in downy stage.
Where found: Y, T. Dry open areas on foothills and mts., well
up toward timberline. Distributed in a rough triangle between

states of Montana, New Mexico, and California. There are about 60 species of *Viguiera*, all native to w. N. America, Mexico, and S. America; this the only species occurring in Rockies except in extreme s. part.

Interesting facts: *Multiflora* means many-flowered. An important value of knowing and using scientific names is that each name applies to one and only one particular plant. The same common name may be given to several or many different plants. For example, this flower is called Goldeneye and so is *Chrysopsis villosa* (p. 201). In such cases — and they are numerous — the scientific name must be known and used if one wishes to designate accurately a particular flower or to discourse intelligently about it.

MULES-EARS *Wyethia amplexicaulis* Nutt.   **Pl. 24**

Family: Compositae (Composite).

Other names: Smooth Dwarf Sunflower, Pik (Indian).

Description: The flowering heads resemble those of the sunflowers (*Helianthus*), with their bright orange-yellow ray- and diskflowers. There are 1 to 5 heads on a stalk, and each measures 2–3 in. broad when fully open. Sometimes these heads are surpassed in height by the erect leaves, which are numerous, glossy green, elliptic, and up to 15 in. long. These plants 1–2 ft. tall, and grow in large, dense, colorful patches.

The plants most easily confused with Mules-ears are the balsamroots (*Balsamorhiza*), but these have few if any leaves

Mules-ears (*Wyethia amplexicaulis* Nutt.)

on the flowering stalks; Mules-ears is densely leaved. Leaves of Mules-ears are glossy, those of balsamroots hairy.

Related species: *W. scabra*, of cent. and s. Rockies, has linear to linear-lanceolate leaves that are rough-hairy to the touch.

Flowering season: May to first part of July. First blooms just prior to early hatchings of sage grouse chicks, reaching its height about time young ravens leave nest.

Where found: Y, T. Moderately dry to moist soil on open hillsides. Grows in higher valleys and in mts. to around 7500 ft. *Wyethia* is a w. N. American genus of about a dozen species; 4 occur in Rocky Mt. area.

Interesting facts: *Wyethia* was named for Captain Nathaniel J. Wyeth, an early fur trader who established the first American fort and fur trading post (Fort Hall) in the Northwest. It was near the present site of Pocatello, Idaho. *Amplexicaulis* means stem-clasping. At the upper-growth elevations of this mules-ears there often occurs another species, White Wyethia, with white rayflowers and sticky, hairy stalks. The two species seem to cross, and fertile hybrids between them are fairly common. The rayflowers of these hybrids are light yellow, and the plants moderately hairy and sticky. These new hybrids then seem to cross with either of the original parents so that plants with all grades of appearance between the two species can be found. This condition, though uncommon, exists in a number of other plants. *Wyethia* is utilized by black bears and deer in early spring; but cattle, horses, and sheep make little use of it. In most areas it is considered a range pest and large-scale eradication programs have been carried out in the West.

WHITE WYETHIA *Wyethia helianthoides* Nutt.   Pl. 24

Family: Compositae (Composite).

Other names: White Mules-ears.

Description: The flower heads look like the sunflowers (*Helianthus*) except that rayflowers are white or cream-colored instead of yellow. Stems coarse, bunched, 8–20 in. tall, and arise from top of a thick woody taproot. Leaves elliptical, basal, and alternate on stem, and may be as much as 1 ft. long.

This showy plant is quite distinctive, and because of its white rayflowers need not be confused with the sunflowers or any of their close relatives. None of our white-flowered species in the Composite family have heads nearly so large (2–5 in. broad).

Flowering season: May to first part of July. First appears about time elk calving reaches peak and young golden eagles are beginning to feather. In full bloom when grizzly bears are mating in mid-June.

Where found: Y, T. Moist to wet soil of meadows, open woods, and seepage areas, from foothills to around 8000 ft. Occurs from Montana to Washington, Oregon, and Wyoming. *Wyethia* is a

w. N. American genus of about a dozen species; 4 occur in Rocky Mt. area.

Interesting facts: *Helianthoides* means helianthus-like. This plant, like the yellow Mules-ears, grows in patches and the flowers usually appear to be turned toward the sun. The flowers and young leaves are eaten by elk, deer, and livestock, and the roots were prepared by the Indians through a process of cooking and fermenting. It apparently increases rapidly with poor range management. It has easily been killed with herbicides, as in Montana and Idaho.

Cocklebur (*Xanthium strumarium* L.)

COCKLEBUR   *Xanthium strumarium* L.

    Family: Compositae (Composite).

    Other names: Clotbur, Sheepbur, Burweed.

    Description: An annual weed growing 1–5 ft. tall, with leaves that may become 6 in. long and almost as broad. Entire plant is rough to the touch. Green male flowers clustered at top; female flowers clustered in axils of leaves below, and lack corollas. These female flowers give rise to oval-shaped, solid burs about 1 in. long that turn brown and are covered with long, stiff, hooked spines; these burs quite conspicuous and often persist throughout winter.

Other plants likely to be confused with this one are the Burdock (*Arctium minus*), whose burs (unlike those of Cocklebur) readily break into small pieces, and the Wild Licorice (*Glycyrrhiza lepidota*), whose burs split open when ripe.

Related species: *X. spinosum* has 3-parted, sharp spines arising from leaf axils.

Flowering season: Latter part of July to first part of Sept. Burs become particularly conspicuous when frosts have thinned and browned the vegetation.

Where found: T, R. Moist to wet soil of fields, waste places, and flooded-silted areas over most of the earth, except high in mts. There are probably only 2 species of *Xanthium* in Rockies, though numerous variations have been described as species.

Interesting facts: *Strumarium* means having cushionlike swellings. This is thought to have been originally an American plant which by means of its burs has been scattered to other continents. It was first found in Europe about 50 years after Columbus discovered America. The burs are a nuisance to both the hunter and his dogs. The seeds within the burs are edible raw and were eaten whole or made into meal by the Indians. Young Cocklebur plants in the tender 2-leaf stage contain a poisonous glucoside (xanthostrumarin) that is fatally poisonous to sheep, cattle, and particularly hogs. The mature burs when eaten by livestock can cause mechanical injury followed by infection of the digestive tract.

Appendixes

APPENDIX I

Key to Plants

WITH the exception of Pteridophyta, Spermatophyta, Gymnospermae, and species of trees included under Angiospermae, the Key has been tailored to include only those genera treated in the text. The characters used in keying the genera have been mainly restricted to those diagnostic of the species treated in this *Field Guide*. To use this Key proceed by a progressive selection of one of repeated pairs of numbers until the genus of your plant is identified (page reference is only to the first page of the genus section). Then turn to the text, and from the descriptions and illustrations determine the species. More than five hundred and ninety of the more conspicuous and commonly observed species in the Rocky Mts. can be identified in this book by using this procedure.

If the first of a pair of numbers does not describe your plant's characters *omit intervening numbers if there are any* and find the second (identical) of the pair; then *go directly to the next-appearing number* (which may or may not be in numerical sequence; the pair of a number already progressed through should of course be skipped) *or its pair* and proceed as before until the genus is named (see also p. xxiv).

If a flowering plant (Angiospermae) is to be keyed, turn directly to page 243, No. 4, and begin the keying process at this point.

1. Plants not producing seeds or flowers but reproducing by single cells; fernlike, mosslike, or rushlike
Division **Pteridophyta**
2. Stems conspicuously jointed, hollow, fluted; leaves reduced to confluent circle of scales at joints; spores borne in terminal pseudocone   **Horsetails**
2. Stems not conspicuously jointed or hollow and fluted; leaves not reduced to scales:
3. Leaves numerous and small, less than ½ in. long; spores borne in an elongated semicone at ends of stems; plants mosslike   **Clubmosses**
3. Leaves few, compound or divided, large, usually many inches long; spores borne in spots on leaf segments or around leaf edges   **Ferns**
1. Plants producing seeds and flowers or cones
Division **Spermatophyta**
4.* Seeds borne in woody or berrylike cones, naked on surface of bracts; leaves are needles or scalelike and overlapping, mostly remain on plant during winter; plants are mostly trees (a few shrubs)   Subdivision **Gymnospermae**
5.* Fruit berrylike; mature leaves scalelike, numerous and overlapping, and less than ½ in. long (*J. communis* has sharp, needlelike leaves)   **Juniperus**

* The second 4 is on page 243. The second 5 is on page 242.

6. Mature leaves needlelike, not overlapping; berrylike cones in axils of branches; plant a low, semiprostrate shrub, usually forming round patches
(Dwarf or Spreading Juniper) **J. communis**
6. Mature leaves scalelike and overlapping; berrylike cones terminal on branches; large upright trees (except *J. horizontalis*):
7. Creeping shrubs; berries on recurved stalks (n. Rocky Mts.)
(Creeping Juniper) **J. horizontalis**
7. Upright, large trees; berries on straight or nearly straight stalks:
8. Scale leaves not toothed (under strong lens); seeds usually 2 in a berry; heartwood reddish; branchlets slender, flattened, often drooping
(Mountain or River Juniper) **J. scopulorum**
8. Scale leaves minutely toothed (under strong lens); seeds mostly 1 in a berry (except in *J. occidentalis*); heartwood brown; branchlets not flattened or drooping:
9. Berries ¼–½ in. in diam., reddish brown or bluish (a waxy bloom), with mealy or fibrous, dry flesh
(Utah Juniper) **J. utahensis**
9. Berries ¼ in. or less in diam., blue or blue-black, rarely copper-colored, with juicy resinous flesh:
10. Limbs usually arising from below or at ground level; foliage inclined to bunch at ends of branches; leaves not glandular; trees or shrubs of s. Rocky Mts.
(One-seed Juniper) **J. monosperma**
10. Limbs usually arising above ground level; foliage not bunched at ends of branches; leaves very glandular; trees from w. Idaho to B.C. and Calif.
(Western Juniper) **J. occidentalis**

5. Fruit a woody cone; mature leaves mostly needlelike or linear, mostly not overlapping (see 1st No. 22, key to *Thuja plicata*, p. 243), usually much more than ½ in. long:
11. Leaves all fall in autumn, 10 to 30 in a cluster on short branch spurs   **Larix**
12. Cones usually less than 1 in. long, subglobose
(American Larch) **L. laricina**
12. Cones usually more than 1 in. long, ovoid:
13. Twigs hairy; leaves 4-angled, with a cross section showing 2 resin ducts   (Alpine Larch) **L. lyallii**
13. Twigs only slightly hairy, this soon falling off; leaves flatly triangular, with a cross section showing no resin ducts
(Western Larch) **L. occidentalis**
11. Leaves persistent throughout winter, single or 5 or less in a cluster:
14. Leaves 2 to 5 in a cluster (except in *Pinus monophylla*), surrounded by papery sheath at base, needlelike; cones maturing 2nd year   **Pinus**
15. Needles 5 in a fascicle:
16. Cones narrowly oblong, 4–10 in. long, long-stalked, pendulous   (Western White Pine) **P. monticola**
16. Cones ovoid or oval, usually 1–8 in. long, short-stalked, not pendulous:

17. Cone scales armed with long slender prickles; seeds shorter
    than the wing   (Bristle-cone Pine) **P. cristata**
17. Cone scales without long slender prickles; seeds longer than
    the wing:
18. Cones opening at maturity, 4–8 in. long, scales not much
    thickened at their tips   (Limber Pine) **P. flexilis**
18. Cones remaining closed, 1–3 in. long, scales very thick at
    their tips   (Whitebark Pine) **P. albicaulis**
15. Needles 3 or less in a fascicle:
19. Needles mostly single   (Single-leaf Pine) **P. monophylla**
19. Needles 2 to 3 in a fascicle:
20. Needles 3–6 in. long, mostly 3 in a fascicle
        (Western Yellow Pine) **P. ponderosa**
20. Needles usually less than 3 in. long, mostly 2 in a fascicle:
21. Seed with long wing; scales of cones with small prickle at
    their tips; sheaths of the leaves persistent
        (Lodgepole Pine) **P. contorta**
21. Seeds without wing; scales of cones without prickles; sheaths
    of leaves deciduous   (Nut Pine, Piñon Pine) **P. edulis**
14. Leaves single, unsheathed at base; cones maturing 1st year:
22. Leaves are minute, flat, overlapping scales, completely
    covering twigs in 4 longitudinal ranks
        (Western Arborvitae) **Thuja plicata**
22. Leaves long, needlelike or linear, not hiding twigs:
23. Cones erect, scales deciduous; leaves not on a stalk   **Abies**
24. Leaves silvery white beneath, dark green above, with lines
    of stomata   (Grand Fir) **A. grandis**
24. Leaves blue-green with stomata on both sides:
25. Scales of cones broader than long; trees with a pyramidal
    crown; found at moderate altitudes   (White Fir) **A. concolor**
25. Scales of cones about as long as broad; trees with spirelike
    crowns; found in high mts.   (Alpine Fir) **A. lasiocarpa**
23. Cones pendulous, scales persistent on the axis; leaves on
    short stalks:
26. Branchlets smooth; bracts of cones longer than the scales,
    2-lobed, a long bristle from between them
        (Douglas Fir) **Pseudotsuga menziesii**
26. Branchlets roughened by persistent peglike leaf bases:
27. Leaves 4-sided and very sharp-pointed   **Picea**
28. Cones usually less than 2 in. long, scales rounded; twigs
    finely hairy   (Engelmann Spruce) **P. engelmanni**
28. Cones 2–4 in. long, scales almost square at ends; twigs
    without hair   (Colorado Blue Spruce) **P. pungens**
27. Leaves flat but narrow and blunt-tipped   **Tsuga**
29. Leaves grooved on upper surface, rounded at tip; cones
    usually less than 1 in. long; branchlets very slender,
    drooping   (Western Hemlock) **T. heterophylla**
29. Leaves convex or ridged above, abruptly pointed at tip;
    cones over 1 in. long; branchlets scarcely or only slightly
    drooping   (Mountain Hemlock) **T. mertensiana**

4. Seeds borne in a closed cavity (ovary) of a true flower;
    leaves mostly flat and broad and fall off during autumn;
    many of these plants are herbs, dying back to ground each
    winter   Subdivision **Angiospermae**

30.* Embryo of seed with a single growing point; leaves mostly parallel-veined; parts of the flowers mostly in 3's or less; vascular bundles scattered in stem (not forming rings)

                                                  Class **Monocotyledoneae**

31. Petals and sepals absent or inconspicuous:

32. Plants without true stems or leaves, small, free-floating, flat aquatics   **page**

                                              Lemna   **13**

32. Plants with true stems and leaves, not flat, free-floating aquatics but usually attached to soil:

33. Flowers all sessile in axils of chaffy imbricated bracts; mostly grasslike plants with jointed stems, sheathing leaves, 1-seeded fruit:

34. Stems usually hollow, round; leaf sheaths split; anthers attached at middle; leaves 2-ranked

                               (Grass Family) **Gramineae**

35. Stems 3–6 ft. tall; spike of flowers erect, dense, without prominent awns   **Elymus**   **6**

35. Stems 1–3 ft. tall; spike of flowers nodding, with awns 1–2 in. long, very prominent   **Hordeum**   **7**

34. Stems solid, more or less triangular; leaf sheaths not split; anthers attached at base; leaves usually 3-ranked

                              (Sedge Family) **Cyperaceae**

36. Male and female flowers in separate spikes; spikes not covered with long silky hairs; seeds enclosed in saclike covering   **Carex**   **8**

36. Male and female flowers in same spike; spikes of flowers covered with white or brown hairs up to 2 in. long; seeds not enclosed in saclike covering:

37. Hairs covering flowers white, about 1 in. long; stems 2 ft. tall or less; grasslike leaves present   **Eriophorum**   **9**

37. Hairs covering flowers brown, less than $\frac{1}{4}$ in. long; stems 3–9 ft. tall; leaves absent   **Scirpus**   **10**

33. Flowers not all sessile, nor in axils of chaffy imbricated bracts; not grasslike plants:

38. Sepals modified to bristles or chaffy scales:

39. Flowers in dense, elongate, terminal spikes; male flowers continuous above female; seeds hidden among bristles

                                          Typha   **1**

39. Flowers in globose, lateral heads, male and female flowers in separate heads; fruit not hidden among bristles

                                     Sparganium   **2**

38. Sepals not modified to bristles or scales; but fleshy or herbaceous and inconspicuous:

40. Plants of bogs; flowers in dense spikes with large, bright yellow spathe enclosing them; leaves 4–16 in. broad

                                   Lysichitum   **11**

40. Plants submerged in water; flowers in small, inconspicuous spikes without any enclosing bract; leaves long, linear

                                 Potamogeton   **2**

31. Petals and sepals present:

41. Petals not conspicuous, green or brownish:

---

* The second 30 is on page 246.

42. Flowers in long, dense spikes; sepals and petals green, fleshy **Triglochin** 4
42. Flowers in heads or panicles; sepals and petals brownish, papery **Juncus** 13
41. Petals conspicuous and bright-colored:
43. Pistils numerous in a head or ring **Sagittaria** 5
43. Pistil 1 in each flower:
44.* Sepals and petals attached below ovary (Lily Family) **Liliaceae**
45. Styles wanting; stigmas sessile:
46. Leaves 3, broadly ovate, forming a whorl just below single flower **Trillium** 30
46. Leaves alternate, slender and elongate **Calochortus** 18
45. Styles present; stigmas terminal:
47. Styles 3; sepals and petals distinct or nearly so (also see 1st No. 55, key to *Brodiaea*):
48. Plants with bulbs **Zigadenus** 32
48. Plants not with bulbs but rootstocks:
49. Plants stout, 3–6 ft. tall; leaves elliptic, large, 5–8 in. broad, covering stem **Veratrum** 31
49. Plants slender, shorter; leaves slender, grasslike, mainly basal or on lower part of stem:
50. Leaves 2 to 6 on lower part of stem; flowers in racemes or almost in a head **Tofieldia** 29
50. Leaves very numerous, mainly in large basal bunches; flowers numerous **Xerophyllum** 31
47. Styles united into 1, at least below; sepals and petals mostly united:
51. Stems from running rootstocks; fruit a berry:
52. Flowers 1; leaves 2 to 5, all basal **Clintonia** 21
52. Flowers few to many; leaves many, alternate:
53. Flowers in axils of leaves and nodding; flower stalk jointed near center, abruptly bent **Streptopus** 28
53. Flowers terminal on stem or branches, their stalks not jointed or bent:
54. Stems branched; flowers 1 to 4 at ends of branches **Disporum** 22
54. Stems unbranched; flowers in racemes or panicles **Smilacina** 27
51. Stems from bulbs; fruit a capsule:
55. Corolla parts united for ⅓ or more of their length, blue **Brodiaea** 17
55. Corolla parts distinct or nearly so:
56. Plants with onionlike odor; flowers in umbel on naked stalk **Allium** 15
56. Plants without onionlike odor; flowers solitary or in a raceme:
57. Flowers with a scarious bract at base, bright blue, usually many in a long raceme **Camassia** 20
57. Flowers without bracts, not blue, usually only 1 to 6:
58. Leaves 2 to 3, arising below surface of ground; bulbs covered with 1 or more fibrous coats **Erythronium** 23
58. Leaves 2 to many, attached above soil; bulbs without fibrous coats but with thickened scales:

* The second 44 is on page 246.

59. Sepals and petals over 1 in. long, red to orange; anthers
    attached in center **Lilium** 26
59. Sepals and petals less than 1 in. long, not red; anthers
    attached at base **Fritillaria** 24

44. Sepals and petals attached at top of the ovary:
60. Flowers regular (parts alike); stamens 3   (Iris Family) **Iridaceae**
61. Sepals and petals similar; style filiform **Sisyrinchium** 35
61. Sepals not like petals; styles petal-like **Iris** 34
60. Flowers irregular (parts not alike); stamens 1 to 2
    (Orchid Family) **Orchidaceae**
62. Plants saprophytic, without green leaves **Corallorhiza** 37
62. Plants not saprophytic, with green, true leaves:
63. Flowers 1 to 3, with leafy bracts:
64. Leaves basal, usually solitary; flowers solitary, pink or rose
    Calypso 36
64. Leaves 2 to several; flowers often more than 1, brownish and
    white, sometimes tinged with purple **Cypripedium** 36
63. Flowers many, in spikes, bracts not leafy:
65. Spike of flowers tending to be twisted; lip (the one odd petal)
    not possessing prominent spur **Spiranthes** 39
65. Spike of flowers not twisted, but usually elongated; lip
    possessing long spur at base **Habenaria** 38

30. Embryo of seed with 2 growing points; leaves mostly netted-
    veined; parts of flowers mostly in 4's or 5's (a few with
    none, or just sepals), vascular bundles forming rings in
    stem Class **Dicotyledoneae**
66. Corolla none; calyx sometimes present; flowers in catkins,
    or catkinlike clusters, stamens and ovaries in separate
    catkins; trees or shrubs:
67. Fruit a single nutlet without long silky hairs; male and
    female catkins on same tree   (Birch Family) **Betulaceae**
68. Bracts of female catkins persistent, thickened, woody, ap-
    pearing conelike; 2 to 4 catkins in cluster **Alnus**
69. Nutlet bordered on each side with membranous wing
    margin as broad as nut; flowers developed with leaves on
    twigs of the season; fruiting stalks slender, longer than
    cones; sepals 6; stamens 6 to 7   (Mountain Alder) **A. sinuata**
69. Nutlet merely acute-margined; flowers developed on last
    year's twigs, opening before leaves in late winter or early
    spring; fruiting stalks shorter than cones; sepals 4;
    stamens 1 to 4:
70. Leaves distinctly lobed and doubly toothed, rounded or
    heart-shaped at base; stamens 4 or 2
    (River Alder) **A. tenuifolia**
70. Leaves not lobed except on vigorous shoots, mostly wedge-
    shaped at base; stamens 2 or 3   (White Alder) **A. rhombifolia**
68. Bracts of female catkins thin and deciduous with the seed;
    female catkins single, erect **Betula**
71. Bark of trunk white or light yellowish brown, separable into
    thin layers   (Paper Birch) **B. papyrifera**
71. Bark of trunk reddish- or grayish-brown, not readily sepa-
    rable into thin layers   (Water Birch) **B. occidentalis**

67. Fruit a capsule; seeds with long silky hairs; a few trees but numerous shrubs   (Willow Family) **Salicaceae**

72. Plants shrubs, usually without a distinct trunk, and less than about 15 ft. tall   (Willows) **Salix**

72. Plants with a distinct trunk, and usually much more than 15 ft. tall (trees)   **Populus**

73. Leaves densely white-woolly beneath, often lobed
(Silver Poplar) **P. alba**

73. Leaves not densely white-woolly beneath:

74. Petioles definitely flattened laterally:

75. Leaves almost round in outline; old bark mostly smooth, whitish, or cream-colored   (Quaking Aspen) **P. tremuloides**

75. Leaves not round; old bark furrowed, rough, not white:

76. Pedicels equaling or longer than capsules; leaves longer than broad, with not more than 10 teeth on each side; no glands present at top of petiole   (Cottonwood) **P. wislizeni**

76. Pedicels shorter than capsules; leaves little longer than broad, if any, with more than 10 teeth on each side; glands usually present at top of petiole:

77. Trees from Canada southward, east of Continental Divide; cup of pistillate flowers about ⅛ in. broad
(Plains Cottonwood) **P. sargentii**

77. Trees of N.M., Ariz., s. Calif.; cup of pistillate flowers about ¼ in. broad   (Fremont Cottonwood) **P. fremontii**

74. Petioles round or slightly flattened on upper surface:

78. Leaves usually ovate to narrowly lance-shaped, wedge-shaped, or rounded at base; fruit noticeably pedicelled (also see 2nd No. 80, key to *P. tacamahaca*):

79. Petioles generally ⅓ or less as long as leaf blades; blades 3 to 7 times as long as broad, gradually coming to long narrow apex   (Narrowleaf Cottonwood) **P. angustifolia**

79. Petioles ½ or more as long as leaf blades; blades only about twice as long as broad, usually abruptly pointed at apex
(Lanceleaf Cottonwood) **P. acuminata**

78. Leaves usually broadly ovate, rounded to heart-shaped at base; fruit without stalk, or very short one:

80. Ovary densely covered with woolly hair, nearly globose, with 3 stigmas; buds only moderately resinous and moderate-sized   (Black Cottonwood) **P. trichocarpa**

80. Ovary without hair, oblong, with 2 stigmas; buds very resinous, large   (Balsam Poplar) **P. tacamahaca**

66. Corolla usually present as well as the calyx, or calyx corolla-like; flowers not in catkins:

81. Calyx corolla-like; leaves usually with stipules and often united around stem at nodes (ocreae)
(Buckwheat Family) **Polygonaceae**

82. Leaves without stipules; flower clusters subtended by partly united bracts; stamens 9   **Eriogonum   40**

82. Leaves with sheathing stipules; flower usually not subtended by partly united bracts; stamens 4 to 8:

83. Sepals commonly 5, all similar and usually erect in fruit; stigmas capitate   **Polygonum   42**

83. Sepals 4 or 6, outer ones spreading or reflexed and remaining small; inner ones usually erect, usually enlarged in fruit; stigmas tufted:
84. Sepals 4; leaves nearly orbicular; styles 2   **Oxyria**   **41**
84. Sepals 6, inner ones with tubercles; leaves elongate; styles 3   **Rumex**   **44**
81. Calyx not corolla-like; leaves not with stipules united around stem:
85.* Corolla of separate petals (none united together):
86.* Stamens usually numerous, at least more than twice as many as sepals:
87.* Ovary superior, calyx entirely free from pistil or pistils:
88. Pistils more than 1 in each flower, entirely distinct or united only at base:
89. Plants aquatic, with broad (3–8 in.), mostly floating leaves; flowers yellow and 3–5 in. broad   **Nuphar**   **51**
89. Plants terrestrial, but often growing in wet places; or if in water, leaves smaller or dissected:
90. Ovaries cohering in ring around a central axis; stamens numerous and filaments united into a tube around the style   (Mallow Family) **Malvaceae**
91. Plants usually 3 ft. or more tall   **Iliamna**   **114**
91. Plants less than 2 ft. tall   **Sphaeralcea**   **115**
90. Ovaries separate or united, but not cohering in a ring; filaments separate or in two groups:
92. Sepals 2; petals 4, outer pair spurred at base and tips recurved   **Dicentra**   **65**
92. Sepals more than 2; petals absent or present, but not as above:
93. Stamens inserted below ovaries; leaves without stipules   (Buttercup Family) **Ranunculaceae**
94. Fruit an achene with 1 ovule:
95. Petals absent but sepals petal-like and mostly pinkish to bluish purple:
96. Leaves all opposite   **Clematis**   **57**
96. Leaves alternate or mostly basal   **Anemone**   **53**
95. Petals present, bright yellow or white   **Ranunculus**   **60**
94. Fruit a follicle or berry, with 2 to many ovules:
97. Flowers irregular (sepals not all alike) mostly deep purplish blue:
98. Upper sepal forming a long narrow spur   **Delphinium**   **59**
98. Upper sepal forming a hooded covering for the other flower parts   **Aconitum**   **51**
97. Flowers regular, mostly not deep purplish blue:
99. Petals conspicuous, each produced backward into long hollow spurs   **Aquilegia**   **55**
99. Petals inconspicuous or absent, not spurred:
100. Leaves compound; fruit a glossy berry   **Actaea**   **52**
100. Leaves simple; fruit a follicle:
101. Petals lacking, sepals petal-like; leaves entire or merely toothed   **Caltha**   **56**

* The second 85 is on page 253; second 86 on page 250; second 87 on page 250.

101. Petals present but small, linear; leaves palmately parted,
     toothed   **Trollius**   63
 93. Stamens inserted on calyx or on a disk; leaves usually with
     stipules   (Rose Family) **Rosaceae**
102. Carpels solitary; fruit a fleshy, 1-seeded drupe; small trees
     or large shrubs   **Prunus**   89
102. Carpels more than 1 (indicated by number of stigmas or its
     lobes) or, if solitary, the fruit an achene:
103. Ovary inferior, enclosed in and grown to fleshy calyx tube;
     fruit a pome; small trees or large shrubs:
104. Leaves pinnately compound; flowers numerous, small, in
     broad clusters   **Sorbus**   94
104. Leaves simple; flowers few, large, never in broad clusters:
105. Plants armed with stout thorns; seeds stony at maturity
                                                          Crataegus 80
105. Plants without thorns; seeds not hard at maturity
                                                        Amelanchier 79
103. Ovary superior, not enclosed in a fleshy calyx tube; fruit of
     achenes, follicles, or berries:
106. Fruit a dry follicle:
107. Stamens well exserted; pods several-seeded, dehiscent
                                                          Spiraea   95
107. Stamens scarcely exserted; pods 1-seeded, indehiscent, or
     tardily so   **Holodiscus**   84
106. Fruit an indehiscent achene or of coherent drupelets:
108. Mature fruit a berry (raspberry) made up of many more or
     less coherent drupelets   **Rubus**   93
108. Mature fruits are dry achenes, sometimes enclosed in the
     fleshy hypanthium:
109. Achenes entirely enclosed in the enlarged hypanthium;
     plants shrubs: **Rosa**   92
110. Leaves compound; flowers large, pink-colored
110. Leaves simple; flowers small and yellow   **Purshia**   90
109. Achenes not enclosed in a hypanthium:
111. Receptacle becoming large, red, pulpy at maturity   **Fragaria**   82
111. Receptacle dry, not enlarged at maturity:
112. Styles persistent on achenes, becoming elongate and
     featherlike:
113. Plants dwarf shrubs; flowers solitary   **Dryas**   82
113. Plants herbs; flowers in cymes   **Geum**   83
112. Styles deciduous and not enlarging:
114. Stamens 5; calyx tube saucer-shaped; upper leaflets confluent
                                                          Ivesia   85
114. Stamens 20 or more; calyx tube none; upper leaflets distinct
                                                        Potentilla   85
 88. Pistils only 1 in each flower, the styles and stigmas often
     more:
115. Leaves punctate with translucent dots   **Hypericum** 115
115. Leaves not punctate:
116. Ovary simple, 1-celled, with 1 style:
117. Fruit a 1-seeded drupe; leaves simple; plant a shrub or
     small tree   **Prunus**   89
117. Fruit a several-seeded berry; leaves compound; plant an herb
                                                          Actaea   52

116. Ovary compound, as shown by number of its styles, stigmas, placentae, or cells:

118. Flowers very irregular, outer 2 petals with rounded knobs at base, long upper part recurved; sepals 2 **Dicentra** 65

118. Flowers regular or nearly so:

119. Sepals and petals 4 each; placentae parietal; stamens 6
Cleome 69

119. Sepals 2 or 5 to 8; placentae basal:

120. Flowers 1 in. or more broad; leaves basal, often withering before flowers open **Lewisia** 46

120. Flowers about ½ in. broad; leaves persisting after flowers wither **Claytonia** 45

87. Ovary inferior (corolla coming from top of ovary):

121. Leaves lacking; stems very fleshy, covered with slender spines; petals numerous **Opuntia** 119

121. Leaves present; stems not fleshy nor covered with spines:

122. Plants herbs, covered with rough barbed hairs **Mentzelia** 117

122. Plants shrubs or small trees; not rough-hairy:

123. Leaves opposite; stipules none **Philadelphus** 77

123. Leaves alternate; stipules present:

124. Leaves pinnately compound; flowers numerous, small, in broad cymes **Sorbus** 94

124. Leaves simple; flowers not in broad cymes:

125. Plants armed with stout thorns; seeds hard at maturity
Crataegus 80

125. Plants unarmed; seeds fairly soft at maturity
Amelanchier 79

86. Stamens not more than twice as many as petals:

126. Stamens of same number as petals and opposite them:

127. Ovary 2- to 4-celled; shrub **Ceanothus** 112

127. Ovary 1-celled; all herbs except *Mahonia*, which has spiny leaves:

128. Plants low shrubs; leaves with spines around edge **Mahonia** 64

128. Plants herbs; leaves not spiny:

129. Calyx 2-parted; style and stigma 2 to 3 **Claytonia** 45

129. Calyx 5-parted; style and stigma 1
(Primrose Family) **Primulaceae**

130. Lobes of corolla reflexed; filaments united; anthers connivent around pistil **Dodecatheon** 143

130. Lobes of corolla erect or spreading; stamens distinct
Primula 143

126. Stamens not of same number as petals, or, if of the same number, alternate with them:

131.* Ovary superior, calyx entirely free from it:

132. Ovaries 2 or more, wholly separate or somewhat united:

133. Plants with milky juice; stamens united with each other and with a large thick stigma common to the 2 ovaries
Asclepias 148

133. Plants without milky juice; stamens free from each other, or at least free from the stigma:

134. Stamens inserted on receptacle, free from calyx:

* The second 131 is on page 252.

135. Pistils entirely separate or united only at very base; leaves fleshy, entire   **Sedum**   **70**

135. Pistils more or less united, at least with a common style; leaves not fleshy or entire (Geranium Family) **Geraniaceae**

136. Leaves mostly elongate and pinnatifid; anthers 5; flowers less than ½ in. broad   **Erodium**   **105**

136. Leaves orbicular and palmately parted; anthers 10; flowers more than ½ in. broad   **Geranium**   **106**

134. Stamens inserted on calyx:

137. Plants shrubs:

138. Fruit a berry; stamens 4 or 5; leaves alternate   **Ribes**   **78**

138. Fruit a capsule; stamens numerous; leaves opposite   **Philadelphus**   **77**

137. Plants herbaceous:

139. Sterile filaments with gland tips present in addition to 5 fertile stamens; scapes 1-flowered   **Parnassia**   **73**

139. Sterile filaments absent; stamens 5 or 10:

140. Stamens 5; plants usually growing on cliffs   **Boykinia**   **72**

140. Stamens 10; plants usually not growing on cliffs:

141. Petals laciniate; leaves palmately lobed; plants not in dense patches   **Lithophragma**   **72**

141. Petals entire; leaves not palmately lobed; plants forming dense patches   **Saxifraga**   **74**

132. Ovary 1 in a flower:

142. Ovary simple, with 1 parietal placenta and 1 style (see also 1st No. 176, key to *Leguminosae*, p. 253):

142. Ovary compound, as shown by number of cells, styles, or stigmas:

143.* Ovary 1-celled:

144. Corolla decidedly irregular   **Viola**   **116**

144. Corolla regular, or nearly so:

145. Ovules solitary; plants shrubs; leaves usually 3-foliate **Rhus**   **110**

145. Ovules more than 1; plants mostly herbs:

146. Ovules attached at center or bottom of cell   (Pink Family) **Caryophyllaceae**

147. Sepals distinct or nearly so:

148. Petals 2-cleft or parted; capsule ovoid, opening with twice as many valves as there are styles   **Arenaria**   **48**

148. Petals entire or notched; capsule elongate, opening with the same number of valves as there are styles   **Cerastium**   **49**

147. Sepals united most of their length into distinct tube with 5 teeth   **Silene**   **50**

146. Ovules attached on 2 or more parietal placentae:

149. Leaves punctate with translucent or black dots **Hypericum** **115**

149. Leaves not punctate:

150. Stamens 4, 5, 8, or 10 (see also both Nos. 134):

150. Stamens 6; petals 4:

151. Stamens 2 short and 4 long   (Mustard Family) **Cruciferae**

152. Mature pods less than 4 times as long as broad   **Draba**   **65**

152. Mature pods more than 4 times as long as broad:

153. Flowers yellow; plants growing on dry soil   **Erysimum**   **66**

153. Flowers white; plants growing in water or in mud   **Rorippa**   **68**

* The second 143 is on page 252.

151. Stamens essentially equal in length   **Cleome**   69

143. Ovary 2- to several-celled:
154. Stamens neither just as many nor twice as many as petals:
155. Plants are trees or shrubs   (Maple Family) **Aceraceae**
155. Plants herbs:
156. Petals 5   **Hypericum**   115
156. Petals 4 (see also 1st No. 151, key to *Cruciferae*, p. 251):
154. Stamens just as many or twice as many as petals:
157. Ovules and seeds only 1 or 2 in each cell:
158. Plants are shrubs or trees, with opposite leaves:
159. Leaves palmately veined and deciduous; large shrubs or
        trees   (Maple Family) **Aceraceae**
159. Leaves pinnately veined, evergreen; low shrubs   **Pachistima**   111
158. Plants herbs:
160. Plants with numerous, coarse, underground rootstocks, thus
        causing stems to grow in dense patches, often covering
        large areas   **Euphorbia**   108
160. Plants without underground rootstocks, stems single or
        clumped together on branching crown: ·
161. Leaves linear and entire; flowers blue   **Linum**   107
161. Leaves orbicular to oblong, but deeply cut; flowers not blue.
        See 2nd No. 135, key to *Geraniaceae*, p. 251
157. Ovules and seeds several to many in each cell:
162. Styles 2 to 5. See 1st No. 146, key to *Caryophyllaceae*, p. 251
162. Styles 1:
163. Plants without green leaves; saprophytes   **Pterospora**   136
163. Plants with green leaves   (Wintergreen Family) **Pyrolaceae**
164. Plants leafy-stemmed   **Chimaphila**   134
164. Plants without leafy stems   **Pyrola**   135

131. Ovary inferior, calyx grown at least to the lower half:
165. Plants small trees or large shrubs; fruit a pome   **Crataegus**   80
165. Plants much smaller and mostly herbs:
166. Stamens 5 or 10; styles 2 to 3:
167. Flowers not in umbels. See both Nos. 134, pp. 250, 251
167. Flowers in umbels   (Parsley Family) **Umbelliferae**
168. Stems densely covered with hair, 3–8 ft. tall; leaflets 4–12 in.
        broad   **Heracleum**   126
168. Stems without conspicuous hair; plants lower; leaflets much
        less than 6 in. broad:
169. Fruit flattened, edges winged   **Lomatium**   127
169. Fruit round in cross section or nearly so:
170. Leaflets very narrow to filiform   **Perideridia**   130
170. Leaflets lanceolate to ovate:
171. Involucre of conspicuous, subfoliaceous bracts   **Sium**   131
171. Involucre wanting or of a few inconspicuous bracts   **Cicuta**   124
166. Stamens 4 or 8; style 1:
172. Plants shrubs; fruit a drupe; style and stigma 1   **Cornus**   132
172. Plants herbs; fruit a capsule or nutlike; either styles or
        stigmas not 1   (Evening Primrose Family) **Onagraceae**
173. Seeds with a tuft of hair at one end; plants 2 ft. or more tall,
        with long raceme of showy, bright pink or lilac-purple
        flowers   **Epilobium**   120

173. Seeds without tuft of hair; plants mostly less than 2 ft. tall and without long raceme of pink flowers:
174. Petals deeply 3-lobed and lavender to purple; anthers attached at base, erect **Clarkia** 120
174. Petals not 3-lobed, white or yellow, sometimes turning pink in age; anthers attached near middle **Oenothera** 121

85. Corolla with at least some of the petals united together:
175. Stamens more numerous than lobes of corolla:
176. Ovary 1-celled; corolla irregular, with only 2 of the petals united (Pea Family) **Leguminosae**
177. Stamens all distinct; leaves trifoliate; corolla yellow **Thermopsis** 102
177. Stamens all, or 9 of them, united:
178. Leaves even-pinnate, the terminal leaflet or leaflets modified into tendrils **Vicia** 104
178. Leaves odd-pinnate, a definite terminal leaflet present, or digitate:
179. Fruit a loment, the pod constricted between the seeds and breaking transversely into 1-seeded segments **Hedysarum** 98
179. Fruit not a loment, not constricted between seeds:
180. Filaments all united; leaves digitate; anthers of 2 forms **Lupinus** 99
180. Filaments all but 1 united:
181. Pods prickly; foliage glandular-dotted **Glycyrrhiza** 98
181. Pods not prickly; foliage not glandular-dotted:
182. Keel (lower petals) abruptly contracted into a distinct beak **Oxytropis** 97
182. Keel not abruptly contracted into a distinct beak:
183. Leaves pinnate, usually several-foliate; margins of leaflets mostly entire **Astragalus** 95
183. Leaves trifoliate (rarely 5 to 9 palmate); margins of leaflets mostly minutely toothed:
184. Flowers in long loose racemes **Melilotus** 100
184. Flowers in dense heads **Trifolium** 102
176. Ovary 3 to several-celled:
185. Plants herbs; styles or stigmas 5 to many; leaves usually incised, not evergreen. See 1st No. 90, key to *Malvaceae*, p. 248
185. Plants shrubs; style and stigma 1; leaves mostly evergreen but not incised (Heath Family) **Ericaceae**
186. Ovary inferior, developing into a bluish-black berry; leaves deciduous **Vaccinium** 140
186. Ovary superior, mostly developing into a dry capsule; leaves evergreen:
187. Plants prostrate and spreading; fruit a fleshy drupe **Arctostaphylos** 139
187. Plants usually erect or nearly so; fruit a dry capsule:
188. Low shrubs with numerous, linear, small leaves; plants heathlike **Phyllodoce** 142
188. Low shrubs with a few large leaves ¼ in. broad and up to 1 in. long **Kalmia** 140
175. Stamens not more numerous than corolla lobes:

189. * Ovary superior, entirely free from calyx:
190. Stamens fewer than corolla lobes; corolla irregular:
191. Ovary separating at maturity into 4 nutlets; stems square; leaves opposite (Mint Family) **Labiatae**
192. Corolla nearly regular; flowers in axillary clusters **Mentha** 162
192. Corolla irregular, distinctly 2-lipped:
193. Calyx distinctly 2-lipped, with saccate protuberance on upper side **Scutellaria** 164
193. Calyx not 2-lipped but 4- to 5-lobed:
194. Flowers in dense capitate clusters; stamens 2 **Monarda** 163
194. Flowers in dense terminal spikes; stamens 4 **Agastache** 161
191. Ovary a 2-celled capsule, usually containing many seeds, not lobed (Figwort Family) **Scrophulariaceae**
195. Corolla saucer-shaped, nearly regular; plants coarse, large, woolly biennials **Verbascum** 179
195. Corolla not saucer-shaped, very irregular; plants not coarse, woolly biennials:
196. Corolla with a long spur at the base, yellow with an orange center **Linaria** 172
196. Corolla not with a distinct spur at base:
197. Flowers with a 5th sterile stamen present, but often rudimentary:
198. Plants annual, small; sterile stamen rudimentary **Collinsia** 170
198. Plants perennials, large; sterile stamen long, conspicuous **Penstemon** 177
197. Flowers with 4 fertile stamens, no 5th sterile stamen:
199. Upper lip of the corolla distinctly lobed and broad **Mimulus** 172
199. Upper lip of corolla very narrow and not lobed or only slightly so:
200. Leaves mostly opposite; anther sacs alike, parallel **Pedicularis** 174
200. Leaves mostly alternate; anther sacs dissimilar:
201. Plants annual; upper lip of corolla little exceeding lower lip **Orthocarpus** 173
201. Plants perennial; upper lip of corolla much longer than lower lip **Castilleja** 168
190. Stamens of same number as corolla lobes; corolla regular:
202. Carpels 2, distinct except at apex; plants with milky juice **Asclepias** 148
202. Carpels united; plants without milky juice:
203. Ovary deeply 4-lobed, separating at maturity into 4 nutlets:
204. Leaves alternate; stems usually round; flowers regular (Borage Family) **Boraginaceae**
205. Fruit with barbed prickles:
206. Nutlets spreading on the low receptacle; biennial, with many broad leaves hiding stem; flowers reddish purple **Cynoglossum** 155
206. Nutlets erect on the elevated receptacle; perennial, with few leaves and these not hiding stem; flowers bright blue **Hackelia** 157
205. Fruit unarmed, without prickles:

* The second 189 is on page 256.

207. Flowers bright yellow, tubular, about 1 in. long
Lithospermum 158
207. Flowers bright blue or reddish in bud:
208. Plants forming gray cushionlike mats; stems 1–4 in. tall
Eritrichium 156
208. Plants not mat-forming; stems taller:
209. Plants hairy, about 1 ft. tall or less; flowers saucer- or bowl-shaped
Myosotis 160
209. Plants without hair, waxy, 1–4 ft. tall; flowers tubular
Mertensia 159
204. Leaves opposite; stems usually square; flowers irregular. See 1st No. 191, key to *Labiatae*, p. 254
203. Ovary not deeply 4-lobed:
210. Ovary 1-celled, with central placentae
(Gentian Family) **Gentianaceae**
211. Corolla whitish or greenish; stems coarse, single, erect, 2–5 ft. tall
Frasera 144
211. Corolla blue or purple; stems slender, several; usually not 2 ft. tall
Gentiana 146
210. Ovary 2-celled or more:
212. Stamens free from corolla. See 2nd No. 185, key to *Ericaceae*, p. 253
212. Stamens on tube of corolla:
213. Stamens 4:
214. Ovary splitting into 4 nutlets at maturity. See 1st No. 191, key to *Labiatae*, p. 254
214. Ovary a capsule with numerous seeds. See 2nd No. 191, key to *Scrophulariaceae*, p. 254
213. Stamens 5:
215. Ovary splitting into 4 nutlets at maturity. See No. 204, key to *Boraginaceae*, p. 254
215. Ovary developing into a capsule or berry:
216. Plants with long, herbaceous, twining, or prostrate stems
Convolvulus 149
216. Plants not with twining stems:
217. Styles or stigmas distinct; fruit a capsule:
218. Styles 2, or 2-lobed   (Waterleaf Family) **Hydrophyllaceae**
219. Flowers in headlike cluster on peduncle   **Hydrophyllum** 153
219. Flowers in distinctly scorpioid or circinate racemes
Phacelia 154
218. Styles 1, but branches of stigma 3
(Phlox Family) **Polemoniaceae**
220. Calyx tube tending to remain unbroken to maturity of capsule:
221. Calyx herbaceous; leaves pinnately compound   **Polemonium** 152
221. Calyx partly scarious; leaves entire   **Collomia** 150
220. Calyx tube tending to split along intercostal membranes:
222. Leaves narrow, entire, at least the lower opposite   **Phlox** 152
222. Leaves greatly dissected   **Gilia** 150
217. Styles and stigmas wholly united; fruit a berry
(Potato Family) **Solanaceae**
223. Fruit a dry capsule; corolla bell-shaped or longer, irregular, about 1 in. long   **Hyoscyamus** 165
223. Fruit a juicy berry; corolla saucer-shaped, ½ in. long or less:

224.   Calyx inflated and bladderlike, enclosing fruit   **Physalis**   166
224.   Calyx not inflated and enclosing fruit   **Solanum**   167

189.   Ovary inferior, calyx tube grown to ovary:
225.   Stamens separate; each flower on its own receptacle:
226.   Stamens free from corolla; leaves alternate   **Campanula**   185
226.   Stamens on corolla; leaves opposite or whorled:
227.   Plants shrubs   (Honeysuckle Family) **Caprifoliaceae**
228.   Stems creeping and very slender; leaves evergreen; flowers
         in pairs   **Linnaea**   181
228.   Stems erect or climbing; leaves deciduous; flowers in clusters:
229.   Flowers tubular; plants vines or shrubs   **Lonicera**   182
229.   Flowers saucer-shaped; plants erect shrubs   **Sambucus**   183
227.   Plants herbs:
230.   Leaves whorled; stem 4-angled, with hooked hairs   **Galium**   180
230.   Leaves opposite; stem round, glabrous   **Valeriana** 184
225.   Stamens united by their anthers into a tube around the
         style; several to many flowers on common receptacle
                                   (Composite Family) **Compositae**
231.   Flowers pink; plants usually rushlike, with leaves often
         reduced to mere scales   **Lygodesmia** 223
231.   Flowers usually not pink, mostly yellow; leaves ample:
232.   Flowers all rayflowers and perfect; plants with milky juice:
233.   Pappus bristles plumose, plume branches interwebbed;
         leaves grasslike   **Tragopogon** 232
233.   Pappus bristles not at all plumose; leaves seldom grass-
         like:
234.   Plants scapose, the leaves all basal; heads solitary on erect
         scapes:
235.   Achenes spinulose, 4- to 5-ribbed; bracts in 2 unequal series
                                                            Taraxacum 229
235.   Achenes not at all spinulose, about 10-ribbed; bracts in
         several series   **Agoseris**   187
234.   Plants not scapose but more or less leafy-stemmed:
236.   Achenes strongly flattened:
237.   Achenes beakless; flowers yellow   **Sonchus**   228
237.   Achenes beaked; flowers blue to lavender   **Lactuca**   223
236.   Achenes not distinctly flattened:
238.   Pappus brownish; plants fibrous-rooted from a caudex
                                                            Hieracium 220
238.   Pappus white; plants taprooted   **Crepis**   206
232.   Flowers all, or some of them, tubular; juice watery:
239.   Style with a ring of hairs below branches; heads discoid and
         often spiny or prickly:
240.   Leaves spiny:
241.   Pappus bristles barbellate; plants rare   **Carduus**   199
241.   Pappus bristles plumose; plants common   **Cirsium**   203
240.   Leaves not spiny:
242.   Bracts about head of flowers hooked at tip; larger leaves
         6–10 in. broad, not lobed   **Arctium**   191
242.   Bracts about head of flowers not hooked; leaves much
         smaller and pinnatifid   **Centaurea** 200
239.   Style without ring of hairs below branches; heads not spiny
         or prickly:

243. Style branches clavate, only flattened at tips, papillate; flowers all tubular, perfect, rose-purple **Liatris** 222

243. Style branches flattened, generally hairy, at least at tips; flowers mostly yellow, different kinds of flowers in heads:

244. Plants white-woolly herbs; corollas all tubular; anthers tailed at base:

245. Pappus bristles of pistillate flowers distinct; basal leaves soon deciduous and scarcely larger than the rest **Anaphalis** 189

245. Pappus bristles of pistillate flowers united at base and tend to fall off together; basal leaves not deciduous but much larger than others **Antennaria** 190

244. Plants mostly not white-woolly herbs; corolla mostly of 2 types, tubular and radiate; anthers truncate to sagittate at base:

246. Style branches with distinct appendages that are glabrous within:

247. Rayflowers yellow:

248. Pappus of not more than 10 scales or awns:

249. Heads ¼ in. or less broad; plants low shrubs; leaves linear, entire **Gutierrezia** 213

249. Heads over ½ in. broad; plants herbs; leaves broad, toothed **Grindelia** 213

248. Pappus of numerous capillary bristles:

250. Pappus double, outer much shorter than inner **Chrysopsis** 201

250. Pappus simple or at least not divided into 2 distinct lengths:

251. Heads small, numerous, tending to be on 1 side of stem **Solidago** 227

251. Heads much larger, few, and not on 1 side of stem **Haplopappus** 214

247. Rayflowers some other color than yellow, or absent:

252. Pappus of long scales; heads about 1–2 in. broad **Townsendia** 231

252. Pappus of capillary bristles; heads usually less than 1 in. broad:

253. Plants shrubs; rayflowers absent; diskflowers yellow **Chrysothamnus** 202

253. Plants herbs; rayflowers present:

254. Involucral bracts about equal in length, not leafy or with a chartaceous base and green tip **Erigeron** 208

254. Involucral bracts graduated in length, either leafy or with chartaceous base and green tip **Aster** 195

246. Style branches without appendages or with appendages hairy on both sides:

255. Pappus of capillary bristles; style branches truncate, with ring of hairs at end:

256. Shrubs; involucral bracts 4 to 6; heads discoid, with 4 to 9 flowers each **Tetradymia** 230

256. Herbs; involucral bracts more than 6; heads radiate:

257. Leaves opposite; flower heads more than 1 in. broad **Arnica** 193

257. Leaves alternate; flower heads less than 1 in. broad **Senecio** 225

255. Pappus chaffy, or of awns, or none:

258. Involucral bracts with scarious or hyaline margins:
259. Plants herbs; receptacle chaffy   **Achillea**   186
259. Plants shrubs; receptacle without chaff   **Artemisia**   193
258. Involucral bracts commonly green, herbaceous:
260. Receptacle naked or bristly:
261. Receptacle evidently bristly   **Gaillardia**   212
261. Receptacle naked:
262. Plants scapose; achenes turbinate   **Hymenoxys**   221
262. Plants with stem leaves; achenes elongate:
263. Heads discoid, flowers all tubular, perfect, not yellow
                                        Chaenactis   200
263. Heads with rayflowers, yellow   **Eriophyllum**   211
260. Receptacle chaffy, at least near margin:
264. Pistillate flowers without corollas; heads unisexual, pistillate
but developing several series of sharp spines   **Xanthium**   237
264. Pistillate flowers with evident corollas, usually ligulate;
heads with some perfect flowers:
265. Achenes of diskflowers flattened parallel to involucral bracts;
bracts not concave; pappus barbed   **Bidens**   198
265. Achenes of diskflowers flattened at right angles to involucral
bracts, or quadrangular; inner bracts mostly concave and
clasping achenes:
266. Receptacle enlarged, conic to columnar:
267. Leaves (at least lower) opposite   **Viguiera**   234
267. Leaves alternate:
268. Seeds quadrangular, not much flattened   **Rudbeckia**   225
268. Seeds flattened, often with 2 sharp and 2 blunt angles
                                        Ratibida   224
266. Receptacle flat to merely convex:
269. Rayflowers neutral, with abortive seeds:
270. Disk achenes strongly flattened, thin-edged   **Helianthella**   216
270. Disk achenes not strongly flattened or thin-edged:
271. Pappus of 2 deciduous awn scales   **Helianthus**   218
271. Pappus none. See 1st No. 267
269. Rayflowers pistillate and fertile:
272. Plants without stem leaves, or these greatly reduced
                                  Balsamorhiza   197
272. Plants with well-developed stem leaves   **Wyethia**   235

Abbreviated Names of Authors

Airy-Shaw — Airy-Shaw, Herbert K.
Ait. — Aiton, William

B. & H. — Bentham, George, and Hooker, Joseph D.
B. & R. — Britton, Nathaniel, and Rusby, Henry
Banks — Banks, Sir Joseph
Bart. — Barton, Benjamin S.
Benth. — Bentham, George
Bieb. — Bieberstein, Friedrich von
Blake — Blake, Sidney
Blank. — Blankinship, Joseph W.
Britt. — Britton, Nathaniel L.
Brown — Brown, Robert

C. & R. — Coulter, John M., and Rose, Joseph N.
Cham. — Chamisso, Adalbert von

DC. — DeCandolle, Augustin
Desf. — Desfontaines, René
Dewey — Dewey, Chester
Dietr. — Dietrich, Albert
Don, D. — Don, David
Don, G. — Don, George
Dougl. — Douglas, David
Dunal — Dunal, Michel
Dur. — Durand, Elias M.

Eat. — Eaton, Amos
Eat., D. C. — Eaton, Daniel Cady
Engelm. — Engelmann, George
Engl. — Engler, Heinrich

Farr — Farr, Edith
Fern. — Fernald, Merritt Lyndon
Fisch. & Mey. — Fischer, Friedrich von, and Meyer, Karl
Forbes — Forbes, James

Graham — Graham, Robert
Gray — Gray, Asa
Greene — Greene, Edward
Griseb. — Grisebach, Heinrich

H. & A. — Hooker, William J., and Arnott, George
H. & S. — Hultén, Eric, and St. John, Harold
HBK. — Humboldt, Friedrich von, Bonpland, Aimé, and Kunth, Carl
Hall — Hall, Harvey
Haw. — Haworth, Adrian
Hill — Hill, John
Hook. — Hooker, Sir William J.
House — House, Homer
Huds. — Hudson, William

James — James, Edwin
Jones — Jones, Marcus
Jtn. — Johnston, Ivan
Juss. — Jussieu, Antoine Laurent de

Keck — Keck, David
Kell. — Kellogg, Albert
Koch — Koch, Karl
Koenig — Koenig, Charles
Kunth — Kunth, Carl
Kuntze — Kuntze, Carl

L. — Linnaeus, Carolus, or Linné, Carl von
Lam. — Lamarck, Jean Baptiste
Lehm. — Lehmann, Johann
Leiberg — Leiberg, John Bernhard
L'Hér. — L'Héritier de Brutelle, Charles
Lindl. — Lindley, John

M. & B. — Mackenzie, Kenneth, and Bush, Benjamin
M. & C. — Mathias, Mildred, and Constance, Lincoln
Mathias — Mathias, Mildred
Maxim. — Maximowicz, Carl Johann
Michx. — Michaux, André
Muhl. — Muhlenberg, Gotthilf H.

Nels. — Nelson, Aven
Nutt. — Nuttall, Thomas

Oakes — Oakes, William

Pall. — Pallas, Peter
Parker — Parker, Kittie
Penn. — Pennell, Francis
Pers. — Persoon, Christiaan
Poir. — Poiret, Jean
Porter — Porter, Thomas
Pursh — Pursh, Frederick

Raf. — Rafinesque-Schmaltz,
   Constantine Samuel
Retz. — Retzius, Anders
Richards. — Richardson, John
Robins. — Robinson, Benjamin L.
Roth — Roth, Albrecht W.
Rydb. — Rydberg, Per Axel

S. & T. — Schinz, Hans, and
   Thelling, A.
Salisb. — Salisbury, Richard A.
Savi — Savi, Gaetano
Schk. — Schkuhr, Christian
Schmidt — Schmidt, Franz
Schult. — Schultes, Joseph
Schum. — Schumann, Karl
Scop. — Scopoli, Johann

Scribn. & Merr. — Scribner,
   Frank L., and Merrill, Elmer
Sheld. — Sheldon, Edmund P.
Sm. — Smith, Sir James Edward
Smiley — Smiley, Frank
Spreng. — Sprengel, Kurt
St. John — St. John, Harold
Suksd. — Suksdorf, Wilhelm
Sw. — Swartz, Olaf

T. & G. — Torrey, John, and
   Gray, Asa
Torr. — Torrey, John

U. & G. — Urban, Ignatz, and
   Gilg, Ernst

W. & S. — Wooten, Elmer, and
   Standley, Paul
Walt. — Walter, Thomas
Wang. — Wangenheim, Friedrich
   von
Wats. — Watson, Sereno
Weber — Weber, Friedrich
Wight — Wight, William
Willd. — Willdenow, Karl

APPENDIX III

Selected Bibliography

Ashton, E. Ruth. *Plants of Rocky Mountain National Park*. Washington: U.S. Govt. Printing Office, 1933.

Coulter, John M., and rev. by Aven Nelson. *New Manual of Botany of the Central Rocky Mountains*. New York, etc.: American Book Company, 1909.

Davis, Ray J. *Flora of Idaho*. Dubuque: W. C. Brown Company, 1952.

Dayton, William A., and Others. *Range Plant Handbook*. Washington: U.S. Govt. Printing Office, 1937.

Harrington, Harold D. *Manual of Plants of Colorado*. Denver: Sage Books, 1954.

Hitchcock, C. Leo, Arthur Cronquist, Marion Ownbey, and J. W. Thompson, eds. *Vascular Plants of the Pacific Northwest*. Part 5 (1955), *Compositae;* Part 4 (1959), *Ericaceae through Campanulaceae;* Part 3 (1961), *Saxifragaceae to Ericaceae*. Seattle: University of Washington Press.

Jepson, E. Carl, and Leland F. Allen. *Wild Flowers of Zion and Bryce Canyon National Parks and Cedar Breaks National Monument*. Bryce Natl. Park: Zion-Bryce Natural History Association, in cooperation with U.S. Natl. Park Service, 1958.

McDougall, Walter B., and Herma A. Baggley. *The Plants of Yellowstone National Park*. Yellowstone Natl. Park: Yellowstone Library and Museum Association, 1956.

Moss, Ezra H. *Flora of Alberta*. Toronto: University of Toronto Press, 1959.

Rydberg, Per Axel. *Flora of the Rocky Mountains and Adjacent Plains* (2nd ed., reprint). New York: Hafner Publishing Company, 1954.

Standley, Paul C. *Plants of Glacier National Park*. Washington: U.S. Govt. Printing Office, 1926.

Index

Index

Achillea lanulosa, 186, **187**
   millefolium, 187
Aconitum columbianum, 51, **Pl. 7**
Actaea arguta, 52, **53**
   rubra, 52
Agastache foeniculum, 161
   urticifolia, 161, **Pl. 20**
Agoseris aurantiaca, 188
   glauca, 187, **188**
   heterophylla, 188
Albert's Penstemon, 178, **Pl. 20**
Alfalfa, 103
Alismaceae, 5
Alkanet, 156, 165
Allium acuminatum, 16
   brevistylum, 16, **16**
   cernuum, 15, **15**, **Pl. 2**
   schoenoprasum, 15, **15**
   textile, 16
Alpine Aster, 195, **Pl. 21**
Alpine Buttercup, 60, **Pl. 6**
Alpine Forget-me-not, 156, **Pl. 17**
Alpine Sunflower, 221, **Pl. 21**
Amelanchier alnifolia, 79, **Pl. 11**
American Bistort, 42, **42**, **Pl. 4**
American Red Raspberry, 93, **93**
American Vetch, 104
Anacardiaceae, 110
Anaphalis margaritacea, 189, **189**
Anchusa officinalis, 156, 165
Anemone, 53, **Pl. 6**
   Candle, 63

Anemone cylindrica, 53, 63
   globosa, 53, **Pl. 6**
   ludoviciana. See *patens*
   parviflora, 54
   patens, 54, **55**, **Pl. 6**
   tetonensis. See *globosa*
Antennaria dimorpha, 190
   luzuloides, 190
   rosea, 190, **191**, **Pl. 22**
Anthemis cotula, 201
apple, Squaw-, 80
Aquilegia coerulea, 55, **Pl. 6**
   flavescens, 56
   formosa, 55
Araceae, 11
Arctium minus, 191, **192**
Arctostaphylos patula, 139
   uva-ursi, 139, **Pl. 15**
Arenaria congesta, **48**, 49
   lateriflora, 49
   obtusiloba, 48, **Pl. 5**
Arnica, 193, **Pl. 19**
Arnica cordifolia, 193, **Pl. 19**
   longifolia, 193
   parryi, 193
   rydbergii, 193
Arrowgrass, 4, **4**
Arrowgrass Family, 4
Arrowhead, 5, **5**, **Pl. 1**
Arrowhead Family, 5
Arrowleaf Balsamroot, 197, **Pl. 20**
Artemisia biennis, 194

Artemisia (*contd.*)
  cana, 194
  ludoviciana, 194
  spinescens, 194
  tridentata, 193, **194**
Arum Family, 11
Asclepiadaceae, 148
Asclepias capricornu, 148
  speciosa, 148, **148**, Pl. 16
  subverticillata, 148
  tuberosa, 148
ash, Mountain-, 94, Pl. 10
Asphodel, False, 29, Pl. 3
Aster, Alpine, 195, Pl. 21
  Engelmann, 197, Pl. 23
  Showy, 195
  Thickstem, 196, **196**, Pl. 23
aster, Golden-, 201, **202**
Aster alpigenus, 195, Pl. 21
  canescens, 195
  conspicuus, 195
  engelmannii, 197, Pl. 23
  frondosus, 195
  integrifolius, 196, **196**, Pl. 23
Astragalus agrestis, 96
  alpinus, 95, **96**
  calycosus, 96
  drummondii, 96
  purshii, 97, Pl. 10
  tegetarius, 96
Avens, Long-plumed, 83, Pl. 11
avens, Mountain-, 82, Pl. 9

Ballhead Sandwort, **48**, 49
Balsamorhiza hookeri, 197, Pl. 21
  incana, 197
  sagittata, 197, Pl. 20
Balsamroot, 197, Pl. 21
  Arrowleaf, 197, Pl. 20
Baneberry, 52, **53**
Barberry Family, 64
Barley, Foxtail, 7, Pl. 1
Barren Strawberry, 83
Batrachium flaccidum. See *Ranunculus aquatilis*
Beardtongue, Crested, 178, Pl. 20
Beargrass, 31, Pl. 1
Bedstraw, 180, Pl. 20
Beeplant, Rocky Mountain, 69, Pl. 8
  Yellow, 69, Pl. 8
Beggarticks, 198, **198**, Pl. 22
Berberidaceae, 64
Berberis repens. See *Mahonia repens*

Bidens cernua, 198, **198**, Pl. 22
  tenuisecta, 199
  vulgata, 199
Big Sagebrush, 193, **194**
Big Whortleberry, 141, **141**
Bighead Clover, 104, Pl. 10
Biscuitroot, 127, Pl. 13
  Mountain, 127, **128**
  Wyeth, 127, Pl. 13
Bistort, American, 42, **42**, Pl. 4
Bitterbrush, 90, **91**, Pl. 9
Bittercress, 68
Bitterroot, 46, **47**, Pl. 5
Bittersweet, 167, 168
Black Nightshade, 167, **167**
Blanketflower, 212, Pl. 20
Blazingstar, 118, Pl. 11
  Ten-petaled, 117, **118**
Bleedingheart Family, 65
Blue Columbine, 55, **Pl. 6**
Blue Penstemon, 178, **Pl. 20**
Bluebell, 160, Pl. 17
  Mountain, 159, Pl. 17
Bluebell Family, 185
Blueberry, 140, Pl. 14
Bluebonnet, 100, Pl. 11
Blue-eyed Grass, 35, Pl. 2
Blue-eyed Mary, 170, **171**
Blueflax, 107, Pl. 14
Blue-flowered Lettuce, 223, Pl. 23
Bog-orchid, White, 38, **39**, Pl. 4
Borage Family, 155
Boraginaceae, 155
Boykinia, James, 72, Pl. 8
Boykinia jamesii, 72, Pl. 8
Bristle Thistle, 199, Pl. 24
Broad-leaved Fireweed, 121, Pl. 13
Brodiaea douglasii, 17, **17**, Pl. 3
  hyacinthina, 18
Brook Saxifrage, 74, **75**
Buckthorn Family, 112
Buckwheat Family, 40
Bull Thistle, 206, Pl. 24
Bulrush, 10, **10**
Bunchberry, 132, Pl. 14
Burdock, 191, **192**
Burreed, 2, Pl. 1
Burreed Family, 2
Bush Penstemon, 177, **177**
Butter-and-Eggs, 108, 172, Pl. 18
Buttercup, Alpine, 60, Pl. 6
  Sagebrush, 62, **62**, Pl. 6
  Subalpine, 60
  Water, 61, Pl. 7

Buttercup Family, 51

Cactaceae, 119
Cactus, 119, Pl. 12
  Plains, 119, Pl. 12
Cactus Family, 119
Calochortus elegans, 18
  macrocarpus, 18
  nitidus, 18, Pl. 3
  nuttallii, 18, **19**, Pl. 3
Caltha leptosepala, 56, Pl. 6
  rotundifolia. See *leptosepala*
Calypso bulbosa, 36, Pl. 4
Camas, 20, **20**, Pl. 2
camas, Death-, 32, Pl. 2
  Mountain Death-, 32, **33**
Camassia cusickii, 21
  howellii, 21
  leichtlinii, 21
  quamash, 20, **20**, Pl. 2
  scilloides, 20
Campanula parryi, 185
  rotundifolia, 185, Pl. 19
  uniflora, 153, 185
Campanulaceae, 185
Campion, Moss, 50, Pl. 6
Canada Thistle, 203, **203**
Candle Anemone, 63
Caper Family, 69
Capparidaceae, 69
Caprifoliaceae, 181
Cardamine breweri, 68
Carduus acanthoides, 199
  nutans, 199, Pl. 24
Carex amplifolia, 8
  festivella, 8
  geyeri, 8
  nebraskensis, 8, Pl. 1
Carum gairdneri. See *Perideridia gairdneri*
Caryophyllaceae, 48
Castilleja chromosa, 170, Pl. 18
  exilis, 170
  flava, 168
  linariaefolia, 169, **169**
  miniata, 170, Pl. 18
  rhexifolia, 170, Pl. 18
  sulphurea, 168, Pl. 18
Cattail, Common, 1, Pl. 1
Cattail Family, 1
Ceanothus fendleri, 113
  sanguineus, 113
  velutinus, 112, **113**
Celastraceae, 111

Centaurea maculosa, 200, Pl. 24
  picris, 200
  solstitialis, 200
Cerastium arvense, 49, Pl. 5
  beeringianum, 49
  nutans, 49
Chaenactis alpina, 201, Pl. 24
  douglasii, 200
  stevioides, 201
Chichorium intybus, 223
Chickweed, Field, 49, Pl. 5
Chicory, 223
Chimaphila menziesii, 134
  umbellata var. *occidentalis*, 134, Pl. 14
Chive, Siberian, 15, **15**
Chokecherry, 89, Pl. 10
Chrysopsis villosa, 201, **202**
Chrysothamnus nauseosus, 202, Pl. 22
  parryi, 202
  viscidiflorus, 202
Cicuta bulbifera, 125, 130
  douglasii, 124, **124**
Cinquefoil, 88, **88**, Pl. 11
  Shrubby, 87, **87**, Pl. 9
Cirsium arvense, 203, **203**
  brevistylum, 204
  foliosum, 204, **205**, Pl. 24
  lanceolatum. See *vulgare*
  undulatum, 204
  vulgare, 206, **206**, Pl. 24
Clammyweed, 69
Clarkia, 120, Pl. 12
Clarkia pulchella, 120, Pl. 12
  rhomboidea, 120
Claytonia chamissoi, 45
  cordifolia, 45
  lanceolata, 45, **46**, Pl. 5
  megarrhiza, 45
  perfoliata, 45
Clematis, 57, Pl. 7
  White, 58, Pl. 7
Clematis columbiana, 57, Pl. 7
  hirsutissima, 57, Pl. 7
  ligusticifolia, 58, Pl. 7
Cleome lutea, 69, Pl. 8
  platycarpa, 69
  serrulata, 69, Pl. 8
Clintonia uniflora, 21, Pl. 3
Clover, 102, **103**
  Bighead, 104, Pl. 10
clover, Owl-, 173, Pl. 18
Cocklebur, 237, **237**

Collinsia grandiflora, 170
  parviflora, 170, **171**
Collomia, 150, **Pl. 14**
Collomia debilis, 150
  grandiflora, 150
  linearis, 150, **Pl. 14**
Columbine, Blue, 55, **Pl. 6**
Common Cattail, 1, **Pl. 1**
Compositae, 186
Composite Family, 186
Coneflower, 224, **Pl. 23**
  Western, 225, **Pl. 22**
Conium maculatum, 125
Convolvulaceae, 149
Convolvulus arvensis, 149, **Pl. 17**
  sepium, 149
Corallorhiza maculata, 37, **37**, **Pl. 4**
  striata, 38, **Pl. 4**
Coralroot, Spotted, 37, **37**, **Pl. 4**
  Striped, 38, **Pl. 4**
Cornaceae, 132
Cornus canadensis, 132, **Pl. 14**
  florida, 133
  nuttallii, 133
  sericea, 133, **Pl. 14**
  stolonifera. See *sericea*
Corydalis aurea, 65
Cotton-sedge, 9, **9**
Coulter's Daisy, 209, **210**
Cow-parsnip, 126, **Pl. 13**
Crassulaceae, 70
Crataegus columbiana, 80
  rivularis, 80, **81**
Crazyweed, **96**, 97, **Pl. 10**
Creeping Wintergreen, 139, **Pl. 14**
Crepis acuminata, 206, **207**
  modocensis, 207
  runcinata, 207
Crested Beardstongue, 178, **Pl. 20**
Cruciferae, 65
Curlydock, 44, **44**
Currant, Golden, 78, **78**
Cutleaf Daisy, 208, **208**, **Pl. 21**
Cut-leaved Nightshade, 168
Cynoglossum boreale, 156
  officinale, 155, **Pl. 17**
Cyperaceae, 8
Cypripedium montanum, 36, **Pl. 4**

Daisy, Coulter's, 209, **210**
  Cutleaf, 208, **208**, **Pl. 21**
  Showy, 210, **Pl. 21**
Dandelion, 229
  False, 187, **188**

Death-camas, 32, **Pl. 2**
  Mountain, 32, **33**
Delphinium bicolor, 59
  nelsoni, 59, **59**, **Pl. 7**
  occidentale, 59
  occidentale var. *cucullatum*, 59
Desert-parsley, 128, **Pl. 13**
Diamondleaf Saxifrage, 76, **76**
Dicentra uniflora, 65, **Pl. 7**
  cucullaria, 65
Disporum oreoganum, 23
  trachycarpum, 22, **22**, **Pl. 3**
Dock, Mexican, 44
Dodecatheon dentatum, 143
  jeffreyi, 143
  pauciflorum, 143, **Pl. 15**
Dogfennel, 201
Dogtooth Violet, 23, **Pl. 2**
Dogwood, Red-osier, 133, **Pl. 14**
Dogwood Family, 132
Draba aurea, 66
  densifolia, 65, **Pl. 8**
  nemorosa, 66
  oligosperma, 66
  reptans, 66
Dryad, 82, **Pl. 9**
Dryas drummondii, 82, **Pl. 9**
  hookeriana, 82, **Pl. 9**
  octopetala. See *hookeriana*
Duckweed, 13
Duckweed Family, 13
Dusty Maiden, 201, **Pl. 24**
Dutchmans-breeches, 65
Dwarf Monkeyflower, 172, 173,
  Pl. 19

Early Paintbrush, 170, **Pl. 18**
Elder, 183
Elderberry, 183, **Pl. 19**
Elephanthead, 176, **Pl. 18**
Elk Thistle, 204, **205**, **Pl. 24**
Elymus canadensis, 6
  cinereus, 6, **Pl. 1**
  condensatus. See *cinereus*
  glaucus, 6
Engelmann Aster, 197, **Pl. 23**
Epilobium adenocaulon, 121
  angustifolium, 120, **Pl. 13**
  latifolium, 121, **Pl. 13**
  paniculatum, 121
  suffruticosum, 121
Ericaceae, 139
Erigeron annuus, 209
  aphanactis, 209

Erigeron (contd.)
  compositus, 208, **208**, Pl. 21
  coulteri, 209, **210**
  simplex 209
  speciosus, 210, Pl. 21
Eriogonum alatum, 40
  deflexum, 40
  dendroideum, 40
  flavum, 40, Pl. 5
  heracleoides var. *subalpinum*, 40,
    Pl. 4
  ovalifolium, 40
  umbellatum, 40
Eriophorum angustifolium, 9, **9**
  gracile, 9
Eriophyllum lanatum var. *integri-
    folium*, 211, **211**, Pl. 23
Eritrichium argenteum. See *elonga-
    tum*
  elongatum, 156, Pl. 17
  howardii, 156
Erodium cicutarium, 105, **105**
Erysimum capitatum, 66, **67**
  repandum, 66
  wheeleri, 66
Erythronium grandiflorum, 23, Pl. 2
Eupatorium maculatum, 222
Euphorbia cyparissias, 109
  esula, 108, **109**, Pl. 15
  serpyllifolia, 109
Euphorbiaceae, 108
Evening Primrose, 121, Pl. 12
  Yellow, 123, **123**
Evening Primrose Family, 120
Everlasting, Pearly, 189, **189**

Fairybells, 22, **22**, Pl. 3
Fairyslipper, 36, Pl. 4
False Asphodel, 29, Pl. 3
False Dandelion, 187, **188**
False Hellebore, 31, Pl. 4
False Lupine, 102, Pl. 11
False Solomonseal, 27, Pl. 2
Falsemallow, Scarlet, 115, Pl. 12
Fernleaf, 174, **174**
Field Chickweed, 49, Pl. 5
Figwort Family, 168
Fireweed, 120, Pl. 13
  Broad-leaved, 121, Pl. 13
Flax Family, 107
Flowering Quillwort, 4
Forget-me-not, 160, Pl. 17
  Alpine, 156, Pl. 17
Foxtail Barley, 7, Pl. 1

Fragaria americana. See *vesca*
  vesca, 82, Pl. 9
  virginiana, 83
  virginiana vars. *glauca, ovalis,
    platypetala*, 83
Franklin Phacelia, 154, **155**
Frasera albicaulis, 145
  fastigiata, 145
  speciosa, 144, **145**, Pl. 15
Fritillaria atropurpurea, 24, Pl. 3
  lanceolata, 24
  pudica, 24, **25**, Pl. 3
Fritillary, Yellow, 24, **25**, Pl. 3
Fumariaceae, 65

Gaillardia aristata, 212, Pl. 20
  pinnatifida, 212
  pulchella, 212
Galium aparine, 180
  boreale, 180, Pl. 20
  triflorum, 180
Garden Sage, 194
Gaultheria humifusa, 139, Pl. 14
Gayfeather, 222
Gentian, Green, 144, **145**, Pl. 15
  Mountain, 146, Pl. 16
  Pleated, 146, **147**
  Western Fringed, 146, Pl. 16
Gentian Family, 144
Gentiana affinis, 146, **147**
  calycosa, 146, Pl. 16
  romanzovii, 147
  strictiflora, 147
  thermalis, 146, Pl. 16
Gentianaceae, 144
Geraniaceae, 105
Geranium, Sticky, 106, **107**, Pl. 10
Geranium carolinianum, 106
  richardsonii, 106
  viscosissimum, 106, **107**, Pl. 10
Geranium Family, 105
Geum macrophyllum, 84
  rossii, 84
  triflorum, 83, Pl. 11
Giant-hyssop, 161, Pl. 20
Gilia, Scarlet, 150, **151**, Pl. 16
Gilia aggregata, 150, **151**, Pl. 16
  congesta, 151
  sinuata, 151
Globeflower, 63, Pl. 7
Glycyrrhiza lepidota, 98, Pl. 11
Goatweed, 115
Golden-aster, 201, **202**
Golden Corydalis, 65

Golden Currant, 78, **78**
Goldeneye, 234, **234**, Pl. 22
Goldenrod, 227, **Pl. 22**
Goldenweed, 215, **216**
  Stemless, 214, **215**
Gooseberry Family, 78
Gramineae, 6
grape, Holly-, 64, **Pl. 7**
Grass, Blue-eyed, 35, **Pl. 2**
grass, Whitlow-, 65, **Pl. 8**
Grass Family, 6
Grass-of-Parnassus, 73, **Pl. 8**
Grass-widows, 35, **Pl. 2**
Greasewood, 194
Great Basin Wild Rye, 6, **Pl. 1**
Green Gentian, 144, **145**, **Pl. 15**
Green Pyrola, 135, **135**
Grindelia aphanactis, 213
  fastigiata, 213
  squarrosa, 213, **Pl. 23**
Gromwell, 158, **Pl. 17**
  Wayside, 158, **159**
Grossulariaceae, 78
Groundcherry, 166, **166**
Groundsel, 225, **226**
Grouse Whortleberry, 141, **141**
Gumweed, 213, **Pl. 23**
Gutierrezia sarothrae, 213

Habenaria dilatata, 38, **39**, **Pl. 4**
  hyperborea, 38
  obtusata, 38
  unalascensis, 38
Hackelia floribunda, 157, **157**
  patens, 158
Haplopappus acaulis, 214, **215**
  macronema, 214
  spinulosus, 214
  uniflorus, 215, **216**
Harebell, 185, **Pl. 19**
  Alpine, 153
Haw, Red, 80
Hawksbeard, 206, **207**
Hawkweed, 220, **220**
Hawthorn, River, 80, **81**
Heath, Mountain, 142, **Pl. 15**
Heath Family, 139
Hedysarum boreale, 99
  occidentale, 98, **Pl. 11**
  sulphurescens, 99
Helianthella, 217, **218**, **Pl. 22**
Helianthella quinquenervis, 217
  218, **Pl. 22**
  uniflora, 216, **217**, **Pl. 22**

Helianthus annuus, 218, **219**, **Pl. 22**
  maximiliani, 219
  nuttallii, 219
  tuberosus, 219
Hellebore, False, 31, **Pl. 4**
hemlock, Poison-, 125
  Water-, 124, **124**
Henbane, 165, **Pl. 17**
Heracleum lanatum, 126, **Pl. 13**
Hieracium albertinum, 220, **220**
  albiflorum, 221
  gracile, 221
  scouleri. See *albertinum*
Holly-grape, 64, **Pl. 7**
Hollyhock, Mountain, 114, **Pl. 12**
Holodiscus discolor, 84, **Pl. 10**
  dumosus, 84
  glabrescens, 84
Honeysuckle, 182, **Pl. 19**
Honeysuckle Family, 181
Hordeum brachyantherum, 7
  jubatum, 7, **Pl. 1**
  pusillum, 7
Horsebrush, 230, **230**
Horsemint, 163, **Pl. 17**
Houndstongue, 155, **Pl. 17**
Hyacinth, Wild, 17, **17**, **Pl. 3**
Hydrangea Family, 77
Hydrangeaceae, 77
Hydrophyllaceae, 153
Hydrophyllum capitatum, 153,
  Pl. 16
  fendleri, 153
Hymenoxys acaulis, 221
  brandegei, 221
  grandiflora, 221, **Pl. 21**
Hyoscyamus niger, 165, **Pl. 17**
Hypericaceae, 115
Hypericum formosum, 116, **Pl. 12**
  majus, 116
  perforatum, 115
hyssop, Giant-, 161, **Pl. 20**

Iliamna longisepala, 114
  rivularis, 114, **Pl. 12**
Indian Paintbrush, 170, **Pl. 18**
Iridaceae, 34
Iris, Rocky Mountain, 34, **Pl. 2**
Iris Family, 34
Iris missouriensis, 34, **Pl. 2**
Ivesia, 85, **Pl. 9**
Ivesia baileyi, 85
  gordonii, 85, **Pl. 9**
  tweedyi, 85

ivy, Poison-, 110, **110**

Jacobs-ladder, 153, **Pl. 16**
James Boykinia, 72, **Pl. 8**
Joe-pye-weed, 222
Juncaceae, 13
Juncaginaceae, 4
Juncus balticus, 13, **14**
    bufonius, 13
    mertensianus, 14
    saximontanus, 13

Kalmia polifolia, 140, **Pl. 15**
Kinnikinnick, 139, **Pl. 15**
Knapweed, Spotted, 200, **Pl. 24**

Labiatae, 161
Lactuca ludoviciana, 223
    pulchella, 223, **Pl. 23**
    scariola, 223
Ladies-tresses, 39, **Pl. 4**
Ladys-slipper, Mountain, 36, **Pl. 4**
Ladysthumb, Water, 43, **Pl. 5**
Larkspur, 59, **59**, **Pl. 7**
laurel, Swamp-, 140, **Pl. 15**
Leafy Spurge, 108, **109**, **Pl. 15**
Leguminosae, 95
Lemna minor, 13
    trisulca, 13
Lemnaceae, 13
Leopard Lily, 24, **Pl. 3**
Lettuce, Blue-flowered, 223, **Pl. 23**
Lewisia, 47, **Pl. 5**
Lewisia pygmaea, 47, **Pl. 5**
    rediviva, 46, **47**, **Pl. 5**
Liatris ligulistylis, 222
    punctata, 222
Licorice, Wild, 98, **Pl. 11**
Ligusticum filicinum, 125, **125**
Lilaea subulata, 4
Liliaceae, 15
Lilium columbianum, 27
    montanum. See *umbellatum*
    umbellatum, 26, **26**
Lily, Leopard, 24, **Pl. 3**
    Red, 26, **26**
    Sego, 18, **19**, **Pl. 3**
    See also Pondlily
Lily Family, 15
Lily-of-the-Valley, Wild, 28, **Pl. 1**
Linaceae, 107
Linaria vulgaris, 108, 172, **Pl. 18**
Linnaea borealis, 181, **181**

Linum kingii, 108
    lewisii, 107, **Pl. 14**
    rigidum, 108
Lithophragma bulbifera, 73
    parviflora, 72, **Pl. 8**
    tenella, 73
Lithospermum angustifolium. See *incisum*
    arvense, 158
    incisum, 158, **Pl. 17**
    ruderale, 158, **159**
Little Penstemon, 178
Little Sunflower, 216, **217**, **Pl. 22**
Loasa Family, 117
Loasaceae, 117
Locoweed, 97, **Pl. 10**
Lodgepole Lupine, 99, **Pl. 11**
Lomatium ambiguum, 127, **Pl. 13**
    dissectum var. *multifidum*, 128, **Pl. 13**
    grayi, 127
    macrocarpum, 127, **Pl. 13**
    montanum, 127, **128**
    simplex, 127
Long-leaved Phlox, 152, **Pl. 16**
Long-plumed Avens, 83, **Pl. 11**
Lonicera ciliosa, 182, **Pl. 19**
    involucrata, **182**, 183
    utahensis, **182**, 183
Loveroot, 125, **125**
Lupine, False, 102, **Pl. 11**
    Lodgepole, 99, **Pl. 11**
Lupinus caespitosus, 100
    laxiflorus, 100
    parviflorus, 99, **Pl. 11**
    pusillus, 100
    sericeus, 100, **Pl. 11**
Lygodesmia grandiflora, 223, **Pl. 24**
    juncea, 224
    spinosa, 224
Lysichitum americanum, 11, **12**, **Pl. 1**

Madder Family, 180
Mahonia aquifolium, 64
    nervosa, 64
    repens, 64, **Pl. 7**
Mallow Family, 114
Malvaceae, 114
Mariposa, Purple-eyed, 18, **Pl. 3**
Marshmarigold, 56, **Pl. 6**
Matchbrush, 213
Meadow Salsify, 232
Medicago sativa, 103

Melilotus alba, 101
  indica, 101
  officinalis, 100, **101**
Mentha arvensis, 162, **162**, **Pl. 20**
  piperita, 162
  spicata, 162
Mentzelia albicaulis, 117
  decapetala, 117, **118**
  laevicaulis, 118, **Pl. 11**
Mertensia alpina, 160
  ciliata, 159, **Pl. 17**
  oblongifolia, 160, **Pl. 17**
Mexican Dock, 44
Milk-thistle, 228, **228**
Milkvetch, 95, **96**
Milkweed, Pink, 148, **148**, **Pl. 16**
Milkweed Family, 148
Mimulus floribundus, 172
  guttatus, 172, **Pl. 18**
  lewisii, 172, **Pl. 19**
  moschatus, 172, **Pl. 19**
  nanus, 172, **173**, **Pl. 19**
Mint, 162, **162**, **Pl. 20**
Mint Family, 161
Monarda menthaefolia, 163, **Pl. 17**
  pectinata, 163
Monkeyflower, Dwarf, 172, 173, **Pl. 19**
  Red, 172, **Pl. 19**
  Yellow, 172, **Pl. 18**
Monkshood, 51, **Pl. 7**
Morning-brides, 200
Morning-glory, 149, **Pl. 17**
Morning-glory Family, 149
Moss Campion, 50, **Pl. 6**
Mountain-ash, 94, **Pl. 10**
Mountain-avens, 82, **Pl. 9**
Mountain Biscuitroot, 127, **128**
Mountain Bluebell, 159, **Pl. 17**
Mountain Death-camas, 32, **33**
Mountain Gentian, 146, **Pl. 16**
Mountain Heath, 142, **Pl. 15**
Mountain Hollyhock, 114, **Pl. 12**
Mountain Ladys-slipper, 36, **Pl. 4**
Mountain-lover, 111, **112**
Mountain Penstemon, 177, 178, **Pl. 21**
Mountain-sorrel, 41, **Pl. 5**
Mountainspray, 84, **Pl. 10**
Mules-ears, 235, **235**, **Pl. 24**
Mullein, 179, **179**
Musk Plant, 172, **Pl. 19**
Myosotis alpestris, 160, **Pl. 17**
  laxa, 161

Myosotis (contd.)
  verna, 160
Mustard Family, 65

Najadaceae, 2
Nightshade, Black, 167, **167**
  Cut-leaved (Three-flowered), 168
Nodding Onion, 15, **15**, **Pl. 2**
Nuphar polysepalum, 51, **Pl. 6**
Nymphaeaceae, 51

oak, Poison-, 111
Oenothera caespitosa, 121, **Pl. 12**
  flava, 122
  heterantha, 122, **122**, **Pl. 13**
  hookeri, 124
  pallida, 122
  rydbergii, 123, **123**
  scapoidea, 122
  strigosa. See *rydbergii*
Onagraceae, 120
Onion, Nodding, 15, **15**, **Pl. 2**
  Shortstyle, 16, **16**
Opuntia fragilis, 119
  polyacantha, 119, **Pl. 12**
  rhodantha, 119, **Pl. 12**
orchid, White Bog-, 38, **39**, **Pl. 4**
Orchid Family, 36
Orchidaceae, 36
Orogenia, 129, **Pl. 14**
Orogenia fusiformis, 129
  linearifolia, 129, **Pl. 14**
Orpine Family, 70
Orthocarpus luteus, 174
  tenuifolius, 173, **Pl. 18**
Owl-clover, 173, **Pl. 18**
Oxyria digyna, 41, **Pl. 5**
Oxytropis besseyi, 96, 97, **Pl. 10**
Oysterplant, 232, **233**

Pachistima myrsinites, 111, **112**
Paintbrush, Early, 170, **Pl. 18**
  Indian, 170, **Pl. 18**
  Wyoming, 169, **169**
  Yellow, 168, **Pl. 18**
Painted-cup, Splitleaf, 170, **Pl. 18**
Parnassia, Wideworld, 73, **74**
Parnassia fimbriata, 73, **Pl. 8**
  palustris, 73, **74**
  parviflora, 73
Parrots-beak, 175, **175**, **Pl. 20**
Parry Primrose, 143, **Pl. 15**
Parry Townsendia, 231, **231**, **Pl. 23**
parsley, Desert-, 128, **Pl. 13**

Parsley Family, 124
parsnip, Cow-, 126, Pl. 13
  Water-, 131, 132, Pl. 13
Pasqueflower, 54, 55, Pl. 6
Pea Family, 95
Pearly Everlasting, 189, 189
Pedicularis bracteosa, 174, 174
  crenulata, 175
  groenlandica, 176, Pl. 18
  hallii, 176
  racemosa, 175, 175, Pl. 20
  siifolia, 175
Penstemon, Albert's, 178, Pl. 20
  Blue, 178, Pl. 20
  Bush, 177, 177
  Little, 178
  Mountain, 177, 178, Pl. 21
Penstemon albertinus, 178, Pl. 20
  bridgesii, 177
  cyaneus, 178, Pl. 20
  deustus, 177
  eriantherus, 178, Pl. 20
  fruticosus, 177, 177
  montanus, 177, 178, Pl. 21
  procerus, 178
  rydbergii, 177
Peraphyllum ramosissimum, 80
Perideridia bolanderi, 130
  gairdneri, 130, 130, Pl. 13
  parishii, 130
Phacelia, Franklin, 154, 155
  Silky, 154, Pl. 16
Phacelia franklinii, 154, 155
  ivesiana, 154
  leucophylla, 154
  linearis, 154
  sericea, 154, Pl. 16
Philadelphus lewisii, 77, Pl. 8
  microphyllus, 77
Phlox, Long-leaved, 152, Pl. 16
  Tufted, 156
  White, 152, Pl. 16
Phlox caespitosa, 156
  hoodii, 152
  kelseyi, 152
  longifolia, 152, Pl. 16
  multiflora, 152, Pl. 16
Phlox Family, 150
Phyllodoce empetriformis, 142, Pl. 15
  glanduliflora, 142
Physalis fendleri, 166
  lobata, 166
  longifolia, 166

Physalis (contd.)
  subglabrata, 166, 166
Pine, Prince's, 134, Pl. 14
Pinedrops, 136, Pl. 15
Pink Family, 48
Pink Milkweed, 148, 148, Pl. 16
Pink Pyrola, 135, 135, Pl. 14
Pink Spirea, 95, Pl. 10
Plains Cactus, 119, Pl. 12
Pleated Gentian, 146, 147
Poison-hemlock, 125
Poison-ivy, 110, 110
Poison-oak, 111
Poison Sumac, 111
Polanisia trachysperma, 69
Polemoniaceae, 150
Polemonium delicatum, 153
  confertum, 153
  occidentale, 153
  pulcherrimum, 153, Pl. 16
  viscosum, 152, Pl. 16
Polygonaceae, 40
Polygonum aviculare, 42
  bistortoides, 42, 42, Pl. 4
  convolvulus, 42
  natans, 43, Pl. 5
  viviparum, 42
Pondlily, Yellow, 51, Pl. 6
Pondweed, 2, 3
Pondweed Family, 2
Portulacaceae, 45
Potamogeton epihydrus, 3
  natans, 3
  pectinatus, 2, 3
  richardsonii, 3
Potato Family, 165
Potentilla anserina, 85, 86
  diversifolia, 85
  fruticosa, 87, 87, Pl. 9
  gracilis ssp. *nuttallii*, 88, Pl. 11
  gracilis var. *pulcherrima*, 88, 89
  norvegica, 85
  palustris, 85
  plattensis, 86
Primrose, 122, 122, Pl. 13
  Evening, 121, Pl. 12
  Parry, 143, Pl. 15
  Yellow Evening, 123, 123
Primrose Family, 143
Primula angustifolia, 144
  incana, 144
  parryi, 143, Pl. 15
Primulaceae, 143
Prince's Pine, 134, Pl. 14

Prunus americana, 89
  melanocarpa, 89, **Pl. 10**
  pensylvanica, 89
Pterospora andromedea, 136, **Pl. 15**
Purple Saxifrage, 74, **75**
Purple-eyed Mariposa, 18, **Pl. 3**
Purshia tridentata, 90, **91**, **Pl. 9**
Purslane Family, 45
Pussytoes, 190, **191**, **Pl. 22**
Pyrola, Green, 135, **135**
  Pink, 135, **135**, **Pl. 14**
Pyrola asarifolia, 135, **135**, **Pl. 14**
  bracteata, 135
  chlorantha, 135, **135**
  uniflora, 135, **135**
Pyrolaceae, 134

Queencup, 21, **Pl. 3**
Quillwort, Flowering, 4

Rabbitbrush, 202, **Pl. 22**
Ranunculaceae, 51
Ranunculus adoneus, 60, **Pl. 6**
  alismaefolius, 62
  aquatilis, 61, **Pl. 7**
  eschscholtzii, 60
  glaberrimus, 62, **62**, **Pl. 6**
Raspberry, American Red, 93, **93**
Ratibida columnifera, 224, **Pl. 23**
  tagetes, 224
Red Haw, 80
Red Lily, 26, **26**
Red Monkeyflower, 172, **Pl. 19**
Red Twinberry, **182**, 183
Red-osier Dogwood, 133, **Pl. 14**
Rhamnaceae, 112
Rhus diversiloba, 111
  glabra, 111
  radicans, 110, **110**
  trilobata, 111, **Pl. 13**
Ribes aureum, 78, **78**
  cereum, 78
  inerme, 78
  viscosissimum, 78
River Hawthorn, 80, **81**
Rocky Mountain Beeplant, 69,
  Pl. 8
Rocky Mountain Iris, 34, **Pl. 2**
Rorippa islandica, 68
  nasturtium-aquaticum, 68, **68**
  sinuata, 68
Rosa arizonica. See *woodsii*
  gymnocarpa, 92
  neomexicana. See *woodsii*

Rosa (contd.)
  nutkana, 92
  woodsii, 92, **Pl. 9**
Rosaceae, 79
Rose, 92, **Pl. 9**
Rose Family, 79
Rosecrown, 70, **70**, **Pl. 8**
Roseroot, 70
Rubiaceae, 180
Rubus idaeus, 93, **93**
  leucodermis, 93
  parviflorus, 93, **Pl. 9**
  spectabilis, 93
Rudbeckia, 225, **Pl. 23**
Rudbeckia hirta, 225
  laciniata, 225, **Pl. 23**
  occidentalis, 225, **Pl. 22**
Rumex acetosella, 44
  crispus, 44, **44**
  maritimus, 44
  mexicanus, 44
  paucifolius, 44
  venosus, 45
Rush Family, 13
Rushpink, 223, **Pl. 24**
Rydbergia grandiflora. See
  Hymenoxys grandiflora
Rye, Great Basin Wild, 6, **Pl. 1**

Sage, Garden, 194
Sagebrush, Big, 193, **194**
Sagebrush Buttercup, 62, **62**, **Pl. 6**
Sagittaria arifolia. See *cuneata*
  cuneata, 5, **5**, **Pl. 1**
  latifolia, 6
St. Johnswort, 116, **Pl. 12**
St. Johnswort Family, 115
Salsify, 232, **Pl. 21**
  Meadow, 232
Salvia officinalis, 194
Sambucus coerulea, 183, **Pl. 19**
  melanocarpa, 183
  pubens, 183
Sandwort, 48, **Pl. 5**
  Ballhead, **48**, 49
Sarcobatus vermiculatus, 194
Saxifraga arguta, 74, **75**
  bronchialis, 74, **75**
  oppositifolia, 74, **75**
  rhomboidea, 76, **76**
Saxifragaceae, 72
Saxifrage, Brook, 74, **75**
  Diamondleaf, 76, **76**
  Purple, 74, **75**

Saxifrage (contd.)
  Yellowdot, 74–76, **75**
Saxifrage Family, 72
Scarlet Falsemallow, 115, **Pl. 12**
Scarlet Gilia, 150, **151**, **Pl. 16**
Scirpus acutus, 10, **10**
  americanus, 11
  paludosus, 11
  validus, 10
Scrophulariaceae, 168
Scutellaria angustifolia, 164
  galericulata, 164, **164**
  lateriflora, 164
Sedge, 8, **Pl. 1**
sedge, Cotton-, 9, **9**
Sedge Family, 8
Sedum debile, 71
  rhodanthum, 70, **70**, **Pl. 8**
  rosea, 70
  stenopetalum, 71, **Pl. 8**
Sego Lily, 18, **19**, **Pl. 3**
Senecio fremontii, 226
  hydrophilus, 226
  integerrimus, 225, **226**
  resedifolius, 226
  triangularis, 226
  vulgaris, 226
  werneriaefolius, 226
Serpentgrass, 42
Serviceberry, 79, **Pl. 11**
Shootingstar, 143, **Pl. 15**
Shortstyle Onion, 16, **16**
Showy Aster, 195
Showy Daisy, 210, **Pl. 21**
Shrubby Cinquefoil, 87, **87**, **Pl. 9**
Siberian Chive, 15, **15**
Sieversia ciliata. See
  Geum triflorum
Silene acaulis, 50, **Pl. 6**
  alba, 50
  drummondii, 50
  menziesii, 50
Silky Phacelia, 154, **Pl. 16**
Silverweed, 85, **86**
Sisyrinchium halophyllum. See
  sarmentosum
  idahoense. See *sarmentosum*
  inflatum, 35, **Pl. 2**
  sarmentosum, 35, **Pl. 2**
Sium suave, 131, **132**, **Pl. 13**
Skullcup, 164, **164**
Skunkcabbage, Yellow, 11, **12**, **Pl. 1**
Sky Pilot, 152, **Pl. 16**

Smilacina racemosa, 27, **Pl. 2**
  stellata, 28, **Pl. 1**
Snowbrush, 112, **113**
Solanaceae, 165
Solanum carolinense, 168
  dulcamara, 167, **167**, 168
  nigrum, 167, **167**
  rostratum, 168
  triflorum, 168
Solidago elongata, 227
  lepida. See *elongata*
  multiradiata, 227
  occidentalis, 227, **Pl. 22**
Solomonseal, False, 27, **Pl. 2**
Sonchus arvensis, 228
  asper, 228, **228**
  uliginosus, 228, **Pl. 23**
Sorbus scopulina, 94, **Pl. 10**
  sitchensis, 94
sorrel, Mountain-, 41, **Pl. 5**
Sow-thistle, 228, **Pl. 23**
Sparganiaceae, 2
Sparganium angustifolium, 2
  eurycarpum, 2
  simplex, 2, **Pl. 1**
Sphaeralcea coccinea, 115, **Pl. 12**
  leptophylla, 115
  munroana, 115
  rivularis. See *Iliamna rivularis*
Spiraea betulifolia, 95
  douglasii, 95, **Pl. 10**
  splendens, 95
Spiranthes romanzoffiana, 39, **Pl. 4**
Spirea, 95
  Pink, 95, **Pl. 10**
Splitleaf Painted-cup, 170, **Pl. 18**
Spotted Coralroot, 37, **37**, **Pl. 4**
Spotted Knapweed, 200, **Pl. 24**
Springbeauty, 45, **46**, **Pl. 5**
Spurge, Leafy, 108, **109**, **Pl. 15**
Spurge Family, 108
Squaw-apple, 80
Squawbush, 111, **Pl. 13**
Staff-tree Family, 111
Starflower, 72, **Pl. 8**
Steershead, 65, **Pl. 7**
Stemless Goldenweed, 214, **215**
Stenotus falcatus. See *Haplopappus acaulis*
Stickseed, 157, **157**
Sticky Geranium, 106, **107**, **Pl. 10**
Stonecrop, 71, **Pl. 8**
Storksbill, 105, **105**
Strawberry, 82, **Pl. 9**

Strawberry (*contd.*)
  Barren, 83
Streptopus amplexifolius, 28, **29**
Striped Coralroot, 38, **Pl. 4**
Subalpine Buttercup, 60
Sugarbowl, 57, **Pl. 7**
Sulphurflower, 40, **Pl. 5**
Sumac, Poison, 111
Sumac Family, 110
Sunflower, 218, **219**, **Pl. 22**
  Alpine, 221, **Pl. 21**
  Little, 216, **217**, **Pl. 22**
Swamp-laurel, 140, **Pl. 15**
Sweetclover, 100, **101**
  White, 100–101
Sweetvetch, 98, **Pl. 11**
Swertia radiata. See *Frasera speciosa*
Syringa, 77, **Pl. 8**

Taraxacum ceratophorum, 229
  eriophorum, 229
  lyratum, 229
  officinale, 229
Ten-petaled Blazingstar, 117, **118**
Tetradymia canescens, 230, **230**
  glabrata, 230
  spinosa, 230
Thermopsis divaricarpa, 102
  montana, 102, **Pl. 11**
  rhombifolia, 102
Thickstem Aster, 196, **196**, **Pl. 23**
Thimbleberry, 93, **Pl. 9**
Thistle, Bristle, 199, **Pl. 24**
  Bull, 206, **Pl. 24**
  Canada, 203, **203**
  Elk, 204, **205**, **Pl. 24**
  thistle, Milk-, 228, **228**
  Sow-, 228, **Pl. 23**
Tofieldia glutinosa, 29, **Pl. 3**
Townsendia, 232, **Pl. 21**
  Parry, 231, **231**, **Pl. 23**
Townsendia incana, 232
  parryi, 231, **231**, **Pl. 23**
  sericea, 232, **Pl. 21**
Toxicodendron radicans. See *Rhus radicans*
Tragopogon dubius, 232, **Pl. 21**
  porrifolius, 232, **233**
  pratensis, 232
Trifolium longipes, 102, **103**
  macrocephalum, 104, **Pl. 10**
Triglochin maritima, 4, **4**
  palustris, 4

Trillium ovatum, 30, **Pl. 2**
  petiolatum, 30
Trollius albiflorus. See *laxus*
  laxus, 63, **Pl. 7**
Troximon glaucum. See *Agoseris glauca*
Twinberry, **182**, 183
  Red, **182**, 183
Twinflower, 181, **181**
Twisted-stalk, 28, **29**
Typha angustifolia, 1
  latifolia, 1, **Pl. 1**
Typhaceae, 1

Umbelliferae, 124
Umbrella Plant, 40, **Pl. 4**

Vaccinium membranaceum, 141, **141**
  occidentale, 141
  oreophilum, 141
  ovalifolium, 140, **Pl. 14**
  scoparium, 141, **141**
Valerian, 184, **184**, **Pl. 19**
Valerian Family, 184
Valeriana acutiloba. See *dioica*
  capitata, 185
  dioica, 184, **184**, **Pl. 19**
  obovata, 185
Valerianaceae, 184
Veratrum californicum, 31
  viride, 31, **Pl. 4**
Verbascum blattaria, 179
  thapsus, 179, **179**
Vetch, 104, **Pl. 10**
  American, 104
Vicia americana, 104
  cracca, 104
  villosa, 104, **Pl. 10**
Viguiera multiflora, 234, **234**, **Pl. 22**
Viola adunca, 116, **Pl. 12**
  nephrophylla, 116
  nuttallii, 116, **Pl. 12**
  praemorsa, 116
Violaceae, 116
Violet, 116, **Pl. 12**
  Dogtooth, 23, **Pl. 2**
  Yellow, 116, **Pl. 12**
Violet Family, 116

Wakerobin, 30, **Pl. 2**
Waldsteinia idahoensis, 83
Wallflower, 66, **67**
Water Buttercup, 61, **Pl. 7**

Water Ladysthumb, 43, **Pl. 5**
Water Lily Family, 51
Watercress, 68, **68**
Water-hemlock, 124, **124**
Waterleaf, 153, **Pl. 16**
Waterleaf Family, 153
Water-parsnip, 131, **132, Pl. 13**
Wayside Gromwell, 158, **159**
Western Coneflower, 225, **Pl. 22**
Western Fringed Gentian, 146, **Pl. 16**
White Bog-orchid, 38, **39, Pl. 4**
White Clematis, 58, **Pl. 7**
White Phlox, 152, **Pl. 16**
White Sweetclover, 100–101
White Wyethia, 236, **Pl. 24**
Whitlow-grass, 65, **Pl. 8**
Whortleberry, Big, 141, **141**
  Grouse, 141, **141**
Wideworld Parnassia, 73, **74**
Wild Hyacinth, 17, **17, Pl. 3**
Wild Licorice, 98, **Pl. 11**
Wild Lily-of-the-Valley, 28, **Pl. 1**
Wintergreen, Creeping, 139, **Pl. 14**
Wintergreen Family, 134
Wiregrass, 13, **14**
Woodnymph, 135, **135**
Woolly Yellowdaisy, 211, **211, Pl. 23**
Wyeth Biscuitroot, 127, **Pl. 13**
Wyethia, White, 236, **Pl. 24**

Wyethia amplexicaulis, 235, **235, Pl. 24**
  helianthoides, 236, **Pl. 24**
  scabra, 236
Wyoming Paintbrush, 169, **169**

Xanthium spinosum, 238
  strumarium, 237, **237**
Xerophyllum tenax, 31, **Pl. 1**

Yampa, 130, **130, Pl. 13**
Yarrow, 186, **187**
  European, 187
Yellow Beeplant, 69, **Pl. 8**
Yellow Evening Primrose, 123, **123**
Yellow Fritillary, 24, **25, Pl. 3**
Yellow Monkeyflower, 172, **Pl. 18**
Yellow Paintbrush, 168, **Pl. 18**
Yellow Pondlily, 51, **Pl. 6**
Yellow Skunkcabbage, 11, **12, Pl. 1**
Yellow Violet, 116, **Pl. 12**
Yellowdaisy, Woolly, 211, **211, Pl. 23**
Yellowdot Saxifrage, 74–76, **75**
Yellowweed, 227

Zigadenus elegans, 32, **33**
  gramineus, 32
  paniculatus, 32, **Pl. 2**
  venenosus, 32